ELEMENTS OF THE THEORY OF COMPUTATION

PRENTICE-HALL SOFTWARE SERIES

Brian W. Kernighan, advisor

ELEMENTS OF THE THEORY OF COMPUTATION

Harry R. Lewis
Harvard University

Christos H. Papadimitriou
Massachusetts Institute of Technology

Prentice-Hall, Inc.
Englewood Cliffs, New Jersey 07632

Library of Congress Cataloging in Publication Data

Lewis, Harry R
Elements of the theory of computation.

(Prentice-Hall software series)
Bibliography: p.
Includes index.
1. Machine theory. 2. Formal languages. 3. Computational complexity. 4. Logic, Symbolic and mathematical. I. Papadimitriou, Christos H., joint author.
II. Title. III. Series.
QA267.L49 511 80-21293
ISBN 0-13-273417-6

Editorial/Production Supervision
and Interior Design by Kathryn Gollin Marshak
Cover Design by Jayne Conte
Manufacturing Buyer: Joyce Levatino

Printed in the United States of America

10 9 8 7 6 5 4 3

Prentice-Hall International, Inc., *London*
Prentice-Hall of Australia Pty. Limited, *Sydney*
Prentice-Hall of Canada, Ltd., *Toronto*
Prentice-Hall of India Private Limited, *New Delhi*
Prentice-Hall of Japan, Inc., *Tokyo*
Prentice-Hall of Southeast Asia Pte. Ltd., *Singapore*
Whitehall Books Limited, *Wellington, New Zealand*

For Marlyn and Xanthippi

CONTENTS

PREFACE

This book is an introduction, on the undergraduate level, to the classical and contemporary theory of computation. The topics covered are, in a few words, the theory of automata and formal languages, computability by Turing machines and recursive functions, uncomputability, computational complexity, and mathematical logic. The treatment is mathematical but the viewpoint is that of computer science; thus the chapter on context-free languages includes a discussion of parsing, and the chapters on logic establish the soundness and completeness of resolution theorem-proving.

In the undergraduate curriculum, exposure to this subject tends to come late, if at all, and collaterally with courses on the design and analysis of algorithms. It is our view that computer science students should be exposed to this material earlier—as sophomores or juniors—both because of the deeper insights it yields on specific topics in computer science, and because it serves to establish essential mathematical paradigms. But we have found teaching a rigorous undergraduate course on the subject a difficult undertaking because of the mathematical maturity assumed by the more advanced textbooks. Our goal in writing this book has been to make the essentials of the subject accessible to a broad undergraduate audience in a way that is mathematically sound but presupposes no special mathematical experience.

The whole book represents about a year's worth of coursework. We have each taught a one-term course covering much of the material in Chapters 1 through 6, omitting on various occasions and in various combinations the sections on parsing, on recursive functions, and on particular unsolvable decision problems. Other selections are also possible; for example, a course emphasizing computability and the foundations of mechanical logic might skip quickly over Chapters 1 through 3 and concentrate on Chapters 4, 6, 8, and 9. However it is used, our fervent hope is that the book will contribute to the intellectual development of the next generation of computer scientists by introducing them at an early stage of their education to crisp and methodical thinking about computational problems.

We take this opportunity to thank all from whom we have learned, both teachers and students. Specific thanks go to Larry Denenberg and Aaron Temin for their proofreading of early drafts, and to Michael Kahl and Oded Shmueli for their assistance and advice as teaching assistants. In the spring of 1980 Albert Meyer taught a course at M.I.T. from a draft of this book, and we thank him warmly for his criticisms and corrections. Of course, the blame for any remaining errors rests with us alone. Renate D'Arcangelo typed and illustrated the manuscript with her characteristic but extraordinary perfectionism and rapidity.

CHAPTER 1

SETS, RELATIONS, AND LANGUAGES

1.1 "IF-THEN" AND ITS RELATIVES

Mathematics deals with true and false statements and the relations between statements. Of course, these statements are *about* objects of one kind or another, and we shall shortly take up the subject matter of the particular branch of mathematics we are studying. But first some remarks are in order about mathematical statements in general.

In mathematics, we often use the English language in ways more precise than those of everyday discourse. Some odd statements may result, but if all the terminology is clearly understood and taken literally, each statement can be seen, without ambiguity, to be either true or false. For example, Sentence (1) should cause no controversy.

The word *watermelon* has more *e*'s than *o*'s. (1)

Neither should Sentence (2).

The word *watermelon* has at least as many *e*'s as *o*'s. (2)

This is patently true, although a bit peculiar in light of the previous statement. It is hard to imagine why one would want to say (2) when one could as easily say (1). That, however, does not affect the *truthfulness* of (2). What about the following sentence?

The word *watermelon* has at least as many *x*'s as *y*'s. (3)

This is another true statement, since zero is at least as big as zero; never mind that one would not ordinarily say such a thing.

The conjunctions *and* and *or* play an important and precise role in the formation of statements. They combine two statements to make a third, which is true or false depending on the truthfulness or falsity of the pieces. In the case of *and*, the compound statement is true if both component statements are true; otherwise the compound statement is false. For example,

the word *watermelon* has more *e*'s than *o*'s and
the word *blueberry* has two consecutive *r*'s (4)

is true since (1) and

the word *blueberry* has two consecutive *r*'s (5)

are both true. In the case of *or*, the compound statement is true if either component statement is true. Thus

the word *blueberry* has two consecutive *r*'s or
the word *peach* is six letters long (6)

is true because (5) is true, in spite of the fact that

the word *peach* is six letters long (7)

is false. Also,

the word *blueberry* has two consecutive *r*'s or
the word *watermelon* has at least as many *e*'s as *o*'s (8)

is true; a combination of statements with the connective *or* is true if one or the other or both of the combined statements is true and false only if both of the statements being combined are false.

Another phrase commonly used as a conjunction is *if . . . then. . . .* In everyday discourse this phrase has overtones of explanation or causality. Such concepts are alien to mathematics, however; we must have a clearer criterion for the truth of an if-then statement. The rule could not be simpler: an if-then statement is true if the first part is false or if the second part is true. By way of shorthand, let us write p and q for the two statements involved. Then *if* p *then* q can be divided into two cases.

Case 1. Statement p is true. Then in order for the compound statement to be true, q must be true as well.

Case 2. Statement p is false. Then the compound statement is automatically true, regardless of whether q is true.

For example,

if the word *watermelon* has more *e*'s than *o*'s,
then the word *blueberry* has two consecutive *r*'s

is true, since Case 1 applies and q is true. The statement

if the word *blueberry* has two consecutive *r*'s,
then the word *peach* is six letters long

is false, since Case 1 applies and q is false. Finally, *any* statement of the form

if the word *peach* is six letters long, then q

is true, regardless of whether q is true or false, since Case 2 applies. In all situations, to show that *if p then q* is true, there is no need to look for a "meaningful" connection between p and q; one merely verifies that they are related by Case 1 or by Case 2.

Mathematics rarely deals with statements about particular objects, such as the words *watermelon* and *blueberry*. Instead, it tends to deal with general statements about classes of objects. To deal with such generalities, we introduce symbols to stand for the objects being discussed, in the way we have used p and q to stand for statements. For example, suppose x stands for any word. Then the statement

$$\text{if } x \text{ has more } e\text{'s than } o\text{'s, then } x \text{ has at least one } e \tag{9}$$

is true. Arguing very carefully, we would break this statement into two cases. If x does not have more e's than o's, then Case 2 applies and Statement (9) is true. On the other hand, if x does have more e's than o's, then Case 1 applies, and to prove that (9) is true, we must show that x has at least one e. Now x cannot have fewer than zero o's, and since it has more e's than o's, it must have at least as many e's as the next number bigger than zero, that is, at least one e. Thus (9) is true.

When the *if* part of an if-then statement can under no circumstances be true, the compound statement is said to be true **vacuously**. For example, let x be any word, l_1 and l_2 any letters, and n_1 and n_2 any numbers, and consider the statement

$$\begin{array}{l}\text{if } x \text{ has } n_1\ l_1\text{'s, } n_2\ l_2\text{'s, and } n_1 < n_2,\\ \text{then } x \text{ has at least } n_1 + n_2 \text{ letters in all.}\end{array} \tag{10}$$

As before, we need consider only the case in which the *if* part is true. But now we must deal with two subcases. If l_1 and l_2 are the same letter, then (10) is vacuously true, since then x cannot have fewer l_1's than l_2's. If l_1 and l_2 are different letters, then x has $n_1 + n_2$ letters which are either l_1's or l_2's, and therefore at least $n_1 + n_2$ letters in all.

Let us go back to Cases 1 and 2 for the truth of an if-then statement. Another way to interpret these cases is to state that *if p then q* is true if it is impossible for p to be true and q to be false simultaneously. One can therefore try to establish a sentence of the form *if p then q* by **contradiction**, that is, by assuming q to be false and p to be true and showing that an inconsistency results. We illustrate this principle by a numerical example. Suppose that x is any number. We might argue as follows to show

$$\text{if } x^2 = 0, \text{ then } x = 0.$$

Suppose that $x^2 = 0$, but $x \neq 0$. Then either $x > 0$ or $x < 0$. But if $x > 0$, then $x^2 > 0$, and if $x < 0$, then $x^2 > 0$. In either case, $x^2 > 0$. This contradicts the assumption that $x^2 = 0$.

In writing mathematics, the phrase

$$p \text{ only if } q$$

means exactly the same thing as

$$\text{if } p, \text{ then } q.$$

Again, we use a numerical example. Let x and y be integers. Then

$$x + y \text{ is odd only if one of } x, y \text{ is odd} \tag{11}$$

means the same thing as

$$\text{if } x + y \text{ is odd, then one of } x, y \text{ is odd}$$

and is a true statement. On the other hand,

$$q \text{ if } p$$

means exactly the same thing as

$$\text{if } p, \text{ then } q.$$

Another way of rephrasing (11) is

$$x \text{ or } y \text{ is odd if } x + y \text{ is odd.}$$

Often *p only if q* (that is, *if p then q*) and *p if q* (that is, *if q then p*) are combined into

$$p \text{ if and only if } q.$$

In order for this statement to be true, p and q must either both be true or both be false. To put it another way, *p if and only if q* means that p and q are true under exactly the same circumstances. To establish that an if-and-only-if statement is true, we usually break it into its two parts and establish each separately. For example, consider

$$x + y \text{ is odd if and only if exactly one}^\dagger \text{ of } x \text{ and } y \text{ is odd.}$$

This can be written in two parts.

(a) If exactly one of x and y is odd, then $x + y$ is odd.

(b) If $x + y$ is odd, then exactly one of x and y is odd.

To establish (a) we may simply write x and y as $2m$ and $2n + 1$ (not necessarily in that order) and note that $2m + 2n + 1$ is odd. To establish (b), it is easiest to argue by contradiction; that is, to assume that $x + y$ is odd but either both or neither of x and y is odd. A contradiction follows immediately.

†*Exactly one* means *one, and not more than one.*

The statement *if q then p* is called the **converse** of the statement *if p then q*. Obviously, the converses of some true statements are true, and the converses of other true statements are false. To argue *p if and only if q*, we may first show *if p then q*, and then show **conversely**, as we shall say, *if q then p*.

1.2 SETS

Mathematics deals with statements about objects. Objects of various kinds have special properties of their own: numbers are even or odd, words are made up of letters, and so on. But some general properties of objects and collections of objects do not depend on what kinds of objects they are; these properties depend only on objects being the same or different from each other, and being grouped together in various ways. The ideas that objects are parts of groups, and that those groups can combine and overlap, have been found to be basic and powerful in many branches of mathematics.

A **set** is a collection of objects. For example, the collection of the four letters a, b, c, and d is a set, which we may name L; we write $L = \{a, b, c, d\}$. The objects comprising a set are called its **elements** or **members**. For example, b is an element of the set L; in symbols, $b \in L$. Sometimes we simply say that b is **in** L, or that L **contains** b. On the other hand, z is not an element of L, and we write $z \notin L$.

In a set we do not distinguish repetitions of the elements. Thus {red, blue, red} is the same set as {red, blue}. Similarly, the order of the elements is immaterial; for example, {3, 1, 9}, {9, 3, 1}, and {1, 3, 9} are the same set. To summarize: *Two sets are equal* (that is, the same) *if and only if they have the same elements*.

The elements of a set need not be related in any way; for example, {3, red, {d, blue}} is a set with three elements, one of which is itself a set. A set may have only one element; it is then called a **singleton**. For example, {1} is the set with 1 as its only element; thus {1} and 1 are quite different. There is also a set with no element at all. Naturally, there can be only one such set: it is called the **empty set**, and is denoted by $\varnothing$. Any set other than the empty set is said to be **nonempty**.

So far we have specified sets by simply listing all their elements, separated by commas and included in braces. Some sets cannot be written in this way, because they are **infinite**. For example, the set $\mathbb{N}$ of natural numbers is infinite; we may suggest its elements by writing $\mathbb{N} = \{0, 1, 2, \ldots\}$, using the three dots and your intuition in place of an infinitely long list. A set that is not infinite is **finite**.†

†This is an informal explanation, since a definition would be beyond the scope of this book.

Another way to specify a set is by referring to other sets and to properties that elements may or may not have. Thus if $I = \{1, 3, 9\}$ and $G = \{3, 9\}$, G may be described as the set of elements of I that are greater than 2. We write this fact as follows.

$$G = \{x: x \in I \text{ and } x \text{ is greater than } 2\}.$$

In general, if a set A has been defined and P is a property that elements of A may or may not have, then we can define a new set

$$B = \{x: x \in A \text{ and } x \text{ has property } P\}.$$

As another example, the set of odd natural numbers is

$$O = \{x: x \in \mathbb{N} \text{ and } x \text{ is not divisible by } 2\}.$$

A set A is a **subset** of a set B—in symbols, $A \subseteq B$—if each element of A is also an element of B. We also say that A **is included in** B. Thus $O \subseteq \mathbb{N}$, since each odd natural number is a natural number. Note that any set is a subset of itself. If A is a subset of B but A is not the same as B, we say that A is a **proper subset** of B and write $A \subsetneq B$. Also note that the empty set is a subset of every set. For if B is any set, then $\varnothing \subseteq B$ vacuously, since each element of $\varnothing$ (of which there are none) is also an element of B.

To prove that two sets A and B are equal, we may prove that $A \subseteq B$ and $B \subseteq A$. Every element of A must then be an element of B and vice versa, so that A and B have the same elements and $A = B$.

Two sets can be combined to form a third by various **set operations**, just as numbers are combined by arithmetic operations such as addition. One set operation is **union**: the union of two sets is that set having as elements the objects that are elements of at least one of the two given sets, and possibly of both. We use the symbol $\cup$ to denote union, so that

$$A \cup B = \{x: x \in A \text{ or } x \in B\}.$$

For example,

$$\{1, 3, 9\} \cup \{3, 5, 7\} = \{1, 3, 5, 7, 9\}.$$

The **intersection** of two sets is the collection of all elements the two sets have in common; that is,

$$A \cap B = \{x: x \in A \text{ and } x \in B\}.$$

For example,

$$\{1, 3, 9\} \cap \{3, 5, 7\} = \{3\}$$

and

$$O \cap \mathbb{N} = O.$$

Finally, the **difference** of two sets A and B, denoted by $A - B$, is the set of all elements of A that are not elements of B.

$$A - B = \{x: x \in A \text{ and } x \notin B\}$$

For example,

$$\{1, 3, 9\} - \{3, 5, 7\} = \{1, 9\}.$$

Certain properties of the set operations follow easily from their definitions. For example, if A, B, and C are sets, the following laws hold.

Idempotency	$A \cup A = A$ $A \cap A = A$
Commutativity	$A \cup B = B \cup A$ $A \cap B = B \cap A$
Associativity	$(A \cup B) \cup C = A \cup (B \cup C)$ $(A \cap B) \cap C = A \cap (B \cap C)$
Distributivity	$A \cup (B \cap C) = (A \cup B) \cap (A \cup C)$ $A \cap (B \cup C) = (A \cap B) \cup (A \cap C)$
Absorption	$A \cap (A \cup B) = A$ $A \cup (A \cap B) = A$
DeMorgan's Laws	$A - (B \cup C) = (A - B) \cap (A - C)$ $A - (B \cap C) = (A - B) \cup (A - C)$

Example 1.2.1

Let us prove the first of DeMorgan's laws. Let

$$L = A - (B \cup C)$$

and

$$R = (A - B) \cap (A - C);$$

we are to show that $L = R$. We do this by showing (a) $L \subseteq R$ and (b) $R \subseteq L$.

(a) Let x be any element of L; then $x \in A$, but $x \notin B$ and $x \notin C$. Hence x is an element of both $A - B$ and $A - C$, and is thus an element of R. Therefore $L \subseteq R$.

(b) Let $x \in R$; then x is an element of both $A - B$ and $A - C$, and is therefore in A but in neither B nor C. Hence $x \in A$ but $x \notin B \cup C$, so $x \in L$. Therefore $R \subseteq L$, and we have established that $L = R$.

Two sets are **disjoint** if they have no element in common, that is, if their intersection is empty.

It is possible to form intersections and unions of more than two sets. If S is any collection of sets, we write $\bigcup S$ for the set whose elements are the elements of the sets in S. For example, if $S = \{\{a, b\}, \{b, c\}, \{c, d\}\}$ then $\bigcup S = \{a, b, c, d\}$; and if $S = \{\{n\} : n \in \mathbb{N}\}$, that is, the collection of all the singleton sets with natural numbers as elements, then $\bigcup S = \mathbb{N}$. In general,

$$\bigcup S = \{x : x \in P \text{ for some set } P \in S\}.$$

Similarly,

$$\bigcap S = \{x : x \in P \text{ for each set } P \in S\}.$$

The collection of all subsets of a set A is itself a set, called the **power set** of A and denoted by 2^A. For example, the subsets of $\{c, d\}$ are $\{c, d\}$ itself, the singletons $\{c\}$ and $\{d\}$, and the empty set $\varnothing$, so

$$2^{\{c,d\}} = \{\varnothing, \{c\}, \{d\}, \{c, d\}\}.$$

A **partition** of a nonempty set A is a subset Π of 2^A such that $\varnothing$ is not an element of Π and such that each element of A is in one and only one set in Π. That is, Π is a partition of A if Π is a set of subsets of A such that

1. each element of Π is nonempty;
2. distinct members of Π are disjoint;
3. $\bigcup \Pi = A$.

For example, $\{\{a, b\}, \{c\}, \{d\}\}$ is a partition of $\{a, b, c, d\}$, but $\{\{a, b, c\}, \{c, d\}\}$ is not. The sets of even and odd natural numbers form a partition of $\mathbb{N}$.

1.3 RELATIONS AND FUNCTIONS

Mathematics deals with statements about objects and the relations between them. It is natural to say, for example, that "less than" is a relation between objects of a certain kind—namely, numbers—which holds between 4 and 7 but not between 4 and itself. But the *general* idea of a relation is, at this point, an intuitive and nonmathematical one; what exactly constitutes a relation? Standard mathematical procedure is to define relations in terms of sets: a relation is a set of objects of a particular kind. The objects that belong to relations are, in essence, the combinations of individuals for which that relation holds in the intuitive sense. So the less-than relation is the set of all pairs of numbers such that the first number is less than the second. Now there is no mystery about less-than as an abstraction; it has been reduced to the set of all its concrete instances.

But we have moved a bit quickly. In a pair that belongs to a relation, we need to be able to distinguish the two parts of the pair, and we have not explained how to do so. We cannot write these pairs as sets, since $\{4, 7\}$ is the same thing as $\{7, 4\}$. It is easiest to introduce a new device for grouping objects called an **ordered pair.**†

We write the ordered pair of two objects a and b as (a, b); a and b are called the *components* of the ordered pair (a, b). The ordered pair (a, b) is not the same as the set $\{a, b\}$. First, the order matters: (a, b) is different from (b, a), whereas $\{a, b\} = \{b, a\}$. Second, the two components of an ordered pair need not be distinct; $(7, 7)$ is a valid ordered pair. Note that two ordered pairs (a, b) and (c, d) are equal only when $a = c$ and $b = d$.

†True fundamentalists would see the ordered pair (a, b) not as a new kind of object, but as identical to $\{a, \{a, b\}\}$.

The **Cartesian product** of two sets A and B, denoted by $A \times B$, is the set of all ordered pairs (a, b) with $a \in A$ and $b \in B$. For example,

$$\{1, 3, 9\} \times \{b, c, d\}$$
$$= \{(1, b), (1, c), (1, d), (3, b), (3, c), (3, d), (9, b), (9, c), (9, d)\}.$$

A **binary relation** on two sets A and B is a subset of $A \times B$. For example, $\{(1, b), (1, c), (3, d), (9, d)\}$ is a binary relation on $\{1, 3, 9\}$ and $\{b, c, d\}$. And $\{(i, j): i, j \in \mathbb{N} \text{ and } i < j\}$ is the less-than relation.

More generally, let n be any natural number. Then if $a_1, \ldots, a_n$ are any n objects, not necessarily distinct, $(a_1, \ldots, a_n)$ is an **ordered n-tuple**; for each $i = 1, \ldots, n$, a_i is the ith **component** of $(a_1, \ldots, a_n)$. An ordered m-tuple $(b_1, \ldots, b_m)$, where m is a natural number, is the same as $(a_1, \ldots, a_n)$ if and only if $m = n$ and $a_i = b_i$ for $i = 1, \ldots, n$. Thus (4, 4), (4, 4, 4), ((4, 4), 4), and (4, (4, 4)) are all distinct. Ordered 2-tuples are the same as the ordered pairs discussed above, and ordered 3-, 4-, 5-, and 6-tuples are called ordered **triples**, **quadruples**, **quintuples**, and **sextuples**, respectively. On the other hand, a **sequence** is an ordered n-tuple for some unspecified n (the **length** of the sequence). If $A_1, \ldots, A_n$ are any sets, then the **n-fold Cartesian product** $A_1 \times \cdots \times A_n$ is the set of all ordered n-tuples $(a_1, \ldots, a_n)$, with $a_i \in A_i$ for $i = 1, \ldots, n$. In case all the A_i are the same set A, the n-fold Cartesian product $A \times \cdots \times A$ of A with itself is also written A^n. For example, $\mathbb{N}^2$ is the set of ordered pairs of natural numbers. An **n-ary relation** on sets $A_1, \ldots, A_n$ is a subset of $A_1 \times \cdots \times A_n$; 1-, 2-, and 3-ary relations are called **unary**, **binary**, and **ternary** relations, respectively.

Another fundamental mathematical idea is that of a **function**. On the intuitive level, a function is an association of each object of one kind with a unique object of another kind: of persons with their ages, dogs with their owners, and so on. But by using the idea of a binary relation as a set of ordered pairs, we can replace the intuitive idea by a concrete definition. A **function from** a set A **to** a set B is a binary relation R on A and B with the following special property: for each element $a \in A$, there is exactly one ordered pair in R with first component a. To illustrate the definition, let C be the set of cities in the United States and let S be the set of states; and let

$$R_1 = \{(x, y): x \in C, y \in S, x \text{ is a city in state } y\}$$
$$R_2 = \{(x, y): x \in S, y \in C, y \text{ is a city in state } x\}.$$

Then R_1 is a function, since each city is in one and only one state, but R_2 is not a function, since some states have more than one city.†

In general, we use letters such as f, g, and h for functions and we write $f: A \longrightarrow B$ to indicate that f is a function from A to B. We call A the **domain**

†Cambridge, Massachusetts, and Cambridge, Maryland, are not the same city; they are different cities that happen to have the same name.

of f. If a is any element of A, we write $f(a)$ for that element b of B such that $(a, b) \in f$; since f is a function, there is exactly one $b \in B$ with this property, so $f(a)$ denotes a unique object. The object $f(a)$ is called the **image of a under** f, or simply f **of** a. To specify a function $f: A \longrightarrow B$, it suffices to specify $f(a)$ for each $a \in A$; for example, to specify the function R_1 above, it suffices to specify, for each city, in which state it is. If $f: A \longrightarrow B$ and A' is a subset of A, then we define

$$f[A'] = \{f(a) : a \in A'\} \qquad \text{(that is, } \{b : b = f(a) \text{ for some } a \in A'\}\text{)}.$$

We call $f[A']$ the **image of A' under** f. The **range** of f is the image of its domain.

Ordinarily, if the domain of a function is a Cartesian product, one set of parentheses is dropped. For example, if $f: \mathbb{N} \times \mathbb{N} \longrightarrow \mathbb{N}$ is defined so that the image under f of an ordered pair (m, n) is the sum of m and n, we would write

$$f(m, n) = m + n$$

rather than

$$f((m, n)) = m + n,$$

simply as a matter of notational convenience.

If $f: A_1 \times A_2 \times \cdots \times A_n \longrightarrow B$ is a function, and $f(a_1, \ldots, a_n) = b$, where $a_i \in A_i$ for $i = 1, \ldots, n$ and $b \in B$, then we sometimes call $a_1, \ldots, a_n$ the **arguments** of f and b the corresponding **value** of f. Thus f may be specified by giving its value for each n-tuple of arguments.

Certain kinds of functions are of special interest. A function $f: A \longrightarrow B$ is **one-to-one** if for any two distinct elements $a, a' \in A$, $f(a) \neq f(a')$. For example, if C is the set of cities in the United States, S is the set of states, and $g: S \longrightarrow C$ is specified by

$$g(s) = \text{the capital of state } s$$

for each $s \in S$, then g is one-to-one since no two states have the same capital. A function $f: A \longrightarrow B$ is **onto** B if each element of B is the image under f of some element of A. The function g just specified is not onto C, but the function $R_1: C \longrightarrow S$ defined above is onto S since each state contains at least one city. Finally a mapping $f: A \longrightarrow B$ is a **bijection between** A **and** B if it is both one-to-one and onto B; for example, if C_0 is the set of capital cities, then the function $g: S \longrightarrow C_0$ specified, as before, by

$$g(s) = \text{the capital of state } s$$

is a bijection between S and C_0.

Any binary relation $R \subseteq A \times B$ has an **inverse** $R^{-1} \subseteq B \times A$ defined by

$$(b, a) \in R^{-1} \quad \text{if and only if} \quad (a, b) \in R.$$

For example, the relation R_2 defined above is the inverse of R_1. Thus, the inverse of a function need not be a function. In the case of R_1, its inverse fails to be a function since some states have more than one city, that is, there are distinct cities c_1 and c_2 such that $R_1(c_1) = R_1(c_2)$. A function $f: A \longrightarrow B$ may also fail to have an inverse if there is some element $b \in B$ such that $f(a) = b$ for no $a \in A$. If $f: A \longrightarrow B$ is a bijection, however, neither of these eventualities can occur and f^{-1} is a bijection between B and A. Moreover $f^{-1}(f(a)) = a$ for each $a \in A$, and $f(f^{-1}(b)) = b$ for each $b \in B$.

When a particularly simple bijection between two sets has been specified, it is sometimes possible to view an object in the domain and its image in the range as virtually indistinguishable: the one may be seen as a renaming or a way of rewriting the other. For example, singleton sets and ordered 1-tuples are, strictly speaking, different, but not much harm is done if we occasionally blur the distinction, because of the obvious bijection f such that $f(\{a\}) = (a)$ for any singleton $\{a\}$. Such a bijection is called a **natural isomorphism**; of course this is not a formal definition since what is "natural" and what distinctions can be blurred depend on the context. Some slightly more complex examples should make the point more clearly.

Example 1.3.1

For any three sets A, B, and C, there is a natural isomorphism of $A \times B \times C$ to $(A \times B) \times C$, namely

$$f(a, b, c) = ((a, b), c)$$

for any $a \in A$, $b \in B$, and $c \in C$.

Example 1.3.2

For any sets A and B, there is a natural isomorphism ϕ from

$$2^{A \times B}$$

that is, the set of all binary relations on A and B, to

$$\{f : f \text{ is a function from } A \text{ to } 2^B\}.$$

Namely, for any relation $R \subseteq A \times B$, let $\phi(R)$ be that function $f: A \longrightarrow 2^B$ such that

$$f(a) = \{b : b \in B \text{ and } (a, b) \in R\}.$$

For example, if S is the set of states and $R \subseteq S \times S$ contains any ordered pair of states with a common border, then the naturally associated function $f: S \longrightarrow 2^S$ is specified by

$$f(s) = \{s' : s' \in S \text{ and } s \text{ and } s' \text{ share a border}\}.$$

Example 1.3.3

Sometimes we regard the inverse of a function $f\colon A \longrightarrow B$ as a function even when f is not a bijection. The idea is to regard $f^{-1} \subseteq B \times A$ as a function from B to 2^A, using the natural isomorphism described under Example 1.3.2. Thus $f^{-1}(b)$ is, for any $b \in B$, the *set* of all $a \in A$ such that $f(a) = b$. For example, if R_1 is as defined above—the function that assigns to each city the state in which it is located—then $R_1^{-1}(s)$, where s is a state, is the set of all cities in that state.

If Q and R are binary relations, then their **composition** $Q \circ R$, or simply QR, is $\{(a, b)\colon \text{for some } c, (a, c) \in Q \text{ and } (c, b) \in R\}$. Note that the composition of two functions $f\colon A \longrightarrow B$ and $g\colon B \longrightarrow C$ is a function h from A to C such that $h(a) = g(f(a))$ for each $a \in A$. For example, if f is the function that assigns to each dog its owner and g assigns to each person his or her age, then $f \circ g$ assigns to each dog the age of its owner.

1.4 SPECIAL TYPES OF BINARY RELATIONS

Binary relations will be found over and over again in these pages; it will be helpful to have convenient ways of representing them and some terminology for discussing their properties. A completely "random" binary relation has no significant internal structure; but many relations we encounter in practice arise out of specific contexts and therefore have important regularities. For example, the less-than and greater-than relations can be pictured as sequential arrangements of the numbers, each number bearing the specified relation to all those on one side of it in the sequence (Figure 1–1). The "shorter-than" relation on words has some of the same properties, except that the words must be clumped together before being arranged in sequence (see Figure 1–2).

Our goal in this section is to use both pictorial and strictly formal methods for describing what such "well-structured" relations as these have in common.

We deal only with binary relations on a set and itself. Thus, let $R \subseteq A \times A$ for some set A. The relation R can be represented by a **directed**

$$\ldots < 1346 < 1347 < 1348 < 1349 < 1350 < \ldots$$

(a) The less-than relation

$$\ldots > 217 > 216 > 215 > 214 > 213 > \ldots$$

(b) The greater-than relation

Figure 1–1

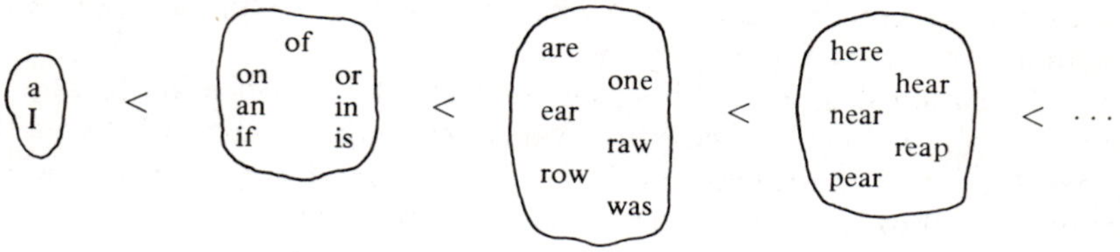

The shorter-than relation

Figure 1–2

graph. Each element of A is represented by a small circle—what we call a **node**—and an arrow is drawn from a to b if and only if $(a, b) \in R$. For example, the relation $R = \{(a, b), (b, a), (a, d), (d, c), (c, c), (c, a)\}$ is represented in Figure 1–3. Note in particular the loop from c to itself, corresponding to the pair $(c, c) \in R$.

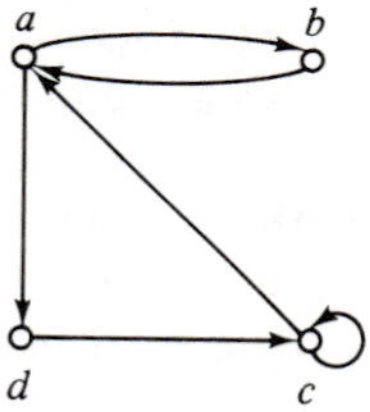

Figure 1–3

To take a less arbitrary example, the less-than-or-equal-to relation $\{(i, j): i, j \in \mathbb{N}, i \leq j\}$ is illustrated in Figure 1–4.

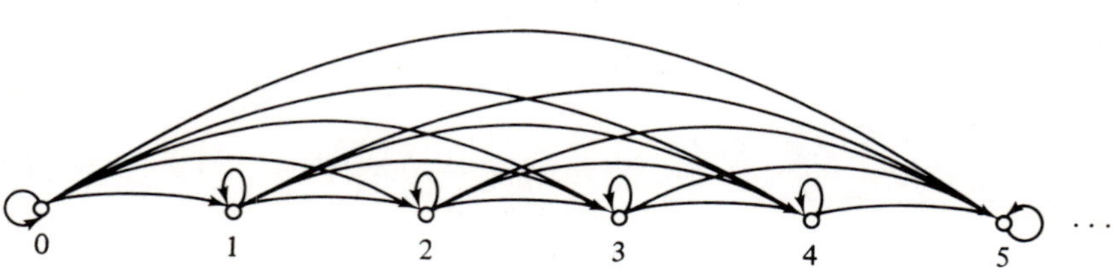

Figure 1–4

Of course, the entire directed graph cannot be drawn, since it would be infinite.

A relation $R \subseteq A \times A$ is **reflexive** if $(a, a) \in R$ for each $a \in A$. The directed graph representing a reflexive relation has a loop from each node to itself. For example, the directed graph of Figure 1–4 represents a reflexive relation, but that of Figure 1–3 does not.

A relation $R \subseteq A \times A$ is **symmetric** if $(b, a) \in R$ whenever $(a, b) \in R$. In the corresponding directed graph, whenever there is an arrow between two nodes, there are arrows between those nodes *in both directions*. For example, the directed graph of Figure 1–5 represents a symmetric relation. This directed

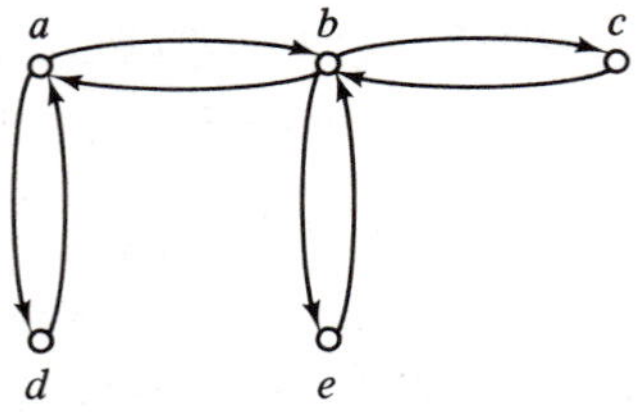

Figure 1–5

graph might depict the relation of "friendship" among five people, since whenever x is a friend of y, y is also a friend of x. The relation of friendship is not reflexive, since we do not regard a person as his or her own friend. Of course, a relation could be both symmetric and reflexive; for example, $\{(a, b)$: a and b are persons with the same father$\}$ is such a relation.

A symmetric relation can be drawn without arrowheads, while combining pairs of arrows going back and forth between the same nodes. Such a depiction is called an **undirected graph**. For example, the relation shown in Figure 1–5 could also be represented by the undirected graph in Figure 1–6.

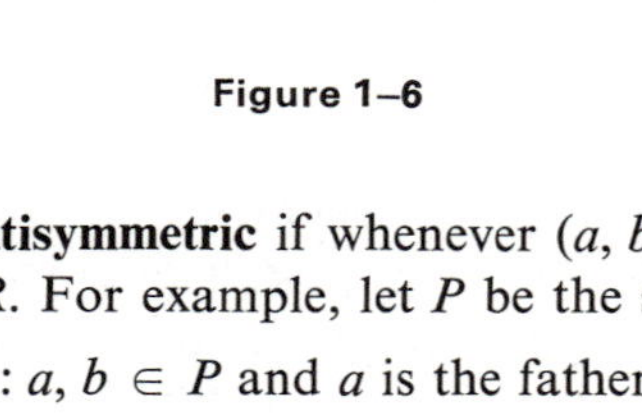

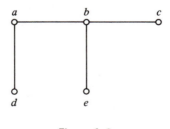

Figure 1–6

A relation R is **antisymmetric** if whenever $(a, b) \in R$ and a and b are distinct, then $(b, a) \notin R$. For example, let P be the set of all persons. Then

$$\{(a, b): a, b \in P \text{ and } a \text{ is the father of } b\}$$

is antisymmetric. A relation may be neither symmetric nor antisymmetric;

for example, the relation

$$\{(a, b): a, b \in P \text{ and } a \text{ is the brother of } b\}$$

and the relation represented in Figure 1–3 are neither.

A binary relation R is **transitive** if whenever $(a, b) \in R$ and $(b, c) \in R$, then $(a, c) \in R$. The relation

$$\{(a, b): a, b \in P \text{ and } a \text{ is an ancestor of } b\}$$

is transitive, since if a is an ancestor of b and b is an ancestor of c, then a is an ancestor of c. So are the less-than and shorter-than relations. In terms of the directed graph representation, transitivity is equivalent to the requirement that whenever there is a sequence of arrows leading from an element a to an element z, there is an arrow directly from a to z. For example, the relation illustrated in Figure 1–7 is transitive.

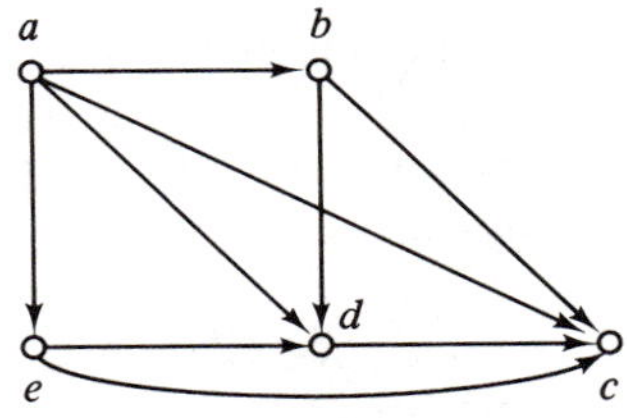

Figure 1–7

A relation that is reflexive, symmetric, and transitive is called an **equivalence relation**. The representation of an equivalence relation by an undirected graph consists of a number of clusters; within each cluster, each pair of nodes is connected by a line (see Figure 1–8). The "clusters" of an equivalence relation are called its **equivalence classes**. We normally write $[a]$ for the

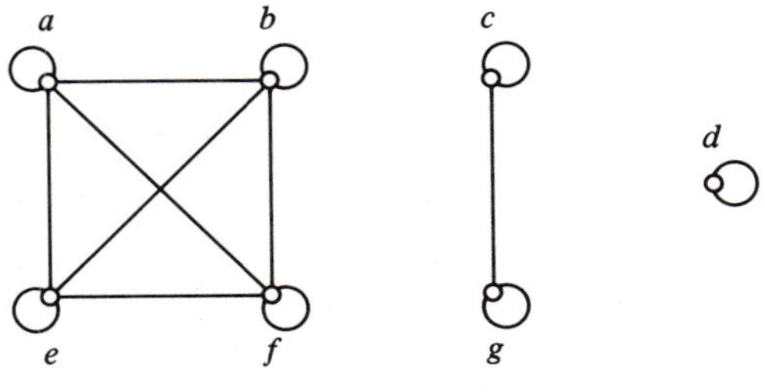

Figure 1–8

equivalence class containing an element a, provided the equivalence relation R is fixed. That is, $[a] = \{b: (a, b) \in R\}$, or since R is symmetric, $[a] = \{b: (b, a) \in R\}$.

Theorem 1.4.1. *Let R be an equivalence relation on a set A. Then the equivalence classes of R constitute a partition of A.*

Proof. Let $\Pi = \{[a]: a \in A\}$. We must show that the sets in Π are nonempty, disjoint and together exhaust A. All equivalence classes are nonempty, since $a \in [a]$ for all $a \in A$, by reflexivity. To show that they are disjoint, consider any two distinct equivalence classes $[a]$ and $[b]$, and suppose that $[a] \cap [b] \neq \emptyset$. Thus there is an element c such that $c \in [a] \cap [b]$. Hence $(a, c) \in R$ and $(c, b) \in R$; since R is transitive, $(a, b) \in R$; and since R is symmetric, $(b, a) \in R$. But now take any element $d \in [a]$; then $(d, a) \in R$ and, by transitivity, $(d, b) \in R$. Hence $d \in [b]$, so that $[a] \subseteq [b]$. Likewise $[b] \subseteq [a]$. Therefore $[a] = [b]$. But this contradicts the assumption that $[a]$ and $[b]$ are distinct.

To see that $\bigcup \Pi = A$, simply notice that $a \in [a]$ since R is reflexive, so that each element of A is in some set in Π. ∎

Thus starting from an equivalence relation R, we can always construct a corresponding partition Π. For example, if

$$R = \{(a, b): a \text{ and } b \text{ are persons and } a \text{ and } b \text{ have the same parents}\}$$

then the equivalence classes of R are groups of siblings. Note that the construction of Theorem 1.4.1 can be reversed: from any partition we can construct a corresponding equivalence relation. Namely, if Π is a partition of A, then

$$\{(a, b): a, b \in A \text{ and } a, b \text{ are in the same set in } \Pi\}$$

is an equivalence relation. Thus there is a natural isomorphism of the set of equivalence relations on a set A to the set of partitions of A.

A relation that is reflexive, antisymmetric, and transitive is called a **partial order**. For example,

$$\{(a, b): a, b \text{ are persons and } a \text{ is an ancestor of } b\}$$

is a partial order (provided we consider each person to be an ancestor of himself or herself).

A partial order $R \subseteq A \times A$ is a **total order** if, for all $a, b \in A$, either $(a, b) \in R$ or $(b, a) \in R$. Thus the ancestor relation is not a total order since siblings are not ancestrally related; but the less-than-or-equal-to relation on numbers is a total order.

Intuitively, what characterizes a partial order, in addition to transitivity, is that by starting from a node and following arrows one cannot get back to that node—except by exploiting the reflexiveness of the relation. It will be useful to sharpen this characterization.

A **chain** in a binary relation R is a sequence $(a_1, \ldots, a_n)$ for some $n \geq 1$ such that $(a_i, a_{i+1}) \in R$ for $i = 1, \ldots, n - 1$; this chain is said to be **from** a_1 **to** a_n. The chain $(a_1, \ldots, a_n)$ is a **cycle** if the a_i are all distinct and also $(a_n, a_1) \in R$. A cycle $(a_1, \ldots, a_n)$ is **trivial** if $n = 1$; otherwise it is **nontrivial**.

Theorem 1.4.2. *A relation is a partial order if and only if it is reflexive and transitive and has no nontrivial cycles.*

Proof. If R has a nontrivial cycle $(a_1, \ldots, a_n)$, where $n \geq 2$, then $(a_n, a_1) \in R$ and also, by transitivity, $(a_1, a_n) \in R$. Since $a_1 \neq a_n$, antisymmetry is violated. Conversely, if R has no nontrivial cycles, it is surely antisymmetric since if $a \neq b$ and both $(a, b) \in R$ and $(b, a) \in R$, then (a, b) is a nontrivial cycle. ■

If $R \subseteq A \times A$ is a partial order, then a **minimal** element of R is an element a such that $(b, a) \in R$ only if $b = a$. We also call a a minimal element of A, if the partial order on A to which we refer is understood from context. For example, a and c are minimal elements in the partial order of Figure 1–9, since no arrow enters a except from a, nor c except

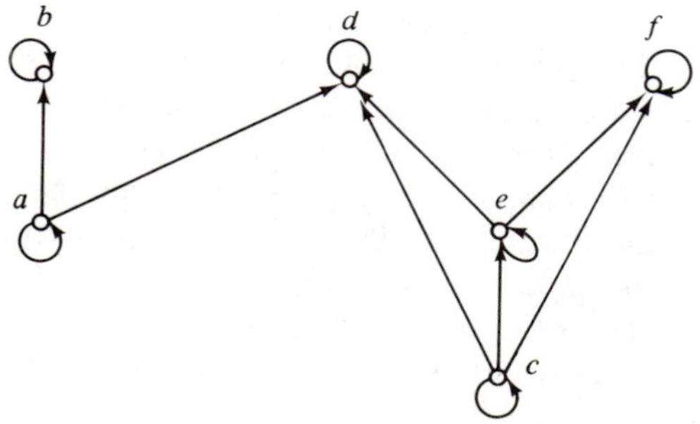

Figure 1–9

from c. Every finite partial order has at least one minimal element. An infinite partial order might or might not have minimal elements. For example, consider the integers or the natural numbers ordered by the less-than-or-equal-to relation; the natural numbers have the minimal element zero, but the integers have none. As another example, if S is any collection of sets then

$$R_S = \{(A, B): A, B \in S \text{ and } A \subseteq B\}$$

is a partial order on S. R_S need not have a minimal element, for example it does not if

$$S = \left\{\left\{x\colon x \text{ is a real number and } 0 \leq x \leq \frac{1}{n}\right\} : n = 1, 2, \ldots\right\}.$$

Also, R_S may have more than one minimal element; for example $S = \{\{a\}, \{b\}, \{a, b\}\}$ has two minimal elements.

One further word on special binary relations. When writing binary relations, particularly transitive ones, we sometimes use **infix notation**: that is, instead of writing $(a, b) \in R$, we write aRb. Equality is one relation that is always written using infix notation: we write $a = b$ instead of $(a, b) \in =$. In general, it is convenient to write transitive relations using infix notation, since aRb and bRc can be combined into the single phrase $aRbRc$ and it can easily be seen that aRc.

1.5 CLOSURES

We say that the natural numbers are closed under addition because the sum of any two natural numbers is again a natural number. The natural numbers are not closed under subtraction, because it is possible to subtract one natural number from another and get a negative number, which is not a natural number. However, the integers are closed under subtraction. Indeed, the integers play a special role with respect to the natural numbers and subtraction. While it is possible to subtract two natural numbers and get a result outside the natural numbers, one cannot get outside the set of integers in this way. At the same time, the integers are in a sense the "smallest" set with this property; one cannot eliminate any of the integers and still have a set containing the natural numbers and closed under subtraction. To put it another way, the integers are neither more nor less than the elements that can be obtained from the natural numbers by repeated subtraction. Thus the integers are called the *closure* of the natural numbers under subtraction.

This sort of relationship among sets is another important and general tool for dealing with sets and relations of many kinds. In this section we develop general properties of closures.

Let D be a set, let $n \geq 0$, and let $R \subseteq D^{n+1}$ be an $(n + 1)$-ary relation on D. Then a subset B of D is said to be **closed under** R if $b_{n+1} \in B$ whenever $b_1, \ldots, b_n \in B$ and $(b_1, \ldots, b_{n+1}) \in R$. Any property of the form "the set B is closed under relations $R_1, \ldots, R_m$" is called a **closure property** of B.

Example 1.5.1

Let $D = 2^{\mathbb{N}}$, let $n = 2$, and let $(S, T, U) \in R$ if and only if $U = S \cap T$. To say that B is closed under R is then to say that any intersection of two sets in B is also in B. For example, B is closed under R, where B is the set of intervals $\{\{x \in \mathbb{N}\colon a \leq x \leq b\}\colon a, b \in \mathbb{N}\}$.

Example 1.5.2

Since relations are sets, we can speak of one relation as being closed under one or more others. Let D be a set, let Q be the ternary relation on D^2 (that is, the subset of $(D \times D)^3$) such that

$$Q = \{((a, b), (b, c), (a, c)) : a, b, c \in D\}.$$

Then a relation $R \subseteq D \times D$ is closed under Q if and only if it is transitive, so transitivity is a closure property. Similarly, if $Q' = \{((a, a)) : a \in D\}$—that is, Q' is a unary relation on $D \times D$—then $R \subseteq D \times D$ is closed under Q' if and only if R is reflexive. (In this case the n in the above definition is zero.)

Example 1.5.3

Let D be any set, $n \geq 0$, and let f be a function from D^n to D. A subset B of D is **closed under** f if $f(b_1, \ldots, b_n) \in B$ for all $b_1, \ldots, b_n \in B$. (For example, let D be the integers and B be the natural numbers, and let f be addition.) Now "closure under a function" is a closure property as previously defined; simply regard $f: D^n \longrightarrow D$ as a relation $R \subseteq D^{n+1}$.

A common type of mathematical construction is to pass from a set A to "the smallest" set B of which A is a subset and which has property P. (Our example of the natural numbers and subtraction is of this type.) Care must be taken, when a definition of this form is used, that the set B is well defined, that is, that "the smallest" has an unambiguous meaning. What is usually meant by "the smallest" is not "having the smallest size," but rather "the minimal, with respect to the partial order by set inclusion." Still, since a set of sets may have several minimal elements or none at all, whether B is well defined also depends on the nature of property P and the set A. For if P is "has either b or c as an element" and $A = \{a\}$, then B is not well defined since both $\{a, b\}$ and $\{a, c\}$ are minimal sets with A as a subset and with property P.

However, if P is a closure property, then the set B is always well defined.

Theorem 1.5.1. *Let P be a closure property defined by relations on a set D and let $A \subseteq D$. Then there is a unique minimal set B of which A is a subset and which has property P.*

Proof. Let P be defined as closure under relations $R_1, \ldots, R_m$, and let each R_i be a subset of D^{n_i+1} for some n_i.

Let S be the set of *all* sets that are closed under $R_1, \ldots, R_m$ and that have A as a subset. S is nonempty since D itself is closed under each R_i and $A \subseteq D$. Now let $B = \bigcap S$; we claim that B is the unique minimal element in S. First, $A \subseteq B$ since $A \subseteq C$ for each $C \in S$. Second, if $1 \leq i \leq m$, $b_1, \ldots,$

$b_{n_i} \in B$ and $(b_1, \ldots, b_{n_i+1}) \in R_i$, then $b_1, \ldots, b_{n_i} \in C$ for each $C \in S$. Hence $b_{n_i+1} \in C$ for each $C \in S$ and $b_{n_i+1} \in B$, so B is closed under each R_i. Finally, if $A \subseteq B'$ and B' is closed under each R_i, then $B' \in S$. Therefore $B \subseteq B'$, so B is minimal. ■

We call B the **closure** of A under the relations $R_1, \ldots, R_m$. A particular case of Theorem 1.5.1 that is of special importance is the formation of the **reflexive, transitive closure** of a binary relation $R \subseteq A \times A$. This relation, denoted by R^*, is the closure of R under the relations

$$Q = \{((a, b), (b, c), (a, c)) : a, b, c \in A\}$$

$$Q' = \{((a, a)) : a \in A\}$$

(a unary relation!). In other words, R^* is the minimal reflexive transitive relation of which R is a subset. For example, let

$$R = \{(a, b) : \text{there is a bus that stops at } a \text{ and, later on, at } b\}.$$

Then

$$R^* = \{(a, b) : b \text{ is reachable by buses from } a\}.$$

The definition of R^* in Theorem 1.5.1 provides a view of it "from above" —R^* is minimal among a class of relations with similar properties. However, R^* can also be characterized "from below," that is, in terms of what ordered pairs must be added to R to obtain R^*.

Theorem 1.5.2. *The reflexive, transitive closure R^* of a binary relation R is equal to*

$$R \cup \{(a, b) : \textit{there is a chain in } R \textit{ from } a \textit{ to } b\}.$$

Proof. Call this latter relation R_0 temporarily; we are to show that $R_0 = R^*$. R_0 is reflexive and transitive; for there is a trivial chain from a to a for any element a, and if $(a_1, \ldots, a_n)$ is a chain from a_1 to a_n and $(a_n, \ldots, a_m)$ is a chain from a_n to a_m then $(a_1, \ldots, a_n, \ldots, a_m)$ is a chain from a_1 to a_m. Also, clearly $R \subseteq R_0$. Since R^* is the unique minimal reflexive, transitive relation that includes R, $R^* \subseteq R_0$. On the other hand, if there is a chain in R from a to b, then (a, b) is a member of any reflexive relation that includes R if $a = b$, and of any transitive relation that includes R if $a \neq b$. Since R_0 contains all such pairs and R^* is both reflexive and transitive, $R_0 \subseteq R^*$. Hence $R_0 = R^*$. ■

The reflexive, transitive closure of a binary relation is only one of several possible closures. In fact, a binary relation has a closure with respect to any combination of reflexivity, transitivity, and symmetry. We have a special notation for only one of these: R^+ is the **transitive closure** of R. (It need not be reflexive, unless R itself happens to be reflexive.) The reflexive, symmetric, transitive closure of a relation is, of course, an equivalence relation. Each of these closures has, like the reflexive, transitive closure, a characterization "from below" as well as "from above."

1.6 FINITE AND INFINITE SETS

A basic property of a finite set is its size, that is, the number of elements it contains. Some facts about the sizes of finite sets are so obvious they hardly need proof. For example, if $A \subseteq B$, then the size of A is less than or equal to that of B; and if $A \subsetneq B$, then the size of A is less than that of B. The size of A is zero if and only if A is the empty set.

However, an extension of the notion of "size" to infinite sets leads to difficulties if we attempt to follow our intuition. Are there more multiples of 17 (0, 17, 34, 51, 68, . . .) than there are perfect squares (0, 1, 4, 9, 16, . . .)? You are welcome to speculate on alternatives, but experience has shown that the only satisfactory convention is to regard these sets as having the same size.

We call two sets A and B **equinumerous** if there is a bijection $f: A \longrightarrow B$. Recall that if there is a bijection $f: A \longrightarrow B$, then there is a bijection $f^{-1}: B \longrightarrow A$; hence equinumerosity is a symmetric relation. In fact, as is easily shown, it is an equivalence relation. For example, $\{8, \text{red}, \{\varnothing, b\}\}$ and $\{1, 2, 3\}$ are equinumerous; let $f(8) = 1$, $f(\text{red}) = 2$, $f(\{\varnothing, b\}) = 3$. So are the multiples of 17 and the perfect squares; a bijection is given by $f(17n) = n^2$ for each $n \in \mathbb{N}$.

In general, a set is finite† if it is equinumerous with $\{1, 2, \ldots, n\}$ for some natural number n. (For $n = 0$, $\{1, \ldots, n\}$ is the empty set, so $\varnothing$ is finite, being equinumerous with itself.) If A and $\{1, \ldots, n\}$ are equinumerous, then we say that the **cardinality** of A (in symbols, $|A|$) is n. The cardinality of a finite set is thus the number of elements in it.

A set is infinite if it is not finite. For example, the set $\mathbb{N}$ of natural numbers is infinite; so are sets such as the set $\mathbb{Z}$ of integers, the set $\mathbb{R}$ of reals, and the set of perfect squares. However, not all infinite sets are equinumerous.

A set is said to be **countably infinite** if it is equinumerous with $\mathbb{N}$, and **countable** if it is finite or countably infinite. A set that is not countable is **uncountable.**

Several techniques are useful for showing a set A to be countably infinite. The most direct way is to exhibit a bijection between some countably

†Once again, this is an explanation, not a definition. The same is true for the term *infinite*.

infinite set B (not necessarily $\mathbb{N}$) and A. Since B and $\mathbb{N}$, and B and A, are then known to be equinumerous, so are $\mathbb{N}$ and A.

Again, suppose that A is an infinite subset of some countably infinite set B; then A must be countably infinite. For we can consider a bijection $f: \mathbb{N} \longrightarrow B$ as a way of listing the elements of B: $B = \{b_0, b_1, b_2, \ldots\}$ where $b_i = f(i)$. A can be listed in the same way, simply by striking out those elements of B that are missing from A. For example, we might have $A = \{b_2, b_7, b_9, b_{13}, \ldots\}$. The required bijection $g: \mathbb{N} \longrightarrow A$ can then be obtained directly: $g(0) = b_2$, $g(1) = b_7$, $g(2) = b_9$, and in general $g(n) = b_m$, where m is the least number such that $|\{b_0, \ldots, b_m\} \cap A| = n + 1$. Such an m exists for each n, since A is an infinite subset of B.

The union of any finite number of countably infinite sets is countably infinite. We show this for three pairwise disjoint, countably infinite sets; a similar argument works in general. Call the sets A, B, and C. The sets can be listed as above: $A = \{a_0, a_1, \ldots\}$, $B = \{b_0, b_1, \ldots\}$, and $C = \{c_0, c_1, \ldots\}$. Then their union can be listed as $A \cup B \cup C = \{a_0, b_0, c_0, a_1, b_1, c_1, \ldots\}$. This listing amounts to a way of "visiting" all the elements in $A \cup B \cup C$ by alternating between different sets, as illustrated in Figure 1–10. The technique of interweaving the enumeration of several sets is called "dovetailing" for reasons that any carpenter can give after looking at Figure 1–10.

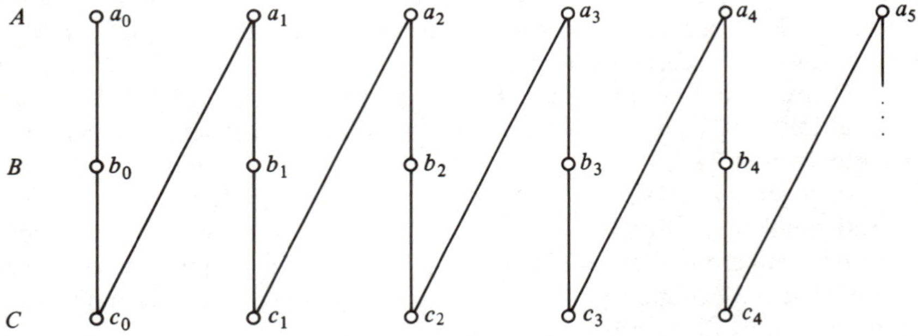

Figure 1–10

The same idea can be used to show that the union of a countably infinite collection of countably infinite sets is countably infinite. For example, let us show that $\mathbb{N} \times \mathbb{N}$ is countably infinite; note that $\mathbb{N} \times \mathbb{N}$ is the union of $\{0\} \times \mathbb{N}$, $\{1\} \times \mathbb{N}$, $\{2\} \times \mathbb{N}$, . . . , that is, the union of a countably infinite collection of countably infinite sets. Dovetailing must here be more subtle than in the example above: we cannot, as we did there, visit one element from each set before visiting the second element of the first set, because with infinitely many sets to visit we could never even finish the first round! Instead we proceed as follows (see Figure 1–11).

1. In the first round, we visit one element from the first set: (0, 0).

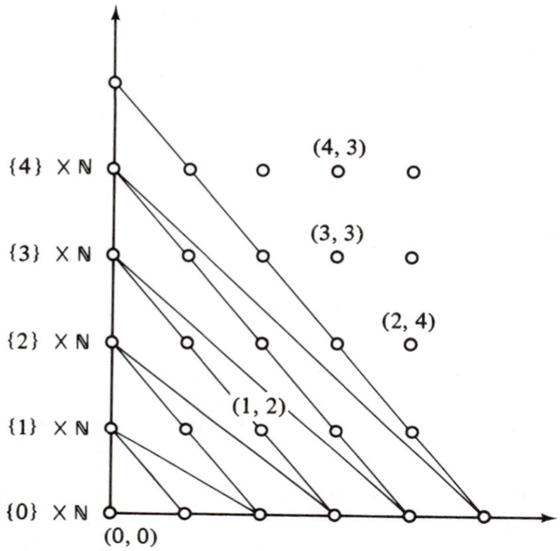

Figure 1-11

2. In the second round, we visit the next element from the first set, (0, 1), and also the first element from the second set, (1, 0).
3. In the third round we visit the next unvisited elements of the first and second sets, (0, 2) and (1, 1), and also the first element of the third set, (2, 0).
4. In general, in the nth round, we visit the nth element of the first set, the $(n - 1)$st element of the second set, . . . , and the first element of the nth set.

Another way of viewing this use of dovetailing is to observe that in the nth round, we visit all pairs $(i, j) \in \mathbb{N} \times \mathbb{N}$ such that $i + j = n - 1$. Since in each round there are only finitely many pairs to visit—in fact, n pairs in the nth round—each round takes only a finitely long time, and any given pair will be visited sooner or later.

At the end of the next section, we present a technique for showing that two infinite sets are *not* equinumerous.

1.7 THREE FUNDAMENTAL PROOF TECHNIQUES

Every proof is different, since every proof is designed to establish a different result. But like games of chess or baseball, observation of many leads one to realize that there are patterns, rules of thumb, and tricks of the trade that can be found and exploited over and over again. The main purpose of this section is to introduce three fundamental principles that recur, under various disguises, in many proofs: mathematical induction, the pigeonhole principle, and diagonalization.

Principle of Mathematical Induction: *Let A be a set of natural numbers such that*

1. $0 \in A$, *and*
2. *for each natural number n, if $\{0, 1, \ldots, n\} \subseteq A$, then $n + 1 \in A$.*

Then $A = \mathbb{N}$.

In less formal terms, the principle of mathematical induction states that any set of natural numbers containing zero, and with the property that it contains $n + 1$ whenever it contains all the numbers up to and including n, must in fact be the set of *all* natural numbers.

The justification for this principle should be clear intuitively; every natural number must wind up in A since it can be "reached" from zero in a finite succession of steps by adding one each time. Another way to argue the same idea is by contradiction; suppose (1) and (2) hold but $A \neq \mathbb{N}$. Then some number is omitted from A. In particular, let n be the first number among 0, 1, 2, . . . that is omitted from $\mathbb{N}$.† Then n cannot be zero, since $0 \in A$ by (1); and since $0, 1, \ldots, n - 1 \in A$ by the choice of n, $n \in A$ by (2), which is a contradiction.

In practice, induction is used to prove assertions of the form, "For all natural numbers n, property P is true." The above principle is applied to the set $A = \{n: P \text{ is true of } n\}$ in the following way.

1. In the **basis step** we show that $0 \in A$, that is, that P is true of 0.
2. The **induction hypothesis** is the assumption that for some fixed but arbitrary $n \geq 0$, P holds of each natural number $0, 1, \ldots, n$.
3. In the **induction step** we show, using the induction hypothesis, that P is true of $n + 1$. By the induction principle, A is then equal to $\mathbb{N}$, that is, P holds of every natural number.

†This is a use of another principle, called the *least number principle*, that is actually equivalent to the principle of mathematical induction, so we are not really "proving" the principle of mathematical induction. The least number principle is: If $A \subseteq \mathbb{N}$ and $A \neq \mathbb{N}$, then there is a unique least number $n \in \mathbb{N} - A$; that is, a unique number n such that $n \notin A$ but $0, 1, \ldots, n - 1 \in A$. A somewhat frivolous example of the least number principle is the fact that there are no uninteresting numbers. For suppose there were; then there would have to be a least such number, say n. But then n would have the remarkable property of being the least uninteresting number, which would surely make n interesting.

Example 1.7.1

Let us show that for any $n \geq 0$, $1 + 2 + \cdots + n = (n^2 + n)/2$.

Basis Step. Let $n = 0$. Then the sum on the left is zero, since there is nothing to add. The expression on the right is $(0^2 + 0)/2 = 0$.

Induction Hypothesis. Assume that, for some $n \geq 0$, $1 + 2 + \cdots + m = (m^2 + m)/2$ whenever $m \leq n$.

Induction Step.

$$
\begin{aligned}
1 + 2 + \cdots + n + (n + 1) \\
&= (1 + 2 + \cdots + n) + (n + 1) \\
&= \frac{n^2 + n}{2} + (n + 1) \qquad \text{by the induction hypothesis} \\
&= \frac{n^2 + n + 2n + 2}{2} \\
&= \frac{n^2 + 2n + 1 + n + 1}{2} \\
&= \frac{(n + 1)^2 + (n + 1)}{2}
\end{aligned}
$$

as was to be shown.

Example 1.7.2

For any finite set A, $|2^A| = 2^{|A|}$; that is, the cardinality of the power set of A is 2 raised to a power equal to the cardinality of A.

Basis Step. Let A be a set of cardinality $n = 0$. Then $A = \varnothing$, and $2^{|A|} = 2^0 = 1$; on the other hand, $2^A = \{\varnothing\}$ and $|2^A| = |\{\varnothing\}| = 1$.

Induction Hypothesis. Let $n \geq 0$, and suppose that $|2^A| = 2^{|A|}$, provided that $|A| \leq n$.

Induction Step. Let A be such that $|A| = n + 1$. Since $n \geq 0$, A contains at least one element a. Let $B = A - \{a\}$; then $|B| = n$. By the induction hypothesis, $|2^B| = 2^{|B|} = 2^n$. Now the power set of A can be divided into two parts, those sets containing the element a and those sets not containing a. The latter part is just 2^B, and the former part is obtained by introducing a into each member of 2^B. Thus

$$2^A = 2^B \cup \{C \cup \{a\}: C \in 2^B\}.$$

This division in fact partitions 2^A into two disjoint equinumerous parts, so the cardinality of the whole is

$$|2^A| = 2^n + 2^n = 2^{n+1} = 2^{|A|}$$

as was to be shown.

We next use induction to establish our second fundamental principle, the *pigeonhole principle.*

The Pigeonhole Principle: *If A and B are nonempty finite sets and $|A| > |B|$, then there is no one-to-one function from A to B.*

In other words, if we attempt to pair off the elements of A (the "pigeons") with elements of B (the "pigeonholes"), sooner or later we will have to put more than one pigeon in a pigeonhole.

Proof. *Basis Step.* Suppose $|B| = 1$, that is, B is a singleton $\{b\}$, and $|A| > 1$. If $f: A \longrightarrow B$, then there are at least two distinct elements $a_1, a_2 \in A$, with $f(a_1) = f(a_2) = b$. Hence f is not one-to-one.

Induction Hypothesis. Suppose that f is not one-to-one, provided that $f: A \longrightarrow B$, $|A| > |B|$, and $|B| \leq n$, where $n \geq 1$.

Induction Step. Suppose that $f: A \longrightarrow B$ and $|A| > |B| = n + 1$. Choose some $b \in B$. (Since $|B| \geq 2$, B is nonempty, and so is the result of removing an element from B.) If $|f^{-1}(b)| \geq 2$, then f is not one-to-one because two members of A have the same image under f, namely, b. If $|f^{-1}(b)| \leq 1$, then consider the function $g: A - f^{-1}(b) \longrightarrow B - \{b\}$ such that $g(a) = f(a)$ for each $a \in A - f^{-1}(b)$. Then $|A - f^{-1}(b)| \geq |A| - 1$, $|B - \{b\}| = n < |A| - 1$, and—by the induction hypothesis—g is not one-to-one. Hence $g(a_1) = g(a_2)$ for some distinct $a_1, a_2 \in A - f^{-1}(b)$; but then $f(a_1) = f(a_2)$ and f is not one-to-one either. ∎

This simple fact is of use in a surprisingly large variety of proofs. We present just one simple application here, but point out other cases as they arise in later chapters.

Theorem 1.7.1. *Let R be a binary relation on a finite set A. If there are arbitrarily long chains† in R, then there is a cycle in R.*

Proof. If there are arbitrarily long chains in R, there is a chain $(a_1, \ldots, a_n)$ for some $n > |A|$. By the pigeonhole principle, the function $f: \{1, \ldots, n\} \longrightarrow A$ such that $f(i) = a_i$ for each i cannot be one-to-one. Hence $f(i) = f(j)$ for some i and j, $1 \leq i < j \leq n$. Let k be the least number such that $k > 0$ and $f(m) = f(m + k)$ for some m, $1 \leq m < n$. Then $(a_m, a_{m+1}, \ldots, a_{m+k-1})$ is a cycle (the trivial cycle (a_m), in case $k = 1$). ∎

Finally, we come to our third basic proof technique, the *diagonalization principle.* It arises less frequently than the induction or pigeonhole principle, but is nonetheless of wide applicability.

†This means, for every $n > 0$, there is a chain of length at least n in R.

The Diagonalization Principle: *Let R be a binary relation on a set A, and let D, the diagonal set for R, be $\{a: a \in A$ and $(a, a) \notin R\}$. For each $a \in A$, let $R_a = \{b: b \in A$ and $(a, b) \in R\}$. Then D is distinct from each R_a.*

If A is a finite set, then R can be pictured as a square array; the rows and columns are labeled with the elements of A and there is a cross in the box with row labeled a and column labeled b just in case $(a, b) \in R$. The diagonal set D corresponds to the complement of the sequence of boxes along the main diagonal, boxes with crosses being replaced by boxes without crosses, and vice versa. The sets R_a correspond to the rows of the array. The diagonalization principle can then be rephrased: the complement of the diagonal is different from each row.

Example 1.7.3

Let $A = \{a, b, c, d, e, f\}$, and $R = \{(a, b), (a, d), (b, b), (b, c), (c, c), (d, b), (d, c), (d, e), (d, f), (e, e), (e, f), (f, a), (f, c), (f, d), (f, e)\}$. R may be pictured like this:

	a	b	c	d	e	f	
a		×		×			$R_a = \{b, d\}$
b		×	×				$R_b = \{b, c\}$
c			×				$R_c = \{c\}$
d		×	×		×	×	$R_d = \{b, c, e, f\}$
e					×	×	$R_e = \{e, f\}$
f	×		×	×	×		$R_f = \{a, c, d, e\}$

The sequence of boxes along the diagonal is

	×	×		×	

Its complement is

×			×		×

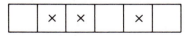

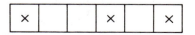

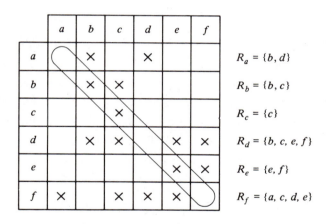

which corresponds to the diagonal set $D = \{a, d, f\}$, and is different from each row of the array. For this row, because of the way it is constructed, differs from the first row in the first position, from the second row in the second position, and so on.

The diagonalization principle holds for infinite sets as well, for similar reasons: The diagonal set D always differs from the set R_a on the question of whether a is an element, and hence cannot be the same as R_a for any a.

We illustrate the use of diagonalization by a classic theorem of Georg Cantor (1845–1918).

Theorem 1.7.2. *The set $2^{\mathbb{N}}$ is uncountable.*

Proof. Suppose that $2^{\mathbb{N}}$ is countably infinite, that is, that there is a bijection $f: \mathbb{N} \longrightarrow 2^{\mathbb{N}}$. Then $2^{\mathbb{N}}$ can be enumerated as

$$2^{\mathbb{N}} = \{S_0, S_1, S_2, \ldots\},$$

where $S_i = f(i)$ for each $i \in \mathbb{N}$. Now consider the set

$$D = \{n \in \mathbb{N} : n \notin S_n\}.$$

D is a set of natural numbers, and therefore should be S_k for some natural number k. Now we ask if $k \in S_k$.

(a) Suppose the answer is yes, $k \in S_k$. Since $D = \{n : n \notin S_n\}$, it follows that $k \notin D$; but $D = S_k$, so $k \notin S_k$, a contradiction.

(b) Suppose the answer is no, $k \notin S_k$; then $k \in D$. But D is S_k, so $k \in S_k$, another contradiction.

Since neither (a) nor (b) is possible, the assumption that $D = S_k$ for some k must have been in error. Hence $2^{\mathbb{N}}$ is uncountable. ■

To recapitulate, let us see how the diagonalization principle, as formulated above, is used in this proof. The set D is in fact that diagonal set for the relation

$$R = \{(i, j) : j \in f(i)\}.$$

Since $S_i = f(i)$, the set

$$R_i = \{j : (i, j) \in R\}$$

is simply S_i. Now, we expect D to differ from each set R_i, that is, from each set S_i, and this is just what is proved by contradiction. Since D is different from each S_i, $D \notin f[\mathbb{N}]$, and the hypothesis that f is a bijection was incorrect.

1.8 ALPHABETS AND LANGUAGES

Until now we have studied sets and relations and general properties of mathematical statements and their proofs. These are the universal paraphenalia of all branches of mathematics. But each branch of mathematics has its own objects of study, and it is time we turned more specifically to those of the theory of computation.

The theory of computation is the mathematical study of computing machines and their capabilities. We must therefore develop a model for the data that computers manipulate. We adopt the mathematically expedient choice of representing data by *strings of symbols*.

We start with the notion of an **alphabet**: a finite set of **symbols**. An example is, naturally, the Roman alphabet $\{a, b, \ldots, z\}$. An alphabet particularly pertinent to the principles on which contemporary computing is based is the **binary alphabet** $\{0, 1\}$. In fact, any object can be in an alphabet; from a formal point of view, an alphabet is simply a finite set of any sort. For simplicity, however, we use as symbols only letters, numerals, and other common characters such as ¢, \$, or #.

A **string** over an alphabet is a finite sequence of symbols from the alphabet. Instead of writing strings with parentheses and commas, as we have written other sequences, we simply juxtapose the symbols. Thus *taxis* is a string over the alphabet $\{a, b, \ldots, z\}$, and \$*ab*¢ is a string over $\{\$, ¢, a, b, c\}$. Also, using the natural isomorphism, we identify a string of only one symbol with the symbol itself; thus the symbol a is the same as the string a. A string may have no symbols at all; in this case it is called the **empty string** and is denoted by e. We generally use u, v, w, x, y, z, and Greek letters to denote strings; for example, we might use w as a name for the string *abc*. Of course, to avoid confusion we shall not use e or any other letter we use as the *name* of a string as a *symbol in* a string. The set of all strings—including the empty string—over an alphabet Σ is denoted by Σ^*.

The **length** of a string is its length as a sequence; thus the length of the string *acrd* is 4. We denote the length of a string w by $|w|$; thus $|101| = 3$ and $|e| = 0$. Alternatively (that is, via a natural isomorphism) a string $w \in \Sigma^*$ can be considered as a function $w: \{1, \ldots, |w|\} \to \Sigma$; the value of $w(j)$, where $1 \leq j \leq |w|$, is the symbol in the jth position of w. For example, if $w = accordion$, then $w(2) = w(3) = c$, $w(4) = w(8) = o$, and $w(1) = a$. This alternative viewpoint brings out a possible point of confusion. Naturally, the symbol c in the second position is identical to that in the third. If, however, we need to distinguish identical symbols at different positions in a string, we shall refer to them as different **occurrences** of the symbol. That is, the symbol $\sigma \in \Sigma$ **occurs** in the jth position of the string $w \in \Sigma^*$ if $w(j) = \sigma$.

Two strings over the same alphabet can be combined to form a third by the operation of **concatenation**. The concatenation of strings x and y, written $x \circ y$ or simply xy, is the string x followed by the string y; formally, $w = x \circ y$ if and only if $|w| = |x| + |y|$, $w(j) = x(j)$ for $j = 1, \ldots, |x|$, and $w(|x| + j) = y(j)$ for $j = 1, \ldots, |y|$. For example, $01 \circ 001 = 01001$, and $beach \circ boy = beachboy$. Of course, $w \circ e = e \circ w = w$ for any string w. And concatenation is **associative**: $(wx)y = w(xy)$ for any strings w, x, and y.

A string v is a **substring** of a string w if and only if there are strings x and y such that $w = xvy$. Both x and y could be e, so every string is a substring of itself; and taking $x = w$ and $v = y = e$, we see that e is a substring of every string. If $w = xv$ for some x, then v is a **suffix** of w; if $w = vy$ for some y, then v is a **prefix** of w. Thus *road* is a prefix of *roadrunner*, a suffix of *abroad*, and a substring of both these and of *broader*. A string may have several occurrences of the same substring; for example, *ababab* has three occurrences of *ab* and two of *abab*.

For each string w and each natural number i, the string w^i is defined as

$$w^0 = e, \text{ the empty string;}$$

$$w^{i+1} = w^i \circ w \qquad \text{for each } i \geq 0.$$

Thus $w^1 = w$, and $(do)^2 = dodo$.

This definition is our first instance of a very common type: **definition by induction**. We have already seen *proofs* by induction, and the underlying idea is much the same. There is a basis case of the definition, here the definition of w^i for $i = 0$; then when that which is being defined has been specified for all $j \leq i$, it is defined for $j = i + 1$. In the example above, w^{i+1} is defined in terms of w^i. To see exactly how any case of the definition can be traced back to the basis case, consider the example of $(do)^2$. According to the definition (with $i = 1$), $(do)^2 = (do)^1 \circ do$. Again according to the definition (with $i = 0$), $(do)^1 = (do)^0 \circ do$. Now the basis case applies: $(do)^0 = e$. So $(do)^2 = (e \circ do) \circ do = dodo$.

The **reversal** of a string w, denoted by w^R, is the string "spelled backwards": for example, $reverse^R = esrever$. A formal definition can be given by induction on the length of a string:

1. If w is a string of length 0, then $w^R = w = e$.
2. If w is a string of length $n + 1 > 0$, then $w = ua$ for some $a \in \Sigma$, and $w^R = au^R$.

Let us use this definition to illustrate how a proof by induction can depend on a definition by induction. We shall show that for any strings w and x, $(wx)^R = x^R w^R$. (For example, $(dogcat)^R = (cat)^R (dog)^R = tacgod$.) We proceed by induction on the length of x.

Basis Step. $|x| = 0$. Then $x = e$, and $(wx)^R = (we)^R = w^R = ew^R = e^R w^R = x^R w^R$.

Induction Hypothesis. If $|x| \leq n$, then $(wx)^R = x^R w^R$.

Induction Step. Let $|x| = n + 1$. Then $x = ua$ for some $u \in \Sigma^*$ and $a \in \Sigma$ such that $|u| = n$.

$(wx)^R$	$= (w(ua))^R$	since $x = ua$
	$= ((wu)a)^R$	since concatenation is associative
	$= a(wu)^R$	by the definition of the reversal of $(wu)a$
	$= au^R w^R$	by the induction hypothesis
	$= (ua)^R w^R$	by the definition of the reversal of ua
	$= x^R w^R$	since $x = ua$

Now we move from the study of individual strings to the study of finite and infinite *sets* of strings. Computing machines—or rather, some simple models of computing machines—will be characterized in terms of regularities in the way they handle many different strings, so it is important first to understand general ways of describing and combining classes of strings.

Any set of strings over an alphabet Σ—that is, any subset of Σ^*—will be called a **language**. Thus Σ^*, $\varnothing$, and Σ are languages. Since a language is simply a special kind of set, we can specify a finite language by listing all its strings. For example, $\{aba, czr, d, f\}$ is a language over $\{a, b, \ldots, z\}$. However, most languages of interest are infinite, so that listing all the strings is not possible. Languages that might be considered are $\{0, 01, 011, 0111, \ldots\}$, $\{w \in \{0, 1\}^*: w$ has an equal number of 0's and 1's$\}$, and $\{w \in \Sigma^*: w = w^R\}$. Thus we can specify infinite languages by the scheme

$$L = \{w \in \Sigma^*: w \text{ has property } P\}$$

following the general form we have used for specifying infinite sets.

If Σ is a finite alphabet, is Σ^* a countably infinite set? It is not hard to see that this is indeed the case. To construct a bijection $f: \mathbb{N} \to \Sigma^*$, first fix some ordering of the alphabet, say $\Sigma = \{a_1, \ldots, a_n\}$, where $a_1, \ldots, a_n$ are distinct. The members of Σ^* can then be enumerated in the following way.

1. For each $k \geq 0$, all strings of length k are enumerated before all strings of length $k + 1$.
2. The n^k strings of length exactly k are enumerated **lexicographically**, that is, $a_{i_1} \ldots a_{i_k}$ precedes $a_{j_1} \ldots a_{j_k}$ provided that, for some m, $0 \leq m \leq k - 1$, $i_l = j_l$ for $l = 1, \ldots, m$, and $i_{m+1} < j_{m+1}$.

For example, if $\Sigma = \{a_1, a_2\}$, the order would be as follows.

$$e$$
$$a_1$$
$$a_2$$
$$a_1a_1$$
$$a_1a_2$$
$$a_2a_1$$
$$a_2a_2$$
$$a_1a_1a_1$$
$$a_1a_1a_2$$
$$a_1a_2a_1$$
$$a_1a_2a_2$$
$$a_2a_1a_1$$
$$\vdots$$

If Σ is the Roman alphabet and the ordering of $\Sigma = \{a_1, \ldots, a_{26}\}$ is the usual one $\{a, \ldots, z\}$, then the lexicographic order for strings of equal length is the order used in dictionaries; however, the ordering described by (1) and (2) for all strings in Σ^* differs from the dictionary ordering by listing shorter strings before longer ones.

Since languages are sets, they can be combined by the set operations of union, intersection, and difference. When a particular alphabet Σ is understood from context, we shall write $\bar{A}$—the **complement** of A—instead of the difference $\Sigma^*—A$.

In addition, certain operations are meaningful only for languages. The first of these is the **concatenation of languages**. If L_1 and L_2 are languages over Σ, their concatenation is $L = L_1 \circ L_2$, or simply L_1L_2, where

$$L = \{w \colon w = x \circ y \text{ for some } x \in L_1 \text{ and } y \in L_2\}.$$

For example, if $\Sigma = \{0, 1\}$, $L_1 = \{w \in \Sigma^* \colon w \text{ has an even number of 0's}\}$ and $L_2 = \{w \colon w \text{ starts with a 0 and the rest of the symbols are 1's}\}$, then $L_1 \circ L_2 = \{w \in \Sigma^* \colon w \text{ has an odd number of 0's}\}$.

Another language operation is the **closure** or **Kleene star** of a single language L, denoted by L^*. L^* is the set of all strings obtained by concatenating zero or more strings from L. (The concatenation of zero strings is e, and the concatenation of one string is the string itself.) Thus,

$$L^* = \{w \in \Sigma^* \colon w = w_1 \circ w_2 \circ \cdots \circ w_k \text{ for some } k \geq 0 \text{ and some } w_1, \ldots, w_k \in L\}.$$

For example, if $L = \{01, 1, 100\}$, then $110001110011 \in L^*$, since it is equal to $1 \circ 100 \circ 01 \circ 1 \circ 100 \circ 1 \circ 1$, a concatenation of strings in L.

Note that the use of Σ^* to denote the set of all strings over Σ is consistent with the notation for the Kleene star of Σ regarded as a finite language. That is, if we let $L = \Sigma$ and apply the definition above, then Σ^* is the set of all strings that can be written as $w_1 \circ w_2 \circ \cdots \circ w_k$ for some $k \geq 0$ and some $w_1, \ldots, w_k \in \Sigma$. Since the w_i are then simply individual symbols in Σ, Σ^* is, as originally defined, the set of all strings whose symbols are in Σ.

For another extreme example, observe that $\varnothing^* = \{e\}$. For let $L = \varnothing$ in the above definition. The only possible concatenation $w_1 \circ \cdots \circ w_k$, with $k \geq 0$ and $w_1, \ldots, w_k \in L$, is that with $k = 0$, that is, the concatenation of zero strings; so the sole member of L^* in this case is e!

As a final example, we show that if $L = \{w \in \{0, 1\}^*: w$ has an unequal number of 0's and 1's$\}$, then $L^* = \{0, 1\}^*$. To see this, first note that for any languages L_1 and L_2, if $L_1 \subseteq L_2$ then $L_1^* \subseteq L_2^*$, as is evident from the definition of Kleene star. Second, $\{0, 1\} \subseteq L$, since both 0 and 1, regarded as strings, have unequal numbers of 0's and 1's. Hence $\{0, 1\}^* \subseteq L^*$; but $L^* \subseteq \{0, 1\}^*$ by definition, so $L^* = \{0, 1\}^*$.

We write L^+ for the set LL^*. Equivalently,

$$L^+ = \{w: w = w_1 \circ w_2 \circ \cdots \circ w_k \text{ for some } k \geq 1 \text{ and some } w_1, \ldots, w_k \in L\}.$$

1.9 FINITE REPRESENTATION OF LANGUAGES

A central issue in the theory of computation is the representation of languages by finite specifications. Naturally, any finite language is amenable to finite representation by exhaustive enumeration of all the strings in the language. The issue becomes challenging only when infinite languages are considered.

Let us be somewhat more precise about the notion of "finite representation of a language." The first point to be made is that any such representation must itself be a string, a finite sequence of symbols over some alphabet Σ. Second, we certainly want different languages to have different representations, otherwise the term *representation* could hardly be considered appropriate. But these two requirements already imply that the possibilities for finite representation are severely limited. For the set Σ^* of strings over an alphabet Σ is countably infinite, so the number of possible representations of languages is countably infinite. (This would remain true even if we were not bound to use a particular alphabet Σ, so long as the total number of available symbols was countably infinite.) On the other hand, the set of all possible languages over a given alphabet Σ—that is, 2^{Σ^*}—is uncountably infinite, since $2^{\mathbf{N}}$, and hence the power set of any countably infinite set, is not countably infinite. With only a countable number of representations and an uncountable number of things to represent, we are unable to represent all languages finitely. Thus, the most we can hope for is to find finite representations, of one sort or another, for at least some of the more interesting languages.

This is our first result in the theory of computation: No matter how powerful are the methods we use for representing languages, only countably many languages can be represented, so long as the representations themselves are finite. There being uncountably many languages in all, uncountably many of them will inevitably be missed under any finite representational scheme.

Of course, this is not the last thing we shall have to say along these lines. We shall describe several ways of describing and representing languages, each more powerful than the last in the sense that each is capable of describing languages the previous one cannot. This hierarchy does not contradict the fact that all these finite representational methods are inevitably limited in scope for the reasons just explained.

We shall also want to derive ways of exhibiting particular languages that cannot be represented by the various representational methods we study. We know that the world of languages is inhabited by vast numbers of such unrepresentable specimens, but, strangely perhaps, it can be exceedingly difficult to catch one, put it on display, and document it. Diagonalization arguments will eventually assist us here.

To begin our study of finite representations, we consider expressions—strings of symbols—that describe how languages can be built up by using the operations described in Section 1.8.

Example 1.9.1

Let $L = \{w \in \{0, 1\}^*: w$ has two or three occurrences of 1, the first and second of which are not consecutive$\}$. This language can be described using only singleton sets and the symbols $\cup$, $\circ$, and $*$ as

$$L = \{0\}^* \circ \{1\} \circ \{0\}^* \circ \{0\} \circ \{1\} \circ \{0\}^* ((\{1\} \circ \{0\}^*) \cup \varnothing^*).$$

The only symbols used in this representation are the braces { and }, the parentheses (and), $\varnothing$, 0, 1, $*$, $\circ$, and $\cup$. In fact, we may dispense with the braces and $\circ$ and write simply

$$L = 0^*10^*010^*(10^* \cup \varnothing^*).$$

Roughly speaking, an expression—such as the one for L in Example 1.9.1—that describes a language exclusively by means of single symbols and $\varnothing$ combined, perhaps with the aid of parentheses, by using the symbols $\cup$ and $*$ is called a *regular expression*. But in order to keep straight the expressions about which we are talking and the "mathematical English" we are using for discussing them, we must tread rather carefully. Instead of using $\cup$, $*$, and $\varnothing$, which are the names in this book for certain operations and sets, we introduce special symbols $\cup$, $\star$, and $\varnothing$, which should be regarded for the moment as completely free of meaningful overtones, just like the symbols a, \$, and ¢ used in earlier examples. In the same way, we introduce special symbols **)** and **(** instead of the parentheses) and (we have been using for *doing* mathematics. The **regular expressions** over an alphabet Σ are the strings over the alphabet $\Sigma \cup \{$**)**, **(**, $\varnothing$, $\cup$, $\star\}$ such that the following hold.

1. $\varnothing$ and each member of Σ is a regular expression.
2. If α and β are regular expressions then so is $(\alpha\beta)$.
3. If α and β are regular expressions then so is $(\alpha \cup \beta)$.
4. If α is a regular expression, then so is $\alpha\star$.
5. Nothing is a regular expression unless it follows from (1) through (4).

Every regular expression represents a language, according to the interpretation of the symbols $\cup$ and $\star$ as set union and Kleene star.

Formally, the relation between regular expressions and the languages they represent is established by a function L, such that if α is any regular expression, then $L(\alpha)$ is the language represented by α. That is, L is a function from strings to languages. The function L is defined as follows.

1. $L(\varnothing) = \varnothing$ and $L(a) = \{a\}$ for each $a \in \Sigma$.
2. If α and β are regular expressions, then $L((\alpha\beta)) = L(\alpha)L(\beta)$.
3. If α and β are regular expressions, then $L((\alpha \cup \beta)) = L(\alpha) \cup L(\beta)$.
4. If α is a regular expression then $L(\alpha\star) = L(\alpha)^*$.

Statement 1 defines $L(\alpha)$ for each regular expression α that consists of a single symbol; if $n > 1$, then (2) through (4) define $L(\alpha)$ for regular expressions of length n in terms of $L(\alpha')$ for one or two regular expressions α' of length $n - 1$ or less. Thus every regular expression is associated in this way with some language.

Example 1.9.2

What is $L(((a \cup b)\star a))$? We have the following.

$$\begin{aligned}
L(((a \cup b)\star a)) &= L((a \cup b)\star)L(a) && \text{by (2)}\\
&= L((a \cup b)\star)\{a\} && \text{by (1)}\\
&= L((a \cup b))^*\{a\} && \text{by (4)}\\
&= (L(a) \cup L(b))^*\{a\} && \text{by (3)}\\
&= (\{a\} \cup \{b\})^*\{a\} && \text{by (1) twice}\\
&= \{a, b\}^*\{a\}\\
&= \{w \in \{a, b\}^* : w \text{ ends with } a\}
\end{aligned}$$

Example 1.9.3

What language is represented by $(c^*(a \cup (bc^*))^*)$? This regular expression represents the set of all strings over $\{a, b, c\}$ that do not have the substring ac. Clearly no string in $L((c^*(a \cup (bc^*))^*))$ can contain the substring ac, since each occurrence of a in such a string is either at the end of the string, or is followed by another occurrence of a, or is followed by an occurrence of b. On the other hand, let w be a string with no substring ac. Then w begins with zero or more c's. If they are removed, the result is a string with no substring ac and not beginning with c. Any such string is in $L((a \cup (bc^*)))$; for it can be read, left to right, as a sequence of a's, b's, and c's, with any blocks of c's immediately following b's (not following a's, and not at the beginning of the string). Therefore $w \in L((c^*(a \cup (bc^*))^*))$.

Example 1.9.4

$(0^* \cup (((0^*(1 \cup (11)))((00^*)(1 \cup (11)))^*)0^*))$ represents the set of all strings over $\{0, 1\}$ that do not have the substring 111.

Every language that can be represented by a regular expression can be represented by infinitely many of them. For example, α and $(\alpha \cup \varnothing)$ always represent the same language; so do $((\alpha \cup \beta) \cup \gamma)$ and $(\alpha \cup (\beta \cup \gamma))$; and so do $((\alpha\beta)\gamma)$ and $(\alpha(\beta\gamma))$. Since set union and concatenation are associative operations—that is, since $(L_1 \cup L_2) \cup L_3 = L_1 \cup (L_2 \cup L_3)$ and $(L_1L_2)L_3 = L_1(L_2L_3)$ for any languages L_1, L_2, L_3—we normally omit the extra (and) symbols in regular expressions; for example, we treat $(a \cup b \cup c)^*$ as a regular expression even though "officially" it is not. For another example, the regular expression of Example 1.9.4 might be rewritten as $0^* \cup 0^*(1 \cup 11)(00^*(1 \cup 11))^*0^*$.

Moreover, we now feel free, when no confusion can result, to blur the distinction between the regular expressions and the "mathematical English" we are using for talking about languages. Thus we may say at one point that a^*b^* is the set of all strings consisting of some number of a's followed by some number of b's—to be precise, we should have written $\{a\}^*\{b\}^*$. At another point, we might say that a^*b^* is a regular expression *representing* that set; in this case, to be precise, we should have written (a^*b^*).

So regular expressions are one method for describing concisely certain infinite languages. We already know that they cannot describe *all* languages; but what are the properties of the languages they *can* describe? We shall spend some time later on this question, but one answer can be given right now—although the "answer" is hardly more than a restatement of the question.

The class of **regular languages** (or **regular sets**) over an alphabet Σ is the minimal set of languages containing $\varnothing$ and the singleton sets $\{a\}$, for $a \in \Sigma$, and closed under the operations of union, concatenation, and Kleene star. That is, the class $\mathcal{R}$ of regular languages is to have the following three properties.

1. $\varnothing \in \mathcal{R}$; and if $a \in \Sigma$, then $\{a\} \in \mathcal{R}$.
2. If $A, B \in \mathcal{R}$, then $A \cup B$, $A \circ B$, and A^* are members of $\mathcal{R}$.
3. If $\mathcal{S}$ is a set of languages containing $\varnothing$ and all languages $\{a\}$, with $a \in \Sigma$ (as in Statement 1) and closed under union, concatenation, and Kleene star (as in Statement 2), then $\mathcal{R} \subseteq \mathcal{S}$.

Since the class of regular languages is defined by a closure property, an application of Theorem 1.5.1 shows that there is a unique class of languages satisfying (1) through (3). Clearly, the class of languages described by regular expressions has all the properties ascribed to $\mathcal{R}$ in (1) through (3). Hence *a language is regular if and only if it can be described by a regular expression.*

Unfortunately, we cannot describe by regular expressions some languages that have very simple descriptions by other means. For example, $\{0^n1^n: n \geq 1\}$ will be shown in Chapter 2 not to be regular. Surely any theory of the finite representation of languages will have to accommodate at least such simple languages as this. Thus regular expressions are an inadequate specification method in general.

In search of a general method for finitely specifying languages, we might return to our general scheme

$$L = \{w \in \Sigma^*: w \text{ has property } P\}.$$

The trouble is that, unless we somehow restrict the kinds of attributes that can be used in describing the property P, we may end up with some bizarre representations of languages. Consider, for example,

$$L = \{w \in \Sigma^*: w \text{ is the name of a cat}\}.$$

L is certainly a language, a finite one in fact, but the representation is not of the sort on which we can expect to build a theory. We might try restricting P to "well-defined mathematical properties" according to some suitable definitions of these terms. But consider

$$L = \{w \in \Sigma^*: \text{for some } x, y, z \in \mathbb{N} - \{0\}, x^{|w|} + y^{|w|} = z^{|w|}\}.$$

L is certainly a language, and the property defining L is certainly mathematical. Indeed, for many purposes such descriptions will be very suitable. But from a *computational* standpoint, this description has a discomforting character: it does not seem to help us determine, given a string w, whether or not it belongs to L. Finding a systematic way to answer this question would settle a mathematical problem that has remained open for centuries!†

So for *computational* purposes, a property P can be considered to be a suitable description of the strings in a language only if we are also given a systematic procedure for deciding, given a string w, whether or not it has property P. Thus we should concentrate on formalizing the notion of a "systematic procedure" or algorithm.

An **algorithm** may be described as a finite sequence of instructions, precisely expressed, that—when confronted with a question of some kind and carried out in the most literal-minded way—will invariably terminate, sooner or later, with the correct answer. For example, the method taught in elementary school for multiplying two integers can be presented as an algorithm. It is designed for answering a particular kind of question, "What is the product of m and n?" If written down in very dry and explicit language it could be carried out mechanically. Finally, we know that, if carried out correctly, it will eventually give the right answer. In general we shall not insist that algorithms be written out in tedious detail; it turns out rarely to be controversial what can and cannot be turned into a fully explicit set of instructions. However, we shall later consider a particular language for stating algorithms, in order to study the limitations of algorithms in general.

An algorithm that is specifically designed, for some language L, to answer questions of the form "Is string w a member of L?" will be called a **language recognition device**. For example, a device for recognizing the language

$$L = \{w \in \{a, b\}^* : w \text{ does not have the substring } bbb\}$$

by reading strings, a symbol at a time, from left to right, might operate like this: Keep a count, which starts at zero and is set back to zero every time an a is encountered in the input; add one every time a b is encountered in the input; stop with a No answer if the count ever reaches three, and stop with a Yes answer if the whole string is read without the count reaching three. On the other hand, a regular expression such as $(e \cup b \cup bb)(a \cup ab \cup abb)^*$ may be viewed as a way of **generating** members of a language: "to produce a member of L, first write down either nothing, or b, or bb; then write down a,

†There are many triples of numbers a, b, and c such that $a^2 + b^2 = c^2$; 3, 4, and 5 are such a triple. Finding such Pythagorean triples is an ancient problem, and is described in the *Arithmetica* of Diophantus as: "To divide a given square number into two squares." The great mathematician Pierre de Fermat (1601–1665) wrote in the margin of his copy of the *Arithmetica*, "On the other hand it is impossible to separate a cube into two cubes, or a biquadrate into two biquadrates, or generally any power except a square into two powers with the same exponent. I have discovered a truly marvelous proof of this, which however the margin is not large enough to contain." But no proof has ever been found, and it is now widely believed that Fermat was mistaken in thinking he had discovered one. The set L contains a string of length greater than 2 if and only if Fermat's assertion is incorrect.

or *ab*, or *abb*, and do this any number of times, including zero; all and only members of L can be produced in this way." Such **language generators** are not algorithms since they are not designed to answer questions and are not completely explicit about what to do. (How are we to choose *which* of a, ab, or abb is to be written down?) The relation between language recognition devices and language generators, both of which are types of finite language specifications, is a major subject of this book.

PROBLEMS

1.1.1. Which of the following are true statements?

(a) Dogs have wings only if cats have wings.

(b) Birds have wings only if cats have wings.

(c) If cats have wings, then birds have wings.

(d) Snakes have legs if and only if guinea pigs have tails.

(e) If frogs have hair and mice have eyes, then sharks do not have teeth.

1.1.2. Finish the argument at the end of Section 1.1.

1.1.3. Prove that, for any integers x and y, xy is odd if and only if both x and y are odd.

1.2.1. Determine whether each of the following is true or false.

(a) $\emptyset \subseteq \emptyset$

(b) $\emptyset \in \emptyset$

(c) $\emptyset \in \{\emptyset\}$

(d) $\emptyset \subseteq \{\emptyset\}$

(e) $\{a, b\} \in \{a, b, \{a, b\}\}$

(f) $\{a, b\} \subseteq \{a, b, \{a, b\}\}$

(g) $\{a, b\} \subseteq 2^{\{a, b, \{a, b\}\}}$

(h) $\{\{a, b\}\} \in 2^{\{a, b, \{a, b\}\}}$

(i) $\{a, b, \{a, b\}\} - \{a, b\} = \{a, b\}$

1.2.2. What are these sets? Write them using braces, commas, and numerals only.

(a) $(\{1, 3, 5\} \cup \{3, 1\}) \cap \{3, 5, 7\}$

(b) $\bigcup \{\{3\}, \{3, 5\}, \bigcap \{\{5, 7\}, \{7, 9\}\}\}$

(c) $(\{1, 2, 5\} - \{5, 7, 9\}) \cup (\{5, 7, 9\} - \{1, 2, 5\})$

(d) $2^{\{7, 8, 9\}} - 2^{\{7, 9\}}$

(e) $2^{\emptyset}$

1.2.3. Prove each of the following.

(a) $A \cup (B \cap C) = (A \cup B) \cap (A \cup C)$

(b) $A \cap (B \cup C) = (A \cap B) \cup (A \cap C)$

(c) $A \cap (A \cup B) = A$

(d) $A \cup (A \cap B) = A$

(e) $A - (B \cap C) = (A - B) \cup (A - C)$

1.2.4. Let $S = \{a, b, c, d\}$.

(a) What partition of S has the fewest members? The most members?

(b) List all partitions of S with exactly two members.

1.3.1. Write each of the following explicitly.

(a) $\{1\} \times \{1, 2\} \times \{1, 2, 3\}$

(b) $\varnothing \times \{1, 2\}$

(c) $2^{\{1,2\}} \times \{1, 2\}$

1.3.2. Let $R = \{(a, b), (a, c), (c, d), (a, a), (b, a)\}$. What is the composition $R \circ R$ of R with itself? What is the inverse R^{-1} of R? Is R, $R \circ R$, or R^{-1} a function?

1.3.3. Let $f: A \longrightarrow B$ and $g: B \longrightarrow C$. Let $h: A \longrightarrow C$ be their composition. In each of the following cases state necessary and sufficient conditions on f and g for h to be as specified.

(a) Onto.

(b) One-to-one.

(c) A bijection.

(C_1 is *necessary* for C_2 if C_1 must hold in order for C_2 to hold. C_1 is *sufficient* for C_2 if C_2 holds whenever C_1 does. So C_1 is *necessary and sufficient* for C_2 provided that C_1 holds if and only if C_2 holds. So you are being asked *under exactly what conditions* on f and g their composition will have the various properties mentioned.)

1.3.4. If A and B are any sets, we write B^A for the set of all functions from A to B. Show that there is a natural isomorphism between $\{0, 1\}^A$ and 2^A.

1.3.5. Let $f: \mathbb{N} \longrightarrow \mathbb{N}$ be defined thus: $f(n) = n + n$ for each $n \in \mathbb{N}$. What is $f[\{n: n \text{ is even}\}]$? What is $f[f[\{n: n \text{ is odd}\}]]$?

1.4.1. Let $R = \{(a, c), (c, e), (e, e), (e, b), (d, b), (d, d)\}$. Draw directed graphs representing each of the following.

(a) R

(b) $R \circ R$

(c) R^{-1}

(d) $R \cap (R \circ R)$

1.4.2. Let R and S be the binary relations on $A = \{1, \ldots, 7\}$ with the graphical representations shown below.

(a) Indicate whether each of R and S is (i) symmetric, (ii) reflexive, and (iii) transitive.

(b) Repeat (a) for the relation $R \cup S$.

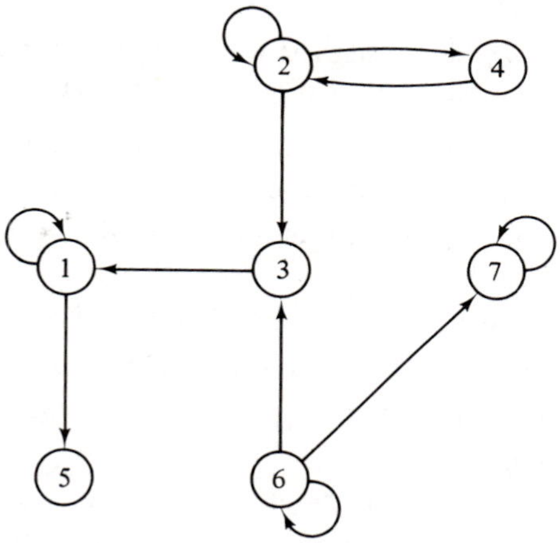

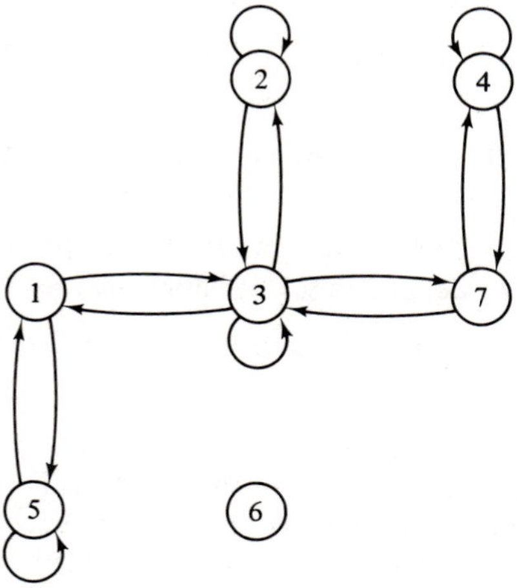

1.4.3. Draw directed graphs representing relations of the following types.

(a) Reflexive, transitive, and antisymmetric.

(b) Reflexive, transitive, and neither symmetric nor antisymmetric.

1.4.4. Let A be a nonempty set and let $R \subseteq A \times A$ be the empty set. Which properties does R have?

(a) Reflexivity.

(b) Symmetry.

(c) Antisymmetry.

(d) Transitivity.

1.4.5. Let $f: A \longrightarrow B$. Show that the following relation R is an equivalence relation on A: $(a, b) \in R$ if and only if $f(a) = f(b)$.

1.4.6. Let $R \subseteq A \times A$ be a binary relation as defined below. In which cases is R a partial order? a total order?

(a) $A =$ the positive integers; $(a, b) \in R$ if and only if b is divisible by a.

(b) $A = \mathbb{N} \times \mathbb{N}$; $((a, b)\ (c, d)) \in R$ if and only if $a \leq c$ or $b \leq d$.

(c) $A = \mathbb{N}$; $(a, b) \in R$ if and only if $b = a$ or $b = a + 1$.

(d) A is the set of all English words; $(a, b) \in R$ if and only if a is no longer than b.

(e) A is the set of all English words; $(a, b) \in R$ if and only if a is the same as b or occurs more frequently than b in the King James Bible.

1.4.7. Let R_1 and R_2 be any two partial orders on the same set A. Show that $R_1 \cap R_2$ is a partial order.

1.4.8. (a) Prove that if S is any collection of sets, then $R_S = \{(A, B): A, B \in S \text{ and } A \subseteq B\}$ is a partial order.

(b) Let $S = 2^{\{1, 2, 3\}}$. Draw a directed graph representing the partial order R_S defined in (a). What element or elements are minimal?

1.4.9. Under what circumstances does a directed graph represent a function?

1.4.10. Let S be any set and let $\mathbf{\Pi}$ be the set of all partitions of S. Let R be the binary relation on $\mathbf{\Pi}$ such that $(\Pi_1, \Pi_2) \in R$ if and only if for every $S_1 \in \Pi_1$, there is an $S_2 \in \Pi_2$ such that $S_1 \subseteq S_2$. Show that R is a partial order on $\mathbf{\Pi}$. What elements of $\mathbf{\Pi}$ are maximal and minimal? Show that, in general, R would not be a partial order on *arbitrary* collections of subsets of S, which need not be *partitions* of S.

1.5.1. Are the following sets closed under the following operations? If not, what are the respective closures?

(a) The odd integers under multiplication.

(b) The positive integers under division.

(c) The negative integers under subtraction.

(d) The negative integers under multiplication.

(e) The odd integers under division.

1.5.2. What is the reflexive, transitive closure R^* of $R = \{(a, b), (a, c), (a, d), (d, c), (d, e)\}$? Draw a directed graph representing R^*.

1.5.3. Is the transitive closure of the symmetric closure of a binary relation necessarily reflexive? Prove it or give a counterexample.

1.5.4. Let $R \subseteq A \times A$ be any binary relation.

(a) Let $Q = \{(a, b)$: $a, b \in A$ and there are chains in R from a to b and from b to $a\}$. Show that Q is an equivalence relation on A.

(b) Let Π be the partition of A corresponding to the equivalence relation Q. Let $\mathbf{R}$ be the relation $\{(S, T)$: $S, T \in \Pi$ and there is a chain from some member of S to some member of $T\}$. Show that $\mathbf{R}$ is a partial order on Π.

1.5.5. Characterize the symmetric closure of a binary relation "from below." Prove that your characterization is equivalent to the definition "from above."

1.5.6. Give an example of a binary relation that is not reflexive but has a transitive closure that is reflexive.

1.6.1. Prove that the following are countable.

(a) The union of any three countable sets, not necessarily infinite or disjoint.

(b) The set of all finite subsets of $\mathbb{N}$.

1.6.2. Explicitly give bijections between each of the following pairs.

(a) $\mathbb{N}$ and the odd natural numbers.

(b) $\mathbb{N}$ and the set of all integers.

(c) $\mathbb{N}$ and $\mathbb{N} \times \mathbb{N} \times \mathbb{N}$.

(We are looking for formulas that are as simple as possible and involve only such operations as addition and multiplication.)

1.6.3. Let C be a set of sets defined as follows.

1. $\varnothing \in C$
2. If $S_1 \in C$ and $S_2 \in C$, then $\{S_1, S_2\} \in C$.
3. If $S_1 \in C$ and $S_2 \in C$, then $S_1 \times S_2 \in C$.
4. Nothing is in C except that which follows from (1), (2), and (3).

(a) Explain carefully why it is a consequence of (1) through (4) that $\{\varnothing, \{\varnothing\}\} \in C$.

(b) Give an example of a set S of ordered pairs such that $S \in C$ and $|S| > 1$.

(c) Does C contain any infinite sets? Explain.

(d) Is C countable or uncountable? Explain.

1.6.4. Show that the dovetailing method of Figure 1–11 visits the pair (i, j) mth where

$$m = \frac{(i + j) \cdot (i + j + 1)}{2} + j + 1.$$

1.7.1. Show by induction that

$$1 \cdot 2 \cdot 3 + 2 \cdot 3 \cdot 4 + \cdots + n \cdot (n + 1) \cdot (n + 2) = \frac{n \cdot (n + 1) \cdot (n + 2) \cdot (n + 3)}{4}.$$

1.7.2. Show by induction that $n^4 - 4n^2$ is divisible by 3 for all $n \geq 0$.

1.7.3. What is wrong with the following purported proof that all horses are the same color?

Proof by induction on the number of horses:

Basis Step. There is only one horse. Then clearly all horses have the same color.

Induction Hypothesis. In any group of up to n horses, all horses have the same color.

Induction Step. Consider a group of $n + 1$ horses. Discard one horse; by the induction hypothesis, all the remaining horses have the same color. Now put that horse back and discard another; again all the remaining horses have the same color. So all the horses have the same color as the ones that were not discarded either time, and so they all have the same color.

1.7.4. By an argument like that of Example 1.7.2, show that there are $|B|^{|A|}$ functions from A to B, if A and B are any finite sets.

1.7.5. Prove by induction: Every partial order on a nonempty finite set has at least one minimal element. Need this statement be true if the requirement of finiteness is lifted?

1.7.6. Prove: If $A_1, \ldots, A_n$ are $n \geq 2$ nonempty finite sets such that $A_1 \subseteq A_2 \subseteq \cdots \subseteq A_n$, f is a function with domain A_n and $|f[A_n]| < n$, then for some i, $1 \leq i \leq n-1$, $f[A_i] = f[A_{i+1}]$. (Use the pigeonhole principle.)

1.7.7. Show that in any group of people there are at least two persons that have the same number of acquaintances within the group. (Use the pigeonhole principle.)

1.7.8. Suppose we try to prove, by an argument exactly parallel to the proof of Theorem 1.7.2, that the set of all *finite* subsets of $\mathbb{N}$ is uncountable. What goes wrong?

1.7.9. Give examples to show that the intersection of two countably infinite sets can be either finite or countably infinite, and that the intersection of two uncountable sets can be finite, countably infinite, or uncountable.

1.7.10. Show that the difference of an uncountable set and a countable set is uncountable.

1.7.11. Show that if S is any set, then there is a one-to-one function from S to 2^S, but not vice versa.

1.8.1. (a) Prove, using the definition of concatenation given in the text, that concatenation of strings is associative.

(b) Give an *inductive* definition of the concatenation of strings.

(c) Using the inductive definition from (b), prove that the concatenation of strings is associative.

1.8.2. Prove each of the following using the inductive definition of reversal given in the text.

(a) $(w^R)^R = w$ for any string w.

(b) If v is a substring of w, then v^R is a substring of w^R.

(c) $(w^i)^R = (w^R)^i$ for any string w and $i \geq 0$.

1.8.3. Let $\Sigma = \{a_1, \ldots, a_{26}\} = \{a, \ldots, z\}$, the Roman alphabet. Carefully define the binary relation $<$ on Σ^* such that $x < y$ if and only if x would precede y in a standard dictionary.

1.8.4. Show each of the following.

(a) $\{e\}^* = \{e\}$

(b) For any alphabet Σ and any $L \subseteq \Sigma^*$, $(L^*)^* = L^*$.

(c) If a and b are distinct symbols, then

$$\{a, b\}^* = \{a\}^*\{\{b\}\{a\}^*\}^*.$$

(d) If Σ is any alphabet, $e \in L_1 \subseteq \Sigma^*$, and $e \in L_2 \subseteq \Sigma^*$, then $(L_1\Sigma^*L_2)^* = \Sigma^*$.

(e) For any language L, $\varnothing L = L\varnothing = \varnothing$.

1.8.5. Give some examples of strings in, and not in, these sets, where $\Sigma = \{a, b\}$.

(a) $\{w\colon \text{for some } u \in \Sigma\Sigma,\ w = uu^Ru\}$

(b) $\{w\colon ww = www\}$

(c) $\{w\colon \text{for some } u \text{ and } v,\ uvw = wvu\}$

(d) $\{w\colon \text{for some } u,\ www = uu\}$

1.8.6. Under what circumstances is $L^+ = L^* - \{e\}$?

1.9.1. What language is represented by the regular expression $(((a^*a)b) \cup b)$? (Proceed as in Example 1.9.2.)

1.9.2. Rewrite each of these regular expressions as a simpler expression representing the same set.

(a) $\varnothing^* \cup a^* \cup b^* \cup (a \cup b)^*$

(b) $((a^*b^*)^*(b^*a^*)^*)^*$

(c) $(a^*b)^* \cup (b^*a)^*$

(d) $(a \cup b)^*a(a \cup b)^*$

1.9.3. Let $\Sigma = \{a, b\}$. Write regular expressions for the following sets:

(a) All strings in Σ^* with no more than three a's.

(b) All strings in Σ^* with a number of a's divisible by three.

(c) All strings in Σ^* with exactly one occurrence of the substring aaa.

1.9.4. Prove that if L is a regular language, then so is $L' = \{w\colon uw \in L \text{ for some string } u\}$. (Show how to construct a regular expression for L' from one for L.)

1.9.5. Which of the following are true? Explain.

(a) $baa \in a^*b^*a^*b^*$

(b) $b^*a^* \cap a^*b^* = a^* \cup b^*$

(c) $a^*b^* \cap c^*d^* = \varnothing$

(d) $abcd \in (a(cd)^*b)^*$

1.9.6. The **star height** $h(\alpha)$ of a regular expression α is defined by induction as follows.

$$h(\varnothing) = 0$$
$$h(a) = 0 \quad \text{for each } a \in \Sigma$$
$$h((\alpha \cup \beta)) = h((\alpha\beta)) = \text{the maximum of } h(\alpha) \text{ and } h(\beta)$$
$$h(\alpha^*) = h(\alpha) + 1$$

For example, if $\alpha = (((ab)^* \cup b^*)^* \cup a^*)$, then $h(\alpha) = 2$. Find, in each case, a regular expression which represents the same language and has star height as small as possible.

(a) $((abc)^*ab)^*$

(b) $(a(ab^*c)^*)^*$

(c) $(c(a^*b)^*)^*$

(d) $(a^* \cup b^* \cup ab)^*$

(e) $(abb^*a)^*$.

1.9.7. A regular expression is in **disjunctive normal form** if it is of the form $(\alpha_1 \cup \alpha_2 \cup \cdots \cup \alpha_n)$ for some $n \geq 1$, where none of the α_i contains an occurrence of $\cup$. Show that every regular language is represented by one in disjunctive normal form. (*Hint:* See Problem 1.8.4(c).)

REFERENCES

Chapter 8 of this text contains a more formal and complete introduction to the theory of propositions and connectives than the one given in Section 1.1.

An excellent source on informal set theory is the book

P. Halmos, *Naïve Set Theory*. Princeton, N.J.: D. Van Nostrand, 1960.

A more elementary introduction to the same subject is

J. Brauer, *Introduction to the Theory of Sets*. Englewood Cliffs, N.J.: Prentice-Hall, 1958.

A splendid book on mathematical induction is

G. Pólya, *Induction and Analogy in Mathematics*. Princeton, N.J.: Princeton University Press, 1954.

A number of examples of applications of the pigeonhole principle appear in the first chapter of

C. L. Liu, *Topics in Combinatorial Mathematics*. Buffalo, N.Y.: Mathematical Association of America, 1972.

Cantor's original diagonalization argument can be found in

G. Cantor, *Contributions to the Foundations of the Theory of Transfinite Numbers*. New York: Dover Publications, 1947. (Cantor's article first appeared in 1895, and is not easy reading.)

Fermat's Last Theorem is discussed in

O. Ore, *Number Theory and its History*. New York: McGraw-Hill, 1948.

Two advanced books on language theory are

A. Salomaa, *Formal Languages*. New York: Academic Press, 1973.

M. A. Harrison, *Introduction to Formal Language Theory*. Reading, Mass.: Addison-Wesley, 1978.

CHAPTER 2

FINITE AUTOMATA

2.1 DETERMINISTIC FINITE AUTOMATA

Modern computers are often viewed as having three main components: the central processing unit, memory, and input-output devices. The **central processing unit** is the "thinker"; it is responsible for such things as individual arithmetical computations and logical decisions based on particular data items. However, the amount of data the unit can handle at any one time is fixed forever by its design; in order to deal with more than this predetermined, limited amount of information, it must ship data back and forth, over time, to and from the memory and input-output devices. The **memory** may in practice be of several different kinds, such as magnetic core, semiconductor, bubble, disks, and tapes. The common feature is that the information capacity of the memory is vastly greater than what can be accommodated, at any one instant of time, in the central processing unit; therefore this memory is sometimes called **auxiliary**, to distinguish it from the limited storage that is part of the central processor. The memory can be expanded, in theory at least, without limit, by adding more core boxes, more tape drives, and so on. Finally, the **input-output** devices are the means by which information is communicated back and forth to the outside world: these are devices such as terminals, card readers, and lineprinters. Of course, tapes could be used for this purpose as well; a tape unit might then be regarded as an input-output device rather than a memory device.

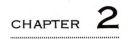

In this chapter we take up a severely restricted model of an actual computer called a **finite automaton**. It shares with a real computer the fact that its "central processor" is of fixed finite capacity, depending on its original design. However, beyond this fixed capacity to handle information, a finite automaton has *no auxiliary memory* at all. It receives its input as a string; the input string is delivered to it on an input tape. It delivers no output at all, except an indication of whether the input is considered acceptable. It is, in other words, a language recognition device, as described at the end of Chapter 1.

Such a simple computational model might at first be considered too trivial to merit serious study: of what use is a computer with no memory? But a finite automaton is not really without memory; it simply has a memory capacity that is fixed "at the factory" and cannot thereafter be expanded. That capacity may, however, be quite large. So we may view machines with many large auxiliary memory units as finite automata, so long as we are content not to require expansion of this memory later on.

Even if the machines with which we are actually concerned have expandable memories, as do real computers, we should first be sure that the theory of finite automata is well understood. It turns out that their theory is rich and elegant, and when we understand it we shall be in a better position to appreciate exactly what the addition of auxiliary memory accomplishes in the way of added computational power. In other words, finite automata are limited in strength, but they are a thoroughly understood subclass of more powerful computational models.

A further reason for studying finite automata is their applicability to the design of several common types of computer algorithms and programs. For example, the lexical analysis phase of a compiler is often based on the simulation of a finite automaton. (A **compiler** is a program for translating programs written in a higher-level programming language into machine language.) The problem of finding an occurrence of one string within another—for example, a particular word within a large text file—can also be solved efficiently by methods originating from the theory of finite automata. (See Problem 2.5.8.)

Let us now describe the operation of finite automata in more detail. The particular subspecies studied in this section are called **deterministic finite automata**, because their operation is completely determined by their input in a way described below. A deterministic finite automaton is, as we have said, a simple language recognition device.

Strings are fed into the device by means of an **input tape**, which is divided into squares, with one symbol inscribed in each tape square (see Figure 2–1). The main part of the machine itself is a "black box" with innards that can be, at any specified moment, in one of a finite number of distinct internal **states**. This black box—called the **finite control**—can sense what symbol is written at any position on the input tape by means of a movable **reading head**. Initially, the reading head is placed at the leftmost square of the tape and the finite control is set in a designated **initial state**. At regular intervals the

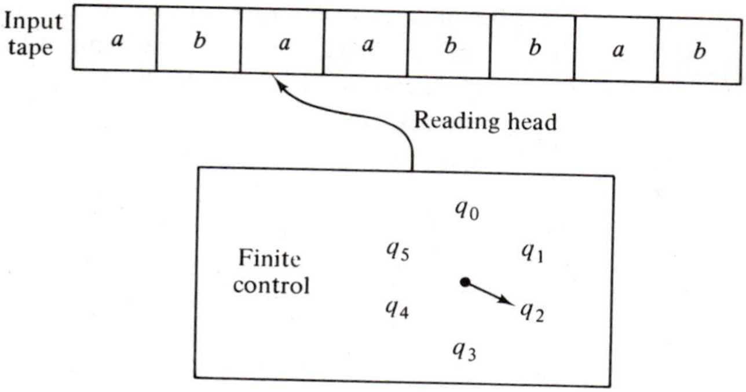

Figure 2–1

automaton reads one symbol from the input tape and then enters a new state that depends only on the current state and the symbol just read. After reading an input symbol, the reading head moves one square to the right on the input tape so that on the next move it will read the symbol in the next tape square. This process is repeated again and again; a symbol is read, the reading head moves to the right, and the state of the finite control changes. Eventually the reading head reaches the end of the input string. The automaton then indicates its approval or disapproval of what it has read by the state it is in at the end: if it winds up in one of a set of **final states** the input string is considered to be **accepted**. The **language accepted** by the machine is the set of strings it accepts.

When this informal account is boiled down to its mathematical essentials, the following formal version is obtained.

Definition 2.1.1

A **deterministic finite automaton** is a quintuple $M = (K, \Sigma, \delta, s, F)$ where

K is a finite set of **states**,

Σ is an alphabet,

$s \in K$ is the **initial state**,

$F \subseteq K$ is the set of **final states**,

and δ, the **transition function**, is a function from $K \times \Sigma$ to K.

The rules according to which the automaton M picks its next state are encoded into the transition function. Thus if M is in state $q \in K$ and the symbol read from the input tape is $\sigma \in \Sigma$, then $\delta(q, \sigma) \in K$ is the uniquely determined state to which M passes.

Having formalized the basic structure of a deterministic finite automaton, we must next render into mathematical terms the notion of a computation by an automaton on an input string. This will be, roughly speaking, a sequence of *configurations* that represent the status of the finite control, reading head, and input tape at successive moments. But since a deterministic finite automaton is not allowed to move its reading head back into the part of the input string that has already been read, the portion of the string to the left of the reading head cannot influence the future operation of the machine. Thus a configuration is determined by the current state and the unread part of the string being processed. In other words, a **configuration of a deterministic finite automaton** $(K, \Sigma, \delta, s, F)$ is any element of $K \times \Sigma^*$. For example, the configuration illustrated in Figure 2–1 is $(q_2, aabbab)$.

The binary relation $\vdash_M$ holds between two configurations of M if and only if the machine can pass from one to the other as a result of a single move. Thus if (q, w) and (q', w') are two configurations of M, then $(q, w) \vdash_M (q', w')$ if and only if $w = \sigma w'$ for some symbol $\sigma \in \Sigma$, and $\delta(q, \sigma) = q'$. In this case we say that (q, w) **yields** (q', w') **in one step**. Note that in fact $\vdash_M$ is a function from $K \times \Sigma^+$ to $K \times \Sigma^*$; that is, for every configuration except those of the form (q, e), there is a uniquely determined next configuration. A configuration of the form (q, e) signifies that M has consumed all its input, and hence its operation ceases at this point.

We denote the reflexive, transitive closure of $\vdash_M$ by $\vdash_M^*$; $(q, w) \vdash_M^* (q', w')$ is read, (q, w) **yields** (q', w') (after some number, possibly zero, of steps). A string $w \in \Sigma^*$ is said to be **accepted** by M if and only if there is a state $q \in F$ such that $(s, w) \vdash_M^* (q, e)$. Finally, **the language accepted by** M, $L(M)$, is the set of all strings accepted by M.

Example 2.1.1

Consider the deterministic finite automaton $M = (K, \Sigma, \delta, s, F)$, where

$$K = \{q_0, q_1\}$$
$$\Sigma = \{a, b\}$$
$$s = q_0$$
$$F = \{q_0\}$$

and δ is the function tabulated below.

q	σ	$\delta(q, \sigma)$
q_0	a	q_0
q_0	b	q_1
q_1	a	q_1
q_1	b	q_0

Then $L(M)$ is the set of all strings in $\{a, b\}^*$ that have an even number of b's. For M passes from state q_0 to q_1 or from q_1 back to q_0 when a b is read, but M essentially ignores a's, always remaining in its current state when an a is read. Thus M counts b's modulo 2, and since q_0 (the initial state) is also the sole final state, M accepts a string if and only if the number of b's is even.

If M is given the input *aabba*, its initial configuration is $(q_0, aabba)$. Then

$$\begin{aligned}(q_0, aabba) &\vdash_M (q_0, abba)\\ &\vdash_M (q_0, bba)\\ &\vdash_M (q_1, ba)\\ &\vdash_M (q_0, a)\\ &\vdash_M (q_0, e).\end{aligned}$$

Therefore $(q_0, aabba) \vdash_M^* (q_0, e)$ and so *aabba* is accepted by M.

The tabular representation of the transition function used in this example is not the clearest description of a machine. We generally use a more convenient graphical representation called the **state diagram** (Figure 2–2). The state diagram is a directed graph, with certain additional information incorporated into the picture. States are represented by nodes, and there is an arrow labeled with σ from node q to q' whenever $\delta(q, \sigma) = q'$. Final states are indicated by double circles, and the initial state is shown by a $>$. Figure 2–2 shows the state diagram of the deterministic finite automaton of Example 2.1.1.

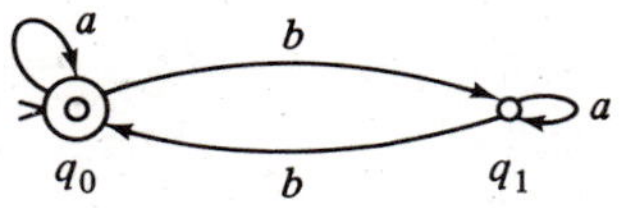

Figure 2–2

Example 2.1.2

Let us design a deterministic finite automaton M that accepts the language $L(M) = \{w: w \in \{a, b\}^* \text{ and } w \text{ does not contain three consecutive } b\text{'s}\}$. We let $M = (K, \Sigma, \delta, s, F)$, where

$$\begin{aligned}K &= \{q_0, q_1, q_2, q_3\}\\ \Sigma &= \{a, b\}\\ s &= q_0\\ F &= \{q_0, q_1, q_2\}\end{aligned}$$

and δ is given by the following table.

q	σ	$\delta(q, \sigma)$
q_0	a	q_0
q_0	b	q_1
q_1	a	q_0
q_1	b	q_2
q_2	a	q_0
q_2	b	q_3
q_3	a	q_3
q_3	b	q_3

The state diagram is shown in Figure 2–3. To see that M does indeed accept the specified language, note that as long as three consecutive b's have not been read, M is in state q_i (where i is 0, 1, or 2) immediately after reading a run of i consecutive b's that either began the input string or was preceded by an a. In particular, whenever an a is read and M is in state q_0, q_1, or q_2, M returns to its initial state q_0. States q_0, q_1, and q_2 are all final, so any input string not containing three consecutive b's will be accepted. However, a run of three b's will drive M to state q_3, which is not final, and M will then remain in this state regardless of the symbols in the rest of the input string. State q_3 is said to be a *dead* state, and if M reaches state q_3 it is said to be *trapped* since no further input can enable it to escape from this state.

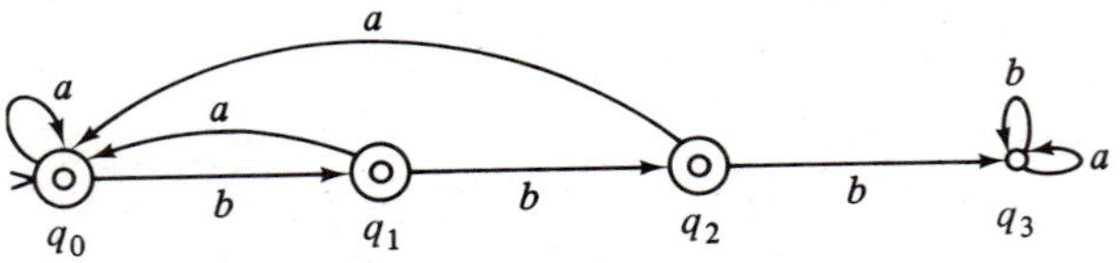

Figure 2–3

2.2 NONDETERMINISTIC FINITE AUTOMATA

In this section we add a powerful, though at first not intuitive, feature to finite automata. This feature is called **nondeterminism**, and is essentially the ability to change states in a way that is only *partially* determined by the current state and input symbol. That is, we shall now permit *several* possible "next states" for a given combination of current state and input symbol. The automaton, as it reads the input string, may choose at each step to go into any one of these legal next states; the choice is not determined by anything in our model, and is therefore said to be *nondeterministic*. On the other hand, the choice is not wholly unlimited either; only those next states that are legal from a given state with a given input symbol can be chosen.

Though nondeterminism is a feature we do not normally associate with real computers, it arises naturally as an extension of the behavior of deterministic finite automata and in some cases greatly simplifies the description of these automata. Moreover, we shall see below that nondeterminism is an inessential feature of finite automata: every nondeterministic finite automaton is equivalent to a deterministic finite automaton. Thus we shall profit from the greater flexibility of nondeterministic finite automata when we wish to design language recognizers without actually extending the class of languages we are able to describe.

To see that a nondeterministic finite automaton can be a much more convenient device to design than a deterministic finite automaton, consider the language $L = (ab \cup aba)^*$, which is accepted by the deterministic finite automaton illustrated in Figure 2–4. Even with the diagram, it takes a few

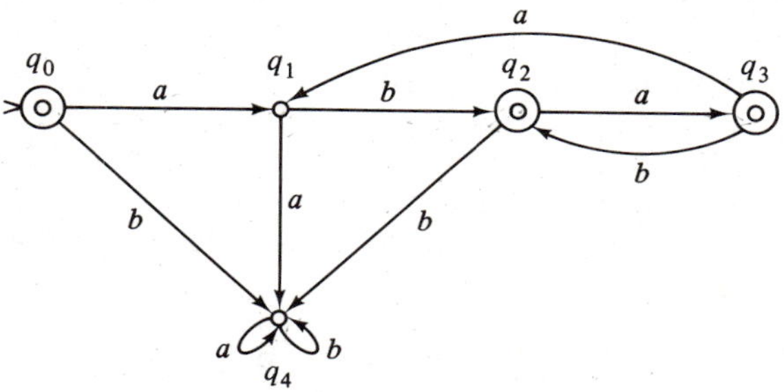

Figure 2-4

moments to ascertain that a deterministic finite automaton is shown; one must check that there are exactly two arrows leaving each node, one labeled a and one labeled b. And some thought is needed to convince oneself that the language accepted by this fairly complex device is the simple language $(ab \cup aba)^*$. One might hope to find a simpler deterministic finite automaton accepting L, but it can be shown formally that this is impossible. However, L is accepted by the simple nondeterministic device shown in Figure 2–5.

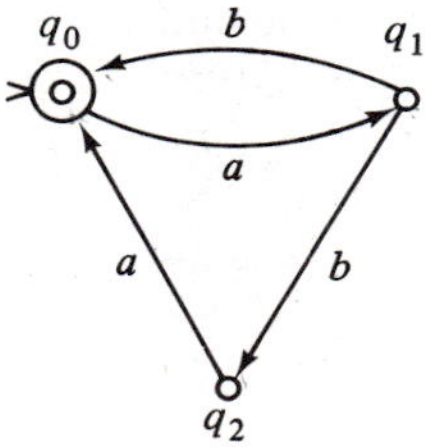

Figure 2–5

When this device is in state q_1 and the input symbol is b, there are two possible next states, q_0 and q_2. Thus Figure 2–5 does not represent a deterministic finite automaton. Nevertheless, there is a natural way to interpret the diagram as a device accepting L. A string is accepted if there is *some* way to get from the initial state (q_0) to a final state (in this case, q_0) while following arrows labeled with the symbols of the string. For example *ab* is accepted by going from q_0 to q_1 to q_0; *aba* is accepted by going from q_0 to q_1 to q_2 to q_0. Of course, the device might guess wrong and go from q_0 to q_1 to q_0 to q_1 on input *aba*, winding up in a nonfinal state; but this does not matter, since there is *some* way of getting from the initial to a final state with this input. On the other hand, the input *abb* is *not* accepted, since there is no way to get from q_0 back to q_0 while reading this string.

Indeed, you will notice that from q_0 there is no state to be entered when the input is b. This is another feature of nondeterministic finite automata: just as from some states with some inputs there may be several possible next states, with other combinations of states and input symbols there may be no possible moves.

Sometimes it is convenient to allow state diagrams in which arrows can be labeled either by symbols in Σ or by the empty string e. For example, the device of Figure 2–6 accepts the same language L. From q_2 this machine can

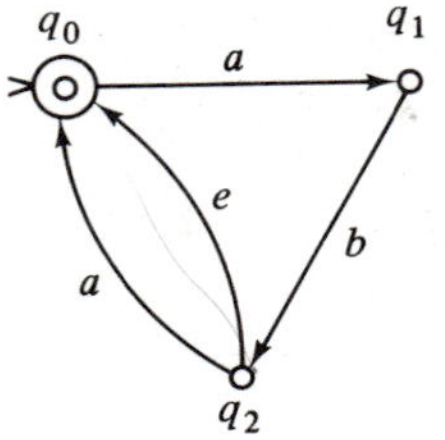

Figure 2–6

return to q_0 either by reading an a or immediately, without consuming any input.

Once we have allowed arrows labeled by e, we may as well generalize our diagrams in the other direction and allow as a label any string in Σ^*. Thus, the language L is also accepted by the one-state device of Figure 2–7.

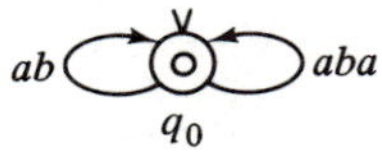

Figure 2–7

The devices illustrated in Figures 2–5, 2–6, and 2–7 are all instances of the following general type.

Definition 2.2.1

A **nondeterministic finite automaton** is a quintuple $M = (K, \Sigma, \Delta, s, F)$, where

K is a finite set of **states,**

Σ is an alphabet,

$s \in K$ is the **initial state,**

$F \subseteq K$ is the set of **final states,**

and Δ, the **transition relation**, is a finite subset of $K \times \Sigma^* \times K$.

The significance of a triple (q, u, p) being in Δ is that M, when in state q, may consume a string u from the input string and enter state p. In other words, $(q, u, p) \in \Delta$ if and only if an arrow $\underset{q}{\circ}\xrightarrow{\;u\;}\underset{p}{\circ}$ appears in the state diagram of M. Each triple $(q, u, p) \in \Delta$ is called a **transition** of M. In keeping with the idea that M is a *finite* device, we have insisted that Δ be a finite set of transitions, even though $K \times \Sigma^* \times K$ is an infinite set.

The formal definitions of computations by nondeterministic finite automata are very similar to those for deterministic finite automata. A **configuration** of M is, once again, an element of $K \times \Sigma^*$. The relation $\vdash_M$ between configurations (**yields in one step**) is defined as follows: $(q, w) \vdash_M (q', w')$ if and only if there is a $u \in \Sigma^*$ such that $w = uw'$ and $(q, u, q') \in \Delta$. Note that $\vdash_M$ need not be a function; for some configurations (q, w), there may be several pairs (q', w')—or none at all—such that $(q, w) \vdash_M (q', w')$. As before, $\vdash_M^*$ is the reflexive, transitive closure of $\vdash_M$, and a string $w \in \Sigma^*$ is **accepted** by M if and only if there is a state $q \in F$ such that $(s, w) \vdash_M^* (q, e)$. Finally $L(M)$, the **language accepted** by M, is the set of all strings accepted by M.

Example 2.2.1

Figure 2–8 shows one of several possible nondeterministic finite automata that accept the set of all strings containing an occurrence of the pattern bab or of the pattern $baab$. Formally, this machine is $(K, \Sigma, \Delta, s, F)$, where

$$K = \{q_0, q_1, q_2, q_3, q_4\}$$

$$\Sigma = \{a, b\}$$

$$s = q_0$$

$$F = \{q_4\}$$

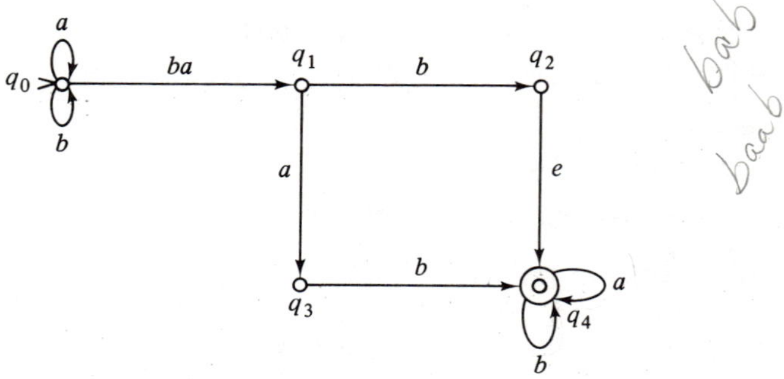

Figure 2–8

and

$$\Delta = \{(q_0, a, q_0), (q_0, b, q_0), (q_0, ba, q_1), (q_1, b, q_2), (q_1, a, q_3), (q_2, e, q_4), (q_3, b, q_4), (q_4, a, q_4), (q_4, b, q_4)\}.$$

When M is given the string *baababaab* as input, several different sequences of moves may ensue. For example, M may wind up in the nonfinal state q_0 in case the only transitions used are (q_0, a, q_0) and (q_0, b, q_0).

$$\begin{aligned}(q_0, baababaab) &\vdash_M (q_0, aababaab)\\ &\vdash_M (q_0, ababaab)\\ &\quad\vdots\\ &\vdash_M (q_0, e)\end{aligned}$$

The same input string may drive M from state q_0 to the final state q_4, and indeed may do so in three different ways. One of these ways is the following.

$$\begin{aligned}(q_0, baababaab) &\vdash_M (q_1, ababaab)\\ &\vdash_M (q_3, babaab)\\ &\vdash_M (q_4, abaab)\\ &\vdash_M (q_4, baab)\\ &\vdash_M (q_4, aab)\\ &\vdash_M (q_4, ab)\\ &\vdash_M (q_4, b)\\ &\vdash_M (q_4, e)\end{aligned}$$

Since a string is accepted by a nondeterministic finite automaton if and only if there is *at least one* sequence of moves leading to a final state, it follows that $baababaab \in L(M)$.

Observe that a deterministic finite automaton is just a special type of a nondeterministic finite automaton: In a deterministic finite automaton, it happens that the transition *relation* $\Delta \subseteq K \times \Sigma^* \times K$ is in fact a *function* from $K \times \Sigma$ to K. In other words, a nondeterministic finite automaton $(K, \Sigma, \Delta, s, F)$ is really a deterministic finite automaton provided that the following condition is satisfied: If $(q, u, q') \in \Delta$ then $|u| = 1$, and for each $q \in K$ and $\sigma \in \Sigma$, there is a unique $q' \in K$ such that $(q, \sigma, q') \in \Delta$.

As in the case of deterministic finite automata, the state of the finite control at any point in a computation is determined only by the portion of the input already read, and not at all by the portion of the input that has not yet been read. This fact makes it possible to combine computations in a way described formally by the next lemma.

Lemma 2.2.1. *Let $M = (K, \Sigma, \Delta, s, F)$ be a nondeterministic finite automaton; let $q, r \in K$ and $x, y \in \Sigma^*$. Then $(q, xy) \vdash_M^* (r, e)$ if, for some $p \in K$, $(q, x) \vdash_M^* (p, e)$ and $(p, y) \vdash_M^* (r, e)$.*

Proof. Suppose that $(q, x) \vdash_M^* (p, e)$ and $(p, y) \vdash_M^* (r, e)$. Since $(q, x) \vdash_M^* (p, e)$, there are $n \geq 0$, $q_0, \ldots, q_n \in K$, and $x_0, \ldots, x_n \in \Sigma^*$, such that

$$(q, x) = (q_0, x_0) \vdash_M (q_1, x_1) \vdash_M \cdots \vdash_M (q_n, x_n) = (p, e).$$

We claim that for $i = 0, \ldots, n-1$, $(q_i, x_i y) \vdash_M (q_{i+1}, x_{i+1} y)$. Since $(q_i, x_i) \vdash_M (q_{i+1}, x_{i+1})$, by definition of $\vdash_M$ there is a string $u_i \in \Sigma^*$ such that $x_i = u_i x_{i+1}$ and $(q_i, u_i, q_{i+1}) \in \Delta$. Also, $x_i y = u_i x_{i+1} y$, so $(q_i, x_i y) \vdash_M (q_{i+1}, x_{i+1} y)$, by definition of $\vdash_M$.

Therefore,

$$(q, xy) = (q_0, x_0 y) \vdash_M (q_1, x_1 y) \vdash_M \cdots \vdash_M (q_n, x_n y) = (p, y)$$

so $(q, xy) \vdash_M^* (p, y)$. Since $(p, y) \vdash_M^* (r, e)$ and $\vdash_M^*$ is transitive, $(q, xy) \vdash_M^* (r, e)$ as was to be shown. ■

2.3 EQUIVALENCE OF DETERMINISTIC AND NONDETERMINISTIC FINITE AUTOMATA

We next show, as promised earlier, that although nondeterministic finite automata appear to be more general than deterministic finite automata, they are nevertheless no more powerful in terms of the languages they accept: A nondeterministic finite automaton can always be converted into a deterministic one.

Definition 2.3.1

Finite automata M_1 and M_2 are said to be **equivalent** if and only if $L(M_1) = L(M_2)$.

Thus two automata are considered to be equivalent if they accept the same language, even though they may "use different methods" to do so. For example, the automata of Figures 2–4, 2–5, 2–6, and 2–7 are all equivalent.

Theorem 2.3.1. *For each nondeterministic finite automaton, there is an equivalent deterministic finite automaton.*

Proof. Let $M = (K, \Sigma, \Delta, s, F)$ be a nondeterministic finite automaton. In order to transform M into an equivalent deterministic finite automaton, various possibilities must be eliminated: transitions $(q, u, q') \in \Delta$ such that $u = e$ or such that $|u| > 1$; transitions that are missing; and multiple transitions that may be applicable to the same configuration. It is relatively easy to eliminate transitions (q, u, q') with $|u| > 1$. In essence, we introduce new states such as those in Figure 2–9(b) to replace an arrow in the state diagram such as that shown in Figure 2–9(a). Formally, if $(q, \sigma_1 \ldots \sigma_k, q')$

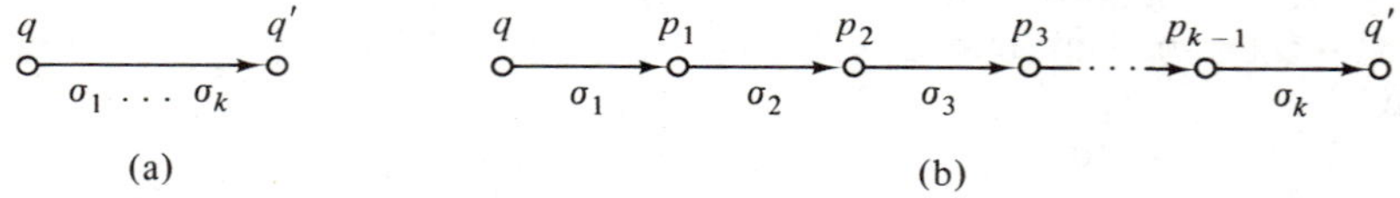

Figure 2–9

is a transition of M and $\sigma_1, \ldots, \sigma_k \in \Sigma$, $k \geq 2$, then add new (nonfinal) states $p_1, \ldots, p_{k-1}$ to K and new transitions $(q, \sigma_1, p_1), (p_1, \sigma_2, p_2), \ldots, (p_{k-1}, \sigma_k, q')$ to Δ. Let $M' = (K', \Sigma, \Delta', s', F')$ be the nondeterministic finite automaton that results from M when this transformation is carried out for each transition (q, u, q') of M such that $|u| > 1$. It should be obvious that M' and M are equivalent, and that $|u| \leq 1$ for each transition (q, u, q') of M'.

Example 2.3.1

When this transformation is carried out on the nondeterministic finite automaton of Figure 2–10(a), the nondeterministic finite automaton of Figure 2–10(b) results.

We shall now construct a deterministic finite automaton $M'' = (K'', \Sigma, \delta'', s'', F'')$ equivalent to M'; this construction will suffice to establish the theorem. The key idea is to view a nondeterministic finite automaton as occupying, at any moment, not a single state but a *set* of states: namely, all the states that can be reached from the initial state by means of the input consumed thus far. Thus if M' had five states $\{q_0, \ldots, q_4\}$ and, after reading a certain input string, it could be in state q_0, q_2, or q_3 but not q_1 or q_4, its state

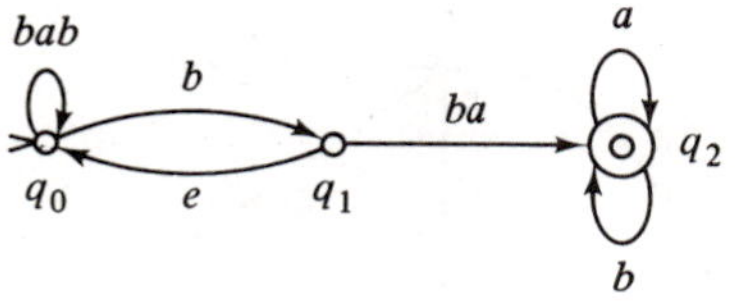

(a)

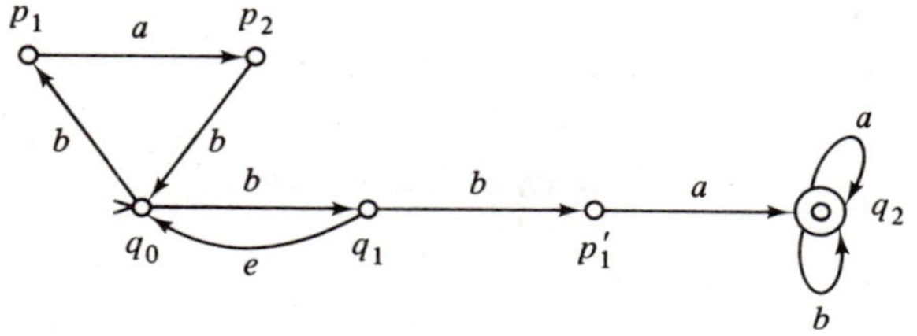

(b)

Figure 2–10

could be considered to be the set $\{q_0, q_2, q_3\}$, rather than an undetermined member of that set. And if the next input symbol could drive M' from q_0 to q_1 or q_2, from q_2 to q_0, and from q_3 to q_2, then the next state of M' could be considered to be the set $\{q_0, q_1, q_2\}$.

The construction formalizes this idea. The set of states of M'' will be $2^{K'}$, the power set of the set of states of M'. The set of final states of M'' will consist of all those subsets of K' that contain at least one final state of M'. The definition of the transition function of M'' will be slightly more complicated. The basic idea is that a move of M'' on reading an input symbol $\sigma \in \Sigma$ imitates a move of M' on input symbol σ, followed by some number of moves of M' on which no input is read. To formalize this idea we need a special definition.

For any state $q \in K'$, let $E(q)$ be the set of all states of M' that are reachable from state q without reading any input. That is,

$$E(q) = \{p \in K' : (q, e) \vdash_{M'}^{*} (p, e)\}.$$

If M' moves without consuming any of its input, its operation does not depend on what that input is. So another way to define $E(q)$ would be to pick *any* string $w \in \Sigma^*$ and write

$$E(q) = \{p \in K' : (q, w) \vdash_{M'}^{*} (p, w)\}.$$

Example 2.3.2

In the automaton of Figure 2–11, $E(q_0) = \{q_0, q_1, q_2, q_3\}$, $E(q_1) = \{q_1, q_2, q_3\}$, $E(q_2) = \{q_2\}$, $E(q_3) = \{q_3\}$, and $E(q_4) = \{q_3, q_4\}$.

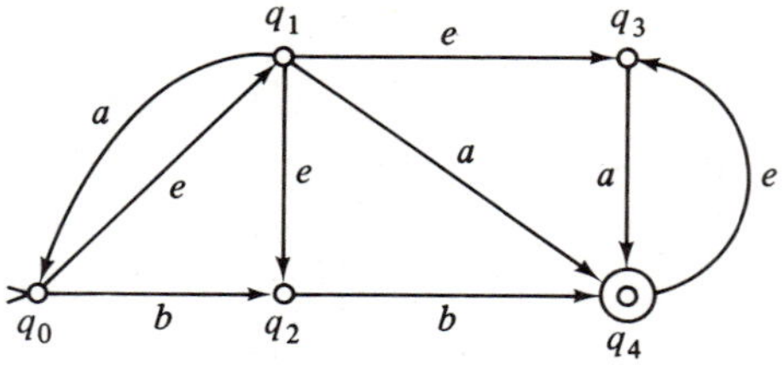

Figure 2–11

Now define

$$M'' = (K'', \Sigma, \delta'', s'', F''),$$

where

$$K'' = 2^{K'}$$
$$s'' = E(s')$$
$$F'' = \{Q \subseteq K' : Q \cap F' \neq \varnothing\}$$

and for each $Q \subseteq K'$ and each symbol $\sigma \in \Sigma$, $\delta''(Q, \sigma) = \bigcup \{E(p): p \in K'$ and $(q, \sigma, p) \in \Delta'$ for some $q \in Q\}$.

For example, if M' is the automaton of Figure 2–11, then $s'' = E(q_0) = \{q_0, q_1, q_2, q_3\}$. Since $(q_1, a, q_0) \in \Delta'$ and $(q_1, a, q_4) \in \Delta'$, it follows that $\delta''(\{q_1\}, a) = E(q_0) \cup E(q_4) = \{q_0, q_1, q_2, q_3, q_4\}$. Similarly, $(q_0, b, q_2) \in \Delta'$ and $(q_2, b, q_4) \in \Delta'$ so $\delta''(\{q_0, q_2\}, b) = E(q_2) \cup E(q_4) = \{q_2, q_3, q_4\}$.

It remains to show that M'' is deterministic and equivalent to M'. The demonstration that M'' is deterministic is straightforward since δ'' is single valued and well defined by the way it was constructed. (It is quite possible that $\delta''(Q, \sigma) = \varnothing$ for some $Q \in K''$, $\sigma \in \Sigma$; indeed $\delta''(\varnothing, \sigma) = \varnothing$ for each $\sigma \in \Sigma$. But $\varnothing$ is just another member of K'' in this context.)

We now claim that for any string $w \in \Sigma^*$, and any states $q, p \in K'$,

$$(q, w) \vdash^*_{M'} (p, e) \quad \text{if and only if} \quad (E(q), w) \vdash^*_{M''} (P, e)$$

for some set P containing p. From this the theorem will follow easily. To show that M' and M'' are equivalent, consider any string $w \in \Sigma^*$. Then $w \in L(M')$ if and only if $(s', w) \vdash^*_{M'} (f', e)$ for some $f' \in F'$ (by definition) and if and only if $(E(s'), w) \vdash^*_{M''} (Q, e)$ for some Q containing f' (by the claim); in other words, if and only if $(s'', w) \vdash^*_{M''} (Q, e)$ for some $Q \in F''$. The last condition is the definition of $w \in L(M'')$.

We prove the claim by induction on $|w|$.

Basis Step. For $|w| = 0$—that is, for $w = e$—we must show that $(q, e) \vdash^*_{M'} (p, e)$ if and only if $(E(q), e) \vdash^*_{M''} (P, e)$ for some set P containing p. The first statement is equivalent to saying that $p \in E(q)$. Since M'' is deterministic and must therefore read an input symbol on every move, the second statement is equivalent to saying that $P = E(q)$ and P contains p, that is, $p \in E(q)$. This completes the proof of the basis step.

Induction Hypothesis. Suppose that the claim is true for all strings w of length k or less for some $k \geq 0$.

Induction Step. We prove the claim for any string w of length $k + 1$. Let $w = va$, where $a \in \Sigma$ and $v \in \Sigma^*$.

First suppose that $(q, w) \vdash_{M'}^{*} (p, e)$. Then there are states r_1 and r_2 such that

$$(q, va) \vdash_{M'}^{*} (r_1, a) \vdash_{M'} (r_2, e) \vdash_{M'}^{*} (p, e).$$

That is, M' reaches state p from state q by some number of moves during which input v is read, followed by one move during which input a is read, followed by some number of moves during which no input is read. Since $(q, va) \vdash_{M'}^{*} (r_1, a)$, then $(q, v) \vdash_{M'}^{*} (r_1, e)$, and since $|v| = k$, by the induction hypothesis $(E(q), v) \vdash_{M''}^{*} (R_1, e)$ for some set R_1 containing r_1. Since $(r_1, a) \vdash_{M'} (r_2, e)$, $(r_1, a, r_2) \in \Delta'$; then by the construction of M'', $E(r_2) \subseteq \delta''(R_1, a)$. But since $(r_2, e) \vdash_{M'}^{*} (p, e)$, $p \in E(r_2)$ and therefore $p \in \delta''(R_1, a)$. Therefore $(R_1, a) \vdash_{M''} (P, e)$ for some P containing p and $(E(q), va) \vdash_{M''}^{*} (R_1, a) \vdash_{M''} (P, e)$.

Now suppose that $(E(q), va) \vdash_{M''}^{*} (R_1, a) \vdash_{M''} (P, e)$ for some P such that $p \in P$ and some R_1 such that $\delta''(R_1, a) = P$. Now by the definition of δ'', $\delta''(R_1, a)$ is the union of all sets $E(r_2)$, where for some state $r_1 \in R_1$, (r_1, a, r_2) is a transition of M'. Since $p \in P = \delta''(R_1, a)$, there is some particular r_2 such that $p \in E(r_2)$ and, for some $r_1 \in R_1$, (r_1, a, r_2) is a transition of M'. Then $(r_2, e) \vdash_{M'}^{*} (p, e)$ by the definition of $E(r_2)$. Also, by the induction hypothesis, $(q, v) \vdash_{M'}^{*} (r_1, e)$, and therefore $(q, va) \vdash_{M'}^{*} (r_1, a) \vdash_{M'} (r_2, e) \vdash_{M'}^{*} (p, e)$.

This completes the proof of the claim and the theorem. ■

Example 2.3.3

This example continues Example 2.3.2. Let M' be the automaton of Figure 2–11. Since M' has 5 states, M'' will have $2^5 = 32$ states. However, only a few of these states will be relevant to the operation of M''—namely, those states that can be reached from state s'' by reading some input string. We shall build this part of M'' by starting from s'' and introducing a new state only when it is needed as the value of $\delta''(q, \sigma)$ for some state q already introduced and some $\sigma \in \Sigma$.

We have already defined $E(q)$ for each state q of M'. Since $s'' = E(q_0) = \{q_0, q_1, q_2, q_3\}$,

$$(q_1, a, q_0)$$
$$(q_1, a, q_4)$$
$$(q_3, a, q_4)$$

are all the transitions (q, a, p) for some $q \in s''$. It follows that

$$\delta''(s'', a) = E(q_0) \cup E(q_4) = \{q_0, q_1, q_2, q_3, q_4\}.$$

Similarly

$$(q_0, b, q_2)$$
$$(q_2, b, q_4)$$

are all the transitions (q, b, p) for some $q \in s''$, so

$$\delta''(s'', b) = E(q_2) \cup E(q_4) = \{q_2, q_3, q_4\}.$$

Repeating this calculation for the newly introduced states, we have the following.

$$\delta''(\{q_0, q_1, q_2, q_3, q_4\}, a) = \{q_0, q_1, q_2, q_3, q_4\}$$
$$\delta''(\{q_0, q_1, q_2, q_3, q_4\}, b) = \{q_2, q_3, q_4\}$$
$$\delta''(\{q_2, q_3, q_4\}, a) = E(q_4) = \{q_3, q_4\}$$
$$\delta''(\{q_2, q_3, q_4\}, b) = E(q_4) = \{q_3, q_4\}$$

Finally,

$$\delta''(\{q_3, q_4\}, a) = E(q_4) = \{q_3, q_4\}$$
$$\delta''(\{q_3, q_4\}, b) = \varnothing$$

and

$$\delta''(\varnothing, a) = \delta''(\varnothing, b) = \varnothing.$$

The relevant part of M'' is illustrated in Figure 2–12. F'', the set of final states, contains each set of states of which q_4 is a member, since q_4 is the sole member of F'; so in the illustration, the three states $\{q_0, q_1, q_2, q_3, q_4\}$, $\{q_2, q_3, q_4\}$, and $\{q_3, q_4\}$ of M'' are final.

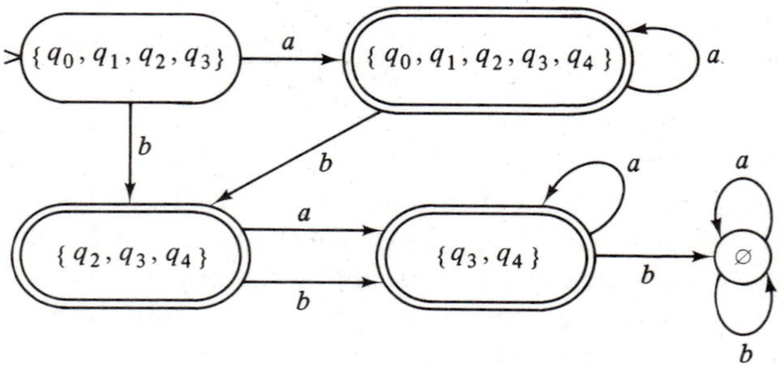

Figure 2–12

2.4 PROPERTIES OF THE LANGUAGES ACCEPTED BY FINITE AUTOMATA

The main result of the last section was that the class of languages accepted by finite automata remains the same even if a new and seemingly powerful feature—nondeterminism—is allowed. In this section we shall show that the class of languages accepted by finite automata is *closed* under certain operations: that is, we show that certain ways of combining languages in the class yield further languages in the class. These results are of interest for several reasons. First, they show that the class of languages accepted by finite automata has a sort of stability: Natural operations for constructing languages from others do not lead outside the class. Second, these results are established by using a very important and a powerful proof technique: **simulation**. The general idea behind a simulation proof is to construct, from one or more automata of one type, an automaton which imitates, to a certain extent, the behavior of the others, perhaps combining, varying, or modifying their behavior to meet certain purposes. (We have already seen one simulation theorem, Theorem 2.3.1, in which we showed how to simulate a nondeterministic finite automaton by a deterministic one.) Third, the results of this section are needed in the next section to establish the relation between finite automata and regular expressions. And finally, since in every case we give explicit constructions, it will follow that algorithms exist for answering many natural questions about finite automata, such as the question of whether two finite automata accept the same language.

Throughout this section, Σ will be a fixed alphabet. Our main result is the following.

Theorem 2.4.1. *The class of languages accepted by finite automata is closed under:*

(a) *union;*

(b) *concatenation;*

(c) *Kleene star;*

(d) *complementation;*

(e) *intersection.*

Proof. In each case we show how to construct an automaton that accepts the appropriate language from one or two given automata.

(a) *Union.* Let L_1 and L_2 be languages accepted by nondeterministic automata M_1 and M_2, respectively. Let $M_1 = (K_1, \Sigma, \Delta_1, s_1, F_1)$ and $M_2 = (K_2, \Sigma, \Delta_2, s_2, F_2)$. Without loss of generality, we may assume that K_1 and K_2 are disjoint sets.

We construct a nondeterministic finite automaton M that accepts $L(M_1) \cup L(M_2)$ as follows (see Figure 2–13): $M = (K, \Sigma, \Delta, s, F)$, where s is a new state not in K_1 or K_2,

$$K = K_1 \cup K_2 \cup \{s\}$$

$$F = F_1 \cup F_2$$

$$\Delta = \Delta_1 \cup \Delta_2 \cup \{(s, e, s_1), (s, e, s_2)\}.$$

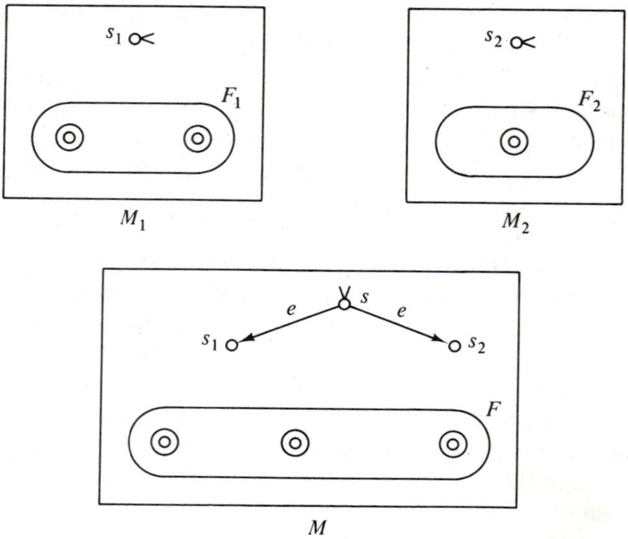

Figure 2–13

That is, M begins any computation by nondeterministically choosing to enter either the initial state of M_1 or the initial state of M_2, and thereafter, M imitates either M_1 or M_2. Formally, if $w \in \Sigma^*$, then $(s, w) \vdash_M^* (q, e)$ for some $q \in F$ if and only if either $(s_1, w) \vdash_{M_1}^* (q, e)$ for some $q \in F_1$ or $(s_2, w) \vdash_{M_2}^* (q, e)$ for some $q \in F_2$. Hence $L(M) = L(M_1) \cup L(M_2)$.

(b) *Concatenation.* Again, let M_1 and M_2 be nondeterministic finite automata; we construct a nondeterministic finite automaton M such that $L(M) = L(M_1) \circ L(M_2)$. The construction is shown schematically in Figure 2–14; M operates by simulating M_1 for a while, and then "jumping" nondeterministically from a final state of M_1 to the initial state of M_2. Thereafter, M imitates M_2.

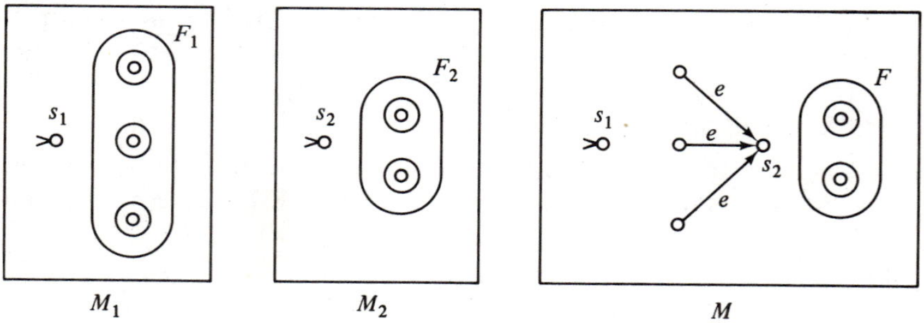

Figure 2–14

Formally, let $M_1 = (K_1, \Sigma, \Delta_1, s_1, F_1)$ and $M_2 = (K_2, \Sigma, \Delta_2, s_2, F_2)$, where K_1 and K_2 are disjoint. Then $M = (K, \Sigma, \Delta, s, F)$ where

$$K = K_1 \cup K_2$$

$$s = s_1$$

$$F = F_2$$

and

$$\Delta = \Delta_1 \cup \Delta_2 \cup (F_1 \times \{e\} \times \{s_2\}).$$

Then $(s, w) \vdash_M^* (q, e)$ for some $q \in F$ if and only if there are $w_1, w_2 \in \Sigma^*$ and there is a $p \in F_1$ such that $w = w_1 w_2$ and $(s_1, w_1) \vdash_{M_1}^* (p, e)$ and $(s_2, w_2) \vdash_{M_2}^* (q, e)$. Hence $L(M) = L(M_1) \circ L(M_2)$.

(c) *Kleene star*. Let M_1 be a nondeterministic finite automaton; we construct a nondeterministic finite automaton M such that $L(M) = L(M_1)^*$. The construction is similar to that for concatenation, and is illustrated in Figure 2–15. M consists of the states of M_1 and all the transitions of M_1; any final state of M_1 is a final state of M. In addition, M has a new initial state s_1'. This new initial state is also final, so that e is accepted; from it, state s_1 can be reached on input e, so that the operation of M_1 can be initiated after M has been started in state s_1'. Finally, transitions on e input are added from each final state of M_1 back to s_1; once a string in $L(M_1)$ has been read, computation can resume from the initial state of M_1.

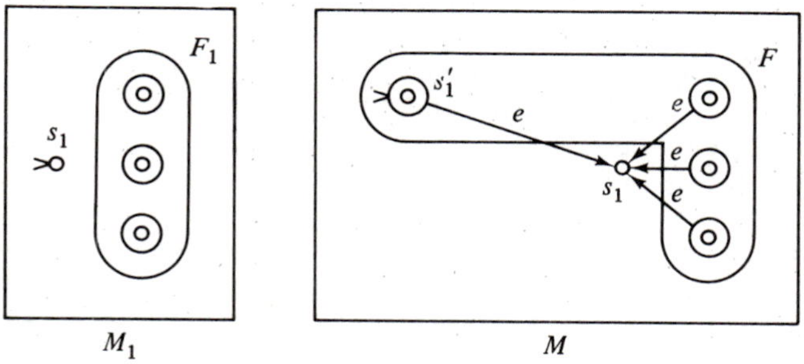

Figure 2–15

Formally, if $M_1 = (K_1, \Sigma, \Delta_1, s_1, F_1)$, then $M = (K, \Sigma, \Delta, s, F)$, where

$$K = K_1 \cup \{s_1'\}$$

$$s = s_1' \text{ is a new state not in } K_1$$

$$F = F_1 \cup \{s_1'\}$$

$$\Delta = \Delta_1 \cup (F \times \{e\} \times \{s_1\}).$$

It follows by inspection of M that if $w \in L(M)$, then either $w = e$ or $w = w_1 \ldots w_k$ for some $k \geq 1$, where for $i = 1, \ldots, k$ there is an $f_i \in F$ such that $(s_1, w_i) \vdash^*_{M_1} (f_i, e)$. Hence $w \in L(M_1)^*$. On the other hand, if $w \in L(M_1)^*$, then either $w = e$ or $w = w_1 \ldots w_k$ for some $w_1, \ldots, w_k \in L(M_1)$; in the former case, $w \in L(M)$ since s'_1 is final, and in the latter case, $w \in L(M)$ since for some $f_1, \ldots, f_k \in F_1$, $(s'_1, w_1 \ldots w_k) \vdash_M (s_1, w_1 \ldots w_k) \vdash^*_M (f_1, w_2 \ldots w_k) \vdash_M (s_1, w_2 \ldots w_k) \vdash^*_M (f_2, w_3 \ldots w_k) \vdash_M (s_1, w_3 \ldots w_k) \vdash^*_M \ldots \vdash^*_M (f_k, e)$. So $L(M) = L(M_1)^*$.

Could the same purpose be accomplished simply by making s_1 final, adding arrows back from the members of F_1 to s_1, and not introducing the new initial state s'_1? If s_1 is a final state of M_1, this procedure has the desired effect, but not if s_1 is not a final state of M_1. We leave it to the reader to see why (see Problem 2.4.2).

(d) *Complementation.* Let $M = (K, \Sigma, \delta, s, F)$ be a *deterministic* finite automaton. Then the complementary language $\Sigma^* - L(M)$ is accepted by the deterministic finite automaton

$$\bar{M} = (K, \Sigma, \delta, s, K - F).$$

That is, $\bar{M}$ is identical to M except that final and nonfinal states are interchanged.

(e) *Intersection.* If L_1 and L_2 are languages accepted by finite automata M_1 and M_2, then

$$L_1 \cap L_2 = \Sigma^* - ((\Sigma^* - L_1) \cup (\Sigma^* - L_2))$$

and $L_1 \cap L_2$ is accepted by a finite automaton by (a) and (d) above. Note that as a practical matter, this construction is rather indirect: Even if M_1 and M_2 start off as deterministic automata, the union construction results in a nondeterministic automaton that must be transformed into a deterministic automaton before the complement construction can be applied. A direct construction is also possible (see Problem 2.4.3). ■

These closure properties can be used to show that there are algorithms for a number of important questions about finite automata. For convenience, we also include in the following theorem two results that do not depend on the closure properties established above.

Theorem 2.4.2. *There are algorithms for answering the following questions about finite automata.*

(a) *Given a finite automaton M and a string w, is $w \in L(M)$?*

(b) *Given a finite automaton M, is $L(M) = \varnothing$?*

(c) *Given a finite automaton M, is $L(M) = \Sigma^*$?*

(d) *Given two finite automata M_1 and M_2, is $L(M_1) \subseteq L(M_2)$?*

(e) *Given two finite automata M_1 and M_2, is $L(M_1) = L(M_2)$?*

Proof. We may assume that the finite automata are in each case deterministic, since nondeterministic finite automata can be converted to deterministic ones by the method of Section 2.3. Question (a) can be answered simply by tracing the operation of M on input w for $|w|$ steps, since M consumes one input symbol on every step. Question (b) can be answered by checking whether there is any sequence of arrows in the state diagram that leads from the initial state to a final state; this can be easily done since the state diagram is finite (see Problem 2.4.11). To answer Question (c), find a finite automation M' such that $L(M') = \Sigma^* - L(M)$, and ask whether $L(M') = \varnothing$. To settle Question (d), ask whether $(\Sigma^* - L(M_2)) \cap L(M_1) = \varnothing$, which can be answered by (b) and closure under intersection. And to settle Question (e), ask whether $L(M_1) \subseteq L(M_2)$ and $L(M_2) \subseteq L(M_1)$. ■

2.5 FINITE AUTOMATA AND REGULAR EXPRESSIONS

It is easy to see that certain simple languages—for example a^*b^* and $\{a, b\}^*$—can be specified either by regular expressions or by finite automata. We now show that any language that can be represented in one way can also be represented in the other. This adds further evidence for the thesis that these languages are a natural, self-contained class with interesting mathematical properties.

Theorem 2.5.1. *A language is regular if and only if it is accepted by a finite automaton.*

Proof. (*Only if*) Recall that the class of regular languages is the smallest class of languages containing the empty set $\varnothing$ and the singletons $\{\sigma\}$, where σ is a symbol, and closed under union, concatenation, and Kleene star. It is evident (see Figure 2–16) that $\varnothing$ and $\{\sigma\}$ are accepted by nondeterministic finite automata. By Theorem 2.4.1 the finite automaton languages are closed under union, concatenation, and Kleene star. Hence every regular language is accepted by some finite automaton.

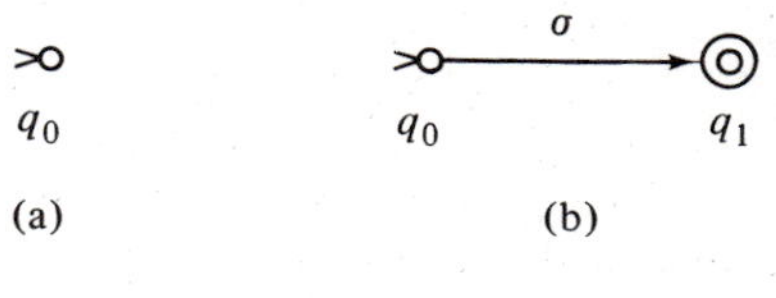

Figure 2–16

Example 2.5.1

Consider the regular expression $(ab \cup aab)^*$. A nondeterministic finite automaton accepting the language denoted by this regular expression can be built up using the methods of Section 2.4 as illustrated in Figure 2–17.

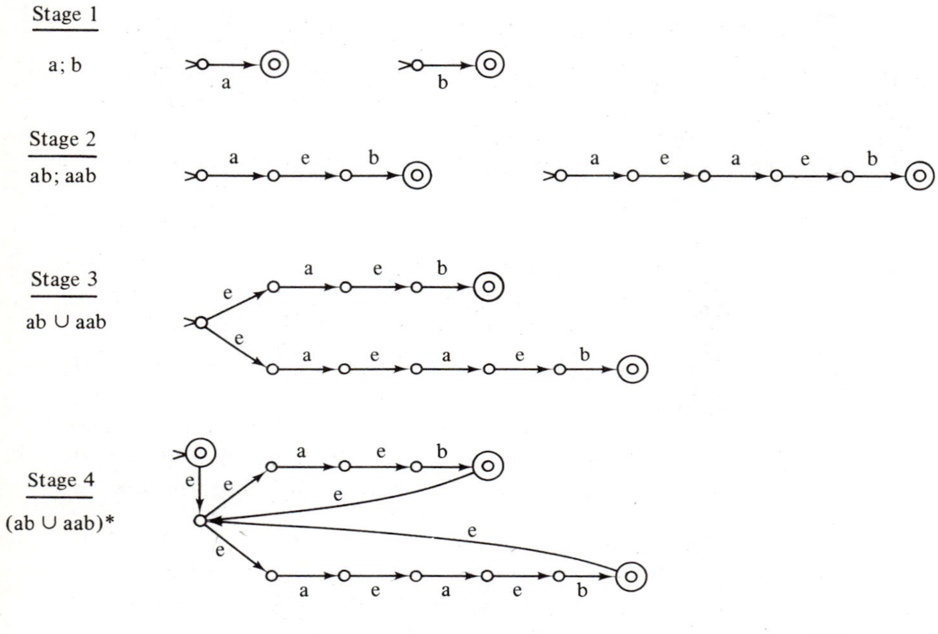

Figure 2–17

(*If*) Let $M = (K, \Sigma, \delta, s, F)$ be a deterministic finite automaton; we need to show that there is a regular language R such that $R = L(M)$. We represent $L(M)$ as the union of many (but a finite number of) simple languages. Let $K = \{q_1, \ldots, q_n\}$, $s = q_1$. For $i, j = 1, \ldots, n$ and $k = 1, \ldots, n + 1$, we let $R(i, j, k)$ be the set of all strings in Σ^* that drive M from q_i to q_j without passing through any state numbered k or greater. Formally,

$$
\begin{aligned}
R(i, j, k) = \{x \in \Sigma^* \colon & (q_i, x) \vdash_M^* (q_j, e), \text{ and, if} \\
& (q_i, x) \vdash_M^* (q_l, y) \text{ for some } y \in \Sigma^*, \\
& \text{then } l < k, \text{ or } y = e \text{ and } l = j, \\
& \text{or } y = x \text{ and } l = i\}.
\end{aligned}
$$

When $k = n + 1$, it follows that

$$R(i, j, n + 1) = \{x \in \Sigma^* \colon (q_i, x) \vdash_M^* (q_j, e)\}.$$

Therefore $$L(M) = \bigcup \{R(1, j, n + 1) \colon q_j \in F\}.$$

The crucial point is that each set $R(i, j, k)$ is regular, and hence so is $L(M)$. The proof is by induction on k. For $k = 1$, we have the following.

$$R(i, j, 1) = \begin{cases} \{\sigma \in \Sigma : \delta(q_i, \sigma) = q_j\} & \text{if } i \neq j \\ \{e\} \cup \{\sigma \in \Sigma : \delta(q_i, \sigma) = q_j\} & \text{if } i = j \end{cases} \tag{1}$$

Each of these sets is finite and therefore regular. For $k = 1, \ldots, n$, provided that all the sets $R(i, j, k)$ have been defined, each set $R(i, j, k + 1)$ can be defined in terms of previously defined languages as

$$R(i, j, k + 1) = R(i, j, k) \cup R(i, k, k)R(k, k, k)^*R(k, j, k). \tag{2}$$

This equation states that to get from q_i to q_j without passing through a state numbered greater than k, M may either

1. go from q_i to q_j without passing through a state numbered greater than $k - 1$; or
2. go (a) from q_i to q_k; then
   (b) from q_k to q_k repeatedly; then
   (c) from q_k to q_j;
   in each case without passing through a state numbered greater than $k - 1$.

Therefore if each language $R(i, j, k)$ is regular, so is each language $R(i, j, k + 1)$. This completes the induction. ∎

Example 2.5.2

Let us construct a regular expression for the language accepted by the deterministic finite automaton of Figure 2–18. This automaton accepts

$$\{w : w \text{ has } 3k + 1\ b\text{'s for some } k \in \mathbb{N}\}.$$

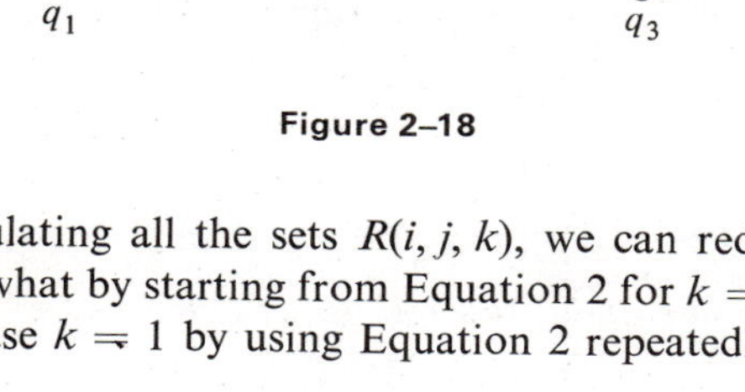

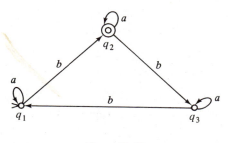

Figure 2–18

Rather than calculating all the sets $R(i, j, k)$, we can reduce the computational labor somewhat by starting from Equation 2 for $k = n + 1$ and working back to the case $k = 1$ by using Equation 2 repeatedly. Since $F = \{q_2\}$, we must find

$$L(M) = R(1, 2, 4).$$

By Equation 1,

$$R(1, 2, 4) = R(1, 2, 3) \cup R(1, 3, 3)R(3, 3, 3)^*R(3, 2, 3).$$

Thus we need four of the sets $R(i, j, k)$ for $k = 3$. These are as follows.

$$R(1, 2, 3) = R(1, 2, 2) \cup R(1, 2, 2)R(2, 2, 2)^*R(2, 2, 2)$$
$$R(1, 3, 3) = R(1, 3, 2) \cup R(1, 2, 2)R(2, 2, 2)^*R(2, 3, 2)$$
$$R(3, 3, 3) = R(3, 3, 2) \cup R(3, 2, 2)R(2, 2, 2)^*R(2, 3, 2)$$
$$R(3, 2, 3) = R(3, 2, 2) \cup R(3, 2, 2)R(2, 2, 2)^*R(2, 2, 2)$$

Expanding further to obtain equations for the required sets $R(i, j, k)$ for $k = 2$ gives these values

$$R(1, 2, 2) = R(1, 2, 1) \cup R(1, 1, 1)R(1, 1, 1)^*R(1, 2, 1)$$
$$R(2, 2, 2) = R(2, 2, 1) \cup R(2, 1, 1)R(1, 1, 1)^*R(1, 2, 1)$$
$$R(1, 3, 2) = R(1, 3, 1) \cup R(1, 1, 1)R(1, 1, 1)^*R(1, 3, 1)$$
$$R(2, 3, 2) = R(2, 3, 1) \cup R(2, 1, 1)R(1, 1, 1)^*R(1, 3, 1)$$
$$R(3, 3, 2) = R(3, 3, 1) \cup R(3, 1, 1)R(1, 1, 1)^*R(1, 3, 1)$$
$$R(3, 2, 2) = R(3, 2, 1) \cup R(3, 1, 1)R(1, 1, 1)^*R(1, 2, 1)$$

The sets $R(i, j, k)$ for $k = 1$ are found using Equation 1.

$$R(1, 1, 1) = R(2, 2, 1) = R(3, 3, 1) = a \cup e$$
$$R(1, 2, 1) = R(2, 3, 1) = R(3, 1, 1) = b$$
$$R(2, 1, 1) = R(3, 2, 1) = R(1, 3, 1) = \varnothing$$

Substituting back into the equations for $k = 2$, we have the following.

$$R(1, 2, 2) = b \cup (a \cup e)(a \cup e)^*b = a^*b$$
$$R(2, 2, 2) = (a \cup e) \cup \varnothing(a \cup e)^*b = (a \cup e)$$
$$R(1, 3, 2) = \varnothing \cup (a \cup e)(a \cup e)^*\varnothing = \varnothing$$
$$R(2, 3, 2) = b \cup \varnothing(a \cup e)^*\varnothing = b$$
$$R(3, 3, 2) = (a \cup e) \cup b(a \cup e)^*\varnothing = (a \cup e)$$
$$R(3, 2, 2) = \varnothing \cup b(a \cup e)^*b = ba^*b$$

The equations for $k = 3$ are as follows.

$$R(1, 2, 3) = a^*b \cup (a^*b)(a \cup e)^*(a) = a^*ba^*$$
$$R(1, 3, 3) = \varnothing \cup (a^*b)(a \cup e)^*(b) = a^*ba^*b$$
$$R(3, 3, 3) = (a \cup e) \cup (ba^*b)(a \cup e)^*b = (a \cup e) \cup ba^*ba^*b$$
$$R(3, 2, 3) = ba^*b \cup (ba^*b)(a \cup e)^*a = ba^*ba^*$$

Finally,

$$L(M) = R(1, 2, 4)$$
$$= a^*ba^* \cup (a^*ba^*b)(a \cup e \cup ba^*ba^*b)^*(ba^*ba^*).$$

We leave it as an exercise (see Problem 2.5.3) to confirm that this regular expression does indeed denote

$$\{w: w \in \{a, b\}^* \text{ and } w \text{ has } 3k + 1\ b\text{'s for some } k \in \mathbb{N}\}.$$

2.6 PROOFS THAT LANGUAGES ARE AND ARE NOT REGULAR

The results of the last two sections establish that the regular languages are closed under a variety of operations and that regular languages may be specified either by regular expressions or by deterministic or nondeterministic finite automata. These facts, used singly or in combinations, provide a variety of techniques for showing languages to be regular.

Example 2.6.1

Let $\Sigma = \{0, \ldots, 9\}$ and let $L \subseteq \Sigma^*$ be the set of decimal representations for nonnegative integers divisible by 2 or 3. For example, 0, 3, 6, 12 $\in L$, but 1, 03, 00 $\notin L$. Then L is regular. We break the proof into four parts.

Let L_1 be the set of decimal representations of nonnegative integers. Then it is easy to see that

$$L_1 = 0 \cup \{1, 2, \ldots, 9\}\Sigma^*$$

which is regular since it is denoted by a regular expression.

Let L_2 be the set of decimal representations of nonnegative integers divisible by 2. Then L_2 is just the set of members of L_1 ending in 0, 2, 4, 6, or 8; that is,

$$L_1 \cap \Sigma^*\{0, 2, 4, 6, 8\}$$

which is regular by Theorem 2.4.1(e).

Let L_3 be the set of decimal representations of nonnegative integers divisible by 3. Recall that a number is divisible by 3 if and only if the sum of its digits is divisible by 3. We construct a finite automaton that keeps track in its finite control of the sum modulo 3 of a string of digits. L_3 will then be the intersection with L_1 of the language accepted by this finite automaton. The automaton is pictured in Figure 2–19.

Finally, $L = L_2 \cup L_3$.

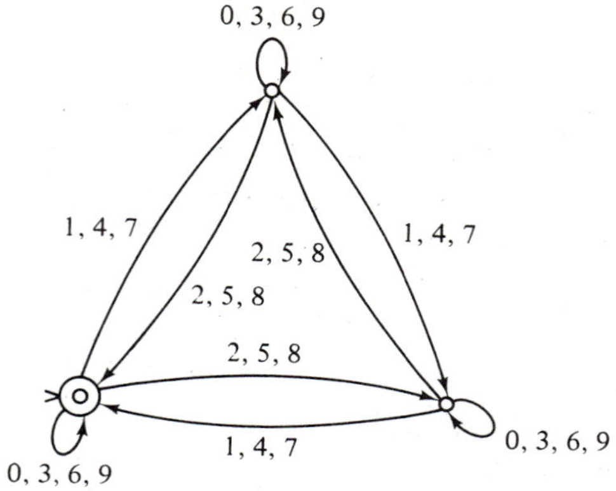

Figure 2–19

Example 2.6.2

Let $\Sigma = \{a, b\}$, and let $L \subseteq \Sigma^*$ be the set of all strings of odd length but containing an even number of a's. Then L is regular, since it is the intersection of two regular languages L_1 and L_2, where

L_1, the set of all strings of odd length, is $\Sigma(\Sigma\Sigma)^*$;

L_2, the set of all strings with an even number of a's, is $b^*(ab^*ab^*)^*$.

Although we now have a variety of powerful techniques for showing that languages are regular, as yet we have none for showing that languages are *not* regular. We know on fundamental principles that nonregular languages do exist, since the number of regular expressions (or the number of finite automata) is countable, whereas the number of languages is uncountable. But to demonstrate that any particular language is not regular requires special tools.

Two properties shared by all regular languages, but not by certain nonregular languages, may be phrased intuitively as follows:

1. As a string is scanned left-to-right, the amount of memory that is required in order to determine at the end whether or not the string is in the language must be bounded—fixed in advance and dependent on the language, not the particular input string. For example, we would expect that $\{a^n b^n : n \geq 0\}$ is not regular, since it is difficult to imagine how a finite state device could be constructed that would correctly remember, upon reaching the border between the a's and the b's, how many a's it had seen so that the number could be compared against the number of b's.

2. Regular languages with an infinite number of strings have infinite subsets with a certain simple repetitive structure that arises from a star in a corresponding regular expression or a cycle in the state diagram of a finite

automaton. This would lead us to expect, for example, that $\{a^n: n \text{ is prime}\}$ is not regular, since there is no simple periodicity in the set of prime numbers.

These intuitive ideas are accurate but not sufficiently precise to be used in formal proofs. We shall now prove a theorem that captures some of this intuition and yields the nonregularity of certain languages as an easy consequence.

Theorem 2.6.1. *Let L be an infinite regular language. Then there are strings x, y, and z such that $y \neq e$ and $xy^nz \in L$ for each $n \geq 0$.*

Proof. Since L is regular, L is accepted by a deterministic finite automaton M. Suppose M has n states. Since L is infinite, M accepts some string w of length n or greater. Let $l = |w|$, $w = \sigma_1 \ldots \sigma_l$, where each $\sigma_i \in \Sigma$, and consider the computation of M on w:

$$(q_0, \sigma_1 \ldots \sigma_l) \vdash_M (q_1, \sigma_2 \ldots \sigma_l) \vdash_M \cdots \vdash_M (q_{l-1}, \sigma_l) \vdash_M (q_l, e)$$

where q_0 is the initial state of M and q_l is a final state of M. Since $l \geq n$ and M has only n states, by the pigeonhole principle there exist i and j, $0 \leq i < j \leq l$, such that $q_i = q_j$. That is, the string $\sigma_{i+1} \ldots \sigma_j$ drives M from state q_i back to state q_i, and this string is nonempty since $i + 1 \leq j$. But then this string could be removed from w, or any number of repetitions of this string could be inserted in w just after the jth symbol of w, and M would still accept this string. That is, M accepts $\sigma_1 \ldots \sigma_i(\sigma_{i+1} \ldots \sigma_j)^n\sigma_{j+1} \ldots \sigma_l$ for each $n \geq 0$; for if $x = \sigma_1 \ldots \sigma_i$, $y = \sigma_{i+1} \ldots \sigma_j$, and $z = \sigma_{j+1} \ldots \sigma_l$, then

$$(q_0, xy^nz) \vdash_M^* (q_i, y^nz) \vdash_M^* (q_i, y^{n-1}z) \vdash_M^* \cdots \vdash_M^* (q_i, z) \vdash_M^* (q_l, e). \quad \blacksquare$$

This theorem is one of a general class called **pumping theorems**, because they assert the existence of certain points in certain strings where a substring can be repeatedly inserted without affecting the acceptability of the string. It follows from this theorem that each of the two languages mentioned earlier in this section is not regular.

Example 2.6.3

The language $L = \{a^nb^n: n \geq 0\}$ is not regular. For L is infinite, so Theorem 2.6.1 applies; so there are strings x, y, and z with $y \neq e$ such that $xy^nz \in L$ for each $n \geq 0$. There are three possibilities for y, and in each case we can show that L must contain some string not of the correct form.

Case 1: y consists entirely of a's. Then $x = a^p$, $y = a^q$, and $z = a^rb^s$, where $p, r \geq 0$ and $q, s > 0$. But then L must contain $xy^nz = a^{p+nq+r}b^s$ for each $n \geq 0$, and at most one of these strings has equal numbers of a's and b's.

Case 2: y consists entirely of b's; this is similar to Case 1.

Case 3: y contains both a's and b's. Then for $n > 1$, xy^nz has an occurrence of b preceding an occurrence of a and therefore cannot be in L.

Example 2.6.4

The language $L = \{a^n: n \text{ is prime}\}$ is not regular. For suppose it were, and let x, y, and z be as specified in Theorem 2.6.1. Then $x = a^p$, $y = a^q$, and $z = a^r$, where $p, r \geq 0$ and $q > 0$. By the theorem, $a^{p+nq+r} \in L$ for each $n \geq 0$, that is, $p + nq + r$ is prime for each $n \geq 0$. But this is impossible. For let $n = p + 2q + r + 2$; then $p + nq + r = (q + 1) \cdot (p + 2q + r)$, which is a product of two natural numbers, each greater than 1.

Theorem 2.6.1 can be strengthened substantially in several ways (see Problems 2.6.4 and 2.6.10). By using these stronger pumping theorems, it is possible to establish many other results about regular languages (see Problems 2.6.5 and 2.6.6).

PROBLEMS

2.1.1. Let M be a deterministic finite automaton. Under exactly what circumstances is $e \in L(M)$? Prove your answer.

2.1.2. Describe informally the languages accepted by the deterministic finite automata shown below.

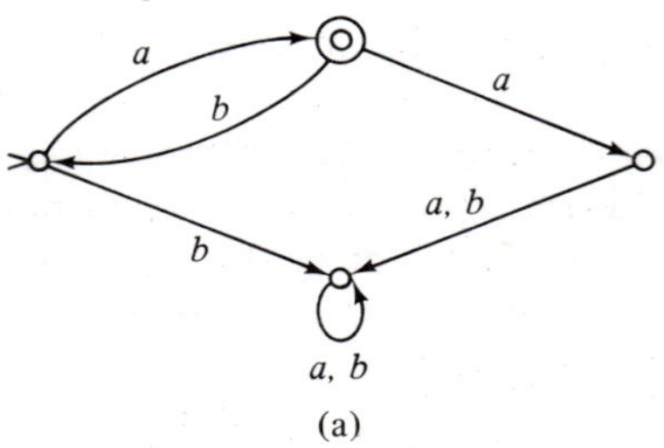

(a)

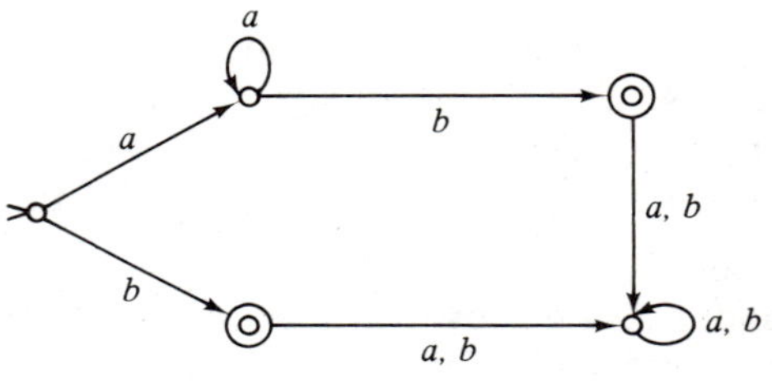

(b)

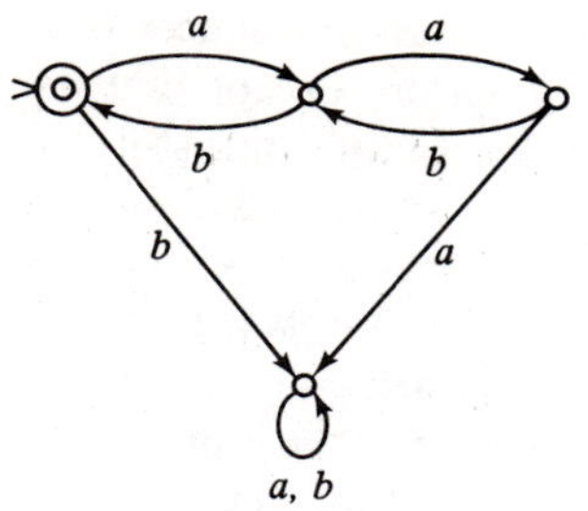

(c)

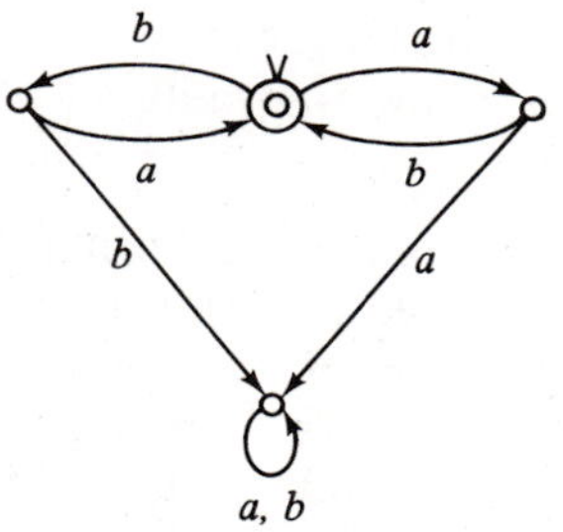

(d)

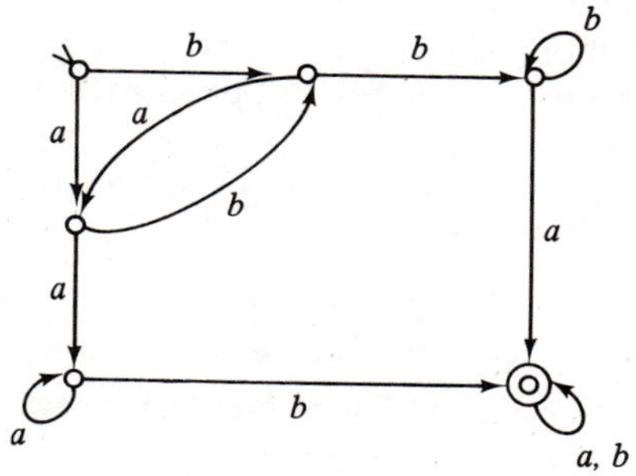

(e)

2.1.3. Construct deterministic finite automata accepting each of the following languages.

(a) $\{w \in \{a, b\}^*$: each a in w is immediately preceded and immediately followed by a $b\}$.

(b) $\{w \in \{a, b\}^*$: w has $abab$ as a substring$\}$.

(c) $\{w \in \{a, b\}^*$: w has neither aa nor bb as a substring$\}$.

(d) $\{w \in \{a, b\}^*$: w has an odd number of a's and an even number of b's$\}$.

(e) $\{w \in \{a, b\}^*$: w has both ab and ba as substrings$\}$.

2.1.4. A **deterministic finite-state transducer** is a device much like a deterministic finite automaton, except that its purpose is not to accept strings or languages but to transform input strings into output strings. Informally, it starts in a designated initial state and moves from state to state, depending on the input, just as a deterministic finite automaton does. On each step, however, it emits (or writes onto an output tape) a string of zero or one or more symbols, depending on the current state and the input symbol. The state diagram for a deterministic finite-state transducer looks like that for a deterministic finite automaton, except that the label on an arrow looks like a/w, which means "if the input symbol is a, follow this arrow and emit output w". For example, the deterministic finite-state transducer over $\{a, b\}$ shown below transmits all b's in the input string but omits every other a.

(a) Draw state diagrams for deterministic finite-state transducers over $\{a, b\}$ which do the following.
  (i) On input w, produce output a^n, where n is the number of occurrences of the substring ab in w.
  (ii) On input w, produce output a^n, where n is the number of occurrences of the substring aba in w.
  (iii) On input w, produce a string of length $|w|$ whose ith symbol is an a if $i = 1$, or if $i > 1$ and the ith and $(i - 1)$st symbols of w are different; otherwise, the ith symbol of the output is a b. Examples are as follows.

Input:	*aabba*	Output:	*ababa*
Input:	*aaaab*	Output:	*abbba*

(b) Formally define
  (i) a **deterministic finite-state transducer**;
  (ii) the notion of a **configuration** for such an automaton;
  (iii) the **yields in one step** relation $\vdash$ between configurations;
  (iv) the notion that such an automaton **produces output** u **on input** w;
  (v) the notion that such an automaton **computes a function** $f: \Sigma^* \rightarrow \Sigma^*$.

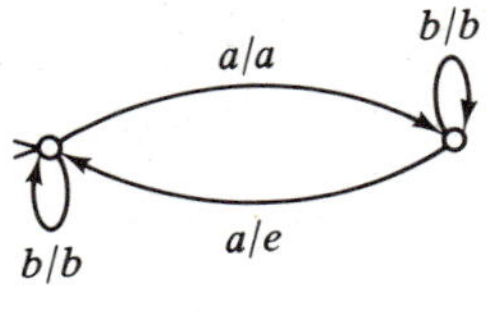

2.1.5. A **deterministic 2-tape finite automaton** is a device like a deterministic finite automaton for accepting *pairs* of strings. Each state is in one of two sets; depending on which set the state is in, the transition function refers to the first or second tape. For example, the automaton shown below accepts all pairs of strings $(w_1, w_2) \in \{a, b\}^* \times \{a, b\}^*$ such that $|w_2| = 2|w_1|$.

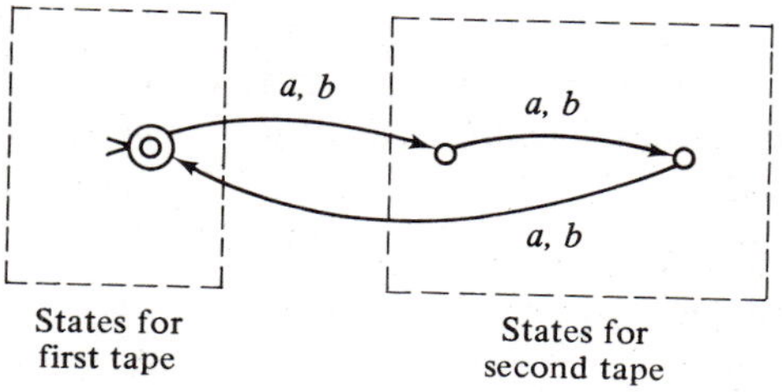

(a) Draw state diagrams for deterministic 2-tape finite automata that accept each of the following.
   (i) All pairs of strings (w_1, w_2) in $\{a, b\}^* \times \{a, b\}^*$ such that $|w_1| = |w_2|$ and $w_1(i) = a$ if and only if $w_2(i) = b$, and vice versa.
   (ii) All pairs of strings $(w_1, w_2) \in \{a, b\}^* \times \{a, b\}^*$ such that the length of w_2 is twice the number of a's in w_1 plus three times the number of b's in w_1.
   (iii) $\{(a^n b, a^n b^m): n, m \geq 0\}$.
   (iv) $\{(a^n b, a^m b^n): n, m \geq 0\}$.

(b) Formally define
   (i) a **deterministic 2-tape finite automaton**;
   (ii) the notion of a **configuration** for such an automaton;
   (iii) the **yields in one step** relation $\vdash$ between configurations;
   (iv) the notion that such an automaton **accepts** an ordered pair of strings;
   (v) the notion that such an automaton **accepts a set** of ordered pairs of strings.

2.1.6. This problem refers to Problems 2.1.4 and 2.1.5. Show that if $f: \Sigma^* \longrightarrow \Sigma^*$ is a function that can be computed by a deterministic finite-state transducer, then $\{(w, f(w)): w \in \Sigma^*\}$ is a set of pairs of strings accepted by some deterministic two-tape finite automaton.

2.1.7. We say that a state q of a deterministic finite automaton $M = (K, \Sigma, \delta, q_0, F)$ is **reachable** if there exists $w \in \Sigma^*$ such that $(q_0, w) \vdash_M^* (q, e)$. Show that if we delete from M any nonreachable state, an automaton results that accepts the same language.

2.1.8. In this problem we show that there is an algorithm for **minimizing** a deterministic finite automaton, that is, finding another deterministic finite automaton accepting the same language with state set that is of minimum size. Assume below that all states are reachable. Let $M = (K, \Sigma, \delta, s, F)$ be any deterministic finite automaton, and for any $q \in K$, let $M_q = (K, \Sigma, \delta, q, F)$. That is, M_q is just M with initial state q. If $k \geq 0$, say that states p and q of M are k-**distinguishable** if there is some input string of length k at most which is accepted by one of M_p or M_q but not the other. Otherwise they are k-**indistinguishable**. Two states are **equivalent** if they are k-indistinguishable for every k.

(a) Show that if a deterministic finite automaton has two equivalent states, one can be eliminated; but if all pairs of distinct states are inequivalent, then the automaton is as small as possible.

(b) Show that states p and q are k-indistinguishable if and only if
  (i) both are final or both are nonfinal; and
  (ii) if $k > 0$, then for each $\sigma \in \Sigma$, $\delta(p, \sigma)$ and $\delta(q, \sigma)$ are $(k - 1)$-indistinguishable.

(c) Define a series of equivalence relations $\equiv_0, \equiv_1, \ldots$ on the states of M as follows.

$p \equiv_0 q$ if and only if both p and q are final or both are nonfinal.

$p \equiv_{k+1} q$ if and only if $p \equiv_k q$ and, for each $\sigma \in \Sigma$, $\delta(p, \sigma) \equiv_k \delta(q, \sigma)$.

Show that $p \equiv_k q$ if and only if p and q are k-indistinguishable.

(d) Show that there is an $n \leq |K|$ such that $\equiv_n$ and $\equiv_{n+1}$ are identical. Then by (c) and the definition of equivalent states, all equivalent states can be discovered by carrying through the inductive definition of $\equiv_{k+1}$ at most $|K|$ times. This information can then be used to minimize the deterministic finite automaton, as shown in (a).

2.1.9. Deterministic finite-state transducers are defined in Problem 2.1.4. A **Mealy automaton** is a deterministic finite-state transducer that emits a single output symbol on each move; thus its output has the same length as its input. Show how to adapt the procedure of Problem 2.1.8 to minimize the number of states of a Mealy automaton.

2.2.1. Which of the following strings are accepted by these nondeterministic finite automata?

(a)

(i) *aa*
(ii) *aba*
(iii) *abb*
(iv) *ab*
(v) *abab*

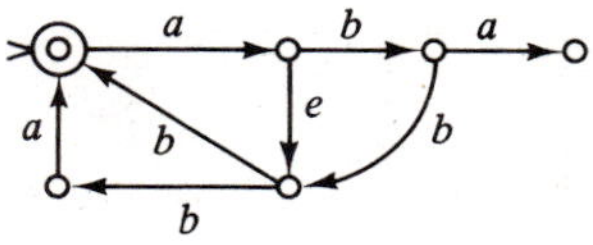

(a)

(b)

(i) *ba*
(ii) *ab*
(iii) *bb*
(iv) *b*
(v) *bba*

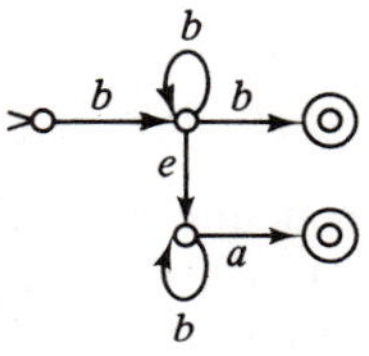

(b)

2.2.2. Draw state diagrams for nondeterministic finite automata accepting these languages.

(a) $(ab)^*(ba)^* \cup aa^*$
(b) $((ab \cup aab)^*a^*)^*$
(c) $((a^*b^*a^*)^*b)^*$
(d) $(ba \cup b)^* \cup (bb \cup a)^*$

2.2.3. Write regular expressions for the languages accepted by these nondeterministic finite automata.

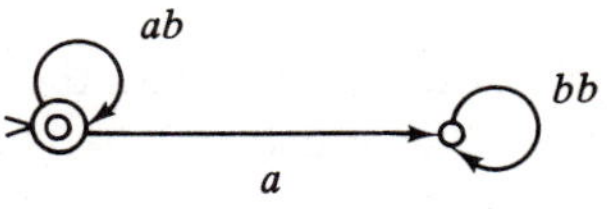

(a)

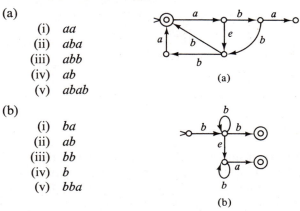

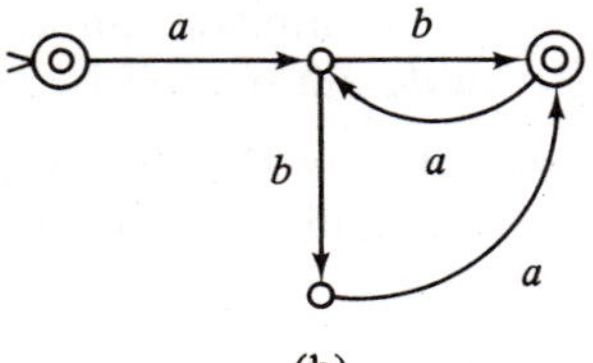

(b)

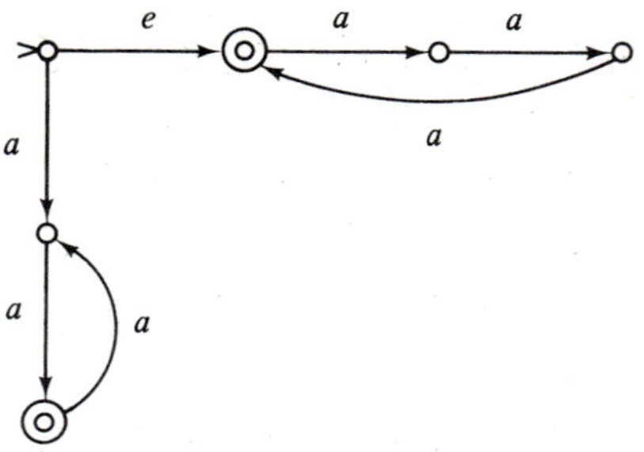

(c)

2.2.4. Suppose we define a **special** finite automaton to be a quintuple $(K, \Sigma, \delta, s, F)$, where K, Σ, s, and F are as described for deterministic or nondeterministic finite automata and δ is a function from a finite subset of $K \times \Sigma^*$ to K. Is a special finite automaton more like a deterministic or a nondeterministic finite automaton? Why?

2.2.5. Some authors define a nondeterministic finite automaton to be a quintuple $(K, \Sigma, \Delta, S, F)$, where K, Σ, Δ, and F are as defined and S is a finite set of initial states, in the same way that F is a finite set of final states. The automaton may nondeterministically begin operating in any of these initial states. Explain why this definition is not more general than ours in any significant way.

2.2.6. What exactly justifies the first sentence of the proof of Lemma 2.2.1?

2.2.7. Prove carefully, by going back to the definition of $\vdash_M$, that if M is a nondeterministic finite automaton then $(q, xy) \vdash_M^* (p, y)$ if and only if $(q, x) \vdash_M^* (p, e)$.

2.2.8. By what sequences of steps, other than the one presented in Example 2.2.1, can the nondeterministic finite automaton of Figure 2–8 accept the input *baababaab*?

2.3.1. (a) Find a simple nondeterministic finite automaton accepting $(ab \cup aab \cup aba)^*$.

(b) Convert the nondeterministic finite automaton of Part (a) to a deterministic finite automaton by the method in Section 2.3.

(c) Try to understand how the machine constructed in Part (b) operates. Can you find an equivalent deterministic machine with fewer states?

2.3.2. Repeat Problem 2.3.1 for the language $(a \cup b)^*aabab$.

2.3.3. Construct deterministic finite automata equivalent to the nondeterministic automata shown below.

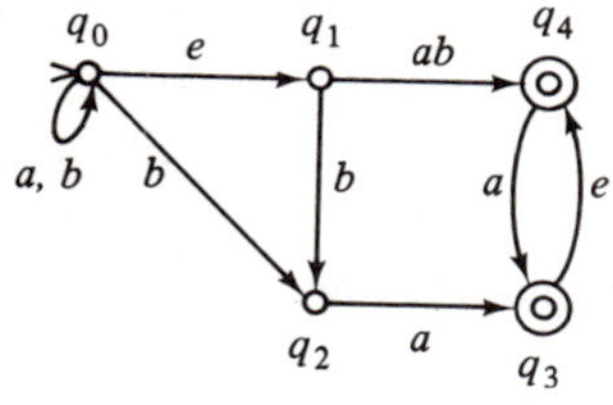

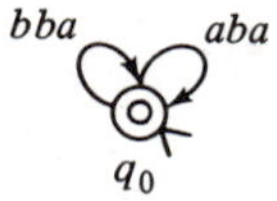

2.3.4. Describe exactly what happens when the construction of Section 2.3 is applied to a finite automaton that is already deterministic.

2.3.5. *Carefully* explain how the set $E(q)$ is actually determined from M' in the proof of Theorem 2.3.1. The definition does not immediately supply an algorithm for finding $E(q)$.

2.3.6. If one applies the construction of Theorem 2.3.1 to a nondeterministic finite automaton $M = (K, \Sigma, \Delta, s, F)$, an equivalent automaton with 2^m states results, where

$$m = |K| + \sum_{\substack{(p, w, q) \in \Delta \\ w \neq e}} (|w| - 1).$$

However, in Example 2.3.2 and Problems 2.3.1 and 2.3.2, we noticed that most of the 2^m states are usually not needed, and therefore there exists a deterministic finite automaton equivalent to M with far fewer than 2^m states. The question arises if there is a nondeterministic finite automaton M such that every deterministic finite automaton equivalent to M has at least 2^m states. In this problem we exhibit such an automaton.

(a) Let $\Sigma = \{a_1, \ldots, a_n\}$, and consider the language $L = \{wa_j: 1 \leq j \leq n, \text{ and } w \in (\Sigma - \{a_j\})^*\}$. Thus L contains all strings that end with the first occurrence of some symbol. Construct a nondeterministic finite automaton M with $n + 2$ states that accepts L. M should have no transition (q, u, p) with $|u| > 1$. (*Hint:* L is the union of n simpler languages.)

(b) Apply to M the construction of Theorem 2.3.1 to obtain an equivalent deterministic finite automaton M''. Show that M'' has $2^{n+1} - 1$ states.

(c) Show that there is no deterministic finite automaton with fewer than $2^{n+1} - 1$ states accepting L. (*Hint:* You may wish to use the results of Problem 2.5.4 here.)

(d) Slightly modify the automaton of Part (a) to yield a nondeterministic finite automaton $N = (K, \Sigma, \Delta, s, F)$ such that N has no transitions on strings of length greater than 1 and there is no deterministic finite automaton equivalent to N with fewer than $2^{|K|}$ states.

2.4.1. In part (d) of the proof of Theorem 2.4.1 why did we insist that M be deterministic? What happens if we interchange the final and nonfinal states of a nondeterministic finite automaton?

2.4.2. What goes wrong in the proof of Part (c) of Theorem 2.4.1 if we use the construction suggested at the end of that part of the proof?

2.4.3. Give a direct construction for the closure under intersection of the languages accepted by finite automata. (*Hint:* If the two automata are deterministic and have state sets K_1 and K_2, consider an automaton with state set $K_1 \times K_2$.)

2.4.4. Construct a simple nondeterministic finite automaton to accept the language $(ab \cup aba)^*a$. Then apply to it the construction of Part (c) of the proof of Theorem 2.4.1 to obtain a nondeterministic finite automaton accepting $((ab \cup aba)^*a)^*$.

2.4.5. Let $L, M \subseteq \Sigma^*$. Define the following languages.

1. $\text{Pref}(L) = \{w \in \Sigma^* : x = wy \text{ for some } x \in L, y \in \Sigma^*\}$ (the set of **prefixes** of L).
2. $\text{Suf}(L) = \{w \in \Sigma^* : x = yw \text{ for some } x \in L, y \in \Sigma^*\}$ (the set of **suffixes** of L).
3. $\text{Subseq}(L) = \{w_1 w_2 \ldots w_k : k \in \mathbb{N}, w_j \in \Sigma^* \text{ for } j = 1, \ldots, k$, and there is a string $x = x_0 w_1 x_1 w_2 \ldots w_k x_k$ in $L\}$ (the set of **subsequences** of L).
4. $L/M = \{w \in \Sigma^* : wx \in L \text{ for some } x \in M\}$ (the **right quotient of** L **by** M).
5. $\text{Max}(L) = \{w \in L : x \neq e \text{ implies } wx \notin L\}$
6. $L^R = \{w^R : w \in L\}$

Show that if L is accepted by some finite automaton then so is each of the following.

(a) $\text{Pref}(L)$

(b) $\text{Suf}(L)$

(c) $\text{Subseq}(L)$

(d) L/M, where M is accepted by some finite automaton.

(e) L/M, where M is *any* language.

(f) Max(L)

(g) L^R

2.4.6. Argue that there are algorithms to answer the following questions about finite automata M_1 and M_2.

(a) Whether $L(M_1)$ and $L(M_2)$ are disjoint.

(b) Whether $L(M_1)$ and $L(M_2)$ are complementary, that is, $L(M_1) = \Sigma^* - L(M_2)$.

(c) Whether $L(M_1)^* = L(M_2)$.

2.4.7. (a) By analogy with Problem 2.1.5, define a **nondeterministic 2-tape finite automaton**, and the notion that such an automaton **accepts** a particular set of ordered pairs of strings.

(b) Show that $\{(a^n b, a^m b^p): n, m, p \geq 0, n = m \text{ or } n = p\}$ is accepted by some nondeterministic 2-tape finite automaton.

(c) We shall see (Problem 2.6.8) that nondeterministic 2-tape finite automata cannot always be converted into deterministic ones. This being the case, which of the constructions used in the proof of Theorem 2.4.1 can be extended to demonstrate closure properties of the following?

(i) The sets of pairs of strings accepted by nondeterministic 2-tape finite automata.

(ii) The sets of pairs of strings accepted by deterministic 2-tape finite automata.

Explain your answers.

2.4.8. A language L is **definite** if there is some k such that, for any string w, whether $w \in L$ depends only on the last k symbols of w.

(a) Rewrite this definition more formally.

(b) Show that every definite language is accepted by a finite automaton.

(c) Show that the class of definite languages is closed under union and complementation.

(d) Give an example of a definite language L such that L^* is not definite.

(e) Give an example of definite languages L_1 and L_2 such that $L_1 L_2$ is not definite.

2.4.9. Let Σ and Δ be alphabets. Consider a function h from Σ to Δ^*. Extend h to a function from Σ^* to Δ^* as follows.

$$h(e) = e$$
$$h(w\sigma) = h(w)h(\sigma), \quad \text{for any } w \in \Sigma^*, \sigma \in \Sigma$$

For example, if $\Sigma = \Delta = \{a, b\}$, $h(a) = ab$, and $h(b) = aab$, then

$$\begin{aligned} h(aab) &= h(aa)h(b) \\ &= h(a)h(a)h(b) \\ &= ababaab. \end{aligned}$$

Any function $h: \Sigma^* \longrightarrow \Delta^*$ defined in this way from a function $h: \Sigma \longrightarrow \Delta^*$ is called a **homomorphism**.

Let h be a homomorphism from Σ^* to Δ^*.

(a) Show that if $L \subseteq \Sigma^*$ is accepted by a finite automaton, so is $h[L]$.

(b) Show that if $L \subseteq \Delta^*$ is accepted by a finite automaton, then so is $\{w \in \Sigma^*: h(w) \in L\}$. (*Hint:* Start from a deterministic finite automaton M accepting L, and construct one which, when it reads an input symbol σ, delivers $h(\sigma)$ in its imagination to M for processing.)

2.4.10. Deterministic finite-state transducers were introduced in Problem 2.1.4. Show that if L is accepted by a finite automaton, and f is computed by a deterministic finite-state transducer, then each of the following is true.

(a) $f[L]$ is accepted by a finite automaton.

(b) $f^{-1}[L]$ is accepted by a finite automaton.

2.4.11. Let $M = (K, \Sigma, \delta, s, F)$ be a deterministic finite automaton. Show that the following method suffices to determine whether $L(M) = \varnothing$: Let $Q_1 = \{s\}$ and, for each i such that $1 \leq i < |K|$, $Q_{i+1} = Q_i \cup \{q \in K: \text{for some } p \in Q_i \text{ and } a \in \Sigma, \delta(p, a) = q\}$. Then $L(M) = \varnothing$ if and only if $F \cap Q_{|K|} = \varnothing$.

2.5.1. Apply the construction of Section 2.5 to obtain regular expressions corresponding to each of the following finite automata. Simplify the resulting regular expressions.

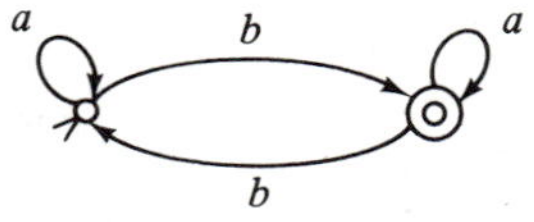

(a)

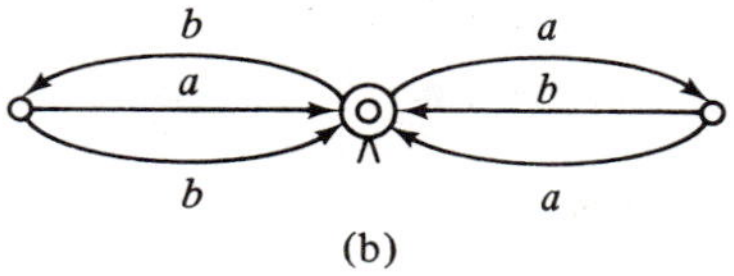

(b)

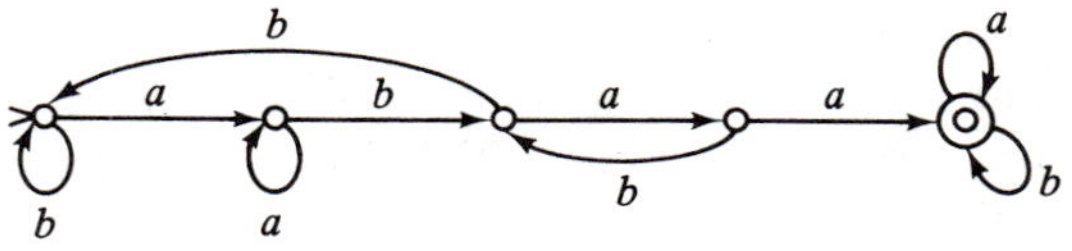

(c)

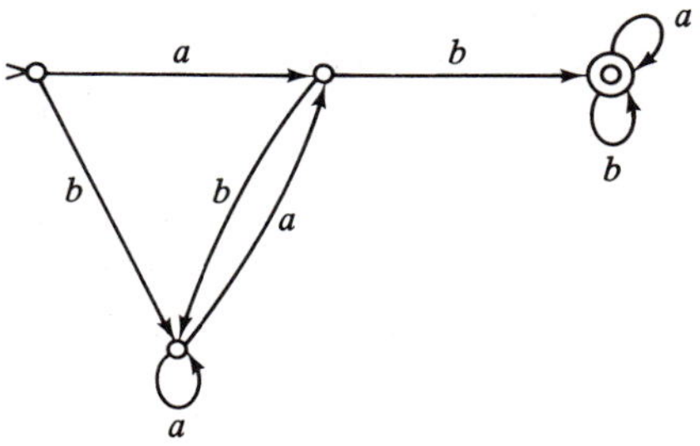

(d)

2.5.2. Using the constructions implicit in the proofs of Theorems 2.5.1 and 2.4.1, construct finite automata accepting these languages.

(a) $a^*(ab \cup ba \cup e)b^*$

(b) $((a \cup b)^*(e \cup c)^*)^*$

(c) $((ab)^* \cup (bc)^*)ab$

2.5.3. Prove that the regular expression given at the end of Section 2.5 denotes the language claimed.

2.5.4. Let Σ be an alphabet and let $L \subseteq \Sigma^*$. Define the binary relation R on Σ^* as follows: xRy if and only if, for all $w \in \Sigma^*$, $xw \in L$ if and only if $yw \in L$.

(a) Show that for any L, R is an equivalence relation on Σ^*.

(b) Show that if the number of equivalence classes of R is finite, then there is a finite automaton that accepts L. (*Hint:* Let the states be the equivalence classes.)

(c) Show that if L is accepted by a finite automaton, then the number of equivalence classes of R is finite.

(d) Show that if L is accepted by a finite automaton, no deterministic finite automaton accepting L has fewer states than that constructed in Part (b).

2.5.5. A **two-way finite automaton** is like a deterministic finite automaton, except that the reading head can go backwards as well as forwards on the input tape. If it tries to back up off the left end of the tape, it stops operating without accepting the input. Formally, a two-way finite automaton M is a quintuple $(K, \Sigma, \delta, s, F)$, where K, Σ, s, and F are as defined for deterministic finite automata and δ is a function from $K \times \Sigma$ to $K \times \{-1, +1\}$; the -1 or $+1$ indicates the direction of head movement. A **configuration** is a member of $K \times \Sigma^* \times \Sigma^*$; configuration (p, u, v) indicates that the machine is in state p with the head on the first symbol of v and with u to the left of the head, as shown below.

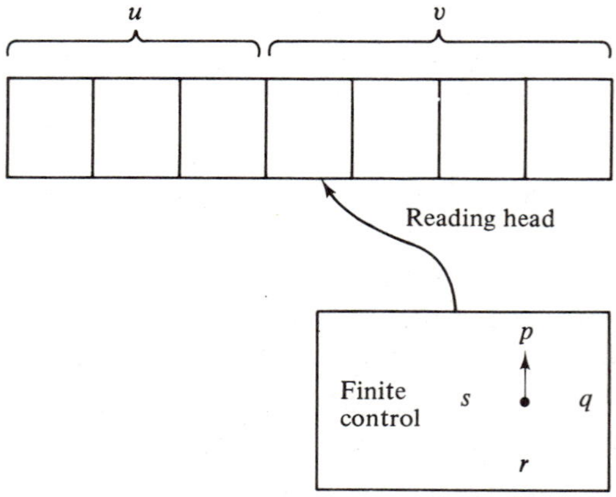

So we write $(p_1, u_1, v_1) \vdash_M (p_2, u_2, v_2)$ if and only if $v_1 = \sigma v$ for some $\sigma \in \Sigma$, $v \in \Sigma^*$, $\delta(p_1, \sigma) = (p_2, \epsilon)$ for $\epsilon = \pm 1$, and either

1. $\epsilon = +1$ and $u_2 = u_1\sigma$, $v_2 = v$, or
2. $\epsilon = -1$, $u_1 = u\sigma'$ for some $u \in \Sigma^*$, $\sigma' \in \Sigma$, $u_2 = u$ and $v_2 = \sigma' v_1$.

As usual, $\vdash_M^*$ is the reflexive, transitive closure of $\vdash_M$; M **accepts** w if and only if $(s, e, w) \vdash_M^* (f, w, e)$ for some $f \in F$. In this problem you will use the result of Problem 2.5.4 (but not the proof) to show that a language accepted by a two-way finite automaton is accepted by a one-way finite automaton. Let M be a two-way finite automaton as just defined.

(a) Let $q \in K$ and $w \in \Sigma^*$. Show that there is at most one $p \in K$ such that $(q, e, w) \vdash_M^* (p, w, e)$.

(b) Let t be some fixed element *not* in K. For any $w \in \Sigma^*$, define a function $\chi_w: K \to K \cup \{t\}$ as follows.

$$\chi_w(q) = \begin{cases} p, & \text{if } (q, e, w) \vdash_M^* (p, w, e) \\ t, & \text{otherwise} \end{cases}$$

By Part (a), χ_w is well defined. Also, for any $w \in \Sigma^*$, define $\theta_w: K \times \Sigma \rightarrow K \cup \{t\}$ as follows:

$$\theta_w(q, a) = \begin{cases} p, \text{ if } (q, w, a) \vdash_M^+ (p, w, a) \text{ but it is not true that} \\ \quad (q, w, a) \vdash_M^+ (r, w, a) \vdash_M^+ (p, w, a) \text{ for any} \\ \quad r \neq p \\ t, \text{ if there is no } p \in K \text{ such that} \\ \quad (q, w, a) \vdash_M^+ (p, w, a). \end{cases}$$

Now suppose that $w, v \in \Sigma^*$, $\chi_w = \chi_v$, and $\theta_w = \theta_v$. Show that, for any $u \in \Sigma^*$, M accepts wu if and only if M accepts vu.

(c) Let R be defined as in Problem 2.5.4 for the language L accepted by M. Show that the number of equivalence classes of R is finite. (Use Part (b) of this problem. How many functions are there from K or $K \times \Sigma$ to $K \cup \{t\}$?) Thus by Part (b) of Problem 2.5.4, L is accepted by some finite automaton.

(d) Can the argument above be adapted to provide an algorithm for *constructing* an equivalent finite automaton from a two-way finite automaton?

(e) Can the argument above be adapted to the case of *nondeterministic* two-way finite automata?

2.5.6. An **arithmetic progression** is the set $\{p + qn: n = 0, 1, 2, \ldots\}$ for some $p, q \in \mathbb{N}$.

(a) (Easy) Show that if $L \subseteq \{a\}^*$ and $\{n: a^n \in L\}$ is an arithmetic progression, then L is regular.

(b) Show that if $L \subseteq \{a\}^*$ and $\{n: a^n \in L\}$ is a union of finitely many arithmetic progressions, then L is regular.

(c) (Harder) Show that if $L \subseteq \{a\}^*$ is regular, then $\{n: a^n \in L\}$ is a union of finitely many arithmetic progressions. (This is the converse of Part (b).)

(d) Show that if Σ is any alphabet and $L \subseteq \Sigma^*$ is regular, then $\{|w|: w \in L\}$ is a union of finitely many arithmetic progressions. (*Hint:* Use Part (c).)

2.5.7. In the "*If*" part of the construction in Section 2.5, we assume that M is deterministic. Can the construction be readily modified to work even when M is nondeterministic? (Naturally, M can be converted into a deterministic machine, but we are interested in a more direct construction.)

2.5.8. Let Σ be an alphabet and $w \in \Sigma^*$. Let $n = |w|$. This problem deals with the construction of a deterministic finite automaton M_w such that

$$L(M_w) = \{u \in \Sigma^*: u = u_1 w u_2 \quad \text{for some} \quad u_1, u_2 \in \Sigma^*\}.$$

(a) Let $i < n$, and $w(1)w(2)\ldots w(i)$ be a prefix of w. Let us define $f_w(i)$—the **failure function**—to be the largest $j < i$ such that $w(1)\ldots w(j) = w(i-j+1)\ldots w(i)$. Describe an algorithm for computing the values of $f_w(i)$, $1 \leq i < n$.

(b) Let $M_w = (K, \Sigma, \delta, s, F)$ where $K = \{q_0, \ldots, q_n\}$, $s = q_0$, $F = \{q_n\}$, and δ is inductively defined as follows, for all $a \in \Sigma$.

1. $$\delta(q_0, a) = \begin{cases} q_1 & \text{if } w(1) = a \\ q_0 & \text{otherwise} \end{cases}$$

2. $$\text{For } j > 0,\ \delta(q_j, a) = \begin{cases} q_{j+1} & \text{if } w(j+1) = a \\ q_n & \text{if } j = n \\ \delta(q_{f_w(j)}, a) & \text{otherwise} \end{cases}$$

Show that $L(M_w) = \{u \in \Sigma^* : u = u_1 w u_2 \text{ for some } u_1, u_2 \in \Sigma^*\}$.

(c) Let $W = \{w_1, \ldots, w_p\} \subseteq \Sigma^*$. Generalize (a) and (b) above to derive a systematic way of constructing a finite automaton M_W that accepts all strings that have at least one string in W as a substring. For example, if $\Sigma = \{a, b\}$ and $W = \{aab, abaa, abb\}$, M_W could be like this:

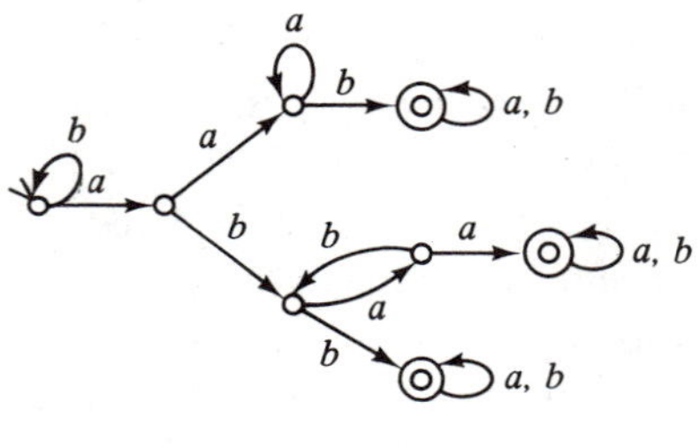

2.6.1. Let $D = \{0, 1\}$ and let $T = D \times D \times D$. A correct addition of two numbers in binary notation can be pictured as a string in T^* if we think of the symbols in T as vertical columns. For example,

$$\begin{array}{r} 0\ 1\ 0\ 1 \\ +0\ 1\ 1\ 0 \\ \hline 1\ 0\ 1\ 1 \end{array}$$

would be pictured as the following string of four symbols.

$$\begin{pmatrix}0\\0\\1\end{pmatrix} \begin{pmatrix}1\\1\\0\end{pmatrix} \begin{pmatrix}0\\1\\1\end{pmatrix} \begin{pmatrix}1\\0\\1\end{pmatrix}$$

Show that the set of all strings in T^* that represent correct additions is a regular language.

2.6.2. Show that each of the following is or is not a regular language. The **decimal notation** for a number is the number written in the usual way, as a string over the alphabet $\{0, 1, \ldots, 9\}$. For example, the decimal notation for 13 is a string of length 2. In **unary notation,** only the symbol I is used; thus 5 would be represented as IIIII in unary notation.

(a) $\{w\colon w$ is the unary notation for a number that is a multiple of 7$\}$

(b) $\{w\colon w$ is the decimal notation for a number that is a multiple of 7$\}$

(c) $\{w\colon w$ is the unary notation for a number n such that there is a pair $p, p + 2$ of twin primes, both greater than $n\}$

(d) $\{w\colon w$ is, for some $n \geq 1$, the unary notation for $10^n\}$

(e) $\{w\colon w$ is, for some $n \geq 1$, the decimal notation for $10^n\}$

(f) $\{w\colon w$ is a sequence of decimal digits that occurs in the infinite decimal expansion of $\frac{1}{7}\}$

(For example, 5714 is such a sequence, since $\frac{1}{7} =$ 0.14285714285714 . . . .)

2.6.3. Prove that $\{a^nba^mba^{n+m}\colon n, m \geq 1\}$ is not regular.

2.6.4. This problem establishes a stronger version of Theorem 2.6.1, which is used in several of the subsequent problems. The proof is similar to that of Theorem 2.6.1. Let $M = (K, \Sigma, \delta, s, F)$ be a deterministic finite automaton, and let w be *any* string in $L(M)$ such that $|w| \geq |K|$. Show that there are strings x, y, and z such that $w = xyz$, $|xy| \leq |K|$, $y \neq e$, and $xy^nz \in L(M)$ for every $n \geq 0$. This result is stronger than Theorem 2.6.1 in two important respects. First, it applies to any sufficiently long string w in the language; in Theorem 2.6.1 the string is chosen for us. Second, the lengths of the initial "unpumped part" x, and the "pumped part" y, are bounded.

2.6.5. Using Problem 2.6.4 and closure under intersection, show that the following are not regular.

(a) $\{ww^R\colon w \in \{a, b\}^*\}$

(b) $\{ww\colon w \in \{a, b\}^*\}$

(c) $\{w\bar{w}\colon w \in \{a, b\}^*\}$, where $\bar{w}$ stands for w with each occurrence of a replaced by b, and vice versa.

2.6.6. Using Problem 2.6.4, show that for any deterministic finite automaton $M = (K, \Sigma, \delta, s, F)$, M accepts an infinite language if and only if M accepts some string of length greater than or equal to $|K|$ and less than $2|K|$.

2.6.7. True or false? Explain your answer in each case. (In each case, a fixed alphabet Σ is assumed.)

(a) Every subset of a regular language is regular.

(b) Every regular language has a regular proper subset.

(c) If L is regular, then so is $\{xy: x \in L \text{ and } y \notin L\}$.

(d) $\{w: w = w^R\}$ is regular.

(e) If L is a regular language, then so is $\{w: w \in L \text{ and } w^R \in L\}$.

(f) If C is any set of regular languages, then $\bigcup C$ is a regular language.

(g) $\{xyx^R: x, y \in \Sigma^*\}$ is regular.

2.6.8. The notion of a deterministic 2-tape finite automaton was defined in Problem 2.1.5. Show that $\{(a^nb, a^mb^p): n, m, p \geq 0, n = m \text{ or } n = p\}$ is not accepted by any deterministic 2-tape finite automaton. (*Hint:* Suppose this set were accepted by some deterministic 2-tape finite automaton M. Then M accepts $(a^nb, a^{n+1}b^n)$ for every n. Show by a pumping argument that it also accepts $(a^nb, a^{n+1}b^{n+q})$ for some $n \geq 0$ and $q > 0$, a contradiction.) By Problem 2.4.7, then, nondeterministic 2-tape finite automata cannot always be converted to deterministic ones, and by Problem 2.1.5, the sets accepted by deterministic 2-tape finite automata are not closed under union.

2.6.9. A **2-head finite automaton** is a finite automaton with *two* tape heads that may move independently, but from left to right only, on the input tape. As with a 2-tape finite automaton (Problem 2.1.5), the state set is divided into two parts; each part corresponds to reading and moving one tape head. A string is accepted if both heads wind up together at the end of the string with the finite control in a final state. Two-head finite automata may be either deterministic or nondeterministic. Using a state-diagram notation of your own design, show that the following languages are accepted by 2-head finite automata.

(a) $\{a^nb^n: n \geq 0\}$

(b) $\{ww: w \in \{a, b\}^*\}$

(c) $\{a^1ba^2ba^3b \ldots a^kb: k \geq 1\}$

In which cases can you make your machines deterministic?

2.6.10. This problem establishes another strengthening of Theorem 2.6.1; in this case, the goal is to make the "pumped" part as *long* as possible, Let $M = (K, \Sigma, \delta, s, F)$ be a deterministic finite automaton, and let w be any string in $L(M)$ of length at least $|K|$. Show that there are strings x, y, and z such that $w = xyz$, $|y| \geq (|w| - |K| + 1)/|K|$, and $xy^nz \in L(M)$ for each $n \geq 0$.

2.6.11. Let $T = D \times D \times D$ where $D = \{0, 1\}$ as in Problem 2.6.1. A correct *multiplication* of two integers can also be represented by a string in T^*. For example, the multiplication $10 \times 5 = 50$, or

$$\begin{array}{r} 0\ 0\ 1\ 0\ 1\ 0 \\ \times\, 0\ 0\ 0\ 1\ 0\ 1 \\ \hline 1\ 1\ 0\ 0\ 1\ 0 \end{array}$$

would be represented by the following string of six symbols.

$$\begin{pmatrix}0\\0\\1\end{pmatrix} \begin{pmatrix}0\\0\\1\end{pmatrix} \begin{pmatrix}1\\0\\0\end{pmatrix} \begin{pmatrix}0\\1\\0\end{pmatrix} \begin{pmatrix}1\\0\\1\end{pmatrix} \begin{pmatrix}0\\1\\0\end{pmatrix}$$

Show that the set of strings in T^* that represent correct multiplications is *not* a regular language. (*Hint:* Consider the multiplication $(2^n + 1)(2^n + 1)$, and use Problem 2.6.4.)

REFERENCES

Some of the first papers on finite automata were

G. H. MEALY, "A Method for Synthesizing Sequential Circuits," *Bell System Technical Journal*, 34, no. 5 (1955), 1045–1079,

and

E. F. MOORE, "Gedanken-Experiments on Sequential Machines," in *Automata Studies*, ed. C. E. Shannon and J. McCarthy, pp. 129–153. Princeton: Princeton University Press, 1956.

The classical paper on finite automata (containing Theorem 2.3.1) is

M. O. RABIN and D. SCOTT, "Finite Automata and their Decision Problems," *IBM Journal of Research and Development*, 3 (1959), 114–125.

Theorem 2.5.1, showing that finite automata accept regular languages, is due to Kleene:

S. C. KLEENE, "Representation of Events by Nerve Nets," in *Automata Studies*, ed. C. E. Shannon and J. McCarthy, pp. 3–42. Princeton: Princeton University Press, 1956.

Our proof of this theorem follows the paper

R. MCNAUGHTON and H. YAMADA, "Regular Expressions and State Graphs for Automata," *IEEE Transactions on Electronic Computers*, EC-9, 1 (1960), 39–47.

Theorem 2.6.1 (known as the Pumping Lemma) *is from*

V. BAR-HILLEL, M. PERLES, and E. SHAMIR, "On Formal Properties of Simple Phrase Structure Grammars," *Zeitschrift für Phonetik, Sprachwissenschaft, und Kommunikationsforschung*, 14 (1961), 143–172.

Finite-state transducers (Problem 2.1.4) were introduced in

S. GINSBURG, "Examples of Abstract Machines," *IEEE Transactions on Electronic Computers*, EC-11, 2 (1962), 132–135.

Two-tape finite state automata (Problems 2.1.5 and 2.4.7) are examined in

M. BIRD, "The Equivalence Problem for Deterministic Two-tape Automata," *Journal of Computer and Systems Sciences*, 7 (1973), 218–236.

Problem 2.1.8 on minimizing finite automata is from Moore's paper cited above. A more efficient algorithm is given in

J. E. HOPCROFT, "An *n* log *n* Algorithm for Minimizing the States in a Finite Automaton," *The Theory of Machines and Computations*, ed. Z. Kohavi. New York: Academic Press, 1971.

The equivalence of one-way and two-way finite automata (Problem 2.5.5) was shown in

J. C. SHEPHERDSON, "The Reduction of Two-Way Automata to One-Way Automata," *IBM Journal of Research and Development*, 3 (1959), 198–200.

CHAPTER 3

CONTEXT-FREE LANGUAGES

3.1 CONTEXT-FREE GRAMMARS

Think of yourself as a language processor. You can recognize a legal English sentence when you hear one; "the cat is in the hat" is at least syntactically correct (whether or not it says anything that happens to be the truth), but "hat the the in is cat" is gibberish. However you manage to do it, you can immediately tell when reading such sentences whether they are formed according to generally accepted rules for sentence structure. In this respect you are acting as a **language recognizer**: a device that accepts valid strings. The finite automata of the last chapter are formalized types of language recognizers.

You also, however, are capable of *producing* legal English sentences. Again, why you would want to do so and how you manage to do it are not our concern; but the fact is that you occasionally speak or write sentences, and in general they are syntactically correct (even when they are lies). In this respect you are acting as a **language generator**. In this section we shall study certain types of formal language generators. Such a device begins, when given some sort of "start" signal, to construct a string. Its operation is not completely determined from the beginning but is nevertheless limited by a set of rules. Eventually this process halts and the device outputs a completed string. The language defined by the device is the set of all strings that it can produce.

Neither a recognizer nor a generator for the English language is at all easy to produce; indeed, from a formal standpoint these tasks may be impossible. Nevertheless the idea of a language generator has some explanatory force in attempts to discuss human language. More important for us, however, is the theory of generators of formal, "artificial" languages, such as the regular languages and the important class of "context-free" languages introduced below. This theory will neatly complement the study of automata, which *recognize* languages, and is also of practical value in the specification and analysis of computer languages.

Regular expressions can be viewed as language generators. For example, consider the regular expression $a(a^* \cup b^*)b$. A verbal description of how to generate a string in accordance with this expression would be the following.

> First output an a. Then do one of the following two things:
> Either output a number of a's or output a number of b's.
> Finally output a b.

The language associated with this language generator—that is, the set of all strings that can be produced by the process just described—is, of course, exactly the regular language defined in the way described earlier by the regular expression $a(a^* \cup b^*)b$.

Regular expressions serve as language generators in such a way that the strings in the language can be produced from left to right—that is, we can imagine each symbol of the generated string to be output as it is determined. However, there are more complex sorts of language generators, called *context-free grammars*, which are based on a more complete understanding of the structure of the strings belonging to the language. To take again the example of the language generated by $a(a^* \cup b^*)b$, note that any string in this language consists of a leading a, followed by a middle part—generated by $(a^* \cup b^*)$—followed by a trailing b. If we let S be a new symbol interpreted as "a string in the language," and M be a symbol standing for "middle part," then we can express this observation by writing

$$S \rightarrow aMb,$$

where $\rightarrow$ is read "can be." We call such an expression a **rule**. What can M, the middle part, be? The answer is: either a string of a's or a string of b's. We express this by adding the rules

$$M \rightarrow A \qquad \text{and} \qquad M \rightarrow B,$$

where A and B are new symbols that stand for strings of a's and b's, respectively. Now, what is a string of a's? It can be the empty string

$$A \rightarrow e,$$

or it may consist of a leading a followed by a string of a's:

$$A \rightarrow aA.$$

Similarly, for B:

$$B \rightarrow e \qquad \text{or} \qquad B \rightarrow bB.$$

The language denoted by the regular expression $a(a^* \cup b^*)b$ can then be defined alternatively by the following language generator.

> Start with the string consisting of the single symbol S. Find a symbol in the current string that appears to the left of $\longrightarrow$ in one of the rules above. Replace an occurrence of this symbol with the string that appears to the right of $\longrightarrow$ in the same rule. Repeat this process until no such symbol can be found.

For example, to generate the string *aaab* we start with S, as specified; we then replace S by aMb according to the first rule, $S \longrightarrow aMb$. To aMb we apply the rule $M \longrightarrow A$ and obtain aAb. We then twice apply the rule $A \longrightarrow aA$ to get the string $aaaAb$. Finally, we apply the rule $A \longrightarrow e$. In the resulting string, *aaab*, we cannot identify any symbol that appears to the left of $\longrightarrow$ in some rule. Thus the operation of our language generator has ended, and *aaab* was produced, as promised.

A context-free grammar is a language generator that operates like the one above, with some such set of rules. Let us pause to explain at this point why such a language generator is called *context-free.* Consider the string $aaAb$, which was an intermediate stage in the generation of *aaab*. It is natural to call the strings *aa* and *b* that surround the symbol A the *context* of A in this particular string. Now, the rule $A \longrightarrow aA$ says that we can replace A by the string aA no matter what the surrounding strings are; in other words, *independently of the context of A*. In a subsequent chapter, we shall examine more general grammars, in which replacements may be conditioned on the existence of an appropriate context.

In a context-free grammar, some symbols appear to the left of $\longrightarrow$ in rules—S, M, A, and B in our example—and some—*a* and *b*—do not. Symbols of the latter kind are called **terminals**, since the production of a string consisting solely of such symbols signals the termination of the generation process. All these ideas are stated formally in Definition 3.1.1.

Definition 3.1.1

A **context-free grammar** G is a quadruple (V, Σ, R, S), where

- V is an alphabet,
- Σ (the set of **terminals**) is a subset of V,
- R (the set of **rules**) is a finite subset of $(V - \Sigma) \times V^*$, and
- S (the **start symbol**) is an element of $V - \Sigma$.

The members of $V - \Sigma$ are called **nonterminals**. For any $A \in V - \Sigma$ and $u \in V^*$, we write $A \underset{G}{\longrightarrow} u$ whenever $(A, u) \in R$. For any strings $u, v \in V^*$, we write $u \underset{G}{\Rightarrow} v$ if and only if there are strings $x, y, v' \in V^*$

and $A \in V - \Sigma$ such that $u = xAy$, $v = xv'y$, and $A \underset{G}{\rightarrow} v'$. The relation $\overset{*}{\underset{G}{\Rightarrow}}$ is the reflexive, transitive closure of $\underset{G}{\Rightarrow}$. Finally, $L(G)$, the **language generated** by G, is $\{w \in \Sigma^* : S \overset{*}{\underset{G}{\Rightarrow}} w\}$; we also say that G **generates** each string in $L(G)$. A language L is said to be a **context-free language** if it is equal to $L(G)$ for some context-free grammar G.

When the grammar to which we refer is obvious, we write $A \rightarrow w$ and $u \Rightarrow v$ instead of $A \underset{G}{\rightarrow} w$ and $u \underset{G}{\Rightarrow} v$.

We call any sequence of the form

$$w_0 \underset{G}{\Rightarrow} w_1 \underset{G}{\Rightarrow} \cdots \underset{G}{\Rightarrow} w_n$$

a **derivation** in G of w_n from w_0. Here $w_0, \ldots, w_n$ may be any strings in V^*, and n, the **length** of the derivation, may be any natural number, including zero. We also say that the derivation has n **steps**.

Example 3.1.1

Consider the context-free grammar $G = (V, \Sigma, R, S)$, where $V = \{S, a, b\}$ and $\Sigma = \{a, b\}$ and R consists of the rules $S \rightarrow aSb$ and $S \rightarrow e$. A possible derivation is

$$S \Rightarrow aSb \Rightarrow aaSbb \Rightarrow aabb.$$

Here the first two steps used the rule $S \rightarrow aSb$, and the last used the rule $S \rightarrow e$. In fact, it is not hard to see that $L(G) = \{a^n b^n : n \geq 0\}$. Hence some context-free languages are not regular.

We shall soon see, however, that all regular languages are context-free.

Example 3.1.2

Let G be the grammar (W, Σ, R, S), where

$$\begin{aligned}
W &= \{S, A, N, V, P\} \cup \Sigma, \\
\Sigma &= \{\text{Jim, big, green, cheese, ate}\}, \\
R &= \{P \rightarrow N, \\
&\quad P \rightarrow AP, \\
&\quad S \rightarrow PVP, \\
&\quad A \rightarrow \text{big}, \\
&\quad A \rightarrow \text{green}, \\
&\quad N \rightarrow \text{cheese}, \\
&\quad N \rightarrow \text{Jim}, \\
&\quad V \rightarrow \text{ate}\}.
\end{aligned}$$

Here G is designed to be a grammar for a part of English; S stands for *sentence*, A for *adjective*, N for *noun*, V for *verb*, and P for *phrase*. The following are some strings in $L(G)$.

Jim ate cheese

big Jim ate green cheese

big cheese ate Jim

Unfortunately, these are also strings in $L(G)$.

big cheese ate green green big green big cheese

green Jim ate green big Jim

Example 3.1.3

Computer programs written in any programming language must satisfy some rigid criteria in order to be syntactically correct and therefore amenable to mechanical interpretation. Fortunately, the syntax of most programming languages can, unlike that of human languages, be captured by context-free grammars. We shall see in Section 3.6 that being context-free is extremely helpful when it comes to **parsing** a program, that is, analyzing it to understand its syntax. Here, we give a grammar that generates a fragment of many common programming languages. This language consists of all strings over the alphabet **(**, **)**, $+$, $*$, x, 1, and 2 that represent syntactically correct arithmetic expressions involving $+$ and $*$ over the variables $x1$ and $x2$. Examples of such strings are $x1$ and $x1*(x2 * x1 + x1)$, but not $*x1 + ($, $x + x2$, $+x1$, or $2 * x1$.

Let

$$G = (V, \Sigma, R, E)$$

where V, Σ, and R are as follows.

$$V = \{x, 1, 2, +, *, (,), T, F, E\}$$

$$\Sigma = \{x, 1, 2, +, *, (,)\}$$

$$R = \{E \to E + T, \quad \text{(R1)}$$

$$E \to T, \quad \text{(R2)}$$

$$T \to T * F, \quad \text{(R3)}$$

$$T \to F, \quad \text{(R4)}$$

$$F \to (E), \quad \text{(R5)}$$

$$F \to x1, \quad \text{(R6)}$$

$$F \to x2\}. \quad \text{(R7)}$$

The symbols E, T, and F are abbreviations for *expression*, *term*, and *factor*, respectively.

The grammar G generates the string $(x1*x2 + x1) * (x1 + x2)$ by the following derivation.

$E \Rightarrow T$	by Rule R2
$\Rightarrow T * F$	by Rule R3
$\Rightarrow T * (E)$	by Rule R5
$\Rightarrow T * (E + T)$	by Rule R1
$\Rightarrow T * (T + T)$	by Rule R2
$\Rightarrow T * (F + T)$	by Rule R4
$\Rightarrow T * (x1 + T)$	by Rule R6
$\Rightarrow T * (x1 + F)$	by Rule R4
$\Rightarrow T * (x1 + x2)$	by Rule R7
$\Rightarrow F * (x1 + x2)$	by Rule R4
$\Rightarrow (E) * (x1 + x2)$	by Rule R5
$\Rightarrow (E + T) * (x1 + x2)$	by Rule R1
$\Rightarrow (E + F) * (x1 + x2)$	by Rule R4
$\Rightarrow (E + x1) * (x1 + x2)$	by Rule R6
$\Rightarrow (T + x1) * (x1 + x2)$	by Rule R2
$\Rightarrow (T * F + x1) * (x1 + x2)$	by Rule R3
$\Rightarrow (F * F + x1) * (x1 + x2)$	by Rule R4
$\Rightarrow (F * x2 + x1) * (x1 + x2)$	by Rule R7
$\Rightarrow (x1 * x2 + x1) * (x1 + x2)$	by Rule R6

Example 3.1.4

Let G be the grammar (V, Σ, R, S), where

$$V = \{a, b, S, A\}$$
$$\Sigma = \{a, b\}$$
$$R = \{S \rightarrow AA,\; A \rightarrow AAA,\; A \rightarrow a,\; A \rightarrow bA,\; A \rightarrow Ab\}.$$

Then $L(G)$ consists of all strings in Σ^* with a number of a's that is even and greater than zero. Since this fact is not obvious, we prove it rather carefully.

First we show that every string in $L(G)$ contains an even, positive number of a's. To do so we prove a stronger fact.

Whenever $w \in V^*$ and $S \overset{+}{\underset{G}{\Rightarrow}} w$, then the sum of the number of A's in w and the number of a's in w is an even, positive number.† (1)

†The relation $\overset{+}{\underset{G}{\Rightarrow}}$ is, of course, the transitive closure of $\underset{G}{\Rightarrow}$.

This fact will hold true in particular when $w \in \Sigma^*$, so it will follow that if $w \in L(G)$, then the number of a's in w is even and positive (since then w contains *no* A's). We prove (1) by induction on the length, k, of a derivation of w from S such as the following.

$$S = w_0 \Rightarrow w_1 \Rightarrow \cdots \Rightarrow w_k = w, \qquad \text{where } k \geq 1.$$

Basis Step. ($k = 1$). Then w can only be AA, since $S \Rightarrow AA$ is the only derivation of length 1. Evidently (1) holds for $w = AA$.

Induction Hypothesis. Suppose that for all w such that $S \overset{*}{\underset{G}{\Rightarrow}} w$ in k or fewer steps, the sum of the number of occurrences of A and a in w is an even, positive number.

Induction Step. If $S \overset{+}{\underset{G}{\Rightarrow}} w$ in $k + 1$ steps, then $S \overset{+}{\underset{G}{\Rightarrow}} w'$ in k steps for some other string $w' \in V^*$, and $w' \underset{G}{\Rightarrow} w$. By the induction hypothesis, w' has an even, positive total number of A's and a's. Furthermore, w is derived from w' by the application of a rule of G. Each rule either adds two additional A's without changing the number of a's (the rules $A \longrightarrow AAA$ and $S \longrightarrow AA$), or replaces one A by one a (the rule $A \longrightarrow a$), or changes neither the number of A's nor the number of a's (the rules $A \longrightarrow Ab$ and $A \longrightarrow bA$). In all cases, (1) holds for w. This completes the induction.

Now we must show that any nonempty string of a's and b's with an even, positive number of a's is in $L(G)$. Let w be any such string. Then w may be written as $b^{m_1}ab^{m_2}a \ldots b^{m_{2n}}ab^{m_{2n+1}}$ for some $n > 0$ and some $m_1, \ldots, m_{2n+1} \geq 0$. (For example, if $w = bbaab$, then $n = 1$, $m_1 = 2$, $m_2 = 0$, and $m_3 = 1$, since $w = b^2ab^0ab^1$.) Then w can be produced as follows.

Derivation	Rule applied	
$S \Rightarrow AA$	$S \longrightarrow AA$	(once)
$\overset{*}{\Rightarrow} A^{2n}$	$A \longrightarrow AAA$	($n - 1$ times)
$\overset{*}{\Rightarrow} b^{m_1}A^{2n}$	$A \longrightarrow bA$	(m_1 times)
$\Rightarrow b^{m_1}aA^{2n-1}$	$A \longrightarrow a$	(once)
$\overset{*}{\Rightarrow} b^{m_1}ab^{m_2}A^{2n-1}$	$A \longrightarrow bA$	(m_2 times)
$\Rightarrow b^{m_1}ab^{m_2}aA^{2n-2}$	$A \longrightarrow a$	(once)
$\vdots$		
$\Rightarrow b^{m_1}ab^{m_2} \ldots b^{m_{2n}}A$		
$\overset{*}{\Rightarrow} b^{m_1}ab^{m_2} \ldots b^{m_{2n}}Ab^{m_{2n+1}}$	$A \longrightarrow Ab$	(m_{2n+1} times)
$\Rightarrow b^{m_1}ab^{m_2} \ldots b^{m_{2n}}ab^{m_{2n+1}}$	$A \longrightarrow a$	(once)

The first part of the proof of this example proceeded in a way typical of proofs involving grammars. To show that every string in $L(G)$ has some property, we may first prove a more general property of strings in V^* (not Σ^*) that are derivable from S. Such a proof is typically by induction on the number of steps in some derivation of the string in V^* from S.

Example 3.1.5

The following grammar generates all strings of properly balanced left and right parentheses: every left parenthesis can be paired with a unique subsequent right parenthesis, and every right parenthesis can be paired with a unique preceding left parenthesis. Moreover, the string between any such pair has the same property. We let $G = (V, \Sigma, R, S)$, where

$$\begin{aligned} V &= \{S, (,)\}, \\ \Sigma &= \{(,)\}, \\ R &= \{S \rightarrow e, \\ &\quad S \rightarrow SS, \\ &\quad S \rightarrow (S)\}. \end{aligned}$$

Two derivations in this grammar are

$$S \Rightarrow SS \Rightarrow S(S) \Rightarrow S((S)) \Rightarrow S(()) \Rightarrow (S)(()) \Rightarrow ()(())$$

and

$$S \Rightarrow SS \Rightarrow (S)S \Rightarrow ()S \Rightarrow ()(S) \Rightarrow ()((S)) \Rightarrow ()(()).$$

Thus the same string may have several derivations in a context-free grammar.

Note also that $L(G)$ is not regular. For if it were, so would $L(G) \cap (^*)^*$ be, by Theorem 2.5.1; but $L(G) \cap (^*)^*$ is $\{(^n)^n : n \geq 0\}$, which we already know not to be regular.

3.2 REGULAR LANGUAGES AND CONTEXT-FREE LANGUAGES

Although we have already seen that not all context-free languages are regular (Example 3.1.1), we prove in this section that every regular language is context-free. In fact, we shall prove a stronger result. We define a very special class of context-free grammars, called the *regular* grammars, and show that the regular languages are exactly the languages generated by such grammars. This result is of importance for two reasons. First, it provides yet another characterization of regular languages, in addition to those in terms of finite automata and regular expressions, and therefore adds to our understanding of the regular languages. Equally important, however, is that the *proof* illustrates the complementary nature of automata and grammars, an idea that will be exploited repeatedly in more complicated situations.

Definition 3.2.1

A context-free grammar $G = (V, \Sigma, R, S)$ is **regular** if and only if $R \subseteq (V - \Sigma) \times \Sigma^*((V - \Sigma) \cup \{e\})$.

That is, a regular grammar is a context-free grammar such that the right-hand side of every rule contains at most one nonterminal, which, if present, must be the last symbol in the string. Intuitively, this nonterminal can be used for remembering the "state" of a derivation.

Example 3.2.1

The grammar $G = (V, \Sigma, R, S)$, with

$$
\begin{aligned}
V &= \{S, A, B, a, b\},\\
\Sigma &= \{a, b\},\\
R &= \{S \longrightarrow bA,\\
&\quad\; S \longrightarrow aB,\\
&\quad\; A \longrightarrow abaS,\\
&\quad\; B \longrightarrow babS,\\
&\quad\; S \longrightarrow e\}
\end{aligned}
$$

is regular, since the right-hand side of each rule is of the form wN or w, where w is a string of terminal symbols and N is a nonterminal.

A derivation in G is

$$S \Rightarrow bA \Rightarrow babaS \Rightarrow babaaB \Rightarrow babaababS \Rightarrow babaabab.$$

Since the only rule with A on the right is $S \longrightarrow bA$ and the only rule with A on the left is $A \longrightarrow abaS$, any part of a derivation involving A is of the form

$$\ldots wS \Rightarrow wbA \Rightarrow wbabaS \Rightarrow \ldots.$$

Similarly, any part of a derivation involving B is of the form

$$\ldots wS \Rightarrow waB \Rightarrow wababS \Rightarrow \ldots.$$

It should then not be hard to convince yourself that

$$L(G) = (abab \cup baba)^*.$$

Theorem 3.2.1 *A language is regular if and only if it is generated by a regular grammar.*

Proof. (*Only if*) Suppose that L is regular; then L is accepted by a deterministic finite automaton $M = (K, \Sigma, \delta, s, F)$. Then let G be the regular grammar (V, Σ, R, S), where

$$V = \Sigma \cup K$$
$$S = s$$
$$R = \{q \longrightarrow ap: \delta(q, a) = p\} \cup \{q \longrightarrow e: q \in F\}.$$

(We assume, without loss of generality, that Σ and K are disjoint sets.) We now show that $L(G) = L(M)$. The rules of G are designed to mimic exactly the moves of M. That is, for any $\sigma_1, \ldots, \sigma_n \in \Sigma$ and $p_0, \ldots, p_n \in K$,

$$(p_0, \sigma_1 \ldots \sigma_n) \vdash_M (p_1, \sigma_2 \ldots \sigma_n) \vdash_M \cdots \vdash_M (p_n, e)$$

if and only if

$$p_0 \underset{G}{\Rightarrow} \sigma_1 p_1 \underset{G}{\Rightarrow} \sigma_1 \sigma_2 p_2 \underset{G}{\Rightarrow} \cdots \underset{G}{\Rightarrow} \sigma_1 \ldots \sigma_n p_n;$$

this is because $\delta(q, a) = p$ if and only if $q \longrightarrow ap$. Then to see that $L(M) \subseteq L(G)$, suppose that $w \in L(M)$; then $(s, w) \vdash_M^* (p, e)$ for some $p \in F$; then $s \overset{*}{\Rightarrow} wp$, and since $p \longrightarrow e$ is also a rule of G, $s \overset{*}{\Rightarrow} w$ and $w \in L(G)$. To see that $L(G) \subseteq L(M)$, suppose that $w \in L(G)$; then $S \underset{G}{\overset{*}{\Rightarrow}} w$, that is, $s \underset{G}{\overset{*}{\Rightarrow}} w$. The rule used at the last step of the derivation must have been of the form $p \longrightarrow e$ for some $p \in F$, so $s \underset{G}{\overset{*}{\Rightarrow}} wp \underset{G}{\Rightarrow} w$. But then $(s, w) \vdash_M^* (p, e)$ and $w \in L(M)$.

(*If*) Let $G = (V, \Sigma, R, S)$ be any regular grammar. We define a nondeterministic finite automaton M such that $L(M) = L(G)$. Let $M = (K, \Sigma, \Delta, s, F)$, where

$$K = (V - \Sigma) \cup \{f\} \qquad \text{where } f \text{ is a new element}$$
$$s = S$$
$$F = \{f\}$$
$$\Delta = \{(A, w, B): A \longrightarrow wB \in R;\ A, B \in V - \Sigma;\ w \in \Sigma^*\}$$
$$\cup \{(A, w, f): A \longrightarrow w \in R;\ A \in V - \Sigma;\ w \in \Sigma^*\}.$$

Once again, derivations are mimicked by moves, in the sense that for any $A_1, \ldots, A_n \in V - \Sigma$, $w_1, \ldots, w_n \in \Sigma^*$,

$$A_1 \underset{G}{\Rightarrow} w_1 A_2 \underset{G}{\Rightarrow} w_1 w_2 A_3 \underset{G}{\Rightarrow} \cdots \underset{G}{\Rightarrow} w_1 \ldots w_{n-1} A_n \underset{G}{\Rightarrow} w_1 \ldots w_n$$

if and only if

$$(A_1, w_1 \ldots w_n) \vdash_M (A_2, w_2 \ldots w_n) \vdash_M \cdots \vdash_M (A_n, w_n) \vdash_M (f, e).$$

Consequently, if $w \in L(G)$, so that $w \in \Sigma^*$ and $S \underset{G}{\overset{*}{\Rightarrow}} w$, then $(S, w) \vdash_M^* (f, e)$, so that $w \in L(M)$. Conversely, if $w \in L(M)$, so that $(S, w) \vdash_M^* (f, e)$, then $S \underset{G}{\overset{*}{\Rightarrow}} w$, so $w \in L(G)$. ■

Example 3.2.2

The nondeterministic finite automaton of Figure 3–1 corresponds to the regular grammar of the Example 3.2.1.

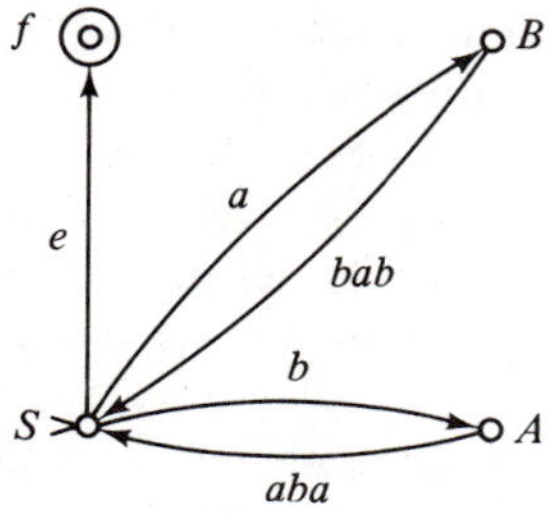

Figure 3–1

3.3 PUSHDOWN AUTOMATA

Not every context-free language can be recognized by a finite automaton, since, as we have already seen, some context-free languages are not regular. Yet the problem of recognizing context-free languages is an important one for both theoretical and practical reasons. What sort of more powerful automaton could be used for recognizing arbitrary context-free languages? Or, to be a bit more specific, what do we need to add to a finite automaton so that the construction in the proof of Theorem 3.2.1 can be generalized to apply to *all* context-free languages?

To take a particular example, consider $\{ww^R: w \in \Sigma^*\}$. It would seem that any automaton that recognizes the strings in this language by reading them from left to right must "remember" the first half of the input string so that it can check it—in reverse order—against the second half of the input. It is not surprising that this function cannot be performed by a finite automaton. If, however, the machine is capable of accumulating its input string as it is read, appending symbols one at a time to a stored string, then it could nondeterministically guess when the center of the input has been reached and thereafter check the symbols off from its memory one at a time (see Figure 3–2).

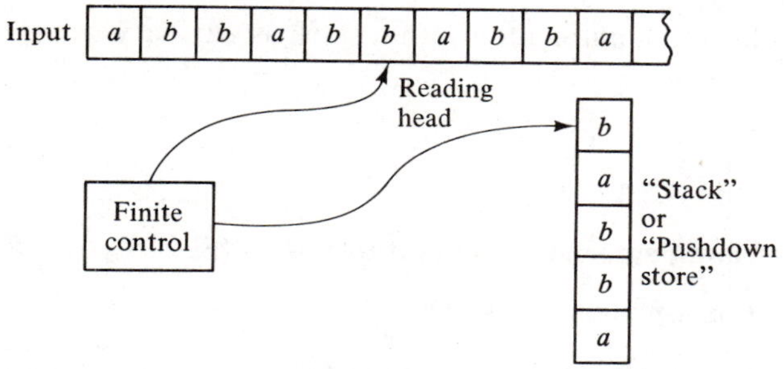

Figure 3–2

To take another example, the set of strings of balanced parentheses (Example 3.1.5) is also nonregular. However, computer programmers are familiar with a simple algorithm for recognizing this language: Start counting at zero, add one for every left parenthesis, and subtract one for every right parenthesis. If the count either goes negative at any time or ends up different from zero, then the string should be rejected as unbalanced; otherwise it should be accepted.

The above examples suggest that finite automata can be extended by the addition of an auxiliary storage device to accept arbitrary context-free languages. However, our goal is to design a class of automata that accept *exactly* the context-free languages; that is, we wish to be able to show that any language accepted by one of these devices is generated by a context-free grammar. With this goal in mind, let us look back at the proof that every language generated by a regular grammar is accepted by some finite automaton. The crux of that construction was to regard the nonterminal symbols as states of an automaton and to mimic every rule $A \longrightarrow wB$ by a transition (A, w, B): "If in state A, read w and go to state B." What if the rule were of the form $A \longrightarrow wBx$? If we "imitated" this generating rule simply by instructing the machine, "If in state A, read w and go to state B," there would be no way to remember that the string to be generated, starting with A, was to *finish* with x. Instead, we equip the machine with a **stack** or **pushdown store** onto which symbols can be placed, and mimic $A \longrightarrow wBx$ by "If in state A, read w, put x on the stack, and go to state B." Later, the symbols on the stack can be removed and checked against the input. The reason for this "last-in-first-out" method of retrieving stored symbols can be seen if we imagine another rule of the grammar to be $B \longrightarrow uCy$, which would be mimicked by "If in state B, read u, put y on the stack, and go to state C." The two grammatical rules together make it possible to generate $wuCyx$ from A; after sequentially carrying through the two corresponding transitions, the machine would have passed from state A, by reading wu, to state C, with y on top of the stack and x underneath it, in the correct order to be removed as the last part of the input is read.

The idea of an automaton with a stack as auxiliary storage can be formalized as follows.

Definition 3.3.1

A **pushdown automaton** is a sextuple $M = (K, \Sigma, \Gamma, \Delta, s, F)$, where

K is a finite set of **states**,

Σ is an alphabet (the **input symbols**),

Γ is an alphabet (the **stack symbols**),

$s \in K$ is the **initial state**,

$F \subseteq K$ is the set of **final states**, and

Δ, the **transition relation**, is a finite subset of

$$(K \times \Sigma^* \times \Gamma^*) \times (K \times \Gamma^*).$$

Intuitively, if $((p, u, \beta), (q, \gamma)) \in \Delta$, then M, whenever it is in state p with β at the top of the stack, may read u from the input tape, replace β by γ on the top of the stack, and enter state q. Such a pair $((p, u, \beta), (q, \gamma))$ is called a **transition** of M; since several transitions of M may be simultaneously applicable, the machines we are describing are nondeterministic in operation. (We shall later alter this definition to define a more restricted class, the deterministic pushdown automata.)

To **push** a symbol is to add it to the top of the stack; to **pop** a symbol is to remove it from the top of the stack. For example, the transition $((p, u, e), (q, a))$ pushes a, while $((p, u, a), (q, e))$ pops a.

As is the case with finite automata, during a computation the portion of the input already read does not affect the subsequent operation of the machine. Accordingly, a configuration is defined to be a member of $K \times \Sigma^* \times \Gamma^*$: The first component is the state of the machine, the second is the portion of the input yet to be read, and the third is the contents of the pushdown store, read top-down. (For example, if the configuration were (q, w, abc), the a would be on the top of the stack and the c on the bottom.) For every transition $((p, u, \beta), (q, \gamma)) \in \Delta$, and for every $x \in \Sigma^*$ and $\alpha \in \Gamma^*$, we define $(p, ux, \beta\alpha) \vdash_M (q, x, \gamma\alpha)$; moreover $\vdash_M$ (**yields in one step**) holds only between configurations that can be represented in this form for some transition, some x, and some α. We denote the reflexive, transitive closure of $\vdash_M$ by $\vdash_M^*$, and say that M **accepts** a string $w \in \Sigma^*$ if and only if $(s, w, e) \vdash_M^* (p, e, e)$ for some state $p \in F$. To put it another way, M accepts a string w if and only if there is a sequence of configurations $C_0, C_1, \ldots, C_n$ $(n \geq 0)$ such that $C_0 \vdash_M C_1 \vdash_M \cdots \vdash_M C_n$, $C_0 = (s, w, e)$, and $C_n = (p, e, e)$ for some $p \in F$. Any sequence of configurations $C_0, C_1, \ldots, C_n$ such that $C_i \vdash_M C_{i+1}$ for $i = 0, \ldots, n-1$ will be called a **computation** by M; it will be said to have **length** n, or to have n **steps**. The **language accepted** by M, denoted $L(M)$, is the set of all strings accepted by M.

When no confusion can result, we write $\vdash$ and $\vdash^*$ instead of $\vdash_M$ and $\vdash_M^*$.

Example 3.3.1

Every finite automaton can be viewed as a pushdown automaton that never operates on its stack. To be precise, let $M = (K, \Sigma, \Delta, s, F)$ be a finite automaton, and let $M' = (K, \Sigma, \Gamma, \Delta', s, F)$, where $\Gamma = \varnothing$ and $\Delta' = \{((p, u, e), (q, e)) : (p, u, q) \in \Delta\}$. Then M and M' accept the same language.

Example 3.3.2

Let us design a pushdown automaton M to accept the language $L = \{wcw^R: w \in \{a, b\}^*\}$. For example, $ababcbaba \in L$, but $abcab \notin L$ and $cbc \notin L$. We let $M = (K, \Sigma, \Gamma, \Delta, s, F)$, where $K = \{s, f\}$, $\Sigma = \{a, b, c\}$, $\Gamma = \{a, b\}$, and $F = \{f\}$, and Δ contains the following five transitions.

1. $((s, a, e), (s, a))$
2. $((s, b, e), (s, b))$
3. $((s, c, e), (f, e))$
4. $((f, a, a), (f, e))$
5. $((f, b, b), (f, e))$

This automaton operates in the following way. As it reads the first half of its input, it remains in its initial state s and uses transitions 1 and 2 to transfer symbols from the input string onto the pushdown store. Note that these transitions are applicable regardless of the current content of the pushdown store, since the "string" to be matched on the top of the pushdown store is the empty string. When the machine sees a c in the input string, it switches from state s to state f without operating on its stack. Thereafter only transitions 4 and 5 are operative; these permit the removal of the top symbol on the stack, provided that it is the same as the next input symbol. If the input symbol does not match the top symbol on the stack, no further operation is possible. If the automaton reaches in this way the configuration (f, e, e)—final state, end of input, empty stack—then the input was indeed of the form wcw^R and the automaton accepts. On the other hand, if the automaton detects a mismatch between input and stack symbols, or if the input is exhausted before the stack is emptied, then it does not accept.

To illustrate the operation of M, we describe a sequence of transitions for the input string *abbcbba*.

State	Unread Input	Stack	Transition Used
s	*abbcbba*	e	–
s	*bbcbba*	a	1
s	*bcbba*	ba	2
s	*cbba*	bba	2
f	*bba*	bba	3
f	*ba*	ba	5
f	a	a	5
f	e	e	4

Example 3.3.3

Now we construct a pushdown automaton to accept $\{ww^R : w \in \{a, b\}^*\}$. That is, the strings accepted by this machine are the same as those accepted by the machine of the previous example, except that the symbol c that marked the center of the strings is missing. Therefore the machine must "guess" when it has reached the middle of the input string and change from state s to state f in a nondeterministic fashion. Thus $M = (K, \Sigma, \Gamma, \Delta, s, F)$, where $K = \{s, f\}$, $\Sigma = \Gamma = \{a, b\}$, $F = \{f\}$ and Δ is the set of the following five transitions.

1. $((s, a, e), (s, a))$
2. $((s, b, e), (s, b))$
3. $((s, e, e), (f, e))$
4. $((f, a, a), (f, e))$
5. $((f, b, b), (f, e))$

Thus this machine is identical to that of the last example, except for transition 3. Whenever the machine is in state s, it can nondeterministically choose either to push the next input symbol onto the stack, or to switch to state f without consuming any input. Therefore even starting from a string of the form ww^R, M has computations that do not lead it to the accepting configuration (f, e, e); but there is *some* computation that leads M to this configuration if and only if the input string is of this form.

Example 3.3.4

This pushdown automaton accepts the language $\{w \in \{a, b\}^* : w$ has the same number of a's and b's$\}$. Either a string of a's or a string of b's is kept by M on its stack. A stack of a's indicates the excess of a's over b's thus far read, if in fact M has read more a's than b's; a stack of b's indicates the excess of b's over a's. In either case, M keeps a special symbol c on the bottom of the stack as a marker. Let $M = (K, \Sigma, \Gamma, \Delta, s, F)$, where $K = \{s, q, f\}$, $\Sigma = \{a, b\}$, $\Gamma = \{a, b, c\}$, $F = \{f\}$, and Δ is listed below.

1. $((s, e, e), (q, c))$
2. $((q, a, c), (q, ac))$
3. $((q, a, a), (q, aa))$
4. $((q, a, b), (q, e))$
5. $((q, b, c), (q, bc))$
6. $((q, b, b), (q, bb))$
7. $((q, b, a), (q, e))$
8. $((q, e, c), (f, e))$

Transition 1 puts M in state q while placing a c on the bottom of the stack. In state q, when M reads an a it either starts up a stack of a's from the bottom, while keeping the bottom marker (transition 2), or pushes an a onto a stack of a's (transition 3), or pops a b from a stack of b's (transition 4). When reading a b from the input, the machine acts analogously, pushing a b onto a stack of b's or a stack consisting of just a bottom marker, and popping an a from a stack of a's (transitions 5, 6, and 7). Finally, when c is the topmost (and therefore the only) symbol on the stack, the machine may remove it and pass to a final state (transition 8). If at this point all the input has been read, then the configuration (f, e, e) has been reached and the input string is accepted.

Here is an illustration of the operation of M.

State	Unread Input	Stack	Transition Used	Comments
s	$abbbabaa$	e	–	Initial configuration.
q	$abbbabaa$	c	1	
q	$bbbabaa$	ac	2	Start a stack of a's.
q	$bbabaa$	c	7	Remove one a.
q	$babaa$	bc	5	Start a stack of b's.
q	$abaa$	bbc	6	
q	baa	bc	4	
q	aa	bbc	6	
q	a	bc	4	
q	e	c	4	
f	e	e	8	Accepts.

3.4 PUSHDOWN AUTOMATA AND CONTEXT-FREE GRAMMARS

It turns out, as we show in this section, that the pushdown automaton is exactly what is needed to carry through a construction like that of Theorem 3.2.1 for arbitrary context-free grammars. This fact is of mathematical and practical significance: mathematical, because it knits together two different formal views of the same class of languages, and practical, because it lays the foundation for the study of syntax analyzers for "real" context-free languages such as programming languages.

Before getting to the proof itself, it will be helpful to introduce some preliminaries. Recall that if $G = (V, \Sigma, R, S)$ is a context-free grammar then $w \in L(G)$ if and only if $w \in \Sigma^*$ and there is a derivation

$$S \underset{G}{\Rightarrow} w_1 \underset{G}{\Rightarrow} w_2 \underset{G}{\Rightarrow} \cdots \underset{G}{\Rightarrow} w_{n-1} \underset{G}{\Rightarrow} w$$

for some strings $w_1, \ldots, w_{n-1} \in V^*$ $(n > 0)$. This derivation will be called a *leftmost* derivation if the nonterminal symbol replaced at every step is the leftmost nonterminal symbol in the string. For example, let G be the grammar of Example 3.1.5, which generates strings of balanced parentheses.

$$V = \{S, (,)\}$$
$$\Sigma = \{(,)\}$$
$$R = \{S \rightarrow e,$$
$$S \rightarrow SS,$$
$$S \rightarrow (S)\}$$

Then

$$S \Rightarrow SS \Rightarrow (S)S \Rightarrow ()S \Rightarrow ()(S) \Rightarrow ()()$$

is a leftmost derivation, but

$$S \Rightarrow SS \Rightarrow S(S) \Rightarrow (S)(S) \Rightarrow ()(S) \Rightarrow ()()$$

is not.

Formally, we write $\alpha \overset{L}{\underset{G}{\Rightarrow}} \beta$, where $\alpha, \beta \in V^*$, if and only if $\alpha = \alpha_1 A \alpha_2$, $\beta = \alpha_1 \gamma \alpha_2$, $A \rightarrow \gamma$ is a rule of G, and $\alpha_1 \in \Sigma^*$. We write $\overset{*L}{\underset{G}{\Rightarrow}}$ for the reflexive, transitive closure of $\overset{L}{\underset{G}{\Rightarrow}}$, and define a **leftmost derivation** to be a sequence of the form

$$w_0 \overset{L}{\underset{G}{\Rightarrow}} w_1 \overset{L}{\underset{G}{\Rightarrow}} \cdots \overset{L}{\underset{G}{\Rightarrow}} w_n$$

for any $n \geq 0$.

The crucial fact about leftmost derivations is given in the following lemma.

Lemma 3.4.1. *For any context-free grammar* $G = (V, \Sigma, R, S)$ *and any string* $w \in \Sigma^*$, $S \overset{*}{\underset{G}{\Rightarrow}} w$ *if and only if* $S \overset{*L}{\underset{G}{\Rightarrow}} w$.

Proof. In one direction this is obvious, since any leftmost derivation is a derivation. To prove the other direction, let

$$w_0 \underset{G}{\Rightarrow} w_1 \underset{G}{\Rightarrow} \cdots \underset{G}{\Rightarrow} w_n$$

be a derivation, not necessarily leftmost, where $w_0 = S$ and $w_n = w \in \Sigma^*$. We show how to transform it little by little into a leftmost derivation. Let k be the least number such that the step $w_k \underset{G}{\Rightarrow} w_{k+1}$ is *not* a leftmost derivation of w_{k+1} from w_k; if there is no such k, then we are done. We define another derivation

$$w'_0 \underset{G}{\Rightarrow} w'_1 \underset{G}{\Rightarrow} w'_2 \underset{G}{\Rightarrow} \cdots \underset{G}{\Rightarrow} w'_n$$

also of n steps and such that $w'_0 = w_0$ and $w'_n = w_n$. This new derivation either is leftmost or has the property that if $w'_{k'} \underset{G}{\Rightarrow} w'_{k'+1}$ is the earliest step in *this* derivation that is not leftmost, then $k' > k$. Since both derivations have the same length, the lemma will follow by induction.

Since $w_k \underset{G}{\Rightarrow} w_{k+1}$ is not leftmost, w_k is of the form $\alpha A \beta B \gamma$ ($\alpha \in \Sigma^*, \beta, \gamma \in V^*, A, B \in V - \Sigma$) and $w_{k+1} = \alpha A \beta \delta \gamma$, where $B \underset{G}{\rightarrow} \delta$. Since $w_n \in \Sigma^*$, $k + 1 < n$, and there is some later step where the indicated occurrence of A is replaced. Thus let l be the least number greater than k such that $w_l = \alpha A \epsilon$ for some $\epsilon \in V^*$ and $w_{l+1} = \alpha \zeta \epsilon$, where $A \underset{G}{\rightarrow} \zeta$. Then $\beta B \gamma \overset{*}{\underset{G}{\Rightarrow}} \epsilon$ in $l - k$ steps. Then we can switch the uses of $B \underset{G}{\rightarrow} \delta$ and $A \underset{G}{\rightarrow} \zeta$ as follows.

$$
\begin{array}{ll}
w_0 \overset{*L}{\underset{G}{\Rightarrow}} w_k = \alpha A \beta B \gamma & k \text{ steps} \\
\overset{L}{\underset{G}{\Rightarrow}} \alpha \zeta \beta B \gamma & 1 \text{ step} \\
\overset{*}{\underset{G}{\Rightarrow}} \alpha \zeta \epsilon & l - k \text{ steps} \\
\overset{*}{\underset{G}{\Rightarrow}} w_n & n - l - 1 \text{ steps}
\end{array}
$$

The new derivation is of length n and begins with at least $k + 1$ leftmost steps. ■

This lemma is used below to permit us to restrict our attention, when considering a property of some string $w \in L(G)$, only to *leftmost* derivations of that string from S.

It will also be useful to be able to combine two computations by a pushdown automaton M into a single computation. While it is obvious that if $(q_1, w_1, \alpha_1) \vdash_M^* (q_2, w_2, \alpha_2)$ and $(q_2, w_2, \alpha_2) \vdash_M^* (q_3, w_3, \alpha_3)$, then $(q_1, w_1, \alpha_1) \vdash_M^* (q_3, w_3, \alpha_3)$, there is a slightly more subtle fact that can be made explicit as follows (compare with Lemma 2.2.1).

Lemma 3.4.2. *If M is a pushdown automaton and $(q_1, w_1, \alpha_1) \vdash_M^* (q_2, e, \alpha_2)$ and $(q_2, w_2, \alpha_2\alpha_3) \vdash_M^* (q_3, e, \alpha_4)$, then $(q_1, w_1w_2, \alpha_1\alpha_3) \vdash_M^* (q_3, e, \alpha_4)$. In particular, if $(q_1, w_1, \alpha_1) \vdash_M^* (q_2, e, e)$ and $(q_2, w_2, \alpha_3) \vdash_M^* (q_3, e, e)$, then $(q_1, w_1w_2, \alpha_1\alpha_3) \vdash_M^* (q_3, e, e)$.*

We leave a formal proof to the reader (Problem 3.4.6). To paraphrase this lemma, during a computation a pushdown automaton neither looks ahead beyond the input it actually reads nor peeks below the part of the stack it actually uses, and its operation is unaffected by any such unseen part of the input or hidden part of the pushdown store.

Theorem 3.4.1. *The class of languages accepted by pushdown automata is exactly the class of context-free languages.*

Proof. We break this proof into two parts, of which the first is easier.

Lemma 3.4.3. *Each context-free language is accepted by some pushdown automaton.*

Proof. Let $G = (V, \Sigma, R, S)$ be a context-free grammar; we must construct a pushdown automaton M such that $L(M) = L(G)$. The machine we construct has only two states, p and q, and remains permanently in state q after its first move. Also, M uses V, the set of terminals and nonterminals, as its stack alphabet. We let $M = (\{p, q\}, \Sigma, V, \Delta, p, \{q\})$, where Δ contains the following transitions.

1. $((p, e, e), (q, S))$
2. $((q, e, A), (q, x))$ for each rule $A \longrightarrow x$ in R.
3. $((q, a, a), (q, e))$ for each $a \in \Sigma$.

The pushdown automaton M begins by pushing S, the start symbol of G, on its initially empty pushdown store, and entering state q (transition 1). On each subsequent step, it either replaces the topmost symbol A on the stack, provided that it is a nonterminal, by the right-hand side x of some rule $A \longrightarrow x$ in R (transitions of type 2), or pops the topmost symbol from the stack, provided that it is a terminal symbol that matches the next input symbol (transitions of type 3). The transitions of M are designed so that the pushdown store during an accepting computation mimics a leftmost derivation of the input string: M intermittently carries out a step of such a derivation on the stack, and between such steps it strips away from the top of the stack any terminal symbols and matches them against symbols in the input string.

Example 3.4.1

Consider the grammar $G = (V, \Sigma, R, S)$ with

$$\begin{aligned} V &= \{S, a, b, c\} \\ \Sigma &= \{a, b, c\} \\ R &= \{S \longrightarrow aSa, \\ &\quad\; S \longrightarrow bSb, \\ &\quad\; S \longrightarrow c\}, \end{aligned}$$

which generates the language $\{wcw^R : w \in \{a, b\}^*\}$. The corresponding pushdown automaton, according to the construction above, is $M = (\{p, q\}, \Sigma, V,$

$\Delta, p, \{q\})$, with

$$\Delta = \{((p, e, e), (q, S)), \quad \text{(T1)}$$
$$((q, e, S), (q, aSa)), \quad \text{(T2)}$$
$$((q, e, S), (q, bSb)), \quad \text{(T3)}$$
$$((q, e, S), (q, c)), \quad \text{(T4)}$$
$$((q, a, a), (q, e)), \quad \text{(T5)}$$
$$((q, b, b), (q, e)), \quad \text{(T6)}$$
$$((q, c, c), (q, e))\}. \quad \text{(T7)}$$

The string *abbcbba* is accepted by *M* through the following sequence of moves.

State	Unread Input	Stack	Transition Used
p	*abbcbba*	*e*	
q	*abbcbba*	*S*	T1
q	*abbcbba*	*aSa*	T2
q	*bbcbba*	*Sa*	T5
q	*bbcbba*	*bSba*	T3
q	*bcbba*	*Sba*	T6
q	*bcbba*	*bSbba*	T3
q	*cbba*	*Sbba*	T6
q	*cbba*	*cbba*	T4
q	*bba*	*bba*	T7
q	*ba*	*ba*	T6
q	*a*	*a*	T6
q	*e*	*e*	T5

Compare this to the operation, on the same string, of the pushdown automaton of Example 3.3.2.

To prove that $L(M) = L(G)$, we prove the following two claims.

Claim I. *If* $S \overset{*L}{\underset{G}{\Rightarrow}} \alpha_1\alpha_2$, *where* $\alpha_1 \in \Sigma^*$ *and* $\alpha_2 \in (V - \Sigma)V^* \cup \{e\}$, *then* $(q, \alpha_1, S) \vdash_M^* (q, e, \alpha_2)$.

Claim II. *If* $(q, \alpha_1, S) \vdash_M^* (q, e, \alpha_2)$, *where* $\alpha_1 \in \Sigma^*$ *and* $\alpha_2 \in V^*$, *then* $S \overset{*L}{\underset{G}{\Rightarrow}} \alpha_1\alpha_2$.

These claims will suffice to establish Lemma 3.4.3, since it will follow (by taking $\alpha_2 = e$) that $S \overset{*L}{\underset{G}{\Rightarrow}} \alpha$, where $\alpha \in \Sigma^*$, if and only if $(q, \alpha, S) \vdash_M^* (q, e, e)$—in other words, $\alpha \in L(G)$ if and only if $\alpha \in L(M)$.

Proof of Claim I. Suppose that $S \overset{*L}{\underset{G}{\Rightarrow}} \alpha$, where $\alpha = \alpha_1\alpha_2$, $\alpha_1 \in \Sigma^*$, and $\alpha_2 \in (V - \Sigma)V^* \cup \{e\}$. We prove the Claim I by induction on the length of a derivation of α from S.

Basis Step. If the derivation is of length 0, then $S = \alpha$, and hence $\alpha_1 = e$ and $\alpha_2 = S$; but then trivially, $(q, \alpha_1, S) \vdash_M^* (q, e, \alpha_2)$.

Induction Hypothesis. Assume that if $S \overset{*L}{\underset{G}{\Rightarrow}} \alpha_1\alpha_2$ by a derivation of length n or less, $n \geq 0$, then $(q, \alpha_1, S) \vdash_M^* (q, e, \alpha_2)$.

Induction Step. Let

$$S = u_0 \overset{L}{\underset{G}{\Rightarrow}} u_1 \overset{L}{\underset{G}{\Rightarrow}} \cdots \overset{L}{\underset{G}{\Rightarrow}} u_{n+1} = \alpha$$

be a leftmost derivation of α from S, and let $\alpha = \alpha_1\alpha_2$ as specified. Clearly, u_n has at least one nonterminal; thus $u_n = \beta_1 A \beta_2$ and $u_{n+1} = \beta_1\gamma\beta_2$, where $\beta_1 \in \Sigma^*$, $A \in V - \Sigma$, and $A \underset{G}{\rightarrow} \gamma$. By the induction hypothesis

$$(q, \beta_1, S) \vdash_M^* (q, e, A\beta_2), \tag{2}$$

but since $A \underset{G}{\rightarrow} \gamma$, $((q, e, A), (q, \gamma))$ is a transition of M of type 2, so

$$(q, e, A\beta_2) \vdash_M (q, e, \gamma\beta_2). \tag{3}$$

Now α is $\beta_1\gamma\beta_2$, where $\beta_1 \in \Sigma^*$, and is also $\alpha_1\alpha_2$, where $\alpha_1 \in \Sigma^*$ and α_2 is either e or begins with a nonterminal. Hence $|\alpha_1| \geq |\beta_1|$ and $|\alpha_2| \leq |\gamma\beta_2|$, and we can write α_1 as $\beta_1\delta$ for some $\delta \in \Sigma^*$ such that $\delta\alpha_2 = \gamma\beta_2$. Therefore

$$(q, \delta, \gamma\beta_2) \vdash_M^* (q, e, \alpha_2) \tag{4}$$

by transitions of type 3. Putting statements (2), (3), and (4) together by Lemma 3.4.2,

$$\begin{aligned}(q, \alpha_1, S) = \; & (q, \beta_1\delta, S)\\ & \vdash_M^* (q, \delta, A\beta_2)\\ & \vdash_M (q, \delta, \gamma\beta_2)\\ & \vdash_M^* (q, e, \alpha_2)\end{aligned}$$

and the induction step is completed.

Proof of Claim II. Now suppose that $(q, \alpha_1, S) \vdash_M^* (q, e, \alpha_2)$, with $\alpha_1 \in \Sigma^*$ and $\alpha_2 \in V^*$; we show that $S \overset{*L}{\underset{G}{\Rightarrow}} \alpha_1\alpha_2$. Again, the proof is by induction, this time on the length of a computation by M.

Basis Step. If $(q, \alpha_1, S) \vdash_M^* (q, e, \alpha_2)$ in zero steps, that is, $(q, \alpha_1, S) = (q, e, \alpha_2)$, then $\alpha_1 = e$, $\alpha_2 = S$, and clearly $S \overset{*L}{\underset{G}{\Rightarrow}} \alpha_1\alpha_2$.

Induction Hypothesis. If $(q, \alpha_1, S) \vdash_M^* (q, e, \alpha_2)$ by a computation of n steps or fewer, $n \geq 0$, then $S \overset{*L}{\underset{G}{\Rightarrow}} \alpha_1\alpha_2$.

Induction Step. Suppose that $(q, \alpha_1, S) \vdash_M^* (q, e, \alpha_2)$ in $n + 1$ steps.

Then for some $\beta \in \Sigma^*, \gamma \in \Gamma^*, (q, \alpha_1, S) \vdash_M^* (q, \beta, \gamma)$ in n steps, and $(q, \beta, \gamma) \vdash_M (q, e, \alpha_2)$. This last move is the result of a transition of type 2 or of type 3.

If the last transition was of type 2, then $\beta = e, \gamma = A\gamma_1$, and $\alpha_2 = \delta\gamma_1$ for some $A \in V - \Sigma, \gamma_1 \in V^*$, and some rule $A \underset{G}{\rightarrow} \delta$. Since $S \overset{*L}{\underset{G}{\Rightarrow}} \alpha_1 A\gamma_1$ by the induction hypothesis, $S \overset{*L}{\underset{G}{\Rightarrow}} \alpha_1\delta\gamma_1 = \alpha_1\alpha_2$.

If the last transition was of type 3, then $\beta = a$, a terminal symbol, and $\gamma = a\alpha_2$. Then $\alpha_1 = \delta a$ for some $\delta \in \Sigma^*$, and $(q, \delta, S) \vdash_M^* (q, e, a\alpha_2)$ in n steps, so by the induction hypothesis $S \overset{*L}{\underset{G}{\Rightarrow}} \delta a\alpha_2 = \alpha_1\alpha_2$.

This completes the proof of Lemma 3.4.3, and with it half the proof of Theorem 3.4.1. ■

We now turn to the proof of the other half of Theorem 3.4.1.

Lemma 3.4.4. *If a language is accepted by a pushdown automaton, it is a context-free language.*

Proof. It will be helpful to restrict somewhat the pushdown automata under consideration. Call a pushdown automaton $(K, \Sigma, \Gamma, \Delta, s, F)$ **simple** if (1) whenever $((q, u, \beta), (p, \gamma))$ is a transition in Δ, $|\beta| \leq 1$; and (2) whenever $((q, u, e), (p, \gamma)) \in \Delta$, then also $((q, u, A), (p, \gamma A)) \in \Delta$ for each $A \in \Gamma$. In other words, (1) if the machine consults its stack at all, it looks at—and possibly removes—only the topmost symbol; and (2) whenever the machine can move without consulting or removing any symbol from the stack, it may also achieve the same effect by removing the top symbol from the stack and then immediately putting it back. We claim that no generality is lost in considering only simple pushdown automata; that is, if a language is accepted by an unrestricted pushdown automaton, then it is accepted by a simple pushdown automaton. To see this, let $M = (K, \Sigma, \Gamma, \Delta, s, F)$ be any pushdown automaton; we construct a simple pushdown automaton that also accepts $L(M)$. We first eliminate from Δ any transition $((q, u, \beta), (p, \gamma))$ with $|\beta| > 1$. This is done by modifying M to pop sequentially the individual symbols of β, rather than removing them all in a single step. Specifically, let $\beta = B_1 \ldots B_n$, where $n > 1$ and $B_1, \ldots, B_n \in \Gamma$; then add to K new states $t_1, \ldots, t_{n-1}$ and replace in Δ the single transition $((q, u, \beta), (p, \gamma))$ by these transitions.

$$((q, e, B_1), (t_1, e))$$
$$((t_1, e, B_2), (t_2, e))$$
$$\vdots$$
$$((t_{n-2}, e, B_{n-1}), (t_{n-1}, e))$$
$$((t_{n-1}, u, B_n), (p, \gamma))$$

A similar modification is carried out for each transition in Δ that violates Condition (1) for simplicity. To satisfy Condition (2), we merely add to Δ the transitions $((q, u, A), (p, \gamma A))$ for each $A \in \Gamma$, whenever $((q, u, e), (p, \gamma))$ is a transition already in Δ. The resulting automaton is simple, and accepts the same language as M accepts.

Now we show that if $M = (K, \Sigma, \Gamma, \Delta, s, F)$ is any *simple* pushdown automaton, then $L(M)$ is the language generated by some context-free grammar G. We let $G = (V, \Sigma, R, S)$, where V contains, in addition to a new symbol S and the symbols in Σ, a new symbol $\langle q, A, p\rangle$ for all $q, p \in K$ and each $A \in \Gamma \cup \{e\}$. To understand the role of the nonterminals $\langle q, A, p\rangle$, remember that G is supposed to generate all strings accepted by M. Therefore the nonterminals of G stand for different parts of the input strings that are accepted by M. In particular, if $A \in \Gamma$ then the nonterminal $\langle q, A, p\rangle$ denotes a portion of the input string that might be read between a point in time when M is in state q with A on top of its stack, and a point in time when M removes that occurrence of A from the stack and enters state p. If $A = e$, then $\langle q, e, p\rangle$ denotes a portion of the input string that might be read between a time when M is in state q and a time when it is in state p with the same stack, without in the interim changing or consulting that part of the stack.

The rules in R are of four types.

1. For each $f \in F$, the rule $S \to \langle s, e, f\rangle$.
2. For each transition $((q, u, A), (r, B_1 \ldots B_n)) \in \Delta$, where $q, r \in K$, $u \in \Sigma^*$, $n > 0$, $B_1, \ldots, B_n \in \Gamma$, and $A \in \Gamma \cup \{e\}$, and for all p, $q_1, \ldots, q_{n-1} \in K$, the rule
$$\langle q, A, p\rangle \to u\langle r, B_1, q_1\rangle\langle q_1, B_2, q_2\rangle \cdots \langle q_{n-1}, B_n, p\rangle.$$
3. For each transition $((q, u, A), (r, e)) \in \Delta$, where $q, r \in K$, $u \in \Sigma^*$, and $A \in \Gamma \cup \{e\}$, and for each $p \in K$, the rule
$$\langle q, A, p\rangle \to u\langle r, e, p\rangle.$$
4. For each $q \in K$, the rule $\langle q, e, q\rangle \to e$.

Note that, because M is simple, either tvpe 2 or type 3 applies to each transition of M.

A rule of type 1 says essentially that the goal is to pass from the initial state to a final state, while leaving the stack in the same condition at the end as it was at the beginning. A rule of type 4 says that no computation is needed to go from a state to itself. A rule of type 2 describes a long computation, with the net effect of going from state q to state p while removing A (possibly e) from the stack. The right-hand side of this single rule of R represents $n + 1 \geq 2$ shorter computations of M, the first of which is a single move to state r while reading input u, and the last n of which are sequences of moves between intermediate states that effect the removal of $B_1, \ldots, B_n$ from the stack. Rules of type 3 are analogous to rules of type 2 for the case in which

$n = 0$, that is, a symbol (or e) is removed from the stack and no symbol is added.

These intuitive remarks are formalized in the proof of the following claim.

Claim. *For any* $q, p \in K$, $A \in \Gamma \cup \{e\}$, *and* $x \in \Sigma^*$,

$$\langle q, A, p\rangle \overset{*}{\underset{G}{\Rightarrow}} x \quad \text{if and only if} \quad (q, x, A) \vdash_M^* (p, e, e).$$

Lemma 3.4.4 follows readily from the claim, since then $\langle s, e, f\rangle \overset{*}{\underset{G}{\Rightarrow}} x$, for some $f \in F$, if and only if $(s, x, e) \vdash_M^* (f, e, e)$; that is, $x \in L(G)$ if and only if $x \in L(M)$.

Proof of Claim. (*Only if*) Suppose that $\langle q, A, p\rangle \overset{*}{\underset{G}{\Rightarrow}} x$; we show by induction on the length of a derivation that $(q, x, A) \vdash_M^* (p, e, e)$.

Basis Step. If the derivation has only one step, that is, if $\langle q, A, p\rangle \underset{G}{\rightarrow} x$, then this rule can only be of type 4; that is, $p = q$ and $A = x = e$. Hence $(q, x, A) \vdash_M^* (p, e, e)$ by the reflexivity of $\vdash_M^*$.

Induction Hypothesis. Assume that if $\langle q, A, p\rangle \overset{*}{\underset{G}{\Rightarrow}} x$ by a derivation of k or fewer steps ($k \geq 1$), then $(q, x, A) \vdash_M^* (p, e, e)$.

Induction Step. Suppose that x is derived from $\langle q, A, p\rangle$ in $k + 1 \geq 2$ steps. Then the first step was of type 2 or of type 3.

If the first step was of type 2, then the derivation has the form

$$\begin{aligned}\langle q, A, p\rangle &\underset{G}{\Rightarrow} u\langle r, B_1, q_1\rangle\langle q_1, B_2, q_2\rangle \cdots \langle q_{n-1}, B_n, p\rangle \\ &\overset{*}{\underset{G}{\Rightarrow}} x,\end{aligned}$$

where $n \geq 1$, $B_1, \ldots, B_n \in \Gamma$, $r, q_1, \ldots, q_{n-1} \in K$, and $((q, u, A), (r, B_1 \ldots B_n)) \in \Delta$. Let us write q_0 for r and q_n for p; then there are strings $z_1, \ldots, z_n \in \Sigma^*$ such that $\langle q_{i-1}, B_i, q_i\rangle \overset{*}{\underset{G}{\Rightarrow}} z_i$ for $i = 1, \ldots, n$, each by derivation of k or fewer steps, and such that $x = uz_1 \ldots z_n$. Then by the induction hypothesis, $(q_{i-1}, z_i, B_i) \vdash_M^* (q_i, e, e)$ for $i = 1, \ldots, n$; combining these computations and the fact that $(q, u, A) \vdash_M (r, e, B_1 \ldots B_n)$ we have the following.

$$\begin{aligned}(q, uz_1 \ldots z_n, A) &\vdash_M (r, z_1 \ldots z_n, B_1 \ldots B_n) \\ &\vdash_M^* (q_1, z_2 \ldots z_n, B_2 \ldots B_n) \\ &\quad\vdots \\ &\vdash_M^* (p, e, e)\end{aligned}$$

If the first step was of type 3, then the derivation has the form $\langle q, A, p\rangle \underset{G}{\Rightarrow} u\langle r, e, p\rangle \overset{*}{\underset{G}{\Rightarrow}} x$, where $((q, u, A), (r, e)) \in \Delta$. An entirely analogous argument then establishes that for some $z \in \Sigma^*$, $x = uz$ and $(q, uz, A) \vdash_M (r, z, e) \vdash_M^* (p, e, e)$. This completes the proof of the only-if direction.

(*If*)

Basis Step. Suppose that $(q, x, A) \vdash_M^* (p, e, e)$ in zero steps, that is, $q = p$, $x = A = e$. Then the claim states that $\langle q, e, q\rangle \overset{*}{\underset{G}{\Rightarrow}} e$; this is true since $\langle q, e, q\rangle \underset{G}{\rightarrow} e$ is a rule of type 4.

Induction Hypothesis. Assume that whenever $(q, x, A) \vdash_M^* (p, e, e)$ in k or fewer steps, $k \geq 0$, $\langle q, A, p\rangle \overset{*}{\underset{G}{\Rightarrow}} x$.

Induction Step. Suppose that $(q, x, A) \vdash_M^* (p, e, e)$ in $k + 1$ steps. Looking at the first step separately, we have $(q, x, A) \vdash_M (r, z, B_1 \ldots B_n) \vdash_M^* (p, e, e)$ for some $z \in \Sigma^*$, $r \in K$, and $B_1, \ldots, B_n \in \Gamma$ $(n \geq 0)$, where the latter part of the computation is of k steps. Then there is a $u \in \Sigma^*$ such that $x = uz$ and $(q, u, A) \vdash_M (r, e, B_1 \ldots B_n)$. This implies either that $((q, u, A), (r, B_1 \ldots B_n))$ is a transition of M, or that $n \geq 1$, $A = B_n$, and $((q, u, e), (r, B_1 \ldots B_{n-1}))$ is a transition. But M is simple, so that the latter case implies the former: $((q, u, A), (r, B_1 \ldots B_n))$ is a transition in either case.

Now if $n > 0$, then each B_i is eventually removed from the stack, and since the machine is simple, there are states $q_1, \ldots, q_{n-1}$ and strings $z_1, \ldots, z_n$ such that $z = z_1 \ldots z_n$ and

$$(q_i, z_{i+1} \ldots z_n, B_{i+1} \ldots B_n) \vdash_M^* (q_{i+1}, z_{i+2} \ldots z_n, B_{i+2} \ldots B_n)$$

for $i = 0, \ldots, n - 1$, where $q_0 = r$ and $q_n = p$, each of the computations having k or fewer steps. Then by the induction hypothesis, $\langle q_i, B_{i+1}, q_{i+1}\rangle \overset{*}{\underset{G}{\Rightarrow}} z_{i+1}$ for $i = 0, \ldots, n - 1$, and since

$$\langle q, A, p\rangle \underset{G}{\rightarrow} u\langle r, B_1, q_1\rangle\langle q_1, B_2, q_2\rangle \ldots \langle q_{n-1}, B_n, p\rangle$$

is a rule of type 2, we have $\langle q, A, p\rangle \overset{*}{\underset{G}{\Rightarrow}} uz_1 \ldots z_n = x$, as was to be shown.

On the other hand, if $n = 0$, then $(r, z, e) \vdash_M^* (p, e, e)$ by a computation of k steps; so by the induction hypothesis, $\langle r, e, p\rangle \overset{*}{\underset{G}{\Rightarrow}} z$. And since $\langle q, A, p\rangle \underset{G}{\rightarrow} u\langle r, e, p\rangle$ is a rule of type 3, we have $\langle q, A, p\rangle \overset{*}{\underset{G}{\Rightarrow}} uz = x$.

This completes the proof of the claim, of Lemma 3.4.4, and of Theorem 3.4.1. ■

3.5 PROPERTIES OF CONTEXT-FREE LANGUAGES

In the last section, two views of context-free languages—as languages generated by context-free grammars and as languages accepted by pushdown automata—were shown to be equivalent. These characterizations enrich our understanding of the context-free languages, since they provide two different methods for comprehending context-freeness. For example, the grammatical representation is more natural and compelling in the case of a programming language fragment such as that of Example 3.1.3; but the representation in terms of pushdown automata is easier to see in the case of $\{w \in \{a, b\}^*: w$ has equal numbers of a's and b's$\}$ (see Example 3.3.4). Nevertheless, any context-free language can in principle be described in either way; the representations are interconvertible.

In this section our goal is to become more familiar with the context-free languages by studying general properties of the class. These properties will provide more tools for recognizing when certain languages are context-free; they will also make it possible to conclude with certainty that certain languages are *not* context-free. They will also enable us to show that there are algorithms for answering certain kinds of questions about context-free languages. And finally, the *proofs* of these properties will give us considerable insight into the internal structure of context-free languages.

Three kinds of properties are considered.

1. *Closure properties.* The results established here are rather similar to some of those shown in Section 2.4 for regular languages.

2. *Periodicity properties.* Here we show that under certain circumstances we can pass, by "pumping," from strings in a context-free language to longer strings with similar structure. This result is analogous to Theorem 2.6.1 for regular languages. We also establish Parikh's Theorem, a periodicity property of a somewhat different sort that applies not to individual strings but to the language as a whole.

3. *Algorithmic properties.* Here we show, by analogy to Theorem 2.4.2 for regular languages, that certain natural questions about context-free languages can be answered by algorithms.

3.5.1 CLOSURE PROPERTIES

Some closure properties of the context-free languages are similar to those of the regular languages.

Theorem 3.5.1. *The context-free languages are closed under union, concatenation, and Kleene star.*

Proof. Let $G_1 = (V_1, \Sigma_1, R_1, S_1)$ and $G_2 = (V_2, \Sigma_2, R_2, S_2)$, and without loss of generality assume that $V_1 - \Sigma_1$ and $V_2 - \Sigma_2$ are disjoint.

Union. Let S be a new symbol and let $G = (V_1 \cup V_2 \cup \{S\}, \Sigma_1 \cup \Sigma_2, R_1 \cup R_2 \cup \{S \rightarrow S_1, S \rightarrow S_2\}, S)$. Then $L(G_1) \cup L(G_2) = L(G)$. For the only rules involving S are $S \rightarrow S_1$ and $S \rightarrow S_2$, so $S \overset{*}{\underset{G}{\Rightarrow}} w$, where

$w \in (\Sigma_1 \cup \Sigma_2)^*$, if and only if either $S_1 \overset{*}{\underset{G}{\Rightarrow}} w$ or $S_2 \overset{*}{\underset{G}{\Rightarrow}} w$; and since G_1 and G_2 have disjoint sets of nonterminals, $S_1 \overset{*}{\underset{G}{\Rightarrow}} w$ if and only if $S_1 \overset{*}{\underset{G_1}{\Rightarrow}} w$; a similar argument can be given for G_2.

Concatenation. The construction is similar: $L(G_1)L(G_2)$ is generated by the grammar

$$(V_1 \cup V_2 \cup \{S\}, \Sigma_1 \cup \Sigma_2, R_1 \cup R_2 \cup \{S \rightarrow S_1S_2\}, S).$$

Kleene Star. $L(G_1)^*$ is generated by

$$(V_1, \Sigma_1, R_1 \cup \{S_1 \rightarrow e, S_1 \rightarrow S_1S_1\}, S_1). \quad \blacksquare$$

As we shall see shortly, the class of context-free languages is *not* closed under intersection or complementation. However, it is closed under intersection with regular sets.

Theorem 3.5.2. *The intersection of a context-free language with a regular language is a context-free language.*

Proof. Here a proof based on finite and pushdown automata is simpler than one based on grammars. If L is a context-free language and R is a regular set, then $L = L(M_1)$ for some pushdown automaton $M_1 = (K_1, \Sigma_1, \Gamma_1, \Delta_1, s_1, F_1)$ and $R = L(M_2)$ for some *deterministic* finite automaton $(K_2, \Sigma_2, \delta_2, s_2, F_2)$. The idea is to combine these machines into a single pushdown automaton M that carries out computations by M_1 and M_2 in parallel and accepts only if both would have accepted. Specifically, let $M = (K, \Sigma, \Gamma, \Delta, s, F)$, where

$K = K_1 \times K_2$, the Cartesian product of the state sets of M_1 and M_2

$\Sigma = \Sigma_1 \cup \Sigma_2$

$\Gamma = \Gamma_1$

$s = (s_1, s_2)$

$F = F_1 \times F_2$

and Δ, the transition relation, is defined by

$$(((q_1, q_2), u, \beta), ((p_1, p_2), \gamma)) \in \Delta$$

if and only if

$$((q_1, u, \beta), (p_1, \gamma)) \in \Delta_1, \tag{4}$$

and

$$(q_2, u) \vdash^*_{M_2} (p_2, e). \tag{5}$$

That is, M passes from state (q_1, q_2) to state (p_1, p_2) in the same way that M_1 passes from state q_1 to p_1, except that in addition M keeps track of the change in the state of M_2 caused by reading the same input. Condition 5 is easy to check, since a deterministic finite automaton reads a single symbol on each move; the argument is like that for Theorem 2.4.1(a). Thus, in practice, we could construct M by repeatedly choosing a transition $((q_1, u, \beta), (p_1, \gamma))$ of M_1 and a state q_2 of M_2 and simulating M_2 for $|u|$ steps on input u to determine what state p_2 it would reach after reading that input. ■

Example 3.5.1

Let L consist of all strings of a's and b's with equal numbers of a's and b's but containing no substring $abaa$ or $babb$. Then L is context-free, since it is the intersection of the language accepted by the pushdown automaton in Example 3.3.4 with the regular language $\{a, b\}^* - \{a, b\}^*\{abaa, babb\}\{a, b\}^*$.

3.5.2 PERIODICITY PROPERTIES

Infinite context-free languages display periodicity of a somewhat subtler form than do regular languages. In order to explore it, we introduce a useful way of representing derivations graphically, which will be used later on for other purposes.

Let G be a context-free grammar. A string $w \in L(G)$ may have many derivations in G. For example, if $G = (\{S, a\}, \{a\}, \{S \rightarrow SS, S \rightarrow a\}, S)$, then the string $aa \in L(G)$ can be derived from S by two distinct derivations, namely,

$$S \Rightarrow SS \Rightarrow aS \Rightarrow aa \quad \text{and} \quad S \Rightarrow SS \Rightarrow Sa \Rightarrow aa.$$

However, these two derivations are in a sense the same. The rules used are the same, and they are applied at the same places in the intermediate string. The only difference is in the order in which the two occurrences of the nonterminal S are replaced by a. Both derivations can be pictured as in Figure 3–3.

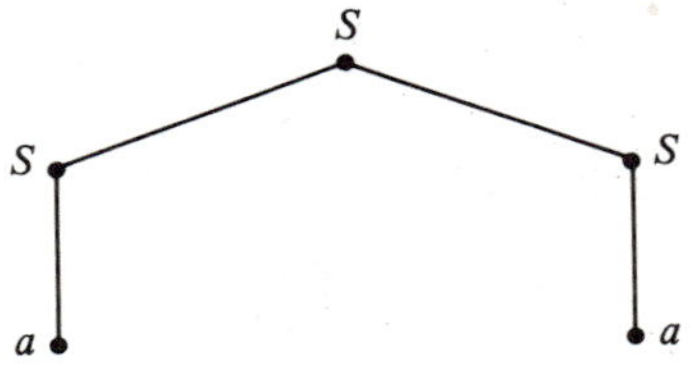

Figure 3–3

Similarly, the derivation

$$S \Rightarrow SS \Rightarrow Sa \Rightarrow SSa \Rightarrow aSa \Rightarrow aaa$$

can be pictured as in Figure 3–4.

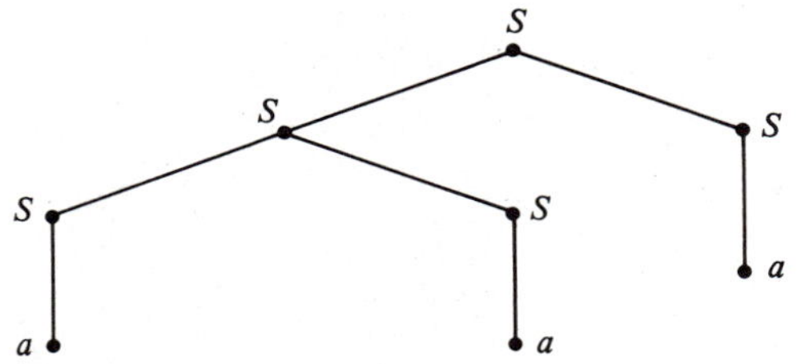

Figure 3–4

We call such a picture a **parse tree**. The points are called **nodes**; the topmost node is called the **root**, and the nodes along the bottom are called **leaves**. By concatenating the labels of the leaves from left to right, we obtain the derived string, which is called the **yield** of the parse tree.

More generally, for an arbitrary context-free grammar $G = (V, \Sigma, R, S)$, we define its *parse trees* and their *roots*, *leaves*, and *yields*, as follows.

1.

This is a parse tree for each $A \in V$. The single node of this parse tree is the root and a leaf. The yield of this parse tree is A.

2. If $A \longrightarrow e$ is a rule in R, then

is a parse tree; its root is the node labeled A, its sole leaf is the node labeled e, and its yield is e.

3. If

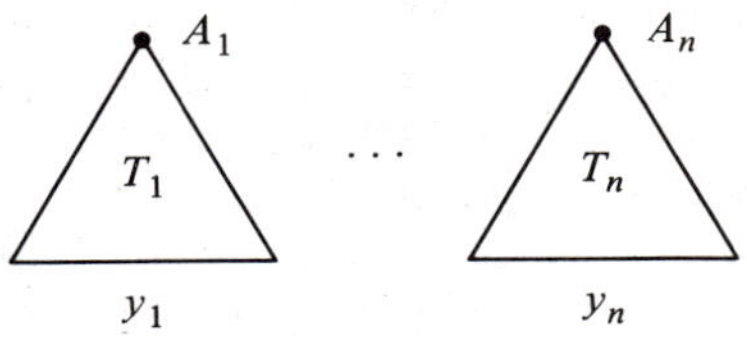

are parse trees ($n \geq 1$) with roots labeled $A_1, \ldots, A_n$, respectively, and with yields $y_1, \ldots, y_n$, and $A \longrightarrow A_1 \ldots A_n$ is a rule in R, then

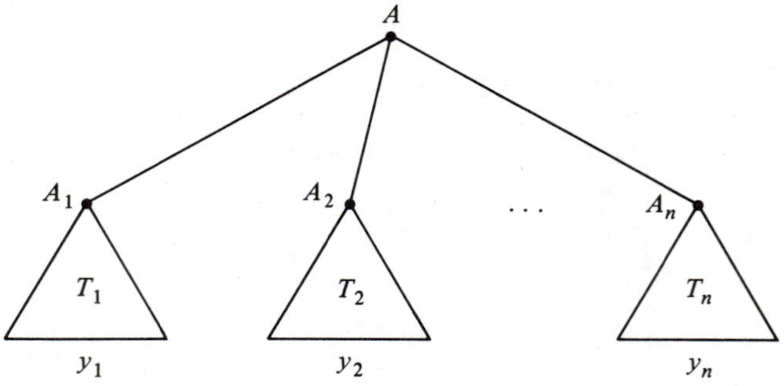

is a parse tree. Its root is the new node labeled A, its leaves are the leaves of $T_1, \ldots, T_n$, and its yield is $y_1 \ldots y_n$.

4. Nothing else is a parse tree.

Example 3.5.2

Let $G = (V, \Sigma, R, S)$, where $V = \{S, (,)\}$, $\Sigma = \{(,)\}$, and $R = \{S \longrightarrow SS, S \longrightarrow (S), S \longrightarrow e\}$. A parse tree with yield (())() is shown in Figure 3–5, together with the order in which the leaves are read to extract that string from the tree.

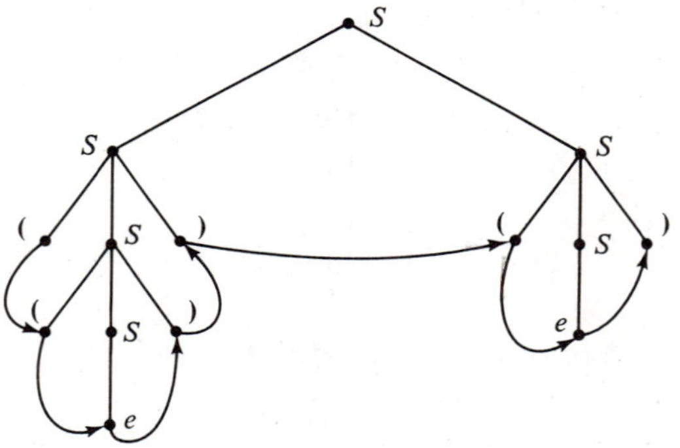

Figure 3–5

A **path** in a parse tree is a sequence of distinct nodes, each connected to the previous one by a line segment; the first node is the root and the last node is a leaf. The **length** of a path is the number of line segments, which is one less than the number of nodes. Thus in Figure 3–5, the longest path has length 4 and the shortest has length 2. The **height** of a parse tree is the length of the longest path, so the tree in Figure 3–5 has height 4.

Theorem 3.5.3. (The Pumping Theorem). *Let G be a context-free grammar. Then there is a number K, depending on G, such that any string w in L(G) of length greater than K can be rewritten as $w = uvxyz$ in such a way that either v or y is nonempty and uv^nxy^nz is in L(G) for every $n \geq 0$.*

Proof. Let $G = (V, \Sigma, R, S)$. It suffices for the theorem to show that there is a K such that any terminal string in $L(G)$ of length greater than K has a derivation of the form

$$S \overset{*}{\Rightarrow} uAz \overset{*}{\Rightarrow} uvAyz \overset{*}{\Rightarrow} uvxyz$$

where $u, v, x, y, z \in \Sigma^*$, $A \in V - \Sigma$, and either v or y is nonempty. Then the derivation $A \overset{*}{\Rightarrow} vAy$ can be repeated any number of times to obtain the various strings uv^nxy^nz.

Let p be the largest number of symbols on the right-hand side of any rule in R, that is,

$$p = \max\{|\alpha|: A \longrightarrow \alpha \text{ is a rule of } G\}.$$

For any $m \geq 1$, a parse tree of height m can have at most p^m leaves, as can easily be shown by induction on m, and can therefore have a yield of length at most p^m. To put it another way, if T is a parse tree with yield of length greater than p^m, then T has some path of length greater than m. Now let $m = |V - \Sigma|$, $K = p^m$, and suppose w has length exceeding K. Let T be a parse tree with root labeled S and with yield w. Then T has at least one path with more than $|V - \Sigma| + 1$ nodes, and therefore at least one path including two nodes labeled with the same member A of $V - \Sigma$. Let us look at such a path in more detail (see Figure 3–6).

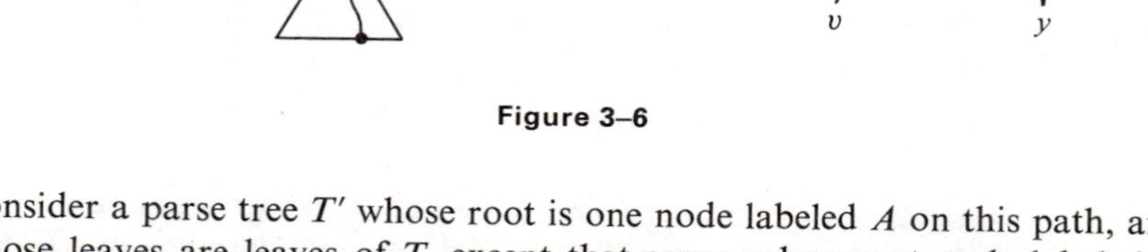

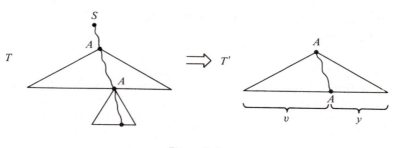

Figure 3–6

Consider a parse tree T' whose root is one node labeled A on this path, and whose leaves are leaves of T, except that some subsequent node labeled A on the path is a leaf. This parse tree T' has root labeled A and has yield of the form vAy for some $v, y \in \Sigma^*$. Now it is possible that $v = y = e$, but this cannot be the case for every choice of the path and two nodes on it with the same label. For if $v = y = e$, then the tree T' can be removed from T, without changing the yield of the tree as a whole, by attaching the parse tree with the lower node as its root at the upper node labeled A. If all paths of length exceeding m could be shortened in this way, without changing the yield of the parse tree, we could obtain a parse tree with yield w and with height less than m, which is impossible. But then we are done; A, u, v, x, y, and z can be determined from T. ■

This theorem is most useful for showing that certain languages are *not* context-free.

Theorem 3.5.4. $L = \{a^n b^n c^n : n \geq 0\}$ *is not context-free.*

Proof. We prove Theorem 3.5.4 by contradiction. Suppose $L = L(G)$ for some context-free grammar G. Let K be a constant for G as specified by the Pumping Theorem and let $n > K/3$. Then $w = a^n b^n c^n$ is in $L(G)$ and has a representation $w = uvxyz$ such that v or y is nonempty and $uv^i xy^i z$ is in $L(G)$ for each $i = 0, 1, 2, \ldots$. But this is impossible; for if either v or y contains two symbols from $\{a, b, c\}$, then uv^2xy^2z contains a b before an a or a c before a b, and if v and y each contain only a's, only b's, or only c's, then uv^2xy^2z cannot contain equal number of a's, b's, and c's. ■

We can now make good on our promise to show that the context-free languages are *not* closed under certain operations.

Theorem 3.5.5. *The context-free languages are not closed under intersection or complementation.*

Proof. Clearly $\{a^n b^n c^m : m, n \geq 0\}$ and $\{a^m b^n c^n : m, n \geq 0\}$ are context-free. The intersection of these two context-free languages is the language $\{a^n b^n c^n : n \geq 0\}$ just shown not to be context-free. And if the context-free languages were closed under complementation, they would be closed under intersection, since

$$L_1 \cap L_2 = \Sigma^* - ((\Sigma^* - L_1) \cup (\Sigma^* - L_2)). \quad ■$$

Unfortunately, there are very simple non-context-free languages which cannot be shown not to be context-free by a direct application of the Pumping Theorem. One example is

$$\{a^m b^n : \text{either } m > n, \text{ or } m \text{ is a prime number and } n \geq m\}.$$

The difficulty is that the Pumping Theorem does not restrict *where* within a string the pumping is to be done. There are various ways of tightening the Pumping Theorem, but we instead establish a related result of a somewhat different type.

Let $\Sigma = \{a_1, \ldots, a_n\}$ be an alphabet. Define $\Psi_\Sigma : \Sigma^* \longrightarrow \mathbb{N}^n$ by $\Psi_\Sigma(w) = (m_1, \ldots, m_n)$, where for $i = 1, \ldots, n$, m_i is the number of occurrences of a_i in w. Thus if $\Sigma = \{a_1, a_2\}$, then $\Psi_\Sigma(a_1a_2a_2a_1a_2) = (2, 3)$. (Where Σ is fixed, we omit the subscript on Ψ.) We shall show that only certain sets of n-tuples of natural numbers can arise as $\Psi[L]$, where L is a context-free language.

Let B and P be finite subsets of $\mathbb{N}^n$. Then define

$$L(B, P) = \{b + p_1 + p_2 + \cdots + p_k : b \in B, k \geq 0, p_1, \ldots, p_k \in P\}.$$

Here addition of n-tuples is done componentwise: $(a_1, \ldots, a_n) + (b_1, \ldots, b_n) = (a_1 + b_1, \ldots, a_n + b_n)$. For example, if $n = 2$,

$$B = \{(0, 0)\} \quad \text{and} \quad P = \{(0, 1), (1, 1)\},$$

then

$$L(B, P) = \{(m, n) : n \geq m\}.$$

Any set $L(B, P)$, where B and P are finite subsets of $\mathbb{N}^n$, is said to be **linear**. A **semilinear** set is a finite union of linear sets.

Theorem 3.5.6 (Parikh's Theorem). *If L is context-free, then $\Psi[L]$ is semilinear.*

Proof. Let $L = L(G)$, where $G = (V, \Sigma, R, S)$. We extend Ψ to domain V^* by ignoring nonterminals; that is, $\Psi(w)$, where $w \in V^*$, is equal to $\Psi(w')$, where w' is the string obtained from w by replacing each nonterminal symbol in w by e.

For each subset Q of $V - \Sigma$, let L_Q be the set of all strings in L that have at least one derivation in which the set of nonterminals used is exactly Q. To be precise, L_Q is defined as follows.

$L_Q = \{w \in L$: w has a derivation

$$S = w_0 \underset{G}{\Rightarrow} w_1 \underset{G}{\Rightarrow} \cdots \underset{G}{\Rightarrow} w_n = w \text{ such that}$$

(a) $w_0, \ldots, w_n \in (Q \cup \Sigma)^*$; and

(b) for each $A \in Q$, there is some $i \leq n$ such that $w_i = uAv$ for some $u, v \in V^*\}$.

Since there are only finitely many sets Q of nonterminals, it suffices for the theorem to show that $\Psi[L_Q]$ is semilinear for each $Q \subseteq V - \Sigma$.

Fix some set $Q \subseteq V - \Sigma$. Let $t = |Q|$. We consider parse trees with the following four properties.

1. The root of the tree is labeled S.
2. The yield of the tree is a string of terminal symbols.
3. The set of nonterminal symbols appearing as labels of nodes of the tree is Q.
4. The tree has height at most t^2.

Let C be the set of all strings w such that w is the yield of a parse tree with Properties 1 through 4. Similarly, we consider parse trees with these four properties.

1′. The root of the tree is labeled with a nonterminal symbol $A \in Q$.

2′. The yield of the tree is in $\Sigma^* A \Sigma^*$, where A is the label of the root.

3′. The set of nonterminal symbols appearing as labels of nodes of the tree is a subset of Q.

4′. The tree has height at most $t^2 + 1$.

Let D be the set of all strings v such that v is the yield of a parse tree with Properties 1′ through 4′. Both C and D are finite sets. We claim that

$$\Psi[L_Q] = L(\Psi[C], \Psi[D])$$

which will establish the theorem.

First we show that $\Psi[L_Q] \subseteq L(\Psi[C], \Psi[D])$. Since every member of L_Q is the yield of a parse tree having Properties 1, 2, and 3, it suffices to show that if w is the yield of such a tree, then $\Psi(w) \in L(\Psi[C], \Psi[D])$. This we do by induction on the number of nodes of the tree.

Basis Step. If the parse tree has t^2 or fewer nodes, then its height is at most t^2 and its yield w is a member of C. Therefore $\Psi(w) \in \Psi[C] \subseteq L(\Psi[C], \Psi[D])$.

Induction Hypothesis. Assume that whenever a parse tree has Properties 1, 2, and 3, k or fewer nodes, and yield w, then $\Psi(w) \in L(\Psi[C], \Psi[D])$.

Induction Step. Let T be a parse tree with $k + 1$ nodes and with Properties 1, 2, and 3, and let w be its yield. If the height of T is at most t^2, then the argument of the basis step applies. So assume that T has height exceeding t^2. Then there is a path in T of length at least $t^2 + 1$, that is, containing at least $t^2 + 2$ nodes (including a leaf). Since the labels of the non-leaf nodes are drawn from a set of cardinality t, there is a path containing at least $t + 1$ nodes labeled with the same member of Q.

Now any node p of T determines a parse tree T_p consisting of p and all nodes below p in T (see Figure 3–7(a)). We claim that for some node p of T, T_p is a parse tree such that:

(a) T_p has a path containing exactly $t + 1$ nodes labeled with the same member of Q; but

(b) there is no node r of T_p, except for p itself, such that T_r contains a path with $t + 1$ or more nodes labeled with the same member of Q.

We have already established that a p exists such that T_p satisfies (a); and if T_p does not also satisfy (b), and $p_1, \ldots p_m$ are the nodes immediately below p in T, then one of $T_{p_1}, \ldots, T_{p_m}$ also satisfies (a), and has height less than that of

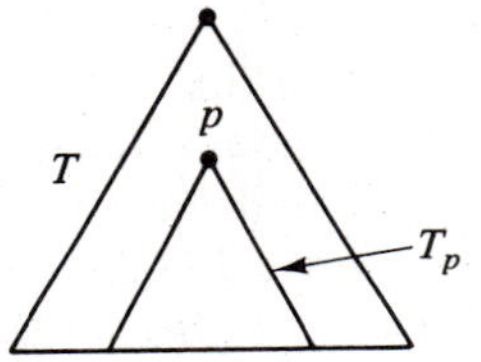

(a)

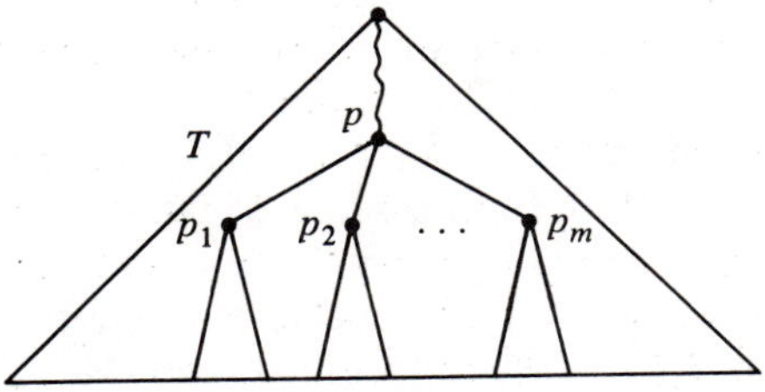

(b)

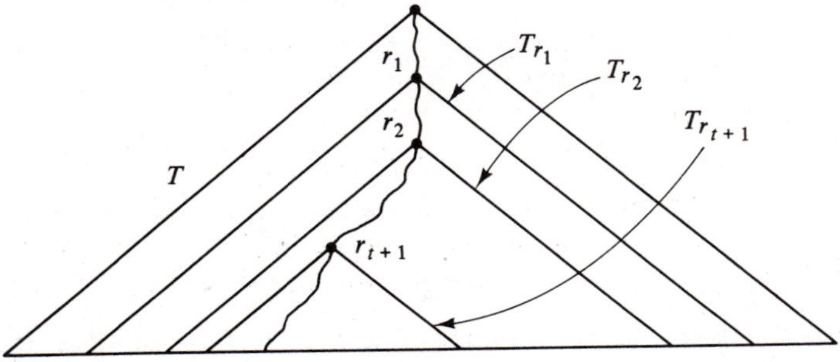

(c)

Figure 3–7

T_p (see Figure 3–7(b)). By repeatedly moving down the tree in this way, we must eventually obtain a tree satisfying both (a) and (b).

Now let $r_1, \ldots, r_{t+1}$ be the $t + 1$ distinct nodes of T_p that are on the same path and are labeled with the same member A of Q. We assume that for each i, r_i is closer to the root than r_{i+1}: $r_1, \ldots, r_{t+1}$ are in order on the path as it would be traversed from the root to a leaf (see Figure 3–7(c)). For each $i = 1, \ldots, t + 1$, let Q_i be that subset of Q containing all nonterminal symbols that are the labels of nodes of T_{r_i}. Clearly $Q_{i+1} \subseteq Q_i$ for each $i = 1, \ldots, t$, and since A is in each Q_i, each Q_i is nonempty. Therefore there is an i, $1 \leq i \leq t$, such that $Q_i = Q_{i+1}$. $T_{r_{i+1}}$ can then be shifted upwards in T by reattaching its root at r_i; call the tree obtained from T in this way T'. Now T' satisfies Properties 1, 2, and 3 and has fewer nodes than T; moreover, by (a) and (b), the part of T deleted in forming T' satisfies Properties 1′, 2′, 3′, and 4′. Thus if w' is the yield of T', then $\Psi(w)$ is equal to $\Psi(w')$ plus $\Psi(v)$ for some $v \in D$. But by the induction hypothesis, $\Psi(w') \in L(\Psi[C], \Psi[D])$, and therefore $\Psi(w) \in L(\Psi[C], \Psi[D])$. This completes the proof of the induction step.

To show that $L(\Psi[C], \Psi[D]) \subseteq \Psi[L_Q]$, let $w \in C$ and $v_1, \ldots, v_k \in D$. Let T be a parse tree with yield w satisfying Properties 1, 2, 3, and 4, and let $V_1, \ldots, V_k$ be parse trees with yields $v_1, \ldots, v_k$, respectively, satisfying Properties 1′, 2′, 3′, and 4′. Let $A_1, \ldots, A_k$ be the nonterminals labeling the roots of $V_1, \ldots, V_k$. Since $A_1, \ldots, A_k \in Q$, each A_i is the label of some node of T. We can therefore form a series of parse trees $T_0, \ldots, T_k$, where $T_0 = T$ and each T_{i+1} is obtained from T_i by opening T_i at a node r labeled A_{i+1}, attaching the root of V_{i+1} at r, and reattaching the part of T_i formerly below r at the leaf of V_{i+1} labeled A_{i+1} (see Figure 3–8). The result is a parse tree T_k satisfying Properties 1, 2, and 3, so its yield y is in L_Q; but $\Psi(y) = \Psi(w) + \Psi(v_1) + \cdots + \Psi(v_k)$. Therefore $L(\Psi[C], \Psi[D]) \subseteq \Psi[L_Q]$. ■

Parikh's Theorem has a number of useful applications. For example, it is now clear that a language such as $\{a^m b^n$: either $m > n$, or m is prime and $n \geq m\}$ cannot be context-free.

Another application is the following result.

Theorem 3.5.7. *Every context-free language over a one-symbol alphabet is regular.*

Proof. If $L \subseteq \{a\}^*$ is context-free, then $\Psi[L] = \{n: a^n \in L\}$ is semilinear. But if S is a semilinear subset of $\mathbb{N}$, then $\{a^n: n \in S\}$ is regular (Problem 3.5.10). Since for $L \subseteq \{a\}^*$, $L = \{a^n: n \in \Psi[L]\}$, it follows that $L \subseteq \{a\}^*$ is regular if it is context-free. ■

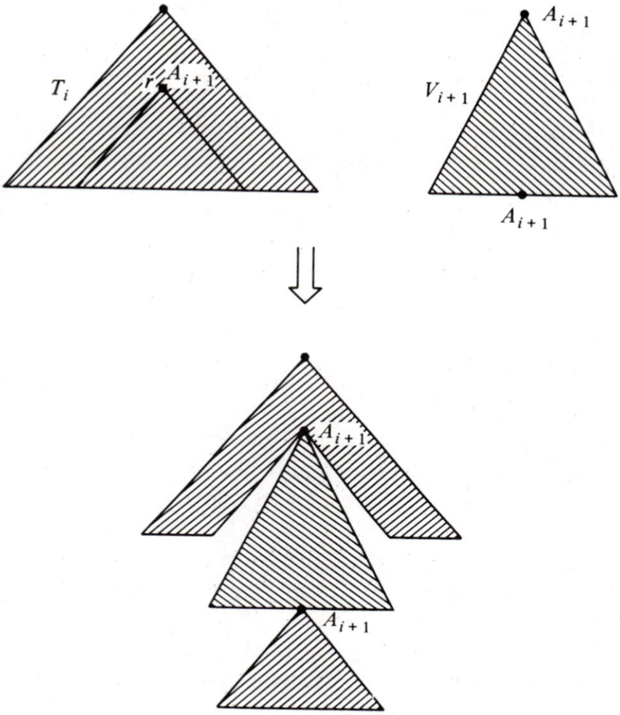

Figure 3–8

3.5.3 ALGORITHMIC PROPERTIES

Although we have studied context-free languages in some detail, there are a number of simple, natural questions we have not addressed. When confronted with a context-free grammar and a string, how can one tell if the string is in the language generated by that grammar? One is tempted at first to follow the line of reasoning used in the proof of Theorem 2.4.2(a): Convert the grammar into an equivalent pushdown automaton, one might argue, and then simply run the automaton on the given input. Unfortunately, this approach does not work, at least directly; a pushdown automaton may compute for a long time without reading any input, and how are we to know when we have let it run long enough to be sure it will not eventually accept? Instead we approach this problem through an analysis of parse trees.

Theorem 3.5.8. *There are algorithms for answering the following questions about context-free grammars.*

(a) *Given a grammar G and a string w, is $w \in L(G)$?*

(b) *Is $L(G) = \varnothing$?*

Before moving to the proof, we make two observations. First, since a pushdown automaton can be converted to an equivalent context-free grammar, these algorithms can also be used for answering the same questions about pushdown automata. And second, the omission of certain questions (for example, "Is $L(G_1) = L(G_2)$?") is no accident; we shall see in Chapter 6 that some questions about context-free grammars are not amenable to solution by algorithms.

Proof of Theorem 3.5.8. Our basic strategy for determining whether $w \in L(G)$ is to inspect all possible derivations up to a certain length, or equivalently all possible parse trees up to a certain size, in search of one for w; if one is found, then $w \in L(G)$, and if one is not found, we can conclude that $w \notin L(G)$. The trick, of course, is to know which derivations or parse trees it suffices to examine.

Now if every rule of G is of the form $A \longrightarrow u$ where u is a terminal symbol or $|u| \geq 2$, then our problem is greatly simplified. For then the derived string becomes longer after each step of a derivation except when a nonterminal is replaced by a single terminal symbol; therefore no derivation with more than $2|w| - 1$ steps need be checked to see if $w \in L(G)$. Or to put it another way, any parse tree with height h must have yield of length at least h; this is easily established by induction (Problem 3.5.14). So to determine whether a particular string w is in $L(G)$, we could simply inspect all parse trees of height at most $|w|$; the number of these trees can be bounded by inspection of G.

So part (a) will be solved if we can convert any grammar into an equivalent one with no rules $A \longrightarrow u$, where u is e or a nonterminal. Actually, this is not quite possible, since if e happens to be in $L(G)$, then it can be generated *only* if there is a rule of the form $A \longrightarrow e$ for some nonterminal A. But we can come close enough to suit our purposes.

First, we eliminate all rules of the form $A \longrightarrow e$, *except* that the rule $S \longrightarrow e$ will have to remain if in fact $e \in L(G)$. The procedure is as follows: Let $G = (V, \Sigma, R, S)$. To begin, whenever $A \longrightarrow e$ is a rule and $B \longrightarrow uAv$ is a rule ($u, v \in V^*$), add $B \longrightarrow uv$ to the set of rules; and repeat this process until no new rules can be added in this way. The process must eventually stop, since the right-hand side of each new rule is a substring of the right-hand side of a rule already in the set. Moreover, the language generated is not changed by this process, since each new rule simply telescopes a derivation implicit in two rules already present. Second, eliminate all rules of the form $A \longrightarrow e$, except the rule $S \longrightarrow e$ if it is present, from the resulting rules.

This too does not change the language generated, since any use of a rule $A \longrightarrow e$ in a derivation would apply to an occurrence of A that had been produced by some other rule $B \longrightarrow uAv$, and the rule $B \longrightarrow uv$ could be used just as well as the two rules $B \longrightarrow uAv$ and $A \longrightarrow e$. Thus even the rule $S \longrightarrow e$, if it remains, need be used only in the single derivation $S \Rightarrow e$ and not in any other derivation in which S may be involved. So the resulting grammar G' has the following properties.

1. $L(G') = L(G)$.
2. If $e \in L(G')$, then $S \longrightarrow e$ is a rule of G'.
3. Any string in $L(G')$ except e has a derivation, and hence a parse tree, in which no rule of the form $A \longrightarrow e$ is used.

Now we must eliminate rules of the form $A \longrightarrow B$, and we shall have settled part (a). To do so, note that we can determine for any two nonterminals A and B whether $A \overset{*}{\underset{G'}{\Rightarrow}} B$; for if $A \overset{*}{\underset{G'}{\Rightarrow}} B$, then there is a derivation of B from A of $|V - \Sigma|$ steps at most. Whenever $A \longrightarrow u$ is a rule of G' and $B \overset{*}{\underset{G'}{\Rightarrow}} A$, add the rule $B \longrightarrow u$; once again, this process does not change the language generated. Finally, eliminate all rules $A \longrightarrow B$; they are no longer needed, since any time a sequence $A \overset{*}{\Rightarrow} B \Rightarrow u$ is used in a derivation, where $u \notin V - \Sigma$, the rule $A \longrightarrow u$ could be used equally well. This completes the proof of part (a).

To answer Question (b), simply note that if $G = (V, \Sigma, R, S)$ generates a nonempty language, then there is a parse tree with yield that is a terminal string and with height at most $|V - \Sigma|$. For a parse tree of height greater than $|V - \Sigma|$ has a path on which two nodes are labeled with the same nonterminal; that path can be shortened by excising the part of the tree between those two nodes (see Figure 3–9). This process can be repeated until a parse

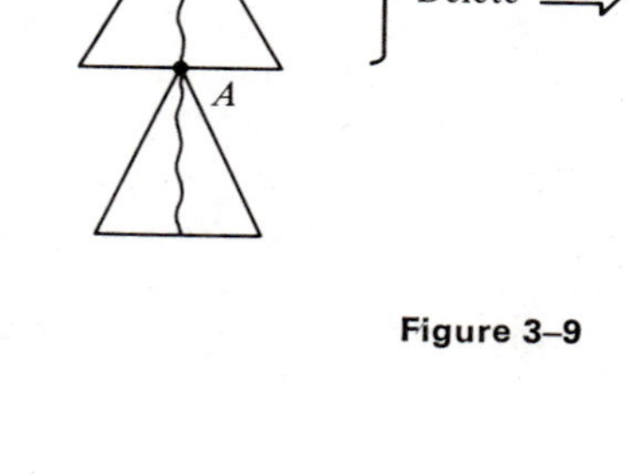

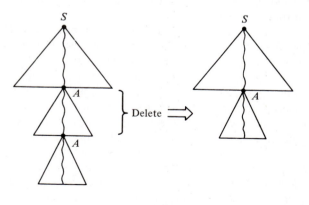

Figure 3–9

tree is obtained with no path longer than $|V - \Sigma|$. Since all parse trees up to height $|V - \Sigma|$ can be explored in search of one whose yield is a terminal string, it can be determined whether $L(G)$ is empty. ■

3.6 DETERMINISM AND PARSING

In the proof of Theorem 3.5.8, we presented a method for determining whether a particular string is generated by a particular context-free grammar. In a few words, the method was to modify the grammar to eliminate certain kinds of "nonproductive" rules, and then to check all parse trees of up to a certain size, depending on the length of the string. This method for determining whether a string is generated by a grammar was not intended to be a *practical* method; it is of theoretical significance only. How, in practice, would we go about answering the question?

This problem has been the subject of a great deal of study, and there are many workable approaches. The ones we discuss here are rooted in the idea of a pushdown automaton. After all, the equivalence of pushdown automata and context-free grammars, which was proved in Section 3.4, should be put to use. We commented, however, before setting out to prove Theorem 3.5.8, that a pushdown automaton is not of immediate practical use for determining whether a string is in a context-free language because it may run for an indefinite period without consuming any input. There is another problem as well, namely, the inherently nondeterministic way in which the pushdown automaton has been defined. With a view towards using Theorem 3.4.1 as the basis for a practical method of accepting context-free languages, can we always make pushdown automata operate deterministically?

Our first objective in this section is to study the question of deterministic pushdown automata. We shall see that there are some context-free languages that *cannot* be accepted by deterministic pushdown automata. This is rather disappointing; it suggests that the conversion of grammars to automata in Section 3.4 may not be the basis for any practical method, for example, for compiling programs written in a context-free programming language such as that suggested by Example 3.1.3. Nevertheless, all is not lost. It turns out that for most programming languages one can construct deterministic pushdown automata that accept all syntactically correct programs. These deterministic devices are used in practice not only for rejecting programs with syntactic errors, but also for the mechanical syntactic analysis of programs, which is an important stage in the process of compilation. Later in this section we shall give two heuristic rules—rules of thumb—that are useful for constructing deterministic pushdown automata from suitable context-free grammars. These rules will not invariably produce a useful pushdown automaton from any context-free grammar; we have already said that that would be impossible. But they are typical of the methods actually used in the construction of compilers for programming languages.

3.6.1 DETERMINISTIC PUSHDOWN AUTOMATA AND CONTEXT-FREE LANGUAGES

A pushdown automaton is *deterministic*, intuitively speaking, if there is at most one transition applicable to each configuration. Formally, M is deterministic if whenever (p, w, γ) is a configuration of M and, for some prefixes w_1 and w_2 of w and γ_1 and γ_2 of γ, both $((p, w_1, \gamma_1), (q_1, \delta_1))$ and $((p, w_2, \gamma_2), (q_2, \delta_2))$ are transitions of M, they are identical transitions: $w_1 = w_2$, $\gamma_1 = \gamma_2$, $q_1 = q_2$, and $\delta_1 = \delta_2$. This condition can be rephrased in an equivalent way. Call two strings **consistent** if the first is a prefix of the second, or vice versa. Call two transitions $((p_1, w_1, \gamma_1), (q_1, \delta_1))$ and $((p_2, w_2, \gamma_2), (q_2, \delta_2))$ **compatible** if $p_1 = p_2$, w_1 and w_2 are consistent, and γ_1 and γ_2 are consistent. Then M is **deterministic** if it has no two distinct compatible transitions.

For example, the machine we constructed in Example 3.3.2 to accept $\{wcw^R\colon w \in \{a, b\}^*\}$ is deterministic: For each choice of state and input symbol, there is only one possible transition. On the other hand, the machine we constructed in Example 3.3.3 to accept $\{ww^R\colon w \in \{a, b\}^*\}$ is not deterministic: Transition 3 is compatible with both transitions 1 and 2. Deterministic context-free languages are essentially those that are accepted by deterministic pushdown automata. However, for reasons that will become clear very soon, we have to modify the acceptance convention slightly. A language is said to be deterministic context-free if it is recognized by a deterministic pushdown automaton that also has the extra capability of sensing the end of the input string. Formally, we call a language $L \subseteq \Sigma^*$ **deterministic context-free** if $L\$ = L(M)$ for some deterministic pushdown automaton M. Here \$ is a new symbol, not in Σ, which is appended to each input string for the purpose of marking its end.

Every deterministic context-free language, as just defined, is a context-free language. To see this, suppose a deterministic pushdown automaton M accepts $L\$$. Then a (possibly nondeterministic) pushdown automaton M' that accepts L can be constructed. At any point, M' may "imagine" a \$ in the input and jump to a new set of states from which it reads no further input.

Formally, if $M = (K, \Sigma \cup \{\$\}, \Gamma, \Delta, s, F)$, then $M' = (K', \Sigma, \Gamma, \Delta', s', F')$, where

$$K' = \{\langle p, i\rangle : p \in K, i = 0, 1\}$$
$$s' = \langle s, 0\rangle$$
$$F' = \{\langle f, 1\rangle : f \in F\}$$

and Δ' contains the following.

$((\langle p, 0\rangle, x, \alpha), (\langle q, 0\rangle, \beta))$ for each $((p, x, \alpha), (q, \beta)) \in \Delta,\quad x \in \Sigma^*$

$((\langle p, 0\rangle, x, \alpha), (\langle q, 1\rangle, \beta))$ for each $((p, x\$, \alpha), (q, \beta)) \in \Delta,\quad x \in \Sigma^*$

$((\langle p, 1\rangle, e, \alpha), (\langle q, 1\rangle, \beta))$ for each $((p, e, \alpha), (q, \beta)) \in \Delta$

It is left as an exercise (Problem 3.6.4) to check that M' does accept L whenever M accepts $L\$$. (It is also possible to use the result of Problem 3.5.6 to show that if $L\$$ is context-free, then so is L.)

If, on the other hand, we had not adopted this special acceptance convention, then many context-free languages that are deterministic intuitively would not be deterministic by our definition. One example is $L = a^* \cup \{a^nb^n : n \geq 0\}$: A deterministic pushdown automaton cannot both remember how many a's it has seen, in order to check the string of b's that may follow, and at the same time be ready to accept with empty stack in case *no* b's follow. However, one can easily design a deterministic pushdown automaton accepting $L\$$: If a \$ is met while the machine is still accumulating a's, then the input was a string in a^*. Then the stack may be emptied and the input accepted.

We have changed the acceptance convention in order to expand the class of context-free languages that can be accepted by deterministic pushdown automata. The natural question at this point is whether *every* context-free language is deterministic—just as every regular language is accepted by a deterministic finite automaton. It would be surprising if this were so. Consider, for example, the language

$$L_0 = \{a^{m_1}ba^{m_2}b \ldots a^{m_n} : n \geq 2, m_1, \ldots, m_n \geq 0, \text{ and } m_i \neq m_j \text{ for some } i, j\}.$$

It would seem that a pushdown automaton could accept this language only by guessing which two blocks of a's to compare. Without so using nondeterminism, it would seem, the machine could not, while reading the first two blocks, compare and at the same time remember their lengths, if they turned out to be equal, for comparison with subsequent blocks. However, to prove that L_0 is not deterministic requires a more delicate argument.

Theorem 3.6.1. *Let $L \subseteq \Sigma^*$ be a context-free language such that*

(a) *for each $u \in \Sigma^*$ there is a $v \in \Sigma^*$ such that $uv \in L$;*

(b) *$\Sigma^* - L$ is not context-free.*

Then L is not deterministic context-free.

Before proceeding to the proof, note that Theorem 3.6.1 immediately implies that the language L_0 just defined is not deterministic context-free, since L_0 has property (a) and $\Sigma^* - L_0 = a^* \cup \{a^mba^mb \ldots a^m : m \geq 0\}$—clearly not a context-free language.

Proof of Theorem 3.6.1. Suppose that $M = (K, \Sigma, \Gamma, \Delta, s, F)$ is a deterministic pushdown automaton accepting $L\$$. As in the proof of Lemma 3.4.4, we may assume that in a single step M examines, and possibly removes, only the topmost symbol on its stack. We may also assume that K consists of two disjoint subsets, K_1 and K_2. K_1 consists of states M can enter before—and only before—\$ is read, and K_2 consists of states M can enter after—and only after—\$ is read; transitions between states in K_2 involve reading no input. This property can be guaranteed by making two copies of the state set of M so that transitions involving \$ input pass from the first copy to the second. We may further assume that $F \subseteq K_2$, since M accepts no input that does not contain \$.

We must now analyze the behavior of M after it reads \$, enters the states in K_2, and reads no further input. Specifically, for $p \in K_2$, consider the set

$$X_p = \{\gamma \in \Gamma^*: (p, e, \gamma) \vdash_M^* (f, e, e) \text{ for some } f \in F\}.$$

We claim that each X_p is a regular set. To see this, let

$$\Theta = \{(r, a, q): r, q \in K_2, a \in \Gamma, \text{ and } (r, e, a) \vdash_M^* (q, e, e)\}.$$

The set Θ can actually be constructed by inspection of M, but for the purposes of this proof we need only observe that Θ is a well-defined set of triples. We claim that X_p is the set of strings accepted by the finite automaton $(K_2, \Gamma, \Theta, p, F)$. This is because, whatever operations M performs on the stack while staying in K_2 and reading no input, M can empty the stack only by a sequence of subcomputations, each of which has the ultimate effect of popping a single symbol. Now since X_p is regular so is $\Gamma^* - X_p$; let $(K'_p, \Gamma, \Delta'_p, p, F'_p)$ be a finite automaton accepting $\Gamma^* - X_p$. Assume, without loss of generality, that K'_p and K'_q are disjoint if $p \neq q$, and that $K'_p \cap K = \{p\}$ for each $p \in K_2$. Let Δ_2 be the set of transitions of M between states in K_2; that is,

$$\Delta_2 = \{((p, e, \gamma_1), (q, \gamma_2)) \in \Delta: p, q \in K_2, \gamma_1, \gamma_2 \in \Gamma^*\}.$$

Then let M' be the pushdown automaton $(K', \Sigma, \Gamma, \Delta', s, F')$, where

$$K' = K \cup \bigcup\{K'_p: p \in K_2\}$$

$$\Delta' = \Delta - \Delta_2 \cup \{((q_1, e, \gamma), (q_2, e)): (q_1, \gamma, q_2) \in \Delta'_p \text{ for some } p \in K_2\}$$

$$F' = \bigcup\{F'_p: p \in K_2\}.$$

That is, M' operates identically with M until \$ is encountered in the input; M' then empties its stack and winds up in a final state if and only if M would have failed to empty its stack or, having emptied it, would not have entered a final state.

Finally, we claim that M' accepts $\Sigma^*\$ - L\$$; this will complete the proof since it contradicts hypothesis (b), that $\Sigma^* - L$ is not context-free. Consider any string $w\$ \in \Sigma^*\$$. M, and hence M', must actually read the entire string and enter a state in K_2 after reading \$; for if M failed to read beyond a certain prefix u of w, then by (a) there would be a string $uv\$ \in L\$$ which M did not accept. But having entered a state in K_2, M' will read no further input, and will accept if and only if M would not. ■

3.6.2 TOP-DOWN PARSING

Having established that not every context-free language can be accepted by a deterministic pushdown automaton, let us now consider some of those that can. Our overall goal for the remainder of this chapter is to study cases in which context-free grammars can be converted into deterministic pushdown automata that can actually be used for language recognition. However, our style here is rather different from that of the rest of this book; there are fewer proofs, and we do not attempt to tie up all the loose ends of the ideas we introduce. We present some guidelines—what we call "heuristic rules"—that will not be useful in all cases, and we do not even attempt to specify exactly *when* they *will* be useful. That is, we aim to introduce some suggestive applications of the theory developed earlier in this chapter, but this venture should not be taken as anything more than an introduction.

Let us begin with an example. The language $L = \{a^n b^n : n \geq 0\}$ is generated by the context-free grammar $G = (\{a, b, S\}, \{a, b\}, R, S)$, where R contains the two rules $S \to aSb$ and $S \to e$. We know how to construct a pushdown automaton that accepts L: just carry out the construction of Lemma 3.4.3 for the grammar G. The result is

$$M_1 = (\{p, q\}, \{a, b\}, \{a, b, S\}, \Delta_1, p, \{q\}),$$

where

$$\Delta_1 = \{((p, e, e), (q, S)), ((q, e, S), (q, aSb)), ((q, e, S), (q, e)),$$
$$((q, a, a), (q, e)), ((q, b, b), (q, e))\}.$$

Since M_1 has two different transitions with identical first components—corresponding to the two rules of G that have identical left-hand sides—it is not deterministic.

Nevertheless, L is a deterministic context-free language, and M_1 can be modified to become a deterministic pushdown automaton M_2 that accepts $L\$$. Intuitively, all the information that M_1 needs at each point in order to decide which of the two transitions to follow is the *next input symbol*. If that symbol is an a, then M_1 should replace S by aSb on its stack if hope of an accepting computation is to be retained. On the other hand, if the next input symbol is a b, then the machine must pop S. M_2 achieves this required anticipation or **lookahead** by consuming an input symbol *ahead of time* and incorporating that information into its state. Formally,

$$M_2 = (\{p, q, q_a, q_b, q_\$\}, \{a, b, \$\}, \{a, b, S\}, \Delta_2, p, \{q_\$\})$$

where Δ_2 contains the following transitions.

1. $((p, e, e), (q, S))$
2. $((q, a, e), (q_a, e))$
3. $((q_a, e, a), (q, e))$
4. $((q, b, e), (q_b, e))$
5. $((q_b, e, b), (q, e))$
6. $((q, \$, e), (q_\$, e))$
7. $((q_a, e, S), (q_a, aSb))$
8. $((q_b, e, S), (q_b, e))$

From state q, M_2 reads one input symbol and, without changing the stack, enters one of the three new states q_a, q_b, or $q_\$$. It then uses that information to differentiate the two compatible transitions $((q, e, S), (q, aSb))$ and $((q, e, S), (q, e))$: The first transition is retained only from state q_a and the second only from state q_b. So M_2 is deterministic. It accepts the input $ab\$$ as follows.

Step	State	Unread Input	Stack	Transition Used	Rule of G
0	p	$ab\$$	e	–	
1	q	$ab\$$	S	1	
2	q_a	$b\$$	S	2	
3	q_a	$b\$$	aSb	7	$S \longrightarrow aSb$
4	q	$b\$$	Sb	3	
5	q_b	$\$$	Sb	4	
6	q_b	$\$$	b	8	$S \longrightarrow e$
7	q	$\$$	e	5	
8	$q_\$$	e	e	6	

So M_2 can serve as a deterministic device for recognizing strings of the form $a^n b^n$. Moreover, by remembering which transitions of M_2 were derived from which rules of the grammar, we can use a trace of the operation of M_2 in order to reconstruct a leftmost derivation of the input string. Specifically, the steps in the computation where a nonterminal is replaced on top of the stack (Steps 3 and 6 in the example) correspond to the construction of a parse tree from the root towards the leaves (see Figure 3–10(a)).

The task of recognizing a context-free language in a deterministic way that also reconstructs the parse trees of the strings is both extremely important and challenging. Devices such as M_2 are called **parsers**. In particular, M_2 is a **top-down parser** because tracing its operation at the steps where nonterminals are replaced on the stack reconstructs a parse tree in a top-down, left-to-right fashion (see Figure 3–10(b)). We shall see a more substantial example shortly.

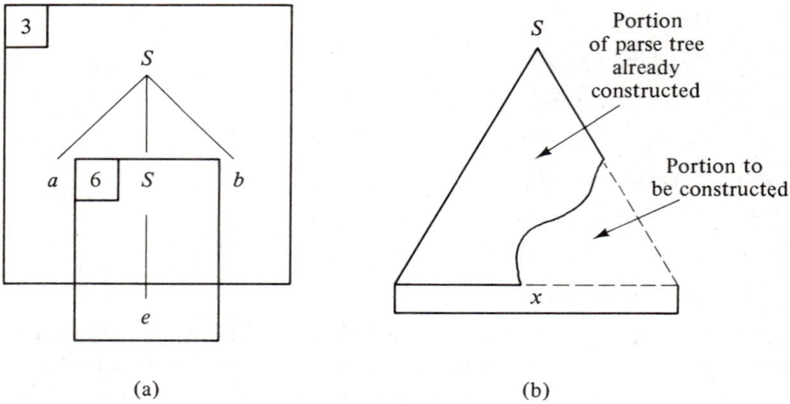

Figure 3–10

Naturally, not all context-free languages have deterministic acceptors that can be derived from the standard nondeterministic one via the lookahead idea. For example, we saw in the previous subsection that some context-free languages are not deterministic to begin with. Even for certain deterministic context-free languages, lookahead of just one symbol may not be sufficient to resolve all uncertainties. Some languages, however, are not amenable to parsing by lookahead for reasons that are superficial and can be removed by slightly modifying the grammar.

Recall the grammar G that generates arithmetic expressions with operations $+$ and $*$ and variables $x1$ and $x2$ (Example 3.1.3). Let us try to construct a top-down parser for this grammar. Our construction of Section 3.4 would give the pushdown automaton

$$M_3 = (\{p, q\}, \Sigma, \Gamma, \Delta, p, \{f\})$$

with

$$\Sigma = \{(,), +, *, x, 1, 2\}$$
$$\Gamma = \Sigma \cup \{E, T, F\}$$

and Δ as given below.

0. $((p, e, e), (q, E))$
1. $((q, e, E), (q, E + T))$
2. $((q, e, E), (q, T))$
3. $((q, e, T), (q, T * F))$
4. $((q, e, T), (q, F))$
5. $((q, e, F), (q, (E)))$
6. $((q, e, F), (q, x1))$
7. $((q, e, F), (q, x2))$

Finally, $((q, \sigma, \sigma), (q, e)) \in \Delta$ for all $\sigma \in \Sigma$. The nondeterminism of M_3 is manifested by the sets of transitions 1–2, 3–4, and 5–6–7 that have identical first components. What is worse, these decisions cannot be made based on the next input symbol. Lets us examine more closely why this is so.

Transitions 6 and 7. Suppose that the configuration of M_3 is $(q, x1, F)$. At this point M_3 could act according to any one of transitions 5, 6, or 7. By looking at the next input symbol—x—M_3 could exclude transition 5, since this transition requires that the next symbol be (. Still, M_3 would not be able to decide between transitions 6 and 7, since they both produce a top of the stack that can be matched to the next input symbol—x. The problem arises because the rules $F \longrightarrow x1$ and $F \longrightarrow x2$ of G have not only identical left-hand sides, but also the same first symbol on their right-hand sides.

There is a very simple way around this problem: Just replace the rules $F \longrightarrow x1$ and $F \longrightarrow x2$ in G by the rules $F \longrightarrow xN$, $N \longrightarrow 1$ and $N \longrightarrow 2$, where N is a new nonterminal (N for *numeral*). This has the effect of "procrastinating" on the decision between the rules $F \longrightarrow x1$ and $F \longrightarrow x2$ until all needed information is available. A modified pushdown automaton M'_3 now results from this modified grammar, in which transitions 6 and 7 are replaced by the following.

6′. $((q, e, F), (q, xN))$

7′. $((q, e, N), (q, 1))$

8′. $((q, e, N), (q, 2))$

Now looking one symbol ahead is enough to decide the correct action. For example, configuration $(q, x1, F)$ would yield $(q, x1, xN)$, $(q, 1, N)$, $(q, 1, 1)$, and finally (q, e, e).

This technique of avoiding nondeterminism is known as **left factoring**. It can be summarized as follows.

Heuristic Rule 1:

Whenever $A \longrightarrow \alpha\beta$ and $A \longrightarrow \alpha\gamma$ are rules with $\alpha \neq e$, then replace them by the rules $A \longrightarrow \alpha A'$, $A' \longrightarrow \beta$, and $A' \longrightarrow \gamma$, where A' is a new nonterminal.

It is easy to see that applying Heuristic Rule 1 does not change the language generated by the grammar.

We now move to examining the second kind of anomaly that prevents us from transforming M_3 into a deterministic parser.

Transitions 1 and 2. These transitions present us with a more serious problem. If the automaton sees x as the next input symbol and the contents of the stack are just E, it could take a number of actions. It could perform transition 2, replacing E by T (this would be justified in case the input is, say, $x1$). Or, it could replace E by $E + T$ (transition 1) and then the top E by T (this should be done if the input is $x1 + x1$). Or, it could perform transition 2 twice and transition 1 once (input $x1 + x1 + x1$), and so on. It seems that there is no bound whatsoever on how far ahead the automaton must peek in order to decide on the right action. The culprit here is the rule $E \longrightarrow E + T$, in which the nonterminal on the left-hand side is repeated as the first symbol of the right-hand side. This phenomenon is called **left recursion,** and can be removed by some further surgery on the grammar.

To remove left recursion from the rule $E \longrightarrow E + T$, we simply replace it by the rules $E \longrightarrow TE'$, $E' \longrightarrow +TE'$, and $E' \longrightarrow e$, where E' is a new nonterminal. It will be shown (see Lemma 3.6.1) that such transformations do not change the language produced by the grammar. The same method must also be applied to the other left recursive rule of G, namely $T \longrightarrow T * F$. We thus arrive at the grammar $G' = (V', \Sigma, R', E)$ where $V' = \Sigma \cup \{E, E', T, T', F, N\}$ and the rules are as follows.

1. $E \longrightarrow TE'$
2. $E' \longrightarrow +TE'$
3. $E' \longrightarrow e$
4. $T \longrightarrow FT'$
5. $T' \longrightarrow *FT'$
6. $T' \longrightarrow e$
7. $F \longrightarrow (E)$
8. $F \longrightarrow xN$
9. $N \longrightarrow 1$
10. $N \longrightarrow 2$

The above technique for removing left recursion can be expressed as follows.†

Heuristic Rule 2:

Let $A \longrightarrow A\alpha_1, \ldots, A \longrightarrow A\alpha_n$ and $A \longrightarrow \beta_1, \ldots, A \longrightarrow \beta_m$ be all rules with A on the left-hand side, where the β's do not start with an A and $n > 0$. Then replace these rules by $A \longrightarrow \beta_1 A', \ldots, A \longrightarrow \beta_m A', A' \longrightarrow \alpha_1 A', \ldots, A' \longrightarrow \alpha_n A'$, and $A' \longrightarrow e$, where A' is a new nonterminal.

Lemma 3.6.1. *Let G be a context-free grammar, and let G' be a grammar resulting from the application of* Heuristic Rule 2 *to G. Then $L(G) = L(G')$.*

†We assume here that there are no rules of the form $A \longrightarrow A$.

Proof. Consider a leftmost derivation $S = \gamma_0 \overset{L}{\underset{G}{\Rightarrow}} \gamma_1 \overset{L}{\underset{G}{\Rightarrow}} \cdots \overset{L}{\underset{G}{\Rightarrow}} \gamma_k = w$ of a string w from S in G. We shall show how to transform it into one in G'. Suppose that $\gamma_j = xA\gamma'$ and $\gamma_{j+1} = x\beta_i\gamma'$, $i \leq m$. Then we can replace this step by $xA\gamma' \overset{L}{\underset{G'}{\Rightarrow}} x\beta_i A'\gamma' \overset{L}{\underset{G'}{\Rightarrow}} x\beta_i\gamma'$. Now suppose that $\gamma_j = xA\gamma'$, $\gamma_{j+i} = xA\alpha_{j_i}\alpha_{j_{i-1}} \ldots \alpha_{j_1}\gamma'$ for $i = 1, \ldots, l$, and $\gamma_{j+l+1} = x\beta_p\alpha_{j_l} \ldots \alpha_{j_1}\gamma'$. Then we replace these $l + 1$ steps by

$$xA\gamma' \overset{L}{\underset{G'}{\Rightarrow}} x\beta_p A'\gamma' \overset{L}{\underset{G'}{\Rightarrow}} x\beta_p\alpha_{j_l}A'\gamma' \overset{L}{\underset{G'}{\Rightarrow}} \cdots$$

$$\overset{L}{\underset{G'}{\Rightarrow}} x\beta_p\alpha_{j_l} \cdots \alpha_{j_1}A'\gamma' \underset{G'}{\Rightarrow} x\beta_p\alpha_{j_l} \cdots \alpha_{j_1}\gamma'.$$

We leave it as an exercise to show that $L(G') \subseteq L(G)$ (see Problem 3.6.7). ■

Still the grammar G' of our example has rules with identical left-hand sides, only now all uncertainties can be resolved by looking ahead at the next input symbol. We can thus construct the following deterministic push-down automaton M_4 that accepts $L(G)\$$.

$$M_4 = (K, \Sigma \cup \{\$\}, V', \Delta, p, \{q_\$\})$$

where

$$K = \{p, q, q_x, q_1, q_2, q_+, q_*, q_), q_(, q_\$\}$$

and Δ is listed below.

$((p, e, e), (q, E))$	
$((q, \sigma, e), (q_\sigma, e))$	for each $\sigma \in \Sigma \cup \{\$\}$
$((q_\sigma, e, \sigma), (q, e))$	for each $\sigma \in \Sigma$
$((q_\sigma, e, E), (q_\sigma, TE'))$	for each $\sigma \in \Sigma \cup \{\$\}$
$((q_+, e, E'), (q_+, +TE'))$	
$((q_\sigma, e, E'), (q_\sigma, e))$	for each $\sigma \in \Sigma - \{+\} \cup \{\$\}$
$((q_\sigma, e, T), (q_\sigma, FT'))$	for each $\sigma \in \Sigma \cup \{\$\}$
$((q_*, e, T'), (q_*, * FT'))$	
$((q_\sigma, e, T'), (q_\sigma, e))$	for each $\sigma \in \Sigma - \{*\} \cup \{\$\}$
$((q_(, e, F), (q_(, (E)))$	
$((q_x, e, F), (q_x, xN))$	
$((q_1, e, N), (q_1, 1))$	
$((q_2, e, N), (q_2, 2))$	

Then M_4 is a parser for G'. For example, the input string $x1 * (x2)\$$ would be accepted as follows.

Step	State	Unread Input	Stack	Rule of G'
0	p	$x1*(x2)\$$	e	
1	q	$x1*(x2)\$$	E	
2	q_x	$1*(x2)\$$	E	
3	q_x	$1*(x2)\$$	TE'	1
4	q_x	$1*(x2)\$$	$FT'E'$	4
5	q_x	$1*(x2)\$$	$xNT'E'$	8
6	q	$1*(x2)\$$	$NT'E'$	
7	q_1	$*(x2)\$$	$NT'E'$	
8	q_1	$*(x2)\$$	$1T'E'$	9
9	q	$*(x2)\$$	$T'E'$	
10	q_*	$(x2)\$$	$T'E'$	
11	q_*	$(x2)\$$	$*FT'E'$	5
12	q	$(x2)\$$	$FT'E'$	
13	$q_($	$x2)\$$	$FT'E'$	
14	$q_($	$x2)\$$	$(E)T'E'$	7
15	q	$x2)\$$	$E)T'E'$	
16	q_x	$2)\$$	$E)T'E'$	
17	q_x	$2)\$$	$TE')T'E'$	1
18	q_x	$2)\$$	$FT'E')T'E'$	4
19	q_x	$2)\$$	$xNT'E')T'E'$	8
20	q	$2)\$$	$NT'E')T'E'$	
21	q_2	$)\$$	$NT'E')T'E'$	
22	q_2	$)\$$	$2T'E')T'E'$	10
23	q	$)\$$	$T'E')T'E'$	
24	$q_)$	$\$$	$T'E')T'E'$	
25	$q_)$	$\$$	$E')T'E'$	6
26	$q_)$	$\$$	$)T'E'$	3
27	q	$\$$	$T'E'$	
28	$q_\$$	e	$T'E'$	
29	$q_\$$	e	E'	6
30	$q_\$$	e	e	3

Here we have indicated the steps in the computation where a nonterminal has been replaced on the stack in accordance with a rule of G'. By applying these rules of G' in sequence, a derivation of the input can be reconstructed; the corresponding parse tree is shown in Figure 3–11. The numbers relate the steps in the computation to the parts of the parse tree.

Thus, given a grammar G, one may try to construct a top-down parser for G as follows: Eliminate left recursion in G by repeatedly applying Heuristic Rule 2 to all left recursive nonterminals A of G. Apply Heuristic Rule 1 to left-factor G whenever necessary. Then examine whether the resulting grammar has the property that one can decide among rules with the same

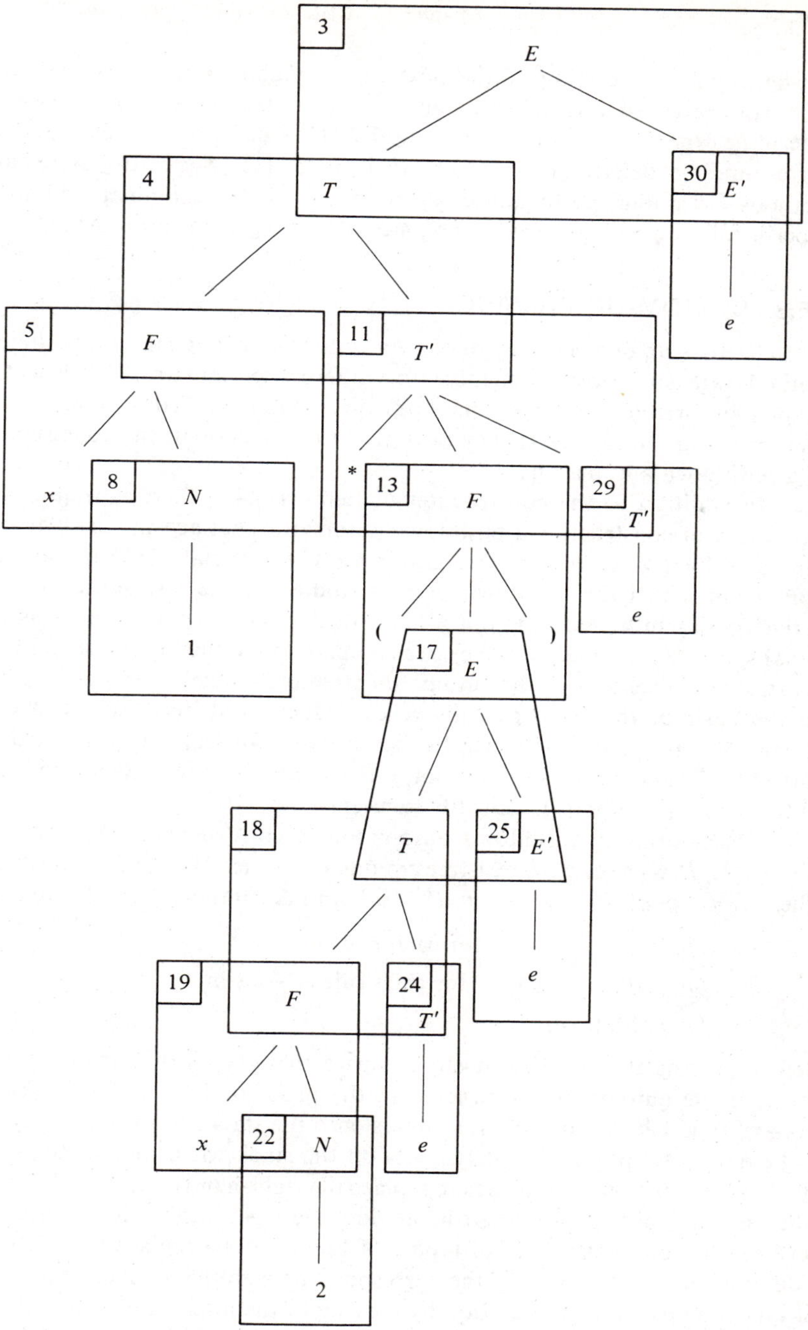

Figure 3–11

left-hand side by looking at the next input symbol. Grammars with this property are called $LL(1)$. Although we have not specified exactly how to determine whether a grammar is indeed $LL(1)$—nor how to construct the corresponding deterministic parser if it is $LL(1)$—there are systematic methods for doing so. In any case, inspection of the grammar and some experimentation will often take the place of more general procedures.

3.6.3 BOTTOM-UP PARSING

There is no one best way to parse a context-free language, and different methods are sometimes preferable for different grammars. We close this chapter by briefly considering methods quite dissimilar from those of top-down parsing. Nevertheless they, too, find their genesis in the construction of a pushdown automaton.

In addition to the construction of Lemma 3.4.3, there is a quite different way of constructing a pushdown automaton that accepts the language generated by a given context-free grammar. The automata of that construction (from which the top-down parsers studied in the last subsection are derived) operate by carrying out a leftmost derivation on the stack; as terminal symbols are generated, they are compared with the input string. In the construction given below, the automaton attempts to read the input first and, on the basis of the input actually read, deduce what derivation it should attempt to carry out. The general effect, as we shall see, is to reconstruct a parse tree from the leaves to the root, rather than the other way around, and so this class of methods is called **bottom-up**.

The bottom-up pushdown automaton is constructed as follows. Let $G = (V, \Sigma, R, S)$ be any context-free grammar; then let $M = (K, \Sigma, \Gamma, \Delta, s, F)$, where $K = \{p, q\}$, $\Gamma = V$, $s = p$, $F = \{q\}$, and Δ contains the following.

1. $((p, \sigma, e), (p, \sigma))$ for each $\sigma \in \Sigma$.
2. $((p, e, \alpha^R), (p, A))$ for each rule $A \longrightarrow \alpha$ in R.
3. $((p, e, S), (q, e))$

Before moving to the proof itself, compare these types of transitions with those of the automaton constructed in the proof of Lemma 3.4.3. Transitions of type 1 here move input symbols onto the stack; transitions of type 3 in Lemma 3.4.3 pop terminal symbols off the stack when they match input symbols. Transitions of type 2 here replace the right-hand side of a rule on the stack by the corresponding left-hand side, the right-hand side being found reversed on the stack; those of type 2 of Lemma 3.4.3 replace the left-hand side of a rule on the stack by the corresponding right-hand side. Transitions of type 3 here end a computation by moving to the final state when only the start symbol remains on the stack; transitions of type 1 of Lemma 3.4.3 start off the computation by placing the start symbol on the initially empty stack.

So the machine of this construction is in a sense perfectly orthogonal to the one of Lemma 3.4.3.

Lemma 3.6.2. *Let G and M be as just presented. Then* $L(M) = L(G)$.

Proof. We need one new definition. A derivation in a context-free grammar will be called **rightmost** if the rightmost nonterminal symbol is replaced at each step. We write $\overset{R}{\underset{G}{\Rightarrow}}$ and $\overset{*R}{\underset{G}{\Rightarrow}}$ for the relations of "yielding in one step of a rightmost derivation" and "yielding by zero or more steps of a rightmost derivation," respectively, by means of the grammar G.

By an argument entirely parallel to the proof of Lemma 3.4.1, any string in $L(G)$ has a rightmost derivation from the start symbol. Therefore proof of the following claim suffices to establish Lemma 3.6.2.

Claim. *For any* $x \in \Sigma^*$ *and* $\gamma \in \Gamma^*$, $(p, x, \gamma) \vdash_M^* (p, e, S)$ *if and only if* $S \overset{*R}{\underset{G}{\Rightarrow}} \gamma^R x$.

For if we let x be an input to M and $\gamma = e$, then since q is the only final state and it can be entered only via transition 3, the claim implies that M accepts x if and only if G generates x.

Proof of Claim. (*Only if*) The proof is by induction on k, the number of steps in the computation by M.

Basis Step. If $k = 0$, then $x = e$, $\gamma = S$, and trivially, $S \overset{*R}{\underset{G}{\Rightarrow}} S$.

Induction Hypothesis. Suppose that the only-if part of the claim holds for computations by M of up to k steps.

Induction Step. Suppose $(p, x, \gamma) \vdash_M^* (p, e, S)$ in $k + 1$ steps. Then for some $w \in \Sigma^*$, $\beta \in \Gamma^*$, $(p, x, \gamma) \vdash_M (p, w, \beta) \vdash_M^* (p, e, S)$, the latter computation being of k steps. By the induction hypothesis, $S \overset{*R}{\underset{G}{\Rightarrow}} \beta^R w$. There are two cases to consider.

Case 1. The transition used in the step $(p, x, \gamma) \vdash_M (p, w, \beta)$ is of type 1. For some $\sigma \in \Sigma$, $x = \sigma w$ and $\beta = \sigma\gamma$; then $\gamma^R x = \gamma^R \sigma w = \beta^R w$ and the only-if part of the claim follows immediately.

Case 2. The transition used in the step $(p, x, \gamma) \vdash_M (p, w, \beta)$ is of type 2. Then for some rule $A \longrightarrow \alpha$ in R and some $\delta \in V^*$, $\beta = A\delta$ and $\gamma = \alpha^R\delta$; and $x = w$. By the induction hypothesis, $S \overset{*R}{\Rightarrow} \beta^R w$; but $\beta^R w = \delta^R A w = \delta^R A x \overset{R}{\underset{G}{\Rightarrow}} \delta^R \alpha x = \gamma^R x$, and the induction is completed.

(*If*) The proof is by induction on k, the number of steps in a rightmost derivation of $\gamma^R x$ from S.

Basis Step. If $k = 0$, then $x = e, \gamma = S$, and trivially, $(p, e, S) \vdash_M^* (p, e, S)$.

Induction Hypothesis. Suppose that the if part of the claim holds for derivations of up to k steps.

Induction Step. Suppose $S \overset{*R}{\underset{G}{\Rightarrow}} \gamma^R x$ by a derivation of $k + 1$ steps, where $x \in \Sigma^*$. Then for some $A \in V - \Sigma$, $w \in \Sigma^*$, and $\beta \in V^*$, $S \overset{*R}{\underset{G}{\Rightarrow}} \beta^R A w \overset{R}{\underset{G}{\Rightarrow}} \beta^R \alpha w = \gamma^R x$, where $A \rightarrow \alpha$ is a rule of G, and where the first part of the derivation has k steps. Since $|x| \geq |w|$, and since $\beta^R \alpha w = \gamma^R x$, there is a $u \in \Sigma^*$ such that $\beta^R \alpha = \gamma^R u$ and $uw = x$. By the induction hypothesis, $(p, w, A\beta) \vdash_M^* (p, e, S)$. By a transition of type 2, $(p, w, \alpha^R \beta) \vdash_M (p, w, A\beta)$, and by $|u|$ transitions of type 1, $(p, x, \gamma) = (p, uw, \gamma) \vdash_M^* (p, w, u^R \gamma) = (p, w, \alpha^R \beta)$. Hence $(p, x, \gamma) \vdash_M^* (p, e, S)$ as was to be shown. ■

Let us consider again the grammar for arithmetic expressions (Example 3.1.3) analyzed in the last section. The rules of this grammar, G, are the following.

$$E \rightarrow E + T \quad \text{(R1)}$$
$$E \rightarrow T \quad \text{(R2)}$$
$$T \rightarrow T * F \quad \text{(R3)}$$
$$T \rightarrow F \quad \text{(R4)}$$
$$F \rightarrow (E) \quad \text{(R5)}$$
$$F \rightarrow x1 \quad \text{(R6)}$$
$$F \rightarrow x2 \quad \text{(R7)}$$

If the construction of Lemma 3.6.2 is applied to this grammar, the following set of transitions is obtained.

$$((p, \sigma, e), (p, \sigma)) \qquad \text{for each } \sigma \in \Sigma \quad (\Delta 0)$$
$$((p, e, T + E), (p, E)) \quad (\Delta 1)$$
$$((p, e, T), (p, E)) \quad (\Delta 2)$$
$$((p, e, F * T), (p, T)) \quad (\Delta 3)$$
$$((p, e, F), (p, T)) \quad (\Delta 4)$$
$$((p, e,)E( ), (p, F)) \quad (\Delta 5)$$
$$((p, e, 1x), (p, F)) \quad (\Delta 6)$$
$$((p, e, 2x), (p, F)) \quad (\Delta 7)$$
$$((p, e, E), (q, e)) \quad (\Delta 8)$$

Let us call this pushdown automaton M. The input $x1 * (x2)$ is accepted by M as follows.

Step	State	Unread Input	Stack	Transition Used	Rule of G
0	p	$x1*(x2)$	e		
1	p	$1*(x2)$	x	$\Delta0$	
2	p	$*(x2)$	$1x$	$\Delta0$	
3	p	$*(x2)$	F	$\Delta6$	R6
4	p	$*(x2)$	T	$\Delta4$	R4
5	p	$(x2)$	$*T$	$\Delta0$	
6	p	$x2)$	$(*T$	$\Delta0$	
7	p	$2)$	$x(*T$	$\Delta0$	
8	p	$)$	$2x(*T$	$\Delta0$	
9	p	$)$	$F(*T$	$\Delta7$	R7
10	p	$)$	$T(*T$	$\Delta4$	R4
11	p	$)$	$E(*T$	$\Delta2$	R2
12	p	e	$)E(*T$	$\Delta0$	
13	p	e	$F*T$	$\Delta5$	R5
14	p	e	T	$\Delta3$	R3
15	p	e	E	$\Delta2$	R2
16	q	e	e	$\Delta8$	

We see that M is certainly not deterministic: Transitions of type $\Delta0$ are compatible with all the transitions of type $\Delta1$ through $\Delta8$. Still, its overall "philosophy" of operation is suggestive. At any point M may **shift** a terminal symbol from its input to the top of the stack (transitions of type $\Delta0$, used in the sample computation at Steps 1, 2, 5, 6, 7, 8, and 12). On the other hand, it may occasionally recognize the top few symbols on the stack as the reverse of the right-hand side of a rule of G, and may then **reduce** this string to the corresponding left-hand side (transitions of types $\Delta2$ through $\Delta7$, used in the sample computation where a "rule of G" is indicated in the rightmost column). The sequence of rules corresponding to the reduction steps turns out to mirror exactly, in reverse order, a rightmost derivation of the input string. In our example, the implied rightmost derivation is as follows.

$$
\begin{aligned}
E &\Rightarrow T \\
&\Rightarrow T * F \\
&\Rightarrow T * (E) \\
&\Rightarrow T * (T) \\
&\Rightarrow T * (F) \\
&\Rightarrow T * (x2) \\
&\Rightarrow F * (x2) \\
&\Rightarrow x1 * (x2)
\end{aligned}
$$

This derivation can be read from the computation by applying the rules mentioned in the right-hand column, from bottom to top, always to the rightmost nonterminal. Equivalently, this process can be thought of as a bottom-to-top, left-to-right reconstruction of parse tree (see Figure 3–12(a); compare to Figure 3–10(a)). In our example, the reconstructed parse tree is shown in Figure 3–12(b); the steps of the computation are shown in the upper left of each box.

In order to construct a practically useful parser for $L(G)$, we must turn M into a deterministic device that accepts $L(G)\$$. As in our treatment of top-down parsers, we shall not give a systematic procedure for doing so. Instead, we carry through the example of G, pointing out the basic heuristic principles that govern this construction.

First, we need a way of deciding between the two basic kinds of moves—namely, *shifting* the next input symbol to the stack and *reducing* the few topmost stack symbols to a single nonterminal according to a rule of the grammar. We decide this by looking at two pieces of information: the next input symbol—call it b—and the top stack symbol—call it a. (The symbol a could be a nonterminal.) The decision between shifting and reducing is done through a relation $P \subseteq (V \cup \{\$\}) \times (\Sigma \cup \{\$\})$, called a **precedence relation**. If a and b are as described above and $(a, b) \in P$, then we reduce; otherwise we shift b. The correct precedence relation for the grammar of our example is given in Figure 3–13. Intuitively, $(a, b) \in P$ means that there exists a rightmost derivation of the form $S \overset{*R}{\underset{G}{\Rightarrow}} \beta Abx \overset{R}{\underset{G}{\Rightarrow}} \beta\gamma abx$; since we are reconstructing rightmost derivations backwards, it makes sense to undo the rule $A \rightarrow \gamma a$ whenever we observe that a immediately precedes b. There are systematic ways to calculate precedence relations as well as to find out when, as is the case in this example, a precedence relation suffices to decide between shifting and reducing.

Now we must confront the other source of nondeterminism: when we decide to reduce, how do we choose which of the prefixes of the pushdown store to replace with a nonterminal? For example, if the pushdown store contains the string $F * T + E$ and we must reduce, we have a choice between reducing F to T (Rule R4) or reducing $F * T$ to T (Rule R3). For our grammar, it suffices to choose the *longest* prefix of the stack contents that matches the reverse of the right-hand side of a rule and reduce it to the left-hand side of that rule. Thus in the case above we should take the second option and reduce $F * T$ to T.

With these two observations it is quite straightforward to construct a deterministic pushdown automaton M' that parses $L(G)\$$. One last detail must be fixed. In order to carry out our second heuristic rule (namely, reduce the longest possible prefix of the stack) the automaton must be able to "sense" the bottom of the stack. This is achieved by placing a special symbol $\#$ on the stack at the beginning of every computation.

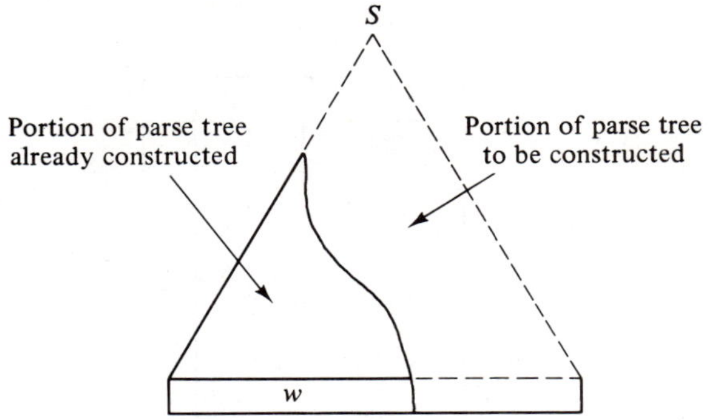

(a)

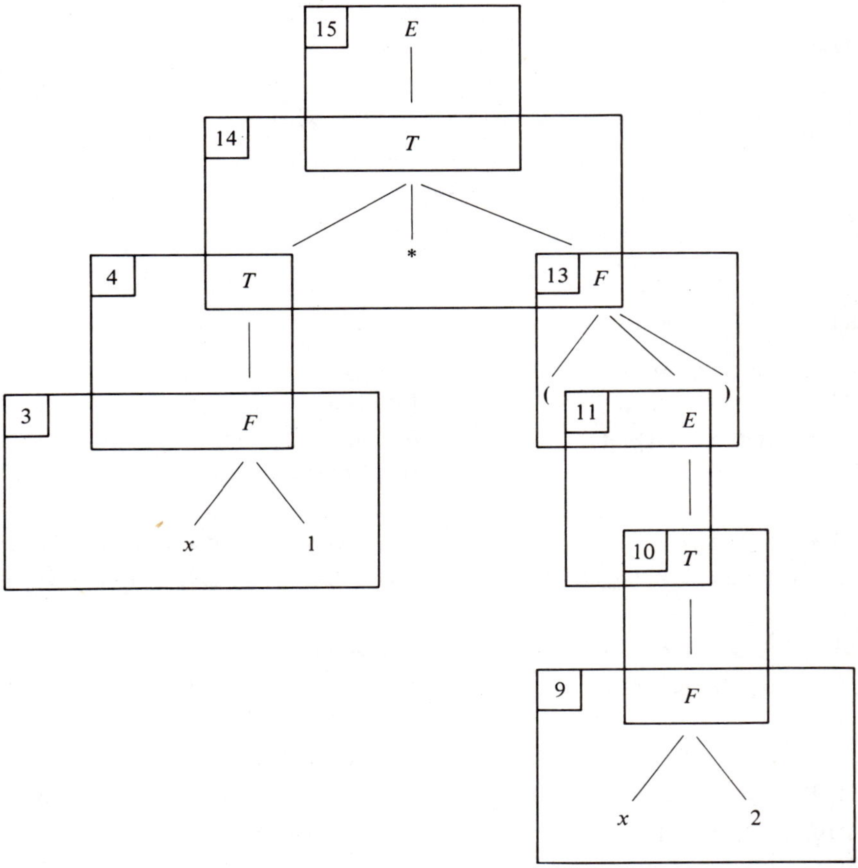

(b)

Figure 3–12

	x	(	)	1	2	+	*	\$
x								
(								
)			X			X	X	X
1			X			X	X	X
2			X			X	X	X
+								
*								
E								
T			X			X		X
F			X			X	X	X

Figure 3–13

Formally, let $M' = (K', \Sigma', \Gamma', \Delta', s, F')$, where

$$K' = \{s, p\} \cup \{p_\sigma : \sigma \in \Sigma'\}$$
$$\Sigma' = \Sigma \cup \{\$\}$$
$$\Gamma' = V \cup \{\$, \#\}$$
$$F' = \{p_\$\}$$

and Δ' is listed below.

$\Delta'1$: $((s, e, e), (p, \#))$

$\Delta'2$: $((p, \sigma, e), (p_\sigma, e))$ for each $\sigma \in \Sigma'$

$\Delta'3$: $((p_\sigma, e, a), (p, \sigma a)$ for each $(a, \sigma) \in (V \cup \{\$\}) \times \Sigma' - P$ (the transitions of type $\Delta'3$ correspond to shifts)

$\Delta'4$: $((p_\sigma, e, T + E), (p_\sigma, E))$ for each $\sigma \in \Sigma'$ such that $(T, \sigma) \in P$

$\Delta'5$: $((p_\sigma, e, Ta), (p_\sigma, Ea))$ for each $\sigma \in \Sigma'$ such that $(T, \sigma) \in P$ and $a \in \Gamma' - \{+\}$

$\Delta'6$: $((p_\sigma, e, F * T), (p_\sigma, T))$ for each $\sigma \in \Sigma'$ such that $(F, \sigma) \in P$

$\Delta'7$: $((p_\sigma, e, Fa), (p_\sigma, Ta))$ for each $\sigma \in \Sigma'$ such that $(F, \sigma) \in P$ and $a \in \Gamma' - \{*\}$

$\Delta'8$: $((p_\sigma, e,)E( ), (p_\sigma, F))$ for each $\sigma \in \Sigma'$ such that $( ), \sigma) \in P$

$\Delta'9$: $((p_\sigma, e, 1x), (p_\sigma, F))$ for each $\sigma \in \Sigma'$ such that $(1, \sigma) \in P$

$\Delta'10$: $((p_\sigma, e, 2x), (p_\sigma, F))$ for each $\sigma \in \Sigma'$ such that $(2, \sigma) \in P$

$\Delta'11$: $((p_\$, e, E\#), (p_\$, e))$

Here M' is deterministic. Furthermore, it can be shown (Problem 3.6.6) that it accepts $L(G)\$$, and in fact, that it is a bottom-up parser for $L(G)\$$.

Once again, bear in mind that the two heuristic rules we have described

—namely, (1) use a precedence relation to decide whether to shift or reduce, and (2) when in doubt, reduce the longest possible string—do not work in all situations. The grammars for which they do work are called **weak precedence grammars**; in practice, many grammars are or can readily be converted into weak precedence grammars.

PROBLEMS

3.1.1. Consider the grammar $G = (V, \Sigma, R, S)$ where

$$V = \{a, b, S, A\}$$
$$\Sigma = \{a, b\}$$
$$R = \{S \to AA,$$
$$A \to AAA,$$
$$A \to a,$$
$$A \to bA,$$
$$A \to Ab\}$$

as given in Example 3.1.4.

(a) Which strings of $L(G)$ can be produced by derivations of four or fewer steps?

(b) Give at least four distinct derivations for the string *babbab*.

(c) For any $m, n, p \geq 0$, describe a derivation in G of the string $b^m a b^n a b^p$.

3.1.2. Consider the grammar (V, Σ, R, S), where V, Σ, and R are defined as follows.

$$V = \{a, b, S, A\}$$
$$\Sigma = \{a, b\}$$
$$R = \{S \to aAa,$$
$$S \to bAb,$$
$$S \to e,$$
$$A \to SS\}$$

(a) Give a derivation of the string *baabbb* in G.

(b) Can you describe $L(G)$ in English?

3.1.3. Construct context-free grammars that generate each of these languages.

(a) $\{wcw^R : w \in \{a, b\}^*\}$

(b) $\{ww^R : w \in \{a, b\}^*\}$

(c) $\{w \in \{a, b\}^* : w = w^R\}$

3.1.4. Consider the alphabet $\Sigma = \{a, b, (,), \cup, *, \varnothing\}$. Construct a context-free grammar that generates all strings in Σ^* that are regular expressions over $\{a, b\}$.

3.1.5. Consider the context-free grammar $G = (V, \Sigma, R, S)$, where

$$\begin{aligned} V &= \{a, b, S, A, B\}, \\ \Sigma &= \{a, b\}, \\ R &= \{S \longrightarrow aB, \\ &\quad S \longrightarrow bA, \\ &\quad A \longrightarrow a, \\ &\quad A \longrightarrow aS, \\ &\quad A \longrightarrow bAA, \\ &\quad B \longrightarrow b, \\ &\quad B \longrightarrow bS, \\ &\quad B \longrightarrow aBB\}. \end{aligned}$$

(a) Show that $ababba \in L(G)$.

(b) Prove that $L(G)$ is the set of all strings in $\{a, b\}^+$ that have equal numbers of occurrences of a and b.

3.1.6. Let G be a context-free grammar and let $k > 0$. We let $L_k(G) \subseteq L(G)$ be the set of all strings that have a derivation in G with k or fewer steps.

(a) What is $L_5(G)$, where G is the grammar of Problem 3.1.5?

(b) Show that, for all context-free grammars G and all $k > 0$, $L_k(G)$ is finite.

3.1.7. Let $G = (V, \Sigma, R, S)$, where $V = \{a, b, S\}$, $\Sigma = \{a, b\}$ and $R = \{S \longrightarrow aSb, S \longrightarrow aSa, S \longrightarrow bSa, S \longrightarrow bSb, S \longrightarrow e\}$. Show that $L(G)$ is regular.

3.1.8. Show that the following languages are context-free by exhibiting context-free grammars generating each.

(a) $\{a^m b^n : m \geq n\}$

(b) $\{a^m b^n c^p d^q : m + n = p + q\}$

(c) $\{w \in \{a, b\}^* : w$ has twice as many b's as a's$\}$

(d) $\{uawb : u, w \in \{a, b\}^*, |u| = |w|\}$

(e) $\{w_1 c w_2 c \ldots c w_k c c w_j^R : k \geq 1, 1 \leq j \leq k, w_i \in \{a, b\}^+$ for $i = 1, \ldots, k\}$

(f) $\{a^m b^n : n \leq m \leq 2n\}$

3.2.1. Consider the regular grammar $G = (V, \Sigma, R, S)$, where

$$V = \{a, b, A, B, S\}$$
$$\Sigma = \{a, b\}$$
$$R = \{S \longrightarrow abA,\ S \longrightarrow B,\ S \longrightarrow baB,\ S \longrightarrow e,$$
$$A \longrightarrow bS,\ B \longrightarrow aS,\ A \longrightarrow b\}.$$

Construct a nondeterministic finite automaton M such that $L(M) = L(G)$. Trace the transitions of M that lead to the acceptance of the string *abba*.

3.2.2. Consider the finite automaton M with the state diagram shown. Find a regular grammar G such that $L(M) = L(G)$. Give a derivation in G for the string *babbbabab*.

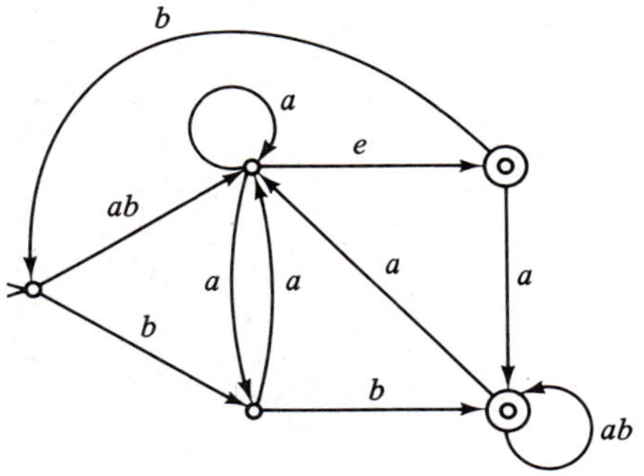

3.2.3. Call a context-free grammar $G = (V, \Sigma, R, S)$ **left-regular** if and only if $R \subseteq (V - \Sigma) \times ((V - \Sigma) \cup \{e\})\Sigma^*$. Show that a language is regular if and only if it is the language generated by some left-regular grammar.

3.2.4. Let G be a regular grammar, and let M be the corresponding automaton, constructed as in the proof of Theorem 3.2.1.

(a) Show that, for any $w \in L(G)$, there is a natural isomorphism between the derivations of w in G and the sequences of transitions leading to acceptance of w by M.

(b) Show that for every regular grammar G there exists another regular grammar G', with $L(G) = L(G')$, such that every string $w \in L(G')$ has a unique derivation in G'.

3.2.5. Suppose that $G = (V, \Sigma, R, S)$ is a context-free grammar such that each rule in R is *either* of the form $A \longrightarrow wB$ *or* of the form $A \longrightarrow Bw$ *or* of the form $A \longrightarrow w$, where in each case $A, B \in V - \Sigma$ and $w \in \Sigma^*$. Is $L(G)$ necessarily regular? Prove it or give a counterexample.

3.2.6. Find a regular grammar generating $\{w \in \{a, b\}^*: w$ does not have the substring $aa\}$.

3.3.1. Consider the pushdown automaton $M = (K, \Sigma, \Gamma, \Delta, s, F)$ where

$$K = \{s, f\},$$
$$F = \{f\},$$
$$\Sigma = \{a, b\},$$
$$\Gamma = \{a\},$$
$$\Delta = \{((s, a, e), (s, a)), ((s, b, e), (s, a)), ((s, a, e), (f, e)),$$
$$((f, a, a), (f, e)), ((f, b, a), (f, e))\}.$$

(a) Trace all possible sequences of transitions of M on input aba.

(b) Show that $aba, aa, abb \notin L(M)$, but $baa, bab, baaaa \in L(M)$.

(c) Describe $L(M)$ in English.

3.3.2. Construct pushdown automata that accept each of the following.

(a) The language generated by $G = (V, \Sigma, R, S)$ where

$$V = \{S, (,), [,]\},$$
$$\Sigma = \{(,), [,]\},$$
$$R = \{S \rightarrow e,$$
$$S \rightarrow SS,$$
$$S \rightarrow [S],$$
$$S \rightarrow (S)\}.$$

(b) The language $\{a^m b^n: m \leq n \leq 2m\}$.

(c) The language $\{w \in \{a, b\}^*: w = w^R\}$.

(d) The language $\{w \in \{a, b\}^*: w$ has twice as many b's as a's$\}$.

3.3.3. Let $M = (K, \Sigma, \Gamma, \Delta, s, F)$ be a pushdown automaton. The **language accepted by** M **by final state** is defined as follows.

$$L_f(M) = \{w \in \Sigma^*: (s, w, e) \vdash_M^* (f, e, \alpha) \text{ for some } f \in F, \alpha \in \Gamma^*\}$$

(a) Show that there is a pushdown automaton M' such that $L(M') = L_f(M)$.

(b) Show that there is a pushdown automaton M'' such that $L_f(M'') = L(M)$.

3.3.4. Let $M = (K, \Sigma, \Gamma, \Delta, s, F)$ be a pushdown automaton. The **language accepted by M by empty store** is defined as follows.

$$L_e(M) = \{w \in \Sigma^*: (s, w, e) \vdash_M^* (q, e, e) \text{ for some } q \in K\}$$

(a) Show that there is a pushdown automaton M' such that $L_e(M') = L(M) \cup \{e\}$.

(b) Show that there is a pushdown automaton M'' such that $L(M'') = L_e(M)$.

(c) Show by a counterexample that it is not necessarily the case that $L(M) = L_e(M) \cap L_f(M)$.

3.4.1. Consider the grammar of Example 3.1.3. Give two derivations of the string $x2 * x2 + x1$, one which is leftmost and one which is not leftmost.

3.4.2. Carry out the construction of Lemma 3.4.3 for the grammar of Example 3.1.5. Trace the operation of the automaton you have constructed on the input string **(()())**.

3.4.3. Carry out the construction of Lemma 3.4.4 for the pushdown automaton of Example 3.3.3, and let G be the resulting grammar. What is the set $\{w \in \{a, b\}^* : \langle q, a, p\rangle \overset{*}{\underset{G}{\Rightarrow}} w\}$? Compare with the proof of Lemma 3.4.4.

3.4.4. Carry out the construction of Lemma 3.4.4 for the pushdown automaton of Example 3.3.4. The resulting grammar will have 25 rules, but many can be eliminated as useless. Show a derivation of the string *aababbba* in this grammar. (You may change the names of the nonterminals for clarity.) Compare with Problem 3.1.5.

3.4.5. Show that if $M = (K, \Sigma, \Gamma, \Delta, s, F)$ is a pushdown automaton, then there is another pushdown automaton $M' = (K', \Sigma, \Gamma, \Delta', s, F)$ such that $L(M') = L(M)$ and for all $((q, u, \beta), (p, \gamma)) \in \Delta'$, $|\beta| + |\gamma| \leq 1$.

3.4.6. Prove Lemma 3.4.2.

3.4.7. A context-free grammar is **linear** if and only if no rule has as its right-hand side a string with more than one nonterminal. A pushdown automaton $(K, \Sigma, \Gamma, \Delta, s, F)$ is said to be **single-turn** if and only if whenever $(s, w, e) \vdash^* (q_1, w_1, \gamma_1) \vdash^* (q_2, w_2, \gamma_2) \vdash^* (q_3, w_3, \gamma_3)$ and $|\gamma_2| < |\gamma_1|$, then $|\gamma_3| \leq |\gamma_2|$. (That is, once the stack starts to decrease in height, it never again increases in height.) Show that a language is generated by a linear context-free grammar if and only if it is accepted by a single-turn pushdown automaton.

3.5.1. Use closure under union to show that the following languages are context-free.

(a) $\{a^m b^n : m \neq n\}$

(b) $\{a, b\}^* - \{a^n b^n : n \geq 0\}$

(c) $\{a^m b^n c^p d^q : n = q, \text{ or } m \leq p, \text{ or } m + n = p + q\}$

(d) $\{a, b\}^* - L$, where L is the language

$$L = \{babaaba^3b \ldots ba^{n-1}ba^nb : n \geq 1\}$$

(e) $\{w \in \{a, b\}^* : w = w^R\}$

3.5.2. Use Theorems 3.5.2 and 3.5.3 to show that the following languages are not context-free.

(a) $\{a^p : p \text{ is a prime}\}$

(b) $\{a^{n^2} : n \geq 0\}$

(c) $\{www : w \in \{a, b\}^*\}$

(d) $\{w \in \{a, b, c\}^* : w$ has equal numbers of a's, b's, and c's$\}$

3.5.3. This problem extends Problem 2.4.9. Recall that a **homomorphism** is a function h from strings to strings such that for any two strings v and w, $h(vw) = h(v)h(w)$. Thus a homomorphism is determined by its values on single symbols: if $w = a_1 \dots a_n$, each a_i a symbol, then $h(w) = h(a_1) \dots h(a_n)$. Note that homomorphisms can "erase": $h(w)$ may be e, even though w is not. Show that if $L \subseteq \Sigma^*$ is a context-free language and $h: \Sigma^* \longrightarrow \Sigma^*$ is a homomorphism then

(a) $h[L]$ is context-free;

(b) $h^{-1}[L]$ (that is, $\{w \in \Sigma^* : h(w) \in L\}$) is context-free. (*Hint:* Start from a pushdown automaton M accepting L. Construct another pushdown automaton, similar to M, except that it reads its input not from the input tape, but from a finite buffer that is occasionally replenished in some way. You supply the rest of the intuition and the formal details.)

3.5.4. Draw parse trees for each of the following.

(a) The grammar of Example 3.1.2 and the string "big Jim ate green cheese."

(b) The grammar of Example 3.1.3 and the strings $(x2 + x1) * x1$ and $x2 + x1 * x1$.

(c) The grammar of Example 3.1.4 and the string *abbabaab*.

3.5.5. Show that the language defined in Problem 3.5.1(d), $L = \{babaab \dots ba^{n-1}ba^nb : n \geq 1\}$, is not context-free

(a) by applying the Pumping Theorem (3.5.3);

(b) by applying the result of Problem 3.5.3. (*Hint:* What is $h[L]$, where $h(a) = aa$ and $h(b) = a$?)

3.5.6. If $L_1 \subseteq \Sigma^*$ and $L_2 \subseteq \Sigma^*$ are languages, the **right quotient of L_1 by L_2** is defined as follows.

$$L_1/L_2 = \{w \in \Sigma^* : \text{there is a } u \in L_2 \text{ such that } wu \in L_1\}$$

(a) Show that if L_1 is context-free and R is regular, then L_1/R is context-free.

(b) Prove that $\{a^m b^n : m \text{ is a prime number and } n \geq m\}$ is not context-free.

3.5.7. Prove the following stronger version of the Pumping Theorem (3.5.3): Let G be a context-free grammar. Then there are numbers K and k such that any string $w \in L(G)$ with $|w| \geq K$ can be rewritten as $w = uvxyz$ with $|vxy| \leq k$ in such a way that either v or y is nonempty and $uv^nxy^nz \in L(G)$ for every $n \geq 0$.

3.5.8. Use Problem 3.5.7 to show that the language $\{ww: w \in \{a, b\}^*\}$ is not context-free.

3.5.9. Give the semilinear set $\Psi[L]$, where L is each of the following context-free languages.

(a) $\{a^m b^n: n \leq m \leq 2n\}$

(b) $\{ww^R: w \in \{a, b\}^*\}$

(c) The language $\{a, b\}^* - L$ of Problem 3.5.1(d).

3.5.10. Let S be a semilinear set. Show that there is a finite automaton M such that $S = \Psi[L(M)]$.

3.5.11. (a) Show that the class of semilinear subsets of $\mathbb{N}^m$ is closed under union, intersection, and complementation.

(b) Is $\mathbb{N}^m$ semilinear?

(c) Show that if $S \subseteq \mathbb{N}^m$ and $T \subseteq \mathbb{N}^n$ are semilinear, then so is $S \times T$.

3.5.12. Give an example of a non-context-free language L such that $\Psi[L]$ is semilinear.

3.5.13. What is wrong with the following argument that $\{a, b\}^* - L$ is *not* context-free, where $L = \{babaaba^3 \ldots ba^{n-1}ba^nb: n \geq 1\}$ (recall Problem 3.5.1(d)):

$$\Psi[L] = \left\{\left(\frac{n(n-1)}{2}, n\right): n \geq 2\right\}$$

is not a semilinear set. Therefore $\Psi[\{a, b\}^* - L] = \mathbb{N}^2 - \Psi[L]$ is also not semilinear, by Problem 3.5.11. Thus $\{a, b\}^* - L$ is not context-free.

3.5.14. Let $G = (V, \Sigma, R, S)$ be a context-free grammar such that, for each $A \to u \in R$, $u \in \Sigma$ or $|u| \geq 2$. Show that for any parse tree of G with height h and yield y, $|y| \geq h$.

3.5.15. Let S be a finite set and $R \subseteq S \times S$ be a binary relation on S. Define the binary relations $R_0, R_1, \ldots, R_s$, where $s = |S|$, inductively as follows.

1. $R_0 = \{(x, x): x \in S\}$
2. $R_{j+1} = \{(x, y)$: there is a $z \in S$ such that $(x, z) \in R_j$ and $(z, y) \in R\}$.

(a) Show that $R_0 \cup R_1 \cup \cdots \cup R_s = R^*$, the reflexive, transitive closure of R.

(b) Based on Part (a), give an algorithm that computes the reflexive, transitive closure of any binary relation on a finite set.

3.5.16. Let $G = (V, \Sigma, R, S)$ be a context-free grammar. Consider the relation $T \subseteq (V - \Sigma) \times (V - \Sigma)$ defined by $(A, B) \in T$ if and only if there exist $u, v \in V^*$ such that $A \underset{G}{\Rightarrow} uBv$. Let T^* be the reflexive, transitive closure of T.

(a) Show that $(A, B) \in T^*$ if and only if there exist $u, v \in V^*$ such that $A \overset{*}{\underset{G}{\Rightarrow}} uBv$.

(b) Show that $L(G) = L(G')$, where G' is the grammar derived from G by omitting all nonterminals A such that $(S, A) \notin T^*$, as well as the rules involving these nonterminals.

(c) Find G' if G is the grammar $G = (V, \Sigma, R, S)$, with $V = \{S, A, B, C, D, a, b\}$, $R = \{S \longrightarrow aA,\ S \longrightarrow Bb,\ C \longrightarrow a,\ B \longrightarrow b,\ A \longrightarrow aBAD,\ A \longrightarrow SBBb\}$.

3.5.17. Let $G = (V, \Sigma, R, S)$ be a context-free grammar. Call a nonterminal $A \in V - \Sigma$ **productive** if $A \overset{*}{\underset{G}{\Rightarrow}} w$ for some $w \in \Sigma^*$. Let $P \subseteq V - \Sigma$ be the set of all productive nonterminals.

(a) Define the sets $P_0, P_1, \ldots, P_n \subseteq V - \Sigma$, where $n = |V - \Sigma|$, inductively as follows.

1. $P_0 = \varnothing$.
2. $P_{j+1} = \{A \in V - \Sigma : A \in P_j \text{ or } A \longrightarrow w \in R \text{ for some } w \in (\Sigma \cup P_j)^*\}$.

Show that $P = P_n$.

(b) Find the set P for the grammar G' of Problem 3.5.16(c).

(c) Use Part (a) to obtain an algorithm for determining whether $L(G) = \varnothing$.

(d) How do you think that your algorithm compares in efficiency with the algorithm given in the proof of Theorem 3.5.8(b)?

3.5.18. Let $G = (V, \Sigma, R, S)$ be a context-free grammar such that $e \notin L(G)$.

(a) Show that there is a grammar $G' = (V', \Sigma, R', S)$ such that $L(G) = L(G')$, and all rules in R' are either of the form $A \longrightarrow a$, $A \in V' - \Sigma$, $a \in \Sigma$, or of the form $A \longrightarrow u$, $A \in V' - \Sigma$, $u \in (V' - \Sigma)^+$.

(b) Based on Part (a), show that there is a grammar $G'' = (V'', \Sigma, R'', S)$ such that $L(G'') = L(G)$ and all rules in R'' are either of the form $A \longrightarrow a$ with $A \in V'' - \Sigma$ and $a \in \Sigma$, or of the form $A \longrightarrow BC$ with $A, B, C \in V'' - \Sigma$. A grammar satisfying this restriction is said to be in **Chomsky normal form.**

(c) Transform the grammar $G = (V, \Sigma, R, S)$ with $V = \{a, b, S, A, B\}$, $\Sigma = \{a, b\}$, and $R = \{S \longrightarrow aA, S \longrightarrow bB, A \longrightarrow Baa, A \longrightarrow ba, B \longrightarrow bAA, B \longrightarrow ab\}$ into an equivalent grammar in Chomsky normal form.

3.5.19. Consider a context-free grammar $G = (V, \Sigma, R, S)$ in Chomsky normal form (see Problem 3.5.18(b)), and a string $w \in \Sigma^*$ with $|w| = n$. Consider the sets of nonterminals $N_{ij}(w)$ with $i = 1, \ldots, n$ and $j = 0, 1, \ldots, n - i$, defined as follows: $N_{ij}(w) = \{A \in V - \Sigma: A \overset{*}{\underset{G}{\Rightarrow}} u$ with $|u| = j + 1$, $w = vux$ and $|v| = i - 1\}$.

(a) What is $N_{i0}(w)$ for $i = 1, \ldots, n$?

(b) Show that $N_{i,j+1}(w) = \{A: A \underset{G}{\longrightarrow} BC$ for some $k \leq j$, $B \in N_{i,k}(w)$, $C \in N_{i+k+1,j-k}(w)\}$ for $i = 1, \ldots, n$ and $j = 0, 1, \ldots, n - i - 1$.

(c) Show that $w \in L(G)$ if and only if $S \in N_{1,n-1}(w)$.

(d) Based on Problem 3.5.18 and Parts (a)–(c), devise an algorithm for testing whether $w \in L(G)$, given any context-free grammar $G = (V, \Sigma, R, S)$ and $w \in \Sigma^*$.

(e) How does your algorithm compare in terms of efficiency to the algorithm given in the proof of Theorem 3.5.8(a)?

3.5.20. Let $G = (V, \Sigma, R, S)$ be a context-free grammar. A nonterminal A of G is called **self-embedding** if and only if $A \overset{+}{\underset{G}{\Rightarrow}} uAv$ for some $u, v \in V^*$.

(a) Give an algorithm to test whether a specific nonterminal of a given context-free grammar is self-embedding.

(b) Show that if G has no self-embedding nonterminal, then $L(G)$ is a regular language.

3.5.21. Let G be a context-free grammar and $w \in L(G)$. Let $D(w)$ be the set of leftmost derivations of w in G, and let $T(w)$ be the set of all parse trees in G that have S as a root and w as yield. Show that there is a natural isomorphism between $D(w)$ and $T(w)$.

3.5.22. A context-free grammar G is called **ambiguous** if there exists a string $w \in L(G)$ with two distinct leftmost derivations in G.

(a) Show that the context-free grammar $G = (V, \Sigma, R, S)$, where $V = \{S, A, a, b\}$, $\Sigma = \{a, b\}$, and $R = \{S \longrightarrow AA, A \longrightarrow AAA, A \longrightarrow bA, A \longrightarrow Ab, A \longrightarrow a\}$ of Example 3.1.4 is ambiguous, because aba has two different leftmost derivations in G.

(b) A language L is **inherently ambiguous** if all context-free grammars G such that $L = L(G)$ are ambiguous. Show that $L(G)$, where G is the context-free grammar in Part (a), is *not* inherently ambiguous.

(c) Show that if L is a regular language, then L is not inherently ambiguous.

3.5.23. Find an algorithm which, given two finite subsets B and P of $\mathbb{N}^n$ and an n-tuple of integers $x \in \mathbb{N}^n$, determines whether $x \in L(B, P)$.

3.5.24. A context-free grammar $G = (V, \Sigma, R, S)$ is said to be in **Greibach normal form** if every rule is of the form $S \longrightarrow e$, or $A \longrightarrow w$ for some $w \in \Sigma(V - \Sigma)^*$.

(a) Show that for every context-free grammar G, there is a context-free grammar G' in Greibach normal form such that $L(G) = L(G')$.

(b) Show that if M is constructed as in the proof of Lemma 3.4.3 from a grammar in Greibach normal form, then the number of steps in any computation of M on an input w can be bounded as a function of the length of w.

3.5.25. Deterministic finite-state transducers were introduced in Problem 2.1.4. Show that if L is context-free and f is computed by a deterministic finite-state transducer, then

(a) $f[L]$ is context-free;

(b) $f^{-1}[L]$ is context-free.

3.5.26. Develop a version of the Pumping Theorem for context-free languages, like that of Problem 2.6.10 for regular languages, in which the length of the "pumped part" is as *long* as possible.

3.5.27. Let M_1 and M_2 be pushdown automata. Show how to construct pushdown automata accepting $L(M_1) \cup L(M_2)$, $L(M_1)L(M_2)$, and $L(M_1)^*$, thus providing another proof of Theorem 3.5.1.

3.5.28. Which of the following languages are context-free? Explain briefly in each case.

(a) $\{a^m b^n c^p : m = n \text{ or } n = p \text{ or } m = p\}$

(b) $\{a^m b^n c^p : m \neq n \text{ or } n \neq p \text{ or } m \neq p\}$

(c) $\{a^m b^n c^p : m = n \text{ and } n = p \text{ and } m = p\}$

(d) $\{w \in \{a, b, c\}^* : w \text{ does not contain equal numbers of occurrences of } a, b, \text{ and } c\}$

(e) $\{w \in \{a, b\}^* : w = w_1 \ldots w_m$ for some $m \geq 2$ and some $w_1, \ldots, w_m$ such that $|w_1| = \cdots = |w_m| \geq 2\}$.

3.5.29. Suppose that L is context-free and R is regular. Is $L - R$ necessarily context-free? What about $R - L$? Justify your answers.

3.5.30. In the proof of Theorem 3.5.2, why did we assume that M_2 was deterministic?

3.6.1. Show that the following languages are deterministic context-free.

(a) $\{a^m b^n : m \neq n\}$

(b) $\{wcw^R : w \in \{a, b\}^*\}$

(c) $\{ca^m b^m : m \geq 0\} \cup \{da^m b^{2m} : m \geq 0\}$

(d) $\{a^m cb^m : m \geq 0\} \cup \{a^m db^{2m} : m \geq 0\}$

(e) $\{w_1 c w_1^R w_2 c w_2^R \cdots w_k c w_k^R : k \geq 1,\ w_i \in \{a, b\}^* \text{ for } i = 1, \ldots, k\}$

3.6.2. Show that the class of deterministic context-free languages is *not* closed under homomorphism. (Compare with Problem 3.5.3.)

3.6.3. Show that if L is a deterministic context-free language, then L is not inherently ambiguous. (Compare with Problem 3.5.22.)

3.6.4. Show that the pushdown automaton M' constructed in Section 3.6.1 accepts the language L, given that M accepts $L\$$.

3.6.5. Consider the context-free grammar $G = (V, \Sigma, R, S)$ where $V = \{(,), ,, a, S, A\}$, $\Sigma = \{(,), ,, a\}$, and R contains these rules.

$$S \rightarrow ()$$
$$S \rightarrow a$$
$$S \rightarrow (A)$$
$$A \rightarrow S$$
$$A \rightarrow A,S$$

(For the reader familiar with the programming language LISP, $L(G)$ contains all atoms and lists, where the symbol a stands for any non-null atom.)

(a) Apply Heuristic Rules 1 and 2 to G. Let G' be the resulting grammar. Argue that G' is $LL(1)$. Construct a deterministic pushdown automaton M accepting $L(G)\$$. Study the computation of M on the string **((())**,a**)**.

(b) Repeat Part (a) for the grammar resulting from G if one replaces the first rule by $A \rightarrow e$.

(c) Repeat Part (a) for the grammar resulting from G if one replaces the last rule by $A \rightarrow S,A$.

3.6.6. Show that the pushdown automaton M' constructed at the end of Section 3.6 is a bottom-up parser for $L(G)\$$.

3.6.7. Complete the proof of Lemma 3.6.1.

3.6.8. Consider again the grammar G of Problem 3.6.5.

(a) Argue that G is a weak precedence grammar, with the precedence relation shown below. Construct a deterministic pushdown automaton that accepts $L(G)\$$.

	a	)	(	,	\$
a		X		X	X
(					
)		X		X	X
,					
A					
S		X		X	

(b) Let $G' = (V, \Sigma, R', S)$ be the grammar with rules

$$S \longrightarrow (A)$$
$$S \longrightarrow a$$
$$A \longrightarrow S,A$$
$$A \longrightarrow e$$

Is G' weak precedence? If so, give an appropriate precedence relation.

3.6.9. Acceptance by final state is defined in Problem 3.3.3. Show that L is deterministic context-free if and only if L is accepted by final state by some deterministic pushdown automaton.

REFERENCES

Context-free grammars are a creation of Chomsky; see

N. Chomsky, "Three Models for the Description of Languages," *IRE Transactions on Information Theory*, 2, no. 3 (1956), 113–124

and also

N. Chomsky, "On Certain Formal Properties of Grammars," *Information and Control*, 2, no. 2 (1959), 137–167. (This paper introduces Chomsky normal form (Problem 3.5.18).)

A closely related notation for the syntax of programming languages, called BNF (for Backus Normal Form or Backus-Naur Form), was also invented in the late 1950's; see

P. Naur, ed., "Revised Report on the Algorithmic Language Algol 60," *Communications of the Association for Computing Machinery*, 6 (1963), 1–17.

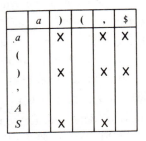

This is reprinted in

S. ROSEN, ed., *Programming Systems and Languages*. New York: McGraw-Hill, 1967, 79–118.

Theorem 3.2.1 on the equivalence of regular grammars and finite automata is from

N. CHOMSKY and G. A. MILLER, "Finite-state Languages," *Information and Control*, 1 (1958), 91–112.

The pushdown automaton was introduced in

A. G. OETTINGER, "Automatic Syntactic Analysis and the Pushdown Store," *Proceedings of Symposia on Applied Mathematics* (Vol. 12). Providence, R.I.: American Mathematical Society, 1961.

Theorem 3.4.1 on the equivalence of context-free languages and pushdown automata was proved independently by Schutzenberger, Chomsky, and Evey.

M. P. SCHUTZENBERGER, "On Context-free Languages and Pushdown Automata," *Information and Control*, 6, no. 3 (1963), 246–264.

N. CHOMSKY, "Context-free Grammar and Pushdown Storage," *Quarterly Progress Report*, 65, (1962) 187–194, M.I.T. Research Laboratory in Electronics, Cambridge, Mass.

J. EVEY, "Application of Pushdown Store Machines," *Proceedings of the 1963 Fall Joint Computer Conference* (215–217). Montreal: AFIPS Press, 1963.

The closure properties presented in subsection 3.5.1, along with many others, can be found in

V. BAR-HILLEL, M. PERLES, and E. SHAMIR, "On Formal Properties of Simple Phrase Structure Grammars," *Zeitschrift für Phonetik, Sprachwissenschaft und Kommunikationsforschung*, 14 (1961), 143–172.

In the same paper one finds a stronger version of Theorem 3.5.3 (the Pumping Theorem for context-free grammars; see also Problem 3.5.7). An even stronger version of that theorem appears in

W. G. OGDEN, "A Helpful Result for Proving Inherent Ambiguity," *Mathematical Systems Theory*, 2 (1968), 191–194.

Parikh's Theorem (Theorem 3.5.6) was first proved in

R. J. PARIKH, "On Context-free Languages," *Journal of the Association for Computing Machinery*, 4 (1966), 570–581.

Efficient algorithms for deciding whether a string belongs to the language generated by a given context-free grammar (compare with Theorem 3.5.8) can be found in the following papers.

J. EARLEY, "An Efficient Context-free Parsing Algorithm," *Communications of the Association for Computing Machinery*, 13 (1970), 94–102.

T. Kasami, "An Efficient Recognition and Syntax Algorithm for Context-free Languages," *Report AFCRL–65–758* (1965), Air Force Cambridge Research Laboratory, Cambridge, Mass.

D. H. Younger, "Recognition and Parsing of Context-free Languages in Time n^3," *Information and Control*, 10, no. 2 (1967), 189–208.

All of these algorithms require about n^3 steps for deciding whether a string of n symbols is generated by a fixed context-free grammar. The first algorithm runs in n^2 steps when the grammar is not ambiguous (Problem 3.5.22), whereas the latter two papers present essentially the algorithm described in Problem 3.5.19. The parsing techniques of subsections 3.6.2 and 3.6.3 suggest even more efficient algorithms for some other restricted classes of context-free grammars. The most efficient general context-free recognition algorithm known is due to Valiant. It runs in time proportional to $n^{2.52\cdots}$, the best time bound known at the time of writing for multiplying two $n \times n$ matrices.

L. G. Valiant, "General Context-free Recognition in Less Than Cubic Time," *Journal of Computer and Systems Sciences*, 10, no. 2 (1975), 308–315.

A complete treatment of parsing techniques can be found in the book

A. V. Aho and J. D. Ullman, *The Theory of Parsing, Translation, and Compiling, Volume I: Parsing*. Englewood Cliffs, N.J.: Prentice-Hall, 1972.

LL(1) parsers (Section 3.6.2) were introduced in

P. M. Lewis II and R. E. Stearns, "Syntax-directed Transduction," *Journal of the Association for Computing Machinery*, 15, no. 3 (1968), 465–488

and also in

D. E. Knuth, "Top-down Syntax Analysis," *Acta Informatica*, 1, no. 2 (1971), 79–110.

Weak precedence parsers were proposed in

J. D. Ichbiah and S. P. Morse, "A Technique for Generating almost Optimal Floyd-Evans Productions for Precedence Grammars," *Communications of the Association for Computing Machinery*, 13, no. 8 (1970), 501–508.

The use of parsers in compiling is explained in the books

P. M. Lewis II, D. J. Rosenkrantz, and R. E. Stearns, *Compiler Design Theory*. Reading, Mass.: Addison-Wesley, 1976

and

A. V. Aho and J. D. Ullman, *Principles of Compiler Design*. Reading, Mass.: Addison-Wesley, 1977.

Problem 3.5.3 (on homomorphisms) is from

S. Ginsburg and G. F. Rose, "Operations which Preserve Definability in Languages," *Journal of the Association for Computing Machinery*, 10, no. 2 (1963), 175–194.

The transitive closure algorithm of Problem 3.5.15 is from

S. WARSHALL, "A Theorem on Boolean Matrices," *Journal of the Association for Computing Machinery*, 9, no. 1 (1962), 11–12.

Ambiguity and inherent ambiguity (Problem 3.5.22) are studied in

N. CHOMSKY and M. P. SCHUTZENBERGER, "The Algebraic Theory of Context Free Languages," in *Computer Programming and Formal Systems* (pp. 118–161), ed. P. Braffort, D. Hirschberg. Amsterdam: North Holland, 1963

and

S. GINSBURG and J. S. ULLIAN, "Preservation of Unambiguity and Inherent Ambiguity in Context-free Languages," *Journal of the Association for Computing Machinery*, 13, no. 1 (1966), 62–88,

respectively.

Greibach normal form (Problem 3.5.24) is due to Greibach.

S. GREIBACH, "A New Normal Form Theorem for Context-free Phrase Structure Grammars," *Journal of the Association for Computing Machinery*, 12, no. 1 (1965), 42–52.

Two advanced books on context-free languages are

S. GINSBURG, *The Mathematical Theory of Context-free Languages*. New York: McGraw-Hill, 1966

and

M. A. HARRISON, *Introduction to Formal Language Theory*. Reading, Mass.: Addison-Wesley, 1978.

CHAPTER 4

TURING MACHINES

4.1 THE DEFINITION OF A TURING MACHINE

We have seen in the last two chapters that neither finite automata nor pushdown automata can be regarded as truly general models for computers, since they are not capable of recognizing even such simple languages as $\{a^nb^nc^n: n \geq 0\}$. In this chapter we take up the study of devices that can recognize this and many more complicated languages. These devices will also be used in ways other than as language recognizers: as computers of functions from strings to strings, for example, and as machines for systematically enumerating the strings in a language.

Although these devices, called **Turing machines** after their inventor Alan Turing (1912–1954), are more general than the automata previously studied, their basic appearance is similar to those automata. A Turing machine consists of a finite control, a tape, and a head that can be used for reading or writing on that tape. The formal definitions of Turing machines and their operation are in the same mathematical style as those used for finite and pushdown automata. So in order to gain the additional computational power and generality of function that Turing machines possess, we shall not move to an entirely new sort of model for a computer.

Nevertheless, Turing machines are not simply one more class of automata, to be replaced later on by a yet more powerful type. We shall see in this chapter that, as primitive as Turing machines seem to be, attempts to strengthen them seem not to have any effect. For example, the addition of extra tapes or extra heads on those tapes results in automata that turn out to be no stronger in terms of computing power than basic Turing machines. We show results of this kind by simulation methods: We can convert any "augmented" Turing machine into a standard machine which functions in an analogous way. Thus any computation that can be carried out on the fancier type of machine can actually be carried out on a Turing machine of the standard variety.

So the Turing machines seem to form a stable and maximal class of automata, in terms of the computations they can perform. In the next chapter we take this idea one step further: we show that Turing machines are equivalent in power to entirely different ways of carrying out computations, not based on the idea of an automaton with states and tapes. Indeed, we shall argue that *any* way of formalizing the idea of a "computational procedure" or an "algorithm" is equivalent to the idea of a Turing machine.

But this is getting ahead of our story. The important points to remember by way of introduction are that Turing machines are designed to satisfy simultaneously these three criteria.

(a) They should be automata; that is, their construction and function should be in the same general spirit as the devices previously studied.

(b) They should be as simple as possible to describe, define formally, and reason about.

(c) They should be as general as possible in terms of the computations they can carry out.

Now let us look more closely at these machines. In essence, a Turing machine consists of a finite-state control unit and a tape (see Figure 4–1).

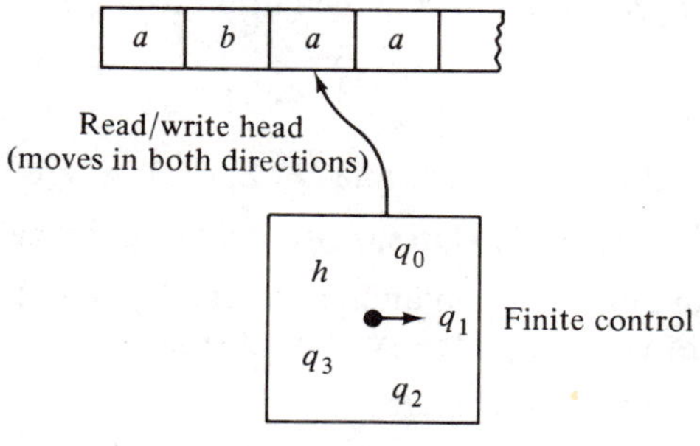

Figure 4–1

Communication between the two is provided by a single head, which reads symbols from the tape and is also used to change the symbols on the tape. The control unit operates in discrete steps; at each step it performs two functions in a way dependent on its current state and the tape symbol currently scanned by the read/write head.

1. Put the control unit in a new state.
2. *Either:*
   (a) Write a symbol in the tape square currently scanned, replacing the one already there; *or*
   (b) Move the read/write head one tape square to the left or right.

The tape has a left end, but it extends indefinitely to the right. Since the machine can move its head only one square at a time, after any finite computation only finitely many tape squares will have been visited. (If the machine attempts to move its head to the left off the end of the tape, it ceases to operate.)

A Turing machine is supplied with input by inscribing that input string on tape squares at the left end of the tape. The rest of the tape initially contains blank symbols. The machine is free to alter its input in any way it sees fit, as well as to write on the unlimited blank portion of the tape to the right.

Because a Turing machine can write on its tape, it can leave an answer on the tape at the end of a computation. Therefore we do not need to provide special "final" states, as we have done for finite and pushdown automata. There is a special **halt state** that is used to signal the end of computation, but no favorable or unfavorable connotation should be inferred. Since this halt state will be the same for all Turing machines, we denote it by h; this symbol will not be used hereafter for any other purpose. Similarly, the blank symbol will be fixed as #. Also, we shall use the distinct symbols L and R to denote movement of the head to the left or right; we assume that these two symbols are not members of any alphabet we consider.

We can now present the formal definition of a Turing machine.

Definition 4.1.1

A **Turing machine** is a quadruple (K, Σ, δ, s), where

K is a finite set of **states,** *not* containing the halt state h;

Σ is an alphabet, containing the blank symbol #, but not containing the symbols L and R;

$s \in K$ is the **initial state**;

δ is a function from $K \times \Sigma$ to $(K \cup \{h\}) \times (\Sigma \cup \{L, R\})$.

If $q \in K$, $a \in \Sigma$, and $\delta(q, a) = (p, b)$, then M, when in state q and scanning symbol a, will enter state p, and (1) if b is a symbol in Σ, rewrite the a as b, or (2) if b is L or R, move its head in direction b. Since δ is a function, the operation of M is deterministic and will stop only when M enters the halt state or attempts to move left off the end of the tape.

Example 4.1.1

Consider the Turing machine $M = (K, \Sigma, \delta, s)$, where

$$K = \{q_0, q_1\}$$
$$\Sigma = \{a, \#\}$$
$$s = q_0$$

and δ is given by the following table.

q	σ	$\delta(q, \sigma)$
q_0	a	$(q_1, \#)$
q_0	$\#$	$(h, \#)$
q_1	a	(q_0, a)
q_1	$\#$	(q_0, R)

When M is started in its initial state q_0, it scans its head to the right, changing all a's to $\#$'s as it goes, until it finds a tape square already containing $\#$; then it halts. (Changing a nonblank symbol to the blank symbol will be called **erasing** the nonblank symbol.) To be specific, suppose that M is started with its head scanning the first of four a's, the last of which is followed by a $\#$. Then M will go back and forth between states q_0 and q_1 four times, alternately changing an a to a $\#$ and moving the head right; the first and last lines of the table for δ are the relevant ones during this sequence of moves. At this point, M will find itself in state q_0 scanning $\#$ and, according to the second line of the table, will halt. Note that the third line of the table, that is, the value of $\delta(q_1, a)$, is irrelevant, since M can never be in state q_1 scanning an a if it is started in state q_0. Nevertheless, some value must be associated with $\delta(q_1, a)$, since δ is required to be a function.

Example 4.1.2

Consider the Turing machine $M = (K, \Sigma, \delta, s)$, where

$$K = \{q_0\}$$
$$\Sigma = \{a, \#\}$$
$$s = q_0$$

and δ is given by the following table.

q	σ	$\delta(q, \sigma)$
q_0	a	(q_0, L)
q_0	$\#$	$(h, \#)$

This machine scans to the left until it finds a # and then halts. If every tape square from the head position back to the leftmost tape square contains an *a*, then *M* will run its tape head off the left end of the tape and cease operating without halting. (In this case we shall say that *M* **hangs**.)

We now formalize the operation of a Turing machine.

To specify the status of a Turing machine computation, we need to specify the state, the contents of the tape, and the position of the head. Since all but a finite initial portion of the tape will be blank, the contents of the tape can be specified by a string. We choose to break that string into three pieces: the part, possibly empty, to the left of the scanned square; the single symbol in the scanned square; and the part, possibly empty, to the right of the scanned square. Moreover, so that no two of these (string, symbol, string) triples will correspond to the same combination of head position and tape contents, we insist that the last string not end with a blank (all tape squares to the right of the last one explicitly represented are assumed to contain blanks anyway). These considerations lead us to the following definitions.

Definition 4.1.2

A **configuration** of a Turing machine $M = (K, \Sigma, \delta, s)$ is a member of

$$(K \cup \{h\}) \times \Sigma^* \times \Sigma \times (\Sigma^*(\Sigma - \{\#\}) \cup \{e\}).$$

Thus (q, e, a, aba), $(h, \#\#, \#, \#a)$, and $(q, \#a\#, \#, e)$ are configurations (see Figure 4–2), but $(q, baa, a, bc\#)$ is not. A configuration whose state component is h will be called a **halted configuration**.

Sometimes we wish to depict the appearance of the tape and the position of the head without indicating the state of the finite control. In this case we write $w\underline{a}u$ instead of the configuration (q, w, a, u): The underlined symbol indicates the head position. For the three configurations illustrated in Figure 4–2, the tapes and head positions would be represented as $\underline{a}aba$, $\#\#\underline{\#}\#a$, and $\#a\#\underline{\#}$. Also, we can write configurations by including the state together with the notation for the tape and head position. That is, we can write (q, w, a, u) as $(q, w\underline{a}u)$. Using this convention, we would write the three configurations shown in Figure 4–2 as $(q, \underline{a}aba)$, $(h, \#\#\underline{\#}\#a)$, and $(q, \#a\#\underline{\#})$. We call this the **abbreviated** notation for configurations.

For Turing machine configurations, **yields in one step** is defined as follows.

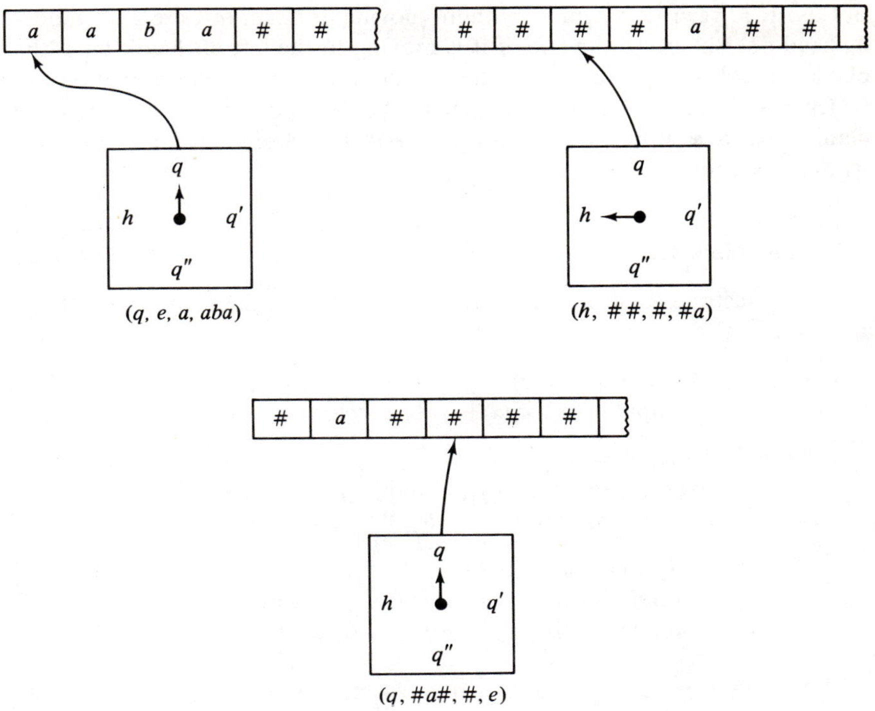

Figure 4–2

Definition 4.1.3

Let $M = (K, \Sigma, \delta, s)$ be a Turing machine and let (q_1, w_1, a_1, u_1) and (q_2, w_2, a_2, u_2) be configurations of M. Then

$$(q_1, w_1, a_1, u_1) \vdash_M (q_2, w_2, a_2, u_2)$$

if and only if, for some $b \in \Sigma \cup \{L, R\}$, $\delta(q_1, a_1) = (q_2, b)$ and either

1. $b \in \Sigma$, $w_1 = w_2$, $u_1 = u_2$, and $a_2 = b$;

or

2. $b = L$, $w_1 = w_2 a_2$, and either
   (a) $u_2 = a_1 u_1$, if $a_1 \neq \#$ or $u_1 \neq e$, or
   (b) $u_2 = e$, if $a_1 = \#$ and $u_1 = e$;

or

3. $b = R$, $w_2 = w_1 a_1$, and either
   (a) $u_1 = a_2 u_2$, or
   (b) $u_1 = u_2 = e$ and $a_2 = \#$.

In Case 1, M rewrites a symbol without moving its head. In Case 2, M moves its head one square to the left; if it is moving to the left off blank tape, the blank symbol on the square just scanned disappears from the configuration. In Case 3, M moves its head one square to the right; if it is moving onto blank tape, a new blank symbol appears in the configuration as the new scanned symbol.

Example 4.1.3

To illustrate these cases, let $w, u \in \Sigma^*$, where u does not end with #, and let $a, b \in \Sigma$.

Case 1. $\delta(q_1, a) = (q_2, b)$
Example: $(q_1, w\underline{a}u) \vdash_M (q_2, w\underline{b}u)$

Case 2. $\delta(q_1, a) = (q_2, L)$
Example for (a): $(q_1, wb\underline{a}u) \vdash_M (q_2, w\underline{b}au)$
Example for (b): $(q_1, wb\underline{\#}) \vdash_M (q_2, w\underline{b})$

Case 3. $\delta(q_1, a) = (q_2, R)$
Example for (a): $(q_1, w\underline{a}bu) \vdash_M (q_2, wa\underline{b}u)$
Example for (b): $(q_1, w\underline{a}) \vdash_M (q_2, wa\underline{\#})$

Note that if $b = L$ and $w_1 = e$, then (q_1, w_1, a_1, u_1) yields no configuration, since there is no $w_2 \in \Sigma^*$ and $a_2 \in \Sigma$ such that $w_1 = w_2a_2$. Such a configuration will be called a **hanging configuration.** On the other hand, every configuration that is not a halted or a hanging configuration yields exactly one configuration in one step.

Definition 4.1.4

For any Turing machine M, $\vdash_M^*$ is the reflexive, transitive closure of $\vdash_M$; we say that configuration C_1 **yields** configuration C_2 if $C_1 \vdash_M^* C_2$. A **computation** by M is a sequence of configurations $C_0, C_1, \ldots, C_n$ for some $n \geq 0$ such that

$$C_0 \vdash_M C_1 \vdash_M C_2 \vdash_M \cdots \vdash_M C_n.$$

We say that the computation is of **length** n or has n **steps.**

Example 4.1.4

Consider the Turing machine M described in Example 4.1.1. If M is started in configuration $(q_0, \underline{a}aaa)$, its computation would be represented formally as follows.

$$
\begin{aligned}
(q_0, \underline{a}aaa) &\vdash_M (q_1, \underline{\#}aaa)\\
&\vdash_M (q_0, \#\underline{a}aa)\\
&\vdash_M (q_1, \#\underline{\#}aa)\\
&\vdash_M (q_0, \#\#\underline{a}a)\\
&\vdash_M (q_1, \#\#\underline{\#}a)\\
&\vdash_M (q_0, \#\#\#\underline{a})\\
&\vdash_M (q_1, \#\#\#\underline{\#})\\
&\vdash_M (q_0, \#\#\#\#\underline{\#})\\
&\vdash_M (h, \#\#\#\#\underline{\#})
\end{aligned}
$$

This computation has nine steps.

Example 4.1.5

Consider again the Turing machine of Example 4.1.2. From the configuration $(q_0, aa\underline{a})$ we have

$$
\begin{aligned}
(q_0, aa\underline{a}) &\vdash_M (q_0, a\underline{a}a)\\
&\vdash_M (q_0, \underline{a}aa).
\end{aligned}
$$

This last configuration (which would be written in full as (q_0, e, a, aa)) is a hanging configuration.

4.2 COMPUTING WITH TURING MACHINES

Turing machines, as we have said, will be used not just as language recognizers but in a number of other ways as well. So far, however, we have merely presented the bare machines without any indication of how they are to be used systematically. It is as though a computer had been delivered with only a wiring diagram but with no advice about the usual procedures for getting information into and out of it. It is time, therefore, to fix some conventions for the use of Turing machines.

First, we adopt the following policy for presenting input to Turing machines: The input string is surrounded by a blank on each side and is written on the leftmost squares of the tape; the head is positioned at the tape square containing the blank that marks the right end of the input; and the machine starts operating in its initial state. Formally, if $M = (K, \Sigma, \delta, s)$ is a Turing machine and $w \in \Sigma^*$, then M is said to **halt on input** w if and only if $(s, \#w\underline{\#})$ yields some halted configuration. Similarly, M is said to **hang on input** w if $(s, \#w\underline{\#})$ yields some hanging configuration.

We start by viewing Turing machines as computers of functions from strings to strings.

Definition 4.2.1

Let Σ_0 and Σ_1 be alphabets *not* containing the blank symbol #. Let f be a function from Σ_0^* to Σ_1^*. A Turing machine $M = (K, \Sigma, \delta, s)$ is said to **compute** f if $\Sigma_0, \Sigma_1 \subseteq \Sigma$ and for any $w \in \Sigma_0^*$, if $f(w) = u$ then

$$(s, \#w\underline{\#}) \vdash_M^* (h, \#u\underline{\#}).$$

If some such Turing machine M exists, then f is said to be a **Turing-computable function**.

Thus when M is presented with input w in the way we have standardized above, M is required to halt eventually with $f(w)$ on the tape, preceded by a blank, and with the input head just to the right of the computed value. The rest of the tape must be blank. Since this is the same as the form in which we required the input to be presented, this convention will facilitate the composition of machines to form more powerful machines. Note, however, that no assurances are given about the behavior of M if it is started in any but the specified way, for example, if the input string contains symbols in $\Sigma - \Sigma_0$.

Note also that a Turing machine that computes a function may not hang on any input in the domain of that function. This is obvious, since a Turing machine that hangs on an input does not halt on that input. It is also critical, however, since it will enable us to assume that a Turing machine that computes a function never attempts to consult any tape square to the left of the blank square that marks the left end of that input.

Example 4.2.1

Let $\Sigma_0 = \Sigma_1 = \{a, b\}$, and let $f: \Sigma_0^* \longrightarrow \Sigma_1^*$ be defined as follows: For any $w \in \Sigma_0^*$, $f(w) = \bar{w}$, where $\bar{w}$ is the result of replacing each occurrence of a in w by b, and vice versa. Then f is computed by a Turing machine M which scans backwards through its input, changing a's to b's and vice versa, until the blank marking the leftmost square is found. In order to leave the tape in the proper format, M must then return its head to the blank marking the right end of the input. Formally, $M = (K, \Sigma, \delta, s)$, where $K = \{q_0, q_1, q_2\}$, $\Sigma = \{a, b, \#\}$, $s = q_0$, and δ is given by the following table.

q	σ	$\delta(q, \sigma)$
q_0	a	(q_1, L)
q_0	b	(q_1, L)
q_0	#	(q_1, L)
q_1	a	(q_0, b)
q_1	b	(q_0, a)
q_1	#	(q_2, R)
q_2	a	(q_2, R)
q_2	b	(q_2, R)
q_2	#	$(h, \#)$

For example, consider the following.

$$\begin{aligned}(q_0, \#aab\underline{\#}) &\vdash_M (q_1, \#aa\underline{b})\\ &\vdash_M (q_0, \#aa\underline{a})\\ &\vdash_M (q_1, \#a\underline{a}a)\\ &\vdash_M (q_0, \#a\underline{b}a)\\ &\vdash_M (q_1, \#\underline{a}ba)\\ &\vdash_M (q_0, \#\underline{b}ba)\\ &\vdash_M (q_1, \underline{\#}bba)\\ &\vdash_M (q_2, \#\underline{b}ba)\\ &\vdash_M (q_2, \#b\underline{b}a)\\ &\vdash_M (q_2, \#bb\underline{a})\\ &\vdash_M (q_2, \#bba\underline{\#})\\ &\vdash_M (h, \#bba\underline{\#})\end{aligned}$$

Note also that

$$\begin{aligned}(q_0, \#\underline{\#}) &\vdash_M (q_1, \underline{\#}\#)\\ &\vdash_M (q_2, \#\underline{\#})\\ &\vdash_M (h, \#\underline{\#})\end{aligned}$$

so that M correctly computes the value $f(e) = e$. Since $(q_0, \#w\underline{\#}) \vdash_M^* (h, \#\bar{w}\underline{\#})$ for all $w \in \Sigma_0^*$, M computes f and f is Turing-computable.

Note also that the behavior of M, when started from a configuration such as $(q_0, \#\#ab\underline{\#}\#ab)$, is totally irrelevant to the question of whether M computes f.

The notion of a Turing-computable function from strings to strings can be extended in several ways. For one, we may consider functions of any number of arguments, including zero. Thus let f be a function from $(\Sigma_0^*)^k$ to Σ_1^*, where $k \geq 0$, and let M be a Turing machine (K, Σ, δ, s), where Σ_0, $\Sigma_1 \subseteq \Sigma$. Suppose that, for any $w_1, \ldots, w_k \in \Sigma_0^*$, if $f(w_1, \ldots, w_k) = u$, then $(s, \#w_1\#w_2\# \ldots \#w_k\underline{\#}) \vdash_M^* (h, \#u\underline{\#})$. Then we again say that M **computes** f and that f is **Turing-computable**.

We shall also wish to discuss the Turing-computable functions from natural numbers to natural numbers. Let I be some fixed symbol other than the blank symbol; then the natural number n may be represented (in **unary notation**, as we shall say) by the string I^n. (Thus zero is represented by the empty string.) Now a function $f: \mathbb{N} \to \mathbb{N}$ is said to be **computed** by a Turing machine M if M computes the function $f'\colon \{I\}^* \to \{I\}^*$, where $f'(I^n) = I^{f(n)}$ for each $n \in \mathbb{N}$. That is, a Turing machine computes a function from numbers to numbers by computing the corresponding function from unary notations to unary notations. More generally, a Turing machine M computes a function $f: \mathbb{N}^k \longrightarrow \mathbb{N}$ if it computes the function $f': (\{I\}^*)^k \longrightarrow \{I\}^*$, where $f'(I^{n_1}, \ldots, I^{n_k}) = I^{f(n_1, \ldots, n_k)}$ for any $n_1, \ldots, n_k \geq 0$. A function from numbers to numbers, or from k-tuples of numbers to numbers, is **Turing-computable** if there is a Turing machine that computes it.

Example 4.2.2

Let f be the successor function: $f(n) = n + 1$ for each $n \in \mathbb{N}$.

We design a Turing machine M which computes f by writing an I in the tape square in which its head is initially located, moving its head one square to the right, and halting. Formally, $M = (K, \Sigma, \delta, s)$, where $K = \{q_0\}$, $\Sigma = \{I, \#\}$, $s = q_0$, and δ is as follows.

q	σ	$\delta(q, \sigma)$
q_0	I	(h, R)
q_0	$\#$	(q_0, I)

For example,

$$(q_0, \#II\underline{\#}) \vdash_M (q_0, \#II\underline{I}) \vdash_M (h, \#III\underline{\#})$$

and in general, $(q_0, \#I^n\underline{\#}) \vdash_M^* (h, \#I^{n+1}\underline{\#})$. (As in Example 4.2.1, M will behave differently if started in a configuration not of the form $(q_0, \#I^n\underline{\#})$ for some n, but this is of no concern.) Note in particular the case $n = 0$.

$$(q_0, \#\underline{\#}) \vdash_M (q_0, \#\underline{I}) \vdash_M (h, \#I\underline{\#})$$

Thus M computes the function $f': \{I\}^* \longrightarrow \{I\}^*$ such that $f'(I^n) = I^{n+1}$ for each n; and therefore M computes the successor function $f: \mathbb{N} \longrightarrow \mathbb{N}$.

Another important derivative of the notion of a Turing-computable function is that of a Turing-decidable language. Let us again fix an alphabet Σ_0 not containing the blank symbol. Let Ⓨ and Ⓝ be two fixed symbols not in Σ_0. Then a language $L \subseteq \Sigma_0^*$ is **Turing-decidable** if and only if the function $\chi_L: \Sigma_0^* \longrightarrow \{Ⓨ, Ⓝ\}$ is Turing-computable, where for each $w \in \Sigma_0^*$,

$$\chi_L(w) = \begin{cases} Ⓨ & \text{if} \quad w \in L \\ Ⓝ & \text{if} \quad w \notin L. \end{cases}$$

If χ_L is computed by a Turing machine M, then M is said to **decide** L, or to be a **decision procedure** for L.

Example 4.2.3

Let $\Sigma_0 = \{a\}$, and let $L = \{w \in \Sigma_0^*: |w| \text{ is even}\}$. Then the following Turing machine $M = (K, \Sigma, \delta, s)$ is a decision procedure for L: $K = \{q_0, \ldots, q_6\}$, $\Sigma = \{a, Ⓨ, Ⓝ, \#\}$, $s = q_0$, and δ is given by the following table.

q	σ	$\delta(q, \sigma)$
q_0	#	(q_1, L)
q_1	a	$(q_2, \#)$
q_1	#	(q_4, R)
q_2	#	(q_3, L)
q_3	a	$(q_0, \#)$
q_3	#	(q_6, R)
q_4	#	$(q_5,$ Ⓨ$)$
q_5	Ⓨ	(h, R)
q_5	Ⓝ	(h, R)
q_6	#	$(q_5,$ Ⓝ$)$

(Omitted entries are irrelevant and may be defined arbitrarily.) Here M erases its input string from right to left, keeping track in its finite control of the parity (odd or even) of the number of symbols it has erased. States q_0, q_1, q_2, and q_3 are used for this purpose. On discovering the blank that marked the left end of the input, M passes from state q_1 to q_4 or from q_3 to q_6, writes Ⓨ or Ⓝ accordingly, moves its head one square to the right, and halts. Thus

$$(q_0, \#a^n\underline{\#}) \vdash_M^* (h, \#\text{Ⓨ}\underline{\#}) \qquad \text{if } n \text{ is even;}$$

$$(q_0, \#a^n\underline{\#}) \vdash_M^* (h, \#\text{Ⓝ}\underline{\#}) \qquad \text{if } n \text{ is odd;}$$

and so M computes χ_L. Therefore L is Turing-decidable.

Yet another way Turing machines can be used is as language *acceptors*. Again, fix some alphabet Σ_0 not containing #. We say that a Turing machine M **accepts** a string $w \in \Sigma_0^*$ if M halts on input w. Thus M accepts a language $L \subseteq \Sigma_0^*$ if and only if $L = \{w \in \Sigma_0^*: M \text{ accepts } w\}$, and a language is said to be **Turing-acceptable** if there is some Turing machine that accepts it. We shall see that every Turing-decidable language is Turing-acceptable, but not vice versa; this distinction will be a major concern of Chapter 6.

Example 4.2.4

Let $\Sigma_0 = \{a, b\}$ and let $L = \{w \in \Sigma_0^*: w \text{ contains at least one } a\}$. Then L is accepted by the Turing machine $M = (K, \Sigma, \delta, s)$, where $K = \{q_0\}$, $\Sigma = \{a, b, \#\}$, $s = q_0$, and δ is given by the following table.

q	σ	$\delta(q, \sigma)$
q_0	a	(h, a)
q_0	b	(q_0, L)
q_0	#	(q_0, L)

This machine, when started in configuration $(q_0, \#w\#)$ for some $w \in \Sigma_0^*$, simply scans left until an a is encountered and then halts. If no a is found, the machine hangs and therefore does not halt. So L is exactly the set of strings w in Σ_0^* such that M halts on input w, and therefore M accepts L.

4.3 COMBINING TURING MACHINES

As an example of computational prowess, none of the examples of the last two sections is especially impressive. Yet we started this chapter by claiming that Turing machines would turn out to be computers of ultimate generality, capable of carrying out enormously complex calculations, in spite of their severely limited mode of operation. Obviously, we have some distance to go in order to justify this claim.

Our goal in this section is to present a method for combining simpler Turing machines into more complex ones, so that Turing machines can be dealt with as "modules" or "subroutines" of other Turing machines. The construction of complicated machines will be facilitated, since sizable submachines can be borrowed in toto from previous constructions. At the same time, we shall develop a graphical notation for these larger machines, akin to flowcharts for computer programs. This notation will then be used exclusively: We shall no longer need to specify Turing machines by presenting their transition functions in detail.

To begin with, we need some formal justification for the idea that two computations by the *same* Turing machine can, under some circumstances, be chained together. Lemma 4.3.1, which is analogous to Lemmas 2.2.1 and 3.4.2, provides that justification.

Lemma 4.3.1. *Let M be a Turing machine and let* $(q_i, w_i\underline{a_i}u_i)$ $(i = 1, 2, 3)$ *be configurations of M. Then if*

$$(q_1, w_1\underline{a_1}u_1) \vdash_M^* (q_2, ww_2\underline{a_2}u_2)$$

for some string w, and

$$(q_2, w_2\underline{a_2}u_2) \vdash_M^* (q_3, w_3\underline{a_3}u_3),$$

then

$$(q_1, w_1\underline{a_1}u_1) \vdash_M^* (q_3, ww_3\underline{a_3}u_3).$$

Proof. See Problem 4.3.4 and the discussion below. ■

This lemma states, in essence, that if a Turing machine can carry out some computation without ever moving its head to the left of a certain square, then it will carry out the same computation, regardless of whether that square is actually the leftmost square of the tape or is some square further to the right on the tape. In the latter case, the contents of the lefthand part of the tape remains unchanged.

The crux of the proof is that since M does not hang during the computation $(q_2, w_2\underline{a_2}u_2) \vdash_M^* (q_3, w_3\underline{a_3}u_3)$ and since M has no direct way of "sensing" the left end of the tape, it must make no attempt during this computation to move its head to the left of the first symbol of $w_2a_2u_2$. But then if started in the configuration $(q_2, ww_2\underline{a_2}u_2)$, it will reach $(q_3, ww_3\underline{a_3}u_3)$ without ever penetrating into the first $|w|$ tape squares.

Lemma 4.3.1 will be useful for combining Turing machines as subroutines. Let us suppose that a Turing machine M_1 has been designed to behave in a certain way; in particular, M_1 is known not to hang when its input is presented according to the conventions we have discussed. Then M_1 can be made part of a larger Turing machine M_2 as follows: M_2 prepares some string as input to M_1, placing it near the right end of the nonblank portion of the tape, passes control to M_1 with the read/write head just beyond the end of that string, and finally retrieves control from M_1 when M_1 has finished computing. The results of any partial computation performed by M_2 before passing control to M_1 will be preserved during the operation of M_1, provided that those partial results were saved on the tape to the *left* of the tape square where the input for M_1 began. It is guaranteed that M_1 will not invade the partial results saved by M_2, since M_1 is known never to attempt to move its head to the left of the blank marking the left end of its input. Accordingly, we shall always design Turing machines in such a way that when properly used they will not hang, if we expect subsequently to make them parts of larger machines.

One further observation is needed before we proceed. As in the proof of Theorem 2.4.1, we shall sometimes need to assume that machines which are being combined do not have any state in common. As is the case for all the automata we have studied, the operation of a Turing machine does not depend in any way on the particular choice of objects used as the states, but only on the way those objects are related to each other by the transition function or by designation as the initial state. It is therefore possible at any point to produce a *copy* of a Turing machine M, indistinguishable from M by inspection of its behavior, but having no state in common with M or with any other Turing machine under consideration at the same time.

We are now ready to describe the construction of certain simple Turing machines and the way they can be combined to form more powerful machines. Fix some alphabet Σ.

The Basic Machines. These are of two types: symbol-writing and head-moving.

1. There are $|\Sigma|$ *symbol-writing machines,* one for each symbol in Σ. Each one simply writes a specified symbol in the currently scanned tape

square and halts. The previous contents of the tape square is ignored, and the head is not moved. Formally, the Turing machine which writes the symbol a is $W_a = (K, \Sigma, \delta, s)$, where $K = \{q\}$ for some arbitrarily chosen state q, $s = q$, and $\delta(q, b) = (h, a)$ for each $b \in \Sigma$. Because these machines are used so often, we abbreviate their names and write a instead of W_a.

2. The *head-moving machines* simply move the head one square to the left or right, and then halt. Again, let q be some fixed state. Let $V_L = (\{q\}, \Sigma, \delta_L, q)$, where $\delta_L(q, a) = (h, L)$ for each $a \in \Sigma$; and let $V_R = (\{q\}, \Sigma, \delta_R, q)$, where $\delta_R(q, a) = (h, R)$ for each $a \in \Sigma$. As above, we abbreviate the names of these machines, writing L and R instead of V_L and V_R.

The Rules for Combining Machines. Turing machines will be combined in a way suggestive of the structure of a finite automaton. Individual machines are like the states of a finite automaton, and the machines may be connected to each other in the way that the states of a finite automaton are connected together. However, the connection from one machine to another is not pursued until the first machine halts; the other machine is then started from its initial state with the tape and head position as they were left by the first machine. So if M_1 and M_2 are any Turing machines, the machine in Figure 4–3 operates as follows: Start in the initial state of M_1; operate as M_1 would operate until M_1 would halt; then initiate M_2 and operate as M_2 would operate.

Figure 4–3

The connection between two machines may be contingent on the symbol in the scanned square at the time the first machine would halt (just as the connection between states of a finite automaton may depend on the next input symbol to be read). Thus if M_1, M_2, and M_3 are Turing machines, then the machine in Figure 4–4 starts by imitating M_1; when M_1 would halt, either M_2 or M_3 is imitated, depending on whether the square scanned at that point contained an a or a b.

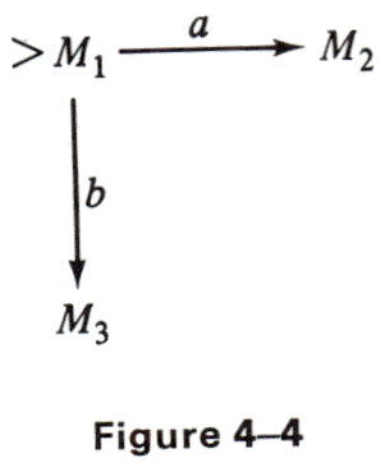

Figure 4–4

Before giving any more complicated examples, let us be more precise about the way machines are combined.

Definition 4.3.1

A **machine schema** is a triple $(\mathfrak{M}, \eta, M_0)$, where

$\mathfrak{M}$ is a finite set of Turing machines with a common alphabet Σ and disjoint state sets;

$M_0 \in \mathfrak{M}$ is the **initial machine**; and

η is a function from a subset of $\mathfrak{M} \times \Sigma$ to $\mathfrak{M}$.

A machine schema $(\mathfrak{M}, \eta, M_0)$ represents a single Turing machine made up of all the individual machines $M \in \mathfrak{M}$. This composite machine—call it $\bar{M}$—starts its operation by imitating that of the initial machine M_0. When and if M_0 would halt, however, $\bar{M}$ may begin to carry out the operation of another machine in $\mathfrak{M}$. Specifically, if M_0 would have halted while scanning symbol a, then

- if $\eta(M_0, a)$ is undefined, then $\bar{M}$ halts; but
- if $\eta(M_0, a) = M \in \mathfrak{M}$, then $\bar{M}$ continues operating from the initial state of M.

The same mode of operation is followed while $\bar{M}$ is imitating M; when M would halt over symbol b, $\bar{M}$ will halt if $\eta(M, b)$ is undefined; otherwise, it will continue from the initial state of $M' = \eta(M, b)$. Of course, it is quite possible that M' is the same as M or M_0, and thus it is possible for $\bar{M}$ to have infinite computations even if the component machines do not.

The next definition provides the formal details corresponding to this informal account.

Definition 4.3.2

Let $\mathfrak{M} = \{M_0, \ldots, M_m\}$ $(m \geq 0)$, where for $i = 0, \ldots, m$, $M_i = (K_i, \Sigma, \delta_i, s_i)$. Let $q_0, \ldots, q_m$ be new states not in any of the K_i. Then if $(\mathfrak{M}, \eta, M_0)$ is a machine schema, it will be said to **represent** the Turing machine M, where $M = (K, \Sigma, \delta, s)$,

$$K = K_0 \cup \cdots \cup K_m \cup \{q_0, \ldots, q_m\}$$

$$s = s_0$$

and δ is defined as follows.

(a) If $0 \leq i \leq m$, $q \in K_i$, $a \in \Sigma$, and $\delta_i(q, a) = (p, b)$, where p is *not* h, then $\delta(q, a) = \delta_i(q, a) = (p, b)$.

(b) If $0 \leq i \leq m$, $q \in K_i$, $a \in \Sigma$, and $\delta_i(q, a) = (h, b)$, then $\delta(q, a) = (q_i, b)$.

(c) If $0 \leq i \leq m$, $a \in \Sigma$, then

$$\delta(q_i, a) = \begin{cases} (h, a) & \text{if } \eta(M_i, a) \text{ is not defined} \\ \delta_j(s_j, a) & \text{if } \eta(M_i, a) = M_j. \end{cases}$$

The states $q_0, \ldots, q_m$ are introduced as temporary stopping points between the various machines; q_i takes the place of the halt state of M_i. In the definition of δ, Part (a) states that each machine functions as expected until it is ready to halt; Part (b) says that M_i enters state q_i instead of halting; and Part (c) says that from state q_i, the combined machine either halts or carries out the first step of the appropriate machine M_j, depending on the contents of the currently scanned square. Note that the state sets K_i are disjoint by Definition 4.3.1, and so δ is a well defined function.

Example 4.3.1

Let $\mathfrak{M}$ consist just of the machine R defined above: $\mathfrak{M} = \{M_0\}$, where $M_0 = R = (\{q\}, \Sigma, \delta_R, q)$. Consider the machine schema $(\mathfrak{M}, \eta, M_0)$, where

$$\eta(M_0, a) = \begin{cases} M_0 & \text{if } a \neq \# \\ \text{undefined} & \text{if } a = \#. \end{cases}$$

Then $(\mathfrak{M}, \eta, M_0)$ represents the machine we denote by $R_\#$, where

$$R_\# = (\{q, q_0\}, \Sigma, \delta, q),$$

and

$$\delta(q, a) = (q_0, R) \qquad \text{for each } a \in \Sigma$$

$$\delta(q_0, a) = \begin{cases} \delta_R(q, a) = (q, R) & \text{if } a \neq \# \\ (h, a) & \text{if } a = \#. \end{cases}$$

This machine, when started on any tape square, moves its head one square to the right, continues moving its head to the right until it finds a blank square, and then halts.

If Σ is the alphabet $\{\#, a, b, c\}$, then the machine $R_\#$ of Example 4.3.1 would be diagrammed as shown in Figure 4–5.

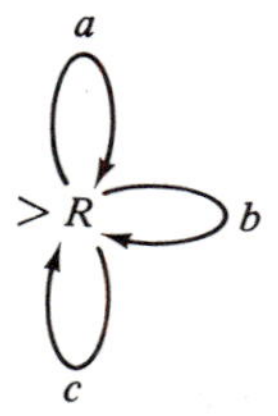

Figure 4–5

The basic rules for depicting a machine schema $(\mathfrak{M}, \eta, M_0)$ are as follows.

1. Each Turing machine $M \in \mathfrak{M}$ is depicted once and only once.

2. The initial machine M_0 is marked with a $>$.
3. Whenever $a \in \Sigma$ and $\eta(M, a)$ is defined, for example, if $\eta(M, a) = M'$, an arrow labeled a is drawn from M to M'. (It is possible, as in Figure 4–5, that $M = M'$.)

Even these three rules become cumbersome to apply, so we abbreviate further. First, there may be two or more occurrences of the same Turing machine (or rather, a symbol denoting that Turing machine) in the same diagram. These represent not the same member of $\mathcal{M}$, but *copies* of the same machine with state sets that are pairwise disjoint and that are disjoint from the state sets of any other illustrated machine. All of these machines are members of $\mathcal{M}$.

Example 4.3.2

Figure 4–6 illustrates a machine schema $(\mathcal{M}, \eta, M_0)$ in which $\mathcal{M}$ consists of two copies of R. The machine represented by this diagram moves its head

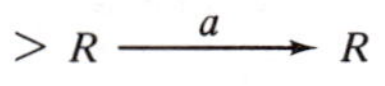

Figure 4–6

right one square; then, if that square contains an a, it moves its head one square further to the right.

Multiple arrows and similar subdiagrams can be eliminated in various ways. An arrow labeled with several symbols takes the place of several arrows, one for each symbol; an unlabeled arrow stands for a bundle of arrows, one for each symbol in Σ.

Example 4.3.3

If $\Sigma = \{a, b, c, \#\}$, the diagram in Figure 4–7(a) can be abbreviated as in Figure 4–7(b) or 4–7(c). This machine moves its head to the right two squares and halts.

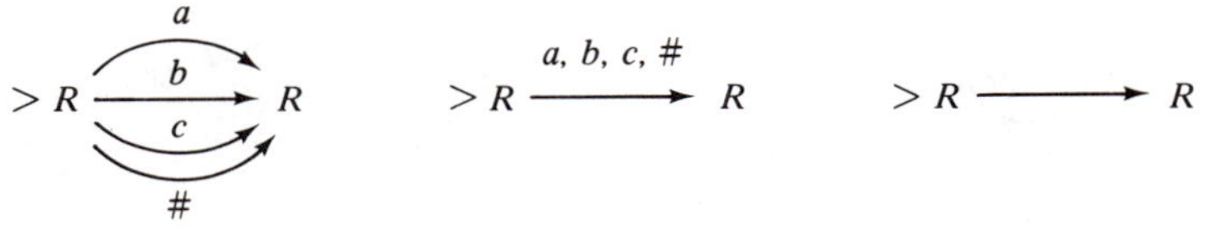

(a) (b) (c)

Figure 4–7

Sometimes the arrow connecting two machines can be omitted entirely, by juxtaposing the representations of the two machines. Under this convention, the machine of Example 4.3.3 (Figure 4–7) becomes simply RR. This machine may also be written as R^2; in general, M^k denotes the same machine as $MM \ldots M$, with k occurrences of M.

If σ is any symbol, we can sometimes eliminate multiple arrows by using $\bar{\sigma}$ to mean "any symbol except σ." With this notation, the machine $R_{\#}$ of Example 4.3.1 and Figure 4–5 would be as illustrated as in Figure 4–8(a). Another shorthand version of the same machine is shown in Figure

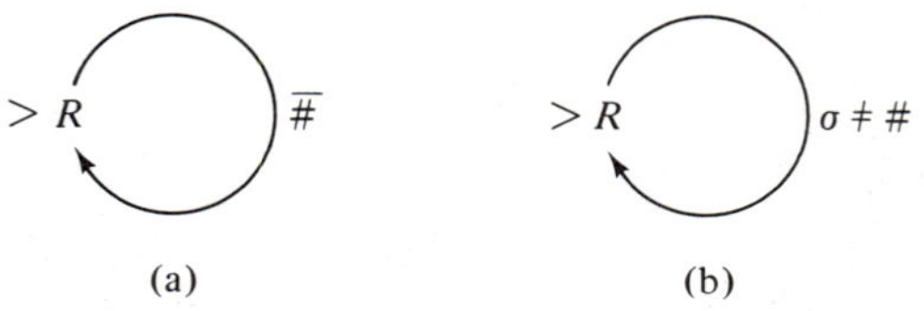

Figure 4–8

4–8(b). Here $\sigma \neq \#$ is read "any symbol σ other than #." The advantage of this notation is that σ may then be used elsewhere in the diagram as the name of a machine.

Example 4.3.4

Figure 4–9(a) depicts a machine that scans to the right until it finds a nonblank square, then copies the symbol in that square onto the square immediately to the left of where it was found. A fuller account of this machine, in the case where $\Sigma = \{a, b, c, \#\}$, is shown in Figure 4–9(b).

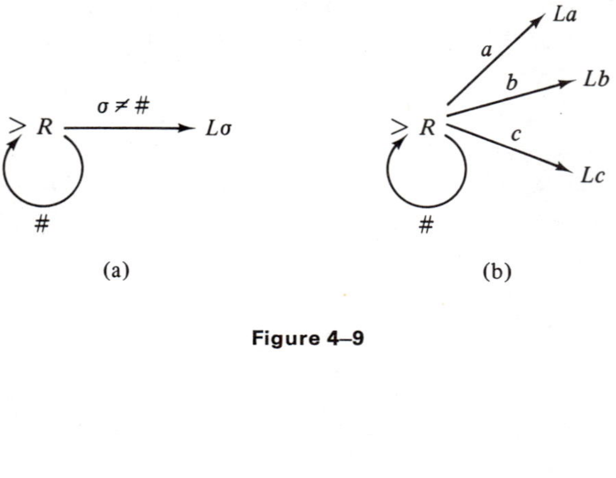

Figure 4–9

4.4 SOME EXAMPLES OF MORE POWERFUL TURING MACHINES

Let us now see how the techniques of the last section enable us to build up Turing machines to accomplish more and more sophisticated functions.

Example 4.4.1

Machines to find marked or unmarked squares are illustrated in Figure 4–10. They are the following.

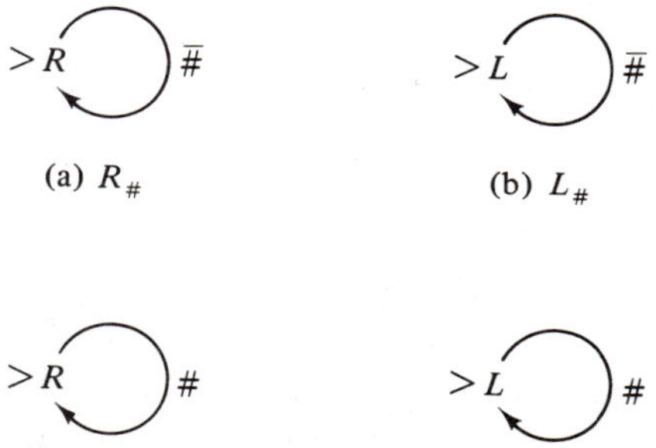

(a) $R_{\#}$ (b) $L_{\#}$

(c) $R_{\overline{\#}}$ (d) $L_{\overline{\#}}$

Figure 4–10

(a) $R_{\#}$, which finds the first blank square to the right of the currently scanned square.

(b) $L_{\#}$, which finds the first blank square to the left of the currently scanned square.

(c) $R_{\overline{\#}}$, which finds the first nonblank square to the right of the currently scanned square.

(d) $L_{\overline{\#}}$, which finds the first nonblank square to the left of the currently scanned square.

Example 4.4.2

The copying machine C performs the following function: If a string w, containing only nonblank symbols but possibly empty, is put on an otherwise blank tape with one blank square to its left, and the head is put on the blank square that marks the end of w, then the machine will eventually stop with $w\#w$ on an otherwise blank tape, with one blank square to the left and the head over the blank square that marks the end of the whole string $w\#w$. Formally, if s is the initial state of C, then $(s, \#w\underline{\#}) \vdash_C^* (h, \#w\#w\underline{\#})$. In order to avoid mentioning the initial state of C explicitly, we say that C **transforms** $\#w\underline{\#}$ **into** $\#w\#w\underline{\#}$, and use similar expressions when describing other machines.

A diagram for C is given in Figure 4–11.

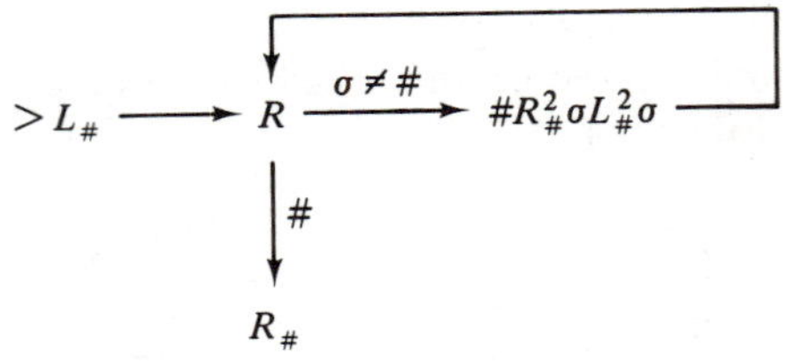

Figure 4–11

Let us follow the operation of C on input $\#abc\underline{\#}$. After $L_\#$, the input has been transformed into $\underline{\#}abc\#$. The head is moved one square to the right, to produce $\#\underline{a}bc\#$. The a is not a blank, so a blank symbol is written ($\#\underline{\#}bc\#$). The second blank symbol to the right of that scanned is found ($\#\#bc\#\underline{\#}$) and an a is written there ($\#\#bc\#\underline{a}$). The second blank symbol to the *left* of that scanned is found ($\#\underline{\#}bc\#a$) and the a is rewritten ($\#\underline{a}bc\#a$). Some of the succeeding configurations of the tape and head may be illustrated as follows.

$\#a\underline{b}c\#a$	
$\#a\underline{\#}c\#a$	
$\#a\#c\#a\underline{\#}$	
$\#a\#c\#a\underline{b}$	
$\#a\underline{\#}c\#ab$	
$\#a\underline{b}c\#ab$	end of another cycle
$\#ab\underline{c}\#ab$	
.	
.	
.	
$\#ab\underline{c}\#abc$	end of a third cycle

At this point, when the head is moved right, a blank symbol is found ($\#abc\underline{\#}abc$). The next blank to the right of that one is found ($\#abc\#abc\underline{\#}$) and the machine halts.

Notice that, by Lemma 4.3.1, C will copy the *last* block of nonblank symbols on the tape if there is more than one such block. For example, if

u, v, and w are strings of nonblank symbols, then C transforms $\#u\#v\#w\underline{\#}$ into $\#u\#v\#w\#w\underline{\#}$. Of course, C will *not* function correctly if it is started with some nonblank symbols to the *right* of the head.

Example 4.4.3

The left-shifting machine S_L transforms $\#w\underline{\#}$, where w contains no blanks, into $w\underline{\#}$. It is illustrated in Figure 4–12.

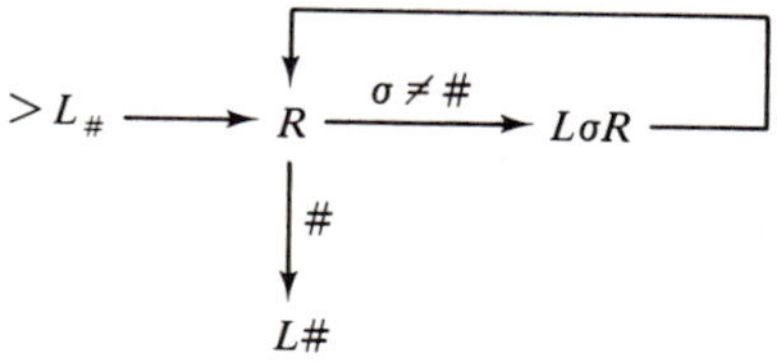

Figure 4–12

To illustrate the operation of S_L, consider a computation starting from $\#ab\underline{\#}$. This is transformed into $\underline{\#}ab$ by $L_\#$. After R, the configuration is $\#\underline{a}b$ and σ is a. The $L\sigma R$ sequence transforms $\#\underline{a}b$ into $a\underline{a}b$; the head moves right and the cycle is repeated with $\sigma = b$. Thus $aa\underline{b}$ is transformed into $ab\underline{b}$. Now a right move puts the head onto a blank square; the head moves left and erases one square, and the machine halts. So the final appearance of the tape and head is $ab\underline{\#}$.

Example 4.4.4

The right-shifting machine S_R transforms $\#w\underline{\#}$, where w contains no blanks, into $\#\#w\underline{\#}$. Its construction is left as an exercise (Problem 4.4.5).

Example 4.4.5

Let Σ be an alphabet containing # and let $\Sigma_0 = \Sigma - \{\#\}$. The function $f: \Sigma_0^* \longrightarrow \Sigma_0^*$ such that $f(w) = ww$ for each $w \in \Sigma_0^*$ is computed by the Turing machine CS_L. This machine simply uses C to copy its input string, leaving a blank between the two copies; it then uses S_L to close up the gap between the copies.

Example 4.4.6

Let Σ and Σ_0 be as in Example 4.4.5 and let $f: \Sigma_0^* \longrightarrow \Sigma_0^*$ be defined by $f(w) = ww^R$. Then f is computed by the Turing machine of Figure 4–13.

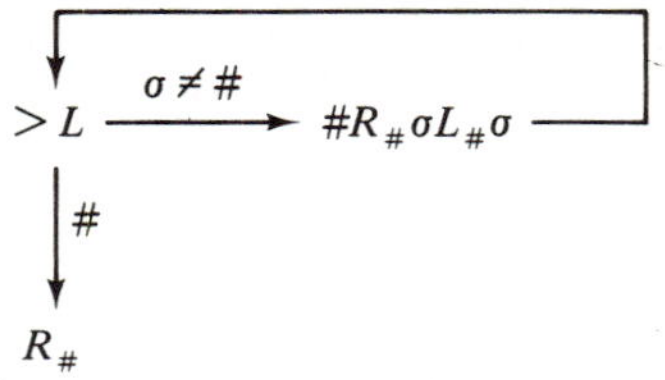

Figure 4–13

This machine transforms the input $\#\sigma_1 \ldots \sigma_n\underline{\#}$ $(\sigma_1, \ldots, \sigma_n \in \Sigma)$ successively into $\#\sigma_1 \ldots \underline{\sigma_i} \ldots \sigma_n\sigma_n\sigma_{n-1} \ldots \sigma_{i+1}$ for $i = n-1, n-2, \ldots, 0$; in the case $i = 0$, this is $\underline{\#}\sigma_1 \ldots \sigma_n\sigma_n \ldots \sigma_1$, which is finally transformed into $\#\sigma_1 \ldots \sigma_n\sigma_n \ldots \sigma_1\underline{\#}$.

Example 4.4.7

Let $\Sigma_0 = \{a, b\}$ and let $L = \{w \in \Sigma_0^*: w = w^R\}$. Then L is decided by the Turing machine of Figure 4–14. This machine first transforms $\#w\underline{\#}$ into $a\underline{\#}w$. It then alternately erases symbols from the ends of w, checking to see

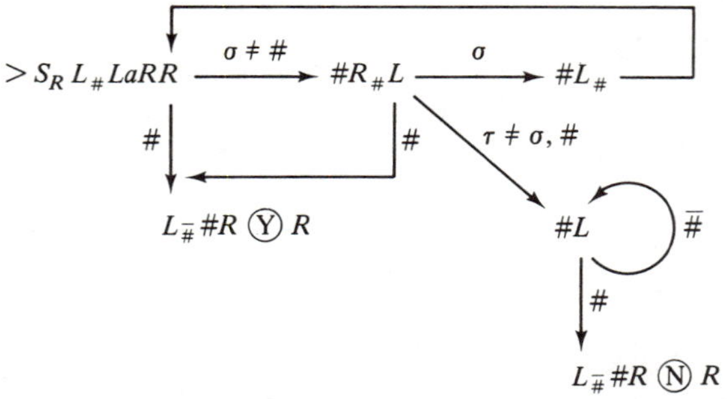

Figure 4–14

that the symbol erased from the right end is the same as that erased just before from the left. If all symbols are erased, the machine returns to the a at the left end of the tape and replaces it with #Ⓨ$\underline{\#}$. If a mismatch is found, the remainder of w is erased and #Ⓝ$\underline{\#}$ is left on the tape.

Example 4.4.8

Let $\Sigma_0 = \{a, b, c\}$, and let $L = \{w \in \Sigma_0^*: w$ has equal numbers of a's, b's, and c's$\}$. Then L is accepted by the Turing machine illustrated in Figure 4–15. In one main cycle of the operation of this machine, it changes one a,

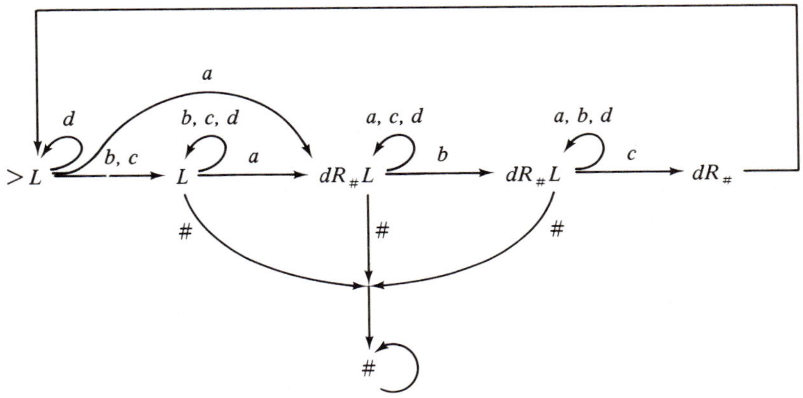

Figure 4–15

one b, and one c on the tape into three d's. It does so by scanning the nonblank part of the tape three times from right to left, once for an a, once for a b, and once for a c, returning each time to the right end of the tape before beginning the next scan. This operation is repeated until the supply of one type of symbol (a, b, or c) is exhausted. If an a was being sought and only d's remain on the nonblank part of the tape, the machine halts and thus accepts the input string. In all other cases, it enters on an unending computation and therefore does not accept the input string.

Example 4.4.9

Subtraction is not defined for all pairs of natural numbers, since the difference between two natural numbers may be negative. However, the very similar function $\dot{-}$ (**monus**) has a natural number as its value for every pair of natural numbers as arguments. The definition of monus is

$$x \dot{-} y = \begin{cases} x - y & \text{if } x \geq y \\ 0 & \text{if } x < y. \end{cases}$$

The function monus is computed by the Turing machine illustrated in Figure 4–16. Here a is some fixed symbol and L_a and R_a are machines which search for the first occurrence of a to the left and right, respectively, of the current head position. The illustrated machine first transforms the input string $\#I^m\#I^n\underline{\#}$ into $\underline{a}I^maI^n$. It then repeatedly removes one I from the end of each block of I's until no more remain in one block or the other. Finally, it erases the a's, erases any remaining I's if it turned out that $n > m$, repositions the head correctly, and halts.

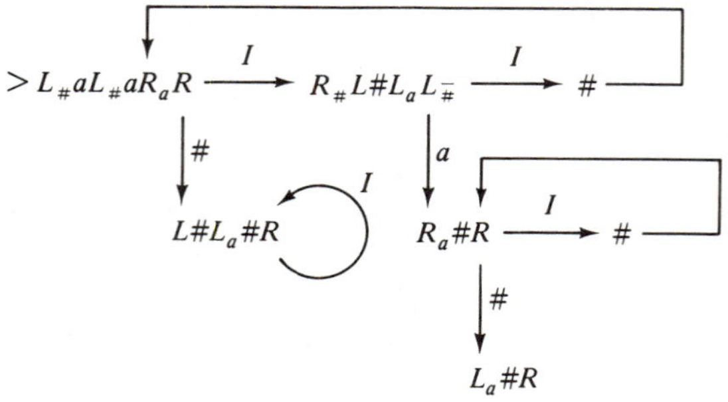

Figure 4–16

Example 4.4.10

The multiplication function $f(n, m) = n \cdot m$ is computed by the Turing machine illustrated in Figure 4–17. This machine first checks whether either

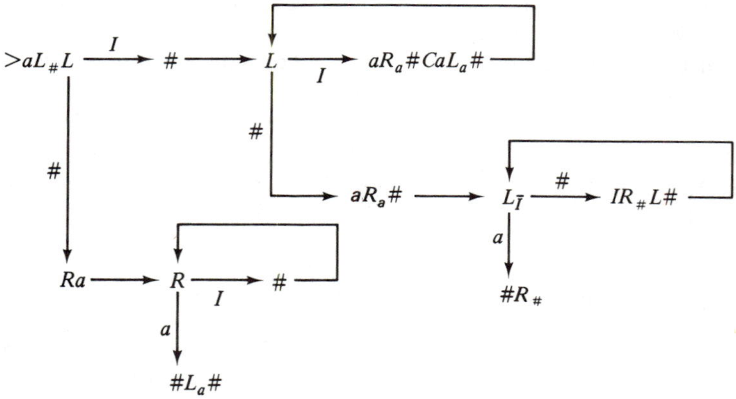

Figure 4–17

argument is zero, and if so halts with the empty string as output. If not, it copies the second string a number of times given by the first string, then finally shifts these copies to the left to remove all the blanks.

4.5 EXTENSIONS OF THE TURING MACHINE

The examples of the previous section make it clear that Turing machines can perform fairly powerful computations, albeit slowly and clumsily. In order to investigate the possibility of designing yet more powerful automata, it is well to consider the effect of extending the Turing machine model in various ways. We shall see that in each case the additional features do not add to the classes of computable functions or decidable languages. A side benefit of these results is that we shall feel free subsequently to use the additional features when designing Turing machines to solve particular problems, secure in the knowledge that our dependency on such features can, if necessary, be eliminated.

The extensions considered in this section are

1. allowing the tape to be infinite in both directions instead of to the right only;
2. allowing several tapes instead of just one;
3. allowing several heads on the tape instead of just one;
4. allowing the "tape" to be two-dimensional instead of one-dimensional.

These additional features can be combined; for example we might also consider machines with several two-way infinite tapes. The exercises for this section introduce several further extensions to the basic Turing machine. And in the next section we deal with an extension of a different kind, nondeterminism.

For each type of extension, we can show that the operation of a seemingly more powerful machine can be imitated, or **simulated**, by a machine of the standard type. A completely rigorous demonstration would in each case

- first, show how to construct a corresponding standard Turing machine for any machine of the extended type; and
- second, prove that the constructed standard Turing machine correctly mimics the behavior of the original machine.

However, these constructions and proofs would be quite tedious to present in detail, so we instead give only sketches and rely on intuition to make up for the lack of formal details. The sketches we present are sufficiently detailed so that there should be no difficulties in seeing that the constructions and proofs could, in principle, be completed.

Two-Way Infinite Tape. A natural extension to the notion of the Turing machine used thus far is to allow the tape to be infinite in both directions (Figure 4–18). The tape now has no distinguished leftmost square, and we could supply an input string by writing it anywhere on the tape and positioning the head on the blank just to its right. Computation would proceed just as for one-way infinite tape machines, except now there is arbitrarily much space to the left as well as to the right for intermediate calculation.

Formally, such a machine is identical to a standard Turing machine: a quadruple (K, Σ, δ, s), as before. The difference is in the notions of configuration and in the definition of the yield relation $\vdash$. Since left and right are

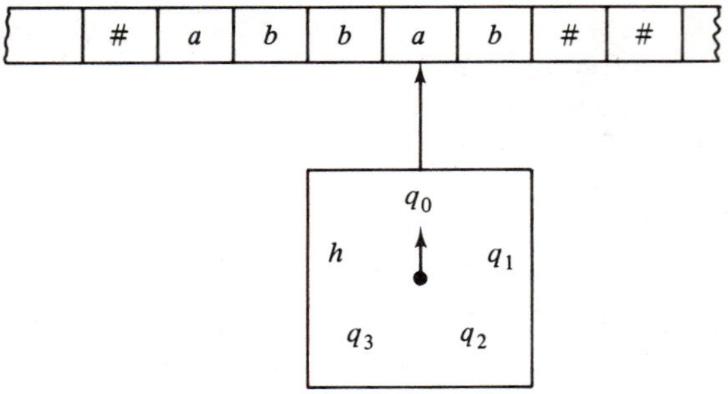

Figure 4–18

symmetric, we would naturally define a configuration of such a machine to be a quadruple (q, w, a, u), where $q \in K$, $w, u \in \Sigma^*$, $a \in \Sigma$, and w does not begin with # and u does not end with #. In keeping with our previous notation, we write this configuration as $(q, w\underline{a}u)$. We do not give the formal definition of the relation $\vdash_M$ between configurations; it is very similar to that for standard Turing machines (Problem 4.5.1). One difference is that if $\delta(q, a) = (p, L)$, then $(q, \underline{a}u) \vdash_M (p, \underline{\#}au)$; that is, blank tape is always available to the left as well as to the right and the machine can never hang. Also, if $\delta(q, a) = (p, R)$, then $(q, \underline{\#}au) \vdash_M (p, \underline{a}u)$. As usual, $\vdash_M^*$ is the reflexive, transitive closure of $\vdash_M$.

Are such machines really any more powerful than Turing machines with one-way infinite tapes? Indeed not; any sort of computation that can be carried out by a two-way infinite tape machine can be carried out by a standard Turing machine. That is the intuitive content of the following lemma.

Lemma 4.5.1. *Let $M_1 = (K_1, \Sigma_1, \delta_1, s_1)$ be any Turing machine with a two-way infinite tape. Then there is a standard Turing machine $M_2 = (K_2, \Sigma_2, \delta_2, s_2)$ such that, for any $w \in (\Sigma_1 - \{\#\})^*$, the following hold.*

(a) *If M_1 halts on input w, that is,*

$$(s_1, w\underline{\#}) \vdash_{M_1}^* (h, u\underline{a}v) \text{ for some } u, v \in \Sigma_1^*, a \in \Sigma_1,$$

then M_2 also halts on input w, and in fact

$$(s_2, \#w\underline{\#}) \vdash_{M_2}^* (h, \#u\underline{a}v).$$

(b) *If M_1 does not halt on input w, then M_2 does not halt on input w.*

Proof. We imagine that M_2 splits its tape down the middle into two **tracks**, so that each tape square can be used for holding two symbols. It then treats its tape as a *folded* version of M_1's tape. To be precise, M_2 will have a "left endmarker" symbol \$, and the correspondence between the tapes of M_1 and M_2 will be as shown in Figure 4–19.

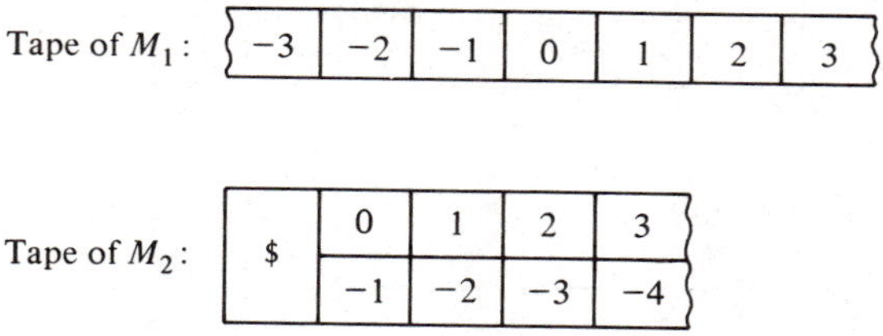

Figure 4–19

On the two-way infinite tape of M_1, the square numbered zero is the leftmost square of those on which the input string is printed. When M_1 would compute on the "righthand" portion of the tape—squares 0, 1, 2, . . .—M_2 will work on the "upper track", and when M_1 would compute on the "lefthand" portion of the tape—squares $-1, -2, -3, \ldots$—M_2 will work on the "lower" track. For example, if M_1 simply scans left down the tape forever, M_2 will scan left until it reaches the leftmost square, then reverse direction and scan right down the tape forever.

Formally, the "two-track" idea is carried through by letting the alphabet of M_2 contain every *ordered pair* (a, b) of symbols in Σ_1. If a tape square of M_2 contains a pair (a, b), we imagine a to be inscribed on the upper track and b on the lower track. We shall also need pairs involving symbols from a disjoint copy of Σ_1,

$$\bar{\Sigma}_1 = \{\bar{a}: a \in \Sigma_1\}.$$

Specifically, we let

$$\Sigma_2 = \{\$\} \cup \Sigma_1 \cup (\Sigma_1 \times \Sigma_1) \cup (\Sigma_1 \times \bar{\Sigma}_1) \cup (\bar{\Sigma}_1 \times \Sigma_1).$$

The use of the symbols with overbars will be explained shortly. M_2 simulates M_1 as follows.

1. Divide the tape into two tracks and copy the input onto the upper track, placing the endmarker $ on the leftmost square.
2. Simulate M_1 on the divided tape.
3. When and if M_1 would halt, restore the tape to "single-track" format.

Step 1 is straightforward. To be precise, the task is to transform an input of the form shown in Figure 4–20(a) into that of Figure 4–20(b), where $a_1 \ldots a_n$ is a string in $(\Sigma_1 - \{\#\})^*$ and the arrows mark the head positions. Let $\mathcal{S}$ be a Turing machine which effects this transformation (Problem 4.5.2(a)).

Step 2, the main part of the simulation, is carried out by a machine M_1' with a state set that contains two copies $\langle q, 1\rangle$ and $\langle q, 2\rangle$ of every state q of M_1. When M_1' is in state $\langle q, 1\rangle$, where q is a state of M_1, it is "working on" the upper track; when M_1' is in state $\langle q, 2\rangle$, it is "working on" the lower

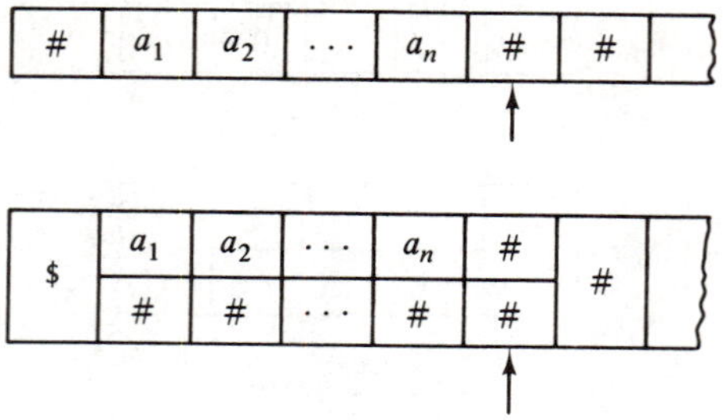

Figure 4–20

track. Also, M'_1 has states called $\langle h, 1\rangle$ and $\langle h, 2\rangle$, corresponding to the halt state of M_1 while M'_1 is working on the upper or lower track. The information about the track on which it was working is passed on to the machine of Step 3 by M'_1 by replacing the scanned symbol on the upper or lower track, for example, a, by its barred correlate $\bar{a}$.

Because the construction of M'_1 illustrates a number of useful techniques, we give it in detail. The state set of M'_1 is $(K_1 \cup \{h\}) \times \{1, 2\}$, as already described; we use brackets, $\langle\ \rangle$, instead of parentheses, ( ), for clarity. Its initial state is $\langle s_1, 1\rangle$; thus it begins simulating M_1 while working on the upper track. Its transition function δ'_1 is as follows.

(a) (Simulate M_1 on the upper track.) If $q \in K_1$, $(a_1, a_2) \in \Sigma_1 \times \Sigma_1$, and $\delta_1(q, a_1) = (p, b)$, then

$$\delta'_1(\langle q, 1\rangle, (a_1, a_2)) = \begin{cases} (\langle p, 1\rangle, L) & \text{if } b \text{ is } L \\ (\langle p, 1\rangle, R) & \text{if } b \text{ is } R \\ (\langle p, 1\rangle, (b, a_2)) & \text{if } b \in \Sigma_1. \end{cases}$$

That is, a move of the tape head to the left or right by M_1 is simulated by a move of the tape head in the same direction by M'_1; and if M_1 would rewrite a tape square, M'_1 changes only the *upper* track.

(b) (Simulate M_1 on the lower track.) If $q \in K_1$, $(a_1, a_2) \in \Sigma_1 \times \Sigma_1$, and $\delta_1(q, a_2) = (p, b)$, then

$$\delta'_1(\langle q, 2\rangle, (a_1, a_2)) = \begin{cases} (\langle p, 2\rangle, R) & \text{if } b \text{ is } L \\ (\langle p, 2\rangle, L) & \text{if } b \text{ is } R \\ (\langle p, 2\rangle, (a_1, b)) & \text{if } b \in \Sigma_1. \end{cases}$$

This part of the definition is symmetric to Part (a); when M_1 would move its head, M'_1 moves its head in the *opposite* direction, and when M_1 would write in a tape square, M'_1 changes only the *lower* track.

(c) (Change tracks.) If $q \in K_1 \cup \{h\}$, then

$$\delta'_1(\langle q, 1\rangle, \$) = (\langle q, 2\rangle, R)$$
$$\delta'_1(\langle q, 2\rangle, \$) = (\langle q, 1\rangle, R).$$

This part of the definition of δ'_1 applies when the head of M'_1 winds up on the leftmost tape square, which is marked with a \$. The head is moved to the right one square, and the information that the other track is being inspected is recorded in the state of M'_1.

(d) (Extend the tape to the right.) If $q \in K_1 \cup \{h\}$, then

$$\delta'_1(\langle q, 1\rangle, \#) = (\langle q, 1\rangle, (\#, \#))$$
$$\delta'_1(\langle q, 2\rangle, \#) = (\langle q, 2\rangle, (\#, \#)).$$

This part of the definition takes care of the case in which M'_1 moves its head to the right onto tape squares which contain ordinary blanks rather than members of the alphabet $\Sigma_1 \times \Sigma_1$. Blanks are changed to pairs of blanks before computation proceeds.

(e) (Halt and record head position.) If $a_1, a_2 \in \Sigma_1$, then

$$\delta'_1(\langle h, 1\rangle, (a_1, a_2)) = (h, (\bar{a}_1, a_2))$$
$$\delta'_1(\langle h, 2\rangle, (a_1, a_2)) = (h, (a_1, \bar{a}_2)).$$

By means of (a) or (b), M'_1 may move into a state $\langle h, 1\rangle$ or $\langle h, 2\rangle$. Neither of these is the "true" halt state; M'_1 moves from these states into the halt state while recording the head position on the upper or lower track.

(f) All other values of δ'_1 may be defined arbitrarily.

Now if M_1 is started on an input $w \in (\Sigma_1 - \{\#\})^*$, and eventually halts with its tape as shown in Figure 4–21(a), where b_1 and b_n are nonblank symbols, then gM'_1, when started on input w, will eventually halt with its tape as shown in Figure 4–21(b), where $c_1c_2 \ldots c_{2k} = \#\# \ldots \#b_1b_2 \ldots b_{i-1}\bar{b}_ib_{i+1} \ldots b_n\# \ldots \#$ (the number of blanks at the beginning and end cannot be predicted).

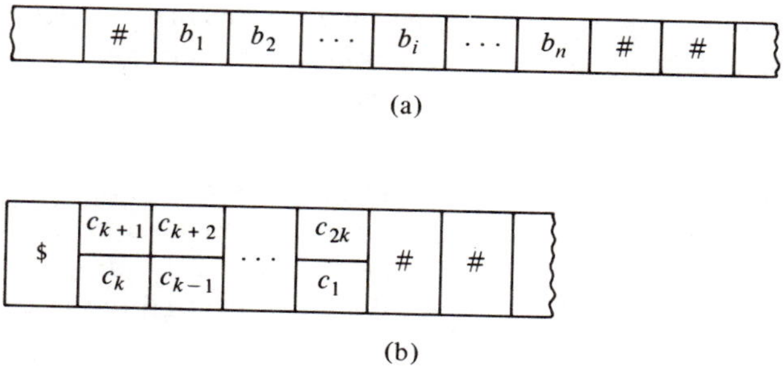

Figure 4–21

Step 3 first transforms the tape shown in Figure 4–21(b) into that shown in Figure 4–22(a), by shifting nonblank symbols from the lower to the upper track or by getting rid of blank symbols at the left end of the upper track.

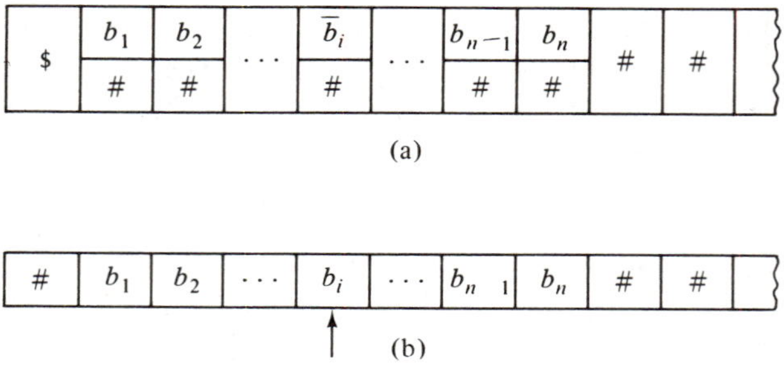

Figure 4–22

Then the tape is converted from two-track to single-track format, and is left as shown in Figure 4–22(b). Let $\mathfrak{F}$ be a Turing machine that achieves these transformations (Problem 4.5.2(b)).

Now if we let M_2 be the Turing machine $\mathcal{S}M'_1\mathfrak{F}$, then M_2 is exactly as specified in the statement of Lemma 4.5.1. ∎

To give a firm answer to the question of whether Turing machines with two-way infinite tapes are more powerful than those with one-way infinite tapes, we must define exactly how these machines are to be used. We give just the definition of computing a function from strings to strings; such notions as deciding a language or accepting a language are defined analogously and left as exercises. We say that a Turing machine $M = (K, \Sigma, \delta, s)$ with a two-way infinite tape **computes a function** $f : \Sigma_0^* \longrightarrow \Sigma_1^*$, where Σ_0 and Σ_1 are alphabets not containing #, if and only if, for any $w \in \Sigma_0^*$, if $f(w) = u$, then $(s, w\underline{\#}) \vdash_M^* (h, u\underline{\#})$.

Theorem 4.5.1. *Any function that is computed or language that is decided or accepted by a Turing machine with a two-way infinite tape is also computed, decided, or accepted, respectively, by a standard Turing machine.*

Proof. Suppose M_1 is a Turing machine with two-way infinite tape that computes a particular function or decides or accepts a particular language. Let M_2 be a standard Turing machine corresponding to M_1 as stated in Lemma 4.5.1. Then M_2 computes the same function or decides or accepts the same language. ∎

Multiple Tapes. For any fixed number $k > 0$, a **k-tape Turing machine** consists of a finite control together with k one-way infinite tapes (see Figure 4–23). Each tape is connected to the finite control by means of a read/write head (one on each tape). The machine can in one step sense the symbols scanned by all its heads and then, depending on those symbols and its current

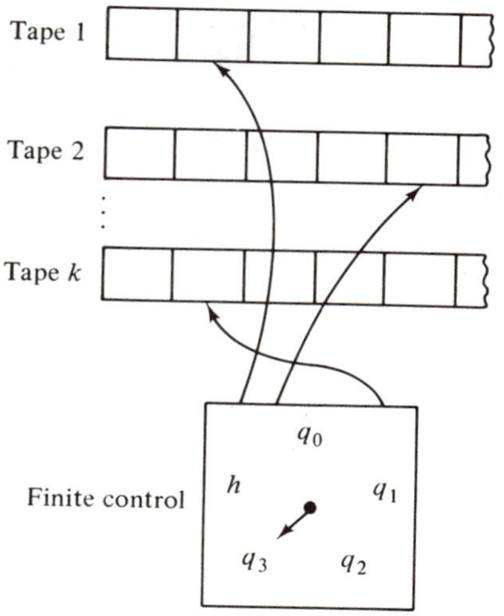

Figure 4–23

state, rewrite some of those scanned squares and move some of the heads to the left or right. Thus a "standard" Turing machine as defined above is a 1-tape Turing machine (that is, a k-tape Turing machine, with $k = 1$).

A k-tape Turing machine can be used for computing a function or deciding a language in any of the ways discussed above for standard Turing machines. We adopt the convention that the input string is placed on the first tape, with the head at the right-hand end, in the same way as it would be presented to a standard Turing machine. The other tapes are initially blank, with the head on the leftmost square of each. At the end of a computation, a k-tape Turing machine is to leave its output on its first tape; the contents of the other tapes are ignored.

With the aid of multiple tapes, it is often easier to construct a Turing machine to perform a particular function. Consider, for example, the task of the copying machine C: to transform $\#w\underline{\#}$ into $\#w\#w\underline{\#}$, where w contains no blanks. A 2-tape Turing machine can accomplish this as follows.

1. Move the head on the first tape left until a blank is found.
2. Move the heads on both tapes to the right, copying each symbol on the first tape onto the second tape, until a blank is found on the first tape. The first square of the second tape should be left blank.
3. Move the head on the second tape to the left until a blank is found.
4. Again move the heads on both tapes to the right, this time copying symbols from the second tape onto the first tape. Halt when a blank is found on the second tape.

This sequence of actions can be pictured as follows.

At the beginning:	First tape	$\#w\underline{\#}$
	Second tape	$\underline{\#}$
After (1):	First tape	$\underline{\#}w\#$
	Second tape	$\underline{\#}$
After (2):	First tape	$\#w\underline{\#}$
	Second tape	$\#w\underline{\#}$
After (3):	First tape	$\#w\underline{\#}$
	Second tape	$\underline{\#}w\#$
After (4):	First tape	$\#w\#w\underline{\#}$
	Second tape	$\#w\underline{\#}$

Turing machines with more than one tape can be depicted in the same way that single-tape Turing machines were depicted in earlier sections. We simply attach as a superscript to the symbol denoting each machine, the number of the tape on which it is to operate; all other tapes are unaffected. For example, $\#^{(2)}$ writes a blank on the second tape, and $L_{\#}^{(1)}$ searches to the left for a blank on the first tape. Using this convention, the 2-tape version of the copying machine might be illustrated as in Figure 4–24. The boxes enclose the submachines performing Functions 1 through 4.

We leave as exercises (Problem 4.5.3) the formal definitions for k-tape Turing machines and their operation, since they are straightforward exten-

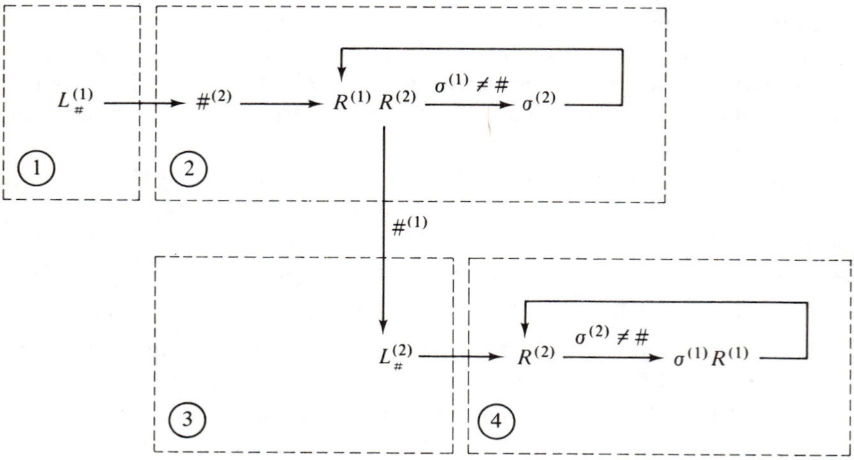

Figure 4–24

sions of those for single-tape Turing machines. We write a configuration of a k-tape Turing machine as $(q, w_1\underline{a_1}u_1, \ldots, w_k\underline{a_k}u_k)$, signifying that the string on the ith tape is $w_i a_i u_i$ with the head on that tape scanning the indicated occurrence of a_i.

We are now ready to show how a k-tape Turing machine can be simulated by a single-tape machine.

Lemma 4.5.2. *Let $k > 0$, and let M_1 be a k-tape Turing machine with alphabet Σ_1 and initial state s_1. Then there is a standard Turing machine $M_2 = (K_2, \Sigma_2, \delta_2, s_2)$ such that $\Sigma_1 \subseteq \Sigma_2$ and for any string $w \in (\Sigma_1 - \{\#\})^*$,*

(a) *If M_1 halts on input w, that is,*

$$(s_1, \#w\underline{\#}, \underline{\#}, \ldots, \underline{\#}) \vdash^*_{M_1} (h, w_1\underline{a_1}u_1, \ldots, w_k\underline{a_k}u_k)$$

for some $w_1, \ldots, w_k$, $u_1, \ldots, u_k$, and $a_1, \ldots, a_k$, then M_2 halts on input w with its tape having the same contents as the first tape of M_1, that is,

$$(s_2, \#w\underline{\#}) \vdash^*_{M_2} (h, w_1\underline{a_1}u_1);$$

(b) *if M_1 hangs on input w, then M_2 hangs on input w;*

(c) *if M_1 neither halts nor hangs on input w, then M_2 neither halts nor hangs on input w.*

As long as only the first tape of M_1 is used for supplying input and producing output, with the other tapes used only for "scratch work," M_2 can reasonably be regarded as equivalent to M_1.

Proof. Except for the leftmost square, which contains a special endmarker \$, and the infinite blank portion of the tape to the right, the single tape of M_2 is split horizontally into $2k$ "tracks." The first, third, . . . , $(2k - 1)$st tracks of the tape of M_2 correspond to the first, second, . . . , kth tapes of M_1. The second, fourth, . . . , $2k$th tracks of the tape of M_2 are used to record the positions of the heads on the first, second, . . . , kth tapes of M_1 in the following way: if the head on the ith tape of M_1 is positioned over the nth tape square, then the $2i$th track of the tape of M_2 contains a 1 in the $(n + 1)$st tape square and a 0 in all tape squares except the $(n + 1)$st. For example, if $k = 2$, then the tapes and heads of M_1 shown in Figure 4–25(a) might correspond to the tape of M_2 shown in Figure 4–25(b).

Of course, the division of the tape of M_2 into tracks is a purely conceptual device; formally, the effect is achieved by letting

$$\Sigma_2 = \Sigma_1 \cup (\Sigma_1 \times \{0, 1\})^k \cup \{\$\}.$$

When given an input $w \in (\Sigma_1 - \{\#\})^*$, M_2 operates as follows.

0. Put an endmarker on the leftmost tape square.

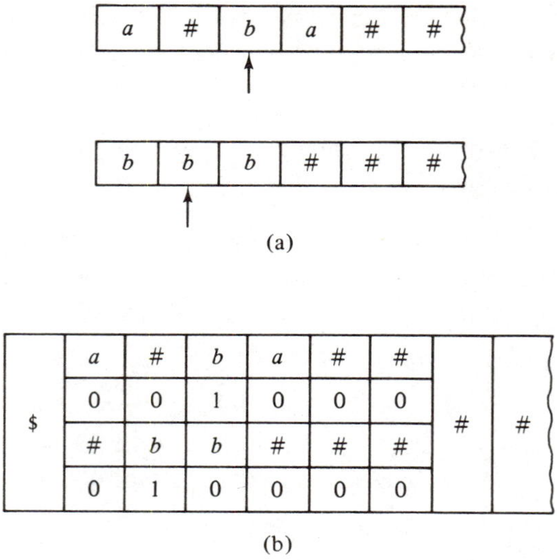

Figure 4–25

1. Divide the next $|w| + 2$ tape squares into $2k$ tracks, putting $\#w\#$ into the first track and marking the positions of the k heads appropriately. At this point, if $k = 2$ and $w = a_1 \ldots a_n$, the tape of M_2 would be as shown in Figure 4–26.

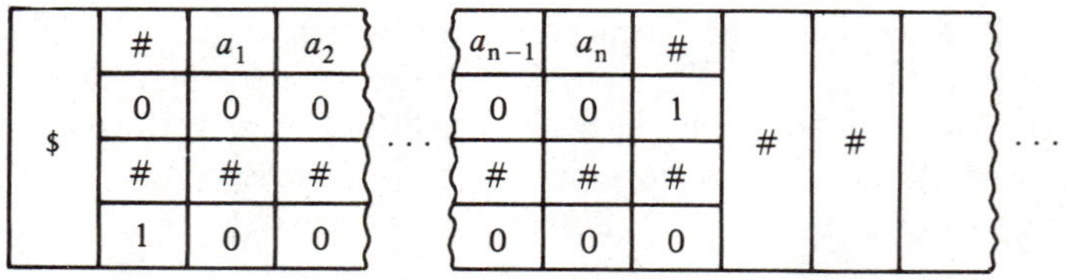

Figure 4–26

2. Simulate the computation by M_1, until M_1 would halt. This involves repeating the following sequence of operations, beginning each time with the tape head at the right end of the portion of the tape that has been divided into tracks:

(a) Scan left down the tape, gathering information about the symbols scanned by the k tape heads of M_1. Return to the right end of the part of the tape that has been divided into tracks. No writing on the tape occurs during this part of the operation of M_2, but when the head has returned to the right end, the state of the finite control has changed to reflect the k-tuple of symbols from Σ_1 in the k tracks at the marked head positions.

(b) Scan left and then right down the tape to update the tracks in accordance with the move of M_1 that is to be simulated. On each pair of tracks, this involves either moving the head position marker one square to the right or left, or rewriting the symbol from Σ_1.

3. When M_1 would halt, M_2 first converts its tape from tracks into single-symbol format, positions its head where M_1 would have placed its first head, and then halts.

Many details have been omitted from this description. Step 2, while by no means conceptually difficult, is rather messy to specify explicitly, and indeed there are several choices as to how the operations described might actually be carried out. As in the construction for Lemma 4.5.1, the division of the tape into tracks must be extended occasionally. Problem 4.5.4 is concerned with completing the construction of M_2. ■

By using the conventions described for the input and output of a k-tape Turing machine, the following theorem is easily derived from Lemma 4.5.2.

Theorem 4.5.2. *Any function that is computed or language that is decided or accepted by a k-tape Turing machine is also computed, decided, or accepted, respectively, by a standard Turing machine.*

Multiple Heads. What if we allow a Turing machine to have several heads on the same tape? In one step, the heads all sense the scanned symbols and move or write independently. (Some convention must be adopted about what happens when two heads that happen to be scanning the same tape square attempt to write different symbols. Perhaps the head with the lower number wins out.)

It is not hard to see that a simulation like that of the last section can be carried out for Turing machines with several heads on a tape. The basic idea is again to divide the tape into tracks, some of which are used solely to record the head positions. To simulate one computational step by the multiple head machine, the tape must be scanned at least twice, once to find the symbols at the head positions, and again to change those symbols or move the heads as appropriate.

The use of multiple heads, like multiple tapes, can sometimes drastically simplify the construction of a Turing machine. A 2-head version of the copying machine C can, for example, function in a way that is much more natural than the one-head version of Example 4.4.2. (See Problem 4.5.7.)

Two-dimensional Tape. Another kind of generalization of the Turing machine is to allow its "tape" to be an infinite two-dimensional grid. (One might even allow a space of higher dimension.) We leave it as an exercise (Problem 4.5.9) to detail the operation of such machines. Once again, however, no fundamental increase in power results.

Theorem 4.5.3. *Turing machines with two-dimensional tapes can be simulated by standard Turing machines.*

4.6 NONDETERMINISTIC TURING MACHINES

We have seen that when finite automata are allowed to act nondeterministically, no increase in computational power results, but that nondeterministic pushdown automata are more powerful than deterministic ones. We can also imagine Turing machines that act nondeterministically: Such machines might have, on certain combinations of state and scanned symbol, more than one possible choice of behavior. Formally, a **nondeterministic Turing machine** is a quadruple (K, Σ, Δ, s), where K, Σ, and s are as for standard Turing machines and Δ is a *subset* of $(K \times \Sigma) \times ((K \cup \{h\}) \times (\Sigma \cup \{L, R\}))$ (rather than a *function* from $K \times \Sigma$ to $(K \cup \{h\}) \times (\Sigma \cup \{L, R\})$). Configurations and the relations $\vdash_M$ and $\vdash_M^*$ are defined in the natural way. But now $\vdash_M$ need not be single-valued: One configuration may yield several others in one step.

When Turing machines are allowed to act nondeterministically, is there any increase in computational power? Since a nondeterministic machine could produce two different outputs from the same input, we have to be careful what is considered to be the end result of a computation by such a machine. We resolve this problem by construing nondeterministic Turing machines only as *acceptors*, so that the only significant fact is whether the machine halts at all, not what is left on the tape.

Before showing that nondeterminism, like the features considered in Section 4.5, can be eliminated from Turing machines, let us consider some examples that demonstrate the power of nondeterminism in Turing machines as a conceptual device.

Example 4.6.1

Let $L = \{w \in \{a, b\}^*: w$ contains an occurrence of the substring $abaab\}$. Of course, L is a regular language, and by the results of Chapter 2 we can design either a nondeterministic or a deterministic finite automaton to accept L. But it is instructive to see how a nondeterministic Turing machine can be designed to accept L, using the conventions we have adopted for supplying input to Turing machines. The machine we design receives its input in the form $\#w\#$, where $w \in \{a, b\}^*$. It first scans from right to left and *nondeterministically guesses* a point in w to start checking for the specified pattern. From here on, its behavior is deterministic. It checks to see that the next five symbols are, from right to left, b, a, a, b, a. If this pattern is detected, the machine halts and therefore accepts the input string. If a violation of this pattern is found, the machine goes into an infinite loop.

By using an obvious extension of the diagrams we have already used for standard Turing machines, this nondeterministic Turing machine can be illustrated as in Figure 4–27.

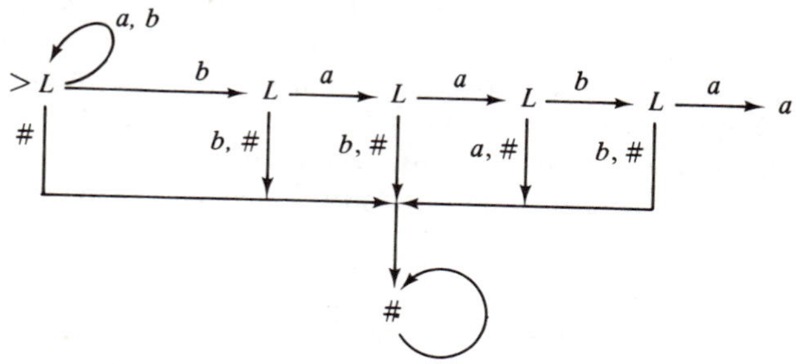

Figure 4–27

The only nondeterministic point in this diagram is in the upper left, where if the scanned symbol is b, there are two possible behaviors: Move the head left and continue the right-to-left scan, or start to check for the desired substring.

As with all nondeterministic devices, there may be several possible computations starting from the same input; in order for the input to be accepted, it is required only that some *one* of them result in the machine halting. On the other hand, the machine can halt on the input *only* if the string *abaab* actually does occur somewhere in the input. Therefore this machine accepts L.

Example 4.6.2

A **composite** number is one that is the product of two natural numbers, each greater than one; for example, 4, 6, 8, 9, 10, and 12 are composite, but 1, 2, 3, 5, 7, and 11 are not. In other words, a composite number is a nonprime other than one or zero.

Let $L = \{I^n : n \text{ is a composite number}\}$. To design a Turing machine to accept L, it would seem to be necessary to find the factors, if any, of a number—a rather complicated task. But if nondeterminism is available, we can design a machine to accept L rather simply, by guessing the factors, if there are any. This machine operates as follows, when given input $\#I^n\underline{\#}$.

1. Nondeterministically choose two numbers $p, q > 1$ and transform the input into $\#I^n\#I^p\#I^q\underline{\#}$.
2. Use the multiplication machine of Example 4.4.10 to transform the result of Step 1 into $\#I^n\#I^{p \cdot q}\underline{\#}$.
3. Check to see that $I^n = I^{p \cdot q}$; this is easy, since only the lengths of these strings need be compared. Halt if the lengths are equal; otherwise continue computing forever in some trivial fashion.

To be explicit, let P be the multiplication machine of Example 4.4.10, and let E be a machine that performs Step 3, that is, for any $w, u \in \{I\}^*$, E halts on input $\#w\#u\underline{\#}$ if and only if $w = u$. Let G be the nondeterministic machine of Figure 4–28, which writes I^p on the tape for some $p \geq 2$. Then L is the language accepted by the machine $GGPE$. Once again, the only nondeterminism in the operation of this machine is at the beginning.

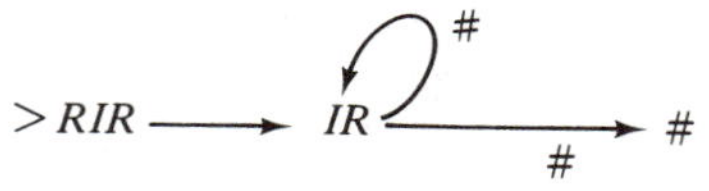

Figure 4–28

Nondeterminism would seem to be a very powerful feature that cannot be eliminated by methods like those of Section 4.5. However, the languages accepted by nondeterministic Turing machines are in fact no different from those accepted by deterministic Turing machines.

Lemma 4.6.1. *For every nondeterministic Turing machine M_1, we can construct a standard Turing machine M_2 such that for any string w not containing a blank,*

(a) *if M_1 halts on input w, then M_2 halts on input w;*

(b) *if M_1 does not halt on input w, then M_2 does not halt on input w.*

Proof. Let $M_1 = (K, \Sigma, \Delta, s)$. Before describing the construction of M_2 in detail, we explain the basic idea informally. Given an input w, M_2 will attempt to run systematically through all possible computations by M_1 in search of one that halts. When and if it discovers one that halts, it too will halt, so M_2 will halt if and only if M_1 halts.

But M_1 may have an infinity of different computations starting from the same input, as in Example 4.6.2; how can M_2 explore them all? It does so by using a *dovetailing procedure*. The crucial observation is the following:

Although for any configuration C of M_1 there may be several configurations C' such that $C \vdash_{M_1} C'$, the *number* of such configurations C' is fixed and bounded in a way that depends only on M_1, not on C. Specifically, the number of quadruples $(q, a, p, b) \in \Delta$ that can be applicable at any point is finite; in fact, it cannot exceed $(|K| + 1)\cdot(|\Sigma| + 2)$, since this is the maximum number of possible combinations (p, b) with $p \in K \cup \{h\}$, $b \in \Sigma \cup \{L, R\}$. Let us call r the maximum number of quadruples that can be applicable at any point; the number r can be determined by inspection of M_1.

Then starting from an initial configuration $C = (s, \#w\#)$, M_1 has at most r computations of one step, for example,

$$C \vdash_{M_1} C_1$$
$$C \vdash_{M_1} C_2$$
$$\vdots$$
$$C \vdash_{M_1} C_r.$$

(If there are actually fewer than r possibilities, we can let some of the C_i be equal.) Similarly, starting from C_1, there are at most r one-step computations

$$C_1 \vdash_{M_1} C_{11}$$
$$C_1 \vdash_{M_1} C_{12}$$
$$\vdots$$
$$C_1 \vdash_{M_1} C_{1r};$$

a similar statement is true for one-step computations starting from any other C_i. So there are at most r^2 two-step computations starting from C. In general, there are at most r^k computations of exactly k steps starting from C.

First M_2 checks all one-step computations of M_1 starting from the given initial configuration, then all two-step computations, and so on, until (and provided that) it finds a computation via which M_1 halts. Since if M_1 halts, it does so in some finite number of steps, M_2 will eventually discover a halting computation of M_1 if one exists. If no sequence of moves of M_1 ends in a halted configuration, then M_2 may run forever.

We now give the details of the Turing machine M_2. It is helpful to assume that M_1 will not hang on any input; we leave it as an exercise (Problem 4.6.6) to modify the construction to accommodate the possibility that M_1 may have computations that end in hanging configurations.

We present M_2 as a 3-tape Turing machine; we know by Lemma 4.5.2 and Theorem 4.5.2 that M_2 can be converted into an equivalent single-tape Turing machine. The three tapes of M_2 are used as follows:

• The first tape is never changed; it always contains the original input w so that each simulated computation of M_1 can begin afresh with the same input

• The second tape is used to simulate the computations of M_1. The first tape is copied onto the second before M_2 begins to simulate each new computation. As it is copied, the input is shifted over one square; the leftmost square of the second tape is marked with a special endmarker \$, which is used to facilitate erasing that tape between simulated computations.

• The third tape is used to direct the particular computation being simulated on the second tape. The string on this tape is over an alphabet $\{d_1, \ldots, d_r\}$, where r is, as defined above, the maximum number of moves M_1 may have from any one configuration. The string $d_3d_5d_1$ on the third tape would correspond to a computation in which the third possible move is taken on the first step of the computation, the fifth possibility on the second step, and the first possibility on the third step. As each simulated computation ends, M_2 generates the next string over $\{d_1, \ldots, d_r\}$ on the third tape, from shortest to longest and in lexicographic order among strings of equal length.

The overall structure of M_2 is illustrated in Figure 4–29.

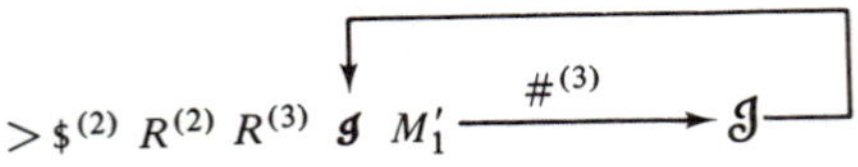

Figure 4–29

At the beginning M_2 configures its second and third tapes as $\$\underline{\#}$ and $\#\underline{\#}$, respectively. The latter is the representation of the empty string, the first string over $\{d_1, \ldots, d_r\}$. Then M_2 enters its main cycle, made up of the three machines $\mathscr{C}$, M'_1, and $\mathscr{G}$. The machine $\mathscr{C}$ copies the first tape onto the second, as described earlier. Using the string on the third tape for directions, M'_1 deterministically simulates one computation by M_1. When it finishes, the head on the third tape will be over a blank if the simulated computation was completed without reaching a halted configuration. In this case, M_2 uses the $\mathscr{G}$ machine to produce the next string in lexicographic order over $\{d_1, \ldots, d_r\}$ on the third tape and then cycles back to simulate another computation by M_1. On the other hand, if the simulated computation by M_1 did end by M_1 moving into the halt state, then the head on the second tape will wind up scanning one of the d_i; in this case, M_2 will itself halt and accept the input.

Thus it remains only to describe $\mathscr{C}$, $\mathscr{G}$, and M'_1. Figure 4–30 illustrates $\mathscr{C}$, which functions as follows.

1. Move the head on the second tape far enough to the right to be beyond any tape square on the second tape that might have been used during

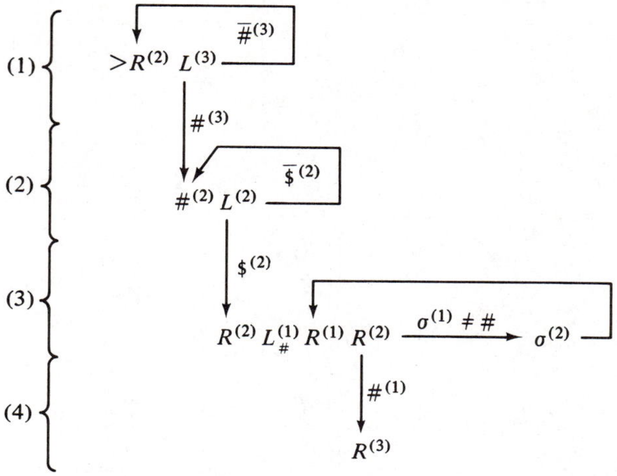

Figure 4–30

the preceding simulated computation of M_1. Since the length of that simulated computation is the length of the string on the third tape, $\mathcal{I}$ can accomplish this by scanning left on the third tape, moving the head on the second tape to the right at the same rate, stopping when a blank is found on the third tape.

2. Erase the second tape from right to left until the \$ endmarker is found on the second tape.

3. Copy the first tape onto the second tape, shifted over one square.

4. Move the head on the third tape to the right one square; this leaves it in the position needed by M'_1.

Figure 4–31 illustrates $\mathcal{J}$. If $\mathcal{J}$ begins with the third tape having the appearance $\#w\#$, where $w \in \{d_1, \ldots, d_r\}^*$, it will end with the third tape as $\#u\#$, where u is the next string after w in lexicographic order, as shown on the next page.

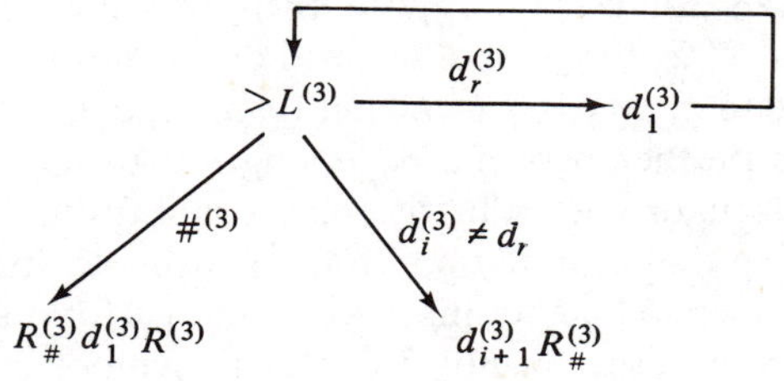

Figure 4–31

$$
\begin{array}{c}
e \\
d_1 \\
d_2 \\
\cdot \\
\cdot \\
\cdot \\
d_r \\
d_1d_1 \\
d_1d_2 \\
\cdot \\
\cdot \\
\cdot \\
d_1d_r \\
d_2d_1 \\
d_2d_2 \\
\cdot \\
\cdot \\
\cdot \\
d_2d_r \\
d_3d_1 \\
\\
\cdot \\
\cdot \\
d_rd_r \\
d_1d_1d_1 \\
d_1d_1d_2 \\
\cdot \\
\cdot \\
\cdot
\end{array}
$$

Finally, we must specify M'_1. The states of M'_1 are the same as those of M_1. The first tape is ignored by M'_1. Regardless of what state it is in, if the symbol scanned on the third tape is $\#$, M'_1 halts: The "directions" on the third tape have been exhausted. Suppose, then, that the symbol scanned on the second tape is $a \in \Sigma$, the symbol scanned on the third tape is d_i $(1 \leq i \leq r)$, and that the state of M'_1 is $q \in K$. Let $(q, a, p_1, b_1), \ldots, (q, a, p_r, b_r)$ be in some fixed order the members of Δ beginning with $(q, a, -, -)$ (if there are fewer than r such quadruples, this list may contain duplicates). Then M'_1 simulates one step in the computation of M_1 by using the particular quadruple (q, a, p_i, b_i). It does so by entering state p_i and performing on the second tape whatever function is specified by b_i (writing a symbol or moving the tape head left or right). In addition, it moves the head on the third tape to the right, unless p_i is the halt state h; in that case the head on the third tape remains stationary. Thus if M_1 would have halted, M'_1 halts with the head on the third tape scanning d_i; otherwise M'_1 will continue operating until the head on the third tape reaches the blank marking the end of the "directions" on the third tape.

This completes the description of M'_1 and hence of M_2. ■

Theorem 4.6.1 follows immediately from Lemma 4.6.1.

Theorem 4.6.1. *Any language accepted by a nondeterministic Turing machine is accepted by a deterministic Turing machine.*

PROBLEMS

4.1.1. Let $M = (K, \Sigma, \delta, s)$, where

$$K = \{q_0, q_1\}$$
$$\Sigma = \{a, b, \#\}$$
$$s = q_0$$

and δ is given by the following table.

q	σ	$\delta(q, \sigma)$
q_0	a	(q_1, b)
q_0	b	(q_1, a)
q_0	$\#$	$(h, \#)$
q_1	a	(q_0, R)
q_1	b	(q_0, R)
q_1	$\#$	(q_0, R)

(a) Trace, as was done in Examples 4.1.4 and 4.1.5, the computation of M starting from the configuration $(q_0, \underline{a}abbba)$.

(b) Describe informally what M does when started in q_0 on any square of a tape.

4.1.2. Repeat Problem 4.1.1 for the machine $M = (K, \Sigma, \delta, s)$, where

$$K = \{q_0, q_1, q_2\}$$
$$\Sigma = \{a, b, \#\}$$
$$s = q_0$$

and δ is given by the following table.

q	σ	$\delta(q, \sigma)$
q_0	a	(q_1, L)
q_0	b	(q_0, R)
q_0	$\#$	(q_0, R)
q_1	a	(q_1, L)
q_1	b	(q_2, R)
q_1	$\#$	(q_1, L)
q_2	a	(q_2, R)
q_2	b	(q_2, R)
q_2	$\#$	$(h, \#)$

Start from the configuration $(q_0, a\underline{b}b\#bb\#\#aba)$.

4.1.3. Repeat Problem 4.1.1 for the machine $M = (K, \Sigma, \delta, s)$, where

$$K = \{q_0, q_1, q_2, q_3, q_4\}$$
$$\Sigma = \{a, b, \#\}$$
$$s = q_0$$

and δ is given by the following table.

q	σ	$\delta(q, \sigma)$
q_0	a	(q_2, R)
q_0	b	(q_3, a)
q_0	$\#$	$(h, \#)$
q_1	a	(q_2, R)
q_1	b	(q_2, R)
q_1	$\#$	(q_2, R)
q_2	a	(q_1, b)
q_2	b	(q_3, a)
q_2	$\#$	$(h, \#)$
q_3	a	(q_4, R)
q_3	b	(q_4, R)
q_3	$\#$	(q_4, R)
q_4	a	(q_2, R)
q_4	b	(q_4, R)
q_4	$\#$	$(h, \#)$

Start from the configuration $(q_0, \underline{a}aabbbaa)$.

4.1.4. Let M be the Turing machine (K, Σ, δ, s), where

$$K = \{q_0, q_1, q_2\}$$

$$\Sigma = \{a, \#\}$$

$$s = q_0$$

and δ is given by the following table.

q	σ	$\delta(q, \sigma)$
q_0	a	(q_1, L)
q_0	$\#$	$(q_0, \#)$
q_1	a	$(q_2, \#)$
q_1	$\#$	$(h, \#)$
q_2	a	(q_2, a)
q_2	$\#$	(q_0, L)

Let $n \geq 0$. Describe carefully what M does when started in the configuration $(q_0, \#a^n\underline{a})$.

4.1.5. In the definition of a Turing machine, we allow rewriting a tape square without moving the head and moving the head left or right without rewriting the tape square. Does it matter that we do not also allow leaving the head stationary without rewriting the tape square?

4.1.6. (a) Which of the following could be configurations?

(i) $(q, a\#a\#, \#, \#a)$
(ii) (q, abc, b, abc)
(iii) $(p, abc, \#, e)$
(iv) (h, e, e, e)
(v) $(q, a\#ab, b, ab\#b\#)$
(vi) (p, a, ab, abc)
(vii) $(q, e, \#, \#\#\#a)$
(viii) (h, abc, a, e)

(b) Rewrite those of Parts (i) through (viii) that are configurations using the abbreviated notation.

(c) Rewrite these abbreviated configurations in full.

(i) $(q, a\underline{b}cd)$
(ii) $(h, \underline{a})$
(iii) $(p, aa\#\underline{\#})$
(iv) $(q, \underline{\#}abc)$

4.1.7. Design and write out in full a Turing machine that scans to the right until it finds two consecutive a's and then halts. The alphabet of the Turing machine should be $\{a, b, \#\}$. Here are some sample starting and ending tapes to illustrate the intended operation.

Start	Finish
$\underline{a}babaab$	$ababa\underline{a}b$
$\underline{a}ab$	$a\underline{a}b$
$\underline{a}ba\#aab$	$aba\#a\underline{a}b$

4.2.1. Let $\Sigma_0 = \{a, b\}$. What function from $\Sigma_0^* \times \Sigma_0^*$ to Σ_0^* is computed by the Turing machine $M = (K, \Sigma, \delta, s)$, where $K = \{q_0, q_1, q_2\}$, $\Sigma = \{a, b, \#\}$, $s = q_0$, and δ is given by the following table?

q	σ	$\delta(q, \sigma)$
q_0	$\#$	(q_1, L)
q_0	a	arbitrary
q_0	b	arbitrary
q_1	a	(q_1, L)
q_1	b	(q_1, L)
q_1	$\#$	(q_2, b)
q_2	a	(q_2, R)
q_2	b	(q_2, R)
q_2	$\#$	$(h, \#)$

4.2.2. What function from $\mathbb{N}$ to $\mathbb{N}$ is computed by the Turing machine $M = (K, \Sigma, \delta, s)$, where $K = \{q_0, q_1, q_2, q_3\}$, $\Sigma = \{I, \#\}$, $s = q_0$, and δ is given by the following table?

q	σ	$\delta(q, \sigma)$
q_0	$\#$	(q_1, L)
q_0	I	arbitrary
q_1	$\#$	(h, R)
q_1	I	$(q_2, \#)$
q_2	$\#$	(q_3, L)
q_2	I	arbitrary
q_3	$\#$	(h, R)
q_3	I	$(h, \#)$

4.2.3. Present a Turing machine that decides the language $\{w \in \{a, b\}^*: w$ contains at least one $a\}$.

4.2.4. Present Turing machines that decide the following languages, where the reference alphabet Σ_0 is $\{a, b\}$.

(a) $\varnothing$

(b) $\{e\}$

(c) $\{a\}$

4.2.5. Suppose $M = (K, \Sigma, \delta, s)$ computes a function f from $\mathbb{N}^k$ to $\mathbb{N}$. In what configuration does M begin when it sets out to compute the value of $f(0, \ldots, 0)$?

4.2.6. Give an example of a Turing machine that does *not* compute a function from strings to strings.

4.2.7. The notion of a **state diagram**, as used extensively for finite automata in Chapter 2, can be generalized as follows for Turing machines: If $\delta(q, a) = (p, b)$, draw an arrow from q to p and label it a/b. For example, the state diagram for the Turing machine of Example 4.1.1 would be

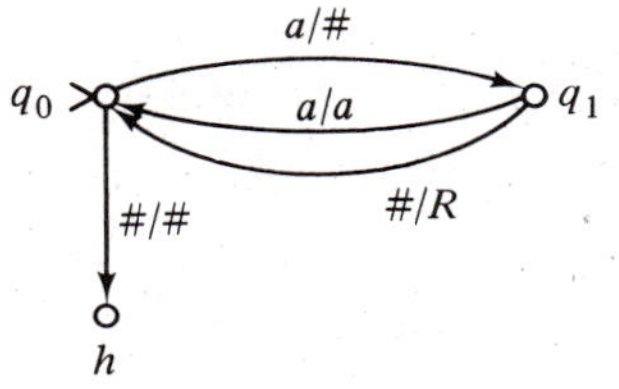

Draw state diagrams for each of these Turing machines.

(a) The machine of Example 4.2.1.

(b) The machine of Example 4.2.3.

4.2.8. Give a Turing machine that accepts the language a^*ba^*b.

4.3.1. Give the full details of the Turing machines illustrated.

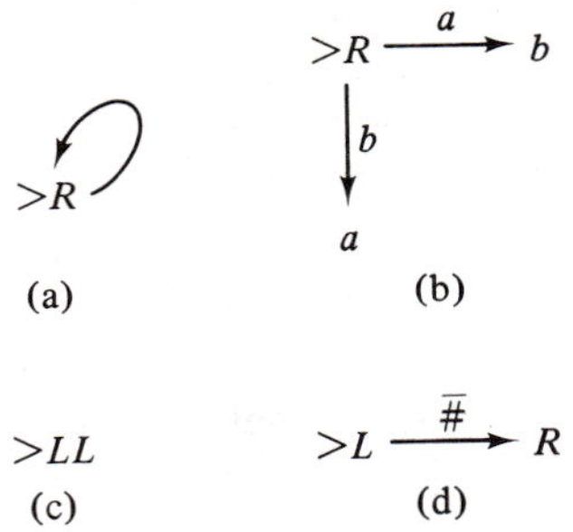

4.3.2. Do the machines LR and RL always accomplish the same thing? Explain.

4.3.3. Explain what this machine does.

$$>R \xrightarrow{\sigma \neq \#} R \xrightarrow{\tau \neq \#} R_{\#}\sigma R_{\#}\tau$$

4.3.4. Prove Lemma 4.3.1.

4.4.1. Consider a computation of the left-shifting machine S_L starting from $\#bab\underline{\#}$. Show the appearance of the tape and the head position on each subsequent step until the machine halts.

4.4.2. Trace the operation of the Turing machine of Example 4.4.6 on the input $\#ab\underline{\#}$.

4.4.3. Trace the operation of the Turing machine of Example 4.4.7 on the input $\#aba\underline{\#}$.

4.4.4. Trace the operation of the Turing machine of Example 4.4.9 on the input $\#I^3\#I\underline{\#}$.

4.4.5. Construct the right-shifting machine S_R of Example 4.4.4.

4.4.6. Construct a Turing machine that decides the language $\{ww: w \in \{a, b\}^*\}$.

4.4.7. Construct Turing machines that compute each function.

(a) The addition function: $f(n, m) = n + m$.

(b) The division function: $f(n, m) =$ the largest integer less than or equal to n/m, if $m > 0$; or 0, if $m = 0$.

4.4.8. Construct a Turing machine that computes the following function from pairs of strings in $\{a, b\}^*$ to strings in $\{a, b\}^*$: $f(u, w) = wu$, for any $u, w \in \{a, b\}^*$.

4.5.1. Let M be a Turing machine with a two-way infinite tape. Define the relation $\vdash_M$ formally, as was done in Definition 4.1.3 for standard Turing machines.

4.5.2. Complete the proof of Lemma 4.5.1 by presenting in detail

(a) the machine $\mathcal{I}$ for Step 1;

(b) the machine $\mathcal{F}$ for Step 3.

Hint: In Part (b), one way to design $\mathcal{F}$ is to construct it as the combination $F_1F_2F_3$, where F_1, F_2, and F_3 perform the following functions:

F_1 shifts nonblank symbols from the lower track to the upper track until no nonblank symbols remain in the lower track;

F_2 removes leading blank symbols from the upper track;

F_3 converts to single-track format and repositions the head correctly.

For example, F_1 might transform

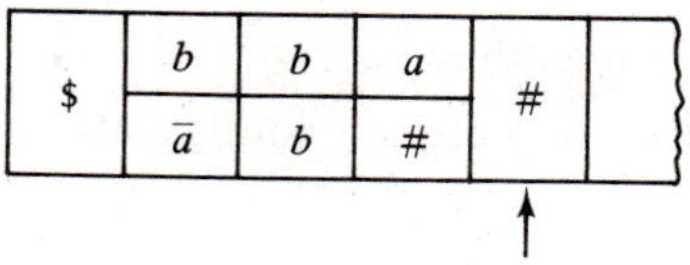

into the following.

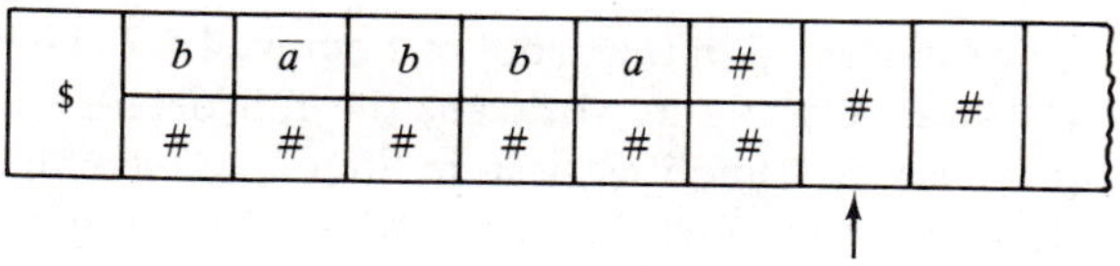

Also, F_2 might transform

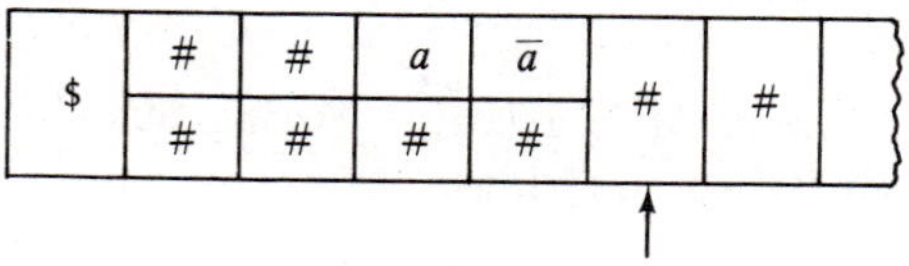

into the following.

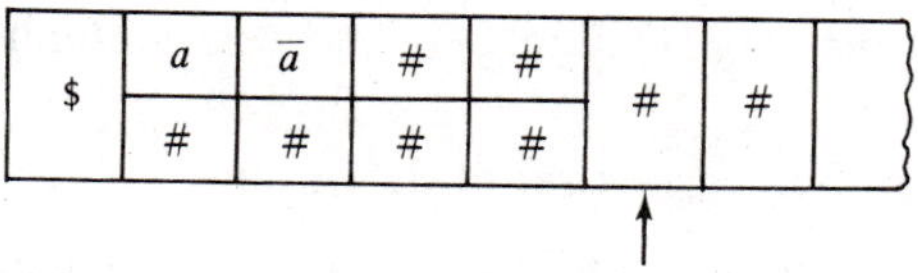

Finally, F_3 might transform

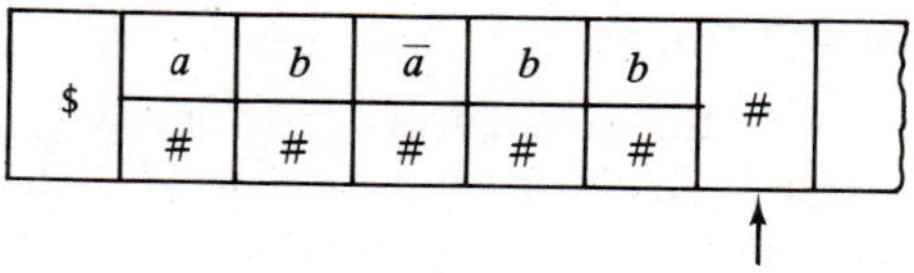

into the following.

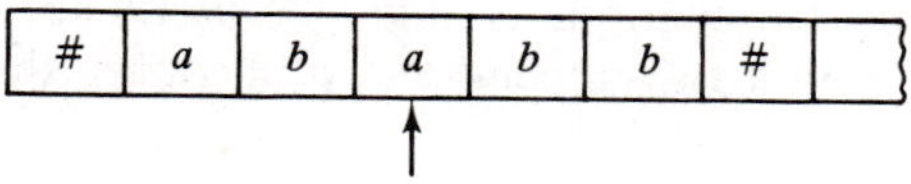

4.5.3. Formally define:

(a) a k-**tape Turing machine**;

(b) a **configuration** of such a machine;

(c) the **yields in one step** relation between configurations for such a machine.

4.5.4. Describe *carefully* the sequence of actions to be taken during

(a) Step 2;

(b) Step 3;

of the machine described in the proof of Lemma 4.5.2. Then specify, as concisely and elegantly as you can, the full details of this machine. (*Hint:* You may find it easiest, in Step 2, to have the machine make k sweeps up and down the tape, rather than trying to update all the tracks in one or two sweeps.)

4.5.5. Formally define:

(a) M **accepts** L, where M is a two-way infinite tape Turing machine;

(b) M **computes** f, where M is a k-tape Turing machine and f is a function from strings to strings.

4.5.6. Formally define:

(a) a k-**head Turing machine** (with a single one-way infinite tape);

(b) a **configuration** of such a machine;

(c) the **yields in one step** relation $\vdash_M$ between configurations of such a machine.

(There is more than one correct set of definitions.)

4.5.7. Describe, informally but carefully, 2-head Turing machines that compute:

(a) the function f: $\{a, b\}^* \longrightarrow \{a, b\}^*$ such that $f(w) = ww$;

(b) the monus function $f(n, m) = n \dot{-} m$.

4.5.8. Show how to construct, for any Turing machine M_1, a Turing machine M_2 such that if M_1 halts on input w, then M_2 halts on input w in the same configuration; and if M_1 does not halt on input w, then M_2 neither halts nor hangs on input w. (In other words, show that "hanging" can be detected and eliminated from Turing machines without otherwise altering their function.)

4.5.9. For some kinds of computations it might be useful for a Turing machine to operate on a two-dimensional grid, rather than a one-dimensional tape.

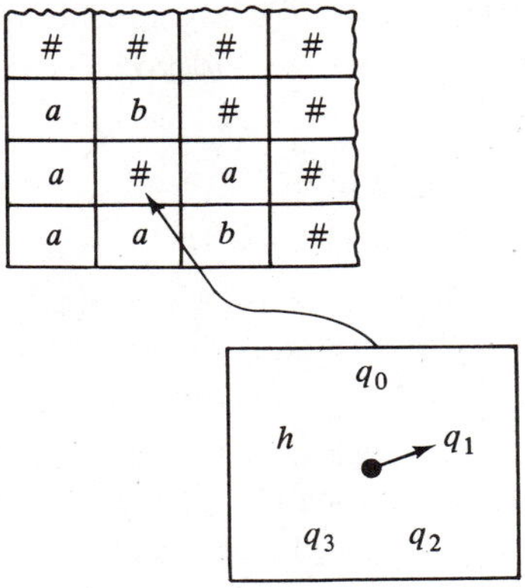

The machine has a single head that can be used for reading and writing in grid cells; on any one step, it can move that head one square up, down, left, or right. Input is supplied as a string on the bottom row of grid squares; the rest of the grid is initially blank.

(a) Define a **two-dimensional Turing machine**, the notion of a **configuration** for such a machine, the relation $\vdash_M$ between configurations of such a machine, and the notion that such a machine **computes** a particular function from strings to strings.

(b) Give an example of a function more conveniently computed by a two-dimensional Turing machine than by a one-dimensional Turing machine.

(c) Explain, carefully but informally, how any two-dimensional Turing machine can be simulated by a standard Turing machine.

4.5.10. Many authors allow a Turing machine both to move the head and to write a symbol at the same time. For them, a Turing machine is a quadruple (K, Σ, δ, s), where K, Σ, and s are as we defined, but δ is a function from $K \times \Sigma$ to $(K \cup \{h\}) \times \Sigma \times \{L, R, S\}$ (S meaning "stay in the same place").

(a) Define carefully the relation $\vdash$ between configurations for these more general machines.

(b) Explain precisely how to convert one of these machines into a Turing machine of the standard type used in this book.

4.6.1. What might be a reasonable definition of "M computes $f: \Sigma_0^* \longrightarrow \Sigma_1^*$," where M is a nondeterministic Turing machine? Can you give an example of a function more conveniently computed by a nondeterministic Turing machine than by a deterministic one?

4.6.2. Describe nondeterministic Turing machines that accept these languages.

(a) $a^*abb^*baa^*$

(b) $\{ww^Ruu^R: w, u \in \{a, b\}^*\}$

(c) $\{I^n: \text{for some } p, q \geq 0, n = p^2 + q^2\}$

4.6.3. Carefully define the notion of a **machine schema** for a nondeterministic Turing machine and the machine represented by such a schema, in the style of Definitions 4.3.1 and 4.3.2.

4.6.4. Strengthen Lemma 4.6.1 as follows: For every nondeterministic Turing machine M_1, we can construct a standard Turing machine M_2 such that for any string w not containing a blank,

(a) if M_1 halts on input w, then M_2 halts on input w in some configuration in which M_1 would have halted;

(b) if M_1 does not halt on input w, then M_2 does not halt on input w.

4.6.5. Trace each of the following.

(a) The operation of the machine $\mathcal{S}$ of Lemma 4.6.1 when the first tape contains $\#ab\underline{\#}$ and the second tape contains $\$b\underline{c}d$.

(b) The operation of the machine $\mathcal{G}$ of Lemma 4.6.1 when $r = 3$ and the third tape contains:

(i) $d_1d_2d_3\underline{\#}$;

(ii) $d_3d_3\underline{\#}$.

4.6.6. Describe modifications to the construction of Lemma 4.6.1 so that it will be correct even if M_1 may hang. Where might the proof as stated go awry if M_1 hangs?

4.6.7. Let $M = (K, \Sigma, \Delta, s)$ be the following nondeterministic Turing machine.

$$K = \{q_0, q_1\}$$
$$\Sigma = \{\#, a\}$$
$$s = q_0$$
$$\Delta = \{(q_0, \#, q_1, a), (q_0, \#, q_1, \#), (q_1, \#, q_1, \#), (q_1, a, q_0, R), (q_1, a, h, R)\}$$

Describe all possible computations of five steps or less by M starting from the configuration $(q_0, \underline{\#})$. Explain in words what M does in general when started from this configuration.

REFERENCES

Turing machines were first conceived by Turing:

A. M. TURING, "On Computable Numbers, with an Application to the Entscheidungsproblem," *Proceedings, London Mathematical Society*, 2, no. 42 (1936), 230–265, and no. 43, 544–546.

Turing introduced this model in order to argue that all detailed sets of instructions that can be carried out by a human calculator can also be carried out by a suitably defined simple machine. For the record, Turing's original machine has one two-way infinite tape and one head (see Section 4.5). A similar model was independently conceived by Post; see

E. L. POST, "Finite Combinatory Processes. Formulation I," *Journal of Symbolic Logic*, 1 (1936), 103–105.

The following books contain interesting introductions to Turing machines:

M. L. MINSKY, *Computation: Finite and Infinite Machines.* Englewood Cliffs, N.J.: Prentice-Hall, 1967.

F. C. HENNIE, *Introduction to Computability.* Reading, Mass.: Addison-Wesley, 1977.

Our notion and notation for combining Turing machines (Section 4.3) was influenced by

H. HERMES, *Enumerability, Decidability, Computability.* New York: Springer Verlag, 1969 (translated from the German edition, 1965).

The following are other advanced books on Turing machines and related concepts introduced in this and the two subsequent chapters:

M. DAVIS, ed., *The Undecidable.* Hewlett, N.Y.: Raven Press, 1965. (This book contains many original articles on several aspects of the subject, including the papers of Turing and Post cited above.)

M. DAVIS, *Computability and Unsolvability.* New York: McGraw-Hill, 1958.

S. C. KLEENE, *Introduction to Metamathematics.* Princeton, N.J.: D. Van Nostrand, 1952.

W. S. BRAINERD and L. H. LANDWEBER, *Theory of Computation.* New York: John Wiley, 1974.

M. MACHTEY and P. R. YOUNG, *An Introduction to the General Theory of Algorithms.* New York: Elsevier North-Holland, 1978.

H. ROGERS, JR., *The Theory of Recursive Functions and Effective Computability.* New York: McGraw-Hill, 1967.

CHAPTER 5

CHURCH'S THESIS

5.1 CHURCH'S THESIS

The main purpose of this book is to come to grips, from a formal, mathematical viewpoint, with the idea of computation. For the most part, the approach we have taken thus far is to regard computation as something done by computers. We have therefore attempted to formalize the idea of a *machine*. Our abstract model of a machine is an automaton: a device with a finite number of distinguishable internal states which operates on a string of symbols in accordance with a fixed finite set of rules. We started with very simple devices of this sort, the finite automata, and then introduced more powerful devices, the pushdown automata and Turing machines, which have memory units where unlimited quantities of information can be saved for subsequent retrieval.

We have seen that Turing machines can be designed to accept quite complicated languages and to calculate the values of nontrivial arithmetical functions. You should be convinced (or will be shortly, if you are not already) that by further compounding the methods already used, it is possible to design Turing machines to carry out even more complex operations. On the other hand, we have also seen that certain additional features that we might consider adding to the basic model do not increase the power of Turing machines. This testifies to the intrinsic power of the basic model, but it also suggests that we have reached a natural upper limit on what a computing machine can be designed to do. This is not to deny that there are aspects of "real-life" computing not captured by the Turing machine model. We have not yet, for example, approached the question of computational efficiency; the methods used by Turing machines surely seem laborious and indirect by comparison with those used on conventional computers. We shall take up this particular issue in Chapter 7.

Nevertheless, if we restrict our attention solely to the question of which languages are or are not decidable and which functions are or are not computable, then any extension of the basic Turing machine model that has been proposed has been shown to be reducible to the basic model. Of course, we are considering only those extensions made "in the same spirit" as the ideas that directed the original design of the Turing machine: The operations must be of a type which could, in principle, be carried out with a finite amount of labor at each step. Under the rules of the game we have been playing, we would not allow a species of automaton which could find the answer to any one of an infinite set of questions in a single step. Unbounded computational power can be achieved only by applying finite resources over an unlimited period of time.

Because the Turing machines can carry out any computation that can be carried out by any similar type of automata, and because these automata seem to capture the essential features of real computing machines, we take the Turing machine to be a precise formal equivalent of the intuitive notion of "algorithm": nothing will be considered an algorithm if it cannot be rendered as a Turing machine. The principle that Turing machines are formal versions of algorithms and that no computational procedure will be considered an algorithm unless it can be presented as a Turing machine is known as Church's Thesis or the Church-Turing Thesis. It is a thesis, not a theorem, because it is not a mathematical result: It simply asserts that a certain informal concept corresponds to a certain mathematical object. It is theoretically possible, however, that Church's Thesis could be overthrown at some future date, if someone were to propose an alternative model of computation that was publicly acceptable as fulfilling the requirement of "finite labor at each step" and yet was provably capable of carrying out computations that cannot be carried out by any Turing machine. No one considers this likely.

But are automata, whether Turing machines or of some other kind, the only possible approach to the idea of computation? Indeed not, and in this chapter we take up two alternatives. The first generalizes an idea we have already pursued in relation specifically to the context-free languages: the idea of a language-generating device or a grammar. We shall show that, just as the context-free grammars are capable of generating all the languages that pushdown automata can accept, there is a more general class of grammars that are as powerful as Turing machines. As general as Turing machines seem to be as computers, they are no more general than systems for producing strings by repeatedly replacing substrings in accordance with fixed sets of rules.

We next make a more radical departure from the previous approaches to the idea of computation. Instead of considering computation from the standpoint of machines or grammars that manipulate strings, we examine a very simple method for defining functions from numbers to numbers. The general idea is that certain very simple functions, such as the successor function, should be regarded as computable; and that certain ways of combining computable functions, such as by composition, should always be regarded as yielding more computable functions, since it is easy to see how to compute the combination if one already knows how to compute the simpler functions. In this way we shall build up a variety of functions from numbers to numbers —called the **μ-recursive functions**—that we are intuitively inclined to accept as computable. But we then show that, as simple as were the basic functions from which we started, any computation that can be carried out by means of a grammar—and therefore, by implication, any computation that can be carried out by a Turing machine—can be imitated by a μ-recursive function.

Finally, we show that Turing machines can compute all the μ-recursive functions, thus completing a cycle of simulations:

> Turing machines can be imitated by grammars,
> which can be imitated by μ-recursive functions,
> which can be imitated by Turing machines.

The only possible conclusion is that *all these approaches to the idea of computation are equivalent.* This is Church's Thesis, extended now to methods quite different from those of the theory of automata.

We close the chapter by considering one aspect of computation by machines on which we have not previously touched: the idea that a single machine can be a general-purpose computer if its writable memory can be used for storing instructions. This notion, familiar to computer programmers, will turn out to be of great importance for the development in Chapter 6 of the theory of *un*computability. But for now, it will close out what might be considered the positive aspects of the theory of computation: the demonstration that certain simple and mathematically precise methods for specifying computations seem to be as general and powerful as those of real computing machines.

5.2 GRAMMARS

Let us recall the essential features of a context-free grammar. Such a language-generating device has an alphabet, V, which is divided into two parts, the set of terminal symbols, Σ, and the set of nonterminal symbols, $V - \Sigma$. It also has a finite set of rules, each of the form $A \rightarrow u$, where A is a nonterminal symbol and $u \in V^*$. It operates by starting from the start symbol S, a nonterminal, and repeatedly replacing the left-hand side of a rule by the corresponding right-hand side until no further such replacements can be made.

In a **grammar** (also called a **rewriting system** or an **unrestricted grammar**) all the same conventions apply, *except that the left-hand sides of rules need not consist of single nonterminals.* Instead, the left-hand side of a rule may consist of any string of terminals and nonterminals containing at least one nonterminal. A single step in a derivation entails removing the entire substring on the left-hand side of a rule and replacing it by the corresponding right-hand side. Before giving some examples, let us fix our definitions.

Definition 5.2.1

A **grammar** is a quadruple $G = (V, \Sigma, R, S)$, where

V is an alphabet;

$\Sigma \subseteq V$ is the set of **terminal** symbols and $V - \Sigma$ is called the set of **nonterminal** symbols;

$S \in V - \Sigma$ is the **start symbol**; and

R, the set of **rules**, is a finite subset of $(V^*(V - \Sigma)V^*) \times V^*$.

We write $u \underset{G}{\rightarrow} v$ if $(u, v) \in R$; we write $u \underset{G}{\Rightarrow} v$ if and only if, for some $w_1, w_2 \in V^*$ and some rule $u' \underset{G}{\rightarrow} v'$, $u = w_1 u' w_2$ and $v = w_1 v' w_2$. As usual, $\overset{*}{\underset{G}{\Rightarrow}}$ is the reflexive, transitive closure of $\underset{G}{\Rightarrow}$. A string $w \in \Sigma^*$ is **generated** by G if and only if $S \overset{*}{\underset{G}{\Rightarrow}} w$; and $L(G)$ is the set of all strings in Σ^* generated by G. We also use other terminology introduced originally for context-free grammars; for example, a **derivation** is a sequence of the form

$$w_0 \underset{G}{\Rightarrow} w_1 \underset{G}{\Rightarrow} \cdots \underset{G}{\Rightarrow} w_n.$$

Example 5.2.1

Any context-free grammar is a grammar; in fact, a context-free grammar is a grammar such that the left-hand side of each rule is a member of $V - \Sigma$, rather than $V^*(V - \Sigma)V^*$. Thus, in an unrestricted grammar, a rule might have the form $uAv \longrightarrow uwv$, which could be read "replace A by w in the context with u on the left and v on the right." Of course, the rules of a grammar may be of a form even more general than this; but it turns out that any language that can be generated by a grammar can be generated by one in which all rules are of this "context-dependent replacement" type (Problem 5.2.9).

Example 5.2.2

Let us design a grammar G that generates $\{w \in \{a, b, c\}^* : w$ has equal numbers of a's, b's, and c's$\}$. The grammar G has nonterminals S (the start symbol) and A, B, and C (which stand for an a, a b, and a c, respectively). To begin with, G has the "context-free" rules

$$S \longrightarrow e$$

$$S \longrightarrow ABCS$$

which generate strings of the form $(ABC)^n$, $n \geq 0$. We must then introduce rules to permute the symbols A, B, and C in any order, and then change A, B, and C into a, b, and c, respectively. One set of rules that suffices is the following.

$$\begin{array}{ccc} AB \longrightarrow BA & AC \longrightarrow CA & BC \longrightarrow CB \\ BA \longrightarrow AB & CA \longrightarrow AC & CB \longrightarrow BC \\ A \longrightarrow a & B \longrightarrow b & C \longrightarrow c \end{array}$$

For example, the following is a derivation of *ccbaba*.

$$\begin{aligned} \underline{S} \Rightarrow ABC\underline{S} \Rightarrow ABCABC\underline{S} & \\ \Rightarrow\ & ABCA\underline{BC} \\ \Rightarrow\ & ABC\underline{AC}B \\ \Rightarrow\ & A\underline{BC}CAB \\ \Rightarrow\ & \underline{AC}BCAB \\ \Rightarrow\ & CA\underline{BC}AB \\ \Rightarrow\ & C\underline{AC}BAB \\ \Rightarrow\ & CC\underline{AB}AB \\ \Rightarrow\ & CCBA\underline{AB} \\ \Rightarrow\ & \underline{C}CBABA \\ \Rightarrow\ & c\underline{C}BABA \\ \Rightarrow\ & cc\underline{B}ABA \\ \Rightarrow\ & ccb\underline{A}BA \\ \Rightarrow\ & ccba\underline{B}A \\ \Rightarrow\ & ccbab\underline{A} \\ \Rightarrow\ & ccbaba \end{aligned}$$

We have underlined the substring to be replaced at each step.

Example 5.2.3

The following grammar G generates all strings of the form $\{a^{2^n}: n \geq 0\}$: $G = (V, \Sigma, R, S)$, where

$$V = \{[,], A, D, S, a\},$$
$$\Sigma = \{a\},$$
$$R = \{S \longrightarrow [A],$$
$$[\longrightarrow [D,$$
$$D] \longrightarrow],$$
$$DA \longrightarrow AAD,$$
$$[\longrightarrow e,$$
$$] \longrightarrow e,$$
$$A \longrightarrow a\}.$$

Intuitively, this grammar operates as follows. Starting from S, the string $[A]$ is produced via the rule $S \longrightarrow [A]$, and then the string $[D^nA]$ is produced by $n \geq 0$ applications of the rule $[\longrightarrow [D$. The D's are "doublers"; every time one passes over an A, from left to right, it replaces that one A by two (by the rule $DA \longrightarrow AAD$). So when all the D's have worked their way to the right end, the string $[D^nA]$ has become $[A^{2^n}D^n]$. The D's can then be "absorbed" by the rule $D] \longrightarrow]$, leaving $[A^{2^n}]$; finally, [and] are erased by the rules $[\longrightarrow e$, $] \longrightarrow e$, and the A's are converted to a's. So G generates all strings of the form a^{2^n}.

We must also show that no string in $\{a\}^*$ not of the form a^{2^n} can be generated by G. The number of D's in the intermediate strings is changed only when the rules $[\longrightarrow [D$ and $D] \longrightarrow]$ are applied, and the symbols [and] can appear only once each, at the left and right ends of the string. If the rule $] \longrightarrow e$ is applied prematurely (before all the D's have been eliminated), no string of terminals can be produced. So the only way to produce a string of terminals is to have all the D's produced at the left end work their way through the A's and disappear at the right end; this process leaves the string in the form

$$\{[, e\}\{A, a\}^{2^n}\{]\}$$

where n is the number of D's produced. The only string of terminals that can be produced is then a^{2^n}.

Evidently, complex computations can be carried out by grammars, even though their operation cannot be controlled in the same way that the operation of a Turing machine can be controlled. We now see that, in a natural sense, *every* Turing machine can be simulated by a grammar. To do so, we start from any Turing machine and represent its configurations as strings; we then construct a grammar that can derive one of these strings from another if and only if the corresponding configurations stand in the "yields" ($\vdash^*$) relation of the Turing machine. This construction is put to immediate use below, to derive a grammatical characterization of the Turing-computable functions, and again in the next chapter, in relation to the Turing-acceptable languages.

Lemma 5.2.1. *Let $M = (K, \Sigma, \delta, s)$ be any Turing machine. Then there is a grammar G such that for any configurations (q, u, a, v) and (q', u', a', v') of M,*

$$(q, u, a, v) \vdash_M^* (q', u', a', v')$$

if and only if

$$[uqav] \overset{*}{\underset{G}{\Rightarrow}} [u'q'a'v'].$$

Here [and] are new symbols not in Σ or K, and it is assumed that K and Σ are disjoint.

Proof. Clearly, the general idea is to represent the configuration (q, u, a, v) by the string $[uqav]$; note that the position of the state within the string also serves as an indication of the head position. This arrangement makes it possible for the left-hand side of each rule to contain as a substring a state and the scanned symbol; except for details related to movement on and off blank tape, only the state, scanned symbol, and head position need be changed when passing from one represented configuration to the next. The symbols [and] appear only at the ends of the representation of a configuration; the symbol] is used to help handle the blank tape detail, while the symbol [is included here only for legibility.

Formally, $G = (V, \Sigma, R, S)$ (the start symbol plays no role in the condition G is required to fulfill), where

$$V = K \cup \Sigma \cup \{[,], h, S\}$$

and R contains the following rules:

(a) For any $q \in K$ and $a \in \Sigma$, if $\delta(q, a) = (p, b)$, where $p \in K \cup \{h\}$ and $b \in \Sigma$, then R contains

$$qa \longrightarrow pb.$$

(b) For any $q \in K$ and $a \in \Sigma$, if $\delta(q, a) = (p, R)$, where $p \in K \cup \{h\}$, then R contains

$$qab \longrightarrow apb$$

for each $b \in \Sigma$, and

$$qa] \longrightarrow ap\#].$$

(c) For any $q \in K$ and $a \in \Sigma$, if $\delta(q, a) = (p, L)$, where $p \in K \cup \{h\}$, then R contains

$$bqac \longrightarrow pbac,$$

for every $b \in \Sigma$ and $c \in \Sigma \cup \{]\}$, such that $a \neq \#$ or $c \neq]$; and

$$bq\#] \longrightarrow pb],$$

for each $b \in \Sigma$, if $a = \#$.

We claim that $(q, u, a, v) \vdash_M (q', u', a', v')$ if and only if $[uqav] \underset{G}{\Rightarrow} [u'q'a'v']$; if this is true, the same will hold for the reflexive, transitive closures $\vdash_M^*$ and $\overset{*}{\underset{G}{\Rightarrow}}$, as asserted in the statement of the lemma. The proof is entirely straightforward and is structured according to the cases in the definition of $\vdash_M$ (Problem 5.2.4). ■

Example 5.2.4

Let $M = (\{q_0, q_1\}, \{a, \#\}, \delta, q_0)$, where δ is given by the following table.

q	σ	$\delta(q, \sigma)$
q_0	a	(q_1, R)
q_0	$\#$	(q_0, a)
q_1	a	(q_0, L)
q_1	$\#$	(q_1, a)

Then the associated grammar G is $(V, \{a, \#\}, R, S)$, where $V = \{q_0, q_1, a, \#, [,], h, S\}$ and R contains the following rules.

(a) 1. $q_0\# \longrightarrow q_0a$
2. $q_1\# \longrightarrow q_1a$

(b) 1. $q_0aa \longrightarrow aq_1a$
2. $q_0a\# \longrightarrow aq_1\#$
3. $q_0a] \longrightarrow aq_1\#]$

(c) 1. $aq_1aa \longrightarrow q_0aaa$
2. $\#q_1aa \longrightarrow q_0\#aa$
3. $aq_1a\# \longrightarrow q_0aa\#$
4. $\#q_1a\# \longrightarrow q_0\#a\#$
5. $aq_1a] \longrightarrow q_0aa]$
6. $\#q_1a] \longrightarrow q_0\#a]$

A computation by M, starting from $(q_0, \#)$, is

$$(q_0, \#) \vdash_M (q_0, \underline{a}) \vdash_M (q_1, a\#) \vdash_M (q_1, a\underline{a}) \vdash_M (q_0, \underline{a}a).$$

The corresponding derivation in G is

$$[q_0\#] \underset{G}{\Rightarrow} [q_0a] \underset{G}{\Rightarrow} [aq_1\#] \underset{G}{\Rightarrow} [aq_1a] \underset{G}{\Rightarrow} [q_0aa];$$

the rules used are (a1), (b3), (a2), and (c5), in that order.

Grammars were introduced as *language-generating devices*. Lemma 5.2.1 indicates that, quite aside from the particular question of which strings of terminal symbols can be derived from the start symbol of a grammar, the general question of deriving one string from another is intimately related to that of when one Turing machine configuration is yielded by another. Accordingly, it is possible to view grammars—like Turing machines—as *computers of functions*. In this chapter our test of computational power is the ability to compute all the Turing-computable functions, so we must adopt a convention for the computation of functions by grammars.

Definition 5.2.2

(a) Let Σ_0 and Σ_1 be alphabets not containing $\#$, and let f be any function from Σ_0^* to Σ_1^*. Then f will be called **grammatically computable** if and only if there is a grammar $G = (V, \Sigma, R, S)$, where $\Sigma_0, \Sigma_1 \subseteq \Sigma$, and there are strings $x, y, x', y' \in V^*$ such that for any $u \in \Sigma_0^*$, $v \in \Sigma_1^*$,

$$f(u) = v$$

if and only if

$$xuy \overset{*}{\underset{G}{\Rightarrow}} x'vy'.$$

In this case we say that G **computes** f.

(b) Let f be any function from $\mathbb{N}$ to $\mathbb{N}$. Then f will be said to be **grammatically computable** if the function $f': \{I\}^* \to \{I\}^*$ is grammatically computable, where

$$f'(I^n) = I^{f(n)} \qquad \text{for each } n \in \mathbb{N}.$$

Thus a grammar is said to compute a function f from strings to strings if two pairs of "endmarkers" x, y and x', y' can be associated with the grammar so that the following holds: For any string u in the domain of f, if u is surrounded by the first pair of endmarkers x, y, then the one and only derivable string of the form $x'vy'$ is that with $v = f(u)$. For computing a function from numbers to numbers, unary encoding is used, as for Turing machines (Section 4.2). Note that the start symbol S plays no role in these definitions.

Example 5.2.5

Let $\Sigma_0 = \{a, b\}$ and let $f: \Sigma_0^* \longrightarrow \Sigma_0^*$ be defined by $f(w) = w^R$. Then f is computed by the grammar (V, Σ_0, R, S), where $V = \{a, b, A, B, *, S, [,]\}$, and R is as follows.

1. $[a \longrightarrow [A, \quad [b \longrightarrow [B$
2. $Aa \longrightarrow aA, \quad Ab \longrightarrow bA, \quad Ba \longrightarrow aB, \quad Bb \longrightarrow bB$
3. $A* \longrightarrow *a, \quad B* \longrightarrow *b$

Let x, y, x', and y' be the strings $[$, $*]$, $[*$, and $]$, respectively. G computes f as follows: Starting from a string $[w*]$, where $w \in \Sigma_0^*$, rules of types 1 and 2 are used to convert terminal symbols (a, b) from the left end of w into the corresponding nonterminals (A, B) and send them off towards the right. As these symbols reach the right end, they are converted back into terminals and the $*$ is used to keep them segregated from the left-hand part of the string; once a symbol has "crossed" the $*$ from left to right, it remains unchanged. Here is a sample derivation of $[*w^R]$ from $[w*]$, marked with the rules used.

$[abb*] \Rightarrow [Abb*]$	Rule 1
$\Rightarrow [bAb*]$	Rule 2
$\Rightarrow [bbA*]$	Rule 2
$\Rightarrow [bb*a]$	Rule 3
$\Rightarrow [Bb*a]$	Rule 1
$\Rightarrow [bB*a]$	Rule 2
$\Rightarrow [BB*a]$	Rule 1
$\Rightarrow [B*ba]$	Rule 3
$\Rightarrow [*bba]$	Rule 3

Theorem 5.2.1. *Every Turing-computable function from strings to strings, or from numbers to numbers, is grammatically computable.*

Proof. Consider first the case of strings. Let $f: \Sigma_0^* \longrightarrow \Sigma_1^*$ be Turing-computable. Then by Definition 4.2.1, there is a Turing machine (K, Σ, δ, s) such that, for any $u \in \Sigma_0^*$, $f(u) = v$ if and only if

$$(s, \#u, \#, e) \vdash_M^* (h, \#v, \#, e).$$

Apply the construction of Lemma 5.2.1 to M, thus obtaining a grammar G, and let x, y, x', and y' be as follows.

$$x = [\#$$
$$y = s\#]$$
$$x' = [\#$$
$$y' = h\#]$$

Then G, x, y, x', and y' are exactly as required.

Exactly the same argument can be used to establish that any Turing-computable function from numbers to numbers is grammatically computable, since we have adopted the convention that both Turing machines and grammars compute functions from numbers to numbers by computing the corresponding functions from strings to strings on the unary encodings of numbers. ■

5.3 THE PRIMITIVE RECURSIVE FUNCTIONS

We shall temporarily move away from the idea of computation as a process on strings. By a *function* we shall now mean a function from $\mathbb{N}^k$ to $\mathbb{N}$ for some $k \geq 0$; such a function will be called **k-place**. We define a large class of such functions, called the μ-recursive functions, each of which is computable in the intuitive sense. By means of an encoding technique, called *Gödel numbering*, we shall show that numbers may be taken as representations of strings, and that any function from strings to strings that is grammatically computable as defined in Definition 5.2.2 can be translated into a μ-recursive function from and to the numerical encodings of strings. The claim that all Turing-computable functions are μ-recursive will then be justified: Given a function from strings to strings that is computed by a Turing machine, we find an equivalent grammar by the method of Theorem 5.2.1, and then use the numerical encoding of strings to compute that function as a μ-recursive function from numbers to numbers.

The methods available for defining μ-recursive functions are very simple, and just as some development was required in Chapter 4 to show that Turing machines were capable of nontrivial calculations, so it will take some time here to show how simple μ-recursive functions can be compounded to yield more complex ones. In fact, we start by considering at some length a proper subset of the μ-recursive functions, called the **primitive recursive functions**; the step from the primitive recursive to the μ-recursive functions is taken in Section 5.5.

The primitive recursive functions are defined by three types of *initial functions* and two *combining rules*. These can all be presented in a straightforward manner.

Definition 5.3.1

The Initial Functions.

(a) The **0-place zero function** ζ is the function from $\mathbb{N}^0$ to $\mathbb{N}$ such that

$$\zeta(\,) = 0.$$

(b) Let $k \geq 1$ and let $1 \leq i \leq k$. Then the ***i*th *k*-place projection function** π_i^k is the function from $\mathbb{N}^k$ to $\mathbb{N}$ such that

$$\pi_i^k(n_1, \ldots, n_k) = n_i \qquad \text{for any } n_1, \ldots, n_k \in \mathbb{N}.$$

Point of notation: Hereafter we write $\bar{n}$ for the sequence $n_1, \ldots, n_k$; sometimes k may be zero. We may also write $\bar{n}$ for the k-tuple $(n_1, \ldots, n_k)$. Thus the above statement would be rewritten

$$\pi_i^k(\bar{n}) = n_i \qquad \text{for any } \bar{n} \in \mathbb{N}^k.$$

(c) The **successor function** σ is the function from $\mathbb{N}$ to $\mathbb{N}$ such that

$$\sigma(n) = n + 1 \qquad \text{for each } n \in \mathbb{N}.$$

(d) An **initial function** is ζ, σ, or one of the π_i^k.

Definition 5.3.2

Composition and Primitive Recursion.

(a) Let $l > 0$ and $k \geq 0$, let g be an l-place function, and let $h_1, \ldots, h_l$ be k-place functions. Let f be the k-place function such that, for every $\bar{n} \in \mathbb{N}^k$,

$$f(\bar{n}) = g(h_1(\bar{n}), \ldots, h_l(\bar{n})).$$

Then f is said to be obtained from $g, h_1, \ldots, h_l$ by **composition**.

(b) Let $k \geq 0$, let g be a k-place function, and let h be a $(k + 2)$-place function. Let f be the $(k + 1)$-place function such that for every $\bar{n} \in \mathbb{N}^k$,

$$f(\bar{n}, 0) = g(\bar{n});$$

and for every $\bar{n} \in \mathbb{N}^k$ and $m \in \mathbb{N}$,

$$f(\bar{n}, m + 1) = h(\bar{n}, m, f(\bar{n}, m)).$$

Then f is said to be obtained from g and h by **primitive recursion.**

Definition 5.3.3

The Primitive Recursive Functions. A function is **primitive recursive** if it is an initial function or can be generated from the initial functions by some sequence of the operations of composition and primitive recursion. More succinctly, the primitive recursive functions are the smallest class of functions containing the initial functions and closed under composition and primitive recursion.

Before investigating the primitive recursive functions in a systematic way, let us look at some very simple examples.

Example 5.3.1

(a) The function $\sigma^2 : \mathbb{N} \to \mathbb{N}$ such that $\sigma^2(n) = n + 2$ for each $n \in \mathbb{N}$ is primitive recursive. For if we let $k = l = 1$ and $g = h_1 = \sigma$, the successor function, in the definition of composition we find that $\sigma^2(n) = g(h_1(n)) = \sigma(\sigma(n))$. Since σ is an initial function, it is primitive recursive, and since σ^2 is obtained from primitive recursive functions by composition, it too is primitive recursive.

(b) Let $\sigma_3 : \mathbb{N}^3 \to \mathbb{N}$ be defined by $\sigma_3(n_1, n_2, n_3) = n_3 + 1$ for all n_1, $n_2, n_3 \in \mathbb{N}$. Then σ_3 is primitive recursive. For if we let $l = 1$; $k = 3$; $h_1 = \pi_3^3$, the third 3-place projection function; and $g = \sigma$, the successor function; then

$$\sigma_3(n_1, n_2, n_3) = g(h_1(n_1, n_2, n_3)) = \sigma(\pi_3^3(n_1, n_2, n_3)) = n_3 + 1.$$

Thus σ_3 is obtained by composition from σ and π_3^3, which are already primitive recursive, and therefore σ_3 itself is primitive recursive.

(c) Let $\text{plus}(n_1, n_2) = n_1 + n_2$. Then plus is primitive recursive. Let $k = 1$; let $g = \pi_1^1$, the first 1-place projection function (that is, the identity function); and let h be the function σ_3 of the previous example. Then plus is obtained from g and h by primitive recursion, since

$$\text{plus}(n, 0) = g(n) = \pi_1^1(n) = n$$

and

$$\begin{aligned}\text{plus}(n, m + 1) &= \sigma_3(n, m, \text{plus}(n, m)) \\ &= \sigma(n + m) = n + m + 1\end{aligned}$$

for all $n, m \in \mathbb{N}$.

(d) Let $\text{plus-3}(n_1, n_2, n_3) = n_1 + n_2 + n_3$. Then plus-3 is primitive recursive; it can be written as

$$\text{plus-3}(n_1, n_2, n_3) = \text{plus}(\pi_1^3(n_1, n_2, n_3), \text{plus}(\pi_2^3(n_1, n_2, n_3), \pi_3^3(n_1, n_2, n_3))).$$

What justifies the notion that, on the intuitive level, every primitive recursive function is computable? The initial functions must surely be viewed as computable. If f is obtained from $g, h_1, \ldots, h_l$ by composition and $g, h_1, \ldots, h_l$ are already known to be computable, then $f(\bar{n})$ can be evaluated by first computing $h_1(\bar{n}), \ldots, h_l(\bar{n})$, yielding, let us say, values $m_1, \ldots, m_l$, and then computing $g(m_1, \ldots, m_l)$. Similarly, if f is obtained from g and h by primitive recursion and g and h are already known to be computable, then $f(\bar{n}, m)$ can be evaluated as follows.

- First compute $f(\bar{n}, 0)$, that is, $g(\bar{n})$. If $m = 0$, we are done. Otherwise, let $g(\bar{n}) = p_0$.
- Compute $f(\bar{n}, 1)$, that is, $h(\bar{n}, 0, p_0)$. Call the result p_1. If $m = 1$, we are done. Otherwise, continue.
- Compute $f(\bar{n}, 2)$, that is, $h(\bar{n}, 1, p_1) \ldots$.

By using each computed value to aid in the next computation, the value of $f(\bar{n}, m)$ can eventually be calculated.

Let us now undertake to study the primitive recursive functions in a more systematic way.

Definition 5.3.4

Constant Functions. For every $k \geq 0$ and $j \geq 0$, we define the **jth k-place constant function** $K_j^k : \mathbb{N}^k \longrightarrow \mathbb{N}$ by $K_j^k(\bar{n}) = j$ for any $\bar{n} \in \mathbb{N}^k$.

Lemma 5.3.1. *The constant functions are all primitive recursive.*

Proof.

$k = 0$: K_0^0 is ζ, which is an initial function;

$$K_{j+1}^0(\ ) = \sigma(K_j^0(\ )) \qquad \text{for each } j \geq 0,$$

so K_{j+1}^0 is obtained from σ and K_j^0 by composition.

$k > 0$: If we have shown for some k that K_j^k is primitive recursive for all $j \geq 0$, then we can also show that K_j^{k+1} is primitive recursive for all $j \geq 0$. For

$$K_j^{k+1}(\bar{n}, 0) = K_j^k(\bar{n})$$
$$K_j^{k+1}(\bar{n}, m + 1) = \pi_{k+2}^{k+2}(\bar{n}, m, K_j^{k+1}(\bar{n}, m))$$

so K_j^{k+1} is obtained from K_j^k and π_{k+2}^{k+2} by primitive recursion. ■

Definition 5.3.5

Let g be a k-place function, and f an l-place function, with $k, l \geq 0$. Suppose that there are functions $h_1, \ldots, h_k : \mathbb{N}^l \longrightarrow \mathbb{N}$, each of which is either one of the l-place projection functions or one of the l-place constant functions, such that for any $\bar{n} \in \mathbb{N}^l$,

$$f(\bar{n}) = g(h_1(\bar{n}), \ldots, h_k(\bar{n})).$$

Then f is said to be obtained from g by **explicit transformation**.

In other words, f is obtained from g by explicit transformation if f is obtained from g by duplicating, permuting, or substituting constant values for arguments of g.

Example 5.3.2

Since plus-3 is primitive recursive (Example 5.3.1(d)), so is the function $f: \mathbb{N} \longrightarrow \mathbb{N}$ such that $f(n) = 2n + 17$; for $f(n) = \text{plus-3}(n, n, 17)$ for any $n \in \mathbb{N}$. Formally, let $k = 3$, $l = 1$, $h_1 = h_2 = \pi_1^1$, and $h_3 = K_{17}^1$ in Definition 5.3.5.

Lemma 5.3.2. *If g is primitive recursive, then so is any function obtained from g by explicit transformation.*

Proof. The lemma follows immediately, since the projection and constant functions are primitive recursive. ■

Explicit transformation enables us to be somewhat less rigid in our demonstrations that functions are primitive recursive.

Example 5.3.3

Consider the predecessor function V as defined below.

$$V(m) = \begin{cases} 0 & \text{if } m = 0 \\ m - 1 & \text{if } m > 0 \end{cases}$$

To show that V is primitive recursive, we write simply

$$V(0) = 0$$
$$V(m + 1) = m$$

instead of the more formal version

$$V(0) = K_0^0(\ )$$
$$V(m + 1) = \pi_1^2(m, V(m))$$

that shows explicitly how V is obtained from K_0^0 and π_1^2 by primitive recursion. In the same spirit, consider the function monus$(n, m) = n \dot{-} m$, defined as follows.

$$n \dot{-} m \quad \begin{cases} 0 & \text{if } n \leq m \\ n - m & \text{if } n > m \end{cases}$$

Here the informal demonstration is

$$n \dot{-} 0 = n$$
$$n \dot{-} (m + 1) = V(n \dot{-} m),$$

and the formal version is

$$\text{monus}(n, 0) = \pi_1^1(n)$$
$$\text{monus}(n, m + 1) = h(n, m, \text{monus}(n, m)),$$

where h is the primitive recursive function obtained from V and π_3^3 by composition as follows.

$$h(n_1, n_2, n_3) = V(\pi_3^3(n_1, n_2, n_3))$$

Example 5.3.4

The following functions are primitive recursive.

(a) The product $n \cdot m$:

$$n \cdot 0 = 0$$

$$n \cdot (m + 1) = n \cdot m + n$$

(b) The power n^m:

$$n^0 = 1$$

$$n^{m+1} = n^m \cdot n$$

(Here we define 0^0 to be 1.)

(c) The sign function sg, where

$$\text{sg}(m) = \begin{cases} 0 & \text{if } m = 0 \\ 1 & \text{if } m > 0 \end{cases}$$

$$\text{sg}(0) = 0$$

$$\text{sg}(m + 1) = 1.$$

Lemma 5.3.3. *Let $k \geq 0$. If g is any $(k + 1)$-place primitive recursive function, then so is f, where*

$$f(\bar{n}, m) = \prod_{i=0}^{m} g(\bar{n}, i) = g(\bar{n}, 0) \cdot g(\bar{n}, 1) \cdot \cdots \cdot g(\bar{n}, m).$$

(In this case we say that f is obtained from g by **bounded product**.)

Proof.

$$f(\bar{n}, 0) = g(\bar{n}, 0) \qquad \text{for any } \bar{n} \in \mathbb{N}^k$$

and

$$f(\bar{n}, m + 1) = f(\bar{n}, m) \cdot g(\bar{n}, m + 1) \qquad \text{for any } \bar{n} \text{ and } m. \quad \blacksquare$$

Example 5.3.5

The factorial function, $f(n) = n!$, is primitive recursive, since

$$n! = \prod_{i=1}^{n} i.$$

Definition 5.3.6

(a) By a **predicate** we mean a relation on the natural numbers, that is, a subset of $\mathbb{N}^k$ for some $k \geq 0$. Such a predicate will be said to be k-**place**. In general, we use uppercase letters for predicates, and write $P\bar{n}$ to indicate that $\bar{n} \in P$.

(b) The **characteristic function** of a k-place predicate P is that k-place function $f: \mathbb{N}^k \longrightarrow \{0, 1\}$ such that the following holds for each $\bar{n} \in \mathbb{N}^k$.

$$f(\bar{n}) = \begin{cases} 1 & \text{if } P\bar{n} \\ 0 & \text{if not } P\bar{n} \end{cases}$$

(c) A predicate is said to be **primitive recursive** if and only if its characteristic function is primitive recursive.

Example 5.3.6

The equality relation $=$ is primitive recursive, since its characteristic function is

$$\epsilon(n, m) = 1 \mathbin{\dot{-}} \mathrm{sg}((n \mathbin{\dot{-}} m) + (m \mathbin{\dot{-}} n)).$$

Likewise the less-than predicate $<$ is primitive recursive, since its characteristic function is

$$\lambda(m, n) = \mathrm{sg}(n \mathbin{\dot{-}} m).$$

We now show how primitive recursive predicates can be used for defining further primitive recursive predicates and primitive recursive functions.

If a predicate P is obtained from a predicate Q by duplicating, permuting, or substituting constant values for the arguments of Q, then P will be said to be obtained from Q by **explicit transformation**. (A formal definition would parallel Definition 5.3.5.)

Example 5.3.7

Let P be the 1-place predicate that holds for a number n if and only if $n = 17$. Then P is obtained from the equality predicate (Example 5.3.6) by explicit transformation.

Lemma 5.3.4. *If Q is primitive recursive, then so is any predicate obtained from Q by explicit transformation.*

Proof. The proof is left to the reader (see Problem 5.3.8). ■

Definition 5.3.7

Let $k, l \geq 0$. If Q is a k-place predicate and R is an l-place predicate, then their **conjunction** is the $(k + l)$-place predicate S such that

$$S\bar{n}\bar{m} \quad \text{if and only if} \quad Q\bar{n} \text{ and } R\bar{m} \qquad \text{for all } \bar{n} \in \mathbb{N}^k, \bar{m} \in \mathbb{N}^l.$$

(Here we write $\bar{m}$ for the sequence $m_1, \ldots, m_l$.) Similarly, their **disjunction** is the $(k + l)$-place predicate T such that

$$T\bar{n}\bar{m} \quad \text{if and only if} \quad Q\bar{n} \text{ or } R\bar{m} \qquad \text{for all } \bar{n} \in \mathbb{N}^k, \bar{m} \in \mathbb{N}^l.$$

Also, the **negation** of Q is the k-place relation P such that

$$P\bar{n} \quad \text{if and only if} \quad \text{not } Q\bar{n}.$$

Lemma 5.3.5. *If Q and R are primitive recursive predicates, then so are their conjunction and disjunction, and so is the negation of Q.*

Proof. If g and h are the primitive recursive characteristic functions of Q and R, then the characteristic functions of the conjunction of Q and R, the disjunction of Q and R, and the negation of Q are f_1, f_2, and f_3, respectively, where

$$f_1(\bar{n}, \bar{m}) = g(\bar{n}) \cdot h(\bar{m})$$
$$f_2(\bar{n}, \bar{m}) = \text{sg}(g(\bar{n}) + h(\bar{m}))$$
$$f_3(\bar{n}) = 1 \mathbin{\dot{-}} g(\bar{n}). \quad \blacksquare$$

Example 5.3.8

Since $=$ and $<$ are primitive recursive, so are all the predicates $=, <, >, \leq, \geq$, and $\neq$. For example, $n \leq m$ if and only if $n = m$ or $n < m$, so $\leq$ is the disjunction of $<$ and $=$.

The operations of conjunction and disjunction can be extended to combine more than two predicates. For example, we may be given three predicates R_1, R_2, and R_3, and we may wish to have a predicate R such that

$$R\bar{m}\bar{n}\bar{p} \qquad \text{if and only if} \qquad R_1\bar{m} \quad \text{and} \quad R_2\bar{n} \quad \text{and} \quad R_3\bar{p}.$$

Clearly any such predicate will be primitive recursive if the predicates from which it is formed are primitive recursive.

Definition 5.3.8

Let $k \geq 0$. If Q is a $(k + 1)$-place predicate, then its **bounded existential quantification** is the $(k + 1)$-place predicate R such that, for any $\bar{n} \in \mathbb{N}^k$ and $m \in \mathbb{N}$, $R\bar{n}m$ if and only if there is an i, $0 \leq i \leq m$, such that $Q\bar{n}i$. More succinctly, we write

$$R\bar{n}m \quad \text{if and only if} \quad \exists i \leq m[Q\bar{n}i].$$

Similarly, the **bounded universal quantification** of Q is that $(k + 1)$-place predicate S such that $S\bar{n}m$ if and only if for every i, $0 \leq i \leq m$, $Q\bar{n}i$ holds, or in brief,

$$S\bar{n}m \quad \text{if and only if} \quad \forall i \leq m[Q\bar{n}i].$$

Lemma 5.3.6. *If Q is primitive recursive, then so are its bounded existential and universal quantifications.*

Proof. If g is the primitive recursive characteristic function of Q, then the characteristic functions f_1 and f_2 of the bounded universal and existential quantifications of Q are

$$f_1(\bar{n}, m) = \prod_{i=0}^{m} g(\bar{n}, i)$$

and

$$f_2(\bar{n}, m) = 1 \dot{-} \prod_{i=0}^{m} (1 \dot{-} g(\bar{n}, i)),$$

respectively. ■

Example 5.3.9

The 4-place predicate $Pn_1n_2n_3k$ that is true if and only if $n_1^k + n_2^k \neq n_3^k$ is primitive recursive, since it is the negation of the predicate whose characteristic function is $\epsilon(n_1^k + n_2^k, n_3^k)$. Therefore the 1-place predicate Q that holds for k if and only if $n_1^k + n_2^k \neq n_3^k$ for all $n_1, n_2, n_3 \leq 1000$ is also primitive recursive; it is obtained by letting $n = 1000$ (explicit transformation) in the definition

$$\forall n_1 \leq n[\forall n_2 \leq n[\forall n_3 \leq n[n_1^k + n_2^k \neq n_3^k]]]$$

(bounded universal quantification, three times).

Lemma 5.3.7. *Let $g_1, \ldots, g_l$ be k-place primitive recursive functions ($k \geq 0, l \geq 2$), and let $P_1, \ldots, P_l$ be k-place primitive recursive predicates such that for every $\bar{n} \in \mathbb{N}^k$, exactly one of $P_1\bar{n}, \ldots, P_l\bar{n}$ holds. Then the k-place function f such that*

$$f(\bar{n}) = \begin{cases} g_1(\bar{n}) & \text{if } P_1\bar{n} \\ \cdot & \\ \cdot & \\ \cdot & \\ g_l(\bar{n}) & \text{if } P_l\bar{n} \end{cases}$$

is also primitive recursive. (The function f is said to be **defined by cases** *from $g_1, \ldots, g_l$ and $P_1, \ldots, P_l$.)*

Proof. If $P_1, \ldots, P_l$ have primitive recursive characteristic functions $h_1, \ldots, h_l$, then

$$f(\bar{n}) = g_1(\bar{n})\cdot h_1(\bar{n}) + \cdots + g_l(\bar{n})\cdot h_l(\bar{n}) \qquad \text{for all } \bar{n} \in \mathbb{N}^k.$$

(For every $\bar{n}$, one and only one of the summands will be nonzero.) ■

Example 5.3.10

Define $f\colon \mathbb{N} \to \mathbb{N}$ by

$$f(n) = \begin{cases} n^2 & \text{if } n \text{ is odd} \\ n^3 & \text{if } n \text{ is even.} \end{cases}$$

Then f is primitive recursive. Clearly g_1, where $g_1(n) = n^2$ for all n, and g_2, where $g_2(n) = n^3$ for all n, are primitive recursive. So are the predicates n *is odd* and n *is even*; they can be defined by

$$\exists m \leq n[n = 2 \cdot m + 1]$$

and

$$\exists m \leq n[n = 2 \cdot m],$$

respectively. (Note the way that the value of m has been bounded.) Thus f is defined by cases from primitive recursive functions and predicates.

Definition 5.3.9

Let $k \geq 0$, and let Q be a $(k + 1)$-place predicate. Then the **bounded minimalization** of Q is the $(k + 1)$-place function f such that

$$f(\bar{n}, m) = \begin{cases} \text{the smallest } p,\ 0 \leq p \leq m, \text{ such that } Q\bar{n}p, \\ \text{if there is such a } p \text{ in the range } 0, \ldots, m; \\ 0 \qquad \text{otherwise.} \end{cases}$$

(The second alternative is chosen arbitrarily; any other value would do as well.) We write $f(\bar{n}, m)$ as $\mu p \leq m[Q\bar{n}p]$.

Lemma 5.3.8. *If Q is primitive recursive, then so is its bounded minimalization.*

Proof. Let h be the $(k + 2)$-place function defined as follows.

$$h(\bar{n}, m, p) = \begin{cases} p & \text{if } \exists i \leq m[Q\bar{n}i] \\ m + 1 & \text{if } Q\,\bar{n}\,m{+}1 \text{ and not } \exists i \leq m[Q\bar{n}i] \\ 0 & \text{if not } \exists i \leq m + 1[Q\bar{n}i] \end{cases}$$

Then h is primitive recursive, being defined by cases from primitive recursive functions and predicates. But f is obtained from h (and a constant function) by primitive recursion:

$$f(\bar{n}, 0) = 0$$

$$f(\bar{n}, m + 1) = h(\bar{n}, m, f(\bar{n}, m)). \quad \blacksquare$$

Example 5.3.11

Let $f(n)$ be the least number between $n/2$ and n that can be expressed as a sum of two perfect nonzero cubes (that is, as $n_1^3 + n_2^3$ for some n_1,

$n_2 > 0$; $f(n) = 0$ if no such n_1, n_2 exist). Then f is primitive recursive, since

$$f(n) = \mu m \leq n[2m \geq n \text{ and } \exists n_1 \leq m[\exists n_2 \leq m[n_1 \neq 0 \text{ and } n_2 \neq 0 \text{ and } m = n_1^3 + n_2^3]]].$$

5.4 GÖDELIZATION

In order to demonstrate that the line of development pursued in the last section ultimately yields a class of functions that includes all the grammatically computable functions—and hence, by Theorem 5.2.1, all the Turing-computable functions—we must take two critical steps. The class of functions must be expanded; the primitive recursive functions are not enough. The reason for this need, and the method for expanding the class of functions under consideration, are explained in the next section. In this section we shall deal with the other missing link in the argument: How can functions from numbers to numbers be regarded as operating on strings?

We have already dealt with a similar problem. Turing machines and grammars are formal systems for operating on strings; and yet, when we wanted to regard them as operating on numbers, we were able to do so by encoding numbers as strings, using unary notation. In order to view the primitive recursive functions or the more general μ-recursive functions of the next section as operating on strings, we must adopt a convention for encoding strings as numbers. This type of encoding is called a *Gödel numbering*, after the logician Kurt Gödel (1906–1978).

There are many ways in which numbers might have been encoded as strings; we could use binary or decimal notation, for example, rather than unary notation. Similarly, there are many possible methods for representing strings as numbers. The one we adopt is very close to that used in conventional computers: we fix some correspondence between individual symbols and numbers, and then regard longer strings as numbers written in a positional notation, the "digits" being the individual symbols. In the data processing industry, the number of individual symbols is usually 256; a number less than 256 represents a single symbol, a number less than 256^2 represents a string of two symbols, and so on.

To see how this correspondence is carried through formally in our particular application, let Δ be any alphabet. Let $\beta = |\Delta| + 1$ and fix some ordering of the symbols in Δ, such as

$$\Delta = \{d_1, \ldots, d_{\beta-1}\}.$$

Each string in Δ^* can be viewed as an integer in base β notation. Specifically, we define a function gn: $\Delta^* \rightarrow \mathbb{N}$ as follows: If $w = d_{i_1} \ldots d_{i_k}$, where $k \geq 0$ and $1 \leq i_j \leq \beta - 1$ for $j = 1, \ldots, k$, then

$$\text{gn}(w) = \beta^{k-1} \cdot i_1 + \beta^{k-2} \cdot i_2 + \cdots + \beta^1 \cdot i_{k-1} + i_k.$$

In particular, $\text{gn}(e) = 0$. We say that $\text{gn}(w)$ is the **Gödel number** of the string w.

Note that gn is a true encoding of strings as numbers, in the sense that every string corresponds to exactly one number and no number corresponds to more than one string (Problem 5.4.5). However, gn is not, as it stands, a bijection: Certain numbers—β, for example—do not correspond to any string. To remedy this, we introduce a new symbol d_0 to correspond to the digit 0. Then gn can be extended in a natural way to become a bijection between $\{e\} \cup \Delta(\Delta \cup \{d_0\})^*$ and $\mathbb{N}$. Let $\mathfrak{D} = \{e\} \cup \Delta(\Delta \cup \{d_0\})^*$, that is, all the strings in $(\Delta \cup \{d_0\})^*$ that do not begin with d_0. Then gn^{-1} is a well-defined function from $\mathbb{N}$ to $\mathfrak{D}$, and $\Delta^* \subsetneq \mathfrak{D} \subsetneq (\Delta \cup \{d_0\})^*$.

Example 5.4.1

Let $\Delta = \{a, b, c\}$. Then $\beta = 4$. If we fix the correspondence

$$d_1 = a$$
$$d_2 = b$$
$$d_3 = c,$$

then

$$\text{gn}(e) = 0$$
$$\text{gn}(a) = \text{gn}(d_1) = 1$$
$$\text{gn}(ba) = \text{gn}(d_2 d_1) = 4^1 \cdot 2 + 1 = 9$$
$$\text{gn}(ccc) = \text{gn}(d_3 d_3 d_3) = 4^2 \cdot 3 + 4^1 \cdot 3 + 3 = 63.$$

The set $\mathfrak{D}$ contains e, a, ba, ccc; ad_0, bd_0a, and $cd_0d_0d_0$; and

$$\text{gn}(ad_0) = \text{gn}(d_1 d_0) = 4^1 \cdot 1 + 0 = 4$$
$$\text{gn}(bd_0a) = \text{gn}(d_2 d_0 d_1) = 4^2 \cdot 2 + 4 \cdot 0 + 1 = 33$$
$$\text{gn}(cd_0d_0d_0) = \text{gn}(d_3 d_0 d_0 d_0) = 4^3 \cdot 3 + 4^2 \cdot 0 + 4 \cdot 0 + 0 = 192.$$

On the other hand, $\mathfrak{D}$ does not contain d_0c or d_0 or d_0ad_0. The first few values of gn^{-1} are as follows.

$$\text{gn}^{-1}(0) = e$$
$$\text{gn}^{-1}(1) = d_1 \quad = a$$
$$\text{gn}^{-1}(2) = d_2 \quad = b$$
$$\text{gn}^{-1}(3) = d_3 \quad = c$$
$$\text{gn}^{-1}(4) = d_1 d_0 = ad_0$$
$$\text{gn}^{-1}(5) = d_1 d_1 = aa$$
$$\text{gn}^{-1}(6) = d_1 d_2 = ab$$
$$\text{gn}^{-1}(7) = d_1 d_3 = ac$$
$$\text{gn}^{-1}(8) = d_2 d_0 = bd_0$$

Lemma 5.4.1.

(a) *The length of a string* $w \in \mathfrak{D}$ *is the smallest number* l *such that* $\beta^l > \text{gn}(w)$.

(b) *If* $x, y \in \Delta^*$ *and* x *is a substring of* y, *then* $\text{gn}(x) \leq \text{gn}(y)$.

Proof.

(a) If $w \in \mathfrak{D}$, then $w = d_{i_1}d_{i_2} \ldots d_{i_l}$, where $0 \leq i_1, \ldots, i_l \leq \beta - 1$ and $i_1 > 0$. Then

$$\text{gn}(w) = \beta^{l-1} \cdot i_1 + \beta^{l-2} \cdot i_2 + \cdots + \beta^1 \cdot i_{l-1} + i_l.$$

This number is less than β^l, since $i_1, \ldots, i_l < \beta$, and is greater than or equal to β^{l-1}, since $i_1 \geq 1$.

(b) If $x = y$, then $\text{gn}(x) = \text{gn}(y)$. If $x \neq y$, then $|x| \leq |y| - 1$, but then by Part (a),

$$\text{gn}(x) < \beta^{|x|} \leq \beta^{|y|-1} \leq \text{gn}(y). \quad \blacksquare$$

With the encoding of strings as numbers thus specified, let us now see how simple functions of strings translate into primitive recursive functions of their Gödel numbers. As we shall shortly wish to apply this development to the computation of functions by grammars, it will be helpful to fix the particular grammar to be considered. Let $G = (V, \Sigma, R, S)$. Also, introduce a new symbol \$, not in V, and let $\Delta = V \cup \{\$\}$; the symbol \$ will be used for encoding derivations in G.

We now introduce a series of functions and predicates, each of which we show to be primitive recursive.

(a) *Length* The 1-place function length is defined as follows: For every $n \in \mathbb{N}$, $\text{length}(n) = |\text{gn}^{-1}(n)|$, that is, the length of the string whose Gödel number is n. Because of Lemma 5.4.1(a), length can be specified by

$$\text{length}(n) = \mu i \leq n[n < \beta^i]$$

and is therefore primitive recursive. The use of bounded minimalization is appropriate since $|w|$ never exceeds $\text{gn}(w)$ for $w \in \mathfrak{D}$ (though they are equal if $\text{gn}(w)$ is 0 or 1). The number β is a constant in this specification.

Example 5.4.2

By inspection of the values in Example 5.4.1, it is evident that

$$\text{length}(0) = 0$$
$$\text{length}(1) = 1$$
$$\text{length}(9) = 2$$
$$\text{length}(63) = 3.$$

(b) *Concatenation* We wish to define a 2-place function concat so that

$$\text{concat}(m, n) = \text{gn}(\text{gn}^{-1}(m)\text{gn}^{-1}(n));$$

that is, concat yields the Gödel number of the concatenation of the two strings whose Gödel numbers are its arguments. This is achieved by defining

$$\text{concat}(m, n) = n + m \cdot \beta^{\text{length}(n)}$$

and so concat is primitive recursive. Moreover, we can define a concatenation function for any fixed number of arguments in the same way. Thus

$$\text{concat}^3(m, n, p) = \text{concat}(m, \text{concat}(n, p))$$

and in general, for each $k \geq 3$, we can define a $(k + 1)$-place function concat^{k+1} by

$$\text{concat}^{k+1}(\bar{n}, m) = \text{concat}(\text{concat}^k(\bar{n}), m).$$

Each of these functions is primitive recursive.

Example 5.4.3

Again referring to Example 5.4.1, we see that

$$\begin{aligned} \text{concat}(\text{gn}(b), \text{gn}(a)) &= \text{concat}(2, 1) \\ &= 1 + 2 \cdot 4^{\text{length}(1)} \\ &= 1 + 2 \cdot 4^1 \\ &= 9 \\ &= \text{gn}(ba). \end{aligned}$$

(c) *Member of* Δ^* The 1-place predicate Δ^* is true if and only if its argument is the Gödel number of string in Δ^*, that is, one not containing the special symbol d_0 introduced to make the Gödel numbering a bijection. That is,

$$\Delta^* n \quad \text{if and only if} \quad \text{gn}^{-1}(n) \in \Delta^*.$$

The predicate Δ^* is primitive recursive, since

$$\Delta^* n \text{ if and only if}$$

$$\forall n_1 \leq n[\forall n_2 \leq n[n \neq \text{concat}(n_1, n_2)] \text{ or } n_1 = 0 \text{ or } \forall n_3 \leq n[n_1 \neq n_3 \cdot \beta]].$$

That is, $\text{gn}^{-1}(n)$ cannot be written as uv, where $u, v \in \mathfrak{D}$ and u ends with d_0; if u ended with d_0, then $\text{gn}(u)$ would be nonzero and divisible by β.

Example 5.4.4

Refer again to Example 5.4.1. Then Δ^*33 is false, since if we let $n_1 = 8 = \text{gn}(bd_0)$, $n_2 = 1 = \text{gn}(a)$, and $n_3 = 2 = \text{gn}(b)$, then

$$\begin{aligned} &33 = \text{concat}(n_1, n_2), \\ &n_1 \neq 0, \text{ and} \\ &n_1 = n_3 \cdot \beta. \end{aligned}$$

(d) *Member of V^** The 1-place predicate V^* is true if and only if its argument is the Gödel number of a string in V^*, that is, one not containing \$ or the special symbol d_0 introduced to make the Gödel numbering a bijection. That is,

$$V^*n \quad \text{if and only if} \quad \text{gn}^{-1}(n) \in V^*.$$

The predicate V^* is primitive recursive, since

$$V^*n \quad \text{if and only if}$$
$$\Delta^*n \text{ and } \forall n_1 \leq n[\forall n_2 \leq n[n \neq \text{concat}^3(n_1, \text{gn}(\$), n_2)]].$$

In this context, gn(\$) is some fixed constant (whatever value happened to have been assigned to the symbol \$ when the Gödel numbering was defined).

(e) *Substitution* Define the 4-place predicate SB as follows: $\text{SB}n_1n_2n_3n_4$ if and only if the strings

$$w_1 = \text{gn}^{-1}(n_1)$$
$$w_2 = \text{gn}^{-1}(n_2)$$
$$w_3 = \text{gn}^{-1}(n_3)$$
$$w_4 = \text{gn}^{-1}(n_4)$$

are in Δ^* and for some strings u and v we have $w_1 = uw_3v$ and $w_2 = uw_4v$. That is, $\text{SB}n_1n_2n_3n_4$ is true if and only if w_2 is obtained from w_1 by substituting w_4 for an occurrence of w_3 (all strings being in Δ^*). Then SB is a primitive recursive predicate, since

$$\text{SB}n_1n_2n_3n_4 \quad \text{if and only if} \quad \Delta^*n_1 \text{ and } \Delta^*n_2 \text{ and } \Delta^*n_3 \text{ and } \Delta^*n_4 \text{ and}$$
$$\exists m \leq n_1[\exists p \leq n_1 \, [n_1 = \text{concat}^3(m, n_3, p) \text{ and } n_2 = \text{concat}^3(m, n_4, p)]].$$

We are using the fact (Lemma 5.4.1(b)) that the Gödel number of a substring is at most that of the string itself.

Example 5.4.5

Refer again to Example 5.4.1. Then SB 5 6 1 2 is true, that is, SB gn(*aa*)gn(*ab*)gn(*a*)gn(*b*). Specifically, let $m = 1$ and $p = 0$; then m, $p \leq 5$ and

$$5 = \text{concat}^3(m, 1, p)$$

and

$$6 = \text{concat}^3(m, 2, p).$$

We now turn to some predicates that refer specifically to the rules of the grammar G.

(f) *Yields in one step* The 2-place predicate Y is defined as follows.

$$Ynm \quad \text{if and only if}$$
$$\text{gn}^{-1}(n), \text{gn}^{-1}(m) \in V^*$$
$$\text{and} \quad \text{gn}^{-1}(n) \underset{G}{\Rightarrow} \text{gn}^{-1}(m).$$

That is, Ynm holds if the string whose Gödel number is n yields the string with Gödel number m in one step. Then Y too is primitive recursive. For let R, the set of rules of G, be $\{(u_1, v_1), \ldots, (u_k, v_k)\}$. Then Ynm is true if and only if V^*n and V^*m and

$$\text{SB}nm\ \text{gn}(u_1)\text{gn}(v_1) \quad \text{or}$$
$$\vdots \quad \text{or}$$
$$\text{SB}nm\ \text{gn}(u_k)\text{gn}(v_k).$$

Once again, the numbers $\text{gn}(u_i)$ and $\text{gn}(v_i)$ are constants.

(g) *Is a derivation* The predicate D is defined as follows: Dn if and only if $\text{gn}^{-1}(n)$ is a string of the form

$$\$x_0\$x_1\$ \ldots \$x_k\$$$

where $k \geq 0$, each $x_i \in V^*$, and $x_i \underset{G}{\Rightarrow} x_{i+1}$ for $i = 0, \ldots, k-1$. That is, Dn holds if and only if n is the encoding of a derivation in G. The symbol \$ was introduced specifically for the purpose of separating the intermediate strings from each other. Then D is primitive recursive, since Dn is true if and only if

$$\Delta^*n \text{ and } \exists m \leq n[n = \text{concat}^3(\text{gn}(\$), m, \text{gn}(\$))]$$
$$\text{and } \forall p \leq n[\forall q \leq n[\forall r \leq n[\forall s \leq n$$
$$[n \neq \text{concat}^7(p, \text{gn}(\$), q, \text{gn}(\$), r, \text{gn}(\$), s)$$
$$\text{or not } V^*q \text{ or not } V^*r \text{ or } Yqr]]]].$$

In other words, if $\text{gn}^{-1}(n)$ can be written as $u\$v\$w\$z$, where v and w do *not* contain \$, then necessarily $v \underset{G}{\Rightarrow} w$.

(h) *Begins a derivation* The 2-place predicate B is defined as: Bpq if and only if p encodes a derivation as in Part (g), and $q = \text{gn}(x_0)$. Then B is primitive recursive, since

$$Bpq \quad \text{if and only if}$$
$$Dp \text{ and } V^*q \text{ and } \exists r \leq p[p = \text{concat}^4(\text{gn}(\$), q, \text{gn}(\$), r)].$$

(i) *Ends a derivation* The 2-place predicate E is defined as: Epq if and only if p encodes a derivation as in Part (g), and $q = \text{gn}(x_k)$. Then E is primitive recursive, since

Epq if and only if

$$Dp \text{ and } V^*q \text{ and } \exists r \leq p[p = \text{concat}^4(r, \text{gn}(\$), q, \text{gn}(\$))].$$

In a few paragraphs we shall use these predicates to define yet more complex ones.

5.5 THE μ-RECURSIVE FUNCTIONS

Let us now turn to the extension of the class of primitive recursive functions mentioned at the beginning of Section 5.4. Why is such an extension needed? The examples of the last section suggest that, to the contrary, quite interesting and complex calculations can be carried out by means of the primitive recursive functions.

This is certainly true. In fact, from a practical standpoint, the primitive recursive functions include far more complex functions than any function we are likely to use. Still, they cannot include all the functions that we are inclined to consider computable from an intuitive standpoint. We now sketch an argument that explains this curious fact. Our argument is informal, and it plays no role in the rest of this chapter except to motivate our introduction of the μ-recursive functions. But it foreshadows a kind of argument that is of critical importance in the next chapter.

Not every function that we would naturally regard as computable can be primitive recursive. To see this, observe that the definitions of primitive recursive functions can be listed systematically. We need merely choose some finite alphabet for representing the initial functions and the equations that define functions in terms of other functions by composition and primitive recursion. We can then imagine listing all the strings over this alphabet and eliminating those which—because of syntactic flaws—do not represent the definitions of primitive recursive functions. (The listing would be done, for example, in lexicographic order.) We are then left with an infinite list $A_1, A_2, A_3, \ldots$, each member of which represents the definition of some primitive recursive function; also, every definition of a primitive recursive function appears somewhere in the list. Let f_i be the primitive recursive function defined by A_i, and consider the 1-place function f such that for every $n \in \mathbb{N}, f(n) = f_n(n, \ldots, n) + 1$. That is, f is to be evaluated on argument n by finding the nth string defining a primitive recursive function, applying that definition to the arguments $n, \ldots, n$ (as many arguments as f_n requires), and then adding 1. This is a perfectly good algorithm for evaluating f, so f must be computable. But f cannot be primitive recursive. For suppose it were; then f must be f_i for some i; that is, some A_i represents a definition of f. But when evaluated with argument i, f and f_i will differ in value by 1, so f cannot be f_i.

This is a diagonalization argument. It depends on our having a sequential listing of all the primitive recursive functions; from that listing one can define a function which differs from all those in the list, and which, therefore, cannot be in the list itself. Compare this argument to our proof in Chapter 1 that $2^{\mathbb{N}}$ is uncountable; there we started from a purported listing of all the members of $2^{\mathbb{N}}$ and obtained a member of $2^{\mathbb{N}}$ not in the listing.

Therefore, in order to obtain all computable functions, some extension must be made to the methods used thus far for defining functions.

Definition 5.5.1

Let $k \geq 0$ and let g be a $(k+1)$-place function. Then the **unbounded minimalization** of g is that k-place function f such that, for any $\bar{n} \in \mathbb{N}^k$,

$$f(\bar{n}) = \begin{cases} \text{the least } m \text{ such that } g(\bar{n}, m) = 0, \\ \qquad\qquad \text{if such an } m \text{ exists;} \\ 0 \qquad \text{otherwise.} \end{cases}$$

The second clause guarantees that f is everywhere defined, regardless of what g is. We write

$$f(\bar{n}) = \mu m[g(\bar{n}, m) = 0]$$

and say that f is obtained from g by **unbounded minimalization.**

In general, the unbounded minimalization of a primitive recursive function need not be primitive recursive, or indeed computable in any intuitive sense. The reason, as we shall show in Chapter 6, is that there is no general method for telling whether an m of the required type exists. However, *if* g has the property that such an m exists for every $\bar{n}$, then f is computable if g is computable; given $\bar{n}$, we need simply evaluate $g(\bar{n}, 0)$, $g(\bar{n}, 1)$, . . . until we find an m such that $g(\bar{n}, m) = 0$. However, in this case f need not, in general, be primitive recursive. These ideas lead to the following definitions.

Definition 5.5.2

A $(k+1)$-place function g is **regular** if and only if, for every $\bar{n} \in \mathbb{N}^k$, there is an m such that $g(\bar{n}, m) = 0$. A function is **μ-recursive** if and only if it can be obtained from the initial functions ζ, π_i^k, and σ by the following operations:

composition;

primitive recursion;

application of unbounded minimalization to regular functions.

Thus every primitive recursive function is μ-recursive. We shall see in Section 5.6 that only one operation of the last type is needed to obtain any μ-recursive function.

We are going to show that every grammatically computable function is μ-recursive. Before proceeding, however, let us comment on what may appear to be a dissatisfying aspect of our definition. When we are presented with what pretends to be a definition of a primitive recursive function, we can check to see that it uses only the initial functions and composition and primitive recursion, and so we can tell whether it is in fact a valid definition. But how can we tell whether something that purports to be the definition of a μ-recursive function actually is one? Specifically, how can we tell whether an application of unbounded minimalization is to a regular or nonregular function?

The answer is that we cannot tell, and moreover, if we could tell, then our definitional method would once again not capture all the computable functions. For if we could tell which definitions represented regular functions and which did not, then all the definitions of μ-recursive functions could be listed in the manner sketched earlier for primitive recursive functions. A similar diagonalization argument would then produce a computable, but not μ-recursive, function. It follows that in any listing of the definitions of μ-recursive functions with the property that we can tell which strings are on the list and which are not by some algorithm, there must also be strings that do not in fact define functions at all. This is a specific case of a choice that must always be faced when dealing with any formalism for computation: If one wants an exhaustive system for representing all the computable functions, then either one must give up the idea that only well defined functions will be represented, or one must accept the fact that the class of legal representations is not defined in terms of simple syntactic criteria alone. In the next chapter we shall pursue the ramifications of such facts as this.

We are nearly ready to complete our proof that the μ-recursive functions are at least as powerful as the grammatically computable functions. We need just one more definition. We continue to regard the alphabet Δ and the Gödel numbering gn as fixed. Thus $\$ \in \Delta$. Let $\Sigma_0, \Sigma_1 \subseteq \Delta - \{\$\}$.

Definition 5.5.3

A function $f: \Sigma_0^* \longrightarrow \Sigma_1^*$ is **μ-recursive** if and only if the function $f': \mathbb{N} \longrightarrow \mathbb{N}$ is μ-recursive, where for each $n \in \mathbb{N}$,

$$f'(n) = \begin{cases} \mathrm{gn}(f(\mathrm{gn}^{-1}(n))) & \text{if } \mathrm{gn}^{-1}(n) \in \Sigma_0^*; \\ 0 & \text{if } \mathrm{gn}^{-1}(n) \notin \Sigma_0^*. \end{cases}$$

In other words, a function f from strings to strings is μ-recursive if the naturally corresponding function f' from Gödel numbers to Gödel numbers is μ-recursive as defined in Definition 5.5.2. When an argument is not a Gödel number, f' is required, somewhat arbitrarily, to have the value zero.

Theorem 5.5.1. *Every grammatically computable function from strings to strings or from numbers to numbers is μ-recursive.*

Proof. Consider first a function from strings to strings. Let $f: \Sigma_0^* \to \Sigma_1^*$ be grammatically computable, and suppose that $G = (V, \Sigma, R, S)$ is a grammar that computes f. We assume that all the development of the last section has been carried out specifically for the grammar G; thus $\$ \notin V$ and $\Delta = V \cup \{\$\}$. Let x, y, x', y' be the strings associated with G and f as specified in Definition 5.2.2. We need three further primitive recursive predicates and one primitive recursive function.

(j) *Member of* Σ_0^*; *member of* Σ_1^* The predicate $\Sigma_0^* n$ is true if and only if $\text{gn}^{-1}(n) \in \Sigma_0^*$. Clearly this predicate can be defined by using the methods of (c) and (d) of Section 5.4. Similarly, $\Sigma_1^* n$ is true if and only if $\text{gn}^{-1}(n) \in \Sigma_1^*$.

(k) *Extract last string* The function extract has as an argument the Gödel number of a derivation encoded as in (g) of the last section and ending with a string of the form $x'vy'$ for some v; its value is gn(v). Formally,

$$\text{extract}(p) = \mu n \leq p[Ep \ \text{concat}^3(\text{gn}(x'), n, \text{gn}(y'))].$$

(l) *Computes* Let C be the following 2-place primitive recursive predicate: Cnp if and only if not $\Sigma_0^* n$ or

$$(Dp \quad \text{and} \quad Bp \ \text{concat}^3(\text{gn}(x), n, \text{gn}(y))$$
$$\text{and} \quad \exists m \leq p[\Sigma_1^* \, m \ \text{and} \ Ep \ \text{concat}^3(\text{gn}(x'), m, \text{gn}(y'))]).$$

If n is the Gödel number of a string u in Σ_0^*, then Cnp says that p encodes a derivation of the form

$$xuy = x_0 \underset{G}{\Rightarrow} x_1 \underset{G}{\Rightarrow} \cdots \underset{G}{\Rightarrow} x_k = x'vy'$$

with $v \in \Sigma_1^*$; specifically, $p = \text{gn}(\$x_0\$x_1 \ldots \$x_k\$)$.

Now for the critical step. Since C is primitive recursive, its characteristic function γ is primitive recursive. And since G computes f, for every $u \in \Sigma_0^*$, there is some $v \in \Sigma_1^*$ such that $xuy \overset{*}{\underset{G}{\Rightarrow}} x'vy'$ (in fact, there is exactly one such v, namely, $v = f(u)$). Thus for every n, there is some p such that $\gamma(n, p) = 1$ (if $\text{gn}^{-1}(n) \notin \Sigma_0^*$ then $Cn0$ is true and so $\gamma(n, 0) = 1$). Then let $\bar{\gamma}(n, p) = 1 \dot{-} \gamma(n, p)$ for all n and p; *then* $\bar{\gamma}$ *is a regular function.* Hence we can apply unbounded minimalization to $\bar{\gamma}$. But if we let

$$f'(n) = \text{extract}(\mu p[\bar{\gamma}(n, p) = 0]),$$

then for any $u \in \Sigma_0^*$,

$$f'(\text{gn}(u)) = \text{gn}(f(u)),$$

and for any n such that $\text{gn}^{-1}(n) \notin \Sigma_0^*, f'(n) = 0$ (Problem 5.5.1). So f' is related to f as stipulated in Definition 5.5.3, and f' is μ-recursive. Therefore f is μ-recursive.

Now consider a function f from $\mathbb{N}$ to $\mathbb{N}$. If f is grammatically computable, then the function $f': \{I\}^* \longrightarrow \{I\}^*$ such that $f'(I^n) = I^{f(n)}$ for each $n \in \mathbb{N}$ is also grammatically computable. By the proof just given, the function f' is also μ-recursive. That is, the function $f'': \mathbb{N} \longrightarrow \mathbb{N}$ such that

$$f''(n) = \begin{cases} \text{gn}(f'(\text{gn}^{-1}(n))) & \text{if gn}^{-1}(n) \in \{I\}^* \\ 0 & \text{if gn}^{-1}(n) \notin \{I\}^* \end{cases}$$

is μ-recursive.

Let enc be the following primitive recursive function from numbers to numbers:

$$\text{enc}(0) = \text{gn}(e) \; (= 0)$$
$$\text{enc}(n + 1) = \text{concat}(\text{gn}(I), \text{enc}(n)).$$

That is, enc(n) is the Gödel number of the unary encoding of n. We claim that

$$f(n) = \text{length}(f''(\text{enc}(n)))$$

for each $n \in \mathbb{N}$, which will establish that f is μ-recursive. For let $n \in \mathbb{N}$; then $\text{enc}(n) = \text{gn}(I^n)$; then $\text{gn}^{-1}(\text{enc}(n)) \in \{I\}^*$, so

$$\begin{aligned} f''(\text{enc}(n)) &= f''(\text{gn}(I^n)) \\ &= \text{gn}(f'(I^n)) \\ &= \text{gn}(I^{f(n)}). \end{aligned}$$

But $\text{length}(\text{gn}(I^{f(n)})) = f(n)$, which completes the proof. ■

5.6 TURING-COMPUTABILITY OF THE μ-RECURSIVE FUNCTIONS

To complete the proof that Turing machines, grammars, and the operations defining the μ-recursive functions are all equally powerful, we must show that every μ-recursive function can be computed by a Turing machine. We laid the groundwork for this task in Chapter 4, where we designed a number of special-purpose Turing machines to search for symbols and copy and shift strings. Let us review the function of some of these machines.

- $R_\#$ searches for the first blank square to the right of the square currently scanned.
- $L_\#$ searches for the first blank square to the left of the square currently scanned.
- S_L shifts left, that is, transforms $\#w\#$ into $w\#$, where w contains no blank.
- S_R shifts right, that is, transforms $\#w\#$ into $\#\#w\#$, where w contains no blank.

Before continuing, let us add to this list two particular machines and one class of machines which will be of great help in the subsequent constructions.

The **erasing machine** E transforms $\#w\underline{\#}$, where w may be empty but contains no blanks, into $\underline{\#}$. It may be diagrammed as shown in Figure 5–1.

Figure 5–1

The **backup machine** B transforms $\#u\#w\underline{\#}$ into $\#w\underline{\#}$; once again, u and w may be empty but contain no blanks. One design for B is shown in Figure 5–2; this machine operates by repeatedly shifting w to the left, one square at a time, until u has been obliterated.

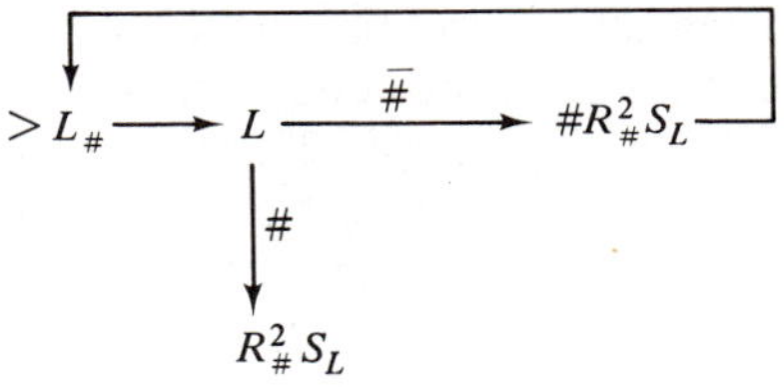

Figure 5–2

The k-**copier** C_k ($k \geq 1$) produces a copy of the kth nonblank string to its left. That is, if $w_1, \ldots, w_k$ contain no blanks, then C_k transforms $\#w_1\#w_2\# \ldots \#w_k\underline{\#}$ into $\#w_1\#w_2\# \ldots \#w_k\#w_1\underline{\#}$. Thus the copying machine C of Example 4.4.2 is equivalent to C_1. One design for C_k is shown in Figure 5–3; note that the design for C in Figure 4–11 is the $k = 1$ case of C_k.

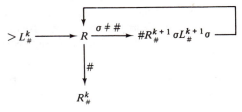

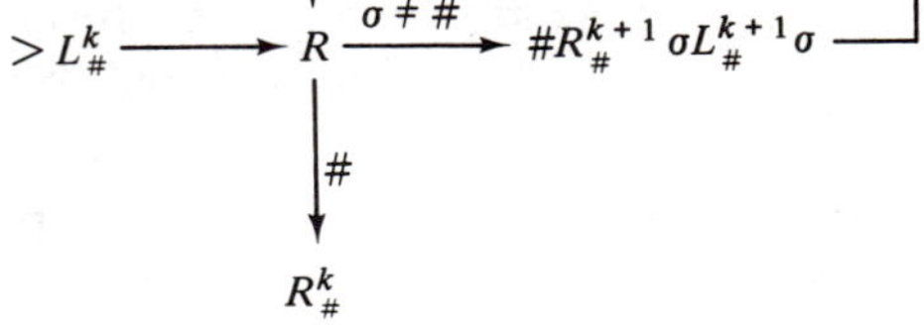

Figure 5–3

Note also that the machine C^l_k (that is, $C_kC_k \ldots C_k$, l copies in all), where $l \leq k$, has the effect of copying the kth through $(k + l - 1)$st nonblank strings to the left of the currently scanned square; that is, C_k^l transforms $\#w_1\#w_2\# \ldots \#w_k\#$ into $\#w_1\#w_2\# \ldots \#w_k\#w_1\#w_2\# \ldots \#w_l\#$.

Now we can move to the main business of this section.

Theorem 5.6.1. *Every μ-recursive function from numbers to numbers or from strings to strings is Turing-computable.*

Proof. We start by considering μ-recursive functions from numbers to numbers; this development takes most of the work. The corresponding result for functions from strings to strings is an easy corollary.

The μ-recursive functions are, by Definition 5.5.2, those that can be obtained from the initial functions ζ, π_i^k, and σ by composition, primitive recursion, and application of unbounded minimalization to regular functions. Our proof that every μ-recursive function is Turing-computable therefore proceeds by first showing that the initial functions are Turing-computable, and then showing that the results of composition, primitive recursion, and unbounded minimalization when applied to Turing-computable functions (to a *regular* Turing-computable function, in the last case) are again Turing-computable. We break this demonstration into a series of lemmas.

Lemma 5.6.1. *The initial functions are Turing-computable.*

Proof.

(a) The ζ function is computed by a Turing machine which, when started, moves its head one square to the right and halts. This is the machine called R in Chapter 4. The R machine, when started in the configuration $(s, \underline{\#})$ (s being its start state) will halt in the configuration $(h, \#\underline{\#})$; this is exactly the behavior required to compute the function $\zeta: \mathbb{N}^0 \longrightarrow \mathbb{N}^1$.

(b) The projection function π_i^k, where $k \geq 1$ and $1 \leq i \leq k$, is computed by the Turing machine $E^{k-i}B^{i-1}$. Here E^{k-i} transforms $\#w_1\#w_2\# \ldots \#w_k\underline{\#}$ into $\#w_1\#w_2 \ldots \#w_i\underline{\#}$, and then B^{i-1} transforms this into $\#w_i\underline{\#}$. In this context, E^0 (if $k = i$) and B^0 (if $i = 1$) should be regarded as trivial machines, which simply halt immediately.

(c) The successor function σ is computed by the Turing machine IR, which transforms $\#I^n\underline{\#}$ $(n \geq 0)$ into $\#I^{n+1}\underline{\#}$. ■

Lemma 5.6.2. *Let $l > 0$ and $k \geq 0$, let g be an l-place Turing-computable function, and let $h_1, \ldots, h_l$ be k-place Turing-computable functions. If f is the function obtained from $g, h_1, \ldots, h_l$ by composition, then f too is Turing-computable.*

Proof. Let $G, H_1, \ldots, H_l$ be Turing machines that compute $g, h_1, \ldots, h_l$, respectively. Then the function f, where $f(\bar{n}) = g(h_1(\bar{n}), \ldots, h_l(\bar{n}))$ for all $\bar{n} \in \mathbb{N}^k$, is computed by the Turing machine

$$C^k_k H_1 C^k_{k+1} H_2 \ldots C^k_{k+l-1} H_l G B^k.$$

For $C^k_k H_1$ transforms $\#w_1\#w_2\# \ldots \#w_k\underline{\#}$ first into $\#w_1\#w_2\# \ldots \#w_k\#w_1\#w_2\# \ldots \#w_k\underline{\#}$ and then into $\#w_1\#w_2\# \ldots \#w_k\#u_1\underline{\#}$, where if $w_i = I^{n_i}$ for $i = 1, \ldots, k$, then $u_1 = I^{h_1(\bar{n})}$. Similarly, after $C^k_k H_1 C^k_{k+1} H_2 \ldots C^k_{k+l-1} H_l$, the tape and head position would be represented by

$$\#w_1\#w_2\# \ldots \#w_k\#u_1\#u_2\# \ldots \#u_l\underline{\#}$$

where $u_i = I^{h_i(\bar{n})}$ for $i = 1, \ldots, l$. This is transformed into $\#w_1\#w_2\# \ldots \#w_k\#v\underline{\#}$, where $v = I^{f(\bar{n})}$, by G, and then into $\#v\underline{\#}$ by B^k. ■

Lemma 5.6.3. *Let $k \geq 0$, let g be a k-place Turing-computable function, and let h be a $(k + 2)$-place Turing-computable function. If f is the function obtained from g and h by primitive recursion, then f too is Turing-computable.*

Proof. Let G and H be Turing machines that compute g and h, respectively. We design a Turing machine F that computes f, where for every $\bar{n} \in \mathbb{N}^k$, $f(\bar{n}, 0) = g(\bar{n})$, and for every $\bar{n} \in \mathbb{N}^k$, $m \in \mathbb{N}$, $f(\bar{n}, m + 1) = h(\bar{n}, m, f(\bar{n}, m))$. An input of the form $\#w_1\#w_2\# \ldots \#w_k\#u\underline{\#}$ is received by F, where for some $n_1, \ldots, n_k, m \in \mathbb{N}$, $w_i = I^{n_i}$ for $i = 1, \ldots, k$ and $u = I^m$. Let us write $\bar{w}$ for $w_1\#w_2\# \ldots \#w_k$. First, F adds a left endmarker \$ to its input, where \$ is a new symbol not used by G or H; that is, the input is transformed into $\$\#\bar{w}\#u\underline{\#}$. This is achieved by the Turing machine $F_1 = (S_R L^2_\#)^{k+1} \$ R^{k+1}_\#$. Next, the tape and head are arranged as follows:

$$\$\#\bar{w}\#I^{m-1}\#\bar{w}\#I^{m-2}\# \cdots \#\bar{w}\#I^1\#\bar{w}\#I^0\#\bar{w}\underline{\#};$$

that is, $\$\#$ followed by $\bar{w}\#I^i\#$ for $i = m - 1, m - 2, \ldots, 0$, followed by $\bar{w}\#$, with the head at the right end. (If $m = 0$, this arrangement is $\$\#\bar{w}\underline{\#}$; if $m = 1$, it is $\$\#\bar{w}\#\#\bar{w}\underline{\#}$.) A Turing machine to effect this transformation is shown in Figure 5–4; let us call this machine F_2.

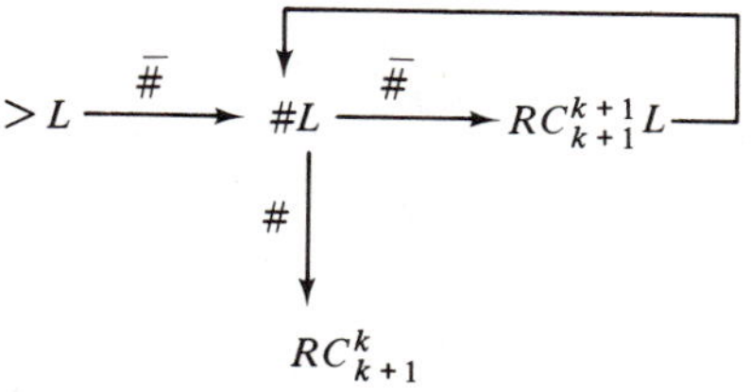

Figure 5–4

Finally, the Turing machines G and H are used to compute the successive values $f(\bar{n}, i)$ for $i = 0, \ldots, m$. Let us write v_i for $I^{f(\bar{n},i)}$; then the appearance of the tape will be, successively, as follows.

$$\$\#\bar{w}\#I^{m-1}\#\bar{w}\#I^{m-2}\# \ldots \#\bar{w}\#I^{1}\#\bar{w}\#I^{0}\#v_0\underline{\#}$$

$$\$\#\bar{w}\#I^{m-1}\#\bar{w}\#I^{m-2}\# \ldots \#\bar{w}\#I^{1}\#v_1\underline{\#}$$

$$\vdots$$

$$\$\#\bar{w}\#I^{m-1}\#\bar{w}\#I^{m-2}\# \ldots \#\bar{w}\#I^{i}\#v_i\underline{\#}$$

$$\vdots$$

$$\$\#\bar{w}\#I^{m-1}\#v_{m-1}\underline{\#}$$

$$\$\#v_m\underline{\#}$$

At the first step, $\bar{w}$ is removed from the right end and is replaced by v_0, by use of the G machine; at each subsequent step, $\bar{w}\#I^i\#v_i$ is removed from the right end and is replaced by v_{i+1}, by use of the H machine. Before each new cycle is initiated, the symbol just to the left of the rightmost string on the tape is checked; if it is not \$, then another cycle must be undertaken, but if it is \$, then the computation is complete, except for shifting the result to the left one square to eliminate the \$. So this part of the computation can be carried out by the Turing machine of Figure 5–5; let us call this machine F_3. The machine F that computes f is then $F_1F_2F_3$. ■

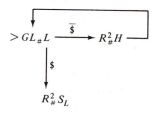

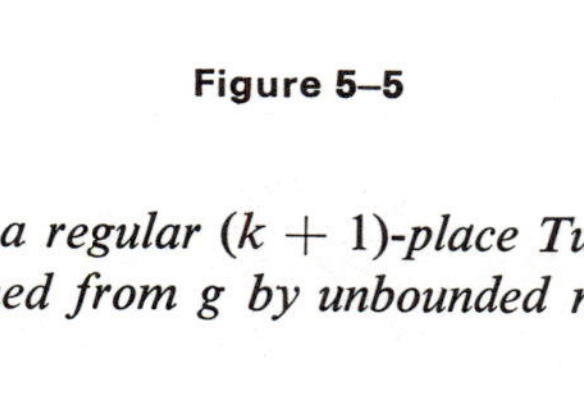

Figure 5–5

Lemma 5.6.4. *Let g be a regular $(k+1)$-place Turing-computable function. If f is the function obtained from g by unbounded minimalization, then f too is Turing-computable.*

Proof. Let G be a Turing machine that computes g; we construct a Turing machine F that computes f, where for all $\bar{n} \in \mathbb{N}^k$,

$$f(\bar{n}) = \text{the least } m \text{ such that } g(\bar{n}, m) = 0.$$

Since g is regular, we are guaranteed that such an m exists for every $\bar{n}$. Machine F receives its input in the form $\#w_1\#w_2\# \ldots \#w_k\underline{\#}$. It first transforms this into $\#w_1\#w_2\# \ldots \#w_k\#\underline{\#}$ (that is, $\#w_1\#w_2\# \ldots \#w_k\#I^0\underline{\#}$), copies this entire string, and applies G to this input. If the result is nonzero, it is erased and one I is appended to the right end of the string remaining on the tape, which now becomes

$$\#w_1\#w_2 \ldots \#w_k\#I^1\underline{\#}.$$

This string is copied, and G is applied to it. The process is repeated until a result of zero is obtained when, for some m, G is applied to $\#w_1\#w_2 \ldots \#w_k\#I^m\underline{\#}$. In this case, the B machine is used to eliminate the unwanted arguments $w_1, \ldots, w_k$ and leave only the result I^m on the tape. The detailed specification of F is shown in Figure 5–6. ■

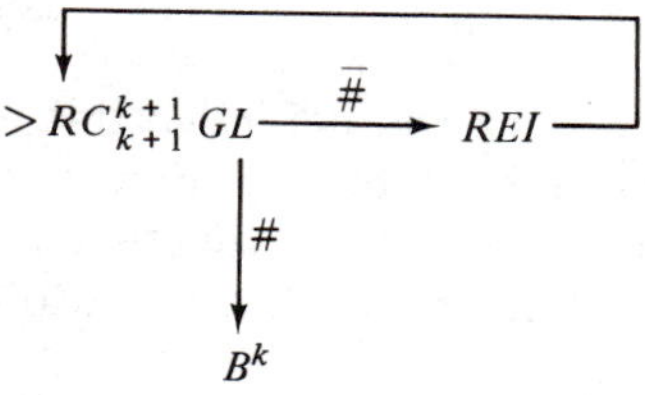

Figure 5–6

Lemmas 5.6.1 through 5.6.4 complete the proof of Theorem 5.6.1 for the case of functions from numbers to numbers. To complete the proof of the theorem, let f be a μ-recursive function from strings to strings. Then the function $f': \mathbb{N} \to \mathbb{N}$ is μ-recursive, where for any n such that $\text{gn}^{-1}(n)$ is a string in the domain of f, $f'(n) = \text{gn}(f(\text{gn}^{-1}(n)))$. By the argument just completed, f' is Turing-computable; suppose that f' is computed by a Turing machine F'. To show that f is Turing-computable, we can design a Turing machine which, when given an input string w in the domain of f,

- first, transforms $\#w\underline{\#}$ into $\#I^{\text{gn}(w)}\underline{\#}$, that is, converts a string into the unary representation of its Gödel number;
- second, uses F' to transform $\#I^{\text{gn}(w)}\underline{\#}$ into $\#I^{f'(\text{gn}(w))}\underline{\#}$, that is, into $\#I^{\text{gn}(f(w))}\underline{\#}$;
- third, transforms $\#I^{\text{gn}(f(w))}\underline{\#}$ into $\#f(w)\underline{\#}$, that is, converts the unary representation of the Gödel number of a string into the string itself.

So the only missing pieces are Turing machines to convert strings back and forth into the unary representations of their Gödel numbers. These machines are entirely straightforward to design and are left as exercises (see Problem 5.6.5). This completes the proof of Theorem 5.6.1. ■

The proof that the Turing-computable, grammatically computable, and μ-recursive functions are all the same is now complete. These functions are most commonly called the **recursive** functions.

We can now make good on a promise we made in Section 5.5 regarding the use of unbounded minimalization in the computation of μ-recursive functions.

Theorem 5.6.2. (Kleene Normal Form.) *Every 1-place μ-recursive function f can be expressed as*

$$f(n) = \alpha(\mu m[\beta(n, m) = 0])$$

where α is a 1-place primitive recursive function and β is a regular 2-place primitive recursive function.

Proof. It was shown in Section 5.5 that this representation is possible for every 1-place Turing-computable function, with α being the function extract and β being the characteristic function $\bar{\gamma}$ of the negation of the 2-place predicate C. But we have just shown that every μ-recursive function is Turing-computable. ∎

5.7 UNIVERSAL TURING MACHINES

One feature that is possessed by contemporary electronic computers, but that Turing machines, as we have described them, do not have, is programmability. That is, we have designed a particular Turing machine for each problem, whereas real computers are "general-purpose" and are not manufactured de novo for every new application. We now show that even Turing machines are in essence programmable. We shall need part of this development in our study of unsolvability in the next chapter; but it also demonstrates that the concept of a general-purpose computer with a program that can be stored as data is at least as old as the theory of Turing machines.

To begin, we must present a general way of specifying Turing machines, so that their descriptions can be used as input to other Turing machines. Each Turing machine is a quadruple (K, Σ, δ, s), and since K and Σ are finite, we could write this quadruple as a string using the symbols in K and Σ and with parentheses, commas, braces, and so on, as punctuation. However, the set of all such strings would not then be a language over a single alphabet (which must, by definition, be finite) since there are Turing machines that have state sets and tape alphabets that may be arbitrarily large. Instead we must *encode* the states and tape symbols as strings over a fixed alphabet. In order to do this, it is convenient to make certain conventions that have not hitherto been necessary but which are now convenient and in no way weaken the theory as it has thus far been developed. We shall assume that there are fixed countably infinite sets

$$K_\infty = \{q_1, q_2, q_3 \dots\}$$

and

$$\Sigma_\infty = \{a_1, a_2, a_3 \dots\}$$

such that for *every* Turing machine, the state set is a finite subset of K_∞ and the tape alphabet is a finite subset of Σ_∞.

Now let us adopt the following correspondence ρ between the component symbols of a Turing machine and strings over the one-symbol alphabet $\{I\}$.

σ	$\rho(\sigma)$
q_i	I^{i+1}
h	I
L	I
R	II
a_i	I^{i+2}

Note that no two members of $K_\infty \cup \{h\}$ are represented in the same way; nor are any two members of $\{L, R\} \cup \Sigma_\infty$. (We assume, as before, that L and R are not tape symbols in Σ_∞ and h is not a state in K_∞.)

Let c be another symbol; we encode Turing machines over the two-symbol alphabet $\{c, I\}$. Let $M = (K, \Sigma, \delta, s)$ be a Turing machine, where now $K \subseteq K_\infty$ and $\Sigma \subseteq \Sigma_\infty$. Thus K may be written as $\{q_{i_1}, q_{i_2}, \dots, q_{i_k}\}$, where $i_1 < i_2 < \cdots < i_k$, and Σ as $\{a_{j_1}, a_{j_2}, \dots, a_{j_l}\}$, where $j_1 < j_2 < \cdots < j_l$; moreover $s = q_{i_m}$ for some m, $1 \leq m \leq k$. Next we define kl strings S_{pr}, where $1 \leq p \leq k$ and $1 \leq r \leq l$; each string S_{pr} encodes the value of the transition function on one state-symbol pair, namely the pair (q_{i_p}, a_{j_r}). Specifically, let $\delta(q_{i_p}, a_{j_r}) = (q', b)$, where $q' \in K \cup \{h\}$ and $b \in \Sigma \cup \{L, R\}$; then let $S_{pr} = cw_1cw_2cw_3cw_4c$, where

$$w_1 = \rho(q_{i_p})$$
$$w_2 = \rho(a_{j_r})$$
$$w_3 = \rho(q')$$
$$w_4 = \rho(b).$$

Example 5.7.1

If M is the Turing machine (K, Σ, δ, s), where $K = \{q_2\}$, $\Sigma = \{a_1, a_3, a_6\}$, $s = q_2$,

$$\delta(q_2, a_3) = \delta(q_2, a_6) = (q_2, R),$$

and

$$\delta(q_2, a_1) = (h, a_3),$$

then

$$k = 1, \qquad i_1 = 2,$$
$$l = 3, \qquad j_1 = 1, \qquad j_2 = 3, \qquad j_3 = 6,$$

and

$$S_{11} = cI^3cI^3cIcI^5c$$
$$S_{12} = cI^3cI^5cI^3cI^2c$$
$$S_{13} = cI^3cI^8cI^3cI^2c.$$

Finally, we write $\rho(M)$ for the single string

$$cS_0cS_{11}S_{12} \ldots S_{1l}S_{21}S_{22} \ldots S_{2l} \ldots S_{k1}S_{k2} \ldots S_{kl}c$$

where $S_0 = \rho(s)$, the encoding of the initial state. This string serves as an encoding of the Turing machine M, in the sense that no two strings correspond to the same machine, and from $\rho(M)$ we can easily reconstruct M. For $\rho(M)$ has the form $cw_0c \ldots$, where $w_0 \in \{I\}^*$; this much of the string determines the initial state. The rest of the string can be broken into blocks of four members of $\{I\}^*$, with each block separated from its neighbors by cc and divided internally by single c's; from these, values of δ can easily be reconstructed. It is, moreover, easy to determine whether a particular string over $\{c, I\}$ is in fact the encoding of a Turing machine; to do so one must check to see that the blocks are organized correctly, that the values of δ are all defined, and so on.

Example 5.7.1 continued.

For the machine M used as an example above, $\rho(M)$ is

$$cI^3ccI^3cI^3cIcI^5ccI^3cI^5cI^3cI^2ccI^3cI^8cI^3cI^2cc.$$

Now we are ready to discuss a **universal Turing machine** U, which uses the encodings $\rho(M)$ of other machines as programs to direct its operation. Intuitively, U takes two arguments, a description of a machine M and an input string w, and performs whatever operations on w would have been performed by M. Naturally, however, w as well as M must be supplied to U in an encoded form, and the end results of the computation (if U halts) will be in the same encoded form. Strings over the tape alphabet of M will be encoded as follows: If $w = b_1 \ldots b_n$, where each $b_i \in \Sigma_\infty$, then $\rho(w) = c\rho(b_1)c\rho(b_2)c \ldots c\rho(b_n)c$. (Note that $\rho(w)$ contains no blanks, even if w does.)

The property that $U = (K_U, \Sigma_U, \delta_U, s_U)$ is to have can then be stated in the following manner.

For any Turing machine $M = (K, \Sigma, \delta, s)$ and for any string $w \in \Sigma^*$,

1. if $(h, u\underline{a}v)$ is a halted configuration of M such that $(s, \#w\underline{\#}) \vdash_M^* (h, u\underline{a}v)$, then $(s_U, \#\rho(M)\rho(w)\underline{\#}) \vdash_U^* (h, \#\rho(uav)\underline{\#})$;
2. if $(s_U, \#\rho(M)\rho(w)\underline{\#}) \vdash_U^* (h, u'\underline{a}'v')$ for some halted configuration $(h, u'\underline{a}'v')$ of U, then $a' = \#$, $v' = e$, and $u' = \#\rho(uav)$ for some u, a, v such that $(h, u\underline{a}v)$ is a halted configuration of M and $(s, \#w\underline{\#}) \vdash_M^* (h, u\underline{a}v)$.

In other words,

1. if M halts on input w, then U halts on an input consisting of the encoding of M followed by the encoding of w, and moreover the tape of U, when U halts, contains the encoding of the string left on the tape of M when M halts; and
2. if U halts on an input consisting of the encoding of M followed by the encoding of w, then M halts on input w, and moreover the contents of the tape of U when U halts is the encoding of the contents of the tape of M when M halts.

We actually describe not the single-tape machine U, but a closely related 3-tape machine U'; from an understanding of how U' works, it follows by Lemma 4.5.2 that U can be constructed. Specifically, U' uses its three tapes as follows: the first tape contains the encoding of the tape of M; the second tape contains the encoding of M itself; and the third tape contains the encoding of the state of M at the current point in the simulated computation.

The machine U' is started with some string $\#\rho(M)\rho(w)$ on its first tape and the other two tapes blank. (It does not matter how U' behaves if its input string is not of this form.) First U' moves $\rho(M)$ onto the second tape and shifts $\rho(w)$ down to the left end of the first tape, preceding it by $c\rho(\#)$ and following it by $\rho(\#)c$. Thus at this point the first tape contains $\#\rho(\#w\#)$. (Note that U' has no difficulty determining where $\rho(M)$ ends and $\rho(w)$ begins; this is the only point in $\rho(M)\rho(w)$ where there are three consecutive c's.) From $\rho(M)$, U' extracts the encoding of the initial state of M, which it copies onto the third tape. Now U' sets about simulating the steps of the computation of M. Between such simulated steps, U' will keep the heads on the second and third tapes at their left ends, and the head on the first tape scanning the c marking the end of the encoded version of the symbol that M would be scanning at the corresponding time. Thus since M starts off scanning the last blank of $\#w\#$, U' should begin its simulation by moving its head on the first tape to the last c on that tape.

Now U' finds on its second tape that block of the form $ccI^icI^jcI^kcI^lcc$ such that I^i is the string of I's ending at the current head position on the third tape and I^j is that on the first tape, and changes the first tape appropriately. If I^l is $\rho(L)$ or $\rho(R)$, this simply involves moving the head a few symbols to the left or right, but if I^l is $\rho(a)$ for some $a \in \Sigma_\infty$, then it may be necessary to shift the right-hand part of the string on the first tape in one direction or the other to put the encoding of one symbol in place of the encoding of another. Finally, U' puts I^k on the third tape and checks whether the third tape now contains $\rho(h)$. If it does not, then U' simulates another computational step by M. If it does, then U' itself halts, after moving the head on the first tape right to the first blank. This completes the description of the operation of U'.

PROBLEMS

5.2.1. (a) Using the grammar of Example 5.2.2, give a derivation of the string *baaccb*.

(b) Find a grammar with fewer rules than that of Example 5.2.2 that generates the same language.

(c) Prove carefully that the grammar of Example 5.2.2 generates $\{w \in \{a, b, c\}^* : w$ has equal numbers of a's, b's, and c's$\}$.

5.2.2. Using the grammar of Example 5.2.3, give a derivation of the string *aaaaaaaa*.

5.2.3. Find grammars that generate each of the following.

(a) $\{a^n b^n c^n : n \geq 0\}$

(b) $\{w \in \{a, b, c\}^* : w$ has more a's than b's and more b's than c's$\}$

(c) $\{a^{n^2} : n \geq 0\}$

(d) $\{ww : w \in \{a, b\}^*\}$

5.2.4. Complete the proof of Lemma 5.2.1 by proving carefully that $(q, u, a, v) \vdash_M (q', u', a', v')$ if and only if $[uqav] \underset{G}{\Rightarrow} [u'q'a'v']$.

5.2.5. (a) Apply the construction of Lemma 5.2.1 to the Turing machine of Example 4.1.1.

(b) Exhibit a halted computation of this machine starting from $(q_0, \underline{a}a)$ and a corresponding derivation using the grammar constructed in Part (a).

5.2.6. Repeat Problem 5.2.5, this time using the Turing machine of Example 4.1.2 and the configuration $(q_0, \#a\underline{a})$.

5.2.7. Show directly (by constructing grammars) that if $f : \Sigma_0^* \rightarrow \Sigma_1^*$ is grammatically computable, then so are f_1 and f_2, where for any $w \in \Sigma_0^*$,

(a) $f_1(w) = f(w)^R$;

(b) $f_2(w) = f(w)f(w)$.

5.2.8. Show that if L is generated by a grammar, then L is generated by a grammar $G = (V, \Sigma, R, S)$ such that $R \subseteq (V - \Sigma)^* \times V^*$ (that is, no terminal symbol appears on the left-hand side of any rule).

5.2.9. Show that if L is generated by a grammar, then L is generated by a grammar G such that each rule is of the form $uAv \longrightarrow uwv$, where A is a single symbol and u, w, and v are strings (possibly empty).

5.2.10. We introduce a variant of the notion of grammar, called a **normal system**. Formally, a normal system is similar to a grammar: it is a quadruple $N = (V, \Sigma, R, S)$, where V is an alphabet, $\Sigma \subseteq V$, $S \in V - \Sigma$, and each rule in R is of the form $u \longrightarrow v$, where u, $v \in V^*$ (note that u or v may be empty and u may consist entirely of symbols in Σ^*). However, the method for deriving strings from each other using normal systems is different from that for a grammar: we write $x \underset{N}{\Rightarrow} y$ if for some $w \in V^*$ and some rule $u \longrightarrow v$, $x = uw$ and $y = wv$. As usual, $\overset{*}{\underset{N}{\Rightarrow}}$ is the reflexive, transitive closure of $\underset{N}{\Rightarrow}$. Show that if L is the language generated by a grammar, then for some normal system $N = (V, \Sigma, R, S)$, $L = \{w \in \Sigma^* : S \overset{*}{\underset{N}{\Rightarrow}} w\}$. (*Hint:* Given a grammar with alphabet V_0, introduce a disjoint copy, V'_0, of V_0; and let N have, among others, rules for removing single symbols in $V_0 \cup V'_0$ from the left end of a string and appending the corresponding symbol from the other half of $V_0 \cup V'_0$ to the right end of a string.)

5.2.11. Let Σ_0 and Σ_1 be alphabets, and let $k > 1$. Define, in some natural way, the idea that a grammar computes a particular function $f: (\Sigma_0^*)^k \longrightarrow \Sigma_1^*$, and argue that any Turing-computable function from $(\Sigma_0^*)^k$ to Σ_1^* can be computed in this way by some grammar.

5.2.12. Modify Definition 5.2.2(a) as follows: Say that $f: \Sigma_0^* \longrightarrow \Sigma_1^*$ is grammatically computable if there is a grammar (V, Σ, R, S), where Σ_0, $\Sigma_1 \subseteq V$, such that for any $u \in \Sigma_0^*$, $v \in \Sigma_1^*$, $uS \overset{*}{\underset{G}{\Rightarrow}} v$ if and only if $v = f(u)$. Show that under this definition, it is still true that every Turing-computable function is grammatically computable.

5.2.13. An oddity in the use of grammars to compute functions is that the order in which rules are applied is indeterminate; in general, more than one rule may be applicable to a given string. In the following alternative, due to A. A. Markov (1903–1979), this possible indeterminacy is avoided, and a simpler version of Definition 5.2.2 is therefore possible. A **Markov system** is a quintuple $G = (V, \Sigma, R, R_1, R_2)$, where V is an alphabet; $\Sigma \subseteq V$; R is a finite *sequence* (not *set*) of rules $(u_1 \longrightarrow v_1, \ldots, u_k \longrightarrow v_k)$ where $u_i, v_i \in V^*$; and (R_1, R_2) is a partition of the rules in R into two disjoint subsets. The relation $u \underset{G}{\Rightarrow} v$, where $u, v \in V^*$, is defined as follows: If there is an i, $1 \leq i \leq k$, such that u_i is a substring of u, then let i be the *least* such number, and let u' be the *shortest* string such that, for some v', $u = u'u_iv'$; then $u \underset{G}{\Rightarrow} v$, provided that $v = u'v_iv'$. Thus if any rule is applicable, there is only one such rule, and the position where it is to be applied is uniquely determined. We write $u \underset{G}{\dot{\Rightarrow}} v$ if there is a sequence $u_0, \ldots, u_n$ of strings such that

$$u = u_0 \underset{G}{\Rightarrow} u_1 \underset{G}{\Rightarrow} u_2 \underset{G}{\Rightarrow} \cdots \underset{G}{\Rightarrow} u_n = v$$

and the one and only use of a rule from the second set R_2 is at the last step, $u_{n-1} \underset{G}{\Rightarrow} u_n$; all rules used at the first $n - 1$ steps are from R_1. We say that G **computes** a function $f: \Sigma^* \longrightarrow \Sigma^*$ if and only if for each $u, v \in \Sigma^*$, $u \underset{G}{\dot{\Rightarrow}} v$ if and only if $v = f(u)$. Show that every Turing-computable function $f: \Sigma^* \longrightarrow \Sigma^*$ is computed by some Markov system. (Lemma 5.2.1 does most of the work, but several changes must be made to the construction given there.)

5.3.1. Show exactly how these functions can be obtained from the initial functions by composition and primitive recursion. Do not take as given any functions except the initial functions.

(a) f, where $f(n)$ is the nth odd number ($f(0) = 1$, $f(1) = 3$, $f(2) = 5, \ldots$).

(b) f, where $f(n, m) = \begin{cases} 0 & \text{if } n \text{ and } m \text{ are both odd or both even;} \\ 1 & \text{otherwise.} \end{cases}$

(c) abs, where $\text{abs}(n, m) = |n - m|$.

(d) $\overline{\text{sg}}$, where $\overline{\text{sg}}(n) = 1$ if $n = 0$, and $\overline{\text{sg}}(n) = 0$ otherwise.

5.3.2. Suppose that f is a 1-place primitive recursive function. Define $F: \mathbb{N} \longrightarrow \mathbb{N}$ by

$$F(n) = \underbrace{f(f(f(\ldots(f}_{n \text{ times}}(n))\ldots))).$$

That is, $F(0) = 0$, $F(1) = f(1)$, $F(2) = f(f(2))$, and so on. Show carefully that F is primitive recursive.

5.3.3. Prove that each of the following functions is primitive recursive. Be sure that your definitions use only the techniques developed in Section 5.3.

(a) $\max(n, m)$ = larger of n and m, or n (or m) if they are equal.

(b) $\text{rem}(n, m)$ = the integer remainder when n is divided by m (zero if m is zero).

(c) quot(n, m) = the integer quotient when n is divided by m (zero if m is zero).

(d) lcm(n, m) = the least common multiple of n and m (zero if either is zero).

(e) gcd(n, m) = the greatest common divisor of m and n.

(f) $p(n)$ = the nth prime number, where $p(0) = 2, p(1) = 3, \ldots$. (If p is a prime number, then the next one cannot be larger than $p! + 1$, since that number always leaves a remainder of 1 when divided by any number less than or equal to p.)

(g) $$\text{prime}(n) = \begin{cases} 0 & \text{if } n \text{ is prime;} \\ 1 & \text{if } n \text{ is not prime.} \end{cases}$$

5.3.4. Suppose that g is a function from $\mathbb{N}^k$ to $\mathbb{N}$ that is known to be primitive recursive. Show that $G: \mathbb{N} \to \mathbb{N}$ is primitive recursive, where for any $n \in \mathbb{N}$,

$$G(n) = \text{the maximum value of } g(n_1, \ldots, n_k) \text{ for any } n_1, \ldots, n_k \leq n.$$

5.3.5. Every natural number n greater than zero can be written in one and only one way as

$$p_1^{e_1} \cdot p_2^{e_2} \cdot \cdots \cdot p_k^{e_k}$$

where each p_i is a prime number, $p_1 < p_2 < \cdots < p_k$, and each $e_i > 0$. This representation is called the **prime factorization** of n, and e_i is called the **exponent** of p_i in the prime factorization of n. For example, the prime factorization of 180 is $2^2 \cdot 3^2 \cdot 5^1$ and the exponent of 3 in this prime factorization is 2. If p is a prime number not among $p_1, \ldots, p_k$, then the exponent of p is considered to be zero; for example, the exponent of 7 in the prime factorization of 180 is 0.

(a) Show that the 2-place function E is primitive recursive, where

$$E(n, p) = \begin{cases} \text{the exponent of } p \text{ in the prime factorization of } n, \text{ if } p \text{ is prime} \\ 0 \quad \text{otherwise.} \end{cases}$$

(b) Let fib (the **Fibonacci function**) be defined by

$$\text{fib}(0) = 0$$
$$\text{fib}(1) = 1$$
$$\text{fib}(n + 2) = \text{fib}(n) + \text{fib}(n + 1),\ n \geq 0.$$

Show that fib is primitive recursive. (*Hint:* Show first, using (a), that f is primitive recursive, where for any $n \in \mathbb{N}$,

$$f(n) = 2^{\text{fib}(n)} \cdot 3^{\text{fib}(n+1)}.)$$

(c) Let $k \geq 1$ and $l \geq 0$, let $g: \mathbb{N}^{k+l+1} \longrightarrow \mathbb{N}$ be primitive recursive, and let $h_0, \ldots, h_{k-1}: \mathbb{N}^l \longrightarrow \mathbb{N}$ be primitive recursive. Let f be that function from $\mathbb{N}^{l+1}$ to $\mathbb{N}$ such that, for any $\bar{n} \in \mathbb{N}^l$,

$$f(\bar{n}, 0) = h_0(\bar{n})$$
$$f(\bar{n}, 1) = h_1(\bar{n})$$
$$\vdots$$
$$f(\bar{n}, k-1) = h_{k-1}(\bar{n})$$

and for any $m \geq k - 1$,

$$f(\bar{n}, m+1) = g(\bar{n}, m, f(\bar{n}, m-k+1), \ldots, f(\bar{n}, m)).$$

(In other words, the value of $f(\bar{n}, m+1)$ depends not just on the previous value $f(\bar{n}, m)$, as in primitive recursion, but on the k previous values.) Show that f is primitive recursive. (*Hint:* Generalize the method used in Part (b).)

5.3.6. (a) Let g be a 1-place primitive recursive function. Show that g' is primitive recursive, where $g'(n, m)$ is the mth digit in the decimal notation for $g(n)$ (zero for large m). (Count left to right, starting from zero.)

(b) Show that d is primitive recursive, where $d(n, m, i)$ is the ith digit to the right of the decimal point in the decimal expansion of the rational number n/m (zero if m is zero). (For example, $d(2, 4, 0) = 5$ and $d(2, 4, 1) = 0$.)

5.3.7. The following are primitive recursive definitions of two familiar functions. What are they? They can be described easily in a few words.

$$A(x, y) = \begin{cases} 0 & \text{if } x = 0 \text{ or } y = 0; \\ \mu z \leq x[\exists w \leq x[w \cdot y + z = x]] & \text{if } x \neq 0 \text{ and } y \neq 0. \end{cases}$$

$$B(x, y) = \begin{cases} 0 & \text{if } x = 0 \text{ or } y = 0; \\ x \mathbin{\dot{-}} (\mu z \leq x[\exists w \leq x[w \cdot (x \mathbin{\dot{-}} z) = x] \\ \quad \text{and } \exists u \leq y[u \cdot (x \mathbin{\dot{-}} z) = y]) & \text{if } x \neq 0 \text{ and } y \neq 0. \end{cases}$$

5.3.8. Define formally: Predicate P is obtained from predicate Q by explicit transformation. Then prove Lemma 5.3.4.

5.3.9. Let f be a 1-place primitive recursive function. Show that the following are primitive recursive.

(a) The 2-place function g, where

$$g(n, m) = \text{the number of values of } i, n \leq i \leq m - 1,$$
$$\text{such that } f(i) = f(i + 1).$$

(b) The 2-place predicate G, such that Gnm is true if and only if there is some i, $n \leq i \leq m - 1$, such that $f(i) < f(i + 1)$.

5.3.10. Suppose that f_1 and f_2 are 1-place functions from $\mathbb{N}$ to $\mathbb{N}$ defined in terms of each other as follows:

$$f_1(0) = a_1$$
$$f_2(0) = a_2$$

where a_1 and a_2 are fixed numbers, and

$$f_1(n + 1) = g_1(n, f_1(n), f_2(n))$$
$$f_2(n + 1) = g_2(n, f_1(n), f_2(n)).$$

Also, g_1 and g_2 are given primitive recursive functions.

(a) Show that f_1 and f_2 are primitive recursive. (*Hint:* Use the result of Problem 5.3.5(a), and show first that f is primitive recursive, where

$$f(n) = 2^{f_1(n)} \cdot 3^{f_2(n)}$$

for all $n \in \mathbb{N}$.)

(b) Generalize the result of Part (a) to functions of more than one argument.

5.4.1. Refer to Examples 5.4.1 through 5.4.3.

(a) What is gn(abc)? gn(ad_0c)?

(b) Of what string is 16 the Gödel number? 19?

(c) What is length(120)?

(d) What is $\text{concat}^3(3, 4, 5)$?

5.4.2. Show that the following are primitive recursive.

(a) The function rev, where

$$\text{rev}(n) = \begin{cases} \text{gn}(\text{gn}^{-1}(n)^R) & \text{if } \text{gn}^{-1}(n)^R \in \mathfrak{D} \\ 0 & \text{if } \text{gn}^{-1}(n)^R \notin \mathfrak{D} \end{cases}$$

That is, rev(n) is the Gödel number of the reversal of the string whose Gödel number is n, unless the string whose Gödel number is n ends with d_0, in which case rev(n) = 0.

(b) The predicate W, where Wnm is true if and only if the symbols of $\text{gn}^{-1}(n)$ can be found, in the same order but perhaps not consecutively, in $\text{gn}^{-1}(m)$. For example, $W\text{gn}(ab)\text{gn}(acbd)$ is true, but $W\text{gn}(ab)\text{gn}(cba)$ is false.

5.4.3. An alternative Gödel numbering, indeed the one used by Gödel and the one most commonly employed, does not require that the alphabet be fixed in advance. Instead, the assumption is made that all symbols to be encoded are drawn from a fixed infinite set $\{a_0, a_1, a_2, \ldots\}$. The string $a_{i_0}a_{i_1}\ldots a_{i_k}$ is encoded by the number $p_0^{i_0}p_1^{i_1}\ldots p_k^{i_k}$, where $p_0, \ldots, p_k$ are the first $k+1$ prime numbers. For example, $a_1a_0a_3$ is encoded as $2^1 \cdot 3^0 \cdot 5^3 = 250$. Using this Gödel numbering, show that each of the following is primitive recursive.

(a) length

(b) concat

You may use the results of Problems 5.3.3(f), 5.3.3(g), and 5.3.5(a).

5.4.4. Show that the 2-place predicate L is primitive recursive, where Lnm is true if and only if n encodes a derivation as in Part (g) of Section 5.4, and the length of the derivation is m.

5.4.5. Prove carefully that if u and w are distinct strings, then $\text{gn}(u) \neq \text{gn}(w)$.

5.5.1. Let γ and f' be as specified in the proof of Theorem 5.5.1. Show that if $\text{gn}^{-1}(n) \notin \Sigma_0^*$, then $f'(n) = 0$.

5.5.2. (For students familiar with convergence of series.) Show that E is μ-recursive, where $E(n)$ is the nth digit to the right of the decimal point in the decimal expansion of e. You may use the result of Problem 5.3.6(b). (*Hint:* $e = \sum_{n=0}^{\infty} 1/n!$. For every n, we can compute an m such that the sum of the infinite series starting after the mth term is less than $10^{-(n+2)}$. If we add m terms of the series and the $(n+1)$st digit is not 9, we are home free; the nth digit of the partial sum is the nth digit of e. If the $(n+1)$st digit is 9, we have to keep calculating digits until we find one which is not 9; but this will happen eventually since e is irrational.)

5.5.3. Suppose that f is a μ-recursive *bijection* of $\mathbb{N}$ to $\mathbb{N}$, so that f has a well defined inverse f^{-1}. Prove that f^{-1} is μ-recursive.

5.5.4. Say that a $(k+1)$-place function f is **superregular** if and only if, for every $\bar{n} \in \mathbb{N}^k$, there is *one and only one* $m \in \mathbb{N}$ such that $f(\bar{n}, m) = 0$. Define the **ι-recursive functions** to be those that can be obtained from the initial functions by repeated uses of composition and primitive recursion and by applications of unbounded minimalization to superregular functions. Clearly every ι-recursive function is μ-recursive; show that every μ-recursive function is ι-recursive by showing that every instance of unbounded minimalization applied to a regular function can be replaced by an application of it to a superregular function.

5.6.1. If $l > k$, what does the Turing machine C_k^l do?

5.6.2. (a) Apply the construction of Lemma 5.6.2 to the function σ_3 as defined in Example 5.3.1(b), and follow the operation of the resulting machine on the input $\#I\#II\#III\#$.

(b) Do the same for the constant function K_1^0 as defined in Lemma 5.3.1.

5.6.3. (a) Apply the construction of Lemma 5.6.3 to the function plus as defined in Example 5.3.1(c). You may assume that a Turing machine which computes σ_3 (compare with Problem 5.6.2(a)) is given. Follow the operation of the resulting machine on the input $\#I\#I\#$.

(b) Do the same for the function V defined in Example 5.3.3, using the input $\#II\#$.

5.6.4. In the Turing machine of Figure 5-6, when G has finished its computation it leaves a value as the rightmost string on the tape. Why does this value not have to be erased before B^k is used to finish a computation?

5.6.5. Complete the proof of Theorem 5.6.1 by designing Turing machines which:

(a) convert a string to the unary representation of its Gödel number; and

(b) convert the unary representation of a Gödel number of a string into that string.

5.6.6. Prove that every function computable by a Markov system (Problem 5.2.13) is Turing-computable.

5.6.7. Prove directly (without using the μ-recursive functions as an intermediary) that every grammatically computable function from strings to strings or from numbers to numbers is Turing-computable.

5.7.1. Let $a_1 = \#$ and $a_2 = I$. Let $M = (\{q_1, q_2\}, \{\#, I\}, \delta, q_2)$, where δ is given by the following table.

q	σ	$\delta(q, \sigma)$
q_1	$\#$	(q_1, L)
q_1	I	$(q_2, \#)$
q_2	$\#$	(q_2, L)
q_2	I	(h, I)

(a) What is $\rho(M)$? What is $\rho(\#II\#)$?

(b) Suppose we used the universal 3-tape machine U' to simulate the computation of M on the input $\#II\#$. What would be the appearance of the three tapes of U' at the beginning of the simulation? At the end? What about the universal 1-tape machine U?

5.7.2. We designed the encodings of Turing machines to facilitate the design of a universal machine. But suppose we had wanted instead to make these encodings as compact as possible, that is, we wished to make $\rho(M)$ very short. Describe a more efficient encoding. (We might even be willing to allow μ to produce identical encodings of distinct machines, as long as it is possible to design a universal machine that correctly simulates machines as described under (1) and (2).)

5.7.3. What modifications to our encoding method, and the design of a universal machine, would be needed if we also wished the universal machine to be able to simulate computations that do not necessarily begin with the head positioned so that only blank tape is to its right? Restate conditions (1) and (2) to describe this more general situation, and describe the modified encoding method and the operation of the universal machine.

5.7.4. Describe in words (precisely, but without constructing a Turing machine to do the job) how to convert, for any Turing machines M_1 and M_2, the encodings $\rho(M_1)$ and $\rho(M_2)$ into the encoding $\rho(M_1 M_2)$.

5.7.5. Using diagrams of the sort introduced in Section 4.5 for Turing machines with several tapes, give the full details of the 3-tape universal machine U'. A little forethought about how to break U' into simpler machines will make its design fairly straightforward. Feel free to change the encoding function ρ if you think it will be helpful to do so.

5.7.6. (a) Design an encoding system for the primitive recursive functions. Like the encoding ρ we have developed for Turing machines, it should use a fixed alphabet; given any string over this alphabet, it should be possible to tell whether or not it actually represents a primitive recursive function, and if it does, it should be possible to determine how the function is obtained from the initial functions by composition and primitive recursion. In principle, therefore, we could design a Turing machine that could compute the values of any primitive recursive function when given its encoding and the arguments for which the value is desired.

(b) Explain carefully, in light of Part (a), the argument at the beginning of Section 5.5 to the effect that not every intuitively computable function can be primitive recursive.

5.7.7. By analogy with a universal Turing machine, a universal finite automaton would accept all strings $\rho(M)\rho(w)$ where M is a finite automaton accepting the input string w. Explain why universal finite automata cannot exist.

REFERENCES

Church's explicit presentation of a formal computational system as an exact substitute for the informal notion of an algorithm appears in

A. Church, "An Unsolvable Problem of Elementary Number Theory," *American Journal of Mathematics*, 58 (1936), 345–363.

This paper is reprinted in The Undecidable, *cited at the end of Chapter 4. Turing's paper, also cited there, proposes the Turing machine as the formalization of the notion of an algorithm, and also describes a universal Turing machine.*

The theory of primitive and μ-recursive functions is developed extensively in

R. Péter, *Recursive Functions*. New York: Academic Press, 1967.

That every μ-recursive function is Turing-computable, and vice versa, was shown in

S. C. Kleene, "General Recursive Functions of Natural Numbers," *Mathematische Annalen*, 112 (1936), 727–742.

Chomsky showed that the class of Turing-computable functions and the class of grammatically computable functions are the same.

N. Chomsky, "On Certain Formal Properties of Grammars," *Information and Control*, 2, no. 2 (1959), 137–167.

Normal systems (Problem 5.2.10) are from

E. L. Post, "Formal Reductions of the General Combinatorial Decision Problem," *American Journal of Mathematics*, 65 (1943), 197–215.

Markov systems (Problem 5.2.13) are from

A. A. Markov, "Theory of Algorithms," *Trudy Mathematicheskogo Instituta imeni V.A. Steklova*, 42 (1954) (in Russian; English Translation, Jerusalem: Israel Program for Scientific Translations, 1961).

Problem 5.5.4 is from

J. Robinson, "General Recursive Functions," *Proceedings of the American Mathematical Society*, 1 (1950), 703–718.

CHAPTER 6

UNCOMPUTABILITY

6.1 THE HALTING PROBLEM

In Chapter 1 we argued that if strings are used to represent languages, not every language can be represented: there are only a countable number of strings over an alphabet, and there are uncountably many languages. Finite automata, pushdown automata, context-free grammars, unrestricted grammars, and Turing machines are all examples of finite objects which can be used for specifying languages. Automata and grammars of each type can be specified by strings; we developed a particular way of doing this for Turing machines in Section 5.7. Accordingly, there are only countably many regular, context-free, Turing-decidable, and Turing-acceptable languages over any alphabet. So although we have worked hard to extend the capabilities of Turing machines as far as possible, in absolute terms they can be used for accepting or deciding only an infinitesimal fraction of all the possible languages. Nevertheless, we have yet to exhibit any particular language that is not Turing-decidable or not Turing-acceptable. In earlier chapters we did succeed in finding certain languages that are not regular or context-free; we now wish to do the same for the Turing-decidable and Turing-acceptable languages.

Our interest in finding such languages is not simply a matter of curiosity about the computational strength of yet one more kind of automaton. For we have argued that the Turing machine should be regarded as a mathematical formalization of the intuitive notion of algorithm. So a language that is not Turing-decidable—**Turing-undecidable**, as we shall say—is not decidable by any algorithm: there can be no general and systematic way to tell which strings are in the language and which are not. Clearly, any demonstration that a particular language is Turing-undecidable will be an achievement of major importance for our theory.

It is equally clear, however, that the methods we shall have to use to find such languages will be different from the "pumping" theorems we used for finding nonregular and non-context-free languages. Turing machines are simply too powerful to permit any clever arguments about simple repetitive patterns in their computations. How then are we to find a language too complicated to be decided by any Turing machine? We shall consider languages whose members encode Turing machines and their inputs, and develop an argument based on the idea that any Turing machine which accepts one of these languages might also appear, in an encoded form, as a *member* of that language. The argument is ingenious, and yet not complicated; as we shall see, it is an instance of the diagonalization principle.

This argument lets us deal in one blow with two Turing-undecidable languages, one that is Turing-acceptable and one that is not. Before finding other examples of such languages, we explore on a more general level the relation between the classes of Turing-acceptable and Turing-decidable languages. We shall find several characterizations of these classes of languages that will give us a more complete picture of the relation between them.

We then turn to the problem of finding other examples of Turing-undecidable languages. The first Turing-undecidable language we find consists of the encodings of certain Turing machines; from a practical standpoint, this is a dissatisfyingly artificial example. But we can show that, as a consequence of the undecidability of this one language, a variety of more natural languages that describe Turing machines and context-free grammars must also be Turing-undecidable. These languages may be viewed as encoding the answers to questions about Turing machines and grammars: Does this Turing machine halt on this input? Do these two context-free grammars generate some of the same strings? By Church's thesis, the Turing-undecidability of these languages implies that the corresponding questions cannot be answered by algorithms of any sort. We call such questions **unsolvable**; this is the intuitive concept corresponding, via Church's Thesis, to the formal notion of Turing-undecidability. We shall give many examples of these unsolvable problems, some for what they tell us about the theory of automata and grammars developed in earlier chapters and some simply as evidence that even very simple types of questions cannot be answered by general and systematic methods.

So we have two primary goals in this chapter: to complete our understanding, on a general level, of the computational abilities of Turing machines, and to explore some specific problems that are not amenable to solution by algorithms. We begin with the first task.

What is the relationship between the classes of Turing-acceptable and Turing-decidable languages? Two facts about these classes are so simple as to be nearly obvious.

Theorem 6.1.1. *Every Turing-decidable language is Turing-acceptable.*

Proof. If L is a language which is decided by a Turing machine M, then L is accepted by the Turing machine M' of Figure 6–1. This machine

Figure 6–1

simply simulates M. When M would halt, M' goes into an infinite loop if M would leave the string Ⓝ on its tape; if M would leave the string Ⓨ on its tape, then M' halts. ■

Theorem 6.1.2. *If L is a Turing-decidable language, then its complement $\bar{L}$ is also Turing-decidable.*

Proof. If L is decided by Turing machine M, then $\bar{L}$ is decided by the Turing machine illustrated in Figure 6–2. This machine simulates M until it would halt, then interchanges the answers Ⓨ and Ⓝ. ■

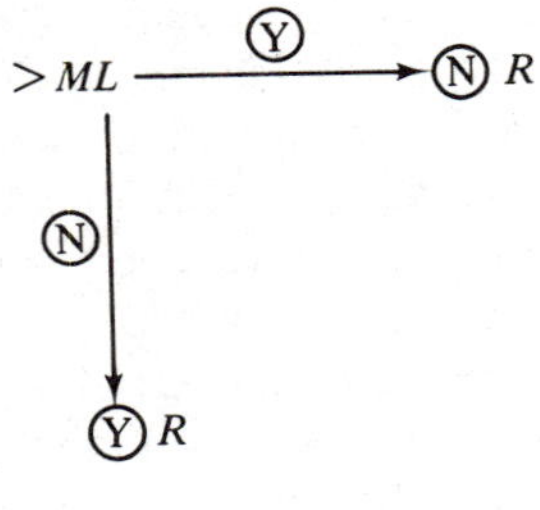

Figure 6–2

But what of the following questions: Is every Turing-acceptable language Turing-decidable? Is the complement of every Turing-acceptable language Turing-acceptable? The answer to both these questions is No. We focus on the first question.

If it were possible to predict for any Turing machine and any input string whether or not that Turing machine would eventually halt on that input, then every Turing-acceptable language would also be Turing-decidable. For then if M_1 were a Turing machine that accepted a language L, we could design a Turing machine M_2 that decided L as follows: M_2 would just perform whatever calculations were necessary to predict the eventual outcome of M_1's computation on input w; M_2 would then halt with Ⓨ or Ⓝ on its tape, depending on whether M_1 would accept w or not. Thus the question of whether every Turing-acceptable language is Turing-decidable comes down to the question of whether there is a "super" Turing machine that can predict the outcome of computations by arbitrary Turing machines on arbitrary inputs.

To be quite specific, if the particular language

$$K_0 = \{\rho(M)\rho(w)\colon \text{ Turing machine } M \text{ accepts input string } w\}$$

is decided by some Turing machine M_0, then every Turing-acceptable language is Turing-decidable. For then given any particular Turing machine M_1 which accepts a language L, we could design a Turing machine M_2 which decides L as follows: First construct a Turing machine M_1^* which, for any input string w, transforms $\#w\#$ into $\#\rho(M_1)\rho(w)\#$; that is, M_1^* shifts its input over $|\rho(M_1)|$ squares, encodes it over the alphabet $\{I, c\}$ in the prescribed way, and writes the fixed string $\#\rho(M_1)$ on the leftmost squares of the tape. Then let $M_2 = M_1^* M_0$. Thus M_2 transforms its input $\#w\#$ into $\#\rho(M_1)\rho(w)\#$ and then passes control to M_0, which by hypothesis decides whether or not M_1 accepts w.

Note, moreover, that the language K_0 is Turing-acceptable: indeed, it is accepted by a variant of the universal machine of the last section (Problem 6.1.5). Thus *every Turing-acceptable language is Turing-decidable if and only if the particular Turing-acceptable language K_0 is Turing-decidable.*

But we can show that K_0 is not Turing-decidable. First, if K_0 were Turing-decidable, then

$$K_1 = \{\rho(M)\colon \text{ Turing machine } M \text{ accepts input string } \rho(M)\}$$

would also be Turing-decidable. If M_0 decided K_0, then a Turing machine M_1 to decide K_1 could be constructed; it would transform its input string $\#w\#$ into $\#w\rho(w)\#$ and then yield control to M_0. Now M_1 would compute the same result on input $\#w\#$ as M_0 would compute on input $\#w\rho(w)\#$; but by the definition of K_0, M_0 would compute the result Ⓨ on input $\#w\rho(w)\#$ if and only if:

(a) w is $\rho(M)$ for some Turing machine M; and

(b) Turing machine M accepts input string w, that is, input string $\rho(M)$.

But this is just the definition of K_1. Therefore, it suffices to show that K is not Turing-decidable.

Second, if K_1 were Turing-decidable, then its complement would also be Turing-decidable:

$$\bar{K}_1 = \{w \in \{I, c\}^*: w \text{ is not the encoding } \rho(M) \text{ of any Turing machine } M, \text{ or } w = \rho(M) \text{ for some Turing machine } M \text{ that does } \textit{not} \text{ accept input } \rho(M)\}.$$

This is an immediate consequence of Theorem 6.1.2.

But $\bar{K}_1$ cannot even be Turing-acceptable. For suppose M^* were a Turing machine that accepted $\bar{K}_1$. Is $\rho(M^*)$ in $\bar{K}_1$? By definition of $\bar{K}_1$, $\rho(M^*) \in \bar{K}_1$ if and only if M^* does not accept input string $\rho(M^*)$. But M^* is supposed to accept $\bar{K}_1$, so $\rho(M^*) \in \bar{K}_1$ if and only if M^* accepts $\rho(M^*)$. Therefore M^* accepts $\rho(M^*)$ if and only if M^* does not accept $\rho(M^*)$. This is absurd, so the assumption that M^* exists must have been in error.

Let us summarize the above argument. We wanted to discover whether every Turing-acceptable language is Turing-decidable. We observed that this would be true if and only if the particular Turing-acceptable language K_0 were Turing-decidable. From K_0 we derived, in two steps, the language $\bar{K}_1$, which has to be Turing-decidable in order for K_0 to be Turing-decidable. But the assumption that $\bar{K}_1$ is Turing-decidable led to a logical contradiction. We have therefore proved the following theorem.

Theorem 6.1.3. *Not every Turing-acceptable language is Turing-decidable.*

This is the answer to the first of the questions we posed after proving Theorem 6.1.2. But the same proof supplies the answer to the other question. It is easy to see that K_1, like K_0, is Turing-acceptable, and we have shown that $\bar{K}_1$ is not Turing-acceptable. Therefore we have also proved Theorem 6.1.4.

Theorem 6.1.4. *The complements of some Turing-acceptable languages are not Turing-acceptable.*

We said that this argument is an instance of the diagonalization principle. To see this, and to underscore the essence of the proof, consider the binary relation R on strings over $\{I, c\}$: $(u, w) \in R$ if and only if $u = \rho(M)$ for some Turing machine M that accepts w. (R is a version of K_0.) If we let

$$R_u = \{w: (u, w) \in R\}$$

for each $u \in \{I, c\}^*$, then for any Turing machine M,

$$R_{\rho(M)} = \{w \in \{I, c\}^*: M \text{ accepts } w\}.$$

Now consider the diagonal set D for R, that is,

$$D = \{w: (w, w) \notin R\}.$$

By definition of R,

$$D = \{w: w \neq \rho(M) \text{ for any Turing machine } M \textit{ or } w = \rho(M) \text{ for some Turing machine } M \text{ such that } M \text{ does not accept } w\}.$$

In other words, D is $\bar{K}_1$. By the diagonalization principle, $D \neq R_w$ for any w; since $D \subseteq \{I, c\}^*$, this means that D is a language not accepted by any Turing machine.

And why is $D \neq R_w$ for any w? Because D differs from each R_w—and therefore from each Turing-acceptable set—on at least one string, namely w: w is in D if and only if it is not in R_w.

Now let us back off a bit from the purely formal aspects of this proof to see what it says on the intuitive level, in light of the Church-Turing thesis. We can view K_0 as an infinite dictionary that gives the answer to every question of the form: does Turing machine M accept input w? Since there is no Turing machine that decides K_0, we can conclude that *there is no algorithm that decides, for an arbitrary given Turing machine M and input string w, whether or not M accepts w*. Thus there are problems about Turing machines —and therefore about algorithms in general—that do not admit algorithmic solution. Such problems are said to be **unsolvable**. A problem that can be solved by an algorithm is called **solvable**, and an algorithm that solves a problem is called a **decision procedure** for that problem.

The most famous of the unsolvable problems is the problem described by K_0. It is generally called the **halting problem for Turing machines**: to determine, for arbitrary given Turing machine M and input w, whether M will eventually halt on input w. Note that this unsolvability result in no way implies that there may not be some circumstances under which it is possible to predict whether a Turing machine will halt on an input string. We might examine the encoding of the Turing machine, for example, to check whether the halt state h is anywhere represented; if not, the machine cannot accept any input string. This and more complex analyses may yield some information; but the results of this section state that any such analysis must ultimately either be inconclusive or yield incorrect results: There is no completely general method that correctly decides all cases.

Moreover, there are certain particular machines for which there is no general method for telling, given an input string, whether the machine will accept or halt on the input string. This follows immediately from the fact that K_0 is Turing-acceptable but not Turing-decidable. So if M_0 is a Turing machine that accepts K_0, then there can be no Turing machine—and hence no algorithm—that determines whether an arbitrary given input string w is accepted by M_0 or not. To summarize, the argument of this section establishes the unsolvability of two particular problems.

Theorem 6.1.5.

(a) *There is no algorithm for determining, given a Turing machine M and an input string w, whether M accepts w.*

(b) *For a certain fixed Turing machine M_0, there is no algorithm for determining, given an input string w, whether M_0 accepts w.*

Let us underscore the distinction between Parts (a) and (b) of this theorem. Naturally, since K_0 is $\{\rho(M)\rho(w)\colon M \text{ accepts } w\}$, K_0 can be split into infinitely many subsets $K_M = \{\rho(M)\rho(w)\colon M \text{ accepts } w\}$, one for each fixed machine M. (Each string in K_M begins the same way, with $\rho(M)$.) It does *not* follow immediately from the fact that K_0 is not Turing-decidable that some one of these subsets K_M is not Turing-decidable. In general, it is quite possible for a language that is not Turing-decidable to be the union of languages that are Turing-decidable. To see this, note that *any* language consisting of a single string is Turing-decidable; it is decided by a Turing machine that simply checks to see whether its input is that particular string and halts with Ⓨ or Ⓝ on its tape accordingly. So *every* language is a union of countably many Turing-decidable languages! However, there is no general method for combining infinitely many decision procedures into one.

In the particular case at hand, however, we know that K_{M_0} is not Turing-decidable, where M_0 is a Turing machine accepting K_0; Theorem 6.1.5(b) follows from this.

6.2 TURING-ENUMERABILITY, TURING-ACCEPTABILITY, AND TURING-DECIDABILITY

In this section we complete our discussion of the basic properties of the Turing-acceptable and Turing-decidable sets. We have already seen that every Turing-decidable language is Turing-acceptable, but the two classes are not the same: The language K_0 is one that bears witness to the difference. Which Turing-acceptable languages are Turing-decidable? There are many ways to answer this question; we present just one here.

Theorem 6.2.1. *A language is Turing-decidable if and only if both it and its complement are Turing-acceptable.*

Proof. If L is Turing-decidable, then L is Turing-acceptable by Theorem 6.1.1; also, $\bar{L}$ is Turing-decidable, and hence Turing-acceptable, by Theorem 6.1.2.

On the other hand, suppose that L is accepted by M_1 and $\bar{L}$ is accepted by M_2. Then we can construct a Turing machine M that decides L. For convenience, we describe M as a 2-tape machine; by Theorem 4.5.2, M can be simulated by a 1-tape machine. The machine M begins by putting its input string w on both tapes and placing its heads at the right ends of both copies of the input. Then M simulates both M_1 and M_2 in parallel: at each step of the operation of M, one step of M_1's computation is carried out on the first tape, and one step of M_2's computation is carried out on the second tape. Since either M_1 or M_2 must accept w, but not both, M eventually reaches a situation in which the simulated version of either M_1 or M_2 is about to halt. When this happens, M determines which of M_1 and M_2 was about to accept w and halts with its tapes appropriately configured to indicate either that $w \in L$ or that $w \notin L$. ∎

Next let us examine the class of Turing-acceptable languages a little more closely. Our original definition was that a language is Turing-acceptable if and only if it is the set of all input strings on which some Turing machine halts. But we can also characterize a language as Turing-acceptable if it is the set of all strings left on the tape at the ends of computations.

Definition 6.2.1

Let Σ_0 be an alphabet not containing $\#$. A language $L \subseteq \Sigma_0^*$ is the **output language** of a Turing machine M if and only if L is the set of all strings w in Σ_0^* such that, for some string $u \in \Sigma_0^*$, $(s, \#u\#) \vdash_M^* (h, \#w\#)$, where s is the initial state of M.

In other words, w is in the output language of M if there is some input string on which M halts, leaving w on the tape in the way we have specified for Turing machines that compute functions.

Theorem 6.2.2. *A language is Turing-acceptable if and only if it is the output language of some Turing machine.*

Proof. First we show that if L is the output language of some Turing machine M, then L is accepted by some Turing machine. By Theorem 4.6.1 it suffices to show that L is accepted by some *nondeterministic* Turing machine M'. A nondeterministic machine M' can be designed to accept L as follows: When given an input string w, M' nondeterministically writes a string u on its tape, saving w on a second track of its tape. Then M' carries out on u whatever computation M would have carried out, ignoring the input string w. When M would have halted, however, M' compares the string M would have left on its tape to w. If they are the same, then M' accepts; otherwise M' goes into an infinite loop. Thus M' accepts w just in case there is some string u from which the output string w would be computed.

Conversely, if L is the set of input strings accepted by some Turing machine M, then we can modify M so that when accepting an input string it halts with that input string on the tape (as above, this requires saving the input somehow during the course of the computation). The set of strings left on the tape at the ends of computations is then exactly the same as the set of input strings M accepts, that is, L. ∎

Another way in which a Turing machine can be used to specify a language is by *generating its members.*

Definition 6.2.2

A Turing machine M **enumerates** the language L if and only if, for some fixed state q of M,

$$L = \{w\text{: for some string } u, (s, \#) \vdash_M^* (q, \#w\#u)\},$$

where s is the initial state of M. A language is **Turing-enumerable** if and only if it is enumerated by some Turing machine.

Thus M enumerates L by starting from blank tape and computing away, periodically passing through a special state q (not the halt state). Entering state q signals that the string to the left of the head is a member of L; M may then leave state q and reenter it later on with some other member of L to the left of its tape head. The string u to the right of the tape head can be used to keep track of how to resume the computation after leaving state q.

Theorem 6.2.3. *A language is Turing-acceptable if and only if it is Turing-enumerable.*

Proof. Suppose that L is accepted by Turing machine M. Then we can design a machine M' which, instead of taking a string as input, starts from the empty tape, systematically generates (for instance, in lexicographic order) all strings over the alphabet of L, and carries out on each the same computation that M would carry out. Unfortunately, the obvious way to achieve this goal may not work: Our new machine M' cannot hope to finish its computation on each string before beginning to work on the next, since it may get "hung up" forever on some string for which the calculation by M does not terminate, even though there are other strings M would accept that have not yet been generated.

The solution is based on the "dovetailing" procedure we used in Section 1.6 to show that a union of countably many sets is countable. Instead of attempting to complete the computation on each string as it is generated, M' carries out the following sequence of operations:

- (Phase 1) First M' carries out one step of the computation of M on the first string over the alphabet of M.
- (Phase 2) Then it carries out two steps of the computation of M on each of the first two strings.
- (Phase 3) Then it carries out three steps of the computation of M on each of the first three strings.

.
.
.

Naturally, any time M' discovers that M would accept a string, M' pauses in state q to signal that fact. Some bookkeeping mechanism must be used in order for M' to keep track of which major phase of its operation is underway, and how far it has progressed; we leave these details to the reader (Problem 6.2.4).

The other direction is somewhat easier. If M enumerates L, then we can modify M to accept L as follows: Redesign M so that it saves any input supplied to it before beginning its enumeration process. Moreover, every time M would enter the distinguished state q, the modified machine compares the current tape contents with the saved input string. If a match is found, the input string is accepted; otherwise, the enumeration process continues. The new machine then accepts exactly the language M enumerates. ■

The way a Turing machine enumerates a language is reminiscent of the way a grammar generates a language. We complete our characterizations of the Turing-acceptable languages by showing that this similarity is no accident.

Theorem 6.2.4. *A language is Turing-acceptable if and only if it is generated by some grammar.*

Proof. First suppose that L is generated by some grammar G. Then we can design a Turing machine M to accept L as follows. Given an input string w, M saves w and then systematically sets about producing all possible derivations using the grammar G. These derivations can be represented by strings over the alphabet of G plus one other symbol used to encode $\Rightarrow$ and to separate the strings in a derivation from each other; M can produce all strings over this combined alphabet in lexicographic order and determine which ones actually represent derivations. Whenever M produces a string which does represent a derivation, it compares the last string in the derivation to the saved input w and halts if they are equal; otherwise it continues to generate lexicographically later derivations.

Now suppose that $L \subseteq \Sigma_0^*$ is Turing-acceptable. Then by Theorem 6.2.2, L is the output language of some Turing machine $M = (K, \Sigma, \delta, s)$. Therefore

$$L = \{w: \text{ for some } u \in \Sigma_0^*, (s, \#u\#) \vdash_M^* (h, \#w\#)\}.$$

Apply the construction of Lemma 5.2.1 to M, and let G_0 be the resulting grammar. Thus G_0 has the property that

$$(s, \#u\#) \vdash_M^* (h, \#w\#)$$

if and only if

$$[\#us\#] \overset{*}{\underset{G_0}{\Rightarrow}} [\#wh\#].$$

Now add the following rules to G_0 to obtain a grammar G.

1. Rules to start derivations and generate an input string:

$$S \rightarrow [\#S_1\#]$$
$$S_1 \rightarrow aS_1 \qquad \text{for each } a \in \Sigma_0$$
$$S_1 \rightarrow s$$

Here S and S_1 are new nonterminals; S will be the start symbol of G. By using these rules alone, any string of the form $[\#us\#]$ can be produced, where $u \in \Sigma_0^*$.

2. Rules to end derivations and erase the endmarkers:

$$h\#] \rightarrow X$$
$$aX \rightarrow Xa \qquad \text{for each } a \in \Sigma_0$$
$$[\#X \rightarrow e$$

Here X is a new nonterminal. Starting from a string of the form $[\#wh\#]$, the first rule yields $[\#wX$; then $|w|$ applications of rules of the second type result in $[\#Xw$; and finally, the last rule results in w.

We leave it to the reader (Problem 6.2.5) to verify that the new rules cannot be used in any but the intended fashion, so that G generates exactly the output language of M. ■

6.3 UNSOLVABLE PROBLEMS ABOUT TURING MACHINES AND μ-RECURSIVE FUNCTIONS

Once we have established, by diagonalization, that the particular language K_0 is not Turing-decidable, the unsolvability of a great variety of problems follows. These results are proved, not by further diagonalizations, but by **reductions**: we show in each case that if some language L_1 were Turing-decidable, then so would be some language L_2 already known *not* to be Turing-decidable. To show that if L_1 were Turing-decidable, then L_2 would be as well, it suffices to show that any algorithm for deciding membership in L_1 could be used, with some modification, to decide membership in L_2.

The reader must take care to understand the "direction" in which a reduction is to be applied. To show that a language L_1 is not Turing-decidable, we must identify a language L_2 which is not Turing-decidable, and then *reduce L_2 to L_1*. To reduce L_1 to L_2 would achieve nothing: it would merely show that L_1 could be decided by a Turing machine if we had a decision procedure for L_2—but L_2 is, by hypothesis, a language already known to have no decision procedure.

We now use reductions to show that several problems about Turing machines are unsolvable.

Theorem 6.3.1. *The following problems about Turing machines are unsolvable.*

(a) *Given a Turing machine M and an input string w, does M halt on input w?*

(b) *For a certain fixed machine M, given an input string w, does M halt on input w?*

(c) *Given a Turing machine M, does M halt on the empty tape?*

(d) *Given a Turing machine M, is there any string at all on which M halts?*

(e) *Given a Turing machine M, does M halt on every input string?*

(f) *Given two Turing machines M_1 and M_2, do they halt on the same input strings?*

(g) *Given a Turing machine M, is the language M accepts regular? Is it context-free? Is it Turing-decidable?*

Proof. Parts (a) and (b) are Theorem 6.1.5.

(c) Suppose that M_0 decided the language

$$\{\rho(M) : M \text{ accepts } e\}.$$

We show that M_0 could be put to use in order to decide K_0; we know that this is impossible, so the assumption that M_0 exists must have been in error. We claim first that there is a systematic way, given any Turing machine M and input string w, to produce a Turing machine M_w that operates as follows: M_w, when started on the empty tape (that is, in configuration $(s, \#\underline{\#})$), writes w on its tape and then starts to simulate M. In other words, if $w = a_1 \ldots a_n$, where each a_i is a single symbol, then M_w is simply

$$a_1Ra_2R \ldots Ra_nRM.$$

Then we could use M_0 to decide K_0 as follows. Given any Turing machine M and input string w, first construct M_w as just described, and then deliver $\rho(M_w)$ as an input to M_0. If M_0 halts with Ⓨ on its tape, then M_w accepts e, and therefore M accepts w. If M_0 halts with Ⓝ on its tape, then M_0 does not accept e, and therefore M does not accept w. So M_0 could be used to answer the general question of whether an arbitrary Turing machine accepts an arbitrary string, and this contradicts Part (a).

To be quite explicit about this argument, we claim that there is a Turing machine T which, on input $\#\rho(M)\rho(w)\underline{\#}$, will eventually halt with $\#\rho(M_w)\underline{\#}$ on its tape. If M_0 decided $\{\rho(M): M \text{ accepts } e\}$, then K_0 would be decided by the Turing machine TM_0.

(d) If Part (d) were a solvable problem, then Part (c) would be solvable as well. For if we could tell whether there were any input on which a Turing machine halted, we could tell whether a Turing machine halted on the empty string, as follows. To tell whether any given Turing machine M halts on the empty string, first modify M so that it erases any input given to it and then proceeds to compute as though it had actually been given the empty string as input. This modified machine M' halts on some input string, if and only if it halts on every input string, if and only if M halts on the empty string. Thus to tell whether M halts on the empty string, we need check only whether M' accepts some string.

Again to be explicit, let E be the Turing machine illustrated in Figure 5–1; E transforms $\#w\underline{\#}$, where w contains no blank, into $\underline{\#}$. Let T_1 be a Turing machine that transforms $\#\rho(M)\underline{\#}$, for any Turing machine M, into $\#\rho(ERM)\underline{\#}$ (ERM is the Turing machine called M' just above). Then if M_1 decided $\{\rho(M): M \text{ halts on some input}\}$, then T_1M_1 would decide $\{\rho(M): M \text{ accepts } e\}$.

(e) The argument for Part (d) works here as well, since M' is constructed so that it accepts some input if and only if it accepts every input.

(f) If we could determine whether two machines halted on the same set of inputs, we could fix one of them to be a trivial machine that halts immediately on every input, and then we would have an algorithm for telling whether an arbitrary machine halts on every input. This is the problem of Part (e), which we already know to be unsolvable.

(g) We show how to modify any Turing machine M' to obtain a Turing machine M such that M halts either on the strings in K_0 or on no strings, depending on whether M' halts on the empty string or not. Since there is no algorithm for telling whether M' halts on the empty string, there can be none for telling whether the set of strings on which M halts is $\varnothing$ (which is regular, context-free, and Turing-decidable) or K_0 (which is none of the three). First, M saves its input string and initiates whatever M' would do on input e. When and if M' would halt, M restores its input and carries out on that input the operation of a machine M_0 that halts exactly on the strings in K_0. Thus M' either halts on no input, because it never finishes imitating M' on input e, or else it halts on an input if and only if M_0 would halt on that input. ∎

The general thrust of Theorem 6.3.1 is that almost any nontrivial question one might like to ask about Turing machines is unlikely to have an answer that can be given by an algorithm. Since we have taken Turing machines to be themselves formal versions of algorithms, this means that many questions *about* algorithms cannot be answered *by* algorithms. A typical such question is that of Part (e). Translated into more general terms, this says that in any sort of language that can be used for stating all computational procedures, there is no systematic way to tell whether a given set of instructions actually describes a procedure that is guaranteed to terminate and deliver an answer, no matter what input it is given. Evidently, such results as these must be considered to imply that the possibilities are inherently limited for computer programs that analyze and predict the behavior of other computer programs. For example, the problem of *program verification*, that is, determining whether a computer program functions correctly under all circumstances, is unsolvable in general, although much effort has gone into the development of methods for verifying restricted types of programs.

We must also be prepared to accept the fact that any formal model of computation will be fraught with the same sort of unsolvable problems as those we have proved for Turing machines. We give but one example, which was foreshadowed in Section 5.6.

Theorem 6.3.2. *There is no algorithm for determining whether a given primitive recursive function is a regular function. Thus there is no general procedure for determining whether a particular application of unbounded minimalization is a legal one or not.*

Proof. Given any Turing machine M, we can adopt a Gödel numbering gn for strings and computations like that developed in Section 5.4 for grammars. We can then define, just as was done for grammars in Chapter 5, a primitive recursive function g such that, for any $n, m \in \mathbb{N}$,

$$g(n, m) = \begin{cases} 0 & \text{if } n \text{ is not the Gödel number of an input string to } M\text{, or if } n = \text{gn}(w) \text{ for some input } w \text{ and } m \text{ is the Gödel number of a halted computation of } M \text{ on input } w; \\ 1 & \text{otherwise.} \end{cases}$$

Then g is a regular function—that is, for every n there is an m such that $g(n, m) = 0$—if and only if M halts on every input. By Theorem 6.3.1(e), this is an unsolvable problem, so the problem of determining which primitive recursive functions are regular must also be unsolvable. ■

6.4 UNSOLVABLE PROBLEMS ABOUT GRAMMARS AND SIMILAR SYSTEMS

In this section we examine a number of problems about strings and objects that combine, substitute, and otherwise operate on them. Our interest in these unsolvability results is threefold. First, they increase our understanding of certain kinds of systems—for example unrestricted grammars—that we have studied in other contexts. Second, where we have observed a direct relationship between some formal objects—such as the context-free grammars—and issues of practical importance in computer science, our unsolvability results warn us not to undertake ambitious programs with impossible goals. And finally, the surprising simplicity of some of the unsolvable problems leaves a lasting impression as a purely mathematical achievement.

6.4.1 UNSOLVABLE PROBLEMS ABOUT UNRESTRICTED GRAMMARS

Because of the close relationship between grammars and Turing machines, the unsolvability of many problems about grammars is easy to demonstrate.

Theorem 6.4.1. *Each of the following problems is unsolvable.*

(a) *For an arbitrary given grammar G and string w, to determine whether $w \in L(G)$.*

(b) *For a certain fixed grammar G_0 and an arbitrary string w, to determine whether $w \in L(G_0)$.*

(c) *For arbitrary grammars G_1 and G_2, to determine whether $L(G_1) = L(G_2)$.*

(d) *For an arbitrary grammar G, to determine whether $L(G) = \varnothing$.*

Proof. Any decision procedure for any of these problems would immediately imply the solvability of a similar unsolvable problem about Turing machines. For example, suppose (a) were solvable. Then we could proceed as follows to determine, for any Turing machine M and string w, whether M accepts w. Simply apply to M the construction given in the proof of Theorem 6.2.4 to produce a grammar G such that $L(G)$ is the language accepted by M. Then instead of asking whether M accepts w, ask instead whether $w \in L(G)$; the two questions have the same answer. So the solvability of (a) would contradict Theorem 6.3.1(a).

In exactly the same way, the solvability of (b), (c), or (d) would contradict the unsolvability of the problems of Theorem 6.3.1(b), (f), and (d). ■

6.4.2 THUE SYSTEMS

A **Thue system** is a finite set of unordered pairs of strings. We can write a Thue system as a list

$$\{w_1, u_1\}$$
$$\{w_2, u_2\}$$
$$\vdots$$
$$\{w_n, u_n\}$$

but remember that the order in which the pairs are listed and the order in which the members of each pair are given are irrelevant.

A Thue system determines an equivalence relation on strings. If J is a Thue system, let Σ be the alphabet consisting of just those symbols appearing in some string in one of the pairs in J. Define two strings in Σ^* to be **equivalent** if and only if one can be transformed into the other by some number of successive replacements of one string in a pair in J by the other. Formally, we define $\equiv_J$ to be the reflexive, transitive closure of the relation $\sim_J$, where $x \sim_J y$ if and only if there is an i, $1 \leq i \leq n$, such that for some $z_1, z_2 \in \Sigma^*$, either $x = z_1 w_i z_2$ and $y = z_1 u_i z_2$, or $x = z_1 u_i z_2$ and $y = z_1 w_i z_2$. Note that, since $\sim_J$ is symmetric, the relation $\equiv_J$ is not only reflexive and transitive, but also symmetric. Therefore $\equiv_J$ is an equivalence relation on strings. The **word problem for Thue systems** is the problem of determining, given a Thue system J and two strings x and y, whether or not x and y are equivalent.

A Thue system may be viewed as a special type of grammar: for every rule $u \longrightarrow w$, $w \longrightarrow u$ is also a rule. (Also, there is no distinguished start symbol.) It is by no means obvious that a proof such as the proof of Theorem 6.4.1 that certain grammatical problems are unsolvable can be modified to show that the corresponding problems for these very special grammars are also unsolvable. However, the word problem for Thue systems is in fact unsolvable, and the proof of Lemma 5.2.1 provides most of the necessary machinery.

Theorem 6.4.2. *The word problem for Thue systems is unsolvable. Moreover, there is a fixed Thue system J_0 and a string w_0 such that the problem of determining whether $w \equiv_{J_0} w_0$ for an arbitrary given string w is also unsolvable.*

Proof. We first observe that the following special version of the halting problem is unsolvable: Given an alphabet Σ_0, a Turing machine M, and a string $w \in \Sigma_0^*$, will M, when started with input w, eventually halt with its tape blank and the head on the leftmost square? In other words, if s is the initial state of M, does $(s, \#w\#) \vdash_M^* (h, \#)$? The only difference between this and the problem of Theorem 6.3.1(a) is that M is required to erase its tape before halting. It should be plausible that the problem of Theorem 6.3.1(a) can be reduced to this special case; we leave the details as an exercise (Problem 6.4.6).

Now let $M = (K, \Sigma, \delta, s)$ be any Turing machine, and let $\Sigma_0 \subseteq \Sigma$. If we apply the construction of Lemma 5.2.1 to M, we obtain a grammar G such that for any $w \in \Sigma_0^*$, $[\#ws\#] \overset{*}{\underset{G}{\Rightarrow}} [h\#]$ if and only if $(s, \#w\#) \vdash_M^* (h, \#)$. Now let J be the Thue system obtained by taking all the rules of G and also all the "inverse rules" $v \longrightarrow u$, where $u \longrightarrow v$ is a rule of G. (Formally, $J = \{\{u, v\} : u \longrightarrow v$ is a rule of $G\}$.) We claim that for any $w \in \Sigma_0^*$, $[\#ws\#] \equiv_J [h\#]$ if and only if $[\#ws\#] \overset{*}{\underset{G}{\Rightarrow}} [h\#]$. This will complete the proof, for then to determine whether $(s, \#w\#) \vdash_M^* (h, \#)$, it would suffice to determine whether the strings $[\#ws\#]$ and $[h\#]$ are equivalent.

Clearly if $[\#ws\#] \overset{*}{\underset{G}{\Rightarrow}} [h\#]$, then $[\#ws\#] \equiv_J [h\#]$, since each rule of G can be paralleled in J. The converse is the hard (and surprising) part: if $[\#ws\#]$ and $[h\#]$ are equivalent, then their equivalence can be established by using the rules of G "in only the forward direction." The key is to use the fact that M is deterministic.

Suppose $[\#ws\#] \equiv_J [h\#]$. Then there is a finite sequence of strings $w_0, \ldots, w_n$ such that $w_0 = [\#ws\#]$, $w_n = [h\#]$, and $w_i \sim_J w_{i+1}$ for each i. Assume further that this sequence is as short as possible: there is no such sequence $u_0, \ldots, u_{n'}$ with $n' < n$. Then we claim that $w_i \underset{G}{\Rightarrow} w_{i+1}$ for each i, that is, all the rules are applied in the forward direction. Clearly this will establish that $w_0 \overset{*}{\underset{G}{\Rightarrow}} w_n$, that is, $[\#ws\#] \overset{*}{\underset{G}{\Rightarrow}} [h\#]$.

To begin with, note that the last rule applied—the one that yields w_n from w_{n-1}—must be applied in the forward direction. For each rule $u \longrightarrow v$ of G, u and v contain states, but the state in u is never h, since M cannot leave the halt state. Therefore, $w_{n-1} \underset{G}{\Rightarrow} w_n$.

Now suppose that for some i, $0 \le i < n - 1$, it is not the case that $w_i \underset{G}{\Rightarrow} w_{i+1}$. Then $w_{i+1} \underset{G}{\Rightarrow} w_i$. Let i be the largest number with this property:

that is, $w_{i+1} \underset{G}{\Rightarrow} w_i$, but $w_{i+1} \underset{G}{\Rightarrow} w_{i+2} \underset{G}{\Rightarrow} \cdots \underset{G}{\Rightarrow} w_n$. But then $w_i = w_{i+2}$. For since M is deterministic, only one rule of G can be applicable to any string $[uqav]$, where $u, v \in \Sigma^*$, $a \in \Sigma$, and $q \in K$, and here we have $w_{i+1} \underset{G}{\Rightarrow} w_i$ and $w_{i+1} \underset{G}{\Rightarrow} w_{i+2}$. But then $w_0, w_1, \ldots, w_{i-1}, w_{i+2}, \ldots, w_n$ is a shorter sequence of which every adjacent pair is related by $\sim_J$ and which begins and ends the same way as $w_0, \ldots, w_n$. This is impossible since n was assumed to be minimal. This completes the proof of the first part of the theorem; the second part is left to the reader (see Problem 6.4.11). ■

6.4.3 POST'S CORRESPONDENCE PROBLEM

This is another problem based on pairs of strings.

Definition 6.4.1

A **correspondence system** is a finite set P of ordered pairs of nonempty strings; that is, P is a finite subset of $\Sigma^+ \times \Sigma^+$ for some alphabet Σ. A **match** of P is any string $w \in \Sigma^+$ such that, for some $n > 0$ and some (not necessarily distinct) pairs $(u_1, v_1), (u_2, v_2), \ldots, (u_n, v_n) \in P$,

$$w = u_1 u_2 \ldots u_n = v_1 v_2 \ldots v_n.$$

Example 6.4.1

If $P = \{(a, ab), (b, ca), (ca, a), (abc, c)\}$, then *abcaaabc* is a match of P, since if the following sequence of five pairs is chosen, the concatenation of the first components and the concatenation of the second components are both equal to *abcaaabc*:

$$(a, ab), (b, ca), (ca, a), (a, ab), (abc, c).$$

Post's correspondence problem is to determine, given a correspondence system, whether that system has a match.

Theorem 6.4.3. *Post's correspondence problem is unsolvable.*

Proof. The proof has two main steps. The first step is to define a *modified* correspondence system in which one of the pairs in the correspondence system is distinguished. This pair must be the first used in the construction of a match. We show that the problem of whether a modified correspondence system has a match can be reduced to the unmodified problem. To show that the unmodified problem is unsolvable, it suffices to show that the modified problem is unsolvable. The second step is to show that the problem of derivability in a grammar can be reduced to the modified problem. Solvability of the correspondence problem would then imply solvability of the grammatical derivability problem, which we know to be unsolvable by Theorem 6.4.1.

Step 1. A **modified correspondence system** is a pair $P' = (P, (x, y))$, where P is a correspondence system and $(x, y) \in P$. A **match** of P' is a string w such that, for some $n \geq 0$ and some pairs $(u_1, v_1), \ldots, (u_n, v_n)$ in P,

$$w = xu_1 \ldots u_n = yv_1 \ldots v_n.$$

We now show how to construct, for each modified correspondence system P'_1, a correspondence system P_2 such that P_2 has a match if and only if P'_1 does as well. Let $P'_1 = (P_1, (x, y))$, where $P_1 \subseteq \Sigma^+ \times \Sigma^+$, and let $*$ and $\$$ be new symbols not in Σ. If P_1 contains k pairs, then P_2 will contain $k + 2$ pairs: one for each pair in P_1 except (x, y); two for (x, y); and one special pair for ending a match. The form of matches of P_2 is this: if $a_1 \ldots a_n$ is a match of P'_1, where $a_1, \ldots, a_n$ are symbols in Σ, then $*a_1*a_2* \ldots *a_n*\$$ will be a match of P_2; that is, the corresponding match of P_2 is obtained by placing a $*$ between each pair of symbols and at the beginning and end, and then terminating with a $\$$. Moreover, each match of P_2 may be decoded to yield a solution of P'_1 by taking the prefix up to and including the first $\$$. This string will be of the form $*a_1*a_2* \ldots *a_n*\$$, and then $a_1 \ldots a_n$ will be a match of P'_1.

If $w = a_1 \ldots a_n$ is any string in Σ^*, let us write $L(w)$ for the string $*a_1*a_2 \ldots *a_n$ in which a $*$ has been inserted just to the left of each symbol, and $R(w)$ for the string $a_1*a_2* \ldots a_n*$.

To force matches of P_2 to begin appropriately, if (x, y) is the starting pair for P'_1, then P_2 contains the pair $(L(x)*, L(y))$. This will be the only pair in P_2 in which both components could begin with the same symbol, so it will have to be used first in constructing any match.

For each pair (u, v) in P_1, including (x, y), P_2 contains the pair $(R(u), L(v))$. Because the two strings in these pairs always begin differently and end differently, they cannot be used at the beginning or end of a match. Finally, P_2 contains the pair $(\$, *\$)$. Because this is the only pair in which each string ends with the same symbol, this is the only pair that can be used to end a match of P_2.

Now if $(x, y), (u_1, v_1), \ldots, (u_n, v_n)$ is a sequence of pairs from P_1, beginning with (x, y), such that $xu_1 \ldots u_n = yv_1 \ldots v_n$, then

$$(L(x)*, L(y)), (R(u_1), L(v_1)), \ldots, (R(u_n), L(v_n)), (\$, *\$)$$

is a sequence of pairs from P_2 such that $L(x)*R(u_1)R(u_2) \ldots R(u_n)\$ = L(y)L(v_1) \ldots L(v_n)*\$$. From this it follows that P_2 has a match if P'_1 has a match. Now if P_2 has a match—for example, if $(u'_1, v'_1), \ldots, (u'_k, v'_k)$ is a sequence of pairs from P_2 such that $u'_1 \ldots u'_k = v'_1 \ldots v'_k$, then as we have said (u'_1, v'_1) must be $(L(x)*, L(y))$ and (u'_k, v'_k) must be $(\$, *\$)$. It is possible that the pair $(\$, *\$)$ appears more than once in the sequence, but since it is the only pair in which \$ appears at all, the subsequence of this sequence of pairs up to and including the first occurrence of $(\$, *\$)$ must also yield a match. So we may assume that $(u'_i, v'_i) \neq (\$, *\$)$ for $i = 1, \ldots, k-1$. But then for $i = 2, \ldots, k-1$, (u'_i, v'_i) must be a pair of the form $(R(u), L(v))$ for some pair $(u, v) \in P_1$, since it follows by induction that for $i = 1, \ldots, k-1$ the string $u'_1 \ldots u'_i$ ends with $*$ but $v'_1 \ldots v'_i$ does not. Thus the sequence $(u'_1, v'_1), \ldots, (u'_k, v'_k)$ has the form indicated at the beginning of this paragraph, where $n = k - 2$ and $xu_1 \ldots u_n = yv_1 \ldots v_n$. Thus if P_2 has a solution, so does P'_1.

Step 2. Now we are ready to show that the problem of determining whether a modified correspondence system has a match is unsolvable. We first note that given a grammar G and strings w and z, it is unsolvable whether $w \overset{*}{\underset{G}{\Rightarrow}} z$, even if G is restricted so that if $u \longrightarrow v$ is a rule of G, then $v \neq e$. To see this, we need merely note that the grammar constructed in Lemma 5.2.1 has exactly this property.

Now let $G = (V, \Sigma, R, S)$ be any grammar with no rules of the form $u \longrightarrow e$, and let w and z be strings in V^*. Let $*$ be a symbol not in V. We define a modified correspondence system $(P, (x, y))$ that has a match if and only if $w \overset{*}{\underset{G}{\Rightarrow}} z$.

1. The initial pair (x, y) is $(*, *w*)$.
2. For each $a \in V \cup \{*\}$, P contains the pair (a, a).
3. For each rule $u \longrightarrow v$ of G, P contains the pair (u, v).
4. P contains the pair $(z**, *)$.

Let us call a **prematch** of $(P, (x, y))$ any pair of strings (u, v) such that

(a) for some $n \geq 0$ and some pairs $(u_1, v_1), \ldots, (u_n, v_n)$ in P, $u = xu_1 \ldots u_n$ and $v = yv_1 \ldots v_n$;

(b) one of u, v is a prefix of the other.

Thus a match of P is a string u such that (u, u) is a prematch, and we may view any match as being built up from a sequence of prematches. The crucial properties of P are the following.

Property I. *If $n \geq 0$, $w_0, \ldots, w_n \in V^*$, and $w = w_0 \underset{G}{\Rightarrow} w_1 \underset{G}{\Rightarrow} \cdots \underset{G}{\Rightarrow} w_n$, then $(*w_0*w_1* \ldots *w_{n-1}*, *w_0*w_1* \ldots *w_n*)$ is a prematch of $(P, (x, y))$.*

Property II. *If (u, v) is a prematch of $(P, (x, y))$ constructed without using pair in (4), then for some $n \geq 0$ and some $w_0, w_1, \ldots, w_n, w'_n, w'_{n+1}$ in V^*,*

$$u = *w_0*w_1* \ldots *w_{n-1}*w'_n,$$

$$v = *w_0*w_1* \ldots *w_{n-1}*w_n*w'_{n+1},$$

$$w = w_0 \overset{*}{\underset{G}{\Rightarrow}} w_1 \overset{*}{\underset{G}{\Rightarrow}} \cdots \overset{*}{\underset{G}{\Rightarrow}} w_n,$$

$$w'_n \text{ is a prefix of } w_n,$$

and

$$w'_n \overset{*}{\underset{G}{\Rightarrow}} w'_{n+1}.$$

Both Properties I and II are proved by induction.

Proof of Property I. The assertion is clearly true if $n = 0$, for then the prematch $(*, *w*)$ is the initial pair. Now suppose that (I) is true up to a certain value of n, and let $w \underset{G}{\Rightarrow} w_1 \underset{G}{\Rightarrow} \cdots \underset{G}{\Rightarrow} w_{n+1}$. Then for some rule $u \longrightarrow v$ of G and some strings $w', w'' \in V^*$, $w_n = w'uw''$ and $w_{n+1} = w'vw''$. By the induction hypothesis, $(*w*w_1* \ldots *w_{n-1}*, *w*w_1* \ldots *w_n*)$ is a prematch. If $w' = a_1 \ldots a_m$, each $a_i \in V$, then by using the pairs $(a_1, a_1), \ldots, (a_m, a_m)$ it follows that $(*w*w_1* \ldots *w_{n-1}*w', *w*w_1* \ldots *w_n*w')$ is a prematch (recall that w' is a prefix of w_n). Since (u, v) is a pair in P, then $(*w*w_1* \ldots *w_{n-1}*w'u, *w*w_1* \ldots *w_n*w'v)$ is a prematch (again note that $w'u$ is a prefix of w_n). If $w'' = b_1 \ldots b_k$, each $b_i \in V$, then using the pairs $(b_1, b_1), \ldots, (b_k, b_k)$ and $(*, *)$, it follows that $(*w*w_1* \ldots *w_{n-1}*w'uw''*, *w*w_1* \ldots *w_n*w'vw''*)$ is a prematch (since $w'uw''* = w_n*$). But $w'vw'' = w_{n+1}$, so the induction is complete.

Proof of Property II. Consider the sequence of pairs in P used in constructing the prematch (u, v). If there is only one pair, then $(u, v) = (x, y) = (*, *w*)$ and the assertion is true with $n = 0$, $w'_n = w'_{n+1} = e$ (since $e \overset{*}{\underset{G}{\Rightarrow}} e$). Proceeding by induction on the length of the sequence of pairs, suppose that (II) holds whenever (u, v) has been constructed using a sequence of $k + 1$ pairs ($k \geq 0$) and consider a prematch (u, v) constructed by means of pairs $(x, y), (u_1, v_1), \ldots, (u_{k+1}, v_{k+1})$. By the induction hypothesis, if we let $w' = xu_1 \ldots u_k$ and $v' = yv_1 \ldots v_k$, then for some $n \geq 0$ and some $w_1, \ldots, w_n, w'_n, w'_{n+1} \in V^*$, $u' = *w*w_1 \ldots *w_{n-1}*w'_n$, $v' = *w*w_1* \ldots *w_n*w'_{n+1}$, $w \overset{*}{\underset{G}{\Rightarrow}} w_1 \overset{*}{\underset{G}{\Rightarrow}} w_2 \overset{*}{\underset{G}{\Rightarrow}} \cdots \overset{*}{\underset{G}{\Rightarrow}} w_n$, w'_n is a prefix of w_n, and $w'_n \overset{*}{\underset{G}{\Rightarrow}} w'_{n+1}$. There are three cases to consider.

(a) $(u_{k+1}, v_{k+1}) = (a, a)$ for some $a \in V$. Then (II) holds for the same value of n, the same $w_1, \ldots, w_n$, and with new values of w'_n and w'_{n+1}, namely w'_na and $w'_{n+1}a$. For in order for $(u'a, v'a)$ to be a prematch, w'_n must be a prefix of w_n, other than w_n itself, and $w'_n a$ must be a prefix of w_n (if w'_n were equal to w_n, then the last symbol of $u'a$ would have to match the last $*$ in $v'a$). And since $w'_n \overset{*}{\underset{G}{\Rightarrow}} w'_{n+1}$, $w'_n a \overset{*}{\underset{G}{\Rightarrow}} w'_{n+1}a$.

(b) $(u_{k+1}, v_{k+1}) = (u'', v'')$ for some rule $u'' \to v''$ of G. Then (II) holds for the same value of n, the same $w_1, \ldots, w_n$, and with new values of w'_n and w'_{n+1}, namely $w'_n u''$ and $w'_{n+1}v''$. The argument is similar to that for (a); $w'_n u''$ must be a prefix of w_n, and $w'_n u'' \overset{*}{\underset{G}{\Rightarrow}} w'_{n+1}v''$, since $w'_n \overset{*}{\underset{G}{\Rightarrow}} w'_{n+1}$ and $u'' \to v''$ is a rule of G.

(c) $(u_{k+1}, v_{k+1}) = (*, *)$. Then (II) holds for a new value of n, namely $n' = n + 1$. For if $(u'*, v'*)$ is a prematch, then $w'_n = w_n$, so $u'* = *w_0*w_1* \ldots *w_n*$ and $v'* = *w_0*w_1* \ldots *w_n*w'_{n+1}*$. Let the new values of $w'_{n'}$ and $w'_{n'+1}$ be e and the induction is complete.

This completes the proof of (I) and (II). Now if in fact there are $w_0, \ldots, w_n$ such that $w = w_0 \underset{G}{\Rightarrow} w_1 \underset{G}{\Rightarrow} \cdots \underset{G}{\Rightarrow} w_n = z$ then by (I), $*w_0*w_1* \ldots *w_n**$ is a match. Conversely, because of (II), no match can be constructed without using the pair in (4). Thus if there is a match, then there is a prematch (u, v) constructed without using the pair in (4) such that $(uz**, v*)$ is also a prematch. Since u is a prefix of v and contains one fewer $*$ than v by (II), and since z contains no $*$, $uz**$ and $v*$ have the same number of $*$'s. Therefore $uz** = v*$ and this string is actually a match. Moreover, v ends with $*$. In (II), then, w'_{n+1} must be e, and hence w'_n must be e. But then z must be w_n, so $w \overset{*}{\underset{G}{\Rightarrow}} z$. This completes the proof. ∎

6.4.4 UNSOLVABLE PROBLEMS ABOUT CONTEXT-FREE GRAMMARS

We have already seen that the intersection of two context-free languages need not be context-free (Theorem 3.5.5). In fact, the situation is much worse than that result suggests: in general, one cannot even tell whether the intersection of two context-free languages is empty, when those languages are presented by means of grammars generating them.

Theorem 6.4.4. *The problem of determining, given two context-free grammars G_1 and G_2, whether $L(G_1) \cap L(G_2) = \varnothing$ is unsolvable. In fact, there is a* particular *context-free grammar G_1 such that the problem of determining, given a context-free grammar G_2, whether $L(G_1) \cap L(G_2) = \varnothing$, is unsolvable.*

Proof. Let P be any correspondence system, and let $P \subseteq \Sigma^+ \times \Sigma^+$. Let $c \notin \Sigma$; let G_1 be a grammar that generates $\{wcw^R : w \in \Sigma^*\}$; and let G_2 be a grammar that generates $\{u_1u_2 \ldots u_n c v_n^R v_{n-1}^R \ldots v_1^R : n \geq 1, (u_1, v_1), \ldots,$

$(u_n, v_n) \in P\}$. Clearly G_1 and G_2 are easy to construct from Σ and P. But $L(G_1) \cap L(G_2) = \{wcw^R: w$ is a match of $P\}$. So if it were possible to determine whether $L(G_1) \cap L(G_2) = \varnothing$, it would also be possible to solve Post's correspondence problem. This we know to be impossible, by Theorem 6.4.3.

To establish the stronger form of this theorem, in which one of the grammars is fixed, note that Post's correspondence problem is unsolvable even if we consider only correspondence systems over the fixed alphabet $\{a, b\}$ (Problem 6.4.3). Therefore G_1 in this construction can be a fixed grammar that generates $\{wcw^R: w \in \{a, b\}^*\}$. ■

The ideas used in the proof of Theorem 6.4.4 yield another unsolvability result about context-free grammars.

Definition 6.4.2

A context-free grammar G is **ambiguous** if there is some string $w \in L(G)$ that has two distinct parse trees.

Ambiguity is a property of natural interest in the study of context-free languages, since if a string can be parsed in two different ways the intended meaning of the string may be in doubt. (See also Problem 3.5.22.)

Example 6.4.2

The following grammar for arithmetic expressions is ambiguous: $G = (V, \Sigma, R, S)$, where $V = \{S, N, x, y, +, *\}$, $\Sigma = \{x, y, +, *\}$, and R consists of the following rules.

$$S \rightarrow N$$

$$S \rightarrow S + S$$

$$S \rightarrow S * S$$

$$N \rightarrow x$$

$$N \rightarrow y$$

For example, $x*y+x$ has the two distinct parse trees shown in Figure 6–3. The reason this grammar would be impractical as a way of describing even a subset of the arithmetic expressions of a real programming language is that it gives no clue as to the intended way of computing an expression such as $x*y+x$: should we multiply $x*y$ first, or add $y+x$ first? The grammar of Example 3.1.3 does not have this failing.

Unfortunately, as desirable as lack of ambiguity might seem to be, there is no general procedure for telling whether a grammar enjoys this property.

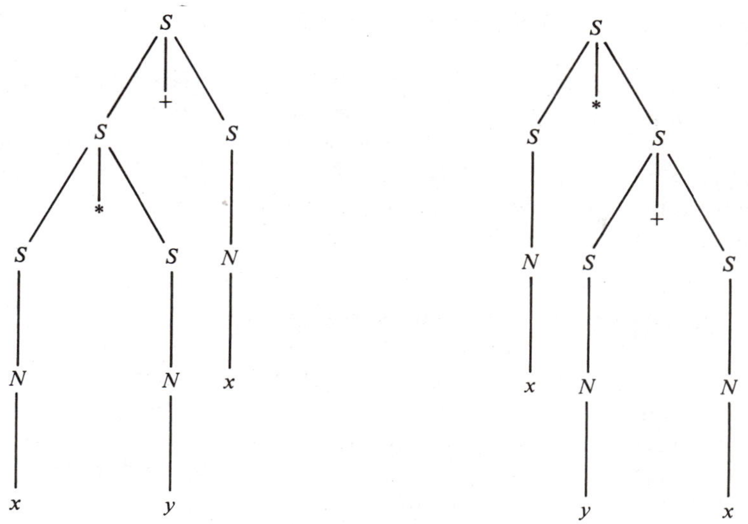

Figure 6–3

Theorem 6.4.5. *It is an unsolvable problem to determine, given a context-free grammar G, whether G is ambiguous.*

Proof. Let P be any correspondence system, with $P \subseteq \Sigma^+ \times \Sigma^+$. Let P contain exactly k pairs, $P = \{(u_1, v_1), \ldots, (u_k, v_k)\}$. Choose k symbols $a_1, \ldots, a_k$ not in Σ. Let $\Delta = \Sigma \cup \{a_1, \ldots, a_k\}$, $V_1 = \Delta \cup \{S_1\}$, and $V_2 = \Delta \cup \{S_2\}$, where S_1 and S_2 are new symbols. Let $G_1 = (V_1, \Delta, R_1, S_1)$, where

$$R_1 = \{S_1 \rightarrow a_i S_1 u_i : i = 1, \ldots, k\} \cup \{S_1 \rightarrow a_i u_i : i = 1, \ldots, k\}.$$

Similarly, let $G_2 = (V_2, \Delta, R_2, S_2)$, where

$$R_2 = \{S_2 \rightarrow a_i S_2 v_i : i = 1, \ldots, k\} \cup \{S_2 \rightarrow a_i v_i : i = 1, \ldots, k\}.$$

Clearly,

$$L(G_1) = \{a_{i_n} \ldots a_{i_1} u_{i_1} \ldots u_{i_n} : n \geq 1, 1 \leq i_1, \ldots, i_n \leq k\}$$

and

$$L(G_2) = \{a_{i_n} \ldots a_{i_1} v_{i_1} \ldots v_{i_n} : n \geq 1, 1 \leq i_1, \ldots, i_n \leq k\}.$$

As in the proof of Theorem 3.5.1, let

$$G = (V_1 \cup V_2 \cup \{S\}, \Delta, R_1 \cup R_2 \cup \{S \rightarrow S_1, S \rightarrow S_2\}, S),$$

where S is a new symbol; then $L(G) = L(G_1) \cup L(G_2)$. We claim that G is ambiguous if and only if P has a match; since there is no algorithm for determining whether a correspondence system has a match, it will follow that there can be none for determining whether a context-free grammar is ambiguous.

If P has a match $u_{i_1} \ldots u_{i_n} = v_{i_1} \ldots v_{i_n}$, then clearly the string $a_{i_n} \ldots a_{i_1}u_{i_1} \ldots u_{i_n} = a_{i_n} \ldots a_{i_1}v_{i_1} \ldots v_{i_n}$ has two different parse trees, one arising from G_1 and one from G_2. Conversely, if w is a string in $L(G)$ with two different parse trees, then $w \in L(G_1)$ and $w \in L(G_2)$, since G_1 and G_2 are both unambiguous separately. But then $w = a_{i_n} \ldots a_{i_1}u_{i_1} \ldots u_{i_n} = a_{i_n} \ldots a_{i_1}v_{i_1} \ldots v_{i_n}$ for some $i_1, \ldots, i_n$, $n \geq 1$, and so w is a match. ■

6.5 AN UNSOLVABLE TILING PROBLEM

We are given a finite set of tiles, each one unit square. We are asked to tile the first quadrant of the plane with copies of these tiles, placing one tile in each square region formed when lines are drawn one unit apart parallel to the horizontal and vertical axes, as shown in Figure 6–4. We have an infinite supply of copies of each tile.

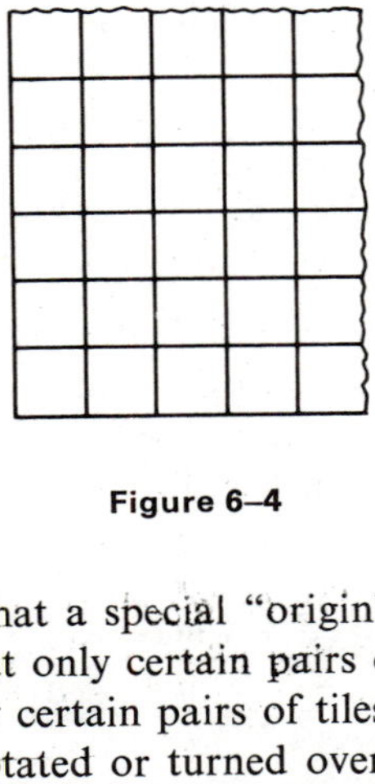

Figure 6–4

The only restrictions are that a special "origin" tile must be placed in the lower left-hand corner; that only certain pairs of tiles may abut each other horizontally; and that only certain pairs of tiles may abut each other vertically. (Tiles may not be rotated or turned over.) Is there an algorithm for determining whether the first quadrant can be tiled, given a finite set of tiles, the origin tile, and the adjacency rules?

This problem can be formalized as follows. A **tiling system** is a quadruple $\mathfrak{D} = (D, d_0, H, V)$, where D is a finite set, $d_0 \in D$, and $H, V \subseteq D \times D$. A **tiling** by $\mathfrak{D}$ is a function $f: \mathbb{N} \times \mathbb{N} \to D$ such that the following hold.

$$f(0, 0) = d_0$$

$$(f(n, m), f(n + 1, m)) \in H \qquad \text{for all } n, m \in \mathbb{N}$$

$$(f(n, m), f(n, m + 1)) \in V \qquad \text{for all } n, m \in \mathbb{N}$$

Theorem 6.5.1. *The problem of determining, given a tiling system, whether there is a tiling by that system is unsolvable.*

Proof. We reduce to this tiling problem the problem of determining, given a Turing machine M, whether M eventually halts when started on the leftmost square of a blank tape. This is a trivial variation on the problem of Theorem 6.3.1(c); there M starts on the *second* square of a blank tape. Clearly this slightly different problem is unsolvable as well. Thus when we have shown that this version of the halting problem is reducible to the tiling problem, we shall have shown that the tiling problem is unsolvable.

The basic idea is to construct from any Turing machine M a tiling system $\mathfrak{D}$ such that a tiling by $\mathfrak{D}$, if one exists, represents an infinite computation by M starting from the blank tape. Configurations of M are represented horizontally in a tiling; successive configurations appear one above the next. If M operates forever, successive rows can be tiled ad infinitum; but if M halts after k steps, it is possible to tile only k rows.

We can think of the edges of the tiles as being marked with certain information; we allow tiles to abut each other horizontally or vertically only if the markings on the adjacent edges are identical. On the horizontal edges, these markings are either a symbol from the alphabet of M or a state-symbol combination. The tiling system is arranged so that if a tiling is possible, then by looking at the markings on the horizontal edges between the kth and $(k + 1)$st rows of tiles, we can read off the configuration of M after $k - 1$ steps of its computation. Thus only one edge along such a border is marked with a state-symbol pair; the other edges are marked with single symbols.

The marking on a vertical edge of a tile is either absent or consists of a state of M, together with a "directional" indicator, which we indicate by an arrowhead. (Two exceptions are given under (e) below.) These markings on the vertical edges are used to communicate a left- or right-hand movement of the head from one tile to the next.

To be specific, let $M = (K, \Sigma, \delta, s)$. Then $\mathfrak{D} = (D, d_0, H, V)$, where D contains the following tiles.

(a) For each $a \in \Sigma$, the tiles illustrated in Figure 6–5, which simply communicate any unchanged symbols upwards from configuration to configuration.

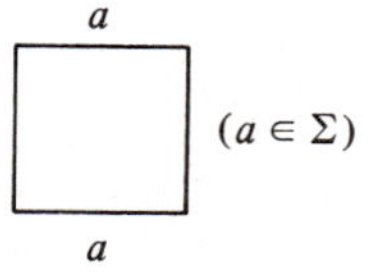

Figure 6–5

(b) For each $a \in \Sigma$ and $q \in K$ such that $\delta(q, a) = (p, b)$, where $p \in K$ and $b \in \Sigma$, the tile shown in Figure 6–6. This tile communicates the head position upwards and also changes the state and scanned symbol appropriately.

Figure 6–6

(c) For each $q \in K$ and $a \in \Sigma$ such that $\delta(q, a) = (p, R)$ for some $p \in K$, the tile shown in Figure 6–7(a) and also, for each $b \in \Sigma$, the tile shown in Figure 6–7(b). These tiles communicate head movement one square from left to right, while changing the state appropriately.

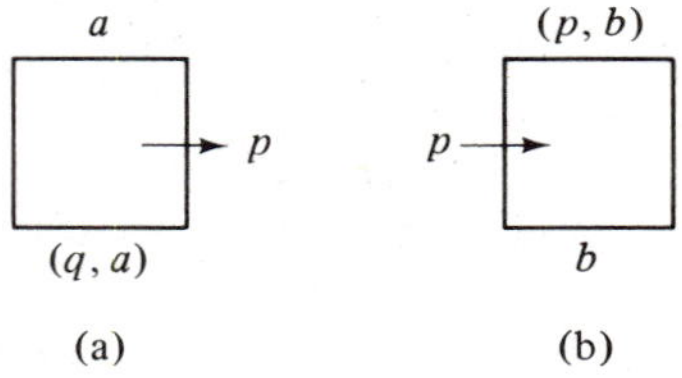

Figure 6–7

(d) Tiles similar to those of (c) for the case in which $\delta(q, a) = (p, L)$ are illustrated in Figure 6–8.

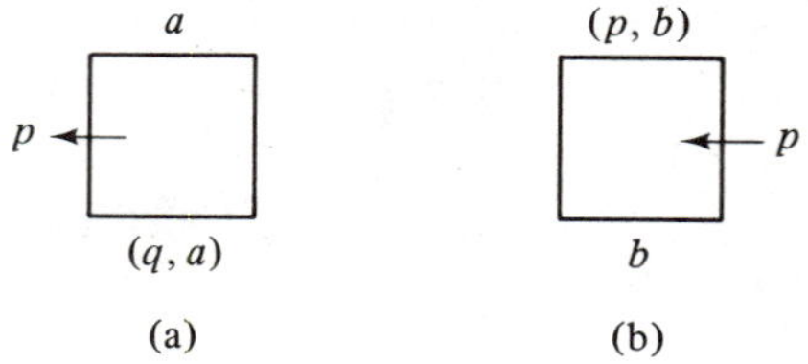

Figure 6–8

These tiles do the bulk of the simulation of M by $\mathfrak{D}$. It remains only to specify some tiles to initiate the computation and ensure that the bottom row is tiled correctly.

(e) The origin tile d_0 is illustrated in Figure 6–9(a). It specifies on its vertical edge the initial state of M and the blank symbol. Its right edge is marked with the blank symbol; this edge can be matched only by the left edge of the final tile, that shown in Figure 6–9(b), which in turn propagates to the right the information that the top edge of every tile in the bottom row is marked with the blank.

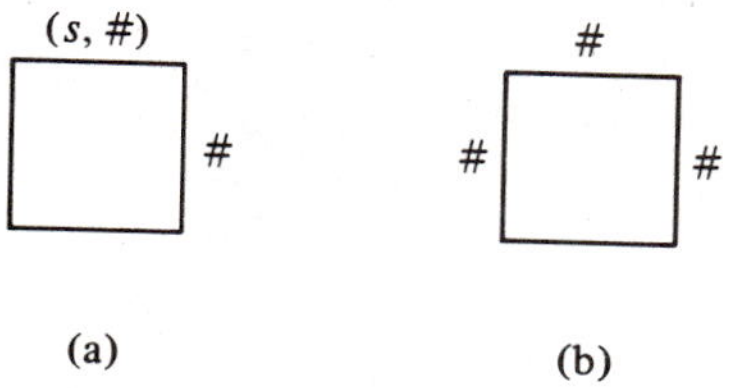

Figure 6–9

This completes the construction of $\mathfrak{D}$. The last set of tiles ensures that the border between the first two rows is marked $(s, \#)\#\#\# \ldots$; the other tiles force each subsequent border to be marked correctly. Note that no tile mentions the halt state, so that if M halts after k steps only k rows can be tiled. ■

Example 6.5.1

Consider the Turing machine (K, Σ, δ, s), where $\Sigma = \{\#\}$, $K = \{s, q\}$, and δ is given by

$$\delta(s, \#) = (q, R)$$
$$\delta(q, \#) = (s, L).$$

This machine simply oscillates its head from left to right and back again, never moving beyond the first tape square. The tiling of the plane associated with the infinite computation of M is shown in Figure 6–10.

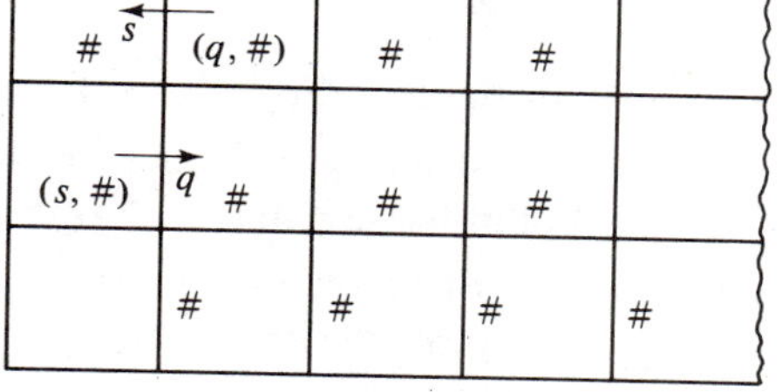

Figure 6–10

The complete set of tiles associated with M is shown in Figure 6–11.

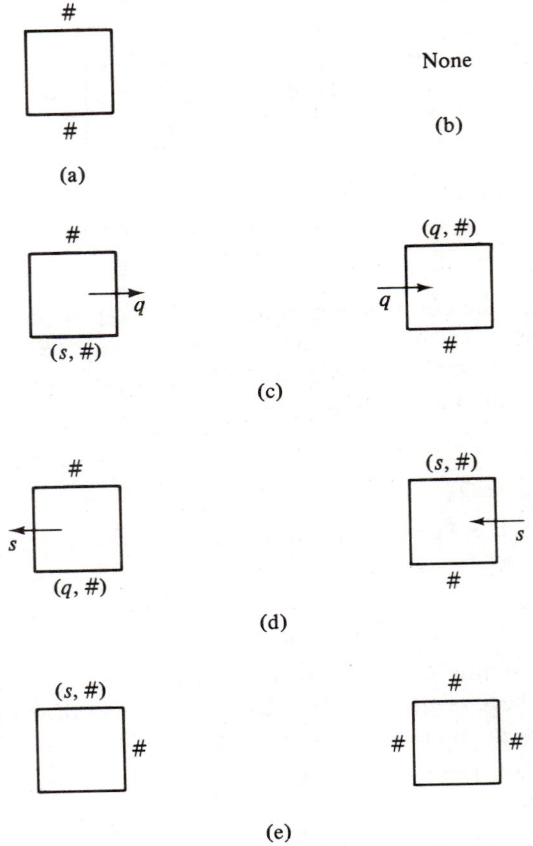

Figure 6–11

PROBLEMS

6.1.1. What is R_u, if u is not the encoding of any Turing machine?

6.1.2. In this problem you will find a particular example of an uncomputable function without using a diagonal argument.

(a) Show that any Turing-computable function from numbers to numbers is computed by a Turing machine with alphabet $\{I, \#\}$.

The **busy-beaver function** $\beta: \mathbb{N} \longrightarrow \mathbb{N}$ is defined as follows: for each $n \geq 0$, $\beta(n)$ is the largest number m such that, for some Turing machine M with alphabet $\{I, \#\}$ and with exactly n states, $(s, \#\underline{\#}) \vdash_M^* (h, \#I^m\underline{\#})$, where s is the initial state of M.

(b) Show that for any n and m, $\beta(n) \geq \beta(m)$ if and only if $n \geq m$. (That is, if more states are available a larger number of I's can be written, starting from the empty tape.)

(c) Show that if $f: \mathbb{N} \longrightarrow \mathbb{N}$ is computed by a Turing machine with alphabet $\{I, \#\}$ and k states, then $\beta(n + k) \geq f(n)$ for all n. In other words, there is a Turing machine M_n with $n + k$ states which writes at least $f(n)$ I's on a blank tape before halting in the conventional way. (*Hint:* It is easy enough to find machines N_n with n states that write n I's. Combine these machines with the fixed machine F which computes f; that is, consider the machines N_nF.)

(d) Show that β is not Turing-computable. (Suppose it were. Then the function γ such that $\gamma(n) = \beta(2n)$ would also be Turing-computable. Using (a), let f in (c) be γ and apply (b) to the resulting inequality.)

(e) Why do we insist throughout this problem that only Turing machines with alphabet $\{I, \#\}$ be considered? (Any other fixed alphabet containing I and $\#$ would do as well.)

6.1.3. According to Theorem 6.1.4, the class of Turing-acceptable languages is not closed under complementation. But show that it is closed under union and intersection.

6.1.4. Show that the class of Turing-decidable languages is closed under union, complementation, intersection, concatenation, and Kleene star.

6.1.5. The universal Turing machine described in Section 5.7 might not accept K_0 because it might accept some strings not of the form $\rho(M)\rho(w)$ for any Turing machine M and string w. Describe carefully the changes that have to be made to the machine of Section 5.7 to obtain one that accepts K_0.

6.1.6. Show that any finite set is Turing-decidable.

6.2.1. Prove that a language is Turing-decidable if and only if it is enumerated *in lexicographic order* by some Turing machine.

6.2.2. Suppose we modify Definition 6.2.2 as follows: M enumerates L if and only if, for some fixed state q of M,

$$L = \{w: (s, \underline{\#}) \vdash_M^* (q, \#w\underline{\#})\},$$

where s is the initial state of M. In other words, M is no longer allowed to retain any "bookkeeping" information. Show that under this definition, it remains true that L is Turing-acceptable if and only if it is enumerated by some Turing machine.

6.2.3. Show that $L \subseteq \Sigma^*$ is Turing-acceptable if and only if, for some nondeterministic Turing machine M, $L = \{w \in \Sigma^*: (s, \#) \vdash_M^* (h, \#w\#)\}$, where s is the initial state of M.

6.2.4. Explain in greater detail how the "dovetailing" machine described in the proof of Theorem 6.2.3 could keep track of the status of its computation.

6.2.5. Prove carefully that the grammar constructed in the proof of Theorem 6.2.4 has the desired properties.

6.2.6. Suppose we drop the restriction that unbounded minimalization be applied only to *regular* functions; and we also redefine it so that if, for some $\bar{n}$, there is *no* m such that $f(\bar{n}, m) = 0$, $\mu m[f(\bar{n}, m) = 0]$ is simply undefined (rather than zero). Now application of unbounded minimalization to a function $f: \mathbb{N}^{k+1} \rightarrow \mathbb{N}$ need not result in a function from $\mathbb{N}^k \rightarrow \mathbb{N}$. It will, nonetheless, result in a function from *some subset* of $\mathbb{N}^k$ to $\mathbb{N}$. Such a function is called a **μ-recursive partial function**. More explicitly, the μ-recursive partial functions are the closure of the set of initial functions under composition, primitive recursion, and unbounded minimalization (as redefined). Show that a language is Turing-acceptable if and only if the Gödel numbers of the strings in the language are:

(a) the domain of a μ-recursive partial function;

(b) the range of a μ-recursive partial function.

6.2.7. Show that if a language is Turing-enumerable, then there is a Turing machine that enumerates it *without ever repeating* an element of the language.

6.2.8. Let Σ be an alphabet not containing the symbol c, and suppose that $L \subseteq \{w_1 c w_2 : w_1, w_2 \in \Sigma^*\}$ is Turing-acceptable. Show that $L' = \{w_1 \in \Sigma^*: \text{for some } w_2 \in \Sigma^*, w_1 c w_2 \in L\}$ is Turing-acceptable. Is L' necessarily Turing-decidable if L is Turing-decidable?

6.2.9. A grammar is said to be **context-sensitive** if and only if each rule is of the form $u \rightarrow v$, where $|v| \geq |u|$. A **context-sensitive language** is one generated by a context-sensitive grammar.

(a) Show that a language is context-sensitive if and only if it does not contain the empty string and it is accepted by some nondeterministic Turing machine with the property that the head never moves to the right of the (blank) square on which it is initially placed. (In other words, if M is such a Turing machine, s is its initial state, and w is an input, then if $(s, \#w\underline{\#}) \vdash_M^* (q, u\underline{a}v)$ for some q, u, a, and v, then $|uav| \leq |\#w\#|$.)

(b) Show that every context-sensitive language is Turing-decidable.

(c) Show that a language is context-sensitive if and only if it is generated by a grammar such that every rule is of the form $uAv \longrightarrow uwv$, where A is a nonterminal and $w \neq e$.

6.2.10. A Turing machine M is said to **cycle** on input w if there is some configuration C such that $(s, \#w\underline{\#}) \vdash_M^* C \vdash_M^+ C$ (where $\vdash_M^+$ means *yields in one or more steps*). Show that if $L \subseteq \Sigma^*$ is Turing-acceptable, then L is accepted by some Turing machine that does not cycle on any input $w \in \Sigma^*$.

6.2.11. Suppose that $f: \Sigma_0^* \longrightarrow \Sigma_1^*$ is a Turing-computable function that is onto Σ_1^*. Show that there is a Turing-computable function $g: \Sigma_1^* \longrightarrow \Sigma_0^*$ such that $f(g(w)) = w$ for each $w \in \Sigma_1^*$.

6.2.12. The Turing-undecidable languages L exhibited in Section 6.1 have the property that $\bar{L}$ is Turing-acceptable.

(a) Show that there is a language L such that neither L nor $\bar{L}$ is Turing-acceptable.

(b) Give an example of such a language.

6.3.1. Show that the following function is not Turing-computable:

$$f: \{I, c\}^* \longrightarrow \{I, c\}^*,$$

where

$$f(w) = \begin{cases} e & \text{if } w \neq \rho(M) \text{ for any Turing machine } M; \\ \rho(M') & \text{if } w = \rho(M) \text{ for some Turing machine } M, \text{ and } M' \text{ is some Turing machine that halts on the same inputs as } M \text{ and such that the number of states of } M' \text{ is as small as possible.} \end{cases}$$

Thus there is no algorithm for minimizing the number of states of a Turing machine (compare with Problem 2.1.8).

6.3.2. Say that Turing machine M **uses** k tape squares on input string w if and only if there is a configuration of M, $(q, u\underline{a}v)$, such that $(s, \#w\underline{\#}) \vdash_M^* (q, u\underline{a}v)$ and $|uav| \geq k$, where s is the initial state of M.

(a) Show that the following problem is solvable: Given a Turing machine M, an input string w, and a number $k > 0$, does M use k tape squares on input w?

(b) Suppose that $f: \mathbb{N} \rightarrow \mathbb{N}$ is Turing-computable, and Σ_0 is an alphabet and M is a Turing machine such that for all input strings $w \in \Sigma_0^*$, M uses at most $f(|w|)$ tape squares on input w. Show that $\{w \in \Sigma_0^*: M \text{ accepts } w\}$ is Turing-decidable.

(c) Show that the following problem is unsolvable: Given a Turing machine M and an input string w, is there a $k > 0$ such that M does *not* use k tape squares on input w? (That is, does M use a finite amount of tape on input w?)

6.3.3. Which of the following problems about Turing machines are solvable, and which are unsolvable? Explain your answers carefully.

(a) To determine, given a Turing machine M, a state q, and a string w, whether M ever reaches state q when started with input w from its initial state.

(b) To determine, given a Turing machine M and a state q, whether there is any configuration $(s, u\underline{a}v)$ which yields a configuration with state q, where s is the initial state of M.

(c) To determine, given a Turing machine M and a state q, whether there is any configuration $(p, u\underline{a}v)$ which yields a configuration with state q, where p is a state of M other than q.

(d) To determine, given a Turing machine M and a symbol a, whether M ever writes the symbol a when started on the empty tape.

(e) To determine, given a Turing machine M, whether M ever writes a nonblank symbol when started on the empty tape.

(f) To determine, given a Turing machine M and a string w, whether M ever moves its head to the left when started with input w.

(g) To determine, given two Turing machines, whether one accepts the complement of the language accepted by the other.

(h) To determine, given two Turing machines, whether there is any string on which each halts.

(i) To determine, given a Turing machine M, whether the language accepted by M is finite.

6.3.4. Show that it is not a solvable problem to determine whether a given primitive recursive function has a given value for any arguments.

6.3.5. Show that it is an unsolvable problem to determine, given a Turing machine M, whether there is some string w such that M enters each of its states during its computation on input w.

6.4.1. Show that the halting problem for Turing machines remains unsolvable even when restricted to Turing machines with some small, fixed number of states. (If the number is required to be fixed but not small, the existence of a universal Turing machine establishes the result. Show how any Turing machine can be simulated, in some suitable sense, by a Turing machine with about half a dozen states but a much larger alphabet. Actually, three states are enough; in fact, two would be enough if we allowed our machines to write and move in a single step.)

6.4.2. Show that any Turing machine can be simulated, in some sense we leave it to you to specify, by an automaton with no tape but with two **counters**. A counter is a pushdown store with only one symbol, except for a distinguishable bottom-marker which is never removed. Thus a counter may be thought of as a register for containing a number. The possible operations on a counter are: add one; see if it contains zero; and if it does not contain zero, subtract one. Conclude that the halting problem for these 2-counter machines is unsolvable. (*Hint:* Reduce any Turing machine to a 2-counter machine as follows.

1. Show how to simulate a Turing machine tape by two pushdown stores.
2. Using a Gödel numbering like that of Chapter 5 of the contents of a pushdown store, show how each pushdown store can be simulated by two counters.
3. Using the following Gödel numbering of four numbers as one, show that four counters can be simulated by two: (p, q, r, s) is encoded as $2^p 3^q 5^r 7^s$.)

6.4.3. Show that Post's correspondence problem is unsolvable, even if restricted to a two-symbol alphabet. What about a one-symbol alphabet?

6.4.4. Let $P = \{(u_1, v_1), \ldots, (u_k, v_k)\}$ be a correspondence system over an alphabet Σ. Let $a_1, \ldots, a_k$ be new symbols, not in Σ. Let $A = \{a_1, \ldots, a_k\}$. Let

$$L_1 = \{u_{i_1} \ldots u_{i_n} a_{i_n} a_{i_{n-1}} \ldots a_{i_1} : n \geq 1, 1 \leq i_1, \ldots, i_n \leq k\}.$$

In other words, L_1 consists of a concatenation of the left-hand sides of pairs in P, followed by a string of symbols which identifies, in reverse order, the pairs from which those strings were chosen. Similarly, let

$$L_2 = \{v_{i_1} \ldots v_{i_n} a_{i_n} a_{i_{n-1}} \ldots a_{i_1} : n \geq 1, 1 \leq i_1, \ldots, i_n \leq k\}.$$

Let c be a new symbol, and let $K = \{wcw^R : w \in \Sigma^* A^*\}$.

(a) Show that $\bar{K}$ is context-free. (*Hint:* Construct a pushdown automaton.)

(b) Show that both L_1 and $\bar{L}_1$ are context-free languages. The same will clearly hold for L_2 and $\bar{L}_2$.

(c) Show, using Part (b) and closure properties of the context-free languages, that if $L = \{ucv^R : u \in L_1, v \in L_2\}$, then $\bar{L}$ is context-free. (*Hint:* $w \in \bar{L}$ if w contains more or less than one c, or if it contains exactly one c which lies between a member of L_1 and a member of $\overline{L_2^R}$, or between a member of $\bar{L}_1$ and a member of L_2^R, or between a member of $\bar{L}_1$ and a member of $\overline{L_2^R}$.)

(d) Show that the context-free language $\bar{K} \cup \bar{L}$ is equal to $(\Sigma \cup A \cup \{c\})^*$ if and only if the correspondence system P has no match. (That is, show that $K \cap L = \varnothing$ if and only if P has no match.)

(e) Conclude that the following problems are unsolvable: To determine, given a context-free grammar (V, Σ, R, S), whether $L(G) = \Sigma^*$; to determine, given a context-free grammar G and a regular grammar R, whether $L(G) = L(R)$; to determine, given two context-free grammars G_1 and G_2, whether $L(G_1) = L(G_2)$.

6.4.5. A (nondeterministic) **2-head finite automaton (THFA)** consists of a finite control, an input tape, and two heads that can read but not write on the tape and move only left to right. The machine is started in its initial state with both heads on the leftmost square of the tape. Each transition is of the form (q, u, v, p) where q and p are states and u and v are strings, and if (q, u, v, p) is a transition of M, then M can, when in state q, read u with its first head and v with its second and enter state p. (See the figure on the next page.) M accepts an input string by moving both heads together off the right end of the tape while entering a designated final state.

(a) Show that it is solvable, given a THFA M and an input string w, whether M accepts w.

(b) Show that it is not solvable, given a THFA M, whether there is any string that M accepts. (Use the correspondence problem.)

(c) A THFA is **deterministic** if it has only one choice of move from any configuration. Is the problem of Part (b) unsolvable even for deterministic THFA's?

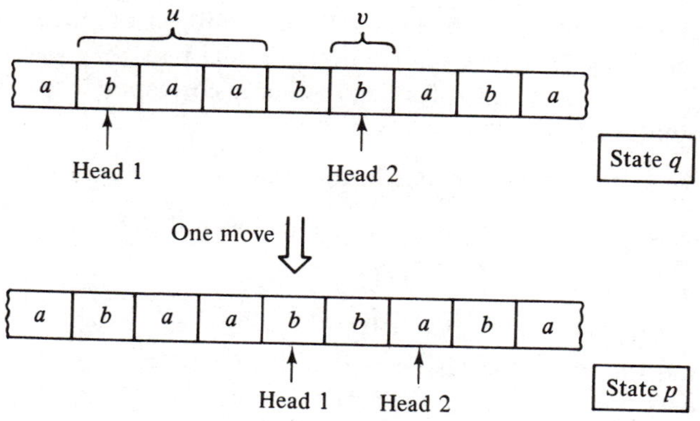

6.4.6. Show that the following problem, used in the proof of Theorem 6.4.2, is unsolvable: Given a Turing machine M with initial state s and a string w, does $(s, \#w\#) \vdash_M^* (h, \#)$?

6.4.7. (a) Find a match for the correspondence system

$$\{(aa, ab), (a, bb), (bba, a), (a, ab), (b, a)\}.$$

(b) Show that the following correspondence system has no match.

$$\{(ab, b), (aba, ba), (ab, ba), (a, abb)\}$$

6.4.8. Let $G = (V, \Sigma, R, S)$, where $V = \{A, B, S\}$, $\Sigma = \varnothing$, and

$$R = \{A \longrightarrow AB, BA \longrightarrow AB\}$$

(a) Follow the construction Step 2 of the proof of Theorem 6.4.3 for the grammar G and the strings $w = AA$ and $z = AABB$ to produce a modified correspondence system P'.

(b) Find a derivation $AA \overset{*}{\underset{G}{\Rightarrow}} AABB$ and a corresponding match of P'.

(c) From P' construct a correspondence system P as in Step 1 of proof of Theorem 6.4.3, and show a match of P.

6.4.9. A **weak match** of a correspondence system $\{(u_1, v_1), \ldots, (u_k, v_k)\}$ is a string w such that, for some $n > 0, i_1, \ldots, i_n, j_1, \ldots, j_n$, where $1 \leq i_1, \ldots, i_n, j_1, \ldots, j_n \leq k$,

$$u_{i_1} \ldots u_{i_n} = v_{j_1} \ldots v_{j_n} = w.$$

That is, w can be gotten both by concatenating n first components and also by concatenating n second components, but the pairs used in the two cases need not be the same. Show that the problem of determining whether a correspondence system has a weak match is solvable.

6.4.10. Suppose that in Problem 6.4.9 the definition of "weak match" is strengthened so that $j_1, \ldots, j_n$ is required to be a *permutation* of $i_1, \ldots, i_n$. Is it still solvable whether a correspondence system has a weak match?

6.4.11. Prove the second sentence in the statement of Theorem 6.4.2.

6.5.1. Let $M = (\{s\}, \{a, \#\}, \delta, s)$, where δ is as follows.

$$\delta(s, \#) = (s, a)$$

$$\delta(s, a) = (s, R)$$

Find the set of tiles associated with M via the construction in Section 6.5, and illustrate the first four rows of a tiling of the plane by means of these tiles.

6.5.2. What will be the appearance of a tiling by $\mathfrak{D}$ if M hangs?

6.5.3. Show that there is some fixed set of tiles D and adjacency rules H and V such that the following problem is unsolvable: Given a **partial tiling**, that is, a mapping $f: S \longrightarrow D$ for some finite subset $S \subseteq \mathbb{N} \times \mathbb{N}$ such that f obeys the adjacency rules, can f be extended to a tiling of the whole plane?

6.5.4. Suppose the rules of the tiling game are changed so that instead of fixing a particular tile to be placed at the origin, we fix instead a particular set of tiles and stipulate that only these tiles may be used in tiling the first row. Show that the tiling problem remains unsolvable.

6.5.5. Prove formally, by induction, the correctness of the construction given in Section 6.5.

6.5.6. Suppose the rules of the tiling game are changed as follows: The tiles are not perfectly square, but may have various bumps and notches along their edges. Two tiles may be laid down next to each other only if their edges fit together perfectly, like pieces of a jigsaw puzzle. Show that the tiling problem remains unsolvable, even if we are now allowed to rotate tiles or turn them over. (There is still a specified "origin tile" which must be put down at position (0, 0) in a fixed orientation.)

6.5.7. Suppose that we think of square tiles as being determined by the *colors* of their four edges, and that two edges may abut provided that they are similarly colored. Show that if we are allowed to rotate tiles and turn them over, then *any* nonempty set of tiles can be used to tile the entire first quadrant (even when we continue to require that one special tile be placed at the origin).

REFERENCES

The unsolvability of the halting problem for Turing machines is shown in Turing's 1936 paper cited at the end of Chapter 4. Church's paper cited at the end of Chapter 5 establishes an unsolvability result for his formal computational system.

Thue systems were introduced in

A. THUE, "Probleme über Veränderungen von Zeichenreihen nach gegebenen Regeln," *Skrifter utgit av Videnskapsselskapet i Kristiana*, I. Matematisk-naturvidenskabelig klasse 1914, 10 (1914), 34 pp.

Their unsolvability was first demonstrated in

E. L. POST, "Recursive Unsolvability of a Problem of Thue," *Journal of Symbolic Logic*, 12 (1947), 1–11.

Correspondence systems and the original proof of their unsolvability can be found in

E. L. POST, "A Variant of a Recursively Unsolvable Problem," *Bulletin of the American Mathematical Society*, 52 (1946), 264–268.

Theorem 6.4.5 and Problem 6.4.4 (unsolvable problems for context-free languages) are from the paper by Bar-Hillel, Perles, and Shamir cited at the end of Chapter 3.

Wang's domino problem is from

H. WANG, "Proving Theorems by Pattern Recognition II," *Bell System Technical Journal*, 40 (1961), 1–141.

Closely related is

J. R. BÜCHI, "Turing-machines and the Entscheidungsproblem," *Mathematische Annalen*, 148 (1962), 201–213.

It turns out that the domino problem remains unsolvable even when the origin constraint is omitted and only the adjacency constraints are imposed. This was first proved by

R. BERGER, "The Undecidability of the Domino Problem," *Memoirs of the American Mathematical Society*, 66 (1966).

A simpler and more readable version may be found in

R. M. ROBINSON, "Undecidability and Nonperiodicity for Tilings of the Plane," *Inventiones Mathematicae*, 12 (1971), 177–209.

Problem 6.4.5 on two-headed finite automata is from the paper by Rabin and Scott cited at the end of Chapter 2.

A celebrated problem, known as "Hilbert's Tenth Problem," asks whether there is a method for finding integer roots of arbitrary multivariate polynomials. The problem was proposed in

D. HILBERT, "Mathematische Probleme," *Proceedings of the International Congress of Mathematicians in Paris 1900*, Göttingen (1900), 253–297 (English translation, *Bulletin of the American Mathematical Society*, 2 (1901–1902), 437–479).

Hilbert's tenth problem was shown unsolvable in

YU. MATIYASEVICH, "Enumerable Sets are Diophantine," *Doklady Akademii Nauk SSSR*, 191 (1970), 279–282 (in Russian; English translation in *Soviet Mathematics—Doklady*, 11 (1970), 354–357).

A good elementary exposition can be found in

M. DAVIS, "Hilbert's Tenth Problem is Unsolvable," *American Mathematical Monthly*, 80 (1973), 233–269.

Problem 6.4.2 is due to Minsky; see his book cited at the end of Chapter 4.

CHAPTER 7

COMPUTATIONAL COMPLEXITY

7.1 TIME-BOUNDED TURING MACHINES

In Chapter 6 we showed that there exist well-defined decision problems that cannot be solved by algorithms, and gave some specific examples of such problems. We can therefore classify all computational problems into two categories: those that can be solved by algorithms and those that cannot. With the great advances in computer technology of the last few years, we might expect that all the problems of the former type could be easily solved by the fast electronic computers now available. Unfortunately, computing practice reveals that many problems, although in principle solvable, cannot be solved in any practical sense by computers due to excessive time requirements.

Suppose that it is your task to schedule the visits of a traveling sales representative to 10 regional offices. You are given a map with the 10 cities and distances in miles, and you are asked to produce the itinerary that minimizes the total distance traversed. This is surely the kind of task that you would like to use a computer to solve. And, from a theoretical standpoint, the problem is certainly solvable. If there are n cities to visit, the number of possible itineraries is finite—to be precise, $(n - 1)!$, that is, $1 \cdot 2 \cdot 3 \cdot \cdots \cdot (n - 1)$. Hence an algorithm can easily be designed that systematically examines all itineraries in order to find the shortest. Naturally, one can even design a Turing machine that computes the shortest tour.

Still, one gets an uneasy feeling about this algorithm. There are too many tours to be examined. For our modest problem of 10 cities, we would have to examine $9! = 362{,}880$ itineraries. With some patience, this can be carried out by a computer, but, what if we had 30 cities to visit? The number of itineraries is now gigantic: $29!$, which is larger than 10^{29}. Even if we could examine a billion tours per second—a pace far beyond the capabilities of existing or projected computers—the required time for completing this calculation would be more than a billion human lifetimes!

Thus, the fact that a problem is solvable in theory does not immediately imply that it can be *realistically* solved. Evidently, our classification of problems into solvable and unsolvable must be refined. Problems that are solvable must be further categorized according to their *complexity* or *difficulty*.

We have already seen such a classification. We know that a Turing-decidable language may be regular, context-free but not regular, or non-context-free. In fact, we know that there are context-free languages that are not deterministic context-free (Section 3.6). We therefore have a hierarchy of Turing-decidable languages: Turing-decidable—context-free—deterministic context-free—regular. This hierarchy reflects *qualitative* or *structural* distinctions between the corresponding automata. For example, a pushdown automaton is essentially a nondeterministic 2-tape Turing machine with severely restricted writing and head-moving capabilities; and a finite automaton is a pushdown automaton that never uses its stack!

Our goal in this chapter is to establish another, *quantitative* classification of decidable languages by considering Turing machines that are restricted, not in their structural capabilities, but in the amount of effort they are allowed to expend when computing on an input string. A natural measure of the amount of effort spent by a Turing machine is the number of steps in the computation or, as we shall say, the amount of time required for the Turing machine to come to a conclusion about its input. Hence, our goal in this chapter will be to characterize the capabilities of Turing machines for deciding languages, when the number of steps performed in each computation is limited.

Among all equivalent versions of Turing machines that we saw in Section 4.5, we shall pick the multiple-tape machine as our basic model. This choice is of purely technical motivation; the use of multiple-tape Turing machines will facilitate a number of proofs below. Just as we saw in Chapter 4 that allowing multiple tapes did not extend the class of Turing-decidable languages, we shall see in this chapter that allowing multiple tapes does not affect, in any way we shall consider of major importance, the amount of *time* a Turing machine needs to decide a language.

Definition 7.1.1

If M is a Turing machine of any variety and $t \in \mathbb{N}$, define the relation $\vdash_M^t$ (*yields in t steps*) between configurations of M as follows:

$$C \vdash_M^0 C'$$

if and only if $C = C'$;

$$C \vdash_M^{t+1} C'$$

if and only if there is a configuration C'' of M such that

$$C \vdash_M^t C'' \text{ and } C'' \vdash_M C'.$$

That is,

$$C \vdash_M^t C'$$

if and only if

$$C \vdash_M^* C'$$

by a computation of exactly t steps.

Now let T be a function from $\mathbb{N}$ to $\mathbb{N}$. Let $L \subseteq \Sigma_0^*$ be a language, and $M = (K, \Sigma, \delta, s)$ be a k-tape Turing machine with $\Sigma_0 \subseteq \Sigma$. We say that M **decides** L **in time** T if the following holds: whenever $w \in L$,

$$(s, \#w\underline{\#}, \underline{\#}, \ldots, \underline{\#}) \vdash_M^t (h, \#\,\text{Ⓨ}\underline{\#}, \underline{\#}, \ldots, \underline{\#}) \text{ for some } t \leq T(|w|);$$

and whenever $w \notin L$,

$$(s, \#w\underline{\#}, \underline{\#}, \ldots, \underline{\#}) \vdash_M^t (h, \#\,\text{Ⓝ}\underline{\#}, \underline{\#}, \ldots, \underline{\#}) \text{ for some } t \leq T(|w|).$$

We say that L is **decidable in time** T if there is some $k > 0$ and some k-tape Turing machine that decides L in time T. The class of all languages decidable in time T is denoted by TIME(T).

Thus we bound the number of steps of a Turing machine not by an absolute constant, but in terms of a *function of the length of the input*. Note that, since a Turing machine must erase its input and write Ⓨ or Ⓝ before it halts, on input w it must always execute $|w| + 1$ writing and $|w| + 3$ head-moving steps; so no function T such that $T(n) < 2n + 4$ for some $n \geq 0$ is a useful time bound.

Example 7.1.1

Consider the language $L = \{w \in \{a, b\}^*: w$ has no occurrence of the string $aa\}$. The 1-tape Turing machine M shown in Figure 7–1 decides L. It does so by reading the input from right to left and acting as a finite automaton, while at the same time erasing the input. In total, it executes just the

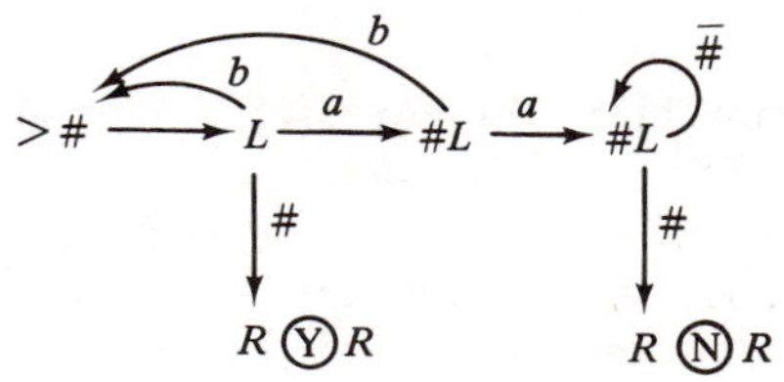

Figure 7–1

minimum possible number of steps: $|w| + 1$ writing and $|w| + 3$ moving steps. Thus M decides L in time T, where $T(n) = 2n + 4$; we conclude that $L \in \text{TIME}(T)$.

A word on notation: We represent functions from $\mathbb{N}$ to $\mathbb{N}$ as usual by single letters such as f, g, or T. When a function can be represented by a simple expression, however, we shall denote the function by the expression, using the variable n to denote the argument. For example, we shall write $n^3 + 2n$ as shorthand for the phrase *the function* $f: \mathbb{N} \to \mathbb{N}$ *such that* $f(n) = n^3 + 2n$ *for all* $n \in \mathbb{N}$. Thus, for the language L of Example 7.1.1, we write $L \in \text{TIME}(2n + 4)$.

Example 7.1.2

Recall the Turing machine of Figure 4–15 which accepts the language $L = \{w \in \{a, b, c\}^* : w$ has the same number of a's, b's, and c's$\}$. This machine can be easily modified to a Turing machine M, shown in Figure 7–2, which *decides* the same language. In fact, we shall immediately show that M decides L within time T, where T is the function $2n^2 + 13n + 9$.

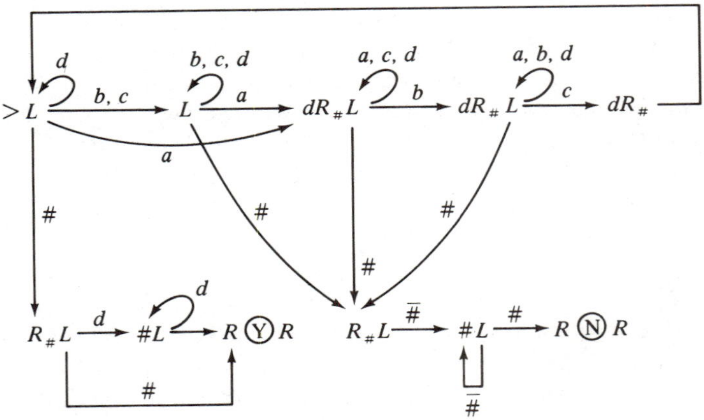

Figure 7–2

Like the Turing machine of Figure 4–15, M operates in stages. At each stage it begins by scanning its input from right to left, until it encounters an a. This a is changed to d by M; M then goes back to the right end of the nonblank part of its tape. Next, it again scans its tape, until a b is found and is changed to a d. This process is repeated for c's, concluding a stage. If M at some stage searches for an a but only finds d's, it erases its tape and halts with the result # Ⓨ # ; in case of any other unsuccessful search, M erases its tape and halts with # Ⓝ #.

Let us carefully count the number of steps that M uses on an input of length n. At each stage, M scans its tape three times; on each scan M examines at most n symbols, changes at most one, and repositions its head to the right end of the tape after at most n more steps—a total of $2n + 1$ steps. Therefore, each stage consists of at most $3 \cdot (2n + 1)$ steps. How many stages are there? There are at most $\lceil n/3 \rceil + 1$, since M is bound to run out of a's, b's, or c's after at most $\lceil n/3 \rceil + 1$ stages.† Finally, M erases its tape and writes Ⓨ or Ⓝ, depending on the condition of termination, in $2n + 4$ more steps. This brings the total number of steps to a number not greater than $(\lceil n/3 \rceil + 1) \cdot 3(2n + 1) + 2n + 4$. To simplify this expression somewhat, notice that for all n, $\lceil n/3 \rceil \leq (n + 2)/3$; hence, after some algebra, the total number of steps of M on an input of length n is found to be no greater than $T(n) = 2n^2 + 13n + 9$. We conclude that M decides L in time T; thus $L \in \text{TIME}(2n^2 + 13n + 9)$.

The step-counting argument of the previous example is quite typical. Since our goal is only to *bound from above* the number of steps by some function T of the input length, our counting need not be exact, as long as it is on the safe (high) side. Our estimate may be grossly pessimistic for certain inputs. In our example, on input b^n, M would perform only $4n + 5$ steps before halting with #Ⓝ#, since it will immediately detect that the input has no a's in it. Thus the bound $T(n)$ reflects the behavior of M in the worst case on *any* input of length n.

Deriving such an upper bound usually involves a careful analysis of the operation of a machine. Naturally, the more careful our analysis, the better estimate we may expect—in Problem 7.1.2, we see that the Turing machine M of Example 7.1.2 decides L in time $n^2 + 4n + 4$, an improvement over the bound T just derived. Obtaining good estimates of the number of steps performed by complex Turing machines sometimes involves ingenious arguments, and there are no simple rules that always work. In fact, Theorem 6.3.1(e) tells us that it is an unsolvable problem even to decide whether a given Turing machine halts on all inputs, let alone to derive an upper bound on the number of steps after which the machine is guaranteed to have halted.

If bounding the time complexity of a given Turing machine from above can be a nontrivial task, then *designing* a Turing machine that accepts a given language L in a desirable time bound T—thus showing that $L \in \text{TIME}(T)$—is even more interesting. The goal of the theory of **computational complexity**, to which this chapter is a brief introduction, is to choose, among

†If X is a real number, $\lceil X \rceil$ denotes the smallest integer m such that $m \geq X$; $\lfloor X \rfloor$ denotes the largest integer m such that $m \leq X$. Thus $\lceil \frac{3}{2} \rceil = 2$, $\lfloor 3.19 \rfloor = 3$, and for $m \in \mathbb{N}$, $\lfloor m \rfloor = \lceil m \rceil = m$.

the many possible Turing machines for deciding a given decidable language, one guaranteed to terminate within T steps, where T is as small as desired—or, if this is not possible, to give a rigorous proof of the impossibility of such a "fast" Turing machine.

Example 7.1.3

Let us ask the following question of the language L in Example 7.1.2: Is there some k-tape Turing machine M' ($k \geq 1$) such that M' decides L, and does so—in the worst case—in considerably fewer steps than M does? In other words, is $L \in \text{TIME}(T')$ for some function T' smaller than T?

We shall now design such a Turing machine M', where M' has four tapes. It first scans its input from right to left, erasing it, while at the same time writing an I on the second tape for each a that it encounters, an I on the third tape for each b, and an I on the fourth tape for each c. Then M' compares the number of I's on its second, third, and fourth tapes by moving the heads on those tapes simultaneously to the left. As long as it sees an I on all three tapes, it erases all three I's and keeps moving left. If it eventually finds the leftmost # on all three tapes simultaneously, then it halts with #Ⓨ# on its first tape; otherwise it halts with #Ⓝ#, after erasing the remaining I's. Figure 7–3 shows M'. Here we have used the notation $[A^{(i)}, B^{(j)}]$, if $A^{(i)}$ and $B^{(j)}$ are actions (such as $L^{(i)}$, $\sigma^{(j)}$, and so on) on the ith and jth tapes that are to be executed *simultaneously*. Similarly, $A^{(i,j,k)}$ stands for $[A^{(i)}, A^{(j)}, A^{(k)}]$. For example, $[\#^{(1)}, I^{(4)}]$ means "simultaneously write # on tape 1 and I on tape 4," and $L^{(2,3,4)}$ means "move the heads on tapes 2, 3, and 4 to the left at the same time."

Intuitively, M' is more efficient than M, but how much? Let us establish a worst-case estimate of the number of steps that M' executes on any input of length n. We break the analysis into three parts, corresponding to the three major submachines (1), (2), (3) illustrated in Figure 7–3.

1. Reading and erasing the input is done in a total of $3n + 1$ steps.
2. Let p be the number of occurrences in the input of the symbol among $\{a, b, c\}$ that occurs in the input the least number of times. Then comparing the number of I's on the three tapes takes $2p + 1$ steps.
3. Erasing the remaining I's and writing the Ⓨ or Ⓝ token takes at most $2(n - 3p) + 2$ more steps.

Thus M' executes at most $3n + 1 + 2p + 1 + 2(n - 3p) + 2 \leq 5n + 4$ steps† on any input of length n. This compares very favorably to the bounds

†In this example and elsewhere, we ignore one unnecessary step at the end of a computation due to the details of Definition 4.3.2.

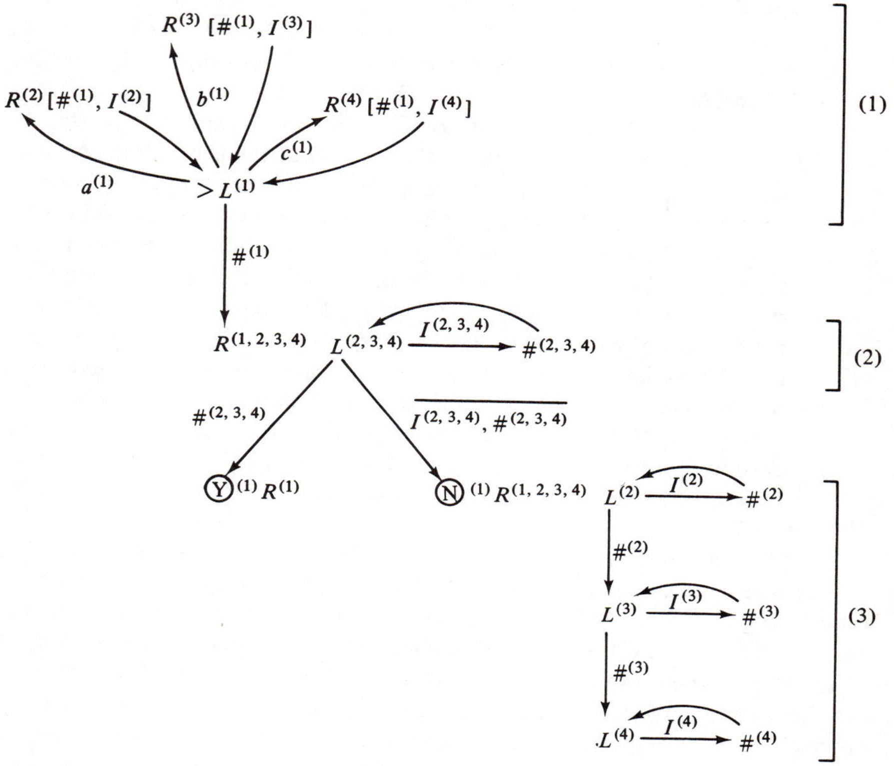

Figure 7–3

of $2n^2 + 13n + 9$ (Example 7.1.2) and $n^2 + 4n + 4$ (Problem 7.1.2) for M. We conclude that $L \in \text{TIME}(5n + 4)$.

Can L be decided any faster? In particular, is $L \in \text{TIME}(cn + d)$ for some constant $c < 5$? Naturally, c cannot be smaller than 2, since, as we said, a minimum of $2n + 4$ steps is required by any Turing machine in order to conform to our input-output conventions when deciding on an input of length n. Our next theorem implies that c can be arbitrarily close to 2. More importantly, this theorem says that questions concerning constant coefficients in a time bound, such as the one above, are meaningless, because constants can always be decreased, essentially at will.

Theorem 7.1.1. *Suppose that $L \in \text{TIME}(T)$, and let ϵ be any positive real number (no matter how small). Then $L \in \text{TIME}(T')$, where for all $n \in \mathbb{N}$, $T'(n) = 2n + 18 + \lceil \epsilon \cdot T(n) \rceil$.*

Proof. Let $M = (K, \Sigma, \delta, s)$ be a k-tape Turing machine that decides L in time T. We shall construct a k'-tape Turing machine $M' = (K', \Sigma', \delta', s')$ that accepts L in time T', where $T'(n) = 2n + 18 + \lceil \epsilon \cdot T(n) \rceil$. If $k = 1$ then $k' = 2$; otherwise $k' = k$.

The operation of M' consists of four phases. In the first phase, M' copies its input from the first tape to the second, at the same time *compressing* and *reversing* it. In the second phase, M' copies the compressed version of its input back to the first tape, in the process undoing the reversal operation of the first phase while maintaining the compression. In the third phase, M' simulates M; the compression of the input makes it possible to simulate many steps of the computation by M with a few steps by M', and this is where the "speedup" is achieved. In the fourth phase, M' performs the steps necessary to leave its tapes with the same appearance as M would have given at the end of its computation. Thus M' may be described as the combination of four machines $M_1 M_2 M_3 M_4$; we now describe those machines in turn. In order to simplify our descriptions, we assume that k, the number of tapes of M, is 1; if $k > 1$ the construction described below can be easily extended (Problem 7.1.4).

Machine M_1 starts with an input string w on its first tape. Then M_1 moves the head on its first tape to the left, erasing w, while at the same time producing a "compressed version" $\kappa(\#w)$ and writing it in reverse on the second tape. For a certain positive integer m (which depends on ϵ and will be fixed later in the proof) $\kappa(\#w)$ is shorter than $\#w$ by a factor of roughly m—to be exact, $|\kappa(\#w)| = \lceil (|w| + 1)/m \rceil$. This compression is achieved by *encoding each m-tuple of symbols of $\#w$ as a single symbol of $\kappa(\#w)$*. (In case $|w| + 1$ is not an exact multiple of m, up to $m - 1$ blanks may have to be introduced into the first symbol of $\kappa(\#w)$.) For example, if $w = abbabaa$ and $m = 3$, then $\kappa(\#w) = (\#, \#, a)(b, b, a)(b, a, a)$ (where the triples are single symbols in the alphabet of M'); at the end of this initial phase of the operation of M', the second tape will contain the reversal of $\kappa(\#w)$, namely $(b, a, a)(b, b, a)(\#, \#, a)$ (with a blank to the left of the first symbol of this string).

Formally, this "compression" phase can be described as follows. Let $w \in \Sigma^*$. If $|w| \leq m$, say $w = \sigma_1 \ldots \sigma_j$ where $j \leq m$ and each $\sigma_i \in \Sigma$, then let $\kappa(w)$ be the m-tuple $(\#, \#, \ldots, \#, \sigma_1, \ldots, \sigma_j)$ ($m - j$ occurrences of $\#$ in all). Otherwise, if $|w| \geq m + 1$—for example, $w = w'\sigma_1 \ldots \sigma_m$, where $w' \in \Sigma^+$ and $\sigma_1, \ldots, \sigma_m \in \Sigma$—then let $\kappa(w) = \kappa(w')\tau$, where τ is the m-tuple $(\sigma_1, \ldots, \sigma_m)$. Then the job of M_1 is to transform $(\#w\underline{\#}, \underline{\#})$ into $(\underline{\#}, \#\kappa(\#w)^R\underline{\#})$. It is possible to design M_1 to perform this function using just $2|w| + 1$ steps; we leave the details of the construction as an exercise (Problem 7.1.5).

Machine M_2 copies $\kappa(\#w)$ to its first tape while erasing $\kappa(\#w)^R$ from the second tape; that is, it transforms $(\underline{\#}, \#\kappa(\#w)^R\underline{\#})$ into $(\#\kappa(\#w)\underline{\#}, \underline{\#})$. Again, M_2 is easy to design; it need use only $2|\kappa(\#w)^R| + 1$ steps, that is,

$2\lceil(|w| + 1)/m\rceil + 1$ steps. Note that M_2 leaves its first tape in the standard arrangement for the beginning of a computation on the input string $\kappa(\#w)$.

The second tape has now served its purpose; neither M_3 nor M_4 uses it at all.

Now M_3 repeatedly *simulates m steps of M by 12 steps of its own*. The first tape of M_3 will—after $12s$ steps—contain $\kappa(x)$, where x is the contents of the first tape of M after ms steps. The state of M_3 after $12s$ steps is of the form (q, j), where $q \in K$ is the state that M would be in after ms steps, and j, $1 \leq j \leq m$, indicates which symbol within the m-tuple currently scanned by M_3 corresponds to the symbol that M would be scanning. For example, if $m = 3$, and $7m = 21$ steps after being started on some input M would be in configuration $(q, aab\underline{b}aba)$, then M_3, when started on the compression of the input to M, would be in configuration $((q, 3), (\#, \#, a)\underline{(a, b, b)}(a, b, a))$ after $7 \cdot 12 = 84$ steps.

The simulation of the next m steps of M proceeds as follows: First the head of M_3 moves one square to the left, two to the right and one to the left, ending where it started. The net effect is that M_3 has now sensed (and encoded in its state) the three m-tuples under and on each side of its head; we call the concatenation of these m-tuples the **active string**. The crucial fact is that now *M_3 has all information necessary for performing the next m steps of M*. This is so because M cannot in m steps read or write on positions out of the active string. So, knowing the active string and the state of M, M_3 can predict exactly what the next m steps of M would be. In fact, this prediction can be performed in *one step* of M_3, since it can be carried out with the help of a finite table, which can be built in advance into the transition function δ_3 of M_3. Now M_3 performs 8 more steps—3 writing steps and 5 head moves—to record the new m-tuples that are to replace the active string, and finally to reposition the head for the next block of 12 steps.

Formally, the states of M_3 are

$$K_3 = K \times \{1, 2, \ldots, m\} \cup K \times \{1, 2, \ldots, m\} \times \Sigma^{3m} \times \{1, 2, \ldots, 11\}.$$

We have already seen the meaning of a state (q, j). State (q, j, x, p), with $x \in \Sigma^{3m}$ and $1 \leq p \leq 11$, is the state to which state (q, j) goes after p of the 12 steps involved in the simulation of m steps of M; x is the known part of the active string, with trailing #'s to mark the unknown part.

In presenting the related transitions, since M_3 does not consult or update its second tape, we shall write $\delta_3(q, \sigma) = (q', \sigma')$ instead of $\delta_3(q, \sigma, \#) = (q', \sigma', \#)$. Then M_3 has the following transitions for all $q \in K$, $1 \leq j \leq m$, and $x, y, z \in \Sigma^m$:

$$\delta_3((q, j), x) = ((q, j, \#^{3m}, 1), L)$$
$$\delta_3((q, j, \#^{3m}, 1), x) = ((q, j, x\#^{2m}, 2), R)$$
$$\delta_3((q, j, x\#^{2m}, 2), y) = ((q, j, xy\#^{m}, 3), R)$$
$$\delta_3((q, j, xy\#^{m}, 3), z) = ((q, j, xyz, 4), L)$$

Now, let $xyz = u\sigma v$, with $|u| = m + j - 1$, and suppose that $(q, u\underline{\sigma}v) \vdash_M^m (q', u'\underline{\sigma}'v')$ (or $(q, u\underline{\sigma}v) \vdash_M^t (q', u'\underline{\sigma}'v')$, where $q' = h$ and $t < m$), and $u'\sigma'v' = x'y'z'$, where $x', y', z' \in \Sigma^m$. Then

$$\delta_3((q, j, xyz, 4), y) = ((q, j, xyz, 5), L)$$
$$\delta_3((q, j, xyz, 5), x) = ((q, j, xyz, 6), x')$$
$$\delta_3((q, j, xyz, 6), x') = ((q, j, xyz, 7), R)$$
$$\delta_3((q, j, xyz, 7), y) = ((q, j, xyz, 8), y')$$
$$\delta_3((q, j, xyz, 8), y') = ((q, j, xyz, 9), R)$$
$$\delta_3(q, j, xyz, 9), z) = ((q, j, xyz, 10), z')$$
$$\delta_3((q, j, xyz, 10), z') = ((q, j, xyz, 11), L)$$

and finally

$$\delta_3((q, j, xyz, 11), y') = \begin{cases} ((q', |u'| + 1), L) & \text{if } |u'| + 1 \leq m \\ ((q', |u'| + 1 - m), y') & \text{if } m < |u'| + 1 \leq 2m \\ ((q', |u'| + 1 - 2m), R) & \text{if } 2m < |u'| + 1. \end{cases}$$

One further detail must be taken care of: What happens when M_3 encounters a new blank? We can force M_3 to treat a blank exactly like an m-tuple of blanks, so that when M_3 encounters a blank, the simulation can proceed without further delays for compression. This effect is achieved by modifying the transition function δ_3 as just defined by replacing $\#^m$ by # everywhere it appears, either as an argument or a value.

Finally, M_4 must convert the result left by M_3, when it halts, back into the output that M would have left on its tape. Since M would leave only Ⓨ or Ⓝ on the tape, M_4 does not need to be a general "decompression" machine; it need merely transform #(#, Ⓨ, #, . . . , #) into #Ⓨ# and #(#, Ⓝ, #, . . . , #) into #Ⓝ#. Thus M_4 takes only two steps.

How many steps, at most, does $M' = M_1M_2M_3M_4$ take on an input w of length n? We have seen that M_1 uses $2n + 1$ steps, M_2 uses $2\lceil (n + 1)/m \rceil + 1$ steps, and M_4 uses 2 steps. At worst, M_3 uses $12\lceil T(n)/m \rceil$ steps, since m steps of M are simulated by 12 of M_3, and M is known never to use more than $T(n)$ steps. So the worst-case total is

$$12\left\lceil \frac{T(n)}{m} \right\rceil + 2\left\lceil \frac{n+1}{m} \right\rceil + 2n + 4$$

steps. Since for any $r, s \in \mathbb{N} - \{0\}$,

$$\left\lceil \frac{r}{s} \right\rceil \leq \frac{r + s - 1}{s},$$

the number of steps is at most

$$\frac{12\,T(n) + 12m - 12 + 2n + 2 + 2m - 2}{m} + 2n + 4;$$

and since $T(n) \geq 2n + 4$ for all n, this number is no larger than

$$\frac{13\,T(n)}{m} + 2n + 18.$$

Finally we can choose a suitable m. If we let $m = \lceil 13/\epsilon \rceil$, then M' decides L in time T', where

$$T'(n) = 2n + 18 + \lceil \epsilon \cdot T(n) \rceil \qquad \text{for all } n \geq 0.$$

This completes the proof of the theorem. ■

7.2 RATE OF GROWTH OF FUNCTIONS

The previous theorem tells us that, when dealing with an upper bound T on the time complexity of a given Turing machine—or of a language—the important thing is the *rate of growth* of the function T, and not details such as constant coefficients and lower-order terms (by lower-order terms we mean terms such as $4n$ or 3 in the expression $n^2 + 4n + 3$). We can formalize this intuitive notion of growth as follows.

Definition 7.2.1

Let f and g be functions from $\mathbb{N}$ to $\mathbb{N}$. We write $f = O(g)$ (read "f is big oh of g") if and only if there is a constant $c > 0$ and an integer $n_0 \in \mathbb{N}$ such that

$$f(n) \leq c \cdot g(n) \quad \text{for all} \quad n \geq n_0.$$

Example 7.2.1

We have that $31n^2 + 17n + 23 = O(n^2)$. To see this, notice that for $n \geq 1$, $n^2 \geq n$ and $n^2 \geq 1$. Thus $31n^2 + 17n + 23 \leq 71n^2$ for $n \geq 1$, and the definition of O is satisfied with $c = 71$ and $n_0 = 1$.

Lemma 7.2.1. *Let $\preccurlyeq$ be the relation defined on the set of functions from $\mathbb{N}$ to $\mathbb{N}$ as follows: $f \preccurlyeq g$ if and only if $f = O(g)$. Then $\preccurlyeq$ is reflexive and transitive.*

Proof. The relation $\preccurlyeq$ is reflexive, since $f = O(f)$ for every function f, with $c = 1$ and $n_0 = 0$. To show that $\preccurlyeq$ is transitive, suppose that $f = O(g)$ and $g = O(h)$. Then there exist $c, c' > 0$ and $n_0, n_0' \in \mathbb{N}$ such that

$$f(n) \leq c \cdot g(n) \qquad \text{for } n \geq n_0$$

and

$$g(n) \leq c' \cdot h(n) \qquad \text{for } n \geq n_0'.$$

Then $f(n) \leq c \cdot c' \cdot h(n)$ for $n \geq \max(n_0, n_0')$, and thus $f = O(h)$. ■

Now define the relation $\asymp$ as follows:

$$f \asymp g \quad \text{if and only if} \quad f = O(g) \quad \text{and} \quad g = O(f).$$

Since $\preccurlyeq$ is reflexive and transitive, $\asymp$ is an equivalence relation.

Definition 7.2.2

The equivalence class of a function $f: \mathbb{N} \rightarrow \mathbb{N}$ under $\asymp$ is called the **rate of growth** of f.

Example 7.2.2

This example is a continuation of Example 7.2.1. Since $31n^2 + 17n + 23 = O(n^2)$ and $n^2 = O(31n^2 + 17n + 23)$, we have that $n^2 \asymp 31n^2 + 17n + 23$, that is, n^2 and $31n^2 + 17n + 23$ have the same rate of growth.

When dealing with rates of growth, one usually tries to distinguish a simple representative of each. This is particularly easy to do with polynomial functions. A **polynomial** p is a function of the form $p(n) = \sum_{j=0}^{d} a_j n^j$, where the a_j are integers and $a_d > 0$. The number d is called the **degree** of p, and the a_j are called its **coefficients**. The following lemma generalizes Examples 7.2.1 and 7.2.2.

Lemma 7.2.2. *Let $f(n) = \sum_{j=0}^{d} a_j n^j$ be a polynomial of degree d. Then:*

(a) $f \asymp n^d$;

(b) $f = O(n^{d+1})$ *and* $f \not\asymp n^{d+1}$.

Proof.

(a) It is immediate that $f(n) \leq (\sum_{j=0}^{d} b_j) \cdot n^d$, where $b_j = \max(a_j, 0)$. Hence $f(n) = O(n^d)$, with $c = \sum_{j=0}^{d} b_j$ and $n_0 = 1$.

Now, let

$$n_0 = 2 \cdot \sum_{j=0}^{d-1} |a_j|.$$

It is not hard to see (Problem 7.2.1) that $n^d \leq 2 \cdot f(n)$ for $n \geq n_0$.

(b) It is obvious that $n^d = O(n^{d+1})$; hence $f = O(n^{d+1})$ since, by (a), $f \asymp n^d$. To show that it is not the case that $n^{d+1} = O(n^d)$, suppose that for all $n \geq n_0$, $n^{d+1} \leq c \cdot n^d$. We immediately discover that this inequality fails for $n = \max(\lceil c \rceil + 1, n_0)$. ■

This lemma shows that the rate of growth of a polynomial can be identified with its degree. Besides polynomials, there are certain rates of growth which, although not polynomial themselves, are bounded from above by polynomials. Examples are $n\lceil \log_2(n+1)\rceil$ and $n^2\lfloor\sqrt{n}\rfloor$. It is readily seen that $n\lceil \log_2(n+1)\rceil = O(n^2)$ (Problem 7.2.3), and $n^2\lfloor\sqrt{n}\rfloor = O(n^3)$.

These polynomial or polynomially bounded rates of growth are particularly interesting when contrasted to **exponential** rates of growth—that is, the rates of growth of functions of the form r^n for some $r > 1$. The fundamental difference between polynomial and exponential functions is stated in the next theorem.

Theorem 7.2.1. *Let* $f(n) = \sum_{j=0}^{d} a_j n^j$ *be any polynomial and let* $r > 1$. *Then* $f = O(r^n)$.

Proof. It suffices to show that $n^d = O(r^n)$. For each $n \geq 0$, let $e_n = r^n$ and $b_n = n^d$. Then $e_{n+1}/e_n = r$, and

$$\frac{b_{n+1}}{b_n} = \frac{(n+1)^d}{n^d} = \left(1 + \frac{1}{n}\right)^d.$$

Hence, the ratio b_{n+1}/b_n decreases with n and is less than r whenever

$$\left(1 + \frac{1}{n}\right)^d < r;$$

that is, whenever

$$n > \frac{1}{r^{1/d} - 1}.$$

Now, take $n_0 = \lceil 1/(r^{1/d} - 1)\rceil$ and $c = n_0^d / r^{n_0}$. Then for any $k \geq 0$, the following holds.

$$\begin{aligned}
(n_0 + k)^d &= n_0^d \cdot \left(\frac{n_0+1}{n_0}\right)^d \cdot \left(\frac{n_0+2}{n_0+1}\right)^d \cdot \cdots \cdot \left(\frac{n_0+k}{n_0+k-1}\right)^d \\
&= n_0^d \cdot \left(1 + \frac{1}{n_0}\right)^d \cdot \left(1 + \frac{1}{n_0+1}\right)^d \cdot \cdots \cdot \left(1 + \frac{1}{n_0+k-1}\right)^d \\
&\leq n_0^d r^k \qquad \text{since} \left(1 + \frac{1}{n}\right)^d \leq r \text{ for } n \geq n_0 \\
&= c r^{n_0} r^k = c r^{n_0+k}
\end{aligned}$$

So $n^d \leq cr^n$ whenever $n \geq n_0$, and $n^d = O(r^n)$. ■

Since for all $d > 0$, n^{d+1} grows strictly faster than n^d (that is, $n^d = O(n^{d+1})$ but $n^d \not\asymp n^{d+1}$), we conclude from Theorem 7.2.1 that *any exponential function grows strictly faster than any polynomial.* Much of the later part of this chapter is centered around this fundamental distinction.

Rates of growth are of obvious relevance and importance to computational complexity. We shall henceforth feel free to express time bounds solely in terms of their rates of growth, since, by Theorem 7.1.1, that is what matters. In fact, we shall henceforth write TIME(f) as a shorthand for

$$\bigcup \{\mathrm{TIME}(g) : g \asymp f\}$$

to denote the class of languages decidable in time with the same rate of growth as f.

7.3 TIME-BOUNDED SIMULATIONS

One of the main advantages of the notion of computational complexity that we are studying in this chapter is that it allows us to revisit the results of Chapters 4, 5, and 6 on Turing machine computation and to derive *time-bounded refinements* of those results. Instead of examining whether a task can or cannot be carried out by a Turing machine, we shall now try to find out in *how much time* it can be carried out. In the following sections, we shall see quantitative analogues of the halting problem and diagonalization arguments of Chapter 6. In this section, we shall start by reexamining the simulation results of Section 4.5, where we showed that certain versions of Turing machines (Turing machines with two-way infinite tape, multiple heads, multiple tapes, or multi-dimensional tape) are equivalent to the standard model (Theorems 4.5.1 to 4.5.3). We shall now see how these simulation arguments affect the number of steps of a computation. Although we have defined what it means to decide a language in time T only for a k-tape Turing machine, the meaning of the notion should be clear for the other versions—two-way infinite tape, single-tape, multiple-head, and two-dimensional tape machines.

Theorem 7.3.1. *Suppose that a language L is decided by a Turing machine M_1 with a two-way infinite tape in time T_1. Then L is decided by a standard 1-tape Turing machine M_2 in time T_2, where for all $n \in \mathbb{N}$, $T_2(n) = 6T_1(n) + 3n + 8$.*

Proof. M_2 is the Turing machine constructed in the proof of Lemma 4.5.1. All we have to prove is that it operates within $T_2(n)$ steps, given that M_1 operates within $T_1(n)$ steps for inputs of length n.

Recall that M_2 operates in three stages. Stage 1 rewrites the input in the 2-track format, and requires $n + 2$ writing steps and $2n + 1$ head moves (refer to Figure 4–20) for an input of length n. Therefore this stage requires only $3n + 3$ steps.

Stage 2 simulates each move of M_1 by one move of M_2. Thus the whole computation of M_1 can be simulated in $T_1(n)$ steps. There is something else, however. Whenever the head of M_1 crosses the line between the square to the left of the input and the square to the left of that one, M_2 performs one extra move to change tracks. But how many times can this line be crossed? At most $T_1(n)$ times, in the very unlikely case that M_1 does nothing else but cross that line. Also, every time that M_1 sees a # for the first time, M_2 does an extra move to convert # to (#, #). Again, this cannot happen more than $T_1(n)$ times, so Stage 2 requires $3T_1(n)$ steps at worst.

At the end of Stage 2, M_2 is left in one of the configurations $((h, 1), \$(\#, \#)^j(\textcircled{Y}, \#)\underline{(\#, \#)}(\#, \#)^k)$ or $((h, 2), \$(\#, \#)^j(\#, \textcircled{Y})\underline{(\#, \#)}(\#, \#)^k)$, or the corresponding rejecting configurations, for some $j, k \geq 0$. The task of Stage 3 is to convert this configuration to the standard halting configuration $(h, \#\textcircled{Y}\underline{\#})$ or $(h, \#\textcircled{N}\underline{\#})$, respectively. This is done by moving right until the first "true" blank symbol is found, and then moving left, erasing all symbols, until \$ is erased. Then M_2 moves right, writes $\textcircled{Y}$ (or $\textcircled{N}$, respectively), moves right once more, and halts.

How many steps can this "cleaning-up" take? The answer depends on the length ($j + k + 3$ in our notation above) of the nonblank portion of the tape of M_2 at the end of Stage 2. The crucial observation here is that each such nonblank symbol, except for \$, was created by the simulation of some step of M_1. Therefore there are at most $T_1(n) + 1$ nonblank symbols and they can be erased in $3T_1(n) + 2$ steps. The rest requires just three steps.

The theorem now follows by adding the counts of steps for the three stages:

$$3n + 3 + 3T_1(n) + 3T_1(n) + 5 = 6T_1(n) + 3n + 8 = T_2(n). \quad \blacksquare$$

Theorem 7.3.2. *Suppose that a language L is decided in time T_1 by a k-tape Turing machine $M_1 = (K_1, \Sigma_1, \delta_1, s_1)$. Then L is decided by a 1-tape Turing machine $M_2 = (K_2, \Sigma_2, \delta_2, s_2)$ in time T_2, where $T_2(n) = 4T_1(n)^2 + (4n + 4k + 3)T_1(n) + 5n + 15$.*

Proof. Again, M_2 is the 1-tape Turing machine described in the proof of Lemma 4.5.2, and M_2 operates in three stages. Stage 1 converts the initial configuration $(s_2, \#w\underline{\#})$ of M_2 into the multi-track format of Figure 4–26. It is easy to see that this can be done in $n + 3$ writing steps and $4n + 7$ head moves, a total of $5n + 10$ steps.

In Stage 2 M_2 simulates one step of M_1 by several steps of its own. Between simulations, the head of M_2 resides at the right end of the $2k$-track portion of the tape. Suppose that this portion of the tape has total length m.

Then M_2 first traverses the whole tape ($2m$ steps) gathering state-symbol information; it then traverses the tape once more ($2m$ moving steps), updating the scanned symbols and head positions in the appropriate tracks. It is straightforward to see that this updating requires four extra steps (two writing steps and two head moves) per tape of M_1, or $4k$ steps in total. Thus the simulation of each step of M_1 can be done in $4m + 4k$ steps, where m is the total length of the $2k$-track portion of the tape before this simulation. This, however, is hardly a satisfying estimate, since it depends on the unknown parameter m. We must bound m from above.

It is immediately obvious that $m \leq T_1(n) + n$. Intuitively, this means that within $T_1(n)$ steps, M_1 cannot visit more than $T_1(n)$ new squares on any tape, and the $2k$-track portion of the tape of M_2 corresponds exactly to the squares that M_1 has visited, plus the input. In fact, this argument is wasteful, since several steps of M_1 must be spent for erasing the tape for acceptance or rejection, and hence not all of the $T_1(n)$ steps of M_1 can involve exploring new tape squares. In any event, it is clear that $m \leq T_1(n) + n$ and hence Stage 2 requires at most $4T_1(n) + 4k + 4n$ steps per simulated step of M_1, or $4T_1^2(n) + 4kT_1(n) + 4nT_1(n)$ steps in all. Finally, the last stage, which erases the tape of M_2 and writes Ⓨ or Ⓝ after the end of the simulation, can take at most $3T_1(n) + 5$ steps, exactly as in the proof of the previous theorem. Adding the three counts one obtains an upper bound for the number of steps of M_2 equal to

$$T_2(n) = 4T_1(n)^2 + (4n + 4k + 3)T_1(n) + 5n + 15. \quad \blacksquare$$

Applying Theorem 7.1.1 and our O notation, we can rephrase Theorem 7.3.2 as follows.

Corollary 7.3.1. *If L is a language decided in time T by some k-tape Turing machine, then L is decided in time $T' = O(T^2)$ by a 1-tape Turing machine.*

One can also prove a similar result for the two-dimensional version of Turing machines (Theorem 4.5.3).

Theorem 7.3.3. *If L is a language decided in time T by some two-dimensional Turing machine, then L is decided in time $T' = O(T^3)$ by a 4-tape Turing machine.*

Proof. See Problem 7.3.1. ■

Another variation on the Turing machine model, which can also be simulated in polynomial time by the standard model, is discussed in Problems 7.3.2 through 7.3.5.

7.4 THE CLASSES $\mathcal{P}$ AND $\mathcal{NP}$

In Sections 7.1 and 7.2, we discussed how Theorem 7.1.1 has the effect of rendering insignificant certain distinctions between time bounds—namely, those distinctions that are based on constant coefficients and lower-order terms. Thus, for a polynomial time bound, what really matters is the *degree* of the polynomial. The three theorems of the previous section have the effect of blurring even boundaries between different degrees. A language that is decidable in time n^2 by a two-dimensional Turing machine is decidable in time n^6 by a 4-tape Turing machine by Theorem 7.3.3, and hence in time n^{12} by a 1-tape Turing machine. After all, our choice of k-tape Turing machines as the basis for defining complexity is arbitrary, and it is a choice that appears to have a significant effect on the degrees of polynomial time bounds. On the other hand, Theorems 7.3.1, 7.3.2, and 7.3.3 above imply that if a language is decidable in time T, a polynomial, by some Turing machine of any of the varieties discussed (single-tape, multiple-tape, two-dimensional), as well as others, then it is decided by a machine of any other variety in time T', where T' is *also a polynomial.* The same holds for some computational models other than Turing machines, which are more similar to real computers. What appears to be important is whether a language is decidable in a polynomial time bound, rather than the degree of this polynomial. This leads us to the following definition.

Definition 7.4.1

We define $\mathcal{P}$ (for polynomial-time decidable) to be the class of languages

$$\mathcal{P} = \bigcup \{\text{TIME}(n^d) : d > 0\}.$$

Notice that by Theorem 7.1.1, TIME(n^d) contains all languages decidable by some Turing machine in a time bound that is a polynomial of degree d. Therefore, taking the union over all degrees, we obtain the class of all languages that are decided by Turing machines in some polynomial time bounds.

Example 7.4.1

Suppose that we want to find out whether there are values zero or one for the variables $x_1, \ldots, x_n$ such that m simultaneous equations of the form

$$\sum_{j=1}^{n} a_{ij}x_j = b_i \qquad i = 1, \ldots, m,$$

are satisfied, where the a_{ij}'s and the b_i's are all nonnegative integers. One usually writes this in a **matrix** notation, capturing all a_{ij} coefficients in an $m \times n$ table (matrix) A, and all the b_i's in an m-tuple (vector) b. For example, if $m = 2, n = 3$, and the equations are

$$x_1 + 2x_3 = 3$$
$$3x_2 + 2x_3 = 2,$$

we have

$$A = \begin{bmatrix} 1 & 0 & 2 \\ 0 & 3 & 2 \end{bmatrix} \quad \text{and} \quad b = \begin{bmatrix} 3 \\ 2 \end{bmatrix}.$$

The above equations are then written succinctly as

$$Ax = b.$$

Recall that in this problem we are looking for solutions to these equations with the x_j's equal to either zero or one. This problem is one version of the important **integer programming** problem arising in various contexts in operations research.

For the purpose of transforming this into a language decision problem, we shall devise an encoding α mapping matrices and vectors of integers to strings over the alphabet $\{I, c\}$. The natural number k is represented by I^{k+1}; vectors are encoded as integers separated by c's, and matrices are encoded as rows separated by cc. Thus, if $m = 2, n = 3$,

$$A = \begin{bmatrix} 1 & 0 & 2 \\ 0 & 3 & 2 \end{bmatrix} \quad \text{and} \quad b = \begin{bmatrix} 3 \\ 2 \end{bmatrix}, \text{ then}$$

$$\alpha(A) = IIcIcIIIccIcIIIIcIII \text{ and}$$
$$\alpha(b) = IIIIcIII.$$

The system of equations $Ax = b$ above does have a **binary solution**, as we say, namely, $x = (1, 0, 1)$.

The problem mentioned above can now be captured formally as the following language:

$$B = \{\alpha(A)@\alpha(b)\colon Ax = b \text{ has a binary solution}\}.^*$$

Is $B \in \mathcal{P}$? Informally, is there an efficient algorithm that would decide for every A and b whether $Ax = b$ has a binary solution? Notice that the restriction that $x \in \{0, 1\}^n$ makes techniques from linear algebra, such as Cramer's rule, inapplicable. Indeed, integer programming is a very well-known hard problem, and, despite intensive research efforts for many decades, no such efficient algorithm is known.

We can, however, show very easily that the following easier version of B is in $\mathcal{P}$:

$$B' = \{\alpha(A)@\alpha(b)\$\alpha(x)\colon x \text{ is a binary solution to } Ax = b\}.^\dagger$$

*Here @ is some fixed symbol other than I, c, and #.
†Again, $ is a new symbol.

We can design a 3-tape Turing machine M' that decides B' in time $T = O(n^2)$. On input $w = \alpha(A)@\alpha(b)\$\alpha(x)$, M' first copies $\alpha(x)$ to its second tape. Then it repeats the following for each row of A. It traverses the row, selectively copying to its third tape only those numbers that correspond to ones in the vector x. After each row is finished, M' works on its third tape, replacing the resulting sequence of integers by a single integer, their sum, the necessary additions being performed by shifting. It can easily be shown that this requires $O(|w|)$ time at most. Thus after all the rows have been processed, the third tape contains the string $\alpha(Ax)$. Hence M' only has to check whether the third tape contains $\alpha(b)$. If it does, M' writes Ⓨ on its first tape and halts; otherwise, it writes Ⓝ. Also, M' writes Ⓝ if at any stage it observes any syntactic error that implies that the input is not of the form $\alpha(A)@\alpha(b)\$\alpha(x)$, with A an $m \times n$ matrix of integers for some m and n, b a vector of m integers, and $x \in \{0, 1\}^n$.

Since processing every row of A requires $O(|w|)$ time, and A cannot have more than $|w|$ rows, we conclude that, by Theorem 7.1.1,

$$B' \in \text{TIME}(n^2)$$

and hence

$$B' \in \mathcal{P}.$$

The class $\mathcal{P}$ introduced above will play a very central role in our further development of complexity theory. It is the quantitative analogue of the class of decidable languages that was discussed and delimited in Chapters 5 and 6. In fact, in Chapter 5, we expressed the opinion, known as Church's Thesis, that the class of decidable languages coincides with the class of decision problems that can be solved by computers. The importance of $\mathcal{P}$ resides in a similar, though somewhat more controversial, opinion that $\mathcal{P}$ *coincides with the class of problems that can be realistically solved by computers.* In other words, exactly as Church's Thesis says that every algorithm can be rendered as a Turing machine, our quantitative version contends that every *practical* or *efficient* algorithm can be rendered as a polynomially time-bounded Turing machine.

We are thus tempted to pursue the analogy further, and to try to exhibit languages that are not in $\mathcal{P}$. Indeed, in Section 7.7 we show that one can use diagonalization to construct quantitative versions of the halting problem, which can formally be shown not to be in $\mathcal{P}$. This, however, is hardly satisfying. The reason is that, unlike the notion of decidability, $\mathcal{P}$ and efficient computation are concepts of earthly, practical motivation. Hence, exhibiting an artificial halting-like problem and arguing that it is not in $\mathcal{P}$ will not fill the bill. What we would like is a "natural" or "reasonable" problem, preferably of practical interest, which is not in $\mathcal{P}$.

In order to explore this desire, we need to sidetrack somewhat. Recall that in the previous section we showed that if a language L is decidable in polynomial time by a Turing machine of one of several varieties (single-tape, multiple-tape, single-tape multiple-head, two-dimensional), then L is decidable in polynomial time by a Turing machine of any of the other kinds. What about the last variant of the Turing machine model that we have introduced, namely the *nondeterministic* Turing machine (Section 4.6)? Is it also equivalent to the remaining kinds, up to a polynomial? In order to discuss this, let us first define formally what we mean by saying that a language is accepted by a nondeterministic Turing machine in a time bound.

Definition 7.4.2

Let T be a function from $\mathbb{N}$ to $\mathbb{N}$. Let $L \subseteq \Sigma_0^*$ be a language, and $M = (K, \Sigma, \Delta, s)$ be a nondeterministic Turing machine. We say that M **accepts** L **in nondeterministic time** T if the following holds. For all $w \in \Sigma_0^*$,

$$w \in L \text{ if and only if } (s, \#w\underline{\#}) \vdash_M^t (h, v\underline{\sigma}u)$$

for some $v, u \in \Sigma^*$, $\sigma \in \Sigma$ and $t \leq T(|w|)$. We say that L is **acceptable in nondeterministic time** T if there is a nondeterministic Turing machine M that accepts L in nondeterministic time T. The class of languages acceptable in nondeterministic time T is denoted by NTIME(T). Finally, we define

$$\mathcal{NP} = \bigcup \{\text{NTIME}(n^d) : d > 0\}.$$

The notion of time-bounded nondeterministic acceptance is therefore an exact quantitative analogue of general nondeterministic acceptance (Section 4.6). We said there that a nondeterministic Turing machine M accepts its input w if there is *some* halting computation of M on input w; it fails to accept its input if all computations are infinite. Here we have exactly the same convention, except that *we regard as infinite any computation that takes more than* $T(|w|)$ *steps* on input w.

Notice a fundamental *asymmetry* in the definition of nondeterministic time-bounded computation. A nondeterministic Turing machine accepts an input w in time T if and only if there are one or more computations that lead to a halting configuration after $T(|w|)$ or fewer steps. The machine fails to accept w if all of its computations continue for more than $T(|w|)$ steps.

Example 7.4.2

The set of all possible computations of a nondeterministic Turing machine on a given input is best pictured by a tree-like structure (see Figure 7–4). Nodes represent configurations, and downward lines are steps. Nondeterministic choices are represented by nodes that have more than one downward line leaving them. In Figure 7–4(a), w is accepted, while in Figure 7–4(b), it is not.

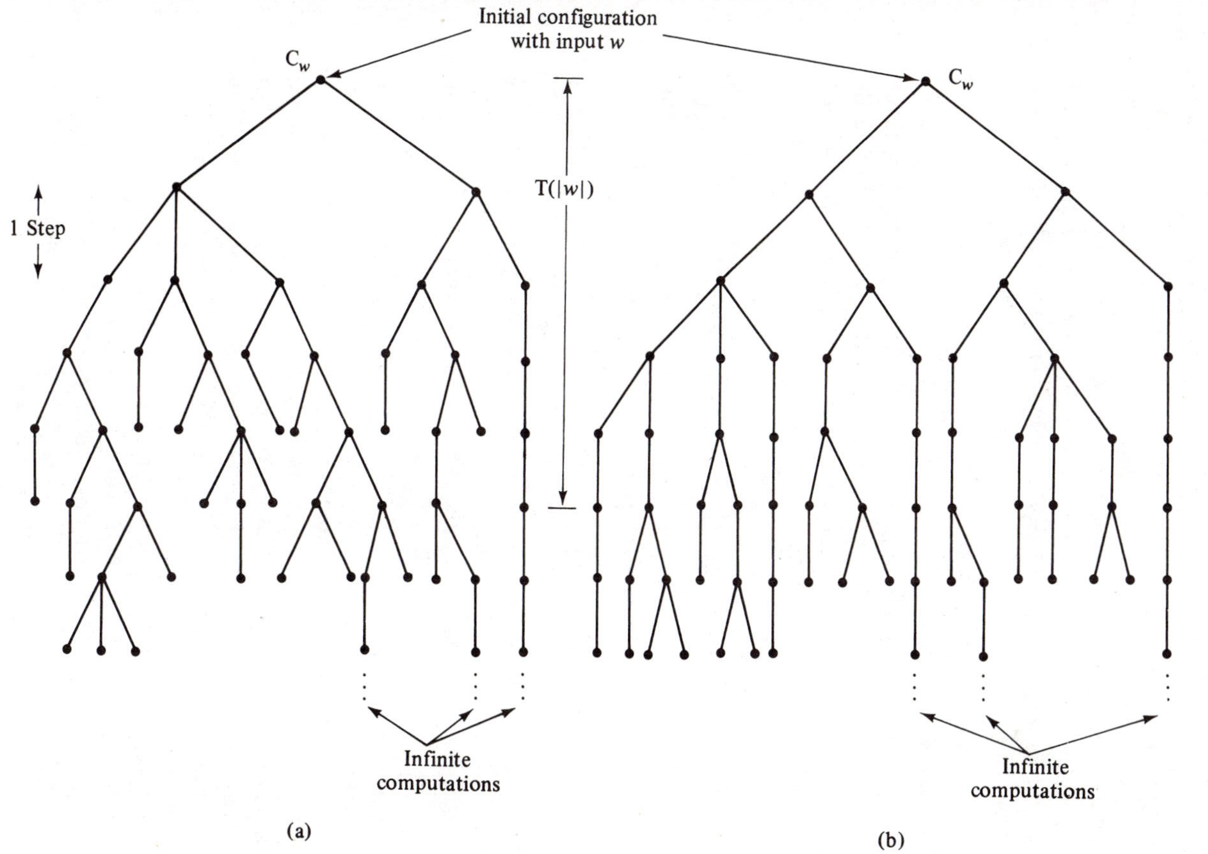
Initial configuration with input w
C_w
C_w
1 Step
$T(|w|)$
Infinite computations
Infinite computations
(a)
(b)

Figure 7–4

One may define k-tape nondeterministic Turing machines in complete analogy to the deterministic case. In fact, the proof of the following is nearly identical to that of Theorem 7.3.2.

Lemma 7.4.1. *If a language L is accepted in nondeterministic time T_1 by a k-tape nondeterministic Turing machine M_1, then there exists a 1-tape nondeterministic Turing machine M_2 that accepts L in nondeterministic time T_2, where $T_2 = O(T_1^2)$.*

Example 7.4.3

The language B of solvable binary equations (Example 7.4.1) which we could not prove to be in $\mathcal{P}$, is easily seen to be in $\mathcal{NP}$, since B is decided in time $T(n) = O(n^2)$ by the following 3-tape nondeterministic Turing machine.

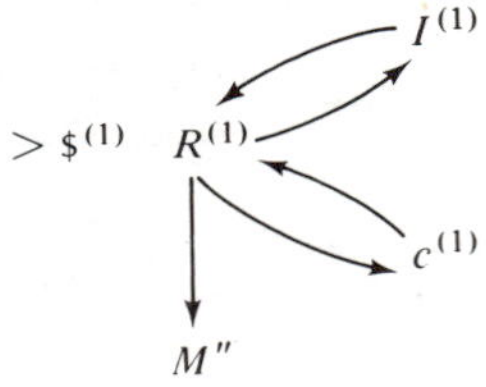

Here M'' is a version of the deterministic 3-tape Turing machine M' that decides B' (Example 7.4.1) in time $T' = O(n^2)$. Machine M'' is identical to M', except that when M' would execute $R\textcircled{N}R$ and halt, M'' executes

$$R\textcircled{N}R\circlearrowleft$$

and loops forever.

Machine M operates by juxtaposing to its input a *nondeterministically chosen* string in $\$\{I, c\}^*$ and then passing control to M''. Thus, if M starts on an input $w = \alpha(A)@\alpha(b)$ such that the corresponding system $Ax = b$ has a binary solution x, it is easy to exhibit an accepting computation of M that has no more than $T'(2|w|) + |w|$ steps: the one that writes $\$\alpha(x)$ before calling M''.

Conversely, if $Ax = b$ has no solution—or if the input is not of the proper form $\alpha(A)@\alpha(b)$—then M will never halt, as M'' would not accept its input, no matter what M juxtaposes to w. It follows that M accepts B in nondeterministic time T, where $T(n) = T'(2n) + n$. Of course, M is 3-tape; by Lemma 7.4.1, $B \in \text{NTIME}(T^2)$, and hence $B \in \mathcal{NP}$.

It is, of course, immediate that $\text{TIME}(T) \subseteq \text{NTIME}(T^2)$—by Lemma 7.4.1—and hence $\mathcal{P} \subseteq \mathcal{NP}$. Is $\mathcal{P}$ equal to $\mathcal{NP}$? In other words, are nondeterministic Turing machines yet another version of Turing machines equivalent to the rest with respect to the class of languages decided in polynomial time? At first glance, one gets the intuitive feeling that nondeterminism is such a strong and "different" feature that this should not be the case. To gain some insight, let us examine how the nondeterministic machine M of Example 7.4.3 manages to decide B in polynomial time. M achieves this by using its nondeterminism in order to "guess" the correct x. If such an x exists, M is bound to succeed. It seems that the only obvious way for a deterministic Turing machine to do the same would be to *try exhaustively* all possibilities for x. The trouble is, of course, that there are too many such possibilities—exactly 2^n—and so this deterministic Turing machine would in the worst case require an exponential amount of time.

A look at Figure 7–4 reveals another aspect of this difficulty. The trees that represent the set of computations of a nondeterministic Turing machine have many nodes (that is, configurations), all at a moderate depth. The only way that a deterministic Turing machine can compete with the nondeterministic one with respect to the number of reachable configurations is by operating for an exponential number of steps.

This difficulty of using a deterministic Turing machine to search a large set of "solutions" was also reflected in the proof of Theorem 4.6.1. It was shown there that a nondeterministic Turing machine can be simulated by a deterministic one; but that simulation was not a direct step-by-step simulation, like the ones of Theorems 4.5.1 through 4.5.3, which lead us to the polynomial bounds of the previous section. By contrast, the simulation of a nondeterministic Turing machine resorted to an exhaustive examination of all possible computations. Again, one gets the intuitive feeling that this is inherent in nondeterminism, since it allows multiple choices at each step, and so there is an exponentially large multitude of possible computations to be checked. The same difficulty is captured in the quantitative version of that simulation, described below. We first need a definition.

Definition 7.4.3

A function $f: \mathbb{N} \to \mathbb{N}$ is a **step-counting function** if there exists a $k \geq 1$ and a k-tape Turing machine M such that for all $w \in \Sigma^*$, M halts in exactly $f(|w|)$ steps on input w, that is,

$$(s, \#w\#, \ldots, \#) \vdash_M^{f(|w|)} (h, u_1\underline{a_1}v_1, \ldots, u_k\underline{a_k}v_k)$$

for some $u_1, \ldots, u_k, v_1, \ldots, v_k \in \Sigma^*$ and $a_1, \ldots, a_k \in \Sigma$.

Lemma 7.4.2. *If p is a polynomial with nonnegative coefficients, then p is a step-counting function.*

Proof. See Problem 7.4.7. ■

Theorem 7.4.1. *Let L be a language accepted in time T_1—where T_1 is a step-counting function—by a nondeterministic Turing machine $M_1 = (K_1, \Sigma_1, \Delta_1, s_1)$. Then there exist integers $k_2 \geq 1$ and $r > 1$ and a k_2-tape deterministic Turing machine $M_2 = (K_2, \Sigma_2, \delta_2, s_2)$ deciding L in time T_2, where $T_2(n) = r^{T_1(n)}$.*

Proof. Our simulation is essentially the same as that in the proof of Theorem 4.6.1. The only difference is that now we have an explicit bound on the length of any accepting computation, and hence we need not dovetail through all possible lengths.

To be more specific, let M be a Turing machine which, on input w, invariably halts after exactly $T_1(|w|)$ steps, in the way prescribed in Definition 7.4.3. Such an M is guaranteed to exist, since T_1 is a step-counting function. If M has k tapes, then let k_2 (the number of tapes of M_2) be $k + 2$.

To begin, M_2 copies its input to its k_2th tape—let $\mathcal{C}$ denote a machine which performs this function. Then M_2 gives control to a version M' of M on input w. In all respects, M' is identical to M, except that it has an extra tape (the $(k_2 - 1)$st), on which it records a symbol d_1 at each step of M. Thus, after the end of the computation of M', the $(k_2 - 1)$st tape contains the string $d_1^{T_1(|w|)}$. Next, M_2 erases its tapes, except for the $(k_2 - 1)$st and k_2nd—let $\mathcal{E}$ be a Turing machine which performs this function. Then M_2 writes a \$ on its first tape, moves right, and enters a loop in which it deterministically simulates computations of M_1 on input w. This loop consists of three machines, $\mathcal{I}$, M_1', and $\mathcal{G}'$. Machine $\mathcal{I}$ copies w from the k_2nd tape to the first. Machine M_1' is a version of M_1 that simulates M_1 deterministically on the first tape, consulting the $(k_2 - 1)$st tape for nondeterministic choices. When and if M_1 would halt, M_1' erases its tapes and halts with #Ⓨ# on the first tape. To pass from one simulated computation of M_1 to the next, M_2 uses machine $\mathcal{G}'$—similar to the machine $\mathcal{G}$ used in the proof of Theorem 4.6.1—which counts in base r_1, where r_1 is the maximum possible number of nondeterministic choices per step of M_1. The only difference between $\mathcal{G}$ and $\mathcal{G}'$ is that the first time $\mathcal{G}'$ tries to increase the length of the string (see the lower left part of Figure 4–31), it erases all tapes and writes Ⓝ on the first tape. In summary, M_2 is shown in Figure 7–5.

One can easily bound from above the number of steps executed by M_2 on input w of length n.

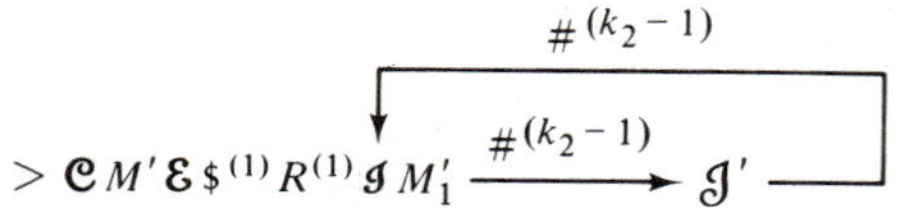

Figure 7–5

1. $\mathcal{C}$ requires $3n + 3$ steps.
2. M' requires, by its definition, $2T_1(n)$ steps.
3. $\mathcal{E}$ requires at most $4T_1(n)$ steps.
4. Each of the (at most $r_1^{T_1(n)}$) cycles of $\mathcal{I}$, M_1', and $\mathcal{J}'$ requires at most $4T_1(n)$ steps.
5. $2T_1(n) + 5$ steps are needed to erase all tapes and write Ⓝ.

The total amounts to $8T_1(n) + 3n + 8 + r_1^{T_1(n)}4T_1(n)$ steps. Now, notice that

$$4T_1(n) \leq 2^{4T_1(n)}$$
$$2T_1(n) \geq 3n + 8,$$

so the upper bound becomes $10T_1(n) + (16r_1)^{T_1(n)} \leq (16r_1 + 1)^{T_1(n)}$. This proves the theorem with $r = 16r_1 + 1$. ■

Corollary 7.4.1. $\mathcal{NP} \subseteq \bigcup \{\text{TIME}(r^{n^d})\colon r, d > 0\}$

Proof. The proof is by Lemma 7.4.2 and Theorem 7.4.1. ■

Corollary 7.4.1 is a far cry from a success in resolving our question of whether $\mathcal{P} = \mathcal{NP}$. This question will be the main theme of the next two sections. We shall end this section by presenting an alternative language-theoretic characterization of $\mathcal{NP}$ which, besides further illuminating the intriguing "guessing" capabilities of nondeterministic machines, is also useful for proving that certain languages are in $\mathcal{NP}$.

Definition 7.4.4

Let $L \subseteq \Sigma^*\$\Sigma^*$ be a language, where $\$ \notin \Sigma$. We say that L is **polynomially balanced** if there exists a polynomial p such that $x\$y \in L$ only if $|y| \leq p(|x|)$.

For any languages L_1 and L_2, we denote the language $\{x\colon$ there is a $y \in L_2$ such that $xy \in L_1\}$ by L_1/L_2. In particular, if $L \subseteq \Sigma^*\$\Sigma^*$ and $\$ \notin \Sigma$, then $L/\$\Sigma^*$ is the set of all $x \in \Sigma^*$ such that $x\$y \in L$ for some $y \in \Sigma^*$.

Theorem 7.4.2. *Let $L \subseteq \Sigma^*$ be a language, where $\$ \notin \Sigma$ and $|\Sigma| \geq 2$. Then $L \in \mathcal{NP}$ if and only if there is a polynomially balanced language $L' \subseteq \Sigma^*\$\Sigma^*$ such that $L' \in \mathcal{P}$ and $L = L'/\$\Sigma^*$.*

Proof. (*If*) Suppose that $L' \in \mathcal{P}$ is a polynomially balanced language. This means two things.

(a) There is a polynomial p such that $x\$y \in L'$ only if $|y| \leq p(|x|)$.

(b) There exists for some k a k-tape deterministic Turing machine M' that decides L' in time q, a polynomial.

We shall exhibit a k-tape nondeterministic Turing machine M that accepts in nondeterministic polynomial time the language $L = L'/\$\Sigma^*$. Let $\Sigma = \{\sigma_1, \ldots, \sigma_l\}$. Then M is simply the machine shown in Figure 7–6, which

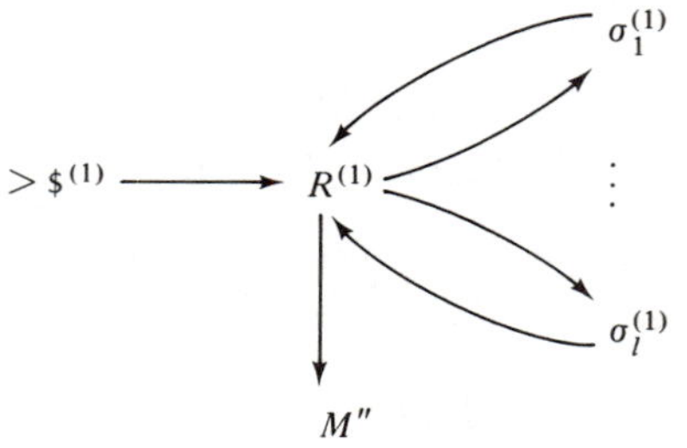

Figure 7–6

operates by juxtaposing a nondeterministically chosen string $y \in \$\Sigma^*$ to its own input, and then passing control to M''. Machine M'' is a simple variant of M': when M' would halt on #Ⓝ#, M'' instead loops forever; in all other respects M'' is identical to M'. It is immediate that $x \in L$ if and only if there is a string $y \in \Sigma^*$ with $|y| \leq p(|x|)$ such that $x\$y \in L'$. This, however, is equivalent to saying that there is a halting computation of M (namely, the one that prints $\$y$ before passing control to M'') with no more than $2p(|x|) + 2 + q(|x| + p(|x|) + 1)$ steps. Hence M accepts L in nondeterministic time T, where $T(n) = 2p(n) + 2 + q(p(n) + n + 1)$—a polynomial.

(*Only If*) Suppose that $L \in \mathcal{NP}$. We shall show that there is a polynomial p and, for each $x \in L$, there exists a nonempty set $Y(x) \subseteq \Sigma^*$, with $|y| \leq p(|x|)$ for all $y \in Y(x)$, such that the language $L' = \{x\$y: x \in L, y \in Y(x)\}$ is in $\mathcal{P}$. It will follow that L' is polynomially balanced and $L = L'/\$\Sigma^*$ as required.

Since $L \in \mathcal{NP}$, there is a nondeterministic Turing machine M and a polynomial q such that M accepts L in nondeterministic time q. Then for every $x \in L$, there is a $t \leq q(|x|)$ and at least one sequence of configurations of M, $C_0 \vdash_M C_1 \vdash_M \cdots \vdash_M C_t$, where $C_0 = (s, \#x\underline{\#})$, and C_t is a halted configuration: $C_t = (h, w\underline{\sigma}u)$ for some $w, u \in \Sigma^*$ and $\sigma \in \Sigma$.

In Chapter 5 we defined a simple function ρ that encodes Turing machines and input strings as strings in $\{I, c\}^*$. The function ρ can easily be extended to encode nondeterministic Turing machines and configurations of those machines. Now the required set $Y(x)$ is the set of all strings $y = \rho(M)@\rho(C_0)@ \ldots @\rho(C_t)$, where M is the nondeterministic Turing machine accepting L and $C_0 \vdash_M C_1 \vdash_M \cdots \vdash_M C_t$, $t \leq q(|x|)$, is one of the possible sequences of configurations of M by which x is accepted. We have to show that $y \in Y(x)$ only if $|y| \leq p(|x|)$ for some polynomial p. But this is straightforward. Each C_j has at most $q(|x|) + |x|$ nonblank tape squares, and hence $|\rho(C_j)| \leq |\rho(M)|(q(|x|) + |x|)$ for $j = 0, 1, \ldots, t$; therefore $|y| \leq p(|x|)$, where $p(n) = |\rho(M)|q(n)(q(n) + n)$—a polynomial, since $|\rho(M)|$ is an a priori known constant, not dependent on $|x|$.

Finally, we show† that $L' = \{x\$y: x \in L, y \in Y(x)\}$ is in $\mathcal{P}$, by designing a 2-tape deterministic Turing machine M' that decides L' in time T, a polynomial. We shall sketch the operation of M': M' first checks whether its input w is of the form $w = x\$\rho(M)@\rho(C_0)@ \ldots @\rho(C_t)$, where

(a) the C_j are configurations of M;

(b) $C_0 = (s, \#x\underline{\#})$;

(c) $C_t = (h, u\underline{\sigma}v)$ for some $u, v \in \Sigma^*$, $\sigma \in \Sigma$.

If not, M' rejects w. Otherwise, M' checks to see whether $C_i \vdash_M C_{i+1}$ for $i = 0, \ldots, t - 1$. It is straightforward to see that M' can perform these checks in time $T(|w|)$, where $T(n) = O(n^2)$. ■

Example 7.4.4

Theorem 7.4.2 provides an alternative proof that the language B of Example 7.4.3 is in $\mathcal{NP}$. For if B' is the language of Example 7.4.1, then $B' \in \mathcal{P}$, $B = B'/\$\Sigma^*$, and B' is polynomially balanced.

Example 7.4.5

Let us now formalize the Traveling Salesman Problem, introduced informally in Section 7.1, as a language decision problem. Our data in this problem are (a) the number n of cities to be traversed—assume that the cities have as names the numbers $1, 2, \ldots, n$—and (b) the distance between any two cities. The latter information is given in terms of an $n \times n$ table called the **distance matrix** D. The entry of D at the ith row and jth column is a natural number d_{ij}, the distance from city i to city j. Notice that we do not insist that D be **symmetric**—that is, $d_{ij} = d_{ji}$ for all i, j. We can represent D using our encoding α for matrices, as described in Example 7.4.1. Naturally $d_{ii} = 0$ for all i.

Once n and D are given, our task is to find the shortest *tour*. Mathematically, a **tour** is an assignment of one of the integers $\{1, 2, \ldots, n\}$ to each

†Since $|\Sigma| \geq 2$, we may assume without loss of generality that $I, c \in \Sigma$.

of the cities $\{1, 2, \ldots, n\}$. If a city i is assigned j, this means that i will be visited jth in the tour. Thus a tour t is formally defined to be a bijection $t: \{1, 2, \ldots, n\} \longrightarrow \{1, 2, \ldots, n\}$. Finally, we can define the length of a tour under D. If t is a tour, then

$$D(t) = \sum_{j=1}^{n-1} d_{t(j),t(j+1)} + d_{t(n),t(1)}.$$

Computing the tour t for which $D(t)$ is smallest is not a language decision problem; rather, it is a problem of function evaluation. To formulate our problem in terms of a language, we assume that we are also given an integer b, the **budget**, and the question is whether there exists a tour t such that $D(t) \leq b$. One can show (Problem 7.4.5) that, if we had a polynomial-time algorithm for deciding whether there is a tour of length within a given limit, we could use that algorithm to develop a new polynomial-time algorithm for computing the shortest tour.

Formally, we define the following language.

$$TSP = \{I^n @ \alpha(D) @ I^b: \text{there is a tour } t \text{ with } D(t) \leq b\}$$

As was the case with the language B, it is not clear at all that $TSP \in \mathcal{P}$. To the contrary, all known algorithms for solving the Traveling Salesman Problem require, like the exhaustive search of all tours discussed in Section 7.1, an exponential amount of time. And this remains true, despite the intensive research effort for many decades towards devising a polynomial-time algorithm for this problem.

It is, however, easy to show that $TSP \in \mathcal{NP}$, using Theorem 7.4.2. To do this, we only have to observe that the language

$$TSP' = \{I^n @ \alpha(D) @ I^b \$ \alpha(t): D(t) \leq b\}$$

is polynomially balanced and in $\mathcal{P}$. Here by $\alpha(t)$ we mean an encoding of the tour t, such as

$$\alpha(t) = I^{t(1)} c I^{t(2)} c \ldots c I^{t(n)}.$$

That TSP' is polynomially balanced is trivial since $|\alpha(t)| \leq n^2$. It is also very easy to see that, given t and D, one can evaluate $D(t)$ and decide whether $D(t) \leq b$ in polynomial time. It follows that $TSP \in \mathcal{NP}$.

Informally speaking, $\mathcal{P}$ is the class of all sets L such that the membership of an element x in L can be tested efficiently. Theorem 7.4.2 considers the class of all sets L such that every element $x \in L$ has a succinct **certificate** y that establishes the membership of x in L. That $\{x\$y: x \in L, y \text{ is a certificate for } x\} \in \mathcal{P}$ simply means that this certificate can be tested efficiently for validity.

This concept of succinct certificates is best illustrated in terms of the set $C \subseteq \mathbb{N}$ of composite numbers. Suppose that we are given a natural number in its usual decimal representation—for instance, 4,294,967,297—and asked whether it is composite. There is no clear way to test efficiently whether this number is in the set C. However, every number in C does have a succinct certificate. For example, the number 4,294,967,297, which happens to be composite, has as a certificate the pair of integers 6,700,417 and 641 that have a product of 4,294,967,297. To check the validity of the certificate, one just has to carry out the multiplication to be convinced that $4{,}294{,}967{,}297 \in C$. And this is the subtlety of a certificate: once you have found it, you can efficiently exhibit its validity. But finding it may be extremely hard: the above factorization of 4,294,967,297 was first discovered by the mathematician Leonard Euler (1707–1783) in 1732, a full 92 years after Pierre de Fermat (1601–1665), another great mathematician, had conjectured that no such factorization existed!

Theorem 7.4.2, by showing that the class of succinctly certifiable languages coincides with $\mathcal{NP}$, has the effect of further establishing $\mathcal{NP}$ as a stable, significant concept. The real importance of $\mathcal{NP}$, however, lies in the fact that it contains a plethora of natural, practical problems for which the membership in $\mathcal{P}$ is in serious doubt—the Traveling Salesman Problem and integer programming are prominent examples. The question whether $\mathcal{P}$ equals $\mathcal{NP}$ is thus the quantitative analogue of the fundamental question (answered in the negative in Chapter 6) of whether the class of Turing-decidable languages is the same as the class of Turing-acceptable languages.

7.5 $\mathcal{NP}$-COMPLETENESS

Now that we have posed the question of whether $\mathcal{P}$ equals $\mathcal{NP}$, we find ourselves in a position similar to that at the beginning of the previous chapter. Indeed, our method for studying the $\mathcal{P} = \mathcal{NP}$ question will in some ways resemble that used in Chapter 6. There we found a particular Turing-acceptable language, K_0, and showed that the question of whether all Turing-acceptable languages are Turing-decidable can be replaced by the question of whether the *specific* Turing-acceptable language K_0 is Turing-decidable. We then used a diagonal argument to show that K_0 is not Turing-decidable. From the undecidability of K_0, a large number of other undecidability results followed.

An important tool in finding the undecidable languages of Chapter 6 was the notion of a *reduction*. We now define formally a *quantitative refinement* of this concept, called *polynomial-time transformation*.

Definition 7.5.1

Let Σ and Δ be alphabets. A function $f: \Sigma^* \longrightarrow \Delta^*$ is said to be **computed in time** T by a k-tape deterministic Turing machine $M = (K, \Sigma', \delta, s)$ if and only if, for all $x \in \Sigma^*$,

$$(s, \#x\#, \#, \ldots, \#) \vdash_M^t (h, \#f(x)\#, \#, \ldots, \#)$$

for some $t \leq T(|x|)$. We say that f is **computable in time** T if there is a Turing machine M that computes f in time T. We say that f is **polynomial-time computable** if there is a polynomial T such that f is computable in time T.

It is immediate that if f is computable in time T, then for all $x \in \Sigma^*$, $|f(x)| \leq T(|x|) + |x|$. This is because the machine computing f cannot in time $T(|x|)$ produce an output $f(x)$ of length greater than $T(|x|) + |x|$.

Example 7.5.1

If L is any language in $\mathcal{P}$, then the function f_L defined by

$$f_L(x) = \begin{cases} \text{Ⓨ} & \text{if } x \in L \\ \text{Ⓝ} & \text{otherwise.} \end{cases}$$

is, by the definition of $\mathcal{P}$, polynomial-time computable.

Definition 7.5.2

Let $L_1 \subseteq \Sigma_1^*$ and $L_2 \subseteq \Sigma_2^*$ be languages. A polynomial-time computable function $\tau: \Sigma_1^* \longrightarrow \Sigma_2^*$ is called a **polynomial-time transformation from** L_1 **to** L_2 if and only if, for each $x \in \Sigma_1^*$, the following holds: $x \in L_1$ if and only if $\tau(x) \in L_2$.

When a polynomial-time transformation exists from L_1 to L_2, it is possible to adapt any decision procedure for L_2 to obtain one for L_1. To see whether any x that is a candidate for membership in L_1 is actually in L_1, one could compute $\tau(x)$ and see whether *that* string is in L_2. Most importantly, if we have a *fast*—that is, polynomial-time—decision procedure for L_2, this method for deciding membership in L_1 is also polynomial-time, since both the transformation step and the test for membership in L_2 can be done in polynomial time.

Like the reductions of Chapter 6, polynomial-time transformations combine in a transitive fashion.

Lemma 7.5.1. *If $\tau_1: \Sigma_1^* \longrightarrow \Sigma_2^*$ and $\tau_2: \Sigma_2^* \longrightarrow \Sigma_3^*$ are polynomial-time transformations from L_1 to L_2 and from L_2 to L_3, respectively, then $\tau_1 \circ \tau_2: \Sigma_1^* \longrightarrow \Sigma_3^*$ is a polynomial-time transformation from L_1 to L_3.*

Proof. Suppose that τ_1 is computed by a Turing machine M_1 in time T_1, a polynomial, and τ_2 is computed by M_2 in time T_2, also a polynomial. Then $\tau_1 \circ \tau_2$ can be computed by $M_1 M_2$. On input $x \in \Sigma_1^*$, $M_1 M_2$ will output $\tau_1 \circ \tau_2(x)$ in time bounded by $T_1(|x|) + T_2(T_1(|x|) + |x|)$—a polynomial.

It remains to show that $x \in L_1$ if and only if $\tau_1 \circ \tau_2(x) \in L_3$. But this is trivial: $x \in L_1$ if and only if $\tau_1(x) \in L_2$, if and only if $\tau_2(\tau_1(x)) = \tau_1 \circ \tau_2(x) \in L_3$. ■

Using the concept of a polynomial-time transformation, we arrive at the following important definition.

Definition 7.5.3

A language $L \subseteq \Sigma^*$ is called **$\mathcal{NP}$-complete** if and only if:

(a) $L \in \mathcal{NP}$;

(b) for every language $L' \in \mathcal{NP}$, there is a polynomial-time transformation from L' to L.

It is surely not obvious that any $\mathcal{NP}$-complete languages exist, though we shall produce one in a few paragraphs. If they do exist, however, they must play a critical role in our theory of $\mathcal{P}$ and $\mathcal{NP}$. For any such language could, if it were decidable in polynomial time, serve as the basis (through polynomial-time transformations) for efficient decision procedures for *every* language in $\mathcal{NP}$. Indeed, just as the decidability of K_0 captured the whole question of the decidability of Turing-acceptable languages, so the question of whether any one $\mathcal{NP}$-complete language is in $\mathcal{P}$ is equivalent to the whole $\mathcal{P} = \mathcal{NP}$ problem.

Theorem 7.5.1. *Let L be an $\mathcal{NP}$-complete language. Then $\mathcal{P} = \mathcal{NP}$ if and only if $L \in \mathcal{P}$.*

Proof. (*Only If*) Suppose that $\mathcal{P} = \mathcal{NP}$. Since L is $\mathcal{NP}$-complete, and hence—by Definition 7.5.3—$L \in \mathcal{NP}$, it follows that $L \in \mathcal{P}$.

(*If*) Suppose that L is decided by a deterministic Turing machine M_1 in time T_1, a polynomial, and let L' be any language in $\mathcal{NP}$; we shall show that $L' \in \mathcal{P}$.

Since L is $\mathcal{NP}$-complete and $L' \in \mathcal{NP}$, then there is a polynomial-time transformation τ from L' to L. Suppose that τ is computed by some Turing machine M_2 in time T_2, a polynomial. Then we claim that the Turing machine $M_2 M_1$ decides L' in polynomial time. To see that $M_2 M_1$ decides L', notice that $M_2 M_1$ halts with Ⓨ on its tape when given input x if and only if $\tau(x) \in L$; and since τ is a polynomial-time transformation, $\tau(x) \in L$ if and only if $x \in L'$. Furthermore, M_2M_1 halts on input x within time $T_2(|x|) + T_1(T_2(|x|) + |x|)$, and this is a polynomial in $|x|$.

Since L' was taken to be *any* language in $\mathcal{NP}$ and we concluded that $L' \in \mathcal{P}$, it follows that $\mathcal{NP} \subseteq \mathcal{P}$—and therefore $\mathcal{P} = \mathcal{NP}$. ∎

As promised, any $\mathcal{NP}$-complete language plays—with respect to the $\mathcal{P} = \mathcal{NP}$ question—the same role that the language K_0 played in Section 6.1 with respect to the question of whether all Turing-acceptable languages are also Turing-decidable. But how are we to find an $\mathcal{NP}$-complete language? Again, the construction of K_0 gives a clue. Since K_0 consisted of the encodings of Turing machines and their accepted inputs, let us now consider instead the encodings of nondeterministic Turing machines, accepted inputs, *and the number of steps needed to accept those inputs*. That is, let

$$N_0 = \{\rho(M)\rho(w)@I^t: \text{ the nondeterministic Turing machine } M \text{ accepts the input } w \text{ in } t \text{ or fewer steps}\}.$$

Theorem 7.5.2. *N_0 is $\mathcal{NP}$-complete.*

Proof. To show that $N_0 \in \mathcal{NP}$, define the language

$$N_0' = \{\rho(M)\rho(w)@I^t\$\rho(C_0)@\rho(C_1)@\ldots@\rho(C_{t'})$$

such that:

(a) $M = (K, \Sigma, \Delta, s)$ is a nondeterministic Turing machine, $w \in \Sigma^*$;

(b) C_i is a configuration of M for $i = 0, \ldots, t'$;

(c) $C_0 = (s, \#w\underline{\#})$, $C_{t'} = (h, u\underline{\sigma}v)$ for some $u, v \in \Sigma^*, \sigma \in \Sigma$;

(d) $C_i \vdash_M C_{i+1}$ for $i = 0, 1, \ldots, t' - 1$;

(e) $t' \leq t\}$.

It can be easily shown—in a manner identical to the *only-if* part of the proof of Theorem 7.4.2—that $N_0' \in \mathcal{P}$, N_0' is polynomially balanced, and $N_0 = N_0'/\$\{I, c, @\}^*$. Hence $N_0 \in \mathcal{NP}$.

We now have to show that for any language $L \subseteq \Sigma^*$ in $\mathcal{NP}$ there is a polynomial-time transformation τ_L from L to N_0. Since $L \in \mathcal{NP}$, there is a nondeterministic Turing machine M_L and a polynomial p_L such that M_L accepts L in nondeterministic time p_L. Then $\tau_L: \Sigma^* \rightarrow \{I, c, @\}^*$ is defined as follows: for every $w \in \Sigma^*$,

$$\tau_L(w) = \rho(M_L)\rho(w)@I^{p_L(|w|)}.$$

The function τ_L is computable in polynomial time, because $\rho(M_L)$ is a constant string, independent of w, $\rho(w)$ can be computed from w in $O(|w|)$ steps, and $I^{p_L(|w|)}$ can easily be computed in $2p_L(|w|)$ steps with the assistance of the machine that counts the polynomial p_L (Lemma 7.4.2). Finally, it is obvious that $w \in L$ if and only if $\tau_L(w) \in N_0$. ∎

Now that we have an example of an $\mathcal{NP}$-complete language, we are tempted to proceed by analogy with the last chapter and to use a diagonalization argument to show that $\mathcal{P} \neq \mathcal{NP}$. Indeed, for the rest of this section we shall succumb to this temptation, *even though the analogy fails* and we shall not succeed in this way in establishing that $\mathcal{P} \neq \mathcal{NP}$. But the effort will give us some insight into the difficulties of the $\mathcal{P} = \mathcal{NP}$ question.

In Chapter 6, just after defining

$$K_0 = \{\rho(M)\rho(w): M \text{ accepts } w\}$$

we identified the input with (the encoding of) the Turing machine by defining

$$K_1 = \{\rho(M): M \text{ accepts input } \rho(M)\}.$$

In the case of N_0 a similar maneuver is not as straightforward, because every string in N_0 has a third component besides $\rho(M)$ and $\rho(w)$: the encoding I^t of the time bound. We can identify all three components by means of a (somewhat awkward) intermediate step. We shall replace N_0 by $\hat{N}_0$, where

$$\hat{N}_0 = \{\rho(M)\rho(w): \text{ the nondeterministic Turing machine } M \text{ accepts } w \text{ in } 3|w| \text{ steps}\}.$$

Notice that, once we know that a language L is $\mathcal{NP}$-complete, we need merely exhibit a polynomial-time transformation from L to L' in order to show that a new language $L' \in \mathcal{NP}$ is $\mathcal{NP}$-complete. Then, by Lemma 7.5.1, there is a polynomial-time transformation from any language in $\mathcal{NP}$ to L'.

Theorem 7.5.3. *$\hat{N}_0$ is $\mathcal{NP}$-complete.*

Proof. That $\hat{N}_0$ is in $\mathcal{NP}$ follows easily from the fact that N_0 is in $\mathcal{NP}$. So it remains only to show that there is a polynomial-time transformation τ from N_0 to $\hat{N}_0$. Given a string $w \in \{I, c, @\}^*$, if w is not of the form $\rho(M)\rho(u)@I^t$, then $\tau(w) = I$—a fixed string not in $\hat{N}_0$. If, however, $w = \rho(M)\rho(u)@I^t$ for some M, u, and t, then define $\tau(w)$ as follows. If $t \geq 3|u| - 2$, then $\tau(w) = \rho(\hat{M})\rho(\hat{u})$, where

$$\hat{u} = u\$^{t+2-3|u|}$$

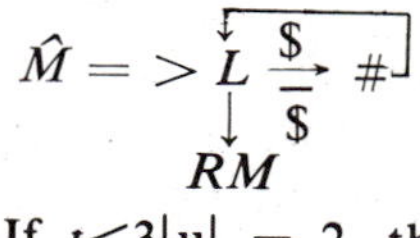

Here \$ is a new symbol. If $t < 3|u| - 2$, then $\tau(w) = \rho(\#^{3|u|-t}M)\ \rho(u)$. It is obvious that τ is a polynomial-time computable. To complete the argument, we must show that $w \in N_0$ if and only if $\tau(w) \in \hat{N}_0$ for every $w \notin (I, c, @\}^*$. If w is not of the form $\rho(M)\rho(u)@I^t$, then $w \notin N_0$ and $\tau(w) = I \notin \hat{N}_0$. Suppose then that $w = \rho(M)\rho(u)@I^t$. If $t \geq 3|u| - 2$, then $\tau(w) = \rho(\hat{M})\rho(\hat{u})$, where $\hat{M}$ and $\hat{u}$ are as defined above. Then $\hat{M}$, when started with input $\hat{u}$, uses $2(t + 3 - 3|u|)$ steps to erase the \$'s and to pass control to M. So $\hat{M}$ accepts $\hat{u}$ within $3|\hat{u}|$ steps (that is, $\tau(w) \in \hat{N}_0$) if and only if M accepts u within $3|\hat{u}| - 2(t + 3 - 3|u|)$ steps. Since $|\hat{u}| = |u| + t + 2 - 3|u|$, $3|\hat{u}| - 2(t + 3 - 3|u|) = t$, and so in this case $\hat{M}$ accepts $\hat{u}$ within $3|\hat{u}|$ steps if and only if M accepts u within t steps. Finally, if $t < 3|u|-2$, then $\tau(w) = \rho(\#^{3|u|-t}M)\rho(u)$. But $\#^{3|u|-t}M$ accepts u in $3|u|$ steps if and only if M accepts u in t steps. ∎

We can now press the analogy between K_0 and $\hat{N}_0$. By analogy with K_1, let

$$N_1 = \{\rho(M)\colon \text{ nondeterministic Turing machine } M \text{ accepts input } \rho(M) \text{ within } 3|\rho(M)| \text{ steps}\}.$$

Naturally, we would like to show that N_1 is in $\mathcal{NP} - \mathcal{P}$ and $\bar{N}_1 \notin \mathcal{NP}$. Alas, the analogy with K_1 and $\bar{K}_1$ breaks down: we cannot use $\bar{N}_1$ to diagonalize over $\mathcal{P}$. Suppose that $\bar{N}_1$ is accepted by a deterministic Turing machine $\bar{M}_1$ in time p, a polynomial. We would hope to derive a contradiction by asking whether $\rho(\bar{M}_1) \in \bar{N}_1$. But no contradiction results; for it could very well be that $\rho(\bar{M}_1) \notin \bar{N}_1$ simply because $\bar{M}_1$ accepts $\rho(\bar{M}_1)$ in exactly $3|\rho(\bar{M}_1)| + 1$ steps and no less!

So this approach fails to prove that $\mathcal{P} \neq \mathcal{NP}$—as, in fact, do far more sophisticated arguments. Although there is sound intuition behind our belief that $\mathcal{P} \neq \mathcal{NP}$, in mathematics we must accept as true only what has been rigorously shown to be true. So far, no one has been able to settle the $\mathcal{P} \stackrel{?}{=} \mathcal{NP}$ enigma either way. There are reasons to suspect that this question may be one of a select class of important mathematical problems that remain unresolved for decades, motivating research and awaiting the development of new and deeper insights and drastically different methodology.

7.6 SOME $\mathcal{NP}$-COMPLETE PROBLEMS

The notion of $\mathcal{NP}$-completeness has failed to provide us with the hoped-for proof that $\mathcal{P} \neq \mathcal{NP}$. Nevertheless, $\mathcal{NP}$-completeness is an important idea, since among all the languages in $\mathcal{NP}$, the $\mathcal{NP}$-complete languages are *least likely* to be decidable in polynomial time. In recent years many interesting languages have been shown to be $\mathcal{NP}$-complete; one detailed census reaches into the hundreds. Some of these languages are string formulations of important practical problems from operations research, number theory, game theory, and other seemingly unrelated areas of mathematics. Prior to the discovery of $\mathcal{NP}$-completeness, much research effort had been devoted in vain to finding polynomial-time algorithms for these problems. The concept of $\mathcal{NP}$-completeness unified the experiences of researchers in these diverse areas by showing that *none* of these problems is solvable by a polynomial-time algorithm unless $\mathcal{P} = \mathcal{NP}$—a circumstance that appears to contradict both intuition and experience. This realization has had the beneficial effect of diverting the research effort previously focussed on solving particular $\mathcal{NP}$-complete problems either towards other, more tractable problems, or towards the resolution of the central $\mathcal{P} \stackrel{?}{=} \mathcal{NP}$ question itself. This redirection of research has been the most profound effect of complexity theory on the practice of computing.

In this section we show a number of languages to be $\mathcal{NP}$-complete. We start with a quantitative version of the tiling problem that was shown to be unsolvable in Chapter 6. We use this $\mathcal{NP}$-complete problem to show that two important practical problems, arising from operations research, are also $\mathcal{NP}$-complete: integer programming and the Traveling Salesman Problem, formalized earlier in this chapter as the languages B and TSP.

7.6.1 A BOUNDED TILING PROBLEM

Consider the tiling systems defined in Section 6.5. It is quite easy to devise an encoding σ of tiling systems as strings over $\{I, c\}$, like the encoding ρ of Turing machines as strings over this alphabet.

Now let $\mathfrak{D} = (D, d_0, H, V)$ be a tiling system and let $s > 0$. An $s \times s$ **tiling by** $\mathfrak{D}$ is a function f: $\{0, 1, \ldots, s-1\} \times \{0, 1, \ldots, s-1\} \to D$ such that

$f(0,0) = d_0$;

$(f(m, n), f(m+1, n)) \in H$ for all m and n, $0 \leq m < s-1, 0 \leq n \leq s-1$;

and

$(f(m, n), f(m, n+1)) \in V$ for all m and n, $0 \leq m \leq s-1, 0 \leq n < s-1$.

That is, an $s \times s$ tiling by $\mathfrak{D}$ is just a tiling of the square of side s in the lower lefthand part of the first quadrant, obeying all the appropriate constraints on the layout of tiles.

Theorem 7.6.1. *The language* $T = \{\sigma(\mathfrak{D})@I^s$: there is an $s \times s$ tiling by $\mathfrak{D}\}$ *is* $\mathcal{NP}$*-complete.*

In order to prove Theorem 7.6.1, we need the following lemma.

Lemma 7.6.1. *The language*

$$N_2 = \{\rho(M)@I^t: \; M \text{ is a nondeterministic Turing machine } (K, \Sigma, \Delta, s), \text{ and } (s, \#) \vdash_M^{t'} (h, u\underline{\sigma}v) \text{ for some } u, v \in \Sigma^*, \; \sigma \in \Sigma, \text{ and } t' \leq t\}$$

is $\mathcal{NP}$*-complete.*

Proof. It is routine to show that $N_2 \in \mathcal{NP}$. We shall give a polynomial-time transformation τ from N_0 to N_2, and thus show that N_2 is $\mathcal{NP}$-complete. Given $w \in \{I, @, c\}^*$, if w is not of the form $\rho(M)\rho(u)@I^t$, then $\tau(w) = I$, a string surely not in N_2. If, however, $w = \rho(M)\rho(u)@I^t$, then $\tau(w) = \rho(M')@I^{t+2|u|+1}$, where M' is the machine

$$Ru(1)Ru(2) \ldots Ru(|u|)RM$$

which writes the string u on its tape and then passes control to M. We leave it as an exercise (Problem 7.6.6) to verify that τ is polynomial-time computable and that, for any $w \in \{I, c, @\}^*$, $w \in N_0$ if and only if $\tau(w) \in N_2$. ■

Proof of Theorem 7.6.1. To show that $T \in \mathcal{NP}$ is left as an exercise (see Problem 7.6.9(a)). In order to show $\mathcal{NP}$-completeness, we shall give a polynomial-time transformation from N_2 to T. Let w be any string in $\{I, c, @\}^*$. As usual, if w is not of the form $\rho(M)@I^t$ for some nondeterministic Turing machine M, then $\tau(w) = I$, a string not in T. On the other hand, if $w = \rho(M)@I^t$, where $M = (K, \Sigma, \Delta, s)$, then $\tau(w) = \sigma(\mathfrak{D})@I^{t+2}$, where $\mathfrak{D}$, described below, is a modification of the tiling system constructed in the proof of Theorem 6.5.1.

Recall that in the proof of that theorem, the horizontal and vertical adjacency constraints were implied by markings on the edges of tiles. In particular, the markings on the upper and lower edges of tiles were of the form a, where $a \in \Sigma$, or (q, a), where $q \in K$ and $a \in \Sigma$. Here we construct in a similar fashion the tiling system $\mathfrak{D} = (D, d_0, H, V)$; but the markings on the upper and lower edges are *augmented to include a number k*. This numerical component of an edge marking stands for *the number of steps executed thus far in the computation by M*; or, alternatively, *the number of the one and only row* in which the tile may be placed.

Formally, there are tiles of the following types:

(a) For each $a \in \Sigma$, and each k, $0 \leq k \leq t$, D contains the tile shown in Figure 7–7.

Figure 7–7

(b) For each $a, b \in \Sigma$ and $q \in K$, $p \in K \cup \{h\}$ such that $(q, a, p, b) \in \Delta$, and for each k, $0 \leq k < t$, D contains the tile shown in Figure 7–8.

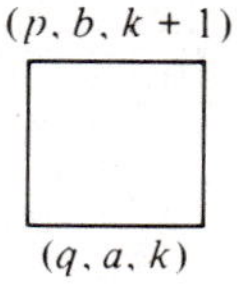

Figure 7–8

(c)–(d) Similarly, D contains the tiles shown in Figures 7–9(a) and 7–9(b) to simulate the move $(q, a, p, R) \in \Delta$; and those in Figures 7–9(c) and 7–9(d) simulate the move $(q, a, p, L) \in \Delta$, for all k, $0 \leq k < t$.

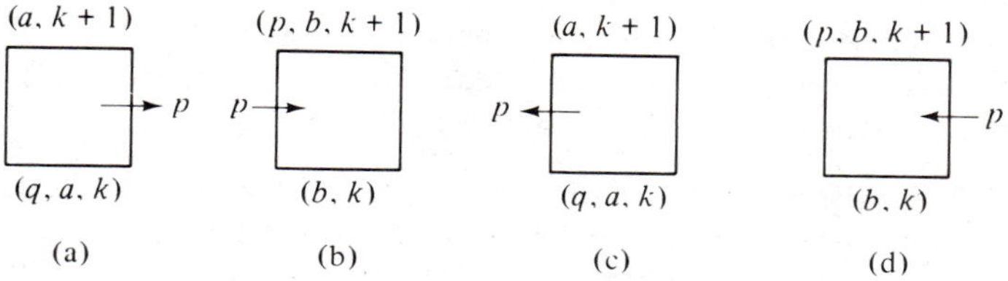

Figure 7–9

(e) For all $a \in \Sigma$ and all k, $0 \leq k \leq t$, D contains the tile shown in Figure 7–10. These permit the propagation of the halt state h, if reached at time t or some time before t, upwards to the $(t + 1)$st row.

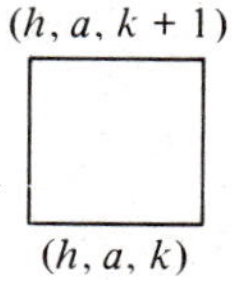

Figure 7–10

(f) The tiles that will fill the 0th row are those shown in Figure 7–11.

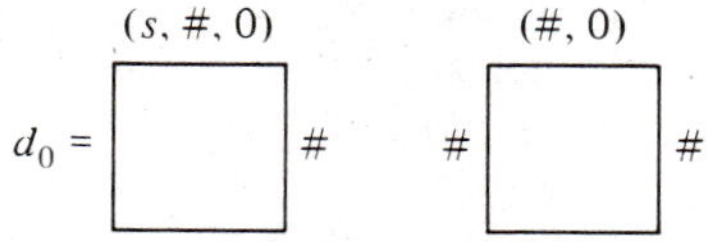

Figure 7–11

It is straightforward to verify the following facts.

1. The markings on top of the 0th row of any $(t + 2) \times (t + 2)$ tiling by $\mathfrak{D}$ are $(s, \#, 0), (\#, 0), \ldots, (\#, 0)$.

2. By induction, one can now show that $t + 1$ markings of the form (a, k) and exactly one of the form (q, a, k) (where $q \in K \cup \{h\}$) appear on top of the kth row in any $(t + 2) \times (t + 2)$ tiling by $\mathfrak{D}$.

3. If the markings on top of each row are interpreted as a configuration, then the $t + 1$ first rows make up a computation of M starting from $(s, \#)$.

4. If *any* marking of the form $(q, a, t + 1)$ appears on the top of the last row—and by (2), one such marking must appear if there is a $(t + 2) \times (t + 2)$ tiling—then q, the state, must be h. This is because in (a)–(d), t is the maximum value of the numerical component of the marking on the upper edge of a tile which has a state component; only in (e) are tiles introduced in which that number can be $t + 1$.

From (1)–(4), it follows that if $\tau(w) \in T$, then $w \in N_2$; that is, if $\tau(w)$ encodes a tiling system $\mathfrak{D}$ and a number s such that there is a $s \times s$ tiling by $\mathfrak{D}$, then w encodes a Turing machine and time bound such that there is a halted computation as described in the definition of N_2. We leave it to the reader to show that, conversely, if the Turing machine encoded by w halts in a time bound as specified by N_2, then $\tau(w)$ encodes a tiling system that has a tiling as specified by T. Finally, it must be shown that τ is polynomial-time computable. This is left as an exercise (see Problem 7.6.9(b)); the critical observation is that the *number* of tiles created in (a)–(f) is only polynomial in t and the size of M. ■

7.6.2 INTEGER PROGRAMMING

The language B was introduced in Examples 7.4.1 and 7.4.3.

Theorem 7.6.2. *B is $\mathcal{NP}$-complete.*

Proof. We already know that $B \in \mathcal{NP}$. We shall show that there is a polynomial-time transformation τ which, given a tiling system $\mathfrak{D}$ and an integer $s > 0$, produces a system of linear equations such that the system has a binary solution $x \in \{0, 1\}^n$ if and only if there is an $s \times s$ tiling by $\mathfrak{D}$.

Let $\mathfrak{D} = (D, d_0, H, V)$ and $D = \{d_0, \ldots, d_{|D|-1}\}$. Our system of equations will have $|D|s^2$ variables x_{ijk}, with $0 \leq i, j \leq s - 1$ and $0 \leq k < |D|$; and also some other variables introduced later in the proof. Intuitively, the intended meaning of each variable x_{ijk} is the following:

$x_{ijk} = 1$ means that $f(i, j) = d_k$, where f is the $s \times s$ tiling to be constructed; $x_{ijk} = 0$ means that $f(i, j) \neq d_k$.

There are four kinds of equations.

(a) For each pair i, j such that $0 \leq i, j < s$, there is the equation

$$\sum_{k=0}^{|D|-1} x_{ijk} = 1.$$

This set of equations states that there is *exactly* one tile in each square, that is, that f is a *function*, as required.

(b) For each i, j, where $0 \leq i < s - 1$ and $0 \leq j < s$, and each k, $0 \leq k < |D|$, there is the inequality

$$x_{ijk} + \sum_{(d_k, d_l) \notin H} x_{i+1,j,l} \leq 1.$$

This means that if $f(i,j) = d_k$—that is, $x_{ijk} = 1$—then no tile d_l for which $(d_k, d_l) \notin H$ can be placed on the square $(i + 1, j)$. That is,

$$\sum_{(d_k, d_l) \notin H} x_{i+1,j,l} = 0.$$

However, if $x_{ijk} = 0$, then the sum is allowed to be one. These inequalities enforce the horizontal adjacency requirements.

However, an inequality has been introduced here, although the problem was defined in terms of equations. One can, fortunately, transform this inequality into an equation by introducing a new variable y_{ijk}, not appearing in any other equation.

$$x_{ijk} + \sum_{(d_k, d_l) \notin H} x_{i+1,j,l} + y_{ijk} = 1.$$

Since this is the only equation in which y_{ijk} participates, we can always satisfy this equation by giving an appropriate value (zero or one) to y_{ijk}, starting from any set of values for the x's that satisfy the above inequality.

(c) Similarly, for each i and j, $0 \leq i < s$, $0 \leq j < s - 1$, and each k, $0 \leq k < |D|$, the equation

$$x_{ijk} + \sum_{(d_k, d_l) \notin V} x_{i,j+1,l} + z_{ijk} = 1$$

where z_{ijk} is a variable playing a role identical to that of y_{ijk} in (b).

(d) Finally, we enforce the initial condition $f(0, 0) = d_0$ by the equation

$$x_{000} = 1.$$

It is routine to check the following.

1. The transformation τ described above can be computed in polynomial time.

2. There is an $s \times s$ tiling by the original system $\mathfrak{D}$ if and only if the resulting set of equations in the variables $\{x_{ijk}, y_{ijk}, z_{ijk}: 0 \leq i, j < s, 0 \leq k < |D|\}$ has a solution with values zero or one. ■

Our proof of Theorem 7.6.2 shows that the problem B of binary equations is $\mathfrak{NP}$-complete *even if we restrict the kinds of coefficients allowed* in A and b. For example, we can impose the restrictions that all entries of A are either zero or one, and that the entries of b are all one. Since the equations constructed in our proof satisfy these restrictions, the resulting restricted problem is also $\mathfrak{NP}$-complete.

Corollary 7.6.1 *The language* $B_R = \{\alpha(A)@\alpha(b)$: *all entries of* A *are in* $\{0, 1\}$ *and all entries of* b *are* 1, *and* $Ax = b$ *has a binary solution*$\}$ *is* $\mathfrak{NP}$*-complete.*

We shall make essential use of this corollary in the next subsection.

7.6.3 THE TRAVELING SALESMAN PROBLEM

Consider first the following problem: Given a Turing machine M, determine whether there is some input to M that will cause it to visit all its states. It is easy to show that this problem is unsolvable (Problem 6.3.5). If we impose a time constraint—that is, we ask instead whether some input causes M to visit all its states *within t steps*—then the problem becomes $\mathfrak{NP}$-complete; this also is not hard to show (Problem 7.6.2). Surprisingly, however, the problem remains $\mathfrak{NP}$-complete even when M is a finite automaton. We shall use an even more restricted version of this problem to show that the Traveling Salesman Problem is $\mathfrak{NP}$-complete.

Suppose that our encoding function ρ for Turing machines is appropriately extended to encode finite automata. Consider the language

$H = \{\rho(M)$: $M = (K, \Sigma, \delta, s, F)$ is a deterministic finite automaton, and there is a string $w \in \Sigma^*$ of length $|K|$ such that $(s, w) \vdash_M^* (s, e)$, and for each $q \in K$, there is a suffix x of w such that $(s, w) \vdash_M^* (q, x)\}$.

Note that because the length of w is required to equal the number of states of M, M may not "waste" any steps: it must visit a new state on each step of its computation on input w. Evidently, then, such a computation defines a set of $|K|$ **transitions**—elements of $K \times \Sigma$, namely $C = \{(q_1, w(1)), \ldots, (q_{|K|}, w(|K|))\}$, such that:

(a) $q_1 = s$;

(b) $\{q_j: 1 \leq j \leq |K|\} = K$; and

(c) $\delta(q_j, w(j)) = q_{j+1}$ for $j = 1, \ldots, |K| - 1$; and $\delta(q_{|K|}, w(|K|)) = s$.

Such a set of transitions will be called a **Hamilton cycle** of M.

Example 7.6.1

The finite automaton M shown in Figure 7–12 has a Hamilton cycle $C = \{(s, a), (q_3, a), (q_2, b), (q_4, b), (q_1, b)\}$ corresponding to the string $w = aabbb$. Hence, $\rho(M) \in H$.

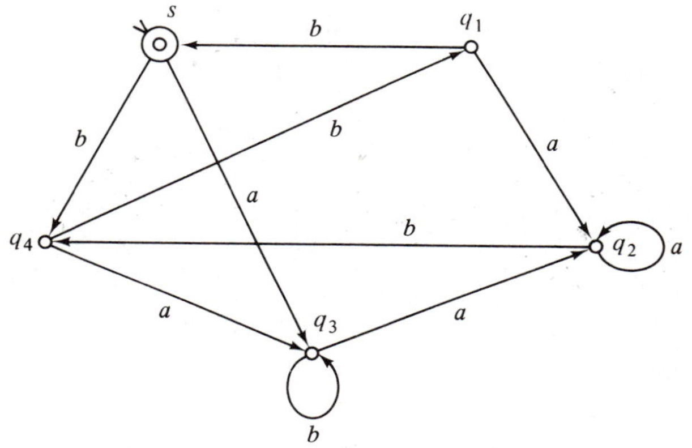

Figure 7–12

The language H can be redefined as follows.

$$H = \{\rho(M):\quad M \text{ has a Hamilton cycle}\}$$

Theorem 7.6.3. *H is $\mathfrak{NP}$-complete.*

Proof. It is left as an exercise (see Problem 7.6.10(a)) to show that $H \in \mathfrak{NP}$. We shall describe a polynomial-time transformation τ from the language B_R of Corollary 7.6.1 to H. Given any $m \times n$ matrix A with coefficients in $\{0, 1\}$ and the vector

$$b = \underbrace{(1, \ldots, 1)}_{m},$$

τ will construct a deterministic finite automaton M such that $Ax = b$ has a binary solution if and only if M has a Hamilton cycle.

We present the construction in two stages. First, we construct a deterministic finite automaton $M_0 = (K_0, \Sigma_0, \delta_0, s_0, F_0)$, and we prove a certain special relationship between the Hamilton cycles of M_0 and the existence of a binary solution to $Ax = b$. Then we shall modify M_0 to obtain M.

The Construction of M_0. The state set of M_0, K_0, contains a state p_j for each column of A (that is, for every variable x_j) and a state q_j for each row of A; it also contains three additional states s_0, p_{n+1}, q_{m+1}. The alphabet Σ_0 contains the symbol b and one symbol a_j for each column of A. Thus $K_0 = \{s_0, p_1, \ldots, p_{n+1}, q_1, \ldots, q_{m+1}\}$, and $\Sigma_0 = \{b, a_1, \ldots, a_n\}$. Then δ_0 is defined as follows.

(a) $\delta_0(s_0, b) = p_1, \delta_0(p_{n+1}, b) = q_1, \delta_0(q_{m+1}, b) = s_0$

(b) $\delta_0(p_j, b) = \delta_0(p_j, a_j) = p_{j+1}$

(c) $\delta_0(q_i, a_j) = q_{i+1}$, for all i, j such that A has a one in its ith row and jth column (that is, x_j has coefficient one in the ith equation)

(d) All the remaining transitions of M_0 are "loops" of the form $\delta(q, a) = q$. Notice that such "loops" can never participate in any Hamilton cycle of M_0, since they represent "wasted" transitions. Hence, they are irrelevant to our problem, and will be disregarded in the subsequent discussion.

Example 7.6.2

Consider the system of equations

$$\begin{aligned} x_1 + x_2 + x_3 \qquad &= 1 \\ x_2 \qquad + x_4 &= 1 \\ x_3 + x_4 &= 1 \end{aligned}$$

with matrix

$$A = \begin{bmatrix} 1 & 1 & 1 & 0 \\ 0 & 1 & 0 & 1 \\ 0 & 0 & 1 & 1 \end{bmatrix}.$$

The corresponding automaton M_0 is shown in Figure 7–13 (with "loops" omitted). There are several Hamilton cycles in M_0. Among these are

$$C_1 = \{(s_0, b), (p_1, b), (p_2, a_2), (p_3, b), (p_4, b), (p_5, b), (q_1, a_1), (q_2, a_2), (q_3, a_3), (q_4, b)\},$$

and

$$C_2 = \{(s_0, b), (p_1, a_1), (p_2, b), (p_3, b), (p_4, a_4), (p_5, b), (q_1, a_1), (q_2, a_4), (q_3, a_4), (q_4, b)\}.$$

Let us define for $1 \le j \le n$ the set $X_j \subseteq K_0 \times \Sigma_0$, where $X_j = \{(q, a_j): q \in K, \delta(q, a_j) \neq q\}$. Therefore X_j contains all nonloop transitions on symbol a_j. In Figure 7–13, $X_3 = \{(p_3, a_3), (q_1, a_3), (q_3, a_3)\}$. Let us call a Hamilton cycle C of M_0 **proper** if $C \cap X_j$ is either X_j or $\varnothing$, for $j = 1, \ldots, n$. In other words, a Hamilton cycle C is proper if, for each a_j, C uses either all or none of the nonloop transitions involving a_j. For example, the Hamilton cycle C_1 of Example 7.6.2 is not proper, while C_2 is.

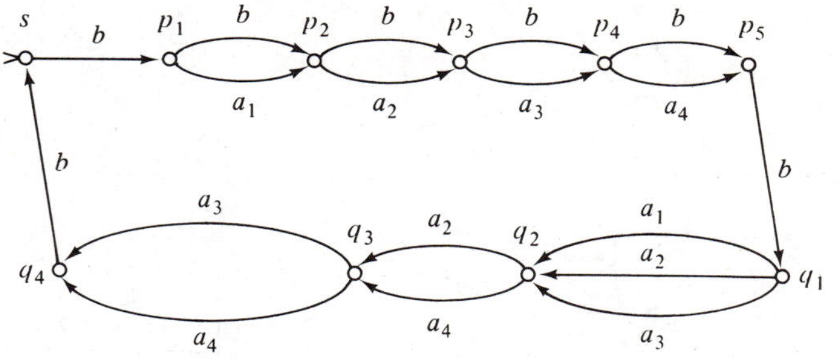

Figure 7–13

Lemma 7.6.2. *M_0 has a proper Hamilton cycle if and only if $Ax = b$ has a binary solution.*

Proof. It is obvious that any Hamilton cycle of M_0 must traverse the states in K_0 in the order $(s_0, p_1, \ldots, p_{n+1}, q_1, \ldots, q_{m+1}, s_0)$. Hence a proper Hamilton cycle exists if and only if there is a choice of a nonloop transition from each state to the next, so that this sequence of choices satisfies the definition of a proper Hamilton cycle.

For the states s_0, p_{n+1}, and q_{m+1}, there is no other choice than b. For the states p_j, $j \leq n$, however, there is a choice between a_j and b. A proper Hamilton cycle exists, therefore, if and only if the choices for $p_1, \ldots, p_n$ can be made in such a way that each of the states $q_1, \ldots, q_m$ has *exactly one* transition with a symbol a_j, such that (p_j, a_j) was chosen. But since the p's correspond to variables and the q's to equations, this means that there is a choice of a subset S of the integers $\{1, \ldots, n\}$ such that in each equation *exactly one* variable x_j with $j \in S$ has coefficient one. However, this is equivalent to saying that the given equations have a binary solution, namely that obtained by setting $x_j = 1$ if $j \in S$ and $x_j = 0$ if $j \notin S$.

Thus there is a proper Hamilton cycle of M_0 if and only if $Ax = b$ has a binary solution, and the lemma is proved. ■

For example, the proper cycle C_2 of Example 7.6.2 corresponds to the solution $x_1 = 1$, $x_2 = 0$, $x_3 = 0$, and $x_4 = 1$.

Now M is constructed from M_0 in such a way that *Hamilton cycles of M correspond exactly to proper Hamilton cycles of M_0.* In order to proceed with the construction, however, we need another lemma. Suppose that N is a deterministic finite automaton $(K, \{a, b\}, \delta, s, F)$ which has among its states and transitions the eight states and transitions shown in Figure 7–14(a). The automaton N may have more states and will certainly have more transitions. However, we know that the states r_1, r_2, and r_3 are "isolated" in that $r_j \neq \delta(q, \sigma)$ for any $(q, \sigma) \in K \times \Sigma - T$, where T is the set of eight transi-

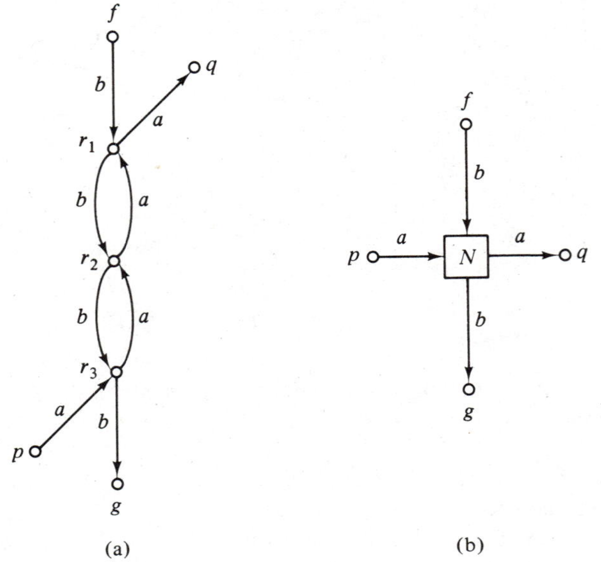

Figure 7–14

tions shown. Let us define $A = \{(p, a), (r_3, a), (r_2, a), (r_1, a)\}$, and $B = \{(f, b), (r_1, b), (r_2, b), (r_3, b)\}$. We can show the following lemma.

Lemma 7.6.3. *If N has a Hamilton cycle C, then either*

(a) $A \cap C = A$ *and* $B \cap C = \varnothing$, *or*

(b) $B \cap C = B$ *and* $A \cap C = \varnothing$.

Proof. Let C be a Hamilton cycle of N. State r_3 can be reached only from p or from r_2, so either $(p, a) \in C$ or $(r_2, b) \in C$. Suppose first that $(p, a) \in C$. It cannot then happen that $(r_3, b) \in C$, that is, that C leaves r_3 to state g; for then state r_2, which must be on the cycle, must be entered from state r_1 (otherwise r_3 would be duplicated), and then r_2 could not be left without duplicating r_1 or r_3 on the cycle. So $(r_3, a) \in C$. It then follows easily that (r_2, a) and (r_1, a) are in C, so $A \subseteq C$ and $B \cap C = \varnothing$. We leave it as an exercise (Problem 7.6.3) to show that if $(r_2, b) \in C$, then $B \subseteq C$ and $A \cap C = \varnothing$. ■

We shall represent the part of automaton N shown in Figure 7–14(a) by the abbreviation in Figure 7–14(b). Lemma 7.6.3 says that this structure behaves as if it consisted of just two transitions—(f, b) and (p, a)—such that every Hamilton cycle must contain *exactly one* of them.

We are now ready to describe the modifications to M_0 that will lead us to M. Notice that a Hamilton cycle of M_0 is proper if and only if it contains *exactly one* of the transitions in each of the pairs $\{(p_j, b), (q_i, a_j)\}$, for all $j \leq n$ and all i such that $\delta(q_i, a_j) \neq q_i$. However, we can now add to M_0 *copies* of the "N-structure" of Figure 7–14 in order to *enforce these conditions explicitly*. Thus for $j = 1, \ldots, n$, we replace the transition (p_j, b) and all (q_{i_l}, a_j) non-loop transitions, $l = 1, \ldots, k$, as shown in Figure 7–15(b), where

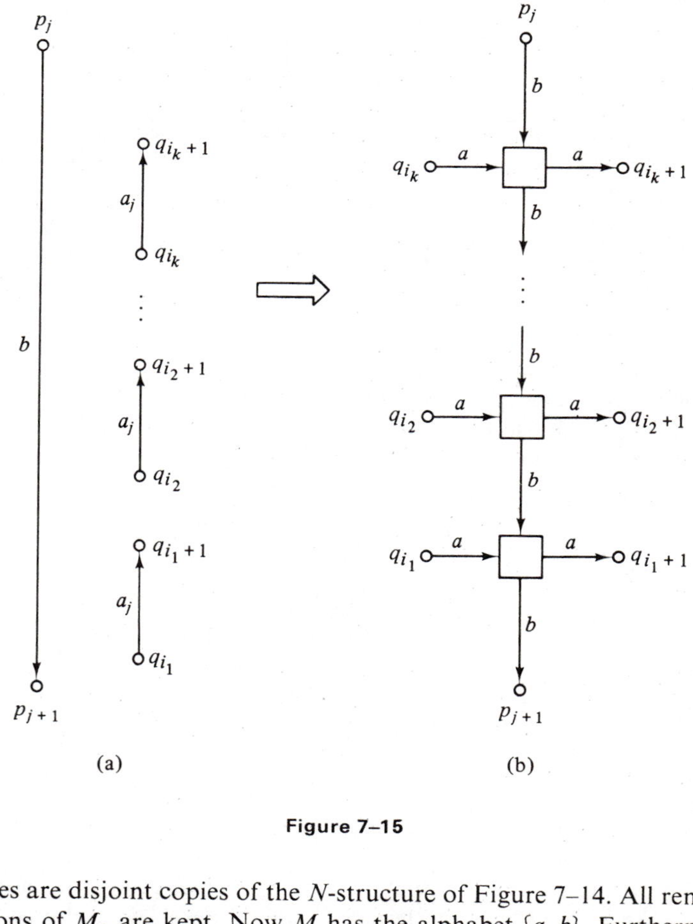

Figure 7–15

the boxes are disjoint copies of the N-structure of Figure 7–14. All remaining transitions of M_0 are kept. Now M has the alphabet $\{a, b\}$. Furthermore, it is immediate by Lemma 7.6.3 that if M has a Hamilton cycle, then it must correspond to a proper Hamilton cycle of M_0; and conversely, if M_0 has a proper Hamilton cycle, then we can devise a Hamilton cycle of M. Thus M has a Hamilton cycle if and only if M_0 has a proper Hamilton cycle, or, by

Lemma 7.6.2, if and only if $Ax = b$ has a binary solution. It is left as an exercise (see Problem 7.6.10(b)) to show that the transformation τ described above is polynomial-time computable. ■

We can now show that the Traveling Salesman Problem, as formulated in Example 7.4.5, is $\mathcal{NP}$-complete.

Theorem 7.6.4. *TSP is $\mathcal{NP}$-complete.*

Proof. We know that $TSP \in \mathcal{NP}$. We shall describe a polynomial-time transformation τ from the language H to TSP. Given the encoding of a finite automaton $M = (K, \Sigma, \delta, s, F)$, τ constructs an integer n, an $n \times n$ distance matrix D with entries d_{ij}, and a budget b such that there exists a tour t of the n cities $\{1, 2, \ldots, n\}$ with $D(t) \leq b$ if and only if M has a Hamilton cycle.

The number n of cities is simply $|K|$—assume for simplicity that $K = \{q_1, \ldots, q_n\}$. The matrix D is defined as follows.

$$d_{ij} = 0 \qquad \text{if there is a } \sigma \in \Sigma \text{ such that } \delta(q_i, \sigma) = q_j$$
$$d_{ij} = 1 \qquad \text{otherwise}$$

Finally, the budget b is set to zero.

Then $\tau(\rho(M)) \in TSP$ if and only if there exists a tour t of the n cities such that $D(t) = 0$. However, this can happen only if $d_{t(j),t(j+1)} = 0$ for $j = 1, \ldots, n-1$, and also $d_{t(n),t(1)} = 0$. If this is the case, however, it is obvious from the definition of d_{ij} that the set

$$\{(q_{t(j)}, \sigma_j): \delta(q_{t(j)}, \sigma_j) = q_{t(j+1)}, j = 1, \ldots, n-1; \delta(q_{t(n)}, \sigma_n) = q_{t(1)}\}$$

is a Hamilton cycle of M.

Conversely, starting from any Hamilton cycle of M, it is clear that we can construct a zero-cost tour, and so, the theorem is proved. ■

It takes somewhat more work to prove that certain "realistic" special cases of the Traveling Salesman Problem are also $\mathcal{NP}$-complete; see Problem 7.6.5 and the references at the end of the chapter.

7.7 THE COMPLEXITY HIERARCHY

One of our motives in studying time-bounded Turing machines, and complexity in general, was the hope of establishing a hierarchy of Turing-decidable languages according to their time complexity. In this section we prove formally that such a hierarchy exists. The results can be interpreted as saying that if one sufficiently increases the time bound on Turing machines, one is guaranteed to obtain new languages, which can be decided within the new bound but not within the old. This situation is not unlike that in which the addition of a stack to a finite automaton, or of nondeterminism to a deterministic pushdown automaton, resulted in the recognition of new languages. There are, however, two major differences: (a) the hierarchy now is infinite, reflecting its quantitative basis, and (b) we are able to exhibit only unnatural, halting-problem-like languages as witnesses to the hierarchy. The results of this section imply, for example, that there exist problems that are solvable in exponential time, but that are not in $\mathcal{P}$. Unfortunately, these problems are not natural and useful ones, like the Traveling Salesman Problem and integer programming—for one thing, they do not seem to be in $\mathcal{NP}$ at all. Proving lower bounds on the complexity of natural problems is the main challenge facing complexity theory today, and the question of whether $\mathcal{P} = \mathcal{NP}$ is a part of this challenge.

Let $f: \mathbb{N} \longrightarrow \mathbb{N}$ be a step-counting function, and let $F: \mathbb{N} \longrightarrow \mathbb{N}$ be another, faster growing step-counting function such that $f^2 = O(F)$ but $f^2 \not\asymp F$. Since F is not $O(f^2)$, it follows that for every $c > 0$ and $n_0 \in \mathbb{N}$, there is an integer $n \geq n_0$ such that $F(n) > cf^2(n)$. We shall make use of this fact in the proof of the following theorem.

Theorem 7.7.1. *Let f and F be as above. Then* TIME(f) $\subsetneq$ TIME(F).

Proof. That TIME(f) $\subseteq$ TIME(F) follows from the fact that $f = O(F)$. What we really have to prove is that the inclusion is proper. We shall do this by exhibiting a language in TIME(F) $-$ TIME(f).

Consider the language

$$L = \{w\colon w = c^j\rho(M);\ j \in S_M;\ \text{and the (deterministic) multi-tape Turing machine } M \text{ rejects } w \text{ in } f(|w|) \text{ steps}\}.$$

By *rejects* w, we mean *halts with* $\#Ⓝ\#$ *on the first tape* when started with input w. Here S_M is a nonempty set of integers that depends on the Turing machine M, and will be specified later in the proof.

We claim that $L \notin$ TIME(f), and yet $L \in$ TIME(F). To show that L is not decidable in time f, suppose that it is. Suppose, that is, that there exists a Turing machine M which decides L in time f. At last we can diagonalize! Choose $j \in S_M$—we can, since S_M is nonempty. Is $c^j\rho(M) \in L$? It is if and only if it is not. Therefore $L \notin$ TIME(f).

It remains to specify how S_M is determined from any Turing machine M, and to show that $L \in$ TIME(F). The intuitive idea is that, since F grows so much faster than f, by "padding" $\rho(M)$ with enough c's, it is possible to determine in $F(|c^j\rho(M)|)$ steps whether or not M rejects $c^j\rho(M)$ in only $f(|c^j\rho(M)|)$ steps, and therefore to determine whether $c^j\rho(M)$ is in L or not. The technical details follow.

One point of notation: If g is any function from $\{I, c\}^*$ to $\mathbb{N}$, we write $\hat{g}$ for that function from $\mathbb{N}$ to $\mathbb{N}$ such that

$$\hat{g}(n) = \max\{g(w): w \in \{I, c\}^n\}.$$

That is, $\hat{g}(n)$ is the maximum value of $g(w)$ for all w of length n.

We shall construct a Turing machine M_L that decides L in time $3F$—by Theorem 7.1.1, this implies that $L \in \text{TIME}(F)$. Since F is a step-counting function, there exists a Turing machine M_F such that M_F halts after $F(|w|)$ steps on any input w. Machine M_L uses M_F as a "clock." At each step of its main computation, M_L also executes (on a disjoint set of tapes) one step of M_F, in parallel. Whenever M_F is about to halt (and therefore $F(|w|)$ steps have been executed) M_L interrupts its own computation, erases its tapes, and halts with #Ⓝ# on its first tape.

The main operation of M_L—in parallel with the "clock" M_F—is as follows.

(a) First M_L examines whether w is of the form $c^j\rho(M)$, where M is, for some k, a k-tape Turing machine. If it is not, M_L rejects w. We can easily design an algorithm for doing so in $O(n^2)$ time for input of length n. It follows that the amount of time M_L spends in this phase of its operation, when presented with an input string w, can be specified exactly as $g_1(w)$ for some function $g_1: \{I, c\}^* \longrightarrow \mathbb{N}$ such that $\hat{g}_1(n) = O(n^2)$.

(b) We would like now to have M_L simulate M on input w, where M is the Turing machine decoded from $c^j\rho(M)$ in the previous step. There is a difficulty, though, since M could have an arbitrarily large number of tapes, and, no matter how many tapes we design M_L to have, there will be M's that have more. In order to simulate M, M_L first produces an encoding $\rho(M')$ of the 1-tape Turing machine M' described in the proof of Theorem 7.3.2, which accepts the same language as M, at a quadratic increase of the number of steps. Since the construction of $\rho(M')$ from $\rho(M)$ can be carried out in time $O(|\rho(M)|^2)$ (see Problem 7.7.2), the time M_L spends in this phase of its operation when the input string is $w = c^j\rho(M)$ can be specified exactly as $g_2(w)$ for some function $g_2: \{I, c\}^* \longrightarrow \mathbb{N}$ such that $\hat{g}_2(n) = O(n^2)$.

(c) Next M_L simulates M' (which in turn simulates M) on the input $w = c^j\rho(M)$; M_L starts a new "clock" M_f—counting up to $f(|w|)$—and advances it once every time that M' has completed the simulation of one step of M. Whenever M_f is about to halt, M_L erases its tapes and halts with #Ⓝ#, rejecting w. Also, if M' is about to halt in a nonrejecting configuration, then M_L rejects w. Finally, M_L accepts w only in the case that M' is about to halt and reject w. Let us write $g_3(w)$ for the number of steps spent by M_L in this stage of its operation on input $w = c^j\rho(M)$. Since the simulation by M' results in only a quadratic increase in the number of steps, and since at most $f(|w|)$ steps of M are simulated, it follows that $\hat{g}_3 = O(f^2)$.

We claim that M_L decides L in time $3F$. First, it is obvious that, with that assistance of M_F, M_L always halts on input w within $3F(|w|)$ steps. Let us now consider a particular Turing machine M. Among all strings of the form $w = c^j\rho(M)$, M_L accepts exactly those that M would reject in $f(|w|)$ steps, and for which the simulation can terminate in $F(|w|)$ steps—that is, those $w = c^j\rho(M)$ for which

$$g_1(c^j\rho(M)) + g_2(c^j\rho(M)) + g_3(c^j\rho(M)) \leq F(|c^j\rho(M)|). \tag{1}$$

The time has come to define S_M. *We define S_M to be exactly the set of integers j for which Inequality* (1) *holds.* It follows immediately that M_L decides L.

It remains only to show that $S_M \neq \varnothing$, for all M.

For each $n \in \mathbb{N}$, let $\gamma(n) = \hat{g}_1(n) + \hat{g}_2(n) + \hat{g}_3(n)$. Then $\gamma = O(f^2)$, and so there is an $n_0 \in \mathbb{N}$ and a $c > 0$ such that $\gamma(n) \leq cf^2(n)$ for all $n \geq n_0$. On the other hand, we know that for all $n'_0 \in \mathbb{N}$ and $c' > 0$, there is an $n > n'_0$ such that $c'f^2(n) < F(n)$. Letting $c' = c$ and $n'_0 = \max(n_0, |\rho(M)|)$, we can conclude that there is an $n \geq |\rho(M)|$ such that $\gamma(n) \leq F(n)$; or, setting $j = n - |\rho(M)| \geq 0$,

$$\gamma(j + |\rho(M)|) \leq F(j + |\rho(M)|).$$

Hence there is a j satisfying (1) and S_M is nonempty. ■

Using Theorem 7.7.1, we can show the following.

Corollary 7.7.1. $\mathcal{P} \subsetneq \text{TIME}(2^n)$.

Proof. Consider the class $\text{TIME}(\lfloor 2^{n/3} \rfloor)$. Since $n^d = O(\lfloor 2^{n/3} \rfloor)$ for all d—by Theorem 7.2.1—we have that $\mathcal{P} \subseteq \text{TIME}(\lfloor 2^{n/3} \rfloor)$. However, letting $f(n) = \lfloor 2^{n/3} \rfloor$ and $F(n) = 2^n$, the previous theorem yields $\text{TIME}(\lfloor 2^{n/3} \rfloor) \subsetneq \text{TIME}(2^n)$. ■

By very different means, a theorem analogous to Theorem 7.7.1 can be proved for *non*deterministic time complexity classes. Thus some knowledge has been gained about the relations between different deterministic time complexity classes on the one hand, and also about the relations between different nondeterministic time complexity classes. But except for disappointingly weak results such as Theorem 7.4.1, the relation between deterministic and nondeterministic time remains largely mysterious.

PROBLEMS

7.1.1. (a) Show that if a language $L \subseteq \Sigma^*$ is regular, then $L \in \text{TIME}(2n + 4)$.
(*Note:* This generalizes Example 7.1.1.)

(b) Show that if $L \in \text{TIME}(2n + 4)$ then L is regular.

7.1.2. Show that the Turing machine M of Example 7.1.2 accepts L in time $n^2 + 6n + 6$, by deriving a more careful estimate for the total number of steps.
(*Hint:* One way of doing this is the following: Consider the jth position to the left of the right end of the input. This position can be "held responsible" for the $2j + 1$ moves required so that the symbol in the position is replaced by a d (if indeed it is eventually replaced); we also need at most $4n + 4$ more moves for the last stage, the erasing, and acceptance or rejection. A summation establishes the bound.)

7.1.3. In Example 7.1.3 we showed that the language L of Example 7.1.2 is accepted in time $5n + 4$ if we use a 4-tape Turing machine. The purpose of this problem is to show how to construct a 1-tape Turing machine M which accepts L in time $c \cdot n \cdot \lceil \log_2 (n + 1) \rceil$ for some integer $c > 0$. This function is not as small as $5n + 4$, but for large n (say, $n \geq c^2$) it becomes smaller than the bound $n^2 + 4n + 4$ of the previous problem. Machine M scans the input from left to right, keeping counts of the numbers of a's, b's, and c's it has seen so far in binary on a second track. After it has thus seen all of its input, M compares the three counts bit by bit, and if they are equal, it accepts. In order to have the counts easily accessible at all times, M shifts the counts one position to the left while incrementing one of them, before it examines the next symbol of the input. Give a reasonably detailed description of M, and carefully analyze its operation to obtain an estimate for c.

7.1.4. How is the construction of M_3 (Proof of Theorem 7.1.1) affected in case M has $k > 1$ tapes?

7.1.5. Give a detailed description of the Turing machine $M_1 = (K_1, \Sigma_1, \delta_1, s_1)$ (see the Proof of Theorem 7.1.1) which condenses its input m-fold in $2n + 1$ steps—that is, for all $w \in \Sigma^*$, $(s_1, \#s\#, \#) \vdash_{M_1}^{2|w|+1} (h, \#, \#\kappa(w)^R\#)$.

7.1.6. Apply Theorem 7.1.1 to show the following.

(a) Suppose that $L \in \text{TIME}(cn^2)$ for some $c > 0$. Then $L \in \text{TIME}(T)$, where $T(n) = \max(n^2, 2n + 20)$.

(b) Suppose that $L \in \text{TIME}(cn)$ for some $c > 2$. Then $L \in \text{TIME}(T)$, where $T = \lceil 2.1n \rceil + 20$.

7.1.7. (a) Suppose that $L_1 \in \text{TIME}(T_1)$ and $L_2 \in \text{TIME}(T_2)$. Show that $L_1 \cup L_2 \in \text{TIME}(T_1 + T_2 + n + 2)$.

(b) Show that if $T_2(n) = 2n + 4$, then the result in (a) can be improved to $L_1 \cup L_2 \in \text{TIME}(T_1 + 2n + 2)$.

7.2.1. Let $f(n) = \sum_{j=0}^{d} a_j n^j$ be a polynomial, with $a_d > 0$ (notice that possibly $a_j \leq 0$ for $0 \leq j < d$). Show that

$$n^d \leq 2 \cdot f(n) \quad \text{for} \quad n \geq 2 \cdot \sum_{j=0}^{d-1} |a_j|.$$

7.2.2. Show that $10^6 n^2 = O(2^n)$. What are appropriate constants c and n_0 in the definition of O for this case?

7.2.3. Show that $\lceil \log_2(n+1) \rceil^k = O(n^\epsilon)$ for all $\epsilon, k > 0$.

7.2.4. (a) Show that $2^{n+1} \asymp 2^n$.

(b) Is it true that $2^{2^{n+1}} \asymp 2^{2^n}$?

7.2.5. Consider the following two functions.

$$f(n) = \begin{cases} n^3 & \text{if } n \text{ is odd;} \\ n^2 & \text{if } n \text{ is even.} \end{cases}$$

$$g(n) = \begin{cases} n^3 & \text{if } n \text{ is prime;} \\ n^2 & \text{if } n \text{ is composite.} \end{cases}$$

Which of the following statements are true?

(a) $f = O(n^2)$

(b) $f = O(n^3)$

(c) $g = O(n^2)$

(d) $g = O(n^3)$

(e) $f = O(g)$

(f) $g = O(f)$

(g) $n^2 = O(f)$

(h) $n^3 = O(f)$

(i) $n^2 = O(g)$

(j) $n^3 = O(g)$

7.3.1. Show that if $L \subseteq \Sigma^*$ is decided in time T by some two-dimensional Turing machine, then L is decided in time $T' = O(T^3)$ by a 4-tape Turing machine.

In our discussions in Chapters 4 and 5 we argued extensively that Turing machines can carry out any task that can be performed by an algorithm. In particular, the reader should be convinced by now that the computational tasks performed by computers can be performed in principle by Turing machines. The operation of all variants of Turing machines, however, suffers from a certain inefficiency and "clumsiness" not found in real computers. A Turing machine is basically a *sequential access* device. Its storage medium, the tape, has a certain fixed geometry (for example, a straight line, k parallel straight lines, a two-dimensional plane, and so on). Each tape square can be reached only from one of the few squares adjacent to it; so, if the machine is currently examining a certain square and wishes to reach a square that is ten squares away, it has to do so through a sequence of ten moves.

In contrast, modern-day computers are equipped with **core memory**; this is a sequence of *memory locations*, each capable of holding a value. The memory of the giant computers of today is so large that its finiteness seems almost besides the point. The fundamental difference between such a memory and the tape of a Turing machine is that each location of the core memory can be addressed at any instant *in one step*, independent of the location or locations that were addressed immediately before. This mode of access is called **random access**.

Again, this difference was not too important when, in Chapters 4 and 5, we were interested in the theoretical capabilities of Turing machines. In the present chapter, however, we are quantitatively evaluating the performance of Turing machines. The question thus remains whether the sequential access Turing machine is an appropriate model for such a quantitative study of random access computers. The purpose of the next four problems is to indicate that the computational capabilities of Turing machines are enhanced only by a polynomial amount if a random access capability is added to the original model.

A **Turing machine with random access** $R = (K, \Sigma, \delta, s, r, 0, 1, \$)$ is an ordinary Turing machine with the following added capability. There is a *special state* $r \in K$ and three special symbols 0, 1 and $\$ \in \Sigma$. The yields relation of R is defined in the ordinary way for configurations $(q, u\underline{a}v)$ with $q \neq r$. However, if R is in the configuration $(r, u\underline{a}v)$ and $v = v_1\$v_2$ for some $v_1 \in 1\{0, 1\}^*$, then

(a) The head of R goes to the n-th square of the tape, where $n \in \mathbb{N}$ is the integer of which the string v_1 is the binary representation; this is done *in one step*.
(b) The state of R becomes the first component of $\delta(r, a)$.

If the string to the right of the head is not in $1\{0, 1\}^*\$\Sigma^*$ and the state of R is r, then R performs its ordinary transition according to δ.

For example, if $\delta(r, b) = (q, L)$, the following hold.

$$(r, \#011\#0a\underline{b}11010\$\#a)$$
$$\vdash_R (q, \#011\#0ab11010\$\#a\#\#\#\#\#\#\#\#\#\underline{\#})$$
$$(r, \#00\underline{b}a1\$\#1) \vdash_R (q, \#0\underline{0}ba1\$\#1)$$

Notice that, in the first example, the second component of $\delta(r, b)$ is ignored.

7.3.2. Give a formal definition of a Turing machine with random access, and of its "yields" relation. What does it mean for such a machine to decide a language $L \in \Sigma_0^*$ in time T?

7.3.3. Repeat the previous problem for a k-tape Turing machine with random access. Such a machine has k special states $r_1, \ldots, r_k$, one for each tape.

7.3.4. Consider the language

$$L = \{w_1\$w_2\$ \ldots \$w_k\$: k > 0, w_1, \ldots, w_k \in \{0, 1\}^*, \text{ and } 1 \leq i < j \leq k \text{ implies } w_i \neq w_j\}.$$

(a) Design a 2-tape Turing machine with random access that decides L in time $T = O(n)$.

(b) Can you find a standard Turing machine (with $k \geq 1$ tapes) that decides L in time $O(n)$?

7.3.5. Suppose that a language L is decided by a k-tape Turing machine with random access in time T. Show that $L \in \text{TIME}(T^2)$.

7.4.1. Suppose that we extend our encoding ρ of Turing machines to include finite automata.

(a) Show that $\{\rho(M): M$ is a finite automaton and $L(M) = \varnothing\}$ $\in \mathcal{P}$.

(b) Show that $\{\rho(M): M$ is a finite automaton and $L(M)$ is infinite$\}$ $\in \mathcal{P}$.

7.4.2. Use Problem 3.5.19 to show that if L is a context-free language then $L \in \mathcal{P}$.

7.4.3. Show that the language $L = \{\rho(M)\rho(w)$: the deterministic Turing machine M halts on input w after at most $|w|^2$ steps$\} \in \mathcal{P}$.

7.4.4. Let $L_1, L_2 \in \mathcal{P}$. Show each of the following.

(a) $L_1 \cup L_2 \in \mathcal{P}$

(b) $L_1 L_2 \in \mathcal{P}$

(c) $L_1^* \in \mathcal{P}$

(d) $\bar{L}_1 \in \mathcal{P}$

7.4.5. (a) Let $f: \Sigma^* \longrightarrow \{I\}^*$ be a function mapping strings in Σ^* to strings of the form $I^j, j \geq 0$, such that there is a polynomial p such that $|f(w)| \leq p(|w|)$ for all $w \in \Sigma^*$. Show that if $\{w@I^j: f(w) \leq j\} \in \mathcal{P}$, then f is polynomial-time computable (see Definition 7.5.1).

(b) Repeat Part (a), but with the assumption $|f(w)| \leq p(|w|)$ relaxed to $|f(w)| \leq 2^{p(|w|)}$.

(c) Use Part (a) above to prove that the function $f: \{I, c, @\}^* \to I^*$ defined as follows is polynomial-time computable if and only if $TSP \in \mathcal{P}$.

$$f(w) = \begin{cases} e & \text{if } w \text{ is not of the form } I^n@\alpha(D)\text{, where } D \text{ is an } n \times n \text{ distance matrix} \\ I^{s+1} & \text{where } s \text{ is the length of the shortest tour through the } n \text{ cities, otherwise} \end{cases}$$

7.4.6. (a) Show that the language $L = \{\rho(M)@I^t: M = (K, \Sigma, \delta, s)$ is a deterministic Turing machine, and for some $w, \alpha, \beta \in \Sigma^*$, $a \in \Sigma$, $(s, \#w\underline{\#}) \vdash_M^t (h, \alpha\underline{a}\beta)\}$ is in $\mathcal{NP}$. Do you think that L is in $\mathcal{P}$?

(b) Repeat Part (a) for nondeterministic Turing machines M.

7.4.7. (a) Show that if a function $f: \mathbb{N} \to \mathbb{N}$ is step-counting, then the functions g and h are also step-counting, where $g(n) = f(2n + 1)$ and $h(n) = f(n + k)$ for some $k \in \mathbb{N}$.

(b) Show that if f is a step-counting function, there is a k-tape Turing machine $M = (K, \Sigma, \delta, s)$ such that for all $w \in \Sigma^*$, $(s, \#w\underline{\#}, \underline{\#}, \ldots, \underline{\#}) \vdash_M^{f(|w|)} (h, u_1\underline{a_1}v_1, \ldots, u_{k-1}\underline{a_{k-1}}v_{k-1}, I^{\lfloor f(|w|)/2 \rfloor}\underline{\#})$ for some $u_1, \ldots, u_{k-1}, v_1, \ldots, v_{k-1} \in \Sigma^*, a_1, \ldots, a_{k-1} \in \Sigma$.

(c) Show that if f_1 and f_2 are step-counting functions, then so are $f_1 + f_2$, $f_1 \cdot f_2$, and $f_1 \circ f_2$.

(d) Show that if p is a polynomial with nonnegative coefficients, then p is a step-counting function.

(e) Show that $n\lfloor \log_2(n + 1) \rfloor$ is a step-counting function.

7.5.1. Define co-$\mathcal{NP}$ to be the following class of languages:

$$\text{co-}\mathcal{NP} = \{\bar{L}: L \in \mathcal{NP}\}.$$

Show that if L is an $\mathcal{NP}$-complete language and $L \in$ co-$\mathcal{NP}$, then $\mathcal{NP} =$ co-$\mathcal{NP}$.

7.5.2. Let $f: \mathbb{N} \to \mathbb{N}$. We say that f is **subexponential** if, for all $\epsilon > 0$, $f = O(2^{n^\epsilon})$, but $f \not\asymp 2^{n^\epsilon}$. Let

$$\mathcal{SUBEXP} = \bigcup \{\text{TIME}(f): f \text{ is subexponential}\}.$$

Show that $L \in \mathcal{SUBEXP}$ for some $\mathcal{NP}$-complete language L, then $\mathcal{NP} \subseteq \mathcal{SUBEXP}$.

7.6.1. (a) We call two systems of binary equations **equivalent** if one has a binary solution if and only if the other does. Let $\sum_{j=1}^{k} x_j = 1$ be one of a set of binary equations $Ax = b$. Show that if we replace this equation by the three equations

$$\sum_{j=1}^{\lfloor k/2 \rfloor} x_j + a = 1$$

$$\sum_{j=\lfloor k/2 \rfloor+1}^{k} x_j + b = 1$$

$$a + b = 1,$$

where a and b are new variables not used in any other equation, then we obtain a system of binary equations that is equivalent to the former one.

(b) Show that the language $B'_R = \{\alpha(A)@\alpha(b)$: all entries of A are 0 and 1, at most three entries in each row of A are 1, all entries of b are 1, and $Ax = b$ has a binary solution$\}$ is $\mathcal{NP}$-complete.

(c) Repeat Part (b), only with *at most* replaced by *exactly* in the definition of B'_R.

(d) Show that $B''_R = \{\alpha(A)@\alpha(b)$: all entries of A are 0 or 1, at most two entries in each row of A are 1, all entries of b are 1, and $Ax = b$ has a binary solution$\}$ is in $\mathcal{P}$.
(*Hint:* Systems of equations modulo 2 *can* be solved by Cramer's rule.)

7.6.2. Show that the language $L = \{\rho(M)@I^t$: $M = (K, \Sigma, \delta, s)$ is a deterministic Turing machine and there is a $w \in \Sigma^*$ such that for every $q \in K$, there is a $t' \leq t$ for which $(s, \#w\#) \vdash_M^{t'} (q, u\underline{\sigma}v)$ for some $u, v \in \Sigma^*$, $\sigma \in \Sigma\}$ is $\mathcal{NP}$-complete.

7.6.3. Complete the proof of Lemma 7.6.3.

7.6.4. Construct the finite automaton M according to the proof of Theorem 7.6.3, starting from the finite automaton M_0 shown in Figure 7–13. You may use the abbreviation of Figure 7–14.

7.6.5. (a) An $n \times n$ distance matrix D is **symmetric** if $d_{ij} = d_{ji}$ for all i, j, $1 \leq i, j \leq n$. Show that *TSP* is $\mathcal{NP}$-complete even if the distance matrices are restricted to be symmetric.

(b) An $n \times n$ distance matrix D is said to **satisfy the triangle inequality** if for all $1 \leq i, j, k \leq n$ we have $d_{ij} + d_{jk} \geq d_{ik}$. Show that the *TSP* remains $\mathcal{NP}$-complete even if the distance matrices are restricted to be symmetric *and* to satisfy the triangle inequality.

7.6.6. Complete the proof of Lemma 7.6.1.

7.6.7. The **exact cover problem** is the following: Given a family $F = \{S_1, \ldots, S_n\}$ of finite sets, is there a subfamily $C \subseteq F$ of *disjoint* sets such that $\bigcup \{S_j: S_j \in C\} = \bigcup \{S_j: S_j \in F\}$?

(a) Formulate the exact cover problem as a language recognition problem.

(b) Show that the exact cover problem is $\mathcal{NP}$-complete.

(*Hint:* View each column of A in B_R (Corollary 7.6.1) as a set of rows.)

7.6.8. The **knapsack problem** is the following: Given $n + 1$ natural numbers $w_1, \ldots, w_n$ (the *weights*) and c (the *capacity*), are there integers $j_1, \ldots, j_k$, $1 \leq j_1 < j_2 < \cdots < j_k \leq n$, such that $\sum_{i=1}^{k} w_{j_i} = c$?

(a) Formulate the knapsack problem as a language recognition problem, with the integers expressed in *unary*. Show that the problem is in $\mathcal{P}$.

(b) Formulate the knapsack problem as a language recognition problem, with the integers expressed in *binary*. Show that the problem is $\mathcal{NP}$-complete.

(*Hint:* View each column of A in B_R (Corollary 7.6.1) as an integer in m-ary notation, for large enough m.)

7.6.9. (a) Show that the language T of Theorem 7.6.1 is in $\mathcal{NP}$.

(b) Show that the transformation τ of Theorem 7.6.1 is polynomial-time computable.

7.6.10. (a) Show that the language H of Theorem 7.6.3 is in $\mathcal{NP}$.

(b) Show that the transformation τ of Theorem 7.6.3 is polynomial-time computable.

7.7.1. Let $g: 1\{0, 1\}^* \to \mathbb{N}$ be the function that maps binary numerals to the integers that they represent. What is $\hat{g}$?

7.7.2. In the proof of Theorem 7.7.1, show that $\rho(M')$ can be constructed from $\rho(M)$ in time $O(|\rho(M)|^2)$.

7.7.3. Let M be a Turing machine and let $t \in \mathbb{N}$. We define the relation $\vdash_{M|t}$ as follows: $(q, u\underline{a}v) \vdash_{M|t} (q', u'\underline{a}'v')$ if and only if $(q, u\underline{a}v) \vdash_M (q', u'\underline{a}'v')$ and $|uav|, |u'a'v'| \leq t$. Let $\vdash^*_{M|t}$ (yields using at most t tape squares) be the reflexive, transitive closure of $\vdash_{M|t}$. If s is the initial state of M, we say that M **uses at most t tape squares on input** w if, whenever $(s, \#w\underline{\#}) \vdash^*_M C$ for some configuration C, then $(s, \#w\underline{\#}) \vdash^*_{M|t} C$.

Now let S be any function from $\mathbb{N}$ to $\mathbb{N}$, let $L \subseteq \Sigma_0^*$ be a language, and let M be a Turing machine. We say that M **decides L in space S** provided that M decides L and uses at most $S(n)$ tape squares on any input of length n in Σ_0^*. We then say that L is **decidable in space S**; we write $L \in \text{SPACE}(S)$.

(a) Show that if $L \in \text{SPACE}(S)$ and $\epsilon > 0$, then $L \in \text{SPACE}(n + 2 + \epsilon S)$ (compare with Theorem 7.1.1).

(b) Define what it means for a language to be decidable in space S by a k-tape Turing machine; then show that if L is such a language, then $L \in \text{SPACE}(S)$ (compare with Corollary 7.3.1).

7.7.4. Let f be any function from $\mathbb{N}$ to $\mathbb{N}$.

(a) Show that $\text{TIME}(f) \subseteq \text{SPACE}(f)$.

(b) Show that if $M = (K, \Sigma, \delta, s)$ is a Turing machine and t is a natural number such that $(q, u\underline{a}v) \vdash_{M|t}^* (h, u'\underline{a}'v')$, where $q \in K$, $u, u', v, v' \in \Sigma^*$, and $a, a' \in \Sigma$, then $(q, u\underline{a}v) \vdash_M^{t'} (h, u'\underline{a}'v')$ for some $t' \leq |K||\Sigma|^t \cdot t$.

7.7.5. (a) Define what it means for a nondeterministic Turing machine M to accept a language L in space S (*notation:* $L \in \text{NSPACE}(S)$). (The definition should combine Definition 7.4.2 and the result of Problem 7.7.3.)

(b) Show that $\text{NSPACE}(S) \subseteq \bigcup\{\text{NTIME}(c^S)\colon c \geq 1\}$.

7.7.6. (a) Let $L \subseteq \Sigma^*\$\Sigma^*$, with $\$ \notin \Sigma$, be a language such that, for some step-counting function $f\colon \mathbb{N} \to \mathbb{N}$, $|y| \leq f(|x|)$ whenever $x\$y \in L$. Suppose that $L \in \text{SPACE}(S)$; show that $L/\$\Sigma^* \in \text{SPACE}(S + f)$.

(b) Define $\mathcal{PSPACE}$ (the class of languages decidable in polynomial space) to be $\bigcup\{\text{SPACE}(n^d)\colon d \geq 1\}$. Using Part (a), show that $\mathcal{NP} \subseteq \mathcal{PSPACE}$.

7.7.7. In this problem we describe a space-efficient implementation, by Turing machines, of an important programming concept: recursion.

Let $L \subseteq \Sigma^*\$I^*$ be a language, where $\$ \notin \Sigma$; for each $i \geq 0$ we denote by L_i the language $L \cap \Sigma^*\$I^i$. Suppose that L has the following properties.

(a) For some function $S_0\colon \mathbb{N} \to \mathbb{N}$, $L_0 \in \text{SPACE}(S_0)$.

(b) There exists a *nondeterministic* Turing machine $M = (K, \Sigma_1, \Delta, s)$, a step-counting function $S_1\colon \mathbb{N} \to \mathbb{N}$, and a number $k \geq 0$ such that, for all $w \in \Sigma^*$ and all halted computations $(s, \#w\#) \vdash_M^* (h, u\underline{a}v)$,

(1) $(s, \#w\underline{\#}) \vdash^{+}_{M|S_1(|w|)} (h, u\underline{a}v)$;

(2) $v = e$, $a = \#$, and $u = w_1\# \ldots \#w_k$ for some $w_1, \ldots, w_k \in \Sigma^*$;

(3) for any $i \geq 0$, $w\$I^{i+1} \in L_{i+1}$ if and only if $w_1\$I^i, \ldots, w_k\$I^i \in L_i$.

Construct a (deterministic) Turing machine M' that decides L, such that for each $i \geq 0$ and $n \geq 0$, M' uses at most $T(n) = S_0(S_1^{(i)}(n)) + \sum_{j=1}^{i} S_1^{(j)}(n)$ tape squares on any input of length n in $\Sigma^*\$I^i$. Here

$$S_1^{(m)}(n) = \underbrace{S_1(S_1(\ldots(S_1}_{m \text{ times}}(n))\ldots)).$$

What is $T(n)$ in case $S_0(n) = S_1(n) = n$? (Intuitively, M' decides a string $w\$I^{i+1}$ by "calling on itself" to decide each of k strings in L_i; to decide the strings in L_i, it "calls on itself" to decide strings in L_{i-1}; and so on. In addition, however, the construction of M' must eliminate the nondeterminism of M.)

7.7.8. Here we establish a relationship between deterministic and nondeterministic space complexity classes, analogous to Theorem 7.4.1 for time complexity classes, but stronger.

Let $S_1 : \mathbb{N} \to \mathbb{N}$ be a step-counting function and suppose that a nondeterministic Turing machine $M_1 = (K_1, \Sigma_1, \Delta_1, s_1)$ accepts the language $L \subseteq \Sigma^*$ in space S_1. If $n \geq 0$ and $C = (q, u\underline{a}v)$ is a configuration of M_1 with $|uav| \leq S_1(n)$, then by $\rho_n(C)$ we denote the string $\rho(C)@^{S_1(n)-|uav|}$, where ρ is some natural encoding of configurations over $\{I, c\}$ as used elsewhere. Then let

$$L' = \{\rho_n(C_1)@\rho_n(C_2)\$I^t : C_1 \text{ and } C_2 \text{ are configurations of } M_1, n \geq 0, C_1 \vdash^{t'}_{M_1|S(n)} C_2, t \geq 0, \text{ and } t' \leq 2^t\}.$$

As in Problem 7.7.7, let $L'_i = L' \cap \{I, c, @\}^*\$I^i$ for each $i \geq 0$.

(a) Suppose that there are functions $f_0, f_1, \ldots : \mathbb{N} \to \mathbb{N}$ and there is a Turing machine M' that decides L' and, for each $i \geq 0$, uses at most $f_i(n)$ tape squares on any input of length n in $\{I, c, @\}^*\$I^i$. Use the results of Problems 7.7.4(b) and 7.7.6(a) to show that, for some constant $k \geq 1$,

$$L \in \text{SPACE}(f_{kS_1(n)}(S_1(n))).$$

(b) Use the implementation of recursion in Problem 7.7.7 to obtain a Turing machine M'' that decides L' and uses, for all $i \geq 0$, at most $(i + 1)\cdot n$ tape squares for any input of length n in $\{I, c, @\}^*\$I^i$.

(c) Conclude that $\text{NSPACE}(S_1) \subseteq \text{SPACE}(S_1^2)$.

(d) Define $\mathcal{NPSPACE} = \bigcup\{\text{NSPACE}(n^d) : d \geq 1\}$. Show that $\mathcal{NPSPACE} = \mathcal{PSPACE}$.

REFERENCES

The following pioneering papers mark the beginning of the theory of computational complexity:

M. O. RABIN, "The Degree of Difficulty of Computing a Function and a Partial Order of Recursive Sets," Hebrew University, Branch of Applied Logic, Report 2, 1960.

M. O. RABIN, "Real-time Computation," *Israel Journal of Mathematics*, 1 (1963), 203–211.

J. HARTMANIS and R. E. STEARNS, "On the Computational Complexity of Algorithms," *Transactions of the American Mathematical Society*, 117 (1965), 285–305.

Theorem 7.1.1 is shown in the latter paper.
The growth of functions (Section 7.2) is of concern to several branches of mathematics; see for example,

G. H. HARDY and E. M. WRIGHT, *An Introduction to the Theory of Numbers*. London: Oxford University Press, 1938.

Our notation is taken partly from this book and partly from

D. E. KNUTH, "Big Omicron and Big Omega and Big Theta," *SIGACT News*, 8, no. 2 (1976), 18–23.

Hennie and Stearns in their article

F. C. HENNIE and R. E. STEARNS, "Two-tape Simulation of Multitape Turing Machines," *Journal of the Association for Computing Machinery*, 13, no. 4 (1966), 533–546

prove a different version of Theorem 7.3.2, stating that if L is decided by a k-tape Turing machine in time T_1, then it is decided by some 2-tape Turing machine in time T_2, where $T_2 = O(T_1 \log T_1)$. Using this result, one can show an improved version of our hierarchy result (see Section 7.7).

Further development of the theory of machines with random-access memory, introduced in Problems 7.3.2 through 7.3.5, appears in

S. A. COOK and R. A. RECKHOW, "Time-Bounded Random-Access Machines," *Journal of Computer and Systems Sciences*, 7, no. 4 (1973), 354–375.

The class $\mathcal{P}$ was first introduced in

A. Cobham, "The Intrinsic Computational Difficulty of Functions," *Proceedings of the 1964 Congress for Logic, Mathematics and the Philosophy of Science* (pp. 24–30). New York: North Holland, 1964

and in

J. Edmonds, "Paths, Trees and Flowers," *Canadian Journal of Mathematics*, 17, no. 3 (1965), 449–467

where also the class $\mathcal{NP}$ was introduced, and it was first conjectured that $\mathcal{P} \neq \mathcal{NP}$. Cook was the first to treat formally the $\mathcal{P} = \mathcal{NP}$ question and to exhibit an $\mathcal{NP}$-complete language in his paper

S. A. Cook, "The Complexity of Theorem-Proving Procedures," *Proceedings of the Third Annual ACM Symposium on the Theory of Computing* (pp. 151–158). New York: Association for Computing Machinery, 1971.

We present Cook's result in Chapter 9 (Theorem 9.6.3).
Karp showed the importance of the concept of $\mathcal{NP}$-completeness in his paper

R. M. Karp, "Reducibility among Combinatorial Problems," in *Complexity of Computer Computations* (pp. 85–104), ed. R. E. Miller and J. W. Thatcher. New York: Plenum Press, 1972

where, among a host of other results, Theorems 7.6.2 and 7.6.3 are proved.
Similar investigations were independently conducted by Levin in

L. A. Levin, "Universal Sorting Problems," *Problemi Peredachi Informatsii*, 9, no. 3 (1973), 265–266 (in Russian).

The importance of the notion of $\mathcal{NP}$-completeness to several areas of pure and applied mathematics and computer science is best demonstrated by the richess and diversity of the results contained in the encyclopedia of the subject, namely

M. R. Garey and D. S. Johnson, *Computers and Intractability: A Guide to the Theory of $\mathcal{NP}$-completeness.* New York: Freeman, 1979.

The $\mathcal{NP}$-complete problems that we mentioned here (Theorems 7.6.1 through 7.6.4, Problems 7.6.1, 7.6.5, 7.6.7, and 7.6.8) can be found in the above sources. It turns out that the Traveling Salesman Problem remains $\mathcal{NP}$-complete even if the cities are restricted to be actual points on the plane and the distance matrix contains their straight line (Euclidean) distances. See

C. H. Papadimitriou, "The Euclidean Traveling Salesman Problem is $\mathcal{NP}$-complete," *Theoretical Computer Science*, 4, no. 3 (1977), 237–244.

Problems 7.7.3 through 7.7.8 on space complexity are based on

W. J. Savitch, "Relationships between Nondeterministic and Deterministic Tape Complexities," *Journal of Computer and Systems Sciences*, 4, no. 2 (1970), 177–192.

A theory has been developed for studying complexity in a more general way, independent of whether the resource considered to be in scarcity and measured is time, space, or any other "reasonable" measure; see

M. Blum, "A Machine-Independent Theory of the Complexity of Recursive Functions," *Journal of the Association for Computing Machinery*, 14, no. 2 (1967), 322–326

and

J. Hartmanis and J. E. Hopcroft, "An Overview of the Theory of Computational Complexity," *Journal of the Association for Computing Machinery*, 18, no. 3 (1971), 444–475.

Books that treat more of complexity theory and its applications are

M. Machtey and P. R. Young, *An Introduction to the General Theory of Algorithms.* New York: Elsevier North-Holland, 1977.

J. E. Hopcroft and J. D. Ullman, *Introduction to Automata Theory, Languages and Computation.* Reading, Mass.: Addison-Wesley, 1979.

C. H. Papadimitriou and K. Steiglitz, *Combinatorial Optimization: Algorithms and Complexity.* Englewood Cliffs, N.J.: Prentice-Hall, in press.

CHAPTER 8

THE PROPOSITIONAL CALCULUS

8.1 INTRODUCTION

We have relied heavily on the notion of a *language* for pressing our development of the theory of computation. We started, in Chapter 1, with the *regular* languages, which are hardly capable of describing the simplest sort of repetitive patterns in strings. The *context-free* languages of Chapter 3 are rich enough to specify more complex patterns, and also have some descriptive power of use in practical situations, such as the syntactic specification of programming languages. With the Turing-decidable and Turing-acceptable languages, we are able not only to specify extremely complex patterns of symbols, but to encode questions and answers of many types, including problems about Turing machines themselves.

But we have not confronted directly the most naïve and natural way in which a language can be used: for making *statements* that might reasonably be viewed as true or false. This chapter and the next are devoted to that aspect of the theory of languages especially as it relates to the theory of automata and of algorithms in general. We shall describe two particular languages, called the *propositional calculus* and the *predicate calculus*, specifically designed for representing the discourse of mathematics in an abstract manner. That is, strings in these languages—what we call *formulas*—will be viewed as making mathematical statements, not necessarily about any of the familiar mathematical objects such as numbers and strings, but on an abstract level about truth and falsity, sets of objects of any sort, and the relations between them. Because a formula in one of these languages may admit several interpretations—it may be true under some, while it may be false under others—the formulas are classified as *satisfiable* or *unsatisfiable*. A satisfiable formula is true under some interpretation; an unsatisfiable formula is true under no interpretation, and must therefore be viewed as invariably false.

Much of the development in these chapters is therefore devoted not to the syntax of the propositional and predicate calculi—syntactically, they are fairly simple context-free languages—but to the way we can *interpret* formulas in these languages as true and false statements. A leading question throughout will be: How can we tell which formulas are satisfiable, that is, correspond to potentially true statements, and which do not? We shall see that the propositional calculus is a weak language, and that algorithms for determining satisfiability are not hard to design. The corresponding problem for the stronger predicate calculus is, however, unsolvable, although the set of unsatisfiable formulas is Turing-acceptable.

Although these results are presented here near the end of our work, historically they are at the very root of the subject matter of this book. The predicate calculus antedated any of the automata we have studied; the Turing machine was invented, as a formalization of the notion of algorithm, specifically to settle the question of whether satisfiability in the predicate calculus was a solvable problem or not. The finite and pushdown automata were later developments, simplifications of the Turing machine. So our presentation has been in almost perfect reverse historical order.

In one respect, however, the material in these chapters is modern. The study of the algorithmic properties of the propositional and predicate calculi has developed into a subject of major importance within computer science. Accordingly, we devote some attention to the *resolution method* for establishing that formulas are unsatisfiable. While in a sense the resolution method does not represent a theoretical advance over what was known before its invention about the propositional and predicate calculi, from the point of view of computer implementation it is a much more adaptable technique than those arising directly from the classical theory.

8.2 SYNTAX OF THE PROPOSITIONAL CALCULUS

The first language we consider is that of the propositional calculus. The strings in this language, called *formulas*, stand for propositions that are either true or false. Formulas are constructed by combining *atomic formulas* with the aid of *logical connectives*. For example, consider the following sentence, used as an example in Section 1.1:

The word *blueberry* has two consecutive *r*'s or
the word *peach* is six letters long.

As rendered in the propositional calculus, the two component sentences,

the word *blueberry* has two consecutive *r*'s

and

the word *peach* is six letters long

would be reduced to atomic formulas, say A and B, and the whole sentence would be abstracted as the formula $(A \vee B)$; here $\vee$ is a logical connective that stands for *or*. The atomic formulas capture none of the "inner meaning" of the sentences they were chosen to represent; all that is left of those sentences is the fact that they are different and individually may be true or false.

One problem that must be confronted immediately is that we do not wish to confine ourselves in advance to any *finite* set of atomic formulas, since there are infinitely many propositions which we may, at some point, wish to discuss; and yet we do want the propositional calculus to be a language in the sense previously used in this book, that is, a set of strings over a fixed finite alphabet. Accordingly, the atomic formulas will themselves be strings. We choose, somewhat arbitrarily, to use strings of the form **AII . . . I$** for atomic formulas, where **A, I,** and **$** are fixed symbols and there can be any number of **I**'s, including zero, between the **A** and the **$**. In what follows, however, atomic formulas are abbreviated by using letters such as A, B, C, A_1, and so on; these are actually names of strings such as **A$**, **AII$**, and **AIIIIIII$**. (We use the **$** at the end of each atomic formula so that no atomic formula will be a substring of any other.) So the formula $(A \vee B)$ might actually be **(AI$ $\vee$ AIII$)**, a string of length 11.

In addition to the logical connective $\vee$, there are two other logical connectives: $\wedge$, which stands for *and*, and $\neg$, which stands for *not*. So if

A stands for "the word *watermelon* has nine letters,"

B stands for "the word *blueberry* has two consecutive *r*'s," and

C stands for "the word *peach* has six letters,"

then the formula $(A \wedge (B \vee \neg C))$ stands for the sentence, "The word *watermelon* has nine letters; and either the word *blueberry* has two consecutive *r*'s, or the word *peach* does not have six letters."

Note that the language of the propositional calculus also includes the left and right parentheses, **(** and **)**. These are obviously necessary; the formula $((A \wedge B) \vee \neg C)$ says something quite different from $(A \wedge (B \vee \neg C))$; indeed, with the atomic formulas A, B, and C understood as we have just stipulated, the first formula represents a true statement, while the second represents a false statement.

To take one final example, consider the sentence, "Either Jim or John is here, but not both." In factual content alone, this sentence says the same thing as, "Jim is here or John is here; and John is not here or Jim is not here." So if we choose the atomic formula A to stand for "Jim is here" and B for "John is here," the sentence as a whole could be rendered as $((A \vee B) \wedge (\neg A \vee \neg B))$. Another English version of the same sentence is, "Jim is here or John is here; and it is not the case that Jim is here and John is here." That version would translate into the propositional calculus as $((A \vee B) \wedge \neg(A \wedge B))$.

In sum, we have the following definition.

Definition 8.2.1

The **formulas of the propositional calculus** are the strings generated by the following context-free grammar (V, Σ, R, S).

$$\Sigma = \{\mathbf{A}, \mathbf{I}, \$, \wedge, \vee, \neg, (,)\}$$

$$V = \Sigma \cup \{S, N\}$$

$$\begin{aligned} R = \{&N \longrightarrow e, \\ &N \longrightarrow N\mathbf{I}, \\ &S \longrightarrow \mathbf{A}N\$, \\ &S \longrightarrow (S \vee S), \\ &S \longrightarrow (S \wedge S), \\ &S \longrightarrow \neg S\} \end{aligned}$$

The **atomic formulas** are those of the form $\mathbf{AI}^n\$$ for some $n \geq 0$. If F and G are any formulas, then the formula $(F \vee G)$ is called the **disjunction** of F and G; $(F \wedge G)$ is called the **conjunction** of F and G; and $\neg F$ is called the **negation** of F. The symbols $\vee, \wedge, \neg$ are called the **disjunction, conjunction**, and **negation signs**, respectively. If one formula is a substring of another, we say that it is a **subformula** of the other—an **atomic subformula**, if it is atomic.

Example 8.2.1

Let A and B be the atomic formulas **AII$** and **AIII$**, respectively. Then $F = ((A \vee B) \wedge (\neg B \vee \neg A))$ is a formula, which would be written in full as

$$((\mathbf{AII\$} \vee \mathbf{AIII\$}) \wedge (\neg\mathbf{AIII\$} \vee \neg\mathbf{AII\$})).$$

The subformulas of F are F itself, $(A \vee B)$, $(\neg B \vee \neg A)$, $\neg B$, $\neg A$, A, and B; of these, the last two are its atomic subformulas. The formula F is the conjunction of $(A \vee B)$ and $(\neg B \vee \neg A)$; the latter of these two formulas is the disjunction of $\neg B$ and $\neg A$; and the latter of these two formulas is the negation of A.

Note that parentheses are not to be used at random; they surround conjunctions and disjunctions, but not negations. Thus $\neg(A)$ and $((A \vee B))$ are not formulas.

It is crucial that parentheses accomplish their intended mission of distinguishing formulas that would be identical if all the parentheses were dropped. We have a name for this concept; recall that a context-free grammar is called *ambiguous* if some string of terminals has more than one parse tree.

Lemma 8.2.1. *The grammar generating the formulas of the propositional calculus is unambiguous.*

Proof. See Problem 8.2.4. ■

And, *or*, and *not* are not the only connectives used in everyday discourse for joining sentences together. One connective of which we made much in Chapter 1 was *if . . . then . . . .* However, the omission of a symbol to represent this connective is not a serious deficiency, since the if-then idea can be conveyed by means of *or* and *not*. We are guided here by the analysis we carried out in Section 1.1: a statement of the form *if p, then q* is true if either *p* is false or *q* is true; but not otherwise. Similarly, *p if and only if q* means the same as *if p, then q; and if q, then p*. We henceforth agree to the following abbreviations.

Definition 8.2.2

If F and G are any formulas, then

$$(F \longrightarrow G) \quad \text{is} \quad (\neg F \vee G)$$

and

$$(F \longleftrightarrow G) \quad \text{is} \quad ((F \longrightarrow G) \wedge (G \longrightarrow F)).$$

The formula $(F \longrightarrow G)$ is called the **conditional** of F and G; $(F \longleftrightarrow G)$ is called their **biconditional**.

Note carefully that while $\vee$, $\wedge$, $\neg$ are symbols in the language of the propositional calculus, $\longrightarrow$ and $\longleftrightarrow$ are not; they are introduced here simply to help us more conveniently describe certain strings involving only the symbols given in Definition 8.2.1. For example, $((A \vee B) \longrightarrow (C \wedge D))$ is an abbreviation for $(\neg(A \vee B) \vee (C \wedge D))$ (which is in turn, perhaps, an abbreviated version of $(\neg(\mathbf{AI\$} \vee \mathbf{A\$}) \vee (\mathbf{AII\$} \wedge \mathbf{AIIII\$})))$. This might be a representation in the propositional calculus of the sentence, "If the president issues an order or the Congress passes a law, there will be gas rationing and prices will be decontrolled."

8.3 TRUTH-ASSIGNMENTS

Now that we have shown how formulas are constructed, we must formalize the idea, which has already been used on the intuitive level, that a sentence is either true or false in a way that depends on the truth or falsity of its atomic subformulas. First we fix two distinct symbols $\top$ and $\bot$ to stand for *true* and *false*, respectively. These two symbols will be called **truth-values.** A **truth-assignment** is a function from a set of atomic formulas to the set $\{\top, \bot\}$ of truth-values. We generally use the letter $\mathcal{A}$ for truth-assignments.

If $\mathcal{A}$ is a truth-assignment and F is a formula, we say that $\mathcal{A}$ is **appropriate to** F if each atomic formula of F is in the domain of $\mathcal{A}$. That is, $\mathcal{A}$ is appropriate to F if $\mathcal{A}$ assigns some truth-value to each atomic formula that appears in F. We next show how to extend a truth-assignment $\mathcal{A}$ to a function that assigns a truth-value to each formula to which $\mathcal{A}$ is appropriate. That is, we extend $\mathcal{A}: S \rightarrow \{\top, \bot\}$, where S is some set of atomic formulas, to a function $\bar{\mathcal{A}}$, which gives a unique truth-value to each formula whose atomic formulas all belong to S. The basic idea is simply to parallel the process, given by rules of the grammar in Definition 8.2.1, by which a formula is constructed from atomic formulas.

Definition 8.3.1

Let $\mathcal{A}$ be any function from a set S of atomic formulas to $\{\top, \bot\}$. Then we define $\bar{\mathcal{A}}$ as follows.

1. $\bar{\mathcal{A}}(A) = \mathcal{A}(A)$ for each atomic formula $A \in S$
2. $\bar{\mathcal{A}}((F \vee G)) = \begin{cases} \top & \text{if } \bar{\mathcal{A}}(F) = \top \text{ or } \bar{\mathcal{A}}(G) = \top \\ \bot & \text{otherwise} \end{cases}$
3. $\bar{\mathcal{A}}((F \wedge G)) = \begin{cases} \top & \text{if } \bar{\mathcal{A}}(F) = \top \text{ and } \bar{\mathcal{A}}(G) = \top \\ \bot & \text{otherwise} \end{cases}$
4. $\bar{\mathcal{A}}(\neg F) = \begin{cases} \top & \text{if } \bar{\mathcal{A}}(F) = \bot \\ \bot & \text{otherwise} \end{cases}$

Example 8.3.1

Let S consist of the three atomic formulas $\{A, B, C\}$, and let $\mathcal{A}$ be the truth-assignment on S such that

$$\mathcal{A}(A) = \top$$
$$\mathcal{A}(B) = \top$$
$$\mathcal{A}(C) = \bot.$$

Let F be the formula $\neg((\neg A \vee B) \wedge C)$. Then $\bar{\mathfrak{A}}(F)$ may be determined as follows.

(a)	$\bar{\mathfrak{A}}(A) = \top$	by (1)
(b)	$\bar{\mathfrak{A}}(\neg A) = \bot$	by (4) and (a)
(c)	$\bar{\mathfrak{A}}(B) = \top$	by (1)
(d)	$\bar{\mathfrak{A}}((\neg A \vee B)) = \top$	by (2), (b), and (c)
(e)	$\bar{\mathfrak{A}}(C) = \bot$	by (1)
(f)	$\bar{\mathfrak{A}}(((\neg A \vee B) \wedge C)) = \bot$	by (3), (d), and (e)
(g)	$\bar{\mathfrak{A}}(\neg((\neg A \vee B) \wedge C)) = \top$	by (4) and (f)

The process by which $\bar{\mathfrak{A}}(F)$ is calculated may be pictured more perspicuously if we look at a parse tree for F. The calculation proceeds by starting with the atomic formulas, which are located at leaves and have truth-values supplied by $\mathfrak{A}$. We then proceed up the tree in the bottom-up fashion, assigning a truth-value to each node whose label is S. The truth-value assigned to the root is $\bar{\mathfrak{A}}(F)$.

Example 8.3.2

This example continues Example 8.3.1. A parse tree for the formula F of Example 8.3.1 is illustrated in Figure 8–1, together with the truth-values associated with the various nodes. (Parse trees for the atomic formulas are omitted.)

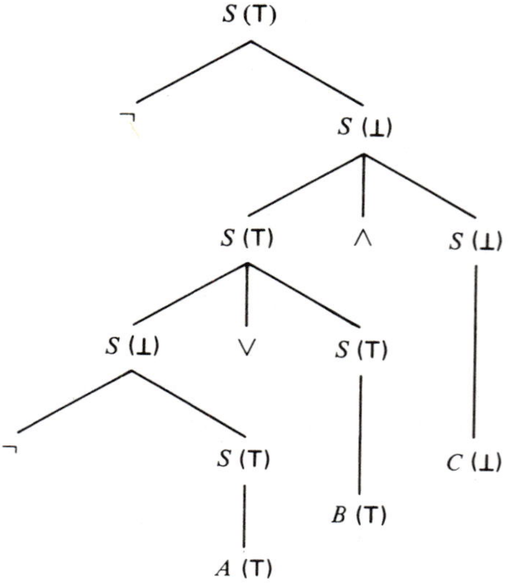

Figure 8–1

Rules 1 through 4 for the definition of $\bar{\mathfrak{A}}$ guarantee a unique value for $\bar{\mathfrak{A}}(F)$, provided that F has only one parse tree with respect to the grammar which generates formulas. But Lemma 8.2.1 guarantees that this grammar is unambiguous. We have therefore shown the following.

Theorem 8.3.1. *Let S be any set of atomic formulas and let $\bar{S}$ be the set of all formulas whose atomic formulas are in S. Given any truth-assignment $\mathfrak{A}$: $S \longrightarrow \{\top, \bot\}$, Rules 1 through 4 of Definition 8.3.1 determine a unique function $\bar{\mathfrak{A}}$: $\bar{S} \longrightarrow \{\top, \bot\}$. Moreover, $\bar{\mathfrak{A}}(A) = \mathfrak{A}(A)$ for each $A \in S$.*

Since $\bar{\mathfrak{A}}$ extends $\mathfrak{A}$ to a larger domain, we shall henceforth refer to both $\bar{\mathfrak{A}}$ and $\mathfrak{A}$ as truth-assignments; and in fact we shall drop the distinction between $\bar{\mathfrak{A}}$ and $\mathfrak{A}$ entirely. In the case of Example 8.3.1 again, we shall write $\mathfrak{A}(\neg((\neg A \vee B) \wedge C)) = \top$, rather than $\bar{\mathfrak{A}}(\neg((\neg A \vee B) \wedge C)) = \top$.

Of course, in actually determining a truth-value, Rules 1 through 4 need not be applied slavishly. It is often possible to save some work by observing that the truth-value of a disjunction $(F \vee G)$ is known to be $\top$ as soon as either F or G is known to have truth-value $\top$. Similarly, the truth-value of a conjunction $(F \wedge G)$ is known to be $\bot$ when either F or G has truth-value $\bot$. In Example 8.3.1, one can conclude very quickly that $\bar{\mathfrak{A}}(F) = \top$ by observing that F is the negation of a conjunction of two formulas, one of which, C, has truth-value $\bot$. The truth-value of $(\neg A \vee B)$ need not be calculated at all.

To Rules 1 through 4 we add two more, for conditionals and biconditionals.

5. $\bar{\mathfrak{A}}((F \longrightarrow G)) = \begin{cases} \top & \text{if } \bar{\mathfrak{A}}(F) = \bot \text{ or } \bar{\mathfrak{A}}(G) = \top \\ \bot & \text{otherwise} \end{cases}$

6. $\bar{\mathfrak{A}}((F \longleftrightarrow G)) = \begin{cases} \top & \text{if } \bar{\mathfrak{A}}(F) = \bar{\mathfrak{A}}(G) \\ \bot & \text{otherwise} \end{cases}$

These are direct consequences of Rules 1 through 4 and the definitions of $\longrightarrow$ and $\longleftrightarrow$. For example,

$$\begin{aligned} \bar{\mathfrak{A}}((F \longrightarrow G)) &= \bar{\mathfrak{A}}((\neg F \vee G)) && \text{by Definition 8.2.2} \\ &= \begin{cases} \top & \text{if } \bar{\mathfrak{A}}(\neg F) = \top \text{ or } \bar{\mathfrak{A}}(G) = \top \\ \bot & \text{otherwise} \end{cases} && \text{by Rule 2} \\ &= \begin{cases} \top & \text{if } \bar{\mathfrak{A}}(F) = \bot \text{ or } \bar{\mathfrak{A}}(G) = \top \\ \bot & \text{otherwise} \end{cases} && \text{by Rule 4} \end{aligned}$$

and this is exactly Rule 5. Note that Rule 6 can be restated as follows: the biconditional of F and G has truth-value $\top$ if F and G both have truth-value $\top$ or both have truth-value $\bot$; if one has truth-value $\top$ and the other has truth-value $\bot$, their biconditional has truth-value $\bot$.

8.4 VALIDITY AND SATISFIABILITY

The last section formalized the relation between a truth-assignment and a formula; that is, it specified how a formula was to be interpreted as true or false relative to a particular truth-assignment. In this section we consider the circumstances under which a formula can be true as an intrinsic property of the formula alone.

Let $\mathcal{A}$ be a truth-assignment and F a formula to which $\mathcal{A}$ is appropriate. If $\mathcal{A}(F) = \top$ then we write $\mathcal{A} \models F$; and if $\mathcal{A}(F) = \bot$ then we write $\mathcal{A} \not\models F$. In the former case, we say that $\mathcal{A}$ **verifies** F; in the latter, that $\mathcal{A}$ **falsifies** F. Also, if S is a set of formulas and $\mathcal{A}$ verifies each formula in S, then $\mathcal{A}$ is said to **verify** S; in symbols, $\mathcal{A} \models S$. If $\mathcal{A}$ verifies a formula or set of formulas, then $\mathcal{A}$ is called a **model** for that formula or set of formulas.

Example 8.4.1

Let $A_0, \ldots, A_n$ be atomic formulas for some $n \geq 0$, and suppose that $\mathcal{A} \models A_0$ but $\mathcal{A} \not\models A_i$ for each $i = 1, \ldots, n$. Then $\mathcal{A} \models (A_0 \vee A_i)$ for $i = 1, \ldots, n$. Let $S = \{(A_0 \vee A_i): i = 1, \ldots, n\}$; then $\mathcal{A}$ is a model for S.

Note in particular that *any* truth-assignment is a model for the empty set, since it is vacuously true that if $F \in \varnothing$ then $\mathcal{A} \models F$.

A formula or set of formulas is **satisfiable** if it has at least one model; otherwise it is **unsatisfiable**. A formula F is **valid** if *every* truth-assignment appropriate to F verifies F; in this case we say that F is a **tautology**.

Example 8.4.2

If F is any formula and A is any atomic formula, then $(A \vee F)$ is satisfiable; for example, $\mathcal{A} \models (A \vee F)$, where $\mathcal{A}$ assigns the truth-value $\top$ to every atomic formula of $(A \vee F)$. The formula $(F \wedge \neg F)$ is unsatisfiable no matter what F is; for if $\mathcal{A}$ is any truth-assignment appropriate to F, then one of $\mathcal{A}(F)$ and $\mathcal{A}(\neg F)$ must be $\bot$. Likewise, one of $\mathcal{A}(F)$ and $\mathcal{A}(\neg F)$ must be $\top$, so $(F \vee \neg F)$ is invariably a tautology.

Obviously every valid formula is satisfiable, so the class of all formulas may be pictured as in Figure 8–2. However, $\mathcal{A} \models F$ if and only if $\mathcal{A} \not\models \neg F$. Therefore a formula has no model if and only if its negation is a tautology; so we have the following.

Theorem 8.4.1. *A formula is valid if and only if its negation is unsatisfiable, and is unsatisfiable if and only if its negation is valid.*

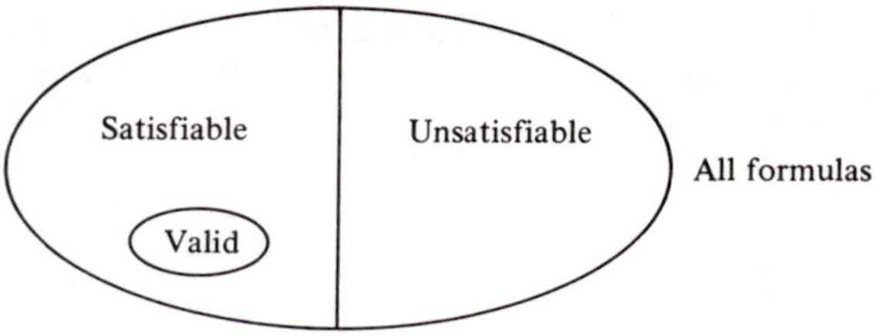

Figure 8–2

It follows that a more symmetric way of drawing Figure 8–2 is shown in Figure 8–3.

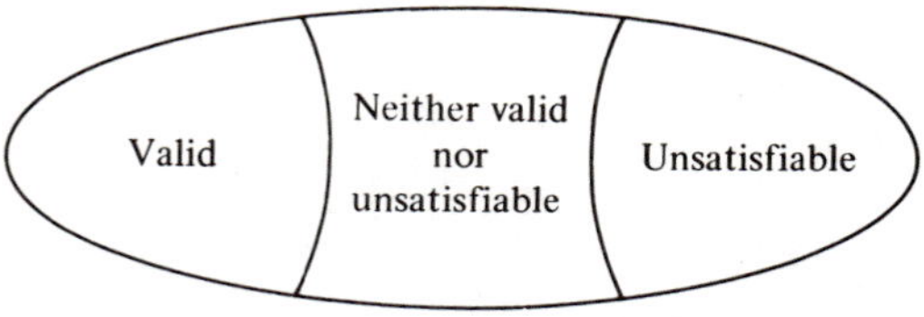

Figure 8–3

The satisfiable formulas make up the two sections on the left, and the two sections on the right consist of the formulas with satisfiable negations. The function that carries a formula to its negation flips the diagram on an axis drawn vertically through its center.

In order to determine whether a formula F is valid or satisfiable, we may compute the truth-value of F under each truth-assignment appropriate to F. Actually, there are infinitely many such truth-assignments, but it suffices to consider only those having domains that include no atomic formula except those appearing in F. There are only a finite number of such truth-assignments—2^n, to be exact, where n is the number of atomic subformulas of F.

These calculations can be carried out systematically using the method of **truth tables**. The first n columns are labeled with the atomic subformulas of F, subsequent columns are labeled with the other subformulas of F that are constructed out of these atomic formulas, and the last column is labeled with F itself. The table has 2^n rows, one for each n-tuple of truth-values for the atomic formulas. The table is then filled with $\top$'s and $\bot$'s, as appropriate. The formula is valid in case the rightmost column consists entirely of $\top$'s, satisfiable if that column contains at least one $\top$, and unsatisfiable if it contains all $\bot$'s.

As examples, let us begin with the truth tables of the connectives $\vee$, $\wedge$, $\neg$, and the defined symbols $\longrightarrow$ and $\longleftrightarrow$. Here A and B may be any distinct atomic formulas.

A	B	$(A \vee B)$
$\top$	$\top$	$\top$
$\top$	$\bot$	$\top$
$\bot$	$\top$	$\top$
$\bot$	$\bot$	$\bot$

A	$\neg A$
$\top$	$\bot$
$\bot$	$\top$

A	B	$(A \wedge B)$
$\top$	$\top$	$\top$
$\top$	$\bot$	$\bot$
$\bot$	$\top$	$\bot$
$\bot$	$\bot$	$\bot$

A	B	$(A \longrightarrow B)$
$\top$	$\top$	$\top$
$\top$	$\bot$	$\bot$
$\bot$	$\top$	$\top$
$\bot$	$\bot$	$\top$

A	B	$(A \longleftrightarrow B)$
$\top$	$\top$	$\top$
$\top$	$\bot$	$\bot$
$\bot$	$\top$	$\bot$
$\bot$	$\bot$	$\top$

To take a somewhat more complex example, consider $(\neg A \longrightarrow (A \longrightarrow B))$.

A	B	$\neg A$	$(A \longrightarrow B)$	$(\neg A \longrightarrow (A \longrightarrow B))$
$\top$	$\top$	$\bot$	$\top$	$\top$
$\top$	$\bot$	$\bot$	$\bot$	$\top$
$\bot$	$\top$	$\top$	$\top$	$\top$
$\bot$	$\bot$	$\top$	$\top$	$\top$

Each column except those labeled by atomic formulas is found from one or two columns to its left with the aid of the tables for $\vee$, $\wedge$, $\neg$, $\longrightarrow$, and $\longleftrightarrow$. In this example, the third column is derived from the first, the fourth from the first and second, and the fifth from the third and fourth. This truth table shows that $(\neg A \longrightarrow (A \longrightarrow B))$ is a tautology.

If we are using the truth-table method to tell whether a formula is satisfiable or whether a formula is a tautology, a little bit of intelligence will in some cases save considerable labor. For example, if there is a column labeled $(F \vee G)$, we may automatically put a $\top$ in any row in which the column labeled F has a $\top$, without finding a truth-value for G. A similar shortcut works for the conjunction of two formulas when one of them has been found to have the truth-value $\perp$.

Unfortunately, these shortcuts are found to be helpful only in special cases; in general, most of the 2^n rows of the truth table have to be worked through in detail, if the goal is to determine whether the rightmost column consists of all $\top$'s or all $\perp$'s, that is, whether the formula is valid or whether the formula is unsatisfiable. On the other hand, if the goal is to show that a formula is satisfiable, we need merely find *one* row in which the rightmost entry is a $\top$, and this can sometimes be done with a single lucky guess of which row to check. Here we have the hallmarks of an $\mathcal{NP}$-complete problem: when a formula is satisfiable, it can be shown to be satisfiable quickly if we are lucky enough to guess the correct truth-assignment; but a demonstration that a formula is *not* satisfiable seems to require an exhaustive search of all truth-assignments, whose number may be exponential in the size of the formula. Indeed, we shall see in Section 9.6 that our intuition is not amiss: telling whether formulas of the propositional calculus are satisfiable is an $\mathcal{NP}$-complete problem. In fact, satisfiability is the granddaddy of all the $\mathcal{NP}$-complete problems; historically, it was the first to be observed.

8.5 EQUIVALENCE AND NORMAL FORMS

If a formula F has n distinct atomic subformulas, there are 2^n truth-assignments with domains that include none but those subformulas. In a sense, the truth-values of F under these 2^n truth-assignments tell us everything about F that we really care about. Some other formula, G, may be syntactically distinct from F, but if G is verified or falsified by the same truth-assignments that verify or falsify F, then for many purposes the distinction between F and G can be ignored. It is useful to be able to transform formulas into others that are equivalent to them in this respect. Thus we have the following formal definition.

Definition 8.5.1

Two formulas are **equivalent** if and only if they are assigned the same truth-value by every truth-assignment appropriate to both.

Formulas with the same atomic subformulas are equivalent in case their truth tables have the same right-hand columns. However, formulas may be equivalent even if they have different atomic subformulas. For example, any two tautologies are equivalent; so are any two unsatisfiable formulas.

Equivalence is, in fact, an equivalence relation. Moreover, replacing one part of a formula by an equivalent subformula does not essentially change the formula as a whole.

Theorem 8.5.1. *Suppose that formulas F and G are equivalent, and that the formula H' results from the formula H by replacing some occurrence of F within H by G. Then H and H' are equivalent.*

Proof. Let $\mathcal{A}$ be any truth-assignment; we must show $\mathcal{A}(H) = \mathcal{A}(H')$. Intuitively speaking, the process of evaluating $\mathcal{A}(H')$ is identical to that of evaluating $\mathcal{A}(H)$, except that $\mathcal{A}(G)$ is evaluated at one point instead of $\mathcal{A}(F)$. But $\mathcal{A}(F) = \mathcal{A}(G)$, so this can make no difference in the result.

More formally, we proceed by induction on k, the number of occurrences of logical connectives in H. If $k = 0$, then H is atomic, and necessarily $F = H$. Then $H' = G$; since F and G are equivalent, so are H and H'.

Now assume that the theorem holds for all H with k or fewer occurrences of logical connectives. Let F, G, H, and H' be as specified in the statement of the theorem, and let H have $k + 1$ occurrences of logical connectives. There are several cases to consider.

(a) If $F = H$, then $G = H'$ and H and H' are equivalent, as in the basis case.

(b) Otherwise $|F| < |H|$, and either (i) $H = \neg J$ for some formula J, (ii) $H = (J_1 \vee J_2)$ for some J_1 and J_2, or (iii) $H = (J_1 \wedge J_2)$ for some J_1 and J_2.

In Case (i), the occurrence of F in H is within J, and $H' = \neg J'$ for some formula J' obtained by replacing an occurrence of F in J by G. But then J has only k occurrences of logical connectives, so $\mathcal{A}(J) = \mathcal{A}(J')$ by the induction hypothesis; therefore $\mathcal{A}(H) = \mathcal{A}(\neg J) = \mathcal{A}(\neg J') = \mathcal{A}(H')$.

In Case (ii) or Case (iii), the occurrence of F is within J_1 or J_2; these cases are treated similarly. ■

Example 8.5.1

The formulas $F = (\neg A \vee B)$ and $G = (B \vee \neg A)$ are equivalent. Consequently we have the following.

$H = \neg(\neg A \vee B)$ and $H' = \neg(B \vee \neg A)$ are equivalent	Case b(i) of the proof, with $J = F$
$H = ((C \wedge (\neg A \vee B)) \vee (D \vee A))$ and $H' = ((C \wedge (B \vee \neg A)) \vee (D \vee A))$ are equivalent	Case b(ii) of the proof, with F occurring within $J_1 = (C \wedge (\neg A \vee B))$

If F and G are equivalent, we write $F \equiv G$. Note carefully that $F \equiv G$ is an abbreviation for the *assertion* that F and G are equivalent formulas; this is quite another type of thing from $(F \leftrightarrow G)$, which is not an assertion, but simply a way of denoting a particular formula. The notations $\equiv$ and $\leftrightarrow$ are not unrelated however; in fact, *$F \equiv G$ if and only if $(F \leftrightarrow G)$ is a tautology*. For if $F \equiv G$, then $\mathfrak{A}(F) = \mathfrak{A}(G)$ for every truth-assignment $\mathfrak{A}$ appropriate to both, and by Rule 6, $\mathfrak{A}((F \leftrightarrow G)) = \top$ for every such truth-assignment, so $(F \leftrightarrow G)$ is a tautology. The converse is equally direct.

We next systematically list some pairs of formulas that are guaranteed to be equivalent. These pairs are described as *laws* of various kinds, since each pair is really a schema into which various subformulas can be substituted.

Theorem 8.5.2. *For any formulas F, G, and H, the following pairs of formulas are equivalent:*

Idempotency	$(F \vee F) \equiv F$	
	$(F \wedge F) \equiv F$	
Commutativity	$(F \vee G) \equiv (G \vee F)$	
	$(F \wedge G) \equiv (G \wedge F)$	
	$(F \leftrightarrow G) \equiv (G \leftrightarrow F)$	
Associativity	$((F \vee G) \vee H) \equiv (F \vee (G \vee H))$	
	$((F \wedge G) \wedge H) \equiv (F \wedge (G \wedge H))$	
Absorption	$(F \vee (F \wedge G)) \equiv F$	
	$(F \wedge (F \vee G)) \equiv F$	
Distributivity	$(F \wedge (G \vee H)) \equiv ((F \wedge G) \vee (F \wedge H))$	
	$(F \vee (G \wedge H)) \equiv ((F \vee G) \wedge (F \vee H))$	
Double Negation	$\neg\neg F \equiv F$	
DeMorgan	$\neg(F \vee G) \equiv (\neg F \wedge \neg G)$	
	$\neg(F \wedge G) \equiv (\neg F \vee \neg G)$	
Tautology	$(F \vee G) \equiv F$	*if F is a tautology*
	$(F \wedge G) \equiv G$	*if F is a tautology*
Unsatisfiability	$(F \vee G) \equiv G$	*if F is unsatisfiable*
	$(F \wedge G) \equiv F$	*if F is unsatisfiable.*

Proof. In every case, these laws follow directly from Rules 1 through 4 for the value of a truth-assignment on a formula. We take just two examples.

The first of the absorption laws states that $(F \vee (F \wedge G)) \equiv F$ for any F and G. To see this, we need to show that $\mathfrak{A}((F \vee (F \wedge G))) = \mathfrak{A}(F)$

for any truth-assignment $\mathfrak{a}$ appropriate to F and G. Since $\mathfrak{a}$ can assume only the two values $\top$ and $\bot$, it suffices to show that $\mathfrak{a}((F \vee (F \wedge G))) = \top$ if and only if $\mathfrak{a}(F) = \top$. Now if $\mathfrak{a}((F \vee (F \wedge G))) = \top$, then by Rule 2, either $\mathfrak{a}(F) = \top$ or $\mathfrak{a}((F \wedge G)) = \top$. But in the latter case, $\mathfrak{a}(F) = \mathfrak{a}(G) = \top$ by Rule 3, so $\mathfrak{a}(F) = \top$ in either case. Conversely, if $\mathfrak{a}(F) = \top$, then $\mathfrak{a}((F \vee (F \wedge G))) = \top$ by Rule 2, regardless of the value of $\mathfrak{a}((F \wedge G))$.

The second of DeMorgan's laws states that $\mathfrak{a}(\neg(F \wedge G)) = \mathfrak{a}((\neg F \vee \neg G))$. Now if $\mathfrak{a}(\neg(F \wedge G)) = \top$, then by Rule 4, $\mathfrak{a}((F \wedge G)) = \bot$, and by Rule 3, $\mathfrak{a}(F) = \bot$ or $\mathfrak{a}(G) = \bot$. But then $\mathfrak{a}(\neg F) = \top$ or $\mathfrak{a}(\neg G) = \top$ by Rule 4, and by Rule 2, $\mathfrak{a}((\neg F \vee \neg G)) = \top$. Conversely, if $\mathfrak{a}((\neg F \vee \neg G)) = \top$, then $\mathfrak{a}(\neg F) = \top$ or $\mathfrak{a}(\neg G) = \top$; hence $\mathfrak{a}(F) = \bot$ or $\mathfrak{a}(G) = \bot$, $\mathfrak{a}((F \wedge G)) = \bot$, and $\mathfrak{a}(\neg(F \wedge G)) = \top$. ■

These laws can often be used in conjunction with Theorem 8.5.1 for simplifying formulas.

Example 8.5.2

Let $F = ((A \vee \neg(B \wedge A)) \wedge (C \vee (D \vee C)))$. Then we have the following.

$F = ((A \vee \neg(B \wedge A)) \wedge (C \vee (D \vee C)))$	
$\equiv ((A \vee (\neg B \vee \neg A)) \wedge (C \vee (D \vee C)))$	by the second of DeMorgan's laws
$\equiv ((A \vee (\neg A \vee \neg B)) \wedge (C \vee (D \vee C)))$	by commutativity of $\vee$
$\equiv (((A \vee \neg A) \vee \neg B) \wedge (C \vee (D \vee C)))$	by associativity of $\vee$
$\equiv ((A \vee \neg A) \wedge (C \vee (D \vee C)))$	by the first tautology law
$\equiv (C \vee (D \vee C))$	by the second tautology law
$\equiv (C \vee (C \vee D))$	by commutativity of $\vee$
$\equiv ((C \vee C) \vee D)$	by associativity of $\vee$
$\equiv (C \vee D)$	by idempotency of $\vee$

In Example 8.5.2, we were intelligent in our choice of which laws to apply; certainly, we could equally well have transformed F into a formula much more complicated than F, if we had applied the laws differently. However, the laws do give us some systematic techniques for simplifying formulas. For example, the law of double negation implies that we need never consider formulas with two or more consecutive negation signs, since adjacent pairs of negation signs can be dropped. The associativity laws imply that in nested conjunctions or disjunctions the grouping of the subformulas is immaterial. Accordingly we write

$$(F_1 \vee \cdots \vee F_n)$$

where $n \geq 3$, for

$$(F_1 \vee (F_2 \vee (\cdots \vee F_n)) \cdots),$$

secure in the knowledge that it does not actually matter whether the F_i are grouped to the right, to the left, or otherwise. Similarly, we write

$$(F_1 \wedge \cdots \wedge F_n)$$

for

$$(F_1 \wedge (F_2 \wedge (\cdots \wedge F_n)) \cdots).$$

The commutativity and idempotency laws can then be used to guarantee that no two F_i are identical. So we will feel free, for example, to reduce $(((A \vee B) \vee (B \vee A)) \vee A)$ to the equivalent formula $(A \vee B)$, without any detailed justification.

Sometimes we use an even shorter notation, analogous to the use of $\sum$ and $\prod$ in mathematics. Just as $\sum_{i=1}^{n} a_i$ is an abbreviation for the sum $a_1 + a_2 + \cdots + a_n$, we write

$$\left(\bigvee_{i=1}^{n} F_i\right) \quad \text{for} \quad (F_1 \vee \cdots \vee F_n)$$

and

$$\left(\bigwedge_{i=1}^{n} F_i\right) \quad \text{for} \quad (F_1 \wedge \cdots \wedge F_n).$$

We use these notations even in the case $n = 1$: then $\left(\bigvee_{i=1}^{n} F_i\right)$ and $\left(\bigwedge_{i=1}^{n} F_i\right)$ are both simply F_1.

Extending our previous terminology, we refer to these formulas as the **disjunction** and **conjunction**, respectively, of $F_1, \ldots, F_n$.

With these abbreviations, and with free use of the associativity and commutativity laws, more general versions of the distributivity laws and DeMorgan's laws can be stated.

Theorem 8.5.3. *Let $m, n \geq 1$ and let $F_1, \ldots, F_m$ and $G_1, \ldots, G_n$ be any formulas. Then we have the following.*

Distributivity

$$\left(\left(\bigvee_{i=1}^{m} F_i\right) \wedge \left(\bigvee_{j=1}^{n} G_j\right)\right) \equiv \left(\bigvee_{i=1}^{m} \left(\bigvee_{j=1}^{n} (F_i \wedge G_j)\right)\right)$$

$$\left(\left(\bigwedge_{i=1}^{m} F_i\right) \vee \left(\bigwedge_{j=1}^{n} G_j\right)\right) \equiv \left(\bigwedge_{i=1}^{m} \left(\bigwedge_{j=1}^{n} (F_i \vee G_j)\right)\right)$$

DeMorgan

$$\neg\left(\bigvee_{i=1}^{m} F_i\right) \equiv \left(\bigwedge_{i=1}^{m} \neg F_i\right)$$

$$\neg\left(\bigwedge_{i=1}^{m} F_i\right) \equiv \left(\bigvee_{i=1}^{m} \neg F_i\right)$$

Proof. See Problem 8.5.5. ■

Although the notation may appear a bit formidable, the idea behind Theorem 8.5.3 is not difficult. In a few words, the first distributivity law states that a conjunction of two disjunctions of formulas can be "multiplied out" to obtain a disjunction of conjunctions of pairs of formulas. This process is quite analogous to the algebraic transformation of a product such as $(a + b + c)\cdot(d + e)$ into the sum $ad + ae + bd + be + cd + ce$. In the propositional calculus, however, $\wedge$ and $\vee$ are symmetric in a way that numerical addition and multiplication are not: hence the second distributivity law. And DeMorgan's laws state that negations can always be "driven into" conjunctions and disjunctions—provided that what was a conjunction becomes a disjunction, and vice versa.

Example 8.5.3

Let

$$H = ((A \vee B \vee C) \wedge (C \vee \neg A)).$$

Let $m = 3$, $n = 2$, $F_1 = A$, $F_2 = B$, $F_3 = C$, $G_1 = C$, and $G_2 = \neg A$; then

$$H = \left(\left(\bigvee_{i=1}^{m} F_i\right) \wedge \left(\bigvee_{j=1}^{n} G_j\right)\right)$$

and, by distributivity,

$$H \equiv \left(\bigvee_{i=1}^{m}\left(\bigvee_{j=1}^{n}(F_i \wedge G_j)\right)\right),$$

that is,

$$H \equiv (((A \wedge C) \vee (A \wedge \neg A)) \vee ((B \wedge C) \vee (B \wedge \neg A)) \vee ((C \wedge C) \vee (C \wedge \neg A))).$$

By means of associativity, commutativity, idempotency, and the first unsatisfiability law, this reduces to

$$((A \wedge C) \vee (B \wedge C) \vee (B \wedge \neg A) \vee C \vee (C \wedge \neg A))$$

and then by absorption to $(C \vee (B \wedge \neg A))$.

Repeated use of the equivalences in Theorem 8.5.3, plus the law of double negation, will transform any formula into an equivalent one in either of two quite special forms. The ability to make this transformation is a standard tool in logical investigations; we shall use it ourselves in Section 8.7 in order to develop an alternative to the truth-table method for establishing satisfiability.

Definition 8.5.2

A **literal** is an atomic formula or the negation of an atomic formula. A formula is in **conjunctive normal form** if it is a conjunction of disjunctions of literals, and is in **disjunctive normal form** if it is a disjunction of conjunctions of literals.

To put it another way, a formula is in conjunctive normal form if and only if it can be written as

$$\left(\bigwedge_{i=1}^{n}\left(\bigvee_{j=1}^{m_i} L_{ij}\right)\right)$$

where $n \geq 1, m_1, \ldots, m_n \geq 1$, and each L_{ij} is a literal. Likewise, a formula is in disjunctive normal form if and only if it can be written as

$$\left(\bigvee_{i=1}^{n}\left(\bigwedge_{j=1}^{m_i} L_{ij}\right)\right)$$

where the L_{ij} are literals.

Example 8.5.4

If A, B, and C are atomic formulas, then A, B, C, $\neg A$, $\neg B$, and $\neg C$ are literals; but $(A \vee B)$, $(A \wedge B)$, and $\neg\neg A$ are not literals. The formula $((A \wedge B) \vee (\neg A \wedge C))$ is in disjunctive normal form, and the formula $((A \vee B) \wedge (B \vee C \vee \neg A) \wedge (A \vee C))$ is in conjunctive normal form. The formulas $(A \vee B)$, $(A \wedge \neg C)$, and A are all in both conjunctive *and* disjunctive normal form; for example, $(A \wedge \neg C)$ is in conjunctive normal form because it is a conjunction of two formulas, each of which is a disjunction of one literal, and it is in disjunctive normal form because it is a disjunction of one formula, which is a conjunction of two literals.

If F and G are formulas, $F \equiv G$, and G is in conjunctive (or disjunctive) normal form, then G is said to be a **conjunctive** (or **disjunctive**) **normal form of** F. Before stating the main fact about conjunctive and disjunctive normal forms, we need one further notational convention. If F is the negation of a formula G, that is, $F = \neg G$, then let $\bar{F} = G$; and if F is not the negation of any formula, then let $\bar{F} = \neg F$. For example, if A is atomic, then $\bar{A} = \neg A$ and $\overline{\neg A} = A$. Thus $\bar{F} \equiv \neg F$ in any case.

Theorem 8.5.4. *Every formula has at least one conjunctive normal form and at least one disjunctive normal form; and there is an algorithm that transforms any formula F into a conjunctive or disjunctive normal form of F, as desired.*

Proof. The proof is by induction on the number of occurrences of logical connectives in the formula. A formula with no logical connectives is atomic and is already in both conjunctive and disjunctive normal form. Now assume the theorem for formulas with k or fewer occurrences of logical connectives, and let F be a formula with $k + 1$ occurrences of logical connectives. There are three cases to consider.

(a) $F = \neg G$ for some formula G with k occurrences of logical connectives. By the induction hypothesis, we can find both a conjunctive and a disjunctive normal form of G. If

$$\left(\bigwedge_{i=1}^{n}\left(\bigvee_{j=1}^{m_i} G_{ij}\right)\right)$$

is a conjunctive normal form of G, then by DeMorgan's laws,

$$\left(\bigvee_{i=1}^{n}\left(\bigwedge_{j=1}^{m_i} \overline{G_{ij}}\right)\right)$$

is a disjunctive normal form of F. Similarly, a conjunctive normal form of F can be obtained from a disjunctive normal form of G.

(b) $F = (G_1 \vee G_2)$ for some formulas G_1 and G_2, each of which has k or fewer occurrences of logical connectives. To obtain a disjunctive normal form of F, we may simply take the disjunction of a disjunctive normal form of G_1 and a disjunctive normal form of G_2. To obtain a conjunctive normal form of F, find conjunctive normal forms of G_1 and G_2, such as $\left(\bigwedge_{i=1}^{m} H_i\right)$ and $\left(\bigwedge_{j=1}^{n} J_i\right)$, where $H_1, \ldots, H_m$ and $J_1, \ldots, J_n$ are disjunctions of literals; then by the first distributivity law

$$\left(\bigwedge_{i=1}^{m}\left(\bigwedge_{j=1}^{n} (H_i \vee J_i)\right)\right)$$

is equivalent to $(G_1 \vee G_2)$. Each formula $(H_i \vee J_j)$ is a disjunction of literals, so this formula is a conjunctive normal form of F.

(c) $F = (G_1 \wedge G_2)$ for some formulas G_1 and G_2. This case is entirely analogous to Case (b). ■

Example 8.5.5

Let $F = \neg((A \wedge B) \vee (C \wedge \neg D))$, and let us find a disjunctive normal form of F. Since F is the negation of a formula, Case (a) applies, so we must find a conjunctive normal form of $((A \wedge B) \vee (C \wedge \neg D))$. Since this is a disjunction of two formulas, Case (b) applies. Now $(A \wedge B)$ and $(C \wedge \neg D)$ are already in conjunctive normal form; applying distributivity we obtain the following conjunctive normal form for $((A \wedge B) \vee (C \wedge \neg D))$.

$$((A \vee C) \wedge (A \vee \neg D) \wedge (B \vee C) \wedge (B \vee \neg D))$$

DeMorgan's laws transform the negation of this formula first into

$$(\neg(A \vee C) \vee \neg(A \vee \neg D) \vee \neg(B \vee C) \vee \neg(B \vee \neg D))$$

and then into

$$((\neg A \wedge \neg C) \vee (\neg A \wedge \neg\neg D) \vee (\neg B \wedge \neg C) \vee (\neg B \wedge \neg\neg D));$$

then the law of double negation reduces this to

$$((\neg A \wedge \neg C) \vee (\neg A \wedge D) \vee (\neg B \wedge \neg C) \vee (\neg B \wedge D)),$$

which is a disjunctive normal form of F.

8.6 COMPACTNESS

Recall that a *set* of formulas, finite or infinite, is called *satisfiable* if there is a single truth-assignment that verifies every formula in the set. Surprisingly, the satisfiability of an infinite set of formulas depends only on the satisfiability of its finite subsets: If each finite subset, however large, is satisfiable, then the set as a whole is satisfiable. In mathematics, any property that can be inferred of an infinite object on the basis of finite "approximations" to that object is called a **compactness** phenomenon; hence the name of this section. This compactness of the propositional calculus is one of its fundamental properties, used several times in this chapter and the next. Moreover, its proof illustrates an interesting technique not used elsewhere in this book.

Theorem 8.6.1. (Compactness Theorem for the Propositional Calculus) *A set of formulas is satisfiable if and only if each of its finite subsets is satisfiable.*

Proof. Clearly if a set of formulas is satisfiable then so is any finite subset. The hard part is the converse.

For each $n \geq 1$, let A_n be the atomic formula $\mathbf{AI}^{n-1}\$$, so that $A_1, A_2, \ldots$ is a listing of all the atomic formulas; and for each $n \geq 0$, let $\mathcal{S}_n$ be the set of all formulas whose atomic formulas are among $A_1, A_2, \ldots, A_n$. (Thus $\mathcal{S}_0 = \varnothing$.) For $n \geq 1$, each $\mathcal{S}_n$ is infinite, but contains only 2^{2^n} mutually inequivalent formulas; that is, $\mathcal{S}_n$ can be partitioned into 2^{2^n} equivalence classes, with all formulas in any class equivalent to each other.

Now let S be an infinite set of formulas, and suppose that each finite subset of S is satisfiable. Then $S \cap \mathcal{S}_n$ is satisfiable for each n. For even though $S \cap \mathcal{S}_n$ may be infinite, we can choose from $S \cap \mathcal{S}_n$ at most 2^{2^n} inequivalent formulas, and any truth-assignment verifying this subset verifies $S \cap \mathcal{S}_n$ as a whole.

Since $S \cap \mathcal{S}_n$ is satisfiable for each n, there is for $n = 0, 1, 2, \ldots$ a truth-assignment $\mathcal{A}_n$ appropriate to $\mathcal{S}_n$ such that $\mathcal{A}_n \models S \cap \mathcal{S}_n$. This does *not* mean that *any* of the $\mathcal{A}_n$ verifies S; indeed, none of the $\mathcal{A}_n$ need even be defined on all the atomic formulas of S. However, we can construct from the set of truth-assignments $\{\mathcal{A}_0, \mathcal{A}_1, \ldots\}$ a truth-assignment $\mathcal{A}$ that does verify S. Specifically, we first construct, for each $n \geq 0$, a set U_n of truth-assignments such that

(a) for $n > 0$, U_n is a subset of U_{n-1};

(b) U_n is a subset of $\{\mathcal{A}_n, \mathcal{A}_{n+1}, \ldots\}$ containing $\mathcal{A}_i$ for infinitely many $i \geq n$;

(c) if $1 \leq m \leq n$, then any two truth-assignments in U_n agree on the truth-value assigned to the atomic formula A_m.

These sets of truth-assignments are obtained by repeatedly "thinning out" the original set $\{\mathcal{A}_0, \mathcal{A}_1, \ldots\}$. Let $U_0 = \{\mathcal{A}_0, \mathcal{A}_1, \ldots\}$; clearly (a) through (c) are true for $n = 0$ ((a) and (c) vacuously). Once U_n has been defined, U_{n+1} can be defined as follows. By (b), U_n contains $\mathcal{A}_i$ for infinitely many $i \geq n + 1$. That is, $\{i: i \geq n + 1 \text{ and } \mathcal{A}_i \in U_n\}$ is infinite. This set can be partitioned into two disjoint subsets: $J_1 = \{i: i \geq n + 1, \mathcal{A}_i \in U_n, \text{ and } \mathcal{A}_i \models A_{n+1}\}$, and $J_2 = \{i: i \geq n + 1, \mathcal{A}_i \in U_n, \text{ and } \mathcal{A}_i \not\models A_{n+1}\}$. Of these two subsets, at least one must be infinite, since the union of two finite sets is finite. Let J be whichever of J_1 and J_2 is infinite (either, if both are infinite), and let $U_{n+1} = \{\mathcal{A}_i: i \in J\}$. Clearly $U_{n+1} \subseteq U_n$ and U_{n+1} contains $\mathcal{A}_i$ for infinitely many $i \geq n + 1$. Moreover, all the truth-assignments in U_{n+1} agree on $A_1, \ldots, A_n$ (by induction, since $U_{n+1} \subseteq U_n$ and U_n satisfies (c)) and on A_{n+1} (by the way U_{n+1} was defined).

Having defined $U_0, U_1, \ldots$ to satisfy (a) through (c), define a truth-assignment $\mathcal{A}: \{A_1, A_2, \ldots\} \to \{\top, \bot\}$ as follows: $\mathcal{A}(A_m)$ is the common value of $\mathcal{B}(A_m)$ for all $\mathcal{B} \in U_n, n \geq m$. (By (a) and (c), all truth-assignments in any of the U_n agree on the truth-value of A_m, if $n \geq m$.) We claim that $\mathcal{A} \models S$. For if $F \in S$, then $F \in S \cap \mathcal{S}_m$ for some m, and so $\mathcal{A}_n \models F$ for all $n \geq m$. Hence $\mathcal{B} \models F$ for all $\mathcal{B} \in U_n$, if $n \geq m$; and hence $\mathcal{A}$, which agrees with all these $\mathcal{B} \in U_n$ for $n \geq m$ on formulas in $\mathcal{S}_m$, also verifies F. ■

Example 8.6.1

Let $S = \{(A_i \vee A_{i+1}): i = 1, 2, \ldots\}$. Clearly S is satisfiable; but we wish to illustrate how this follows from the satisfiability of the finite subsets of S. Now $S \cap \mathcal{S}_n = \{(A_i \vee A_{i+1}): 1 \leq i \leq n - 1\}$ for each $n \geq 0$, and each such set is finite. Define for each n a truth-assignment $\mathcal{A}_n$ as follows.

- If n is even, then

$$\mathcal{A}_n \models A_i \quad \text{if } 1 \leq i \leq n \text{ and } i \text{ is even;}$$
$$\mathcal{A}_n \not\models A_i \quad \text{if } i > n \text{ or } i \text{ is odd.}$$

- If n is odd, then

$$\mathcal{A}_n \models A_i \quad \text{if } 1 \leq i \leq n \text{ and } i \text{ is odd;}$$
$$\mathcal{A}_n \not\models A_i \quad \text{if } i > n \text{ or } i \text{ is even.}$$

Now $\mathcal{A}_n \models S \cap \mathcal{S}_n$ for each n, since each formula $(A_i \vee A_{i+1})$, where $i \leq n - 1$, contains an atomic formula A_j for some even $j \leq n$ and an atomic formula A_j for some odd $j \leq n$. Nevertheless, no $\mathcal{A}_n$ verifies S, even though each $\mathcal{A}_n$ is defined for all atomic formulas; and what is worse, the $\mathcal{A}_n$ disagree quite extensively among themselves on the truth-values to be assigned to the various atomic formulas.

Let us see how a single truth-assignment $\mathcal{A}$ is constructed from the $\mathcal{A}_n$. To begin, we let $U_0 = \{\mathcal{A}_0, \mathcal{A}_1, \ldots\}$. To define U_1, we split $\{i: i \geq 1$ and

$\mathcal{A}_i \in U_0\}$, that is $\{1, 2, \ldots\}$, into the two subsets

$$J_1 = \{i: i \geq 1, \mathcal{A}_i \in U_0, \text{ and } \mathcal{A}_i \models A_1\}$$

and

$$J_2 = \{i: i \geq 1, \mathcal{A}_i \in U_0, \text{ and } \mathcal{A}_i \not\models A_1\}.$$

Here J_1 contains all odd numbers and J_2 contains all even numbers greater than zero. Both J_1 and J_2 are infinite, so we arbitrarily let $J = J_1$ and

$$U_1 = \{\mathcal{A}_i: i \in J_1\} = \{\mathcal{A}_1, \mathcal{A}_3, \mathcal{A}_5, \ldots\}.$$

Next, to define U_2, we split $\{3, 5, \ldots\}$ into the subsets

$$J_1' = \{i: i \geq 2, \mathcal{A}_i \in U_1, \text{ and } \mathcal{A}_i \models A_2\}$$

and

$$J_2' = \{i: i \geq 2, \mathcal{A}_i \in U_1, \text{ and } \mathcal{A}_i \not\models A_2\}.$$

Now $J_1' = \varnothing$ and $J_2' = \{3, 5, \ldots\}$, so we are forced to let

$$U_2 = \{\mathcal{A}_i: i \in J_2'\} = \{\mathcal{A}_3, \mathcal{A}_5, \ldots\}.$$

Continuing in the same way, we discover that the only possibility for $n \geq 1$ is to let

$$U_n = \{\mathcal{A}_i: i \text{ is odd and } i \geq n\}.$$

If $\mathcal{B} \in U_n$ and $m \leq n$, then $\mathcal{B} \models A_m$ if and only if m is odd. Thus the combined truth-assignment $\mathcal{A}: \{A_1, A_2, \ldots\} \rightarrow \{\top, \bot\}$ is defined by

$$\mathcal{A} \models A_i \quad \text{if and only if} \quad i \text{ is odd } (i = 1, 2, \ldots),$$

and $\mathcal{A} \models S$ as required.

8.7 RESOLUTION IN THE PROPOSITIONAL CALCULUS

We now undertake to use the sorts of transformations developed in Section 8.5 in order to derive an alternative to the truth-table method for establishing unsatisfiability. Bear in mind that *any* method for establishing unsatisfiability can be used equally well for establishing validity, since a formula is valid if and only if its negation is unsatisfiable.

We have seen that for formulas in conjunctive normal form the order of the formulas around the connectives $\wedge$ and $\vee$ is irrelevant, in the sense that all permutations are equivalent formulas. For example, $((A \vee B) \wedge \neg C)$, $(\neg C \wedge (A \vee B))$, $((B \vee A) \wedge \neg C)$, and $(\neg C \wedge (B \vee A))$ are all equivalent. Since we are concerned with the distinctions between formulas only insofar as they may make those formulas inequivalent, it is convenient to regard a disjunction of literals as a *set* of literals, and a formula in conjunctive normal form as a *set of sets* of literals. Thus all four of the formulas just listed would be regarded as the set $\{\{A, B\}, \{\neg C\}\}$.

Formally, a **clause** is any finite set of literals, possibly empty. Each disjunction of literals corresponds to some clause, and each nonempty clause corresponds to one or more disjunctions of literals. Although the empty clause does not directly correspond to any formula, we shall see that it is a useful concept. We write $\square$ for the empty clause.

A **clause set** is a set of clauses, possibly containing the empty clause, possibly empty itself, and possibly infinite. Every formula in conjunctive normal form corresponds to a clause set in a natural way, and every finite clause set not containing the empty clause and not itself empty corresponds to one or more formulas in conjunctive normal form. The empty clause set is to be distinguished from the empty clause, although as sets they are identical. (There is, after all, only one empty set!) We use $\varnothing$ to denote the empty clause set.

Example 8.7.1

Let A, B, C, and D be atomic formulas. Then $\{A, B, C\}$, $\{A, \neg A\}$, $\square$, and $\{\neg A\}$ are clauses, but $\varnothing$, $\{\{A\}\}$, and $\{\neg\neg A\}$ are not. Also, $\{\{A\}\}$, $\{\square\}$, $\{\{A, B\}, \{\neg B, \neg C\}, \{D\}\}$, $\{\{A\}, \square\}$, and $\varnothing$ are clause sets, but $\{\{\square\}\}$, $\square$, $\{\varnothing\}$, $\{A\}$, and $\{\{A, B\}, C\}$ are not. Here $\{\{A\}\}$ is the representation of the formula A as a clause set; and $\{\{A, B\}, \{\neg B, \neg C\}, \{D\}\}$ is the representation of the formula $((A \vee B) \wedge (\neg B \vee \neg C) \wedge D)$, among others, as a clause set.

We can now ascribe some of the properties possessed by formulas to clauses and clause sets. A truth-assignment $\mathfrak{A}$ is **appropriate** to a clause set S if every atomic formula appearing in some clause in S is in the domain of $\mathfrak{A}$. Suppose, then, that $\mathfrak{A}$ is appropriate to S. We can determine a truth-value for each clause in S, and then for S as a whole, by analogy with the way we would determine the truth-value of a corresponding formula in conjunctive normal form. Since $\mathfrak{A}$ verifies a disjunction of literals just in case $\mathfrak{A}$ verifies one of the literals, we define:

I. $\mathfrak{A}$ verifies a clause if and only if $\mathfrak{A}$ verifies at least one of its members.

Similarly, since $\mathfrak{A}$ verifies a conjunction of formulas just in case $\mathfrak{A}$ verifies each of those formulas, we define

II. $\mathfrak{A}$ verifies a clause set if and only if $\mathfrak{A}$ verifies each of its members.

For example, let S be the clause set $\{\{A, B\}, \{\neg C\}\}$ which corresponds to each of the formulas used at the beginning of this section. If $\mathfrak{A} \models A$, $\mathfrak{A} \models \neg B$, and $\mathfrak{A} \models \neg C$, then $\mathfrak{A} \models S$. On the other hand, if $\mathfrak{A} \models A$, $\mathfrak{A} \models B$ and $\mathfrak{A} \models C$, then $\mathfrak{A} \not\models S$, since then $\mathfrak{A} \not\models \{\neg C\}$.

It is now apparent why the empty clause set and the empty clause must be regarded as distinct. By Rule I, $\mathfrak{A} \not\models \square$ for each truth-assignment $\mathfrak{A}$, because $\square$ has no members for $\mathfrak{A}$ to verify, so $\mathfrak{A}$ cannot verify one or more. But by Rule II, $\mathfrak{A} \models \varnothing$ for each $\mathfrak{A}$, since $\mathfrak{A}$ verifies each clause in $\varnothing$ (of which there happen to be none). On the other hand, $\mathfrak{A} \not\models \{\square\}$ for each $\mathfrak{A}$.

A clause or clause set may be satisfiable, unsatisfiable, or a tautology in the same way that a formula may be. For example, the empty clause set is a tautology, but the empty clause is unsatisfiable. Any clause set containing the empty clause is unsatisfiable, but there are other unsatisfiable clause sets as well. For example, $\{\{A\}, \{\neg A\}\}$ is unsatisfiable, just as the formula $(A \wedge \neg A)$ is unsatisfiable.

Naturally two clause sets are **equivalent** if any truth-assignment appropriate to each assigns both the same truth-value.

Now let us begin to investigate ways in which we might try to extract additional, implicit information from a clause set, beyond what it states explicitly. The information sought is going to be found as new clauses, which must also be verified by any truth-assignment verifying the original clauses. To start, we take an example.

Consider the clause set $\{\{A, B, \neg C\}, \{\neg B, \neg D\}\}$. In order for a truth-assignment $\mathcal{A}$ to verify this clause set, $\mathcal{A}$ must verify A, B, or $\neg C$, as well as either $\neg B$ or $\neg D$. To a certain extent these objectives are incompatible, since $\mathcal{A}$ cannot verify the first clause by verifying B *and also* verify the second clause by verifying $\neg B$. Thus whether $\mathcal{A}$ verifies B or not, in order to verify the whole it must verify A or $\neg C$ (one of the literals other than B in the first clause), or it must verify $\neg D$ (the only literal other than $\neg B$ in the second clause). It follows that the clause set $\{\{A, B, \neg C\}, \{\neg B, \neg D\}\}$ is equivalent to $\{\{A, B, \neg C\}, \{\neg B, \neg D\}, \{A, \neg C, \neg D\}\}$; the third clause is a consequence of the other two. Formally, $\{A, \neg C, \neg D\}$ is said to be a *resolvent* of the other two clauses.

More generally, we have the following definition.

Definition 8.7.1

Let C_1 and C_2 be clauses. Then D is a **resolvent** of C_1 and C_2 if and only if, for some literal L, $L \in C_1$, $\bar{L} \in C_2$, and $D = (C_1 - \{L\}) \cup (C_2 - \{\bar{L}\})$.

That is, a resolvent of two clauses is any clause obtained by striking out a complementary pair of literals, one from each, and merging the remaining literals into a single clause. Note that two clauses may have more than one resolvent; for example, $\{A, B\}$ and $\{\neg A, \neg B\}$ have the resolvents $\{A, \neg A\}$ and $\{B, \neg B\}$. Also, two nonempty clauses may have the empty clause as a resolvent; this is the case whenever one clause is $\{A\}$ and the other is $\{\neg A\}$ for some atomic formula A.

Intuitively, adding a resolvent of two clauses to a clause set does not strengthen that clause set. This idea is formalized in Lemma 8.7.1.

Lemma 8.7.1. (The Resolution Rule) *Let S be a clause set and let D be a resolvent of two clauses in S. Then S and $S \cup \{D\}$ are equivalent.*

Proof. Let $\mathfrak{A}$ be a truth-assignment appropriate to S. If $\mathfrak{A} \models S \cup \{D\}$ then clearly $\mathfrak{A} \models S$. Now suppose $\mathfrak{A} \models S$ and $D = (C_1 - \{L\}) \cup (C_2 - \{\bar{L}\})$, where $C_1, C_2 \in S$, and L is a literal such that $L \in C_1$ and $\bar{L} \in C_2$. Then $\mathfrak{A} \models D$. For $\mathfrak{A}$ cannot verify both L and $\bar{L}$, so in order for $\mathfrak{A}$ to verify both C_1 and C_2, $\mathfrak{A}$ must verify some literal in either $(C_1 - \{L\})$ or $(C_2 - \{\bar{L}\})$, that is, some literal in D. ∎

To restate the intuitive idea once more, two clauses that have a resolvent are at odds over the truth-value of some atomic formula, in a way that the formation of the resolvent makes explicit.

Note carefully that the resolution rule does *not* state that a clause set is equivalent to the result of adding a resolvent and discarding the clauses from which it was formed. This, in general, is false. For example, $\{\{A, B\}, \{\neg B\}\}$ is not equivalent to $\{\{A\}\}$, since if $\mathfrak{A} \models A$ and $\mathfrak{A} \models B$, then $\mathfrak{A}$ verifies the second clause set but not the first.

By the resolution rule, the operation of adding to a clause set all the resolvents of clauses in that set results in an equivalent clause set. Therefore we define, for any clause set S,

$$R(S) = S \cup \{C\colon C \text{ is a resolvent of two clauses in } S\}.$$

Then $S \equiv R(S)$.

Example 8.7.2

Let

$$S = \{\{A, \neg B, \neg C\}, \{B, D\}, \{\neg A, \neg D\}\}.$$

From the first two clauses, the resolvent $\{A, \neg C, D\}$ is obtained; from the last two, the resolvent $\{\neg A, B\}$ is obtained, and from the first and last, $\{\neg B, \neg C, \neg D\}$ is obtained. Hence

$$R(S) = \{\{A, \neg B, \neg C\}, \{B, D\}, \{\neg A, \neg D\}, \{A, \neg C, D\}, \{\neg A, B\}, \{\neg B, \neg C, \neg D\}\}.$$

Similarly, $R(R(S))$ consists of $R(S)$ and the following clauses.

$\{\neg C, D, \neg D\}$	from $\{\neg A, \neg D\}$ and $\{A, \neg C, \neg D\}$
$\{A, \neg A, \neg C\}$	also from $\{\neg A, \neg D\}$ and $\{A, \neg C, \neg D\}$; or from $\{A, \neg B, \neg C\}$ and $\{\neg A, B\}$
$\{B, \neg B, \neg C\}$	from $\{A, \neg B, \neg C\}$ and $\{\neg A, B\}$
$\{B, \neg C, D\}$	from $\{A, \neg C, D\}$ and $\{\neg A, B\}$
$\{\neg A, \neg C, \neg D\}$	from $\{\neg A, B\}$ and $\{\neg B, \neg C, \neg D\}$

Now let

$$R^0(S) = S$$
$$R^{i+1}(S) = R(R^i(S)) \qquad \text{for each } i \geq 0$$

and let $R^*(S) = \bigcup \{R^i(S): i \geq 0\}$. In other words, $R^*(S)$ is the closure of S under the operation R of adding all resolvents of clauses already present.

Now if S is finite, then since each clause *in* S is also finite, there are only a finite number of clauses that can be formed from the atomic formulas appearing in S. Hence there is only a finite number of resolvents that can ever be formed starting from the clauses in S. So there must be an $i \geq 0$ such that $R^{i+1}(S) = R^i(S)$; then $R^*(S) = R^i(S)$. On the other hand, if S is infinite, then it is quite possible that $R^i(S) \subsetneq R^{i+1}(S)$ for each $i \geq 0$.

Example 8.7.3

Let $S = \{\{A, B\}, \{\neg B, \neg C\}, \{C, \neg D\}\}$. Then $R(S) = S \cup \{\{A, \neg C\}, \{\neg B, \neg D\}\}$; $R^2(S) = R(S) \cup \{\{A, \neg D\}\}$; and $R^3(S) = R^2(S) = R^*(S)$. On the other hand, if $A_0, A_1, \ldots$ are distinct atomic formulas and $S = \{\{\neg A_j, A_{j+1}\}: j = 0, 1, 2, \ldots\}$, then $R^i(S) = \{\{\neg A_j, A_k\}: j + 1 \leq k \leq j + i + 1\}$, and $R^*(S) = \{\{\neg A_j, A_k\}: j + 1 \leq k\}$.

In any case, S and $R^*(S)$ are equivalent. For if $C \in R^*(S)$, then $C \in R^i(S)$ for some i, and $S \equiv R(S) \equiv R^2(S) \equiv \cdots \equiv R^i(S)$.

The main importance of the resolution rule is that its repeated application to finite sets of clauses can be used to determine whether a clause set is satisfiable. Naturally, this provides us with an algorithm for determining whether a formula is satisfiable: put it into conjunctive normal form, and then repeatedly apply resolution to the corresponding set of clauses. The basis for these methods is the following important theorem.

Theorem 8.7.1. (Resolution Theorem) *A clause set S is unsatisfiable if and only if* $\square \in R^*(S)$.

Proof. If $\square \in R^*(S)$, then S is unsatisfiable, since $S \equiv R^*(S)$. The hard part is to show the converse. So assume that S is unsatisfiable. By Theorem 8.6.1, the Compactness Theorem, some finite subset of S is unsatisfiable.

As in the proof of the Compactness Theorem, let us write A_n $(n \geq 1)$ for the atomic formula $\mathbf{AI}^{n-1}\$$; and let us write $\mathcal{C}_n$ $(n \geq 0)$ for the set of all clauses that can be constructed using $A_1, A_2, \ldots, A_n$ alone. In particular, $\mathcal{C}_0 = \{\square\}$. Then there is an $n \geq 0$ such that $S \cap \mathcal{C}_n$, and hence $R^*(S) \cap \mathcal{C}_n$, is unsatisfiable. We prove the following claim by induction on k.

Claim. For each $k = n, n - 1, \ldots, 0$, and each truth-assignment $\mathfrak{a}$ appropriate to $\{A_1, \ldots, A_k\}$, there is some clause C in $R^*(S) \cap \mathcal{C}_k$ such that $\mathfrak{a} \not\models C$.

That is, for every truth-assignment that assigns a truth-value to each of the first k atomic formulas, there is some clause in $R^*(S)$ that contains none but these atomic formulas and is falsified by $\mathcal{A}$. Since the only clause that can be falsified in the case $k = 0$ is $\square$, it follows that $\square \in R^*(S)$.

For $k = n$, the claim is immediate, since any truth-assignment $\mathcal{A}$ violating the claim would verify $R^*(S) \cap \mathcal{C}_n$, which is known to be unsatisfiable.

Now suppose that the claim holds for $k + 1 \leq n$ but fails for k; we derive a contradiction. Then there is some truth-assignment $\mathcal{A}$ appropriate to $\{A_1, \ldots, A_k\}$ such that $\mathcal{A} \models R^*(S) \cap \mathcal{C}_k$. Let $\mathcal{A}_1$ and $\mathcal{A}_2$ be the two truth-assignments that have the same values as $\mathcal{A}$ on the atomic formulas $A_1, \ldots, A_k$, and such that

$$\mathcal{A}_1 \models A_{k+1}$$

$$\mathcal{A}_2 \not\models A_{k+1}.$$

By the induction hypothesis there are clauses $C_1, C_2 \in R^*(S) \cap \mathcal{C}_{k+1}$ such that $\mathcal{A}_1 \not\models C_1$ and $\mathcal{A}_2 \not\models C_2$. Now both C_1 and C_2 must actually contain occurrences of the atomic formula A_{k+1}, since otherwise one of them would be in $R^*(S) \cap \mathcal{C}_k$ and would be falsified by $\mathcal{A}$ as well as $\mathcal{A}_1$ or $\mathcal{A}_2$. In fact, C_1 must contain $\neg A_{k+1}$ as a member but not A_{k+1}, while C_2 must contain A_{k+1} and not $\neg A_{k+1}$; under any other circumstances either $\mathcal{A}_1 \models C_1$ or $\mathcal{A}_2 \models C_2$. But then C_1 and C_2 have a resolvent

$$D = (C_1 - \{\neg A_{k+1}\}) \cup (C_2 - \{A_{k+1}\})$$

which is in $R^*(S) \cap \mathcal{C}_k$: D is in $\mathcal{C}_k$ because all occurrences of A_{k+1} and $\neg A_{k+1}$ are discarded from C_1 and C_2 in forming D, and $D \in R^*(S)$ because it is a resolvent of clauses in $R^*(S)$. Moreover, $\mathcal{A} \not\models D$; for if $\mathcal{A} \models D$, then either $\mathcal{A} \models C_1 - \{\neg A_{k+1}\}$ or $\mathcal{A} \models C_2 - \{A_k\}$, and then either $\mathcal{A}_1 \models C_1$ or $\mathcal{A}_2 \models C_2$. But this is the desired contradiction; we assumed that $\mathcal{A} \models R^*(S) \cap \mathcal{C}_k$, and here we have found a $D \in R^*(S) \cap \mathcal{C}_k$ such that $\mathcal{A} \not\models D$. This completes the induction and the proof of the theorem. ■

The Resolution Theorem can be used for determining satisfiability of individual formulas. The steps of the procedure are as follows.

1. Put the formula into conjunctive normal form.
2. Form a set of clauses by taking the literals in each disjunction as a clause. Call this set S.
3. Form $R(S)$, $R^2(S)$, . . . until $R^i(S) = R^{i+1}(S)$ for some i. This will eventually happen since S is finite.
4. If $\square \in R^i(S)$, then S is unsatisfiable; otherwise S is satisfiable.

This might be called the brute-force approach to resolution. However, one can also attempt slightly greater subtlety. Every clause in $R^i(S)$ has a "family tree" that traces its descent from the clauses in S. For example, the tree in Figure 8–4 shows that $\{\{A, B\}, \{A, \neg B\}, \{\neg A, B\}, \{\neg A, \neg B\}\}$ is unsatisfiable.

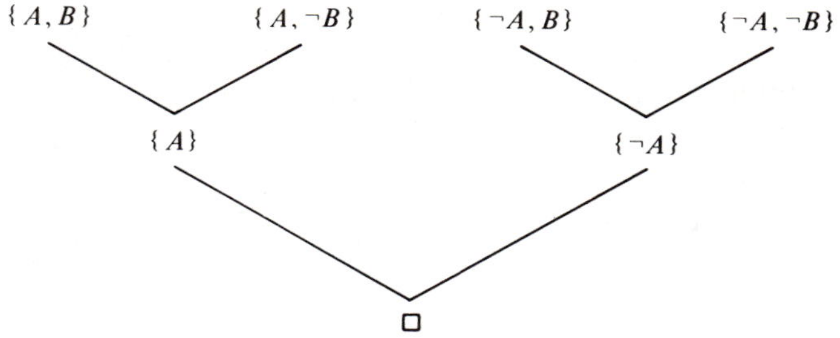

Figure 8–4

So rather than forming all possible resolvents, we can try to form only those needed to produce the empty clause. (For example, the resolvent $\{B\}$ is not needed in this example.) This leads us to the following idea.

Definition 8.7.2

A **deduction** from a clause set S is a sequence of clauses $C_1, \ldots, C_n$ such that each C_i is either a member of S or a resolvent of C_j and C_k for some $j, k < i$. The deduction is said to be a deduction of C_n, the last clause in the sequence.

The Resolution Theorem may then be restated: a set of clauses is unsatisfiable if and only if there is a deduction of the empty clause from it. This formulation is the basis of many computer programs for determining whether formulas of the propositional calculus are satisfiable.

Example 8.7.4

Let $S = \{\{A, B, \neg C\}, \{\neg A\}, \{A, B, C\}, \{A, \neg B\}\}$. One deduction of $\square$ from S is the following.

$C_1 = \{A, B, \neg C\}$	member of S
$C_2 = \{A, B, C\}$	member of S
$C_3 = \{A, \neg B\}$	member of S
$C_4 = \{A, C\}$	resolvent of C_2 and C_3
$C_5 = \{A, B\}$	resolvent of C_1 and C_4
$C_6 = \{A\}$	resolvent of C_3 and C_5
$C_7 = \{\neg A\}$	member of S
$C_8 = \square$	resolvent of C_6 and C_7

This deduction is depicted in Figure 8–5; note that the clause $\{A, \neg B\}$ is used twice.

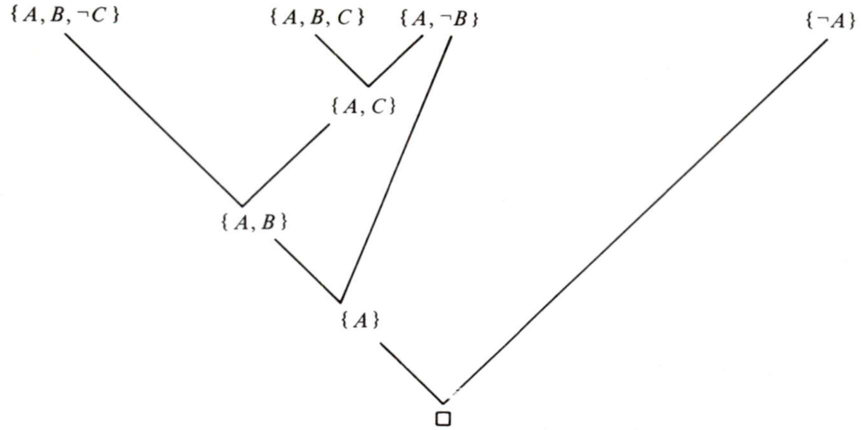

Figure 8–5

Unfortunately, none of the variations on the resolution approach has yet yielded a polynomial-time algorithm for determining satisfiability. The number of clauses generated in an attempt to determine whether $\square \in R^*(S)$ grows exponentially in the original size of S. So while the resolution method is a convenient one for computer implementation, it does not meet the theoretical criteria for efficiency that we established in Chapter 7.

PROBLEMS

8.2.1. Choose some atomic formulas to represent the component subsentences of each of the following sentences, and then render the sentences as formulas of the propositional calculus.

(a) Either he has a rash or he is running a temperature; and he is sick if he is running a temperature, but he is not sick if he has a rash. (*But* should be treated as if it were *and.*)

(b) If Jane is sick and Mary is sick, then they can share a room. But if one is sick and one is not sick, they cannot share a room.

(c) The disease can be treated with penicillin only if the patient is not allergic and has not been sick for more than a week.

(d) One, and only one, of Alice, Ann, and Abigail is a lawyer.

8.2.2. Which of the following are formulas? Draw parse trees of those that are formulas, and explain why those that are not formulas are malformed. (A, B, C, and D are atomic formulas.)

(a) $\neg\neg\neg A$

(b) $\neg B \vee \neg A$

(c) $\neg(B \vee A)$

(d) $(\neg B \rightarrow \neg A)$

(e) $(A \wedge (B \vee (C \wedge A)))$

(f) $\neg(A \vee (B \wedge (C \vee D) \wedge (A \wedge (C \wedge \neg A) \vee (D \vee A)))$

8.2.3. What are the subformulas of each formula?

(a) $((\neg A \vee (\neg B \vee \neg C)) \wedge (B \vee C))$

(b) $\neg(A \vee \neg(A \vee \neg A))$

8.2.4. Prove Lemma 8.2.1. (*Hint:* First show that every formula contains equal numbers of occurrences of left and right parentheses, and that every occurrence of a conjunction or disjunction sign in a formula is preceded by more left parentheses than right. Then show that if there is a formula with two parse trees, the shortest such formula can be written as $(F \between G)$ and as $(F' \between G')$, where F, G, F', and G' are formulas, $F \neq F'$, and $\between$ is in each case a conjunction or disjunction sign. One of F or F' must then be a proper prefix of the other; derive a contradiction.)

8.3.1. Let A, B, and C be atomic formulas and let $\mathfrak{A}$ be a truth-assignment such that $\mathfrak{A}(A) = \mathfrak{A}(B) = \mathfrak{A}(C) = \bot$. Find the truth-values of the following formulas. Show how you found them.

(a) $\neg(A \vee \neg(A \vee \neg B))$

(b) $((A \leftrightarrow \neg B) \rightarrow (C \rightarrow A))$

(c) $(\neg A \rightarrow (\neg B \rightarrow \neg C))$

(d) $((\neg A \wedge \neg B) \rightarrow (\neg A \vee C))$

8.3.2. Prove Rule 6 (for the truth-value of a biconditional).

8.3.3. Many authors do not include the conjunction sign as a symbol in the propositional calculus, but introduce it as an abbreviation, as we have done with $\rightarrow$ and $\leftrightarrow$. Explain carefully why this can be done.

8.3.4. Find a formula F involving the three atomic subformulas A, B, and C with the following property: for any truth-assignment $\mathfrak{A}$: $\{A, B, C\} \rightarrow \{\top, \bot\}$, changing any one of $\mathfrak{A}(A)$, $\mathfrak{A}(B)$, or $\mathfrak{A}(C)$ changes the truth-value of F.

8.4.1. Let $A_1, A_2, \ldots$ be distinct atomic formulas. Give models for each of the following.

(a) $\{(A_i \vee A_{i+1}), (\neg A_i \vee \neg A_{i+1}): i = 1, 2, \ldots\}$

(b) $\{(A_i \vee A_{i+1}), (\neg A_i \vee (\neg A_{i+1} \vee \neg A_{i+2})), (A_i \leftrightarrow A_{i+3}): i = 1, 2, \ldots\}$

(c) $\{\neg A_2, A_3\} \cup \{((A_i \wedge A_j) \leftrightarrow A_{i \cdot j}): i, j = 1, 2, \ldots\}$

8.4.2. Construct truth-tables for the following formulas.

(a) $((A \wedge B) \wedge (\neg B \vee C))$

(b) $(A \longrightarrow (B \vee C))$

(c) $\neg(\neg A \vee \neg(\neg B \vee \neg A))$

(d) $(A \leftrightarrow (B \leftrightarrow C))$

(e) $(A \leftrightarrow (B \leftrightarrow A))$

8.4.3. Show, as succinctly as possible, that the following are tautologies.

(a) $(((A \wedge B) \leftrightarrow A) \longrightarrow B)$

(b) $((A \vee (A \wedge B)) \longrightarrow (A \wedge (A \vee B)))$

(c) $((\neg A \longrightarrow \neg B) \longrightarrow (B \longrightarrow A))$

(d) $(((A \vee B) \wedge (\neg B \vee C)) \longrightarrow (A \vee C))$

8.4.4. Prove, or give a counterexample.

(a) If $(F \longrightarrow G)$ is valid and F is valid, then G is valid.

(b) If $(F \longrightarrow G)$ is satisfiable and F is satisfiable, then G is satisfiable.

(c) If $(F \vee G)$ is satisfiable, then F is satisfiable or G is satisfiable.

(d) If $(F \wedge G)$ is valid, then F is valid and G is valid.

8.4.5. Let $A_1, \ldots, A_n$ be distinct atomic formulas and let $\mathfrak{A}: \{A_1, \ldots, A_n\} \longrightarrow \{\top, \bot\}$ be any truth-assignment. Show that there is a formula F such that for any truth-assignment $\mathfrak{B}: \{A_1, \ldots, A_n\} \longrightarrow \{\top, \bot\}$, $\mathfrak{B} \models F$ if and only if $\mathfrak{A} = \mathfrak{B}$.

8.4.6. Suppose that the propositional calculus had been defined, not with the three logical connectives $\vee$, $\wedge$, $\neg$, but with $\leftrightarrow$, $\oplus$, and $\neg$ as logical connectives, where for any formulas F and G and any truth-assignment appropriate to them,

$$\mathfrak{A}((F \oplus G)) = \begin{cases} \top & \text{if } \mathfrak{A}(F) \neq \mathfrak{A}(G) \\ \bot & \text{otherwise.} \end{cases}$$

Show that for formulas with these connectives, there is a polynomial-time decision procedure for satisfiability.

8.5.1. Complete the proof of Theorem 8.5.1 in Cases (ii) and (iii).

8.5.2. Show that if $(F \leftrightarrow G)$ is a tautology, then $F \equiv G$.

8.5.3. Prove each of the following for any formulas F, G, and H.

(a) $(F \vee (G \wedge H)) \equiv ((F \vee G) \wedge (F \vee H))$
(b) $\neg(F \vee G) \equiv (\neg F \wedge \neg G)$
(c) $(F \vee G) \equiv G$, if F is unsatisfiable.
(d) $(F \wedge (F \vee G)) \equiv F$

8.5.4. Is it true that $(F \leftrightarrow (G \leftrightarrow H)) \equiv ((F \leftrightarrow G) \leftrightarrow H)$? Prove it or give a counterexample.

8.5.5. Prove Theorem 8.5.3.

8.5.6. (a) Convert to disjunctive normal form.
(i) $((A \vee B) \wedge (C \vee D))$
(ii) $\neg((A \vee B) \rightarrow C)$
(b) Convert to conjunctive normal form.
(i) $((A \vee B) \rightarrow (C \wedge D))$
(ii) $(A \vee (\neg B \wedge (C \vee (\neg D \wedge E))))$.

8.5.7. Prove: If F is a formula with n atomic subformulas, and there are k truth-assignments on these atomic formulas which verify F ($k > 0$), then there is a disjunctive normal form of F which is a disjunction of exactly k conjunctions of literals.

8.5.8. Show that there is a sequence of formulas $F_1, F_2, \ldots$ with the following properties: there is a k such that for every n, F_n has at most kn occurrences of logical connectives; but for every n, no disjunctive normal form of F_n has fewer than 2^n occurrences of logical connectives.

8.5.9. If a formula is in disjunctive normal form, there is an easy way to tell whether it is satisfiable. What is this procedure?

8.5.10. (a) Show that the following is a polynomial-time transformation which yields, for any formula F, a formula G in conjunctive normal form that is satisfiable if and only if F is satisfiable. (You must show how to obtain a truth-assignment verifying G from any verifying F, and vice versa.) Let $F_1, \ldots, F_n$ be the subformulas of F, with $F_n = F$. Let $A_1, \ldots, A_n$ be distinct atomic formulas. Let G be the conjunction of A_n and conjunctive normal forms of all of the following formulas:

$((A_i \vee A_j) \leftrightarrow A_k)$ whenever F_k is $(F_i \vee F_j)$;
$((A_i \wedge A_j) \leftrightarrow A_k)$ whenever F_k is $(F_i \wedge F_j)$;
$(\neg A_i \leftrightarrow A_k)$ whenever F_k is $\neg F_i$.

(b) Would you expect that it might be possible in the same way to transform any formula F quickly into *disjunctive* normal form in such a way as to preserve satisfiability?

8.5.11. Suppose that, instead of building the propositional calculus around the three logical connectives $\vee$, $\wedge$, $\neg$, we had instead used the single logical connective $|$, where the rule for finding the truth-value of a formula involving $|$ is

$$\mathcal{A}((F\,|\,G)) = \begin{cases} \top & \text{if } \mathcal{A}(F) = \bot \text{ and } \mathcal{A}(G) = \bot \\ \bot & \text{otherwise.} \end{cases}$$

(a) Show that $\wedge$, $\vee$, and $\neg$ can then be introduced by definition; that is, if A and B are distinct atomic formulas, then there are formulas involving $|$ alone equivalent to $(A \vee B)$, $(A \wedge B)$, and $\neg A$.

(b) If the definitions of Part (a) are used to rewrite arbitrary formulas as formulas involving $|$ alone, might the translation of a formula grow exponentially, as a function of its original length? If so, can you come up with alternative definitions of $\wedge$, $\vee$, and $\neg$ in terms of $|$ that avoid exponential growth?

8.5.12. Let $F = ((A \wedge B) \vee (B \wedge C) \vee (A \wedge C))$. Show that $\neg F \equiv ((\neg A \wedge \neg B) \vee (\neg B \wedge \neg C) \vee (\neg A \wedge \neg C))$.

8.6.1. Let $S = \{((A_i \wedge A_{i+1}) \vee (A_{i+1} \wedge A_{i+2}) \vee (A_{i+2} \wedge A_{i+3})) : i = 1, 2, \ldots\}$. For $i = 1, 2, \ldots$, define a truth-assignment $\mathcal{A}: \{A_1, A_2, \ldots\} \rightarrow \{\top, \bot\}$ by

$$\mathcal{A}_i \models A_j \quad \text{if and only if} \quad j \leq i \text{ and } i \not\equiv j \pmod 3.$$

(Here $i \not\equiv j \pmod 3$ means that the remainders are different when i and j are divided by 3.) Show that $\mathcal{A}_n \models S \cap \mathcal{S}_n$ for each n. Then construct from the $\mathcal{A}_i$ a truth-assignment verifying S by the method of the proof of Theorem 8.6.1.

8.6.2. Show that if L is an infinite language (over a finite alphabet), then there is an infinite set of distinct strings in L, say $w_1, w_2, \ldots$, such that w_i is a prefix of w_{i+1} for $i = 1, 2, \ldots$.

8.6.3. An undirected graph, finite or infinite, is said to be k-**colorable** if and only if there is a function c from the nodes to $\{1, \ldots, k\}$ (the "colors") such that $c(u) \neq c(v)$ whenever there is an edge connecting u and v. Show that if every *finite* subgraph of a graph is k-colorable, then so is the entire graph. (A subgraph of a graph G is a subset of the nodes of G together with those edges of G that join nodes in the subset.) (*Hint:* Construct, for each finite subgraph of the given infinite graph, a formula that is satisfiable if and only if that subgraph is k-colorable. A typical atomic subformula is to be interpreted as true if and only if a particular node has a particular color.)

8.6.4. Show that there is a tiling by a given tiling system if and only if there are $n \times n$ tilings for every n.

8.7.1. Rewrite as clause sets.

(a) $(A \wedge B)$

(b) $(A \vee B)$

(c) $\neg(A \wedge B \wedge \neg C)$

(d) $((A \wedge \neg B \wedge C) \vee (\neg A \wedge B \wedge \neg C))$

(e) $(A \leftrightarrow (\neg B \wedge \neg C))$

8.7.2. Which of the following clause sets are satisfiable? Give models of those that are, and explain why those that are not satisfiable, are not.

(a) $\{\{A, B\}, \{\neg A, \neg B\}, \{\neg A, B\}\}$

(b) $\{\{\neg A\}, \{A, \neg B\}, \{B\}\}$

(c) $\{\{A\}, \square\}$

(d) $\{\square\}$

(e) $\{\{A_i, A_{i+1}\}, \{\neg A_i, \neg A_{i+1}\}: i = 1, 2, \ldots\}$

(f) $\{\{A_1\}, \{\neg A_1, \neg A_2\}, \{A_1, A_2, A_3\}, \{\neg A_1, \neg A_2, \neg A_3, \neg A_4\}, \ldots\}$

8.7.3. Find all resolvents of these pairs of clauses.

(a) $\{A, B\}, \{\neg A, \neg B\}$

(b) $\{A, \neg B\}, \{B, C, D\}$

(c) $\{\neg A, B, \neg C\}, \{B, C\}$

(d) $\{A, \neg A\}, \{A, \neg A\}$

8.7.4. Find $R(S)$ for these clause sets S.

(a) $\{\{A, \neg B\}, \{A, B\}, \{\neg A\}\}$

(b) $\{\{A, B, C\}, \{\neg B, \neg C\}, \{\neg A, \neg C\}\}$

(c) $\{\{\neg A, \neg B\}, \{B, C\}, \{\neg C, A\}\}$

(d) $\{\{A\}, \{B\}, \{A, B\}\}$

(e) $\{\{\neg A\}, \{A, B, \neg C\}, \{C, \neg A\}\}$

8.7.5. Find deductions of the empty clause from each of the following clause sets.

(a) $\{\{A, \neg B, C\}, \{B, C\}, \{\neg A, C\}, \{B, \neg C\}, \{\neg B\}\}$

(b) $\{\{A, \neg B\}, \{A, C\}, \{\neg B, C\}, \{\neg A, B\}, \{B, \neg C\}, \{\neg A, \neg C\}\}$

(c) $\{\{\neg A\}, \{A, B\}, \{A, C\}, \{\neg B, \neg C, A\}\}$

(d) $\{\{\neg A, B\}, \{\neg B, C\}, \{\neg C, A\}, \{A, B, C\}, \{\neg A, \neg B, \neg C\}\}$

8.7.6. Use resolution to show that each of these formulas is unsatisfiable.

(a) $((A \leftrightarrow (B \rightarrow C)) \wedge (A \leftrightarrow B) \wedge (A \leftrightarrow \neg C))$

(b) $\neg(((A \rightarrow B) \rightarrow \neg B) \rightarrow \neg B)$

(c) $(((A \wedge B) \vee (A \wedge C) \vee (B \wedge C)) \vee ((\neg A \wedge \neg B) \vee (\neg A \wedge \neg C) \vee (\neg B \wedge \neg C)))$

8.7.7. A clause is called a **tautology** if it contains both A and $\neg A$ for some atomic formula A. Define $R_0(S) = S \cup \{C\colon C$ is a resolvent of two clauses in S, neither of which is a tautology$\}$. Define $R_0^0(S) = S$; $R_0^{i+1}(S) = R_0(R_0^i(S))$ for each $i \geq 0$; $R_0^*(S) = \bigcup \{R_0^i(S)\colon i \geq 0\}$. Show that S is unsatisfiable if and only if $\square \in R_0^*(S)$.

8.7.8. Clause C_1 **subsumes** clause C_2 if $C_1 \subsetneqq C_2$. Define $R_1(S) = R(S) - \{C\colon C$ is subsumed by some clause in $R(S)\}$. As before, define $R_1^0(S) = S$; $R_1^{i+1}(S) = R_1(R_1^i(S))$ for each $i \geq 0$; $R_1^*(S) = \bigcup \{R_1^i(S)\colon i \geq 0\}$. Show that S is unsatisfiable if and only if $\square \in R_1^*(S)$.

8.7.9. Consider finite clause sets S such that $|C| \leq 2$ for each $C \in S$. Show that the resolution method provides a polynomial-time decision procedure for satisfiability for such clause sets.

8.7.10. Let $\circledless$ be any partial ordering of the set of all atomic formulas; and also say that two literals are related by $\circledless$ if their atomic subformulas are related by $\circledless$. For any clause set S, let $R_2(S) = S \cup \{C\colon C = (C_1 - \{L\}) \cup (C_2 - \{\bar{L}\})$ for some clauses $C_1, C_2 \in S$ and some literal L such that $L \in C_1$, $\bar{L} \in C_2$, and $L \circledless L'$ for no literal $L' \in C\}$. Let $R_2^0(S) = S$, $R_2^{i+1}(S) = R_2(R_2^i(S))$ for $i \geq 0$, and $R_2^*(S) = \bigcup \{R_2^i(S)\colon i \geq 0\}$. Show that S is unsatisfiable if and only if $\square \in R_2^*(S)$.

8.7.11. For any clause set S, let $R_3(S) = \{C\colon C$ is a resolvent of two clauses in $S\}$. Define $R_3^0(S) = S$, $R_3^{i+1}(S) = R_3(R_3^i(S))$ for $i \geq 0$, $R_3^*(S) = \bigcup \{R_3^i(S)\colon i \geq 0\}$. Give an example of an unsatisfiable clause set S such that $\square \notin R_3^*(S)$.

8.7.12. Give a natural definition of the resolvent of *any number* of clauses (not just two), and prove an analogue of Lemma 8.7.1 (the Resolution Rule).

8.7.13. Let $R_4(S) = S \cup \{C\colon C$ is a resolvent of two clauses in S, one of which is a singleton (contains only one literal)$\}$. Define $R_4^*(S)$ in the usual way. If $T \subseteq S$, let $R_5(S, T) = S \cup \{C\colon C$ is a resolvent of a clause in T and a clause in $S\}$. Define $R_5^0(S) = S$, $R_5^{i+1}(S) = R_5(R_5^i(S), S)$, $R_5^*(S) = \bigcup \{R_5^i(S)\colon i \geq 0\}$. Show that $\square \in R_4^*(S)$ if and only if $\square \in R_5^*(S)$. (*Hint:* Proceed by induction on $|S|$.)

8.7.14. A **Horn formula** is a formula in conjunctive normal form such that in each conjunct, at most one disjunct is an atomic formula (rather than the negation of an atomic formula). Show that there is a polynomial-time decision procedure for satisfiability of Horn formulas.

REFERENCES

The References section at the end of Chapter 9 includes references for both Chapters 8 and 9.

CHAPTER 9

THE PREDICATE CALCULUS

9.1 THE PREDICATE CALCULUS: SYNTAX

As a language for stating mathematical ideas, the propositional calculus is severely limited. For one thing, there is no direct way to talk about individual objects, and therefore no way to assert that objects stand in certain relations to each other; every assertion about an object must be rendered as a separate atomic formula. For another, there is no way of making an assertion in a single formula that covers an infinite set of similar cases: the language is essentially finite in its expressive power.

In the predicate calculus we can make general statements about all objects in a fixed set, called the **universe**. On one level, formulas of the predicate calculus resemble those of the propositional calculus: They are built up from atomic formulas by means of logical connectives. However, the language is richer in two important respects. First, the atomic formulas are themselves constructed out of *names for relations* and *names for individual objects* in the universe. For example, Pxy is an atomic formula; it states that a certain binary relation, denoted by P, holds for the pair of objects (x, y). Here P is called a **predicate sign** and x and y are called **variables**. Second, there are two special symbols $\forall$ and $\exists$, called the **universal** and **existential quantifiers**, respectively.

These symbols are used for converting statements about particular objects, denoted by variables, into general statements about all the objects in the universe. For example, $\forall x \forall y Pxy$ states that whatever x and y are, the relation P holds of the pair (x, y); this formula would be read, "For all x and y, Pxy." On the other hand, $\forall x \exists y Pxy$ states that for any x in the universe, there is some y in the universe such that P holds for (x, y); in words, "For all x, there is a y such that Pxy." To take two more simple examples, $\forall x \forall y(Pxy \leftrightarrow Pyx)$ states that P is a symmetric relation: for any x and y, P holds for (x, y) if and only if P holds for (y, x). And $\exists x \neg Pxx$ states that P is not reflexive: there is at least one x such that P does not hold for (x, x).

In addition to the predicate signs—such as P in the examples just given—and variables—such as x and y in the examples—the predicate calculus also has signs that stand for functions. Thus if f is a function sign denoting a binary function, then $f(xy)$, where x and y are variables, names an object in the universe, specifically the value of the function denoted by f on the pair of objects named by x and y. (The comma is not a symbol of the predicate calculus; we design the language to make it unnecessary to separate by commas the arguments of a function.) To take another simple example, $\forall x \forall y Pf(xy)f(yf(yx))$ is a legal formula; thus occurrences of function signs can be nested.

One important characteristic of relations is that every object that belongs to a relation is a k-tuple for the same value of k. Similarly, the domain of a function is a set of k-tuples for some fixed value of k. These regularities must be maintained in the predicate calculus: for example, a formula cannot use a function sign in one place with one argument, and elsewhere with two arguments. To ensure that such inconsistencies do not arise, every function sign and every predicate sign is fixed, once and for all, to have a particular number of argument places; it can be used in a formula only with that number of arguments.

In the propositional calculus, individual formulas turn out to be true or false in a way that depends on the interpretations of the atomic formulas. The same holds for the predicate calculus, only now predicate and function signs must be interpreted. We shall have much more to say about this idea in the next section; for now, we content ourselves with a few simple examples. Naturally, $\exists x \neg Pxx$ is true if and only if the predicate sign P is interpreted as a binary relation that is not reflexive. If P, Q, and R are predicate signs standing for 1-place relations, then $\forall x(Px \vee Qx \vee Rx)$ states that one of the three properties denoted by P, Q, and R must hold of every object in the universe; this might be the rendition, in the predicate calculus, of the statement "Every Latin noun is masculine, feminine, or neuter." The formula $(\forall x(Px \vee Qx) \wedge \exists y(\neg Py \wedge \neg Qy))$ must be regarded as invariably false, no matter what relations P and Q represent; the first half says that each object has either property P or property Q, while the second half says that something has neither property. On the other hand, $(\forall x(Px \vee Qx) \wedge \exists y \neg Py \wedge \exists z \neg Qz)$ is true under some interpretations, but not others. For example, if the universe consists of the natural numbers, and if Px states that a number is even and Qx states that the number is odd, then the formula comes out true: every number is either even or odd, but some numbers are not even and some are not odd.

Now let us focus more specifically on the syntax of the language. There are infinitely many predicate signs, function signs, and variables in the predicate calculus. However, as we did for the atomic formulas of the propositional calculus, we construe these signs as strings over a fixed finite alphabet. In fact, the formulas of the predicate calculus comprise a context-free language. However, it is not too enlightening to write a context-free grammar that generates this set of formulas, so we instead define the language in English.

Definition 9.1.1

(a) The symbols of the predicate calculus are the following:

P	used for forming predicate signs
v	used for forming variables
f	used for forming function signs
I	used for forming numerals in unary notation
$	used as a separator and endmarker
$\wedge$, $\vee$, $\neg$	logical connectives
$\forall$, $\exists$	quantifiers
(,)	parentheses

(b) For each $n \geq 0$, $\mathbf{vI}^n\$$ is a **variable**.

(c) For each $n \geq 0$ and $m \geq 0$, $\mathbf{PI}^n\$\mathbf{I}^m\$$ is an ***n*-place predicate sign**.

(d) For each $n \geq 0$ and $m \geq 0$, $\mathbf{fI}^n\$\mathbf{I}^m\$$ is an ***n*-place function sign**.

(e) **Terms** are defined inductively as follows.

(i) Every variable is a term.

(ii) If f is an n-place function sign and $t_1, \ldots, t_n$ are terms, then $f(t_1 \ldots t_n)$ is a term.

(f) **Atomic formulas** are defined as follows.

If P is an n-place predicate sign and $t_1, \ldots, t_n$ are terms, then $Pt_1 \ldots t_n$ is an atomic formula.

(g) **Formulas** are defined as follows.

(i) Atomic formulas are formulas.

(ii) If F and G are formulas, then so are $(F \vee G)$, $(F \wedge G)$, and $\neg F$.

(iii) If F is a formula and x is a variable, then $\forall x F$ and $\exists x F$ are formulas.

Just as we rarely wrote an atomic formula of the propositional calculus in full—as, for example, **AII$**—we shall rarely write predicate signs, function signs, or variables in full. Instead, we use letters such as P and Q to stand for predicate signs, f and g to stand for function signs, and x and y to stand for variables. Bear in mind, however, that these are simply the names of certain strings that are actually several symbols in length.

A 0-place function sign stands for a particular element in the universe, so we call such function signs **constant signs**. Instead of using the abbreviations f, g, and so on, for constant signs, we use a, b, and c; moreover, we omit the empty pair of parentheses which should, according to Definition 9.1.1(e), follow them when they are used in the construction of terms. In sum, then, we might write the term whose function sign is **fII** simply as a or b, rather than $f(\,)$ or $g(\,)$.

Example 9.1.1

- Let x be the variable **vII$** and y the variable **v$**.
- Let P be the 1-place predicate sign **PIIII** and Q the 2-place predicate sign **PIII**.
- Let f be the 2-place function sign **fII$$** and c the constant sign **fII**.
- Then the following are terms:

$f(xy)$	in full:	**fII$$(vIIv)**
c	in full:	**fII( )**
$f(cf(yy))$	in full:	**fII$$(fII( )fII$$(vv))**.

- The following are formulas:

Qxy	in full:	**PIIIvIIv**
$\neg\forall xPf(cx)$	in full:	**¬∀vIIPIIII$fII$$(fII( )vII$)**

Let us now state the essential properties of the language of the predicate calculus.

Lemma 9.1.1. *Every formula of the predicate calculus can be constructed, by means of the rules in Definition 9.1.1, in one and only one way.*

We do not prove this lemma; instead, we leave as an exercise (Problem 9.1.5) the stronger fact that the set of formulas of the predicate calculus is generated by an unambiguous context-free grammar. But let us note one or two of the more important features of the language that contribute to this "unique readability." No variable, function sign, or predicate sign is a proper substring of any other, so any occurrence of the symbol **v**, **P**, or **f** in a formula begins a variable, function sign, or predicate sign which is ended by a uniquely determined occurrence of $. Likewise, no proper substring of an atomic formula is an atomic formula, since each predicate symbol must be followed by a particular number of terms, and there can be no ambiguity about where those terms begin or end.

One further property that will prove convenient is that there can be no "chance combinations" of symbols in a formula to form variables, predicate signs, or function signs that are not part of the unique decomposition of that formula according to Lemma 9.1.1. So a phrase such as "the set of predicate letters appearing in the formula F" means exactly the same thing as "the set of predicate letters used in the construction of F by the process described in Definition 9.1.1."

Just as in the propositional calculus, we call $(F \vee G)$ the **disjunction** of F and G, $(F \wedge G)$ the **conjunction** of F and G, and $\neg F$ the **negation** of F. We also call $\forall x F$ and $\exists x F$ the **universal** and **existential quantification**, respectively, of F with respect to the variable x.

We introduce the notions of the **conditional** and **biconditional** of two formulas just as was done for the propositional calculus; $(F \longrightarrow G)$ is an abbreviation for $(\neg F \vee G)$, and $(F \longleftrightarrow G)$ is an abbreviation for $((F \longrightarrow G) \wedge (G \longrightarrow F))$.

A **subformula** of a formula is a substring of that formula which is itself a formula. Once again, the language has been so designed that the subformulas of a formula are exactly those formulas that partake in the uniquely determined construction of the formula as specified in Definition 9.1.1 and Lemma 9.1.1. To put it another way, the subformulas of a formula are

1. the formula itself; and
2. if the formula is $(F \vee G)$ or $(F \wedge G)$ for some formulas F and G, the subformulas of F and the subformulas of G; and
3. if the formula is $\neg F$ for some formula F or $\forall x F$ or $\exists x F$ for some variable x and some formula F, the subformulas of F.

Example 9.1.2

The following is a list of all subformulas of $\neg(\forall x Pxy \vee (\exists x Qx \wedge \exists x \neg Qx))$.

$$\neg(\forall x Pxy \vee (\exists x Qx \wedge \exists x \neg Qx))$$
$$(\forall x Pxy \vee (\exists x Qx \wedge \exists x \neg Qx))$$
$$\forall x Pxy$$
$$(\exists x Qx \wedge \exists x \neg Qx)$$
$$Pxy$$
$$\exists x Qx$$
$$\exists x \neg Qx$$
$$\neg Qx$$
$$Qx$$

Here, of course, P must be a 2-place predicate sign and Q a 1-place predicate sign.

Another syntactic notion for the predicate calculus is that of the **scope** of an occurrence of the negation sign or a quantifier in a formula. Any such occurrence in a formula F refers to or embraces a particular subformula of F. Formally, this notion is justified by Lemma 9.1.1. The scope of an occurrence of $\neg$ in F is that uniquely determined subformula G such that the occurrence of $\neg$ is the leftmost symbol of $\neg G$. Similarly, the scope of an occurrence of $\forall$ or $\exists$ is that formula G such that, for some variable x, the occurrence of $\forall$ or $\exists$ is the leftmost symbol of $\forall x G$ or $\exists x G$. In Example 9.1.2, the scope of the first occurrence of $\neg$ is $(\forall x Pxy \vee (\exists x Qx \wedge \exists x \neg Qx))$; the scope of the second occurrence of $\neg$ is Qx; the scope of the (only) occurrence of $\forall$ is Pxy; the scope of the first occurrence of $\exists$ is Qx; and the scope of the second occurrence of $\exists$ is $\neg Qx$.

Finally, the **matrix** of a formula is the result of deleting all occurrences of quantifiers and the occurrences of variables immediately following those occurrences of quantifiers. It is easily seen that the result of this process is indeed a formula. For example, the matrix of the formula in Example 9.1.2 is $\neg(Pxy \vee (Qx \wedge \neg Qx))$.

9.2 STRUCTURES AND SATISFIABILITY

A formula of the propositional calculus is "brought to life" by specifying a truth-assignment that gives a truth-value to each atomic subformula. For the predicate calculus, the task is somewhat more complicated. To determine whether a formula is true or false, we must have interpretations for the predicate and function signs as relations and functions, respectively. We may also have to have interpretations for some of the variables as particular objects. But let us start with the predicate and function signs.

Definition 9.2.1

A **structure** is a pair $\mathfrak{A} = ([\mathfrak{A}], \mathcal{I}_{\mathfrak{A}})$, where $[\mathfrak{A}]$ is any nonempty set called the **universe** of $\mathfrak{A}$ and $\mathcal{I}_{\mathfrak{A}}$ is a function having as its domain a set of predicate and function signs. Specifically,

- if P is an n-place predicate sign in the domain of $\mathcal{I}_{\mathfrak{A}}$, then $\mathcal{I}_{\mathfrak{A}}(P)$ is an n-ary relation on $[\mathfrak{A}]$, that is, a subset of $[\mathfrak{A}]^n$;
- if f is an n-place function sign in the domain of $\mathcal{I}_{\mathfrak{A}}$, then $\mathcal{I}_{\mathfrak{A}}(f)$ is a function from $[\mathfrak{A}]^n$ to $[\mathfrak{A}]$.

For $\mathcal{I}_{\mathfrak{A}}(P)$ we also write $P^{\mathfrak{A}}$ and for $\mathcal{I}_{\mathfrak{A}}(f)$ we write $f^{\mathfrak{A}}$. Moreover, in case the domain of $\mathcal{I}_{\mathfrak{A}}$ is finite, say $\{P_1, \ldots, P_m, f_1, \ldots, f_n\}$, we may write $\mathfrak{A}$ as the $(m + n + 1)$-tuple $([\mathcal{A}], P_1^{\mathcal{A}}, \ldots, P_m^{\mathcal{A}}, f_1^{\mathcal{A}}, \ldots, f_n^{\mathcal{A}})$. Note, however, that this form of expression is somewhat imprecise, since it does not explicitly indicate which predicate or function sign is associated with which relation or function. Nevertheless it is convenient when confusion cannot arise.

If $\mathcal{A}$ is a structure and F is a formula such that each predicate letter and function sign of F is assigned a value by $\mathcal{I}_{\mathcal{A}}$, then $\mathcal{A}$ is said to be **appropriate** to F.

Example 9.2.1

Let P be a 2-place predicate sign and f be a 1-place function sign, and let F be the formula $\forall x Pxf(x)$. Then $\mathcal{A} = ([\mathcal{A}], P^{\mathcal{A}}, f^{\mathcal{A}})$ is a structure appropriate to F, where

$[\mathcal{A}] = \mathbb{N}$,

$P^{\mathcal{A}} = \{(m, n): m, n \in \mathbb{N}, m < n\}$,

$f^{\mathcal{A}}$ is the successor function: $f(n) = n + 1$ for each $n \in \mathbb{N}$.

Also, $\mathcal{B}$ is a structure appropriate to F, where

$[\mathcal{B}] = \mathbb{N}$,

$P^{\mathcal{B}} = \{(m, n): m, n \in \mathbb{N}, n < m\}$,

$f^{\mathcal{B}}$ is the successor function.

We regard F as true in the structure $\mathcal{A}$ since every number is less than its successor, whereas F is false in $\mathcal{B}$. On the other hand, the opposite holds for $G = \forall x \exists y Pyx$, to which the structures $\mathcal{A}$ and $\mathcal{B}$ are also appropriate. Finally, the formula $Pxf(y)$ cannot immediately be considered true or false in either structure; we must first know what x and y are. Our next task is to formalize these ideas.

Definition 9.2.2

Let F be a formula and $\mathcal{A}$ a structure appropriate to F. If ξ is a function with a domain that includes all the variables of F and with a range that is a subset of $[\mathcal{A}]$, then ξ is said to be **appropriate** to F and $\mathcal{A}$. For each such F, $\mathcal{A}$, and ξ, and for each term t or formula G that can be constructed by using the variables, predicate signs, and function signs of F, we define a value $\mathcal{A}(t)_\xi$ in $[\mathcal{A}]$ or $\mathcal{A}(G)_\xi$ in $\{\top, \bot\}$ as follows.

1. (a) If x is a variable of F, then $\mathcal{A}(x)_\xi = \xi(x)$.
   (b) If $t_1, \ldots, t_n$ are terms and f is an n-place function sign of F, then

$$\mathcal{A}(f(t_1 \ldots t_n))_\xi = f^{\mathcal{A}}(\mathcal{A}(t_1)_\xi, \ldots, \mathcal{A}(t_n)_\xi);$$

that is, $\mathcal{A}(f(t_1 \ldots t_n))_\xi$ is calculated by first finding

$\mathfrak{A}(t_1)_\xi, \ldots, \mathfrak{A}(t_n)_\xi$, which are members of $[\mathfrak{A}]$, and then applying to these values the function $f^{\mathfrak{A}}: [\mathfrak{A}]^n \longrightarrow [\mathfrak{A}]$.

Before proceeding, we need one auxiliary definition. If ξ is a function of the sort described, and x is a variable of F and a is a member of $[\mathfrak{A}]$, then $\xi[x/a]$ is the function ξ' that is identical to ξ except that $\xi'(x) = a$ (whatever $\xi(x)$ might be). With this notation, we can define the value of $\mathfrak{A}(G)_\xi$ by cases, depending on whether G is atomic, or is a disjunction, conjunction, negation, or universal or existential quantification of one or two subformulas.

2. (a) If $t_1, \ldots, t_n$ are terms and P is an n-place predicate sign of F, then

$$\mathfrak{A}(Pt_1 \ldots t_n)_\xi = \begin{cases} \top & \text{if } (\mathfrak{A}(t_1)_\xi, \ldots, \mathfrak{A}(t_n)_\xi) \in P^{\mathfrak{A}} \\ \bot & \text{otherwise.} \end{cases}$$

(b) $$\mathfrak{A}((G \vee H))_\xi = \begin{cases} \top & \text{if } \mathfrak{A}(G)_\xi = \top \text{ or } \mathfrak{A}(H)_\xi = \top \\ \bot & \text{otherwise.} \end{cases}$$

(c) $$\mathfrak{A}((G \wedge H))_\xi = \begin{cases} \top & \text{if } \mathfrak{A}(G)_\xi = \top \text{ and } \mathfrak{A}(H)_\xi = \top \\ \bot & \text{otherwise.} \end{cases}$$

(d) $$\mathfrak{A}(\neg G)_\xi = \begin{cases} \top & \text{if } \mathfrak{A}(G)_\xi = \bot \\ \bot & \text{otherwise.} \end{cases}$$

(e) $$\mathfrak{A}(\forall x G)_\xi = \begin{cases} \top & \text{if } \mathfrak{A}(G)_{\xi[x/a]} = \top \text{ for each } a \in [\mathfrak{A}] \\ \bot & \text{otherwise.} \end{cases}$$

(f) $$\mathfrak{A}(\exists x G)_\xi = \begin{cases} \top & \text{if } \mathfrak{A}(G)_{\xi[x/a]} = \top \text{ for some } a \in [\mathfrak{A}] \\ \bot & \text{otherwise.} \end{cases}$$

Finally, we write $\mathfrak{A} \models_\xi G$ if and only if $\mathfrak{A}(G)_\xi = \top$.

The subcases of (2) other than (a), (e), and (f) are similar to those for the propositional calculus. Case (a) says that to determine $\mathfrak{A}(Pt_1 \ldots t_n)_\xi$, find the values $\mathfrak{A}(t_1)_\xi, \ldots, \mathfrak{A}(t_n)_\xi$, all of which are in $[\mathfrak{A}]$, and then see whether that n-tuple is in the relation $P^{\mathfrak{A}}$. Case (e) says that $\mathfrak{A}(\forall xG)_\xi$ is to be $\top$ if and only if $\mathfrak{A}(G)_{\xi'}$ is $\top$ for every function ξ' identical to ξ except, possibly, for its value on x. Case (f) is similar, except that $\mathfrak{A}(G)_{\xi'}$ need be $\top$ for only one such ξ'.

Example 9.2.2

Consider again the structure $\mathfrak{A}$ of Example 9.2.1. First consider $Pxf(y)$, and let ξ be the function from $\{x, y\}$ to $\mathbb{N} = [\mathfrak{A}]$ such that

$$\xi(x) = 5$$
$$\xi(y) = 7.$$

Then $\mathfrak{A}(y)_\xi = \xi(y) = 7$, and $\mathfrak{A}(f(y))_\xi = f^{\mathfrak{A}}(\mathfrak{A}(y)_\xi) = f^{\mathfrak{A}}(7) = 7 + 1 = 8$. Next, $\mathfrak{A}(Pxf(y))_\xi = \top$ if and only if $(\mathfrak{A}(x)_\xi, \mathfrak{A}(f(y))_\xi) \in P^{\mathfrak{A}}$, that is, if and only if $(5, 8) \in P^{\mathfrak{A}}$; since this is the case, $\mathfrak{A} \models_\xi Pxf(y)$.

Now consider $\forall xPxf(x)$. By 2(e), $\mathfrak{A}(\forall xPxf(x))_\xi = \top$ if and only if $\mathfrak{A}(Pxf(x))_{\xi[x/a]} = \top$ for each $a \in \mathbb{N}$. Now $\mathfrak{A}(Pxf(x))_{\xi[x/a]} = \top$ if and only if $(\mathfrak{A}(x)_{\xi[x/a]}, \mathfrak{A}(f(x))_{\xi[x/a]}) \in P^{\mathfrak{A}}$. But $\mathfrak{A}(x)_{\xi[x/a]} = a$, and $\mathfrak{A}(f(x))_{\xi[x/a]} = f^{\mathfrak{A}}(\mathfrak{A}(x)_{\xi[x/a]}) = f^{\mathfrak{A}}(a) = a + 1$. Since $(a, a+1) \in P^{\mathfrak{A}}$ for each $a \in \mathbb{N}$, $\mathfrak{A} \models_\xi \forall xPxf(x)$.

Finally, consider $\forall x\exists yPyx$. Again, $\mathfrak{A}(\forall x\exists yPyx)_\xi = \top$ if and only if $\mathfrak{A}(\exists yPyx)_{\xi[x/a]} = \top$ for each $a \in \mathbb{N}$. In turn, $\mathfrak{A}(\exists yPyx)_{\xi[x/a]} = \top$ if and only if $\mathfrak{A}(Pyx)_{\xi[x/a][y/b]} = \top$ for some $b \in \mathbb{N}$. And $\mathfrak{A}(Pyx)_{\xi[x/a][y/b]} = \top$ if and only if $(\mathfrak{A}(y)_{\xi[x/a][y/b]}, \mathfrak{A}(x)_{\xi[x/a][y/b]}) \in P^{\mathfrak{A}}$. Now $\mathfrak{A}(y)_{\xi[x/a][y/b]} = b$ and $\mathfrak{A}(x)_{\xi[x/a][y/b]} = a$, so $\mathfrak{A}(\forall x\exists yPyx) = \top$ if and only if, for each $a \in \mathbb{N}$, there is a $b \in \mathbb{N}$ such that $(b, a) \in P^{\mathfrak{A}}$, that is, such that $b < a$. This is false, since no such b exists for $a = 0$, so $\mathfrak{A} \not\models_\xi \forall x\exists yPyx$.

In one respect Definition 9.2.2 seems overly cumbersome. In determining the value of $\mathfrak{A}(\forall xPxf(x))_\xi$, for example, there is no need for ξ to be defined on the variable x; for x does not refer to any particular object in the universe, but is simply being used as a "place holder." The formula $\forall yPyf(y)$ says exactly the same thing as $\forall xPxf(x)$. On the other hand, the variables in the formula $Pyf(x)$ must be associated with particular objects in the universe before the formula can be construed as true or false. This distinction is made precise as follows.

Definition 9.2.3

The **free variables** of a formula are defined by induction as follows:

(a) The free variables of an atomic formula are all the variables occurring in it.

(b) The free variables of $(F \vee G)$ or of $(F \wedge G)$ are the free variables of F and the free variables of G; the free variables of $\neg F$ are the free variables of F.

(c) The free variables of $\forall xF$ or $\exists xF$ are the free variables of F, except for x (if x happens to be a free variable of F).

An occurrence of a variable x in a formula G is a **bound occurrence** if it is an occurrence within a subformula of G of the form $\forall xF$ or $\exists xF$; any other occurrence of x in G is a **free occurrence**. We say that the indicated occurrence of $\forall$ or $\exists$ **binds** each free occurrence of x in F.

For example, the occurrences of x in $\forall xPxf(xy)$ are bound, while the occurrence of y is free. Note that a variable may have both free and bound occurrences in the same formula; this is the case, for example, in $(Qx \vee \forall xPx)$.

The following lemma captures the idea that no particular value need be assigned to a variable that has only bound occurrences.

Lemma 9.2.2. *If x has no free occurrences in F, then the value of $\mathfrak{A}(F)_\xi$ is independent of the value of $\xi(x)$.*

Proof. See Problem 9.2.8. ∎

As a special case, consider formulas in which there are *no* free occurrences of variables; such formulas are said to be **closed**. If F is a closed formula, then $\mathfrak{A} \models_\xi F$ for some appropriate ξ if and only if $\mathfrak{A} \models_\xi F$ for every appropriate ξ, so we write simply $\mathfrak{A} \models F$ and call $\mathfrak{A}$ a **model** for F.

If $\mathfrak{A} \models F$ for every $\mathfrak{A}$ appropriate to F, then F is said to be **valid**. A closed formula is said to be **satisfiable** if it has at least one model, otherwise **unsatisfiable**. As with the propositional calculus, a closed formula F is valid if and only if $\neg F$ is unsatisfiable.

These notions directly extend similar notions for the propositional calculus; simply regard the atomic formulas of the propositional calculus as 0-place predicate signs. However, it is no longer straightforward to determine whether a formula is satisfiable; there is no "truth-table" method for the predicate calculus. One problem is that the number of structures that must be considered is not limited in advance; in the propositional calculus, one could by inspection draw up a finite list of truth-assignments to be checked, and know that if a verifying truth-assignment was not discovered on that list then none existed. What is worse, one must consider single structures which are themselves infinite, that is, have infinite universes; some formulas have infinite models but no finite models.

Example 9.2.3

Let F be

$$((\forall x(Pxf(x) \wedge \neg Pxx) \wedge \forall x\forall y\forall z((Pxy \wedge Pyz) \longrightarrow Pxz)).$$

Then F is satisfiable; for example, F is true in the universe $\mathbb{N}$ if P is interpreted as *less than* and f is interpreted as the successor function. That is, $\mathfrak{A} = ([\mathfrak{A}], P^{\mathfrak{A}}, f^{\mathfrak{A}})$ is a model for F, where $[\mathfrak{A}] = \mathbb{N}$, $P^{\mathfrak{A}} = \{(m, n) : m, n \in \mathbb{N}, m < n\}$, and $f(n) = n + 1$ for each n. But F has no finite model. For suppose $\mathfrak{B}$ were a model for F and $[\mathfrak{B}]$ were finite. Let b be any element of $[\mathfrak{B}]$ and consider the elements $b, f^{\mathfrak{B}}(b), f^{\mathfrak{B}}(f^{\mathfrak{B}}(b)), \ldots$; call them $b_0, b_1, \ldots$. Because $\mathfrak{B}$ is a model of F, $P^{\mathfrak{B}}$ is a relation which is transitive but antireflexive (that is, not true of any pair (b, b)), and $(b_i, b_{i+1}) \in P^{\mathfrak{B}}$ for each $i = 0, 1, \ldots$;

therefore $(b_i, b_j) \in P^{\mathcal{B}}$ whenever $i < j$. But because $[\mathcal{B}]$ is finite, $b_i = b_j$ for some $i, j, i < j$, so $(b_i, b_i) \in P^{\mathcal{B}}$ for some i; and this contradicts the fact that $P^{\mathcal{B}}$ is antireflexive.

We shall see in Section 9.6 that the apparent difficulty in determining whether a formula is satisfiable is quite real; in fact, there is *no* algorithm for determining whether a formula of the predicate calculus is satisfiable. That is, determining satisfiability in the predicate calculus is an unsolvable problem.

9.3 EQUIVALENCE

The truth-assignments appropriate to a formula of the propositional calculus tell us everything of importance about that formula. A similar situation obtains for the predicate calculus.

Definition 9.3.1

Let F and G be formulas. Then F and G are **equivalent**—in symbols, $F \equiv G$—if and only if, for every structure $\mathcal{A}$ and function ξ appropriate to both F and G, $\mathcal{A}(F)_\xi = \mathcal{A}(G)_\xi$.

An analogue to Theorem 8.5.1 follows easily; we leave the proof as an exercise.

Theorem 9.3.1. *Let F and G be equivalent formulas, and suppose H' results from H by replacing some occurrence of F by G. Then H and H' are equivalent.*

Proof. See Problem 9.3.1. ∎

All the equivalences in Theorem 8.5.2 involving the logical connectives apply equally to the predicate calculus. These include the associativity and commutativity laws for $\wedge$ and $\vee$, DeMorgan's laws, the law of double negation, and so on. The reason these laws continue to be true is that the rules for determining the truth-values of disjunctions, conjunctions, and negations are the same in the predicate calculus as in the propositional calculus (Definitions 8.3.1 and 9.2.2). Accordingly, every formula without quantifiers can be put into either conjunctive normal form (a conjunction of disjunctions of atomic formulas and their negations) or disjunctive normal form (a disjunction of conjunctions of atomic formulas and their negations).

In addition, there are important equivalences involving the position of the quantifiers.

Lemma 9.3.1.

(a) *For any formula F and variable x,*

$$\neg\forall xF \equiv \exists x\neg F$$
$$\neg\exists xF \equiv \forall x\neg F.$$

(b) *Let F and G be any formulas, and suppose that x has no free occurrence in G. Then*

$$(\forall xF \vee G) \equiv \forall x(F \vee G)$$
$$(\forall xF \wedge G) \equiv \forall x(F \wedge G)$$
$$(\exists xF \vee G) \equiv \exists x(F \vee G)$$
$$(\exists xF \wedge G) \equiv \exists x(F \wedge G).$$

(c) *For any formulas F and G and any variable x,*

$$\forall x(F \wedge G) \equiv (\forall xF \wedge \forall xG)$$
$$\exists x(F \vee G) \equiv (\exists xF \vee \exists xG).$$

Proof.

(a) $\mathfrak{A}(\neg\forall xF)_\xi = \top$

if and only if $\quad \mathfrak{A}(\forall xF)_\xi = \bot$

if and only if $\quad \mathfrak{A}(F)_{\xi[x/a]} = \bot$ for some $a \in [\mathfrak{A}]$

if and only if $\quad \mathfrak{A}(\neg F)_{\xi[x/a]} = \top$ for some $a \in [\mathfrak{A}]$

if and only if $\quad \mathfrak{A}(\exists x\neg F)_\xi = \top$.

The other equivalence is proved similarly.

(b) We take just the first formula.

$$\mathfrak{A}((\forall xF \vee G))_\xi = \top$$

if and only if $\quad \mathfrak{A}(\forall xF)_\xi = \top$ or $\mathfrak{A}(G)_\xi = \top$

if and only if $\quad \mathfrak{A}(F)_{\xi[x/a]} = \top$ for each $a \in [\mathfrak{A}]$, or $\mathfrak{A}(G)_\xi = \top$

if and only if, for each $a \in [\mathfrak{A}]$, either

$$\mathfrak{A}(F)_{\xi[x/a]} = \top$$

or $\quad \mathfrak{A}(G)_\xi = \top$

if and only if, for each $a \in [\mathfrak{A}]$, either

$$\mathfrak{A}(F)_{\xi[x/a]} = \top$$

or $\quad \mathfrak{A}(G)_{\xi[x/a]} = \top$, by Lemma 9.2.2

if and only if, for each $a \in [\mathfrak{A}]$,

$$\mathfrak{A}((F \vee G))_{\xi[x/a]} = \top$$

if and only if

$$\mathcal{A}(\forall x(F \vee G)) = \top.$$

(c) Again, we prove only the first formula.

$$\mathcal{A}(\forall x(F \wedge G))_\xi = \top$$

if and only if $\mathcal{A}((F \wedge G))_{\xi[x/a]} = \top$ for each $a \in [\mathcal{A}]$

if and only if $\mathcal{A}(F)_{\xi[x/a]} = \top$

and $\mathcal{A}(G)_{\xi[x/a]} = \top$ for each $a \in [\mathcal{A}]$

if and only if $\mathcal{A}(F)_{\xi[x/a]} = \top$ for each $a \in [\mathcal{A}]$

and $\mathcal{A}(G)_{\xi[x/a]} = \top$ for each $a \in [\mathcal{A}]$

if and only if $\mathcal{A}(\forall xF)_\xi = \top$

and $\mathcal{A}(\forall xG)_\xi = \top$

if and only if $\mathcal{A}((\forall xF \wedge \forall xG))_\xi = \top$. ■

These equivalences should be noted as well for what they do *not* state. It is not true, in general, that $\forall x(F \vee G) \equiv (\forall xF \vee \forall xG)$; nor that $\exists x(F \wedge G) \equiv (\exists xF \wedge \exists xG)$ (see Problem 9.3.4).

If all the quantifiers of F are at the left end, that is, F is of the form $Qv_1 \ldots Qv_nG$, where each Q is $\forall$ or $\exists$ and G has no quantifiers, then F is said to be **prenex** and $Qv_1 \ldots Qv_n$ is the **prefix**. Prenex form is useful for many purposes, and Parts (a) and (b) of Lemma 9.3.1 can be used to move quantifiers gradually towards the left end of a formula. There can be obstacles to this procedure, however. For example, if F is $(\forall xPx \vee Qx)$, then (b) does not apply and F cannot be converted to the form $\forall x(Px \vee Qx)$—perhaps for good reasons, as we just noted. The difficulty clearly has to do with variables that happen to have both free and bound occurrences in the same formula. But the bound occurrences can be changed systematically to eliminate conflicts, as the next lemma states.

First we introduce some new notation. Let $F[x/t]$, where x is a variable and t is a term, be the result of replacing each free occurrence of x in F by t. More generally, we write $F[x_1/t_1, \ldots, x_n/t_n]$ for the result of *simultaneously* replacing all free occurrences of x_1 by $t_1, \ldots, x_n$ by t_n.

Example 9.3.1

$Pxy[x/z]$ is Pzy;

$(Qx \vee \forall xPx)[x/y]$ is $(Qy \vee \forall xPx)$;

$(\forall xPxy \vee \exists yQy)[y/f(x)]$ is $(\forall xPxf(x) \vee \exists yQy)$;

and

$Pxy[x/y, y/z]$ is Pyz.

Note that $F[x_1/t_1][x_2/t_2]$ is not necessarily the same as $F[x_1/t_1, x_2/t_2]$. For example, if

$$F = Px$$

$$x_1 = x \qquad t_1 = y$$

$$x_2 = y \qquad t_2 = z$$

then

$$F[x_1/t_1, x_2/t_2] \text{ is } Py,$$

but

$$F[x_1/t_1][x_2/t_2] \text{ is } Py[y/z],$$

that is, Pz.

Lemma 9.3.2. *Suppose that y does not occur in F. Then* $\forall xF \equiv \forall yF[x/y]$.

Proof. See Problem 9.3.9. ■

Now we can transform any formula into an equivalent prenex one. The steps of the algorithm are as follows.

1. Rename variables so that no variable has both free and bound occurrences, and so that there is at most one occurrence of a quantifier with any particular variable.
2. Apply the equivalences from (a) and (b) to "pull" the quantifiers to the left end.

A formula is called **rectified** if it is as provided by Step (1), that is, no variable has both free and bound occurrences and there is at most one occurrence of a variable with any particular quantifier. Naturally, any formula that has any quantifier at all has infinitely many equivalent rectified forms. Similarly, it may be possible to apply Step (2) in different ways, to come up with different end results.

Example 9.3.2

(a) To convert $(Qx \vee \forall xPxx)$ to prenex form, we first select a new variable, say y, and replace the bound occurrences of x by y. The result is the rectified formula $(Qx \vee \forall yPyy)$. Part (b) of Lemma 9.3.1 applies to yield the prenex form $\forall y(Qx \vee Pyy)$. (Commutativity of $\vee$ has been used twice implicitly.)

(b) Let us convert $(\exists x(Qx \wedge (\forall yPxy \vee \neg\forall yQy)) \wedge Rx)$ to prenex form. Here x has both free and bound occurrences, and there are two occurrences of $\forall$ with the variable y. Introducing new variables, z and w, we obtain the rectified form

$$(\exists z(Qz \wedge (\forall yPzy \vee \neg\forall wQw)) \wedge Rx).$$

By moving the $\exists z$ outwards, this becomes

$$\exists z((Qz \wedge (\forall y Pzy \vee \neg \forall w Qw)) \wedge Rx).$$

Next we apply Part (a) of Lemma 9.3.1 to obtain

$$\exists z((Qz \wedge (\forall y Pzy \vee \exists w \neg Qw)) \wedge Rx).$$

Next we can work on $\forall y$ or $\exists w$. We choose the former; using Part (b) three times, we obtain

$$\exists z \forall y((Qz \wedge (Pzy \vee \exists w \neg Qw)) \wedge Rx).$$

Finally we use Part (b) three times more on $\exists w$ and obtain, finally,

$$\exists z \forall y \exists w((Qz \wedge (Pzy \vee \neg Qw)) \wedge Rx).$$

The following theorem summarizes the results of this section.

Theorem 9.3.2. *Every formula of the predicate calculus is equivalent to at least one rectified formula and to at least one formula in prenex form. Every formula without quantifiers is equivalent to at least one formula in conjunctive normal form and at least one formula in disjunctive normal form. Hence every formula is equivalent to at least one formula in prenex form with matrix in conjunctive normal form, and also to at least one formula in prenex form with matrix in disjunctive normal form. Moreover, there exist algorithms for transforming a formula into an equivalent one in any of these forms.*

9.4 THE EXPANSION THEOREM

The propositional calculus may be viewed as a special case of the predicate calculus; we can simply regard the 0-place predicate signs as atomic formulas of the propositional calculus, and then every formula of the propositional calculus becomes a formula of the predicate calculus that happens to involve no variables, function signs, or quantifiers. The definitions of *truth-assignment* and *model* mesh so that a formula of this type has a model if and only if it has a verifying truth-assignment. There is no such simple reduction in the other direction, however. That is, one cannot generally reduce formulas of the predicate calculus to single formulas of the propositional calculus. However, a fundamental fact is that each formula of the predicate calculus can be reduced in a systematic way to a *countable set* of formulas without quantifiers or variables. These formulas can be viewed as formulas of the propositional calculus; the collection of all the quantifier-free formulas corresponding to a particular formula F is called the **Herbrand**

expansion of F and is denoted by $E(F)$. The crucial facts about the Herbrand expansion are

1. that it is generated in a systematic way from F, and one can easily tell what is and is not in $E(F)$; and
2. F is satisfiable (as a formula of the predicate calculus) if and only if $E(F)$ is satisfiable (as a countable set of formulas of the propositional calculus).

Before giving the general definition of the Herbrand expansion, we present a particular example. Let

$$F = (\forall y \exists x Pyx \wedge \exists z \forall w \neg Pwz).$$

Here F is satisfiable; for example $\mathfrak{A} \models F$, where $[\mathfrak{A}] = \mathbb{N}$ and $P^{\mathfrak{A}} = \{(m, n): m < n\}$. The subformula $\forall y \exists x Pyx$ is true, since whatever numerical value the variable y assumes—for example, m—there is a greater value, say $m + 1$, for x. The subformula $\exists z \forall w \neg Pwz$ is also true since there is a value for z, namely, 0, such that no number is less than that value.

In the Herbrand expansion, it is made explicit that in order for a structure $\mathfrak{A}$ to be a model for F, there must be ways of selecting values for the existentially quantified variables corresponding to various ways of substituting values for the universally quantified variables so that the matrix comes out true in each case. In the particular example of F, we first select a 1-place function sign f and a 0-place function sign a, and replace F by its **functional form**

$$(\forall y Pyf(y) \wedge \forall w \neg Pwa).$$

Here $f(y)$ denotes a choice for the object x, corresponding to y, such that Pyx holds. Of course in any model for F, there could be more than one such choice for x; in the functional form, however, we merely acknowledge that for each value of y there must be at least one choice for x. Similarly, a stands for some fixed object such that $\neg Pwa$ holds, whatever the value of w; a is not a function of w, since the choice of z should be independent of the value of w.

The **Herbrand universe** of F is the set of terms that can be formed from a and f, namely, $\{a, f(a), f(f(a)), \ldots\}$. It turns out that in order to test whether F is satisfiable, it suffices to consider the functional form, and to consider only values for y and w drawn from the Herbrand universe. Moreover, it is not necessary to consider arbitrary interpretations for the function signs f and a; it suffices to **interpret** f **syntactically**, that is, to consider f simply as a function from the Herbrand expansion to itself. For example, the function f yields the term $f(f(a))$ when applied to the term $f(a)$.

The Herbrand expansion is derived from the matrix of the functional form by substituting terms from the Herbrand universe for the free variables in all possible ways. In our example, the matrix of the functional form is

$$F^* = Pyf(y) \wedge \neg Pwa$$

and the Herbrand expansion is

$$\begin{aligned}
\{&Paf(a) \wedge \neg Paa, && = F^*[y/a, w/a] \\
&Pf(a)f(f(a)) \wedge \neg Paa, && = F^*[y/f(a), w/a] \\
&Paf(a) \wedge \neg Pf(a)a, && = F^*[y/a, w/f(a)] \\
&Pf(a)f(f(a)) \wedge \neg Pf(a)a, && = F^*[y/f(a), w/f(a)] \\
&\ldots\}.
\end{aligned}$$

The first formula is obtained by substituting a for both y and w; the second is found by substituting $f(a)$ for y and a for w; and so on.

Now each atomic formula $Paf(a)$, Paa, $Pf(a)f(f(a))$, and so on, is treated as an atomic formula of the propositional calculus. We see that F is satisfiable since there is a truth-assignment that verifies each formula in the expansion, namely the truth-assignment $\mathfrak{A}$ such that

$\mathfrak{A} \models Pst$ if s and t are terms in the Herbrand universe and $t = f(s)$

$\mathfrak{A} \models \neg Pst$ otherwise.

Notice that if we consider the formula

$$G = (\forall y \exists x Pyx \wedge \exists z \forall w \neg Pzw),$$

instead of F, then the functional form is

$$(\forall y Pyf(y) \wedge \forall w \neg Paw)$$

and the Herbrand expansion begins

$$\begin{aligned}
\{&Paf(a) \wedge \neg Paa, \\
&Pf(a)f(f(a)) \wedge \neg Paa, \\
&Paf(a) \wedge \neg Paf(a), \\
&\ldots\}.
\end{aligned}$$

But G is unsatisfiable since in the Herbrand expansion both $Paf(a)$ and $\neg Paf(a)$ must be true.

We now give the general definitions relevant to the Herbrand expansion. In defining the functional form, it is not sufficient to treat existential quantifiers in one way and universal quantifiers in another. The important thing is the distribution of negation signs around quantifiers. An occurrence of the universal quantifier is called **positive** if it is in the scope of an even number of occurrences of negation signs, otherwise it is **negative**. For existential quantifiers the situation is just the opposite, since an existential quantifier corresponds to a universal quantifier preceded and followed by a negation sign. Thus in a prenex formula, the positive quantifiers are universal and the negative quantifiers are existential. In general, an occurrence of $\forall$ is positive if it would remain universal when the formula is put into prenex form, and is negative if it would turn into an existential quantifier. For example, in $\forall x(Px \wedge \neg\exists y \neg\exists z Rxyz)$, the occurrence of $\forall$ is positive, being a universal quantifier in the scope of zero negation signs; the first occurrence of $\exists$ is positive, being an existential quantifier in the scope of one negation sign; and the second occurrence of $\exists$ is negative, being an existential quantifier in the scopes of two negation signs. A prenex form of this formula is $\forall x \forall y \exists z(Px \wedge \neg\neg Rxyz)$.

The **functional form** of a closed formula F is defined as follows.

1. If F is not already rectified, apply Theorem 9.3.2 to make it rectified.

2. For each negative occurrence of a quantifier Q, let x be the variable bound by that occurrence, let G be the scope of that occurrence, and let $y_1, \ldots, y_n$ be in order the variables bound by those positive occurrences of quantifiers in whose scopes the subformula QxG occurs. Then choose a new n-place function sign f_x not used elsewhere in the formula and replace the subformula QxG by $G[x/f_x(y_1 \ldots y_n)]$.

Step 2 is to be carried out repeatedly until no more negative occurrences of quantifiers remain. Note that the order in which the negative occurrences are chosen is irrelevant to the final result, except possibly for the choice of the new function signs. These new function signs are called **indicial function signs**, and the term $f_x(y_1 \ldots y_n)$ that replaces x is called the **indicial term** for x in F.

Example 9.4.1

Let $F = \forall y_1(Py_1 \vee \neg\forall x_1 \exists y_2(Qx_1y_1y_2 \vee \neg\exists x_2 Qx_2y_1y_2))$. Here y_1 and y_2 are bound by positive occurrences of quantifiers and x_1 and x_2 by negative occurrences. Then the functional form is $\forall y_1(Py_1 \vee \neg\exists y_2(Qf_{x_1}(y_1)y_1y_2 \vee \neg Qf_{x_2}(y_1y_2)y_1y_2))$; $f_{x_1}(y_1)$ and $f_{x_2}(y_1y_2)$ are the indicial terms for x_1 and x_2, respectively, in F.

Now define F^* to be the matrix of the functional form. We next define a set of terms associated with F called its **Herbrand universe** $D(F)$. One special constant sign ł is set aside for the sole purpose of beginning the construction of the Herbrand universe, in case F^* contains no 0-place function sign.

1. ł $\in D(F)$, if F^* contains no constant sign.
2. If $t_1, \ldots, t_n \in D(F)$ $(n \geq 0)$ and f is any n-place function sign (indicial or not) occurring in F^*, then $f(t_1 \ldots t_n) \in D(F)$.

Finally we can define the Herbrand expansion. Let $y_1, \ldots, y_n$ be the variables of F^*. (These are the variables which in F were bound by positive occurrences of quantifiers.) Then the **Herbrand expansion** $E(F)$ is the set of all formulas

$$F^*[y_1/t_1, \ldots, y_n/t_n]$$

with $t_1, \ldots, t_n \in D(F)$. These formulas, which have neither quantifiers nor variables, are now to be regarded as formulas of the propositional calculus.

Example 9.4.2

This example continues Example 9.4.1. Let F be as in Example 9.4.1. Then

$$F^* = (Py_1 \wedge \neg(Qf_{x_1}(y_1)y_1y_2 \vee \neg Qf_{x_2}(y_1y_2)y_1y_2))$$

and

$$D(F) = \{\dagger, f_{x_1}(\dagger), f_{x_2}(\dagger\dagger), f_{x_1}(f_{x_1}(\dagger)), f_{x_1}(f_{x_2}(\dagger\dagger)), f_{x_2}(f_{x_1}(\dagger)\dagger), \ldots\}$$

and

$$\begin{aligned} E(F) = \{&(P\dagger \wedge \neg(Qf_{x_1}(\dagger)\dagger\dagger \vee \neg Qf_{x_2}(\dagger\dagger)\dagger\dagger)), \\ &(Pf_x(\dagger) \wedge \neg(Qf_{x_1}(f_{x_1}(\dagger))f_{x_1}(\dagger)\dagger \vee \neg Qf_{x_2}(f_{x_1}(\dagger)\dagger)f_{x_1}(\dagger)\dagger)), \\ &\ldots\}. \end{aligned}$$

Here $E(F)$ is satisfiable; a truth-assignment verifying $E(F)$ is $\mathcal{A}$, where

$\mathcal{A} \models Pt$ for each term $t \in D(F)$

$\mathcal{A} \models Qt_1t_2t_3$ where $t_1, t_2, t_3 \in D(F)$, if and only if $t_1 = f_{x_2}(s_1s_2)$ for some $s_1, s_2 \in D(F)$.

Every formula in $E(F)$ has the form

$$(Pt_1 \wedge \neg(Qf_{x_1}(t_1)t_1t_2 \vee \neg Qf_{x_2}(t_1t_2)t_1t_2))$$

for some t_1, t_2 in $D(F)$. By the definition of $\mathcal{A}$, this formula is of the form $(A \wedge \neg(B \vee \neg C))$, where $\mathcal{A} \models A, \mathcal{A} \models \neg B$, and $\mathcal{A} \models C$, and so $\mathcal{A} \models (A \wedge \neg(B \vee \neg C))$; thus $\mathcal{A} \models E(F)$.

We can now state and prove the main result.

Theorem 9.4.1. (Expansion Theorem) *A closed formula is satisfiable if and only if its Herbrand expansion is satisfiable.*

Proof. The proof is in two steps. We first show that a closed formula is satisfiable if and only if its functional form is satisfiable. We then show that any closed formula without negative quantifiers—any functional form is of this type—is satisfiable only if it has what we call a *free* model. A free model is tantamount to a truth-assignment verifying the Herbrand expansion, so this second step establishes the Expansion Theorem for the special case of functional forms; when combined with the first step, it establishes the theorem for all closed formulas.

Lemma 9.4.1. *A closed formula is satisfiable if and only if its functional form is satisfiable.*

Proof. A formula and its functional form cannot have exactly the same models, since the functional form contains, in general, function signs not appearing in the formula itself. Thus we define one structure to be an **extension** of the other if the former is obtained from the latter by possibly adding interpretations of one or more function signs. We shall see that every model of a closed formula has an extension that is a model of its functional form; and every model of the functional form is a model of the formula itself.

We first note that it suffices to prove the lemma for formulas with the property that no quantifier is in the scope of a negation sign. For if F does not have this property, then F can be transformed into an equivalent formula F_1 that does, by means of DeMorgan's laws, the law of double negation, and the laws of Lemma 9.3.1(a). Not only is F equivalent to F_1, but the functional form of F (call it $\hat{F}$) is equivalent to the functional form of F_1 (call it $\hat{F}_1$): the same laws that transform F into F_1 also transform $\hat{F}$ into $\hat{F}_1$, except that Lemma 9.3.1(a) need never be applied to negative occurrences of quantifiers. For example, let $F = (\neg\exists x \neg\exists y Pxy \vee \neg\exists z Pzz)$; then $F_1 = (\forall x \exists y Pxy \vee \forall z \neg Pzz)$, $\hat{F} = (\neg\exists x \neg Pxf_y(x) \vee \neg\exists z Pzz)$, and $\hat{F}_1 = (\forall x Pxf_y(x) \vee \forall z \neg Pzz)$. Since $F \equiv F_1$ and $\hat{F} \equiv \hat{F}_1$, to show that F is satisfiable if and only if $\hat{F}$ is satisfiable it suffices to show that F_1 is satisfiable if and only if $\hat{F}_1$ is satisfiable.

So we may assume that each subformula of F is either

1. a formula without quantifiers; or
2. a disjunction or conjunction of two subformulas of F; or
3. of the form $\forall x F'$ or $\exists x F'$ for some variable x and some subformula F'.

Thus an occurrence of a quantifier is negative if and only if that quantifier is existential and positive if and only if it is universal.

Note that if F has this structure and G is a subformula of F, then any occurrence of a quantifier in G is positive or negative depending on whether it is positive or negative as a quantifier of F. If G is such a subformula of F, define $\hat{G}$ to be the formula that results from G by deleting each existential quantifier of G and the occurrence of a variable that follows it, and replacing all other occurrences of that variable by the indicial term in F for that variable. Free occurrences of variables in G are not changed. For example, let F be $(\forall x \exists y Pxy \vee \forall z \neg Pzz)$, so that $\hat{F}$ is $(\forall x Pxf_y(x) \vee \forall z \neg Pzz)$. Then if G

is $\forall x \exists y Pxy$, then $\hat{G}$ is $\forall x Pxf_y(x)$; if G is $\exists y Pxy$, then $\hat{G}$ is $Pxf_y(x)$; if G is Pxy, then $\hat{G}$ is Pxy; if G is $\forall z \neg Pzz$, then $\hat{G}$ is $\forall z \neg Pzz$; and if G is Pzz, then $\hat{G}$ is Pzz.

To show that a structure appropriate to F is a model of that formula if and only if some extension of that structure is a model of the functional form $\hat{F}$, we proceed by induction on the subformulas of F. We need one further definition.

Let us call a structure $\mathfrak{A}$ **narrowly appropriate** to a formula G if the domain of $\mathcal{I}_{\mathfrak{A}}$ is *exactly* the set of predicate and function signs actually appearing in G.

Sublemma 9.4.1. *Let G be a subformula of F.*

(a) *For any structure $\mathfrak{A}$ appropriate to $\hat{G}$ and function ξ appropriate to $\hat{G}$ and $\mathfrak{A}$, if $\mathfrak{A} \models_\xi \hat{G}$ then $\mathfrak{A} \models_\xi G$.*

(b) *For any structure $\mathfrak{A}$ narrowly appropriate to G, there is an extension $\mathfrak{B}$ of $\mathfrak{A}$ such that, for any mapping ξ appropriate to G and $\mathfrak{A}$, if $\mathfrak{A} \models_\xi G$ then $\mathfrak{B} \models_\xi \hat{G}$.*

Note that this sublemma implies Lemma 9.4.1, since in the case $G = F$, it states that any model for F yields one for its functional form, and vice versa.

Proof. The proof proceeds by induction on the structure of G, which has the special structure previously assumed of F.

Basis Step. G has no quantifier. Then $G = \hat{G}$ and both (a) and (b) are trivial.

Induction Step.

1. Let $G = (G_1 \wedge G_2)$, where G_1 and G_2 are formulas for which the sublemma holds; the case $G = (G_1 \vee G_2)$ is similar. Then $\hat{G} = (\hat{G}_1 \wedge \hat{G}_2)$.
   (a) If $\mathfrak{A} \models_\xi \hat{G}$, then $\mathfrak{A} \models_\xi \hat{G}_1$ and $\mathfrak{A} \models_\xi \hat{G}_2$; then $\mathfrak{A} \models_\xi G_1$ and $\mathfrak{A} \models_\xi G_2$ by the induction hypothesis; and hence $\mathfrak{A} \models_\xi (G_1 \wedge G_2)$.
   (b) Let $\mathfrak{A}$ be a structure narrowly appropriate to G. By the induction hypothesis there are extensions $\mathfrak{B}_1$ and $\mathfrak{B}_2$ of $\mathfrak{A}$ defined on the function signs of $\hat{G}_1$ and $\hat{G}_2$, respectively, such that, for any ξ, if $\mathfrak{A} \models_\xi (G_1 \wedge G_2)$, then $\mathfrak{B}_1 \models_\xi \hat{G}_1$ and $\mathfrak{B}_2 \models_\xi \hat{G}_2$. Now $\mathfrak{B}_1$ and $\mathfrak{B}_2$ can be merged into a single structure $\mathfrak{B}$ that has the same interpretation as $\mathfrak{B}_1$ or $\mathfrak{B}_2$ whenever either or both are defined. For both $\mathfrak{B}_1$ and $\mathfrak{B}_2$ are extensions of $\mathfrak{A}$, and hence have the same interpretations for any predicate sign

or function sign of F on which both are defined. And the indicial function signs in $\hat{G}_1$ are disjoint from those in $\hat{G}_2$, since F is rectified and the indicial function signs appearing in $\hat{G}_1$ or $\hat{G}_2$ arise from quantifiers within $\hat{G}_1$ or $\hat{G}_2$. Then $\mathfrak{B} \models_\xi (\hat{G}_1 \wedge \hat{G}_2)$, so $\mathfrak{B}$ is the required extension of $\mathfrak{A}$.

2. Let $G = \forall x G_1$; then $\hat{G} = \forall x \hat{G}_1$.
   (a) If $\mathfrak{A} \models_\xi \hat{G}$, then $\mathfrak{A} \models_{\xi[x/a]} \hat{G}_1$ for each $a \in [\mathfrak{A}]$. By the induction hypothesis, $\mathfrak{A} \models_{\xi[x/a]} G_1$ for each $a \in [\mathfrak{A}]$, so $\mathfrak{A} \models_\xi \forall x G_1$, that is, $\mathfrak{A} \models_\xi G$.
   (b) If $\mathfrak{A} \models_\xi G$ then $\mathfrak{A} \models_{\xi[x/a]} G_1$ for each $a \in [\mathfrak{A}]$. By the induction hypothesis, there is an extension $\mathfrak{B}$ of $\mathfrak{A}$ such that for any ξ', if $\mathfrak{A} \models_{\xi'} G_1$ then $\mathfrak{B} \models_{\xi'} \hat{G}_1$. This same $\mathfrak{B}$ is the required extension for $\hat{G}$.
3. Let $G = \exists x G_1$, and let $f(y_1 \ldots y_n)$ be the indicial term for x in F. Then

$$\hat{G} = \hat{G}_1[x/f(y_1 \ldots y_n)].$$

   (a) If $\mathfrak{A} \models_\xi \hat{G}$ then $\mathfrak{A} \models_{\xi[x/a]} \hat{G}_1$, where $a = f^{\mathfrak{A}}(\xi(y_1), \ldots, \xi(y_n))$. By the induction hypothesis, $\mathfrak{A} \models_{\xi[x/a]} G_1$, and therefore $\mathfrak{A} \models_\xi \exists x G_1$. Hence $\mathfrak{A} \models_\xi G$.
   (b) Let $\mathfrak{B}$ be the structure provided by the induction hypothesis for $\hat{G}_1$. To extend $\mathfrak{B}$ to a structure $\mathfrak{C}$ for $\hat{G}$ we need to define $f^{\mathfrak{C}}$ for n-tuples $(a_1, \ldots, a_n) \in [\mathfrak{A}]^n$. Let ξ be any function appropriate to G_1 and $\mathfrak{A}$ such that $\xi(y_i) = a_i$ for $i = 1, \ldots, n$, and define

$$f^{\mathfrak{C}}(a_1, \ldots, a_n) = \begin{cases} \text{some } a \text{ such that } \mathfrak{A} \models_{\xi[x/a]} G_1, \text{ if there} \\ \text{is such an } a \in [\mathfrak{A}]; \\ \text{arbitrary otherwise.} \end{cases}$$

   Note that the only variables with free occurrences in G_1 are x and $y_1, \ldots, y_n$, so that the only values of ξ significant in determining whether there is such an a are the values at $y_1, \ldots, y_n$. So this is a proper definition of $f^{\mathfrak{C}}$, not affected by the choice of values for ξ on variables other than $y_1, \ldots, y_n$.

   Now $\mathfrak{C}$ is the required extension. For if $\mathfrak{A} \models_\xi G$, then $\mathfrak{A} \models_{\xi[x/a]} G_1$ for some a, and hence $\mathfrak{A} \models_{\xi[x/a]} G_1$ for $a = f^{\mathfrak{C}}(\xi(y_1), \ldots, \xi(y_n))$ in particular. By the induction hypothesis $\mathfrak{B} \models_{\xi[x/a]} \hat{G}_1$, and hence $\mathfrak{C} \models_\xi \hat{G}$.

   This completes the proofs of Sublemma 9.4.1 and Lemma 9.4.1. ■

Now call a formula **positive** if all occurrences of its quantifiers are positive; thus any functional form is a positive formula. A structure $\mathfrak{A}$ for a positive formula F will be called **free** if $[\mathfrak{A}] = D(F)$ and for each n-place function sign f occurring in F, and any $t_1, \ldots, t_n \in D(F)$, $f^{\mathfrak{A}}(t_1, \ldots, t_n)$ is the term $f(t_1 \ldots t_n)$.

Lemma 9.4.2. *A closed positive formula has a model if and only if it has a free model.*

Proof. A free model is a model, so in one direction this result is trivial. Now let F be closed and positive. Without loss of generality, we may again assume that no occurrence of a quantifier in F is within the scope of a negation sign. If F does not have this property, we can find as before a positive formula F_1 equivalent to F, having the same Herbrand universe as F, and having no occurrence of a quantifier within the scope of a negation sign. Since any free model of F_1 will then be a free model of F, it suffices to show that F_1 has a free model if F_1 has any model; it will follow that F has a free model if F has any model.

So let F be a closed, positive formula such that no quantifier of F is in the scope of a negation sign, and let $\mathfrak{A}$ be a model of F. We define a function $\mu\colon D(F) \longrightarrow [\mathfrak{A}]$ which "embeds" the Herbrand universe in the universe of the model $\mathfrak{A}$:

If $\text{ł} \in D(F)$, then $\mu(\text{ł})$ is any fixed member of $[\mathfrak{A}]$;

For each n-place function sign f and any $t_1, \ldots, t_n \in D(F)$,

$$\mu(f(t_1 \ldots t_n)) = f^{\mathfrak{A}}(\mu(t_1), \ldots, \mu(t_n)).$$

Now let $\mathfrak{B}$ be the free structure such that $(t_1, \ldots, t_n) \in P^{\mathfrak{B}}$, where P is an n-place predicate sign, if and only if $(\mu(t_1), \ldots, \mu(t_n)) \in P^{\mathfrak{A}}$.

The proof that $\mathfrak{B}$ is a model of F proceeds by induction on the subformulas of F.

Sublemma 9.4.2. *Let G be any subformula of F. Then for any appropriate ξ, if $\mathfrak{A} \models_{\xi\circ\mu} G$, then $\mathfrak{B} \models_{\xi} G$.*

Proof.

Basis Step. If G is without quantifiers, then the sublemma follows immediately from the definition of $\mathfrak{B}$.

Induction Step.

(a) If G is of the form $(G_1 \vee G_2)$ or $(G_1 \wedge G_2)$ and $\mathfrak{A} \models_{\xi\circ\mu} G$, then it follows immediately from the induction hypothesis and the definition of $\models$ that $\mathfrak{B} \models_{\xi} G$.

(b) G is of the form $\exists x G'$. This case cannot arise, since then F would have a negative occurrence of a quantifier.

(c) $G = \forall x G'$. Then if $\mathfrak{A} \models_{\xi \circ \mu} G$,

then	$\mathfrak{A} \models_{\xi \circ \mu} \forall x G'$	
then	$\mathfrak{A} \models_{\xi \circ \mu[x/a]} G'$	for each $a \in [\mathfrak{A}]$
then	$\mathfrak{A} \models_{\xi \circ \mu[x/\mu(t)]} G'$	for each $t \in D(F)$, since $\mu(t) \in [\mathfrak{A}]$ for each $t \in D(F)$
then	$\mathfrak{B} \models_{\xi[x/t]} G'$	for each $t \in D(F)$, by the induction hypothesis
then	$\mathfrak{B} \models_{\xi} G$.	

This completes the proofs of Sublemma 9.4.2 and Lemma 9.4.2. ■

The last step in the proof of the Expansion Theorem is to show that a closed positive formula has a free model if and only if its expansion is truth-functionally satisfiable. But this is an immediate consequence of the definitions. If $\mathfrak{A}$ is a free model of F, then $\mathfrak{A}$ determines a truth-assignment verifying $E(F)$: $\mathfrak{A} \models Pt_1 \ldots t_n$ (as a truth-assignment) if and only if $(t_1, \ldots, t_n) \in P^{\mathfrak{A}}$. Conversely, if $\mathfrak{A}$ is a truth-assignment verifying $E(F)$, let $P^{\mathfrak{A}}$, for any n-place predicate sign P of F, be $\{(t_1, \ldots, t_n): \mathfrak{A} \models Pt_1 \ldots t_n\}$; then $\mathfrak{A} \models F$.

This completes the proof of Theorem 9.4.1. ■

By retracing our steps through the proof of the Expansion Theorem, we can strengthen it in a way that is useful in the next section. We now undertake to extend the Expansion Theorem to infinite sets of formulas. A *set* of formulas is satisfiable if and only if there is some single structure that is a model for each formula in the set.

The **free universe** generated by a set of function signs is the set of all terms that can be constructed from those function signs—plus the special constant sign ł, if no other constant sign is present. Thus the Herbrand universe of a formula is the free universe generated by the function signs of its functional form. The **expansion of a formula** F without quantifiers **over a free universe** D, denoted by $E(F, D)$, is the set of all formulas $F[y_1/t_1, \ldots, y_n/t_n]$, where $y_1, \ldots, y_n$ are the variables of F and $t_1, \ldots, t_n \in D$. Thus the Herbrand expansion $E(F)$ of a closed formula F is $E(F^*, D(F))$.

Theorem 9.4.2. *Let S be any set of closed formulas of the predicate calculus. Assume that when the functional forms of these formulas are chosen, no two distinct formulas are assigned any indicial function sign in common. Let D be the free universe generated by the set of function signs appearing in the functional forms of the formulas in S. Then S is satisfiable if and only if the union of all the expansions $E(F^*, D)$ is satisfiable, where F is a formula in S.*

Proof. First we extend Lemma 9.4.1 by showing that S is satisfiable if and only if the set of functional forms of formulas in S is satisfiable. In one direction this is easy: since we showed that any model for the functional form of a formula is a model for the formula itself, it follows immediately that any model for a *set* of functional forms is a model for the *set* of formulas of which they are the functional forms. In the other direction, we showed in Lemma 9.4.1 that any model for a closed formula can be extended to yield a model for its functional form by assigning appropriate interpretations to the indicial function signs. Now if S has a model, that is there is a structure $\mathfrak{A}$ such that $\mathfrak{A} \models F$ for each $F \in S$, then for each $F \in S$ there is an extension $\mathfrak{A}_F$ which is a model for the functional form of F; $\mathfrak{A}_F$ assigns interpretations to the predicate and function signs of all the formulas in S, and, in addition, to the indicial function signs of the functional form of F. But no two functional forms have any indicial function sign in common, so the structures $\mathfrak{A}_F$ are nowhere incompatible with each other; they can be merged to yield a model for the set of all functional forms of formulas in S.

To complete the argument we must show that if S' is a set of closed positive formulas, then S' is satisfiable if and only if $\bigcup \{E(F^*, D) : F \in S'\}$ is satisfiable, where D is the free universe generated by the function signs of the formulas in S'. Let us say that a structure appropriate to each formula in S' is a *free* structure if its universe is D and the function signs are interpreted syntactically. As before, any free model for S' yields immediately a truth-assignment verifying $\bigcup \{E(F^*, D) : F \in S'\}$ and vice versa, so it suffices to show that S' has a model if and only if S' has a free model. In one direction this is trivial; and in the other direction, the construction given in Lemma 9.4.2 extends directly to provide a free model for S' derived from any model for S'. ■

9.5 THREE APPLICATIONS OF THE EXPANSION THEOREM

In this section we present three fundamental facts about the predicate calculus that follow directly from the two versions of the Expansion Theorem (Theorems 9.4.1 and 9.4.2). These results indicate that the predicate calculus is perhaps not as strong a language as one might think: its formulas can be interpreted by means of models which may be uncountably infinite in size, and yet several important properties of these formulas are directly related to the Herbrand expansion, which is countable.

Theorem 9.5.1. *The set of unsatisfiable formulas of the predicate calculus is Turing-acceptable; so is the set of valid formulas of the predicate calculus.*

Proof. Since a formula is valid if and only if its negation is unsatisfiable, it suffices to consider the case of unsatisfiable formulas. By the Expansion Theorem (Theorem 9.4.1), a formula is unsatisfiable if and only if its Herbrand expansion is unsatisfiable; by the Compactness Theorem for the Propositional Calculus (Theorem 8.6.1) the expansion is unsatisfiable if and only if some finite subset is unsatisfiable. These two facts in conjunction suggest the following procedure for testing unsatisfiability: generate the Herbrand expansion a little bit at a time, in some systematic way; at regular intervals, stop and test (using truth tables, for example) whether the finite portion generated thus far is unsatisfiable. If the original formula is unsatisfiable, then that fact will be discovered at some point, but if the original formula is satisfiable, this procedure may not halt. ■

Theorem 9.5.2. (Skolem-Löwenheim Theorem) *Any satisfiable formula of the predicate calculus has a countable model. Moreover, any satisfiable countably*† *infinite set of formulas of the predicate calculus has a countable model.*

Proof. If F is satisfiable then its Herbrand expansion is satisfiable; but any truth-assignment verifying the Herbrand expansion of a formula F immediately yields a model of F with universe $D(F)$, which is countable. Likewise, if S is a countable set of formulas, then the free universe D described in the statement of Theorem 9.4.2 is countable, since each formula has only finitely many function signs and so there are only countably many function signs in all. Thus a truth-assignment verifying the union of the expansions $E(F^*, D)$, where $F \in S$, provides a countable model for S. ■

So although there are formulas with infinite models but no finite models (Example 9.2.3), there are no formulas with uncountable models but no countable models. Indeed, we cannot escape from the countable even if we use countable *sets* of formulas to determine models.

Finally, we show that the predicate calculus obeys a compactness property like that of the propositional calculus. For this we first need a lemma, which says, in essence, that the inclusion of *extra* function signs does not affect the satisfiability of the expansion of a formula.

Lemma 9.5.1. *Let F be any closed formula and let D_0 be a free universe of which $D(F)$ is a subset. If $E(F)$ is satisfiable, then so is $E(F^*, D_0)$.*

Proof. Let t_0 be any fixed term in $D(F)$. Define a function $\mu: D_0 \longrightarrow D(F)$ as follows.

†According to our formulation of the predicate calculus, any set of formulas must be countable. However, this is not invariably the rule obeyed by other authors, so we add the word *countably* here for emphasis.

(a) $\mu(t) = t_0$, if $t = f(t_1 \dots t_n)$ for some terms $t_1, \dots, t_n \in D_0$ and some function sign f that does *not* appear in F^* ($n \geq 0$).

(b) $\mu(t) = f(\mu(t_1) \dots \mu(t_n))$, if $t = f(t_1 \dots t_n)$ for some terms $t_1, \dots, t_n \in D_0$ and some function sign f that *does* appear in F^* ($n \geq 0$).

In particular, $\mu(t) = t$ for any term $t \in D(F)$, since then only Clause (b) applies. On the other hand, if $t = f(f(g(f(\text{ł}))))$, where f appears in F^* but g does not, then $\mu(t) = f(f(t_0))$. (A natural choice for t_0 would be ł, or some other constant sign.)

Now suppose that $E(F)$ is satisfiable, say $\mathfrak{A} \models E(F)$. For any atomic formula $Pt_1 \dots t_n$ appearing in $E(F^*, D_0)$, extend $\mathfrak{A}$ by defining

$$\mathfrak{A} \models Pt_1 \dots t_n \quad \text{if and only if} \quad \mathfrak{A} \models P\mu(t_1) \dots \mu(t_n).$$

No value of $\mathfrak{A}$ need be redefined, since $\mu(t) = t$ if $t \in D(F)$. Moreover, now $\mathfrak{A} \models E(F^*, D_0)$. For if we take a typical formula in this set, say $F^*[y_1/t_1, \dots, y_n/t_n]$, then $\mathfrak{A}$ assigns to each atomic subformula the same truth-value it assigns to the atomic formula in the corresponding position in the formula $F^*[y_1/\mu(t_1), \dots, y_n/\mu(t_n)]$. So $\mathfrak{A}(F^*[y_1/t_1, \dots, y_n/t_n]) = \mathfrak{A}(F^*[y_1/\mu(t_1), \dots, y_n/\mu(t_n)])$. But $F^*[y_1/\mu(t_1), \dots, y_n/\mu(t_n)]$ is a member of $E(F)$ and is therefore verified by $\mathfrak{A}$; so $F^*[y_1/t_1, \dots, y_n/t_n]$ is also verified by $\mathfrak{A}$. Since $t_1, \dots, t_n$ were chosen arbitrarily, $\mathfrak{A} \models E(F^*, D_0)$, and $E(F^*, D_0)$ is satisfiable. ■

Example 9.5.1

If $F^* = Pyf(y) \wedge \neg Qg(yz)$, and $s, t \in D_0$, then $F^*[y/t, z/s] = Ptf(t) \wedge \neg Qg(ts)$, and the truth-value $\mathfrak{A}$ assigns to this formula is by definition the truth-value it assigns to $P\mu(t)\mu(f(t)) \wedge \neg Q\mu(g(ts))$. But f and g appear in F^*, so by definition of μ the latter formula is $P\mu(t)f(\mu(t)) \wedge \neg Qg(\mu(t)\mu(s))$; but this is $F^*[y/\mu(t), z/\mu(s)]$, a member of $E(F)$. Hence $\mathfrak{A}$ verifies both $F^*[y/\mu(t), z/\mu(s)]$ and, by extension, $F^*[y/t, z/s]$.

Now we are ready for the main theorem.

Theorem 9.5.3. (Compactness Theorem for the Predicate Calculus) *A countable set of formulas of the predicate calculus has a model if and only if each finite subset has a model.*

Proof. A model for a set is a model for each finite subset, so in one direction the theorem is trivial. So let S be a countably infinite set of formulas of the predicate calculus, say $S = \{F_0, F_1, \dots\}$. For each $i = 0, 1, 2, \dots$, let G_i be the formula $(F_0 \wedge F_1 \wedge \cdots \wedge F_i)$. By a suitable choice of indicial function signs, we may assume that $G_i^* = (F_0^* \wedge \cdots \wedge F_i^*)$. Let D be the free universe generated by the function signs appearing in the F_i^* (or, equivalently, the G_i^*). Suppose that S is unsatisfiable. Then the following are true.

1. $\{G_0, G_1, \ldots\}$ is unsatisfiable, since any model for this set would be a model for S.
2. $\bigcup \{E(G_i^*, D): i = 0, 1, \ldots\}$ is unsatisfiable, by Theorem 9.4.2.
3. Some finite subset of $\bigcup \{E(G_i^*, D): i = 0, 1, \ldots\}$ is unsatisfiable by the Compactness Theorem for the Propositional Calculus (Theorem 8.6.1).
4. $\bigcup \{E(G_i^*, D): i = 0, 1, \ldots, k\}$ is unsatisfiable for some fixed k, since a finite subset of $\{E(G_i^*, D): i = 0, 1, \ldots\}$ must be derived from some finite number of the G_i.
5. $E(G_k^*, D)$ is unsatisfiable, since any formula in $E(G_i^*, D)$, $i < k$, would be verified by any truth-assignment verifying $E(G_k^*, D)$.
6. $E(G_k)$ is unsatisfiable, by Lemma 9.5.1.
7. G_k is unsatisfiable, by the Expansion Theorem (Theorem 9.4.1).
8. $\{F_0, \ldots, F_k\}$ is unsatisfiable, since any model for the set of these formulas would be a model for G_k. ■

9.6 UNSOLVABILITY AND $\mathcal{NP}$-COMPLETENESS

The three theorems of the last section point up limitations or weaknesses of the predicate calculus: unsatisfiability is a Turing-acceptable at worst, models of formulas need be countable at worst, and satisfiability of an infinite set of formulas can be reduced to the case of finite sets of formulas. In this section we give the other side of the coin, at least as far as the first of these results is concerned: satisfiability is not a solvable problem for the predicate calculus, even if formulas are not allowed to have function signs. As an immediate corollary of this proof, we show that in the propositional calculus satisfiability is $\mathcal{NP}$-complete. Thus the results of this section have a dual purpose: to establish the unsolvability of satisfiability for the predicate calculus and its $\mathcal{NP}$-completeness for the propositional calculus; and to underscore once more the general parallelism between unsolvability and $\mathcal{NP}$-completeness by showing that in some cases essentially the same proof can establish both.

Theorem 9.6.1. *The problem of satisfiability in the predicate calculus is unsolvable.*

Proof. We reduce the tiling problem of Theorem 6.5.1 to the satisfiability problem. That is, we give an effective procedure that yields, for each tiling system $\mathfrak{D}$, a formula $F_{\mathfrak{D}}$ such that there is a tiling by $\mathfrak{D}$ if and only if $F_{\mathfrak{D}}$ is satisfiable. Since it is unsolvable whether there is a tiling by a tiling system, it must also be unsolvable whether a formula is satisfiable.

Let $\mathfrak{D} = (D, d_0, H, V)$ be any tiling system. The formula $F_{\mathfrak{D}}$ has a 2-place predicate sign corresponding to each tile; that is, if d is a tile in D, then P_d will be a 2-place predicate sign of $F_{\mathfrak{D}}$. The model that $F_{\mathfrak{D}}$ is intended to have (in case $F_{\mathfrak{D}}$ is satisfiable) has universe $\mathbb{N}$, and the atomic formula P_dxy is intended to signify that that the values of the variables x, y—numbers $m, n \in \mathbb{N}$—designate a position (m, n) in the plane at which a tile of type d is located.

The formula $F_{\mathfrak{D}}$ has four parts:

1. an assertion that every lattice-point position contains at most one tile;
2. an assertion that at position (0, 0) tile d_0 is located;
3. an assertion that every horizontally adjacent pair of positions is covered with a pair of tiles from H;
4. an assertion that every vertically adjacent pair of positions is covered with a pair of tiles from V.

Note that Condition 1 plus either 3 or 4 implies that every position is covered by exactly one tile; that is, we do not need to assert separately that there is a tile at each position.

In addition to the 2-place predicate signs, $F_{\mathfrak{D}}$ uses a constant sign a, which stands for the numerical value $0 \in \mathbb{N}$, and a 1-place function sign f, which stands for the successor function.

The formula $F_{\mathfrak{D}}$ is then as follows:

$$\forall x \forall y \, (\bigwedge_{\substack{d_1, d_2 \in D \\ d_1 \neq d_2}} \neg(P_{d_1}xy \wedge P_{d_2}xy) \tag{1}$$

$$\wedge \; P_{d_0}aa \tag{2}$$

$$\wedge \bigvee_{(d_1, d_2) \in H} (P_{d_1}xy \wedge P_{d_2}f(x)y) \tag{3}$$

$$\wedge \bigvee_{(d_1, d_2) \in V} (P_{d_1}xy \wedge P_{d_2}xf(y))) \tag{4}$$

Here we have used $\bigwedge$ and $\bigvee$ in a natural extension of the way they were introduced in Section 8.5. For example, in (1) the conjunction of $\neg(P_{d_1}xy \wedge P_{d_2}xy)$ is taken over all pairs of distinct tiles d_1, d_2 in D.

First suppose there is a tiling by $\mathfrak{D}$. Then the model we informally described above is indeed a model for $F_{\mathfrak{D}}$. To be precise, suppose

$$\tau : \mathbb{N} \times \mathbb{N} \rightarrow D$$

is a tiling such that

$$\tau(0, 0) = d_0$$
$$(\tau(m, n), \tau(m + 1, n)) \in H \qquad \text{for all } m, n \in \mathbb{N}$$
$$(\tau(m, n), \tau(m, n + 1)) \in V \qquad \text{for all } m, n \in \mathbb{N}.$$

Then from τ we define a structure $\mathfrak{A}$ for F as follows.

$$[\mathfrak{A}] = \mathbb{N}$$
$$P_d^{\mathfrak{A}} = \{(m, n) : \tau(m, n) = d\} \qquad \text{for each } d \in T$$
$$f^{\mathfrak{A}}(m) = m + 1 \qquad \text{for } m \in \mathbb{N}$$
$$a^{\mathfrak{A}} = 0$$

Then $\mathfrak{A}$ is a model for $F_{\mathfrak{D}}$, since

1. for every $m, n \in \mathbb{N}$ and every distinct $d_1, d_2 \in D$, it cannot happen both that $\tau(m, n) = d_1$ and that $\tau(m, n) = d_2$;
2. $\tau(0, 0) = d_0$;
3. for all $m, n \in \mathbb{N}$, there is a pair $(d_1, d_2) \in H$ such that $\tau(m, n) = d_1$ and $\tau(m + 1, n) = d_2$;
4. for all $m, n \in \mathbb{N}$, there is a pair $(d_1, d_2) \in V$ such that $\tau(m, n) = d_1$ and $\tau(m, n + 1) = d_2$.

Now for the converse. Suppose F is satisfiable. By the Expansion Theorem, $E(F_{\mathfrak{D}})$ is satisfiable, so there is a truth-assignment $\mathfrak{A}$ such that $\mathfrak{A} \models E(F_{\mathfrak{D}})$. Now $F_{\mathfrak{D}}$ is a positive formula, so $D(F_{\mathfrak{D}}) = \{a, f(a), f(f(a)), \ldots, f^n(a), \ldots\}$ and $E(F_{\mathfrak{D}})$ is the set of all quantifier-free formulas that can be derived from the matrix of $F_{\mathfrak{D}}$ by substituting terms $f^m(a)$ and $f^n(a)$ for x and y in the matrix of $F_{\mathfrak{D}}$. Each such quantifier-free formula must be verified by $\mathfrak{A}$.

We claim that a mapping $\tau: \mathbb{N} \times \mathbb{N} \to D$ can be defined by

$$\tau(m, n) = d \quad \text{if and only if} \quad \mathfrak{A} \models P_d f^m(a) f^n(a).$$

In order for this to be a proper definition it is required that for each $m, n \in \mathbb{N}$ there be exactly one $d \in D$ such that $\mathfrak{A} \models P_d f^m(a) f^n(a)$. If there were more than one such d for some m and n, then one of the formulas in $E(F_{\mathfrak{D}})$ would have a subformula

$$\neg(P_{d_1} f^m(a) f^n(a) \wedge P_{d_2} f^m(a) f^n(a))$$

that was falsified by $\mathfrak{A}$. To show that such a d exists for each (m, n), note that Condition 3 alone requires that for any terms $t_1, t_2 \in D(F_{\mathfrak{D}})$ there is a $d \in D$ such that $\mathfrak{A} \models P_d t_1 t_2$.

We claim further that the mapping τ so defined does in fact satisfy the stipulations of the system $\mathfrak{D}$. For example, let $m, n \in \mathbb{N}$; to show that

$(\tau(m, n), \tau(m+1, n)) \in H$, note that $\mathfrak{A}$ must verify the disjunction

$$\bigvee_{(d_1,d_2)\in H} (P_{d_1} f^m(a) f^n(a) \wedge P_{d_2} f^{m+1}(a) f^n(a)),$$

so $\mathfrak{A}$ must verify some formula

$$P_{d_1} f^m(a) f^n(a) \wedge P_{d_2} f^{m+1}(a) f^n(a)$$

for some $(d_1, d_2) \in H$, so $\mathfrak{A} \models P_{d_1} f^m(a) f^n(a)$ and also $\mathfrak{A} \models P_{d_2} f^{m+1}(a) f^n(a)$. Thus, by the definition of τ, $\tau(m, n) = d_1$ and $\tau(m+1, n) = d_2$ with $(d_1, d_2) \in H$. The origin and vertical adjacency conditions may be checked similarly. ■

The proof of the above theorem uses the Expansion Theorem only in a special case, when the formula to be considered is positive and so the formula is identical to its functional form. However, if we wish to show that even for restricted sets of formulas, satisfiability is unsolvable, we must use the full strength of the Expansion Theorem.

Theorem 9.6.2. *The problem of satisfiability in the predicate calculus is unsolvable, even for formulas without function signs.*

Proof. If the formula $F_{\mathfrak{D}}$ of the previous proof had been the functional form of a formula $G_{\mathfrak{D}}$ without function signs, then this theorem would follow directly, since $F_{\mathfrak{D}}$ would be satisfiable if and only if $G_{\mathfrak{D}}$ was satisfiable. However, $F_{\mathfrak{D}}$ is not of the correct form, since no formula without function signs could have a functional form with prefix $\forall x \forall y$ and both $f(x)$ and $f(y)$ in the matrix. However $F_{\mathfrak{D}}$ is easily rearranged to avoid this problem; replace (4) by

$$\bigvee_{(d_1,d_2)\in V} (P_{d_1} yx \wedge P_{d_2} y f(x))$$

The resulting formula, call it $F'_{\mathfrak{D}}$, is equivalent to $F_{\mathfrak{D}}$. Moreover, $F'_{\mathfrak{D}}$ may be viewed as the functional form of the following formula $G_{\mathfrak{D}}$.

$$\begin{aligned} \exists z \forall x \exists v \forall y \, (& \bigwedge_{\substack{d_1, d_2 \in D \\ d_1 \neq d_2}} \neg(P_{d_1} xy \wedge P_{d_2} xy) \\ & \wedge P_{d_0} zz \\ & \wedge \bigvee_{(d_1,d_2)\in H} (P_{d_1} xy \wedge P_{d_2} vy) \\ & \wedge \bigvee_{(d_1,d_2)\in V} (P_{d_1} yx \wedge P_{d_2} yv)) \end{aligned}$$

When the functional form of $G_{\mathfrak{D}}$ is formed, a constant sign a replaces the variable z in the matrix and the indicial term $f(x)$ replaces v in the matrix, so the functional form of $G_{\mathfrak{D}}$ is $F'_{\mathfrak{D}}$ as desired. ■

We close this section by showing that satisfiability in the propositional calculus is $\mathcal{NP}$-complete. To do so we reduce the bounded version of the tiling problem given in Theorem 7.6.1. In that problem we are given both a tiling system $\mathfrak{D} = (D, d_0, H, V)$ and a number n in unary notation and are asked to determine whether there is an $n \times n$ tiling by $\mathfrak{D}$. Given $\mathfrak{D}$ and n, let us form a formula $\alpha_{\mathfrak{D},n}$ of the propositional calculus as follows. Construct the formula $F_{\mathfrak{D}}$ exactly as in the proof of Theorem 9.6.1; then instead of considering the full Herbrand expansion $E(F_{\mathfrak{D}})$, let $E^n(F_{\mathfrak{D}})$, for each $n \geq 0$, be the subset of $E(F_{\mathfrak{D}})$ consisting of all those formulas in which the terms substituted for x and y in $F^*_{\mathfrak{D}}$ are $f^i(a)$ and $f^j(a)$, where i and j are less than or equal to n. That is,

$$E^n(F_{\mathfrak{D}}) = \{F^*_{\mathfrak{D}}[x/f^i(a), y/f^j(a)]: 0 \leq i, j \leq n\}.$$

This is a finite set, so that conjunction of all the formulas in it is a formula, which may be viewed as a formula of the propositional calculus. Exactly as in the proof of Theorem 9.6.1, it follows that $\alpha_{\mathfrak{D},n}$ is satisfiable if and only if there is an $(n + 2) \times (n + 2)$ tiling by $\mathfrak{D}$. It remains only to show that the transformation from $\mathfrak{D}$ and n to $\alpha_{\mathfrak{D},n}$ is a polynomial-time transformation. Now the length of $F^*_{\mathfrak{D}}$ is polynomial in the size of $\mathfrak{D}$; in fact, if $|D| = k$, then $|F^*_{\mathfrak{D}}| = O(k^3)$, since each of the major subformulas (1) through (4) of $F_{\mathfrak{D}}$ involves, at worst, a conjunction of two atomic formulas for each pair of members of D, and each predicate sign has length $O(k)$. Each member of the set $E^n(F_{\mathfrak{D}})$ of $(n + 1)^2$ formulas is longer than $F^*_{\mathfrak{D}}$ by a factor that is the length of the terms, $f^i(a)$ and $f^j(a)$, substituted for x and y. But the length of these terms is at worst proportional to n, since the longest of them are $f^n(a)$ and $f^n(a)$. So each member of $E^n(F_{\mathfrak{D}})$ is of length $O(k^3n)$; since there are $(n + 1)^2$ members in all, the length of $\alpha_{\mathfrak{D},n}$ is polynomial in the sizes of $\mathfrak{D}$ and n. It is also easy to see that $\alpha_{\mathfrak{D},n}$ can actually be constructed from $\mathfrak{D}$ and n in polynomial time.

Finally, it was argued in Section 8.4 that the satisfiability problem for the propositional calculus is in $\mathcal{NP}$. This completes the proof of Theorem 9.6.3.

Theorem 9.6.3. *The satisfiability problem for the propositional calculus is $\mathcal{NP}$-complete.*

9.7 RESOLUTION IN THE PREDICATE CALCULUS

Theorem 9.5.1 suggests a method for establishing that a formula of the predicate calculus is unsatisfiable: Generate its Herbrand expansion a little bit at a time, occasionally pausing to check, by truth tables for example, whether the finite portion thus far produced is unsatisfiable. When and if a finite unsatisfiable portion of the Herbrand expansion is found, we can conclude that the original formula is unsatisfiable; and if the formula is unsatisfiable, such an unsatisfiable subset of the Herbrand expansion will eventually be discovered.

Of course, there is no reason why the truth-table method is preferable to any other for testing satisfiability of the partially generated Herbrand expansion. We could use resolution instead, for example. The resolution method requires that the formulas in the Herbrand expansion be converted to clause form, and since each of these formulas has the same structure (only the atomic formulas being different from one to the other) it is apparent that a good deal of effort is wasted by making the same conversion repeatedly. The idea naturally occurs, then, of converting the matrix of the functional form of the original formula to clause form, and making substitutions into these clauses, rather than making substitutions and then converting to clause form.

So let us extend to the predicate calculus the notions of clauses and clause sets. A **literal** is now any atomic formula, possibly containing variables, or the negation of such an atomic formula. If L is a literal, we write $\bar{L}$ for $\neg L$ if L is an atomic formula, and for M if L is the literal $\neg M$, where M is atomic. A clause is a finite set of literals (possibly the empty clause $\square$) and a clause set is a set of clauses (possibly the empty clause set $\varnothing$). Any formula without quantifiers can be converted to a clause set by putting it in conjunctive normal form and then regarding the disjunctions of literals as clauses.

Next, suppose that D is a free universe (specifically, the Herbrand universe of a formula). Then from any clause we can form a set of clauses without variables by substituting terms from D for the variables of the clause. These variable-free clauses will be called **ground** clauses, and will be called **ground instances** over D of the clause from which they were derived. **Ground literals** are defined similarly. If S is a clause set, we write $E(S, D)$ for the set of all ground instances of clauses in S, when the terms substituted for the variables are drawn from the free universe D.

Example 9.7.1

Let $F = \forall y \exists x (Pxy \vee (\neg Pyx \wedge \neg Pxx))$. Then F^* is $(Pf(y)y \vee (\neg Pyf(y) \wedge \neg Pf(y)f(y)))$. In conjunctive normal form, this becomes $((Pf(y)y \vee \neg Pyf(y)) \wedge (Pf(y)y \vee \neg Pf(y)f(y)))$; as a clause set, $\{\{Pf(y)y, \neg Pyf(y)\}, \{Pf(y)y, \neg Pf(y)f(y)\}\}$. With $D = D(F) = \{\dagger, f(\dagger), f(f(\dagger)), \ldots\}$, some of the ground instances of clauses in this clause set are $\{Pf(\dagger)\dagger, \neg P\dagger f(\dagger)\}$, $\{Pf(\dagger)\dagger, \neg Pf(\dagger)f(\dagger)\}$, and $\{Pf(f(\dagger))f(\dagger), \neg Pf(\dagger)f(f(\dagger))\}$.

Now a resolution-based satisfiability-testing method for the propositional calculus might be described as follows: Given a formula F, convert F^*

to a clause set S; form larger and larger finite subsets $D_1, D_2, \ldots$ of $D(F)$; form the expansions $E(S, D_1), E(S, D_2), \ldots$; test each in sequence for satisfiability by computing $R^*(E(S, D_1)), R^*(E(S, D_2)), \ldots$, in an attempt to find some $R^*(E(S, D_i))$ that contains the empty clause.

But again one would find that a good deal of effort is wasted in this process. The reason this time is that many similar resolvents are formed with different instances of the same clauses.

Example 9.7.2

Let S be the clause set $\{\{Pxy, Qx\}, \{\neg Pxf(x)\}\}$. Some of the ground instances are

$$\{P\dagger\dagger, Q\dagger\}, \{\neg P\dagger f(\dagger)\},$$
$$\{P\dagger f(\dagger), Q\dagger\}, \{\neg Pf(\dagger)f(f(\dagger))\},$$
$$\{Pf(\dagger)\dagger, Qf(\dagger)\}, \{Pf(\dagger)f(\dagger), Qf(\dagger)\}, \ldots.$$

In particular, for every n, both

$$\{Pf^n(\dagger)f^{n+1}(\dagger), Qf^n(\dagger)\} \quad \text{and} \quad \{\neg Pf^n(\dagger)f^{n+1}(\dagger)\}$$

are ground instances; these can be resolved to yield $\{Qf^n(\dagger)\}$ for each n. But in some sense (made precise below), to form all these resolvents would really be to perform the *same resolution* over and over gain; once one sees the pattern, it is clear that no progress is ever made in this way towards producing the empty clause.

The thought then occurs to treat a clause containing variables as a *bundle* of similar clauses, namely all its ground instances. Instead of resolving ground instances, resolve the bundles to yield another bundle; one can always form ground instances later, if desired. The whole trick in carrying through this idea is to come up with the right notion of the *resolvent* of two clauses containing variables. We work backwards from the goal towards the definition in two lemmas.

Let S be a finite or infinite clause set and let D be a set of terms. Hereafter by an *instance* of a clause or literal we shall mean a ground clause or literal which is a ground instance of that clause or literal over D.

Lemma 9.7.1. *Suppose that the* resolvents *of two clauses are defined in such a way that*

(a) *for* ground *clauses the old definition* (*Definition 8.7.1*) *agrees with the new;*

and for any clauses C_1 and C_2,

(b1) *every resolvent of an instance of C_1 and an instance of C_2 is an instance of some resolvent of C_1 and C_2, and* (b2) *every instance of a resolvent of C_1 and C_2 contains as a subset some resolvent of an instance of C_1 and an instance of C_2.*

Define, as before,

$$R(S) = S \cup \{C\colon C \text{ is a resolvent of two clauses in } S\};$$
$$R^0(S) = S;$$
$$R^{n+1}(S) = R(R^n(S)) \qquad \text{for } n \geq 0;$$
$$R^*(S) = \bigcup \{R^n(S)\colon n \geq 0\}.$$

Then $\square \in R^*(E(S, D))$ *if and only if* $\square \in R^*(S)$.

That is, to see whether the empty clause can be obtained by repeated resolutions of *ground instances* of clauses in S, it suffices to see whether it can be obtained by repeated resolutions of the clauses themselves.

Proof. We first show that for each $n \geq 0$, $R^n(E(S, D)) \subseteq E(R^n(S), D)$; it will follow that if $\square$ is in the former set, it is in the latter. This we do by induction on n. For $n = 0$ the two sets are the same. Now let $n \geq 0$.

If $C \in R^{n+1}(E(S, D))$,

then $C \in R(R^n(E(S, D)))$ by definition of R^{n+1},

then C is a resolvent of two clauses in $R^n(E(S, D))$ by definition of R,

then C is a resolvent of two clauses in $E(R^n(S), D)$ by the induction hypothesis,

then C is an instance of a resolvent of two clauses in $R^n(S)$ by (b1),

then C is in $E(R(R^n(S)), D) = E(R^{n+1}(S), D)$.

To complete the proof, we shall use the fact that for each $n \geq 0$, every clause in $E(R^n(S), D)$ includes as a subset some clause in $R^n(E(S, D))$. Since the empty clause has only itself as a subset, it will follow that if $\square \in E(R^n(S), D)$, then $\square \in R^n(E(S, D))$. This proof of this fact resembles the previous proof (see Problem 9.7.2). ∎

Before stating the second lemma, we need a bit more notation. We henceforth use Greek letters such as η and θ for **substitutions**, that is, expressions of the form $[v_1/t_1, \ldots, v_n/t_n]$, where the v_i are distinct variables and the t_i are terms. These expressions have up to now been used simply as a notational convenience, but we shall now recognize them as mathematical objects in their own right; shortly we shall develop some rules for manipulating them.

Now fix a free universe D and assume that all substitutions mentioned below are of the form $[v_1/t_1, \ldots, v_n/t_n]$, where $t_1, \ldots, t_n \in D$. For any clauses B_1, B_2, C_1, and C_2, let us define the following set of clauses.

$$r(B_1, B_2; C_1, C_2) = \{B_1\theta_1 \cup B_2\theta_2 : C_1\theta_1 = C_2\theta_2 = \{L\} \text{ for some literal } L, \text{ and } L, B_1\theta_1, \text{ and } B_2\theta_2 \text{ are all ground}\}$$

That is, in order for $r(B_1, B_2; C_1, C_2)$ to be nonempty, C_1 and C_2 must both be sets of atomic formulas or must both be sets of negations of atomic formulas. By substituting for the variables of C_1, all the literals in C_1 collapse to the same ground literal; and by substituting in another way for the variables in C_2, all the literals in C_2 also become that same ground literal. Then $r(B_1, B_2; C_1, C_2)$ contains the clause obtained from B_1 and B_2 by substituting for the variables of B_1 as was done for C_1 and by substituting for the variables of B_2 as was done for C_2.

Example 9.7.3

Let $B_1 = \{Px\}$, $B_2 = \{Qf(y)\}$, $C_1 = \{Rxf(z)\}$, $C_2 = \{Rg(w)y\}$. Then $C_1\theta_1 = C_2\theta_2 = \{Rg(t_1)f(t_2)\}$ whenever $\theta_1 = [x/g(t_1), z/t_2]$ and $\theta_2 = [w/t_1, y/f(t_2)]$ for some terms t_1 and t_2. So

$$r(B_1, B_2; C_1, C_2) = \{\{Pg(t_1), Qf(f(t_2))\} : t_1, t_2 \in D\}.$$

Lemma 9.7.2. *Suppose that for any clauses B_1, B_2, C_1, and C_2 such that $r(B_1, B_2; C_1, C_2) \neq \varnothing$, there is a clause B such that*

$$r(B_1, B_2; C_1, C_2) = E(B, D).$$

Then there is a definition of resolvent *that satisfies Conditions* (a) *and* (b) *of Lemma 9.7.1.*

Proof. Define B to be a resolvent of B_1 and B_2 provided that B is a clause such that, for some nonempty subsets $C_1 \subseteq B_1$ and $C_2 \subseteq B_2$,

$$E(B, D) = r(B_1 - C_1, B_2 - C_2; C_1, \{\bar{L} : L \in C_2\}).$$

If B_1 and B_2 are ground clauses already, then B is a ground clause, $E(B, D) = B$, C_1 and C_2 must be singletons, and so a resolvent of B_1 and B_2 in this sense is a resolvent in the sense of the propositional calculus, and vice versa. Thus (a) is satisfied.

To show (b1), consider a resolvent of instances $B_1\theta_1$ and $B_2\theta_2$; namely $B_0 = (B_1\theta_1 - \{L_0\}) \cup (B_2\theta_2 - \{\bar{L}_0\})$. Then let $C_1 = \{L \in B_1 : L\theta_1 = L_0\}$ and $C_2 = \{L \in B_2 : L\theta_2 = \bar{L}_0\}$. Then

$$B_0 = (B_1 - C_1)\theta_1 \cup (B_2 - C_2)\theta_2 \in r(B_1 - C_1, B_2 - C_2; C_1, \{\bar{L} : L \in C_2\}) = E(B, D)$$

for some resolvent B of B_1 and B_2, as was to be shown.

To show (b2), suppose $B_0 \in E(B, D)$ for some resolvent B of B_1 and

B_2, and let

$$E(B, D) = r(B_1 - C_1, B_2 - C_2; C_1, \{\bar{L} : L \in C_2\}),$$

where $C_1 \subseteq B_1$ and $C_2 \subseteq B_2$. Then $B_0 = (B_1 - C_1)\theta_1 \cup (B_2 - C_2)\theta_2$ for some θ_1 and θ_2 such that $C_1\theta_1 = \{\bar{L}\theta_2 : L \in C_2\} = \{L_0\}$ for some ground literal L_0. Now for *any* clauses A_1 and A_2 and any substitution θ, $A_1\theta - A_2\theta \subseteq (A_1 - A_2)\theta$; that is, any instance of a literal in A_1 that does not coincide, under the same substitution, with any literal of A_2 must be an instance under that substitution of some literal in A_1 that is not a literal in A_2. (The converse fails, which is why (b1) and (b2) are asymmetric; see Problem 9.7.4.) Therefore

$$(B_1\theta_1 - C_1\theta_1) \bigcup (B_2\theta_2 - C_2\theta_2) \subseteq (B_1 - C_1)\theta_1 \cup (B_2 - C_2)\theta_2 = B_0.$$

But $(B_1\theta_1 - C_1\theta_1) \cup (B_2\theta_2 - C_2\theta_2)$ is a resolvent of instances of B_1 and B_2, since $C_1\theta_1 = \{\bar{L}\theta_2 : L \in C_2\} = \{L_0\}$ for some single literal L_0; so (b2) is established. ■

It thus remains only to show that $r(B_1, B_2; C_1, C_2) = \{B_1\theta_1 \cup B_2\theta_2 : C_1\theta_1 = C_2\theta_2 = \{L\}$ for some literal $L\}$ can always be expressed as the expansion of some single clause.

Before proceeding, let us introduce the small calculus of substitutions mentioned above. First, to be precise, a **substitution** is an expression $[y_1/t_1, \ldots, y_n/t_n]$ where the y_i are distinct variables, the t_i are terms, and no $t_i = y_i$. The individual expressions y_i/t_i are the **components** of the substitution, and we treat the substitution as the *set* of these components, so that two substitutions differing only in the *order* of their components will be considered identical. Substitutions can be composed, and there is an identity substitution ϵ, namely, the empty substitution [ ]. The composition operation is denoted by juxtaposition and is defined via the rule that for any clause or literal A and any substitutions η and θ, $A(\eta\theta) = (A\eta)\theta$. Formally, the composition of $\eta = [x_1/t_1, \ldots, x_n/t_n]$ and $\theta = [y_1/s_1, \ldots, y_m/s_m]$ is formed from the list $[x_1/t_1\theta, \ldots, x_n/t_n\theta, y_1/s_1, \ldots, y_m/s_m]$ by deleting any y_i/s_i with y_i among $x_1, \ldots, x_n$ and any $x_i/t_i\theta$ with $x_i = t_i\theta$.

A **variant** of a clause is any clause that can be obtained from it by a one-to-one replacement of variables. Variants are easy to produce but should not be dismissed lightly; they play a crucial role later. In particular, we shall occasionally need what we call a **separating pair of substitutions** for a pair of clauses B_1 and B_2. By this we mean a pair of substitutions ξ_1 and ξ_2 such that $B_1\xi_1$ is a variant of B_1, $B_2\xi_2$ is a variant of B_2, and $B_1\xi_1$ and $B_2\xi_2$ have no variable in common. Naturally, if B_1 and B_2 already have no variable in common, ξ_1 and ξ_2 can both be empty; otherwise one or the other must contain a substitution component x/y for any variable x they have in common, where y is some new variable for each such x. We assume that lexicographic ordering is used to distinguish some particular separating pair of substitutions ξ, η for any pair of clauses B_1 and B_2; we call ξ, η *the* separating pair of substitutions for B_1 and B_2.

Now back to the problem of writing $r(B_1, B_2; C_1, C_2)$ as $E(B, D)$ for some clause B. We can easily express $r(B_1, B_2; C_1, C_2)$ as *a* set of ground instances of *some* single clause. Simply let ξ, η be the separating pair of substitutions for $B_1 \cup C_1$ and $B_2 \cup C_2$, and then for any θ_1 and θ_2, we can readily find a substitution θ such that $B_1\theta_1 \cup B_2\theta_2 = (B_1\xi \cup B_2\eta)\theta$. (For example, if $B_1 = \{Px\}$ and $B_2 = \{Qx\}$, then perhaps $\xi = [x/y]$ and $\eta = \epsilon$, so $B_1\xi \cup B_2\eta = \{Py, Qx\}$. Then if $\theta_1 = [x/f(a)]$ and $\theta_2 = [x/a]$, θ would be $[y/f(a), x/a]$.) Then $r(B_1, B_2; C_1, C_2)$ can be expressed as $\{B\theta : |C\theta| = 1\}$, where $B = B_1\xi \cup B_2\eta$ and $C = C_1\xi \cup C_2\eta$, and it is understood that $B\theta$ and $C\theta$ must be ground clauses. Now suppose we can show that *every* substitution θ such that $C\theta$ is a clause containing a single ground literal may be gotten as $C\sigma\theta'$, for some θ', where σ is a *fixed* substitution such that $C\sigma$ is a clause containing a single, not necessarily ground, literal. Since then $|C\sigma\theta'| = 1$ for *any* θ', we shall have $r(B_1, B_2; C_1, C_2) = E(B\sigma, D)$ as desired.

Call a substitution θ such that $|C\theta| = 1$ a **unifier** of C. Then the whole problem comes down to proving the following theorem.

Theorem 9.7.1. (Unification Theorem) *Any clause C that has a unifier has a* **most general** *unifier, that is, a unifier σ such that every unifier θ of C is $\sigma\theta'$ for some θ'.*

Proof. We prove this theorem by stating an algorithm, then proving that the algorithm determines correctly whether or not a clause, C, has a unifier, and, if it does, constructs a most general unifier. Say that C is **unifiable** if it has a unifier.

Unification Algorithm.

1. If some of the literals in C are atomic formulas and some are the negations of atomic formulas, halt; C is not unifiable.

2. If the literals in C do not all have the same predicate sign, halt; C is not unifiable.

3. Let $i = 0$ and let σ_0 be ϵ, the empty substitution.

4. If $|C\sigma_i| = 1$ then halt; C is unifiable and σ_i is a most general unifier.

5. Since $|C\sigma_i| > 1$, $C\sigma_i$ contains distinct literals L_1 and L_2. Scan L_1 and L_2 from left to right until the first discrepancy is found. If the discrepancy arises because L_1 and L_2 have different function signs at corresponding positions, halt; C_1 and C_2 are not unifiable.

6. The discrepancy discovered in (5) must have occurred because one literal has a variable where the other has a function sign or a distinct variable. Let v be the variable at the position under scrutiny in one of the literals, and let t be the term beginning at the same position in the other literal (t might also be a variable). If v occurs in t, halt; C is not unifiable.

7. Let $\sigma_{i+1} = \sigma_i[v/t]$ and $i = i + 1$, and go back to Step (4).

We must show: that the algorithm always terminates; that if it does so via (1), (2), (5), or (6), then C is indeed not unifiable; and that otherwise σ_k is a most general unifier of C, where k is the final value of i. There should be no argument about Step (1) or (2); clearly a substitution cannot change negation signs or predicate signs. So we need be concerned only with the main part of the algorithm, Steps (3) through (7). We show by induction that for each value of i, if C is unifiable then so is $C\sigma_i$. Now if the algorithm terminates via (5) or (6) then $C\sigma_i$ cannot be unifiable; in the former case a unifier would have to make distinct function signs identical, and in the latter case any substitution would produce two terms of different lengths. So to complete the proof, it suffices to assume that C is unifiable and to show that $C\sigma_i$ is unifiable for each i and that the algorithm eventually terminates via (4).

Since C is unifiable, there is a substitution θ such that $|C\theta| = 1$. We find, for each i, a substitution θ_i such that $\sigma_i\theta_i = \theta$. For $i = 0$ we have $\sigma_0 = \epsilon$ and $\theta_0 = \theta$; thus $\sigma_0\theta_0 = \theta$ and $C\sigma_0$ is unifiable by assumption.

Now assume as the induction hypothesis that $C\sigma_i$ is unifiable and $\sigma_i\theta_i = \theta$. Suppose that the algorithm reaches Step (6), and let v and t be as specified there. Since $|(C\sigma_i)\theta_i| = 1$, $v\theta_i = t\theta_i$. Now the component $v/t\theta_i$ need not be part of θ_i, since $t\theta_i$ might be the variable v. However, if θ_i has a component with v on the left, then the term on the right must be $t\theta_i$. For otherwise, if θ_i had a component v/t' where $t' \neq t\theta_i$, then $v\theta_i$—which is t'—would be different from $t\theta_i$.

Let θ_{i+1} be the result of removing from θ_i the component $v/t\theta_i$, if it occurs. Then no component of θ_{i+1} has v on the left. Moreover,

$$\begin{aligned}
\sigma_{i+1}\theta_{i+1} &= \sigma_i[v/t]\theta_{i+1} \\
&= \sigma_i\theta_{i+1}[v/t\theta_{i+1}] && \text{since } v \text{ is not on the left-hand side of any component in } \theta_{i+1} \\
&= \sigma_i\theta_{i+1}[v/t\theta_i] && \text{since } v \text{ does not occur in } t\text{, by (6)} \\
&= \sigma_i\theta_i && \text{by definition of } \theta_{i+1}.
\end{aligned}$$

Since $\sigma_{i+1}\theta_{i+1} = \sigma_i\theta_i$ and $C\sigma_i$ is unifiable, so is $C\sigma_{i+1}$. Thus it remains only to show that the algorithm eventually terminates. But since both v and t occur in $C\sigma_i$ but v does not occur in t, $C\sigma_{i+1}$ has fewer variables than $C\sigma_i$.

So the algorithm repeats Steps (3) through (7) a number of times at most equal to the number of variables in C. ■

Example 9.7.4

Let $C = \{Pxf(x)y, Pg(z)wy, Pxuu\}$. Clearly Steps (1) and (2) are passed successfully. The first two literals are chosen and a discrepancy is found with $v = x$ and $t = g(z)$; we let $\sigma_1 = [x/g(z)]$. Then $C\sigma_1 = \{Pg(z)f(g(z))y, Pg(z)wy, Pg(z)uu\}$. Going back to Step (5), a discrepancy is found in the first two literals, with $v = w$ and $t = f(g(z))$. So $\sigma_2 = \sigma_1[w/f(g(z))] = [x/g(z), w/f(g(z))]$ and $C\sigma_2 = \{Pg(z)f(g(z))y, Pg(z)uu\}$. The next time around, $v = u$ and $t = f(g(z))$; $\sigma_3 = [x/g(z), w/f(g(z)), u/f(g(z))]$ and $C\sigma_3 = \{Pg(z)f(g(z))y, Pg(z)f(g(z))f(g(z))\}$. Finally, on the fourth iteration, $v = y$ and $t = f(g(z))$, so $\sigma_4 = [x/g(z), w/f(g(z)), u/f(g(z)), y/f(g(z))]$. Now $C\sigma_4 = \{Pg(z)f(g(z))f(g(z))\}$ and the algorithm terminates successfully with the most general unifier σ_4.

Clearly all most general unifiers are equally useful; we assume that one, called *the* most general unifier, is chosen by the algorithm in some fixed way.

We can now pull the threads together and describe the resolution method for the predicate calculus quite simply. Let B_1 and B_2 be clauses, and let their separating substitutions be ξ and η. If there are nonempty subsets $C_1 \subseteq B_1$ and $C_2 \subseteq B_2$ such that $C_1\xi \cup \{\bar{L} : L \in C_2\eta\}$ is unifiable with most general unifier σ, then $((B_1 - C_1)\xi \cup (B_2 - C_2)\eta)\sigma$ will be called a **resolvent** of B_1 and B_2. If S is any set of clauses, then $R(S)$ consists of S and all resolvents of clauses in S, $R^0(S) = S$, $R^{n+1}(S) = R(R^n(S))$ for each $n \geq 0$, and $R^*(S) = \bigcup \{R^n(S) : n \geq 0\}$. Then we have proved the following theorem.

Theorem 9.7.2. (Resolution Theorem for the Predicate Calculus) *A clause set S is unsatisfiable if and only if $\square \in R^*(S)$.*

This theorem, together with the algorithm for finding most general unifiers, is the basis for many computer programs which test formulas for satisfiability. To recapitulate, the method is this: given a formula F, put F^* into conjunctive normal form and consider it to be a set S of clauses. Repeatedly find all possible resolvents of clauses in S and add them to S; since there are only finitely many clauses and each clause has only finitely many subsets, there are only finitely many resolvents at each stage. If $\square$ is ever generated, then the original formula was unsatisfiable. .

Many refinements and extensions to this method have been proposed and implemented as computer programs. However, any discussion of these methods would lead us well beyond the scope of this book.

Example 9.7.5

Let F be the formula

$$(\forall y \exists x(Txy \wedge (Ey \leftrightarrow \neg Ex))$$
$$\wedge \forall x \forall y \forall z((Txy \wedge Tyz) \rightarrow Txz)$$
$$\wedge \forall x \neg \exists y(Ex \wedge Ey \wedge Txy)).$$

Rectifying, forming F^*, and converting to conjunctive normal form, we obtain

$$(Ty_1 f(y_1) \wedge (\neg Ey_1 \vee \neg Ef(y_1)) \wedge (Ey_1 \vee Ef(y_1))$$
$$\wedge (\neg Tx_2 y_2 \vee \neg Ty_2 z_2 \vee Tx_2 z_2)$$
$$\wedge (\neg Ex_3 \vee \neg Ey_3 \vee \neg Tx_3 y_3)),$$

or, as a clause set,

1. $\{\{Ty_1 f(y_1)\},$
2. $\{\neg Ey_1, \neg Ef(y_1)\},$
3. $\{Ey_1, Ef(y_1)\},$
4. $\{\neg Tx_2 y_2, \neg Ty_2 z_2, Tx_2 z_2\},$
5. $\{\neg Ex_3, \neg Ey_3, \neg Tx_3 y_3\}\}.$

Let us show that F is unsatisfiable by selectively forming resolvents. We indicate, in each case, which clauses were used and which subsets of these clauses led to the formation of a resolvent.

6.	$\{\neg Tf(y)z, Tyz\}$	(1), (4)	$\{Ty_1 f(y_1)\}$	$\{\neg Tx_2 y_2\}$
7.	$\{Ty' f(f(y'))\}$	(1), (6)	$\{Ty_1 f(y_1)\}$	$\{\neg Tf(y)z\}$
8.	$\{\neg Ey', \neg Ef(f(y'))\}$	(5), (7)	$\{\neg Tx_3 y_3\}$	$\{Ty' f(f(y'))\}$
9.	$\{\neg Ey', Ef(y')\}$	(3), (8)	$\{Ef(y_1)\}$	$\{\neg Ef(f(y'))\}$
10.	$\{\neg Ey'\}$	(2), (9)	$\{\neg Ef(y_1)\}$	$\{Ef(y')\}$
11.	$\{Ey_1\}$	(3), (10)	$\{Ef(y_1)\}$	$\{\neg Ey'\}$
12.	$\square$	(10), (11)	$\{\neg Ey'\}$	$\{Ey_1\}$

PROBLEMS

9.1.1. Write the following assertions as formulas of the predicate calculus.

(a) P stands for a reflexive binary relation.

(b) P stands for a transitive binary relation.

(c) f stands for an onto function.

(d) f stands for a one-to-one function. (Introduce a 2-place predicate sign E to stand for the relation of equality.)

(e) The value of the function represented by the 2-place function sign f does not depend on the second argument.

9.1.2. Let C be a 3-place predicate sign standing for the relation between a child and his or her two parents. Write formulas stating that:

(a) no pair of siblings has any children;

(b) no pair of first cousins has any children;

(c) there are second cousins who have children.

9.1.3. Let M be a 2-place predicate sign standing for the relation between a set and a member of that set. Let S be a 2-place predicate sign standing for the relation between a set and a subset of that set. Write formulas that state each of the following.

(a) Unions exist; that is, for any two sets, there is a third set that is their union.

(b) Every set has a complement.

(c) Any member of a subset of a set is a member of that set.

(d) There is a set with no members, which is a subset of every set.

(e) Power sets exist.

9.1.4. Let $P, f,$ and x be the following predicate sign, function sign, and variable, respectively:

P is **PIII**,

f is **fIII**,

x is **v$**.

Write the following in full.

(a) The term $f(f(x))$.

(b) The atomic formula Pxx.

(c) The atomic formula $Pf(x)f(f(x))$.

(d) The formula $(\forall xPxf(x) \wedge \exists x\neg Pf(x)x)$.

9.1.5. (a) Present a context-free grammar generating the formulas of the predicate calculus.

(b) Show that the grammar of Part (a) is unambiguous.

9.1.6. What are the subformulas of these formulas?

(a) $\forall x\forall y(Pxy \wedge \neg Pyx)$

(b) $\forall x(Pxf(x) \wedge \exists y\neg Pyx)$

(c) $\forall x\forall y(Pxy \leftrightarrow \neg Rxy)$.

9.1.7. What is the scope of each occurrence of the negation sign in these formulas?

(a) $(\neg \forall x Pxx \wedge \exists x(\neg Pxy \vee Rxy))$

(b) $\neg(Rxy \wedge \neg \forall z(Pyz \vee (Pzy \wedge \neg \forall y Pyy)))$

9.1.8. What is the scope of each occurrence of a quantifier in the formulas of Problem 9.1.7?

9.1.9. What are the matrices of the formulas of Problem 9.1.7?

9.1.10. Under exactly what circumstances is the matrix of a formula a subformula of that formula?

9.2.1. Let L be a 2-place predicate sign, E a 1-place predicate sign, and f a 2-place function sign. Let x, y, and z be variables. Let $\mathfrak{A}$ be the structure such that

$$[\mathfrak{A}] = \mathbb{N};$$
$$L^{\mathfrak{A}} = \{(m, n): m < n\};$$
$$E^{\mathfrak{A}} = \{m: m \text{ is even}\};$$
$$f^{\mathfrak{A}}(m, n) = m + n.$$

Let ξ be the function from $\{x, y, z\}$ to $\mathbb{N}$ such that

$$\xi(x) = 5$$
$$\xi(y) = 2$$
$$\xi(z) = 0.$$

What are the values of the following? Explain your reasoning.

(a) $\mathfrak{A}(f(xy))_\xi$

(b) $\mathfrak{A}(f(yf(yf(yy))))_\xi$

(c) $\mathfrak{A}(Lxy)_\xi$

(d) $\mathfrak{A}(\forall x \forall y Lxf(xy))_\xi$

(e) $\mathfrak{A}(\forall z Lzf(xz))_\xi$

(f) $\mathfrak{A}(\forall x \forall y((Ex \wedge Ey) \longrightarrow Ef(xy)))_\xi$

(g) $\mathfrak{A}(\forall y((Ex \wedge Ey) \longrightarrow Ef(xy)))_\xi$

(h) $\mathfrak{A}(\forall x \exists y(Ey \wedge Lxy))_\xi$

(i) $\mathfrak{A}(\forall y(\neg Ef(xy) \longleftrightarrow Ef(yz)))_\xi$

(j) $\mathfrak{A}(\forall x(Lzx \longrightarrow \exists y(Lzy \wedge Lyz)))_\xi$

9.2.2. Which of the following are models for the formula $\exists x \exists y \exists z(Pxy \wedge (Pzy \wedge (Pxz \wedge \neg Pzx)))$?

(a) $[\mathfrak{A}] = \mathbb{N}$, $P^{\mathfrak{A}} = \{(m, n): m < n\}$

(b) $[\mathfrak{A}] = \mathbb{N}$, $P^{\mathfrak{A}} = \{(m, m+1): m \geq 0\}$

(c) $[\mathfrak{A}] = \{a, b\}^*$, $P^{\mathfrak{A}} = \{(u, v): u$ is lexicographically earlier than $v\}$

(d) $[\mathfrak{A}] = \{a, b\}^*$, $P^{\mathfrak{A}} = \{(u, ua), (u, ub): u \in \{a, b\}^*\}$

(e) $[\mathfrak{A}] = 2^{\mathbb{N}}$, $P^{\mathfrak{A}} = \{(A, B): A \subseteq B\}$

9.2.3. For which of the following structures $\mathfrak{A}$ is $\mathfrak{A}(F)_\xi = \top$ for some ξ, where F is $(\forall xPxf(x) \wedge (\neg\exists xPxz \wedge (Pzz \rightarrow \forall xPzx)))$?

(a) $[\mathfrak{A}] = \mathbb{N}$, $P^{\mathfrak{A}} = \{(m, n): m < n\}$, $f^{\mathfrak{A}}(m) = m + 3$

(b) $[\mathfrak{A}] = \mathbb{N} - \{0\}$, $P^{\mathfrak{A}} = \{(m, n): m$ divides $n\}$, $f^{\mathfrak{A}}(m) = 2 \cdot m$

(c) $[\mathfrak{A}] = \{a, b, c\}$, $P^{\mathfrak{A}} = \{(a, b), (a, c), (b, c)\}$, $f^{\mathfrak{A}}(a) = b$, $f^{\mathfrak{A}}(b) = c$, $f^{\mathfrak{A}}(c) = a$

9.2.4. Find models for these formulas.

(a) $\forall x\exists y\exists zPxyz \wedge \forall x\forall y(Pxxy \rightarrow \neg Pyyx)$

(b) $((\forall x(Px \leftrightarrow \neg Pf(x)) \wedge (Qx \leftrightarrow \neg Qf(f(x)))) \wedge \exists y(Py \wedge \neg Qy))$

(c) $\forall x\exists y\forall z((Pxy \leftrightarrow Pyz) \wedge (Pxy \leftrightarrow \neg Pyx))$

9.2.5. What are the free variables of each of the subformulas of $\forall x(Pxy \vee \neg\exists x\forall yQxy)$?

9.2.6. Which of the following formulas are closed?

(a) $(\forall xPx \vee \forall xQx)$

(b) $\forall x(\forall yPxy \vee \forall yPyy)$

(c) $(\forall yPyy \vee Qyy)$

(d) $(Pz \leftrightarrow (\exists xQxz \wedge \forall zRzz))$

9.2.7. Prove that the following formula has no finite model.

$$(\forall x(\forall y(Pxy \rightarrow \neg Pyx) \wedge \exists yPxy) \wedge \forall x\forall y\forall z((Pxy \wedge Pyz) \rightarrow Pxz))$$

9.2.8. Prove Lemma 9.2.2.

9.2.9. Suppose it is known that F has a finite model. Describe a procedure that would find one.

9.2.10. Suppose we did not insist, as we do in Definition 9.2.1, that the universe of a structure be *nonempty*. Would anything of importance be changed? For example, would the sets of satisfiable and unsatisfiable formulas remain the same?

9.2.11. Classify the following formulas as (i) valid; (ii) unsatisfiable; (iii) neither valid nor unsatisfiable.

(a) $(\forall x \forall y(Px \vee Qy) \wedge \exists x \exists y(\neg Px \wedge \neg Qy))$

(b) $(\neg \exists x \exists y Pxy \vee \forall x Pxx)$

(c) $(\neg \exists x Pxx \vee \forall x \forall y Pxy)$

(d) $\forall x \forall y(Pxy \wedge \neg Pyx)$

(e) $(\forall x Pxx \wedge \exists x \forall y(Pxy \wedge \neg Pyx))$

(f) $(\forall x Pxx \wedge \forall y \exists x(Pxy \wedge \neg Pyx))$

9.2.12. Let F be a tautology of the propositional calculus with atomic formulas $A_1, \ldots, A_n$. Let $G_1, \ldots, G_n$ be closed formulas of the predicate calculus. Let G be the formula of the predicate calculus that is obtained from F by replacing each occurrence of A_i by G_i for $i = 1, \ldots, n$. Prove that G is valid.

9.2.13. Let $\mathcal{A}$ be a model for a closed formula F of the predicate calculus with no function signs and with 1-place predicate signs only. Define an equivalence relation $\sim$ on $[\mathcal{A}]$ by: $a \sim b$ if and only if, for each predicate sign P occurring in F, $a \in P^{\mathcal{A}}$ if and only if $b \in P^{\mathcal{A}}$. Show that the set of equivalence classes of $\sim$ also form a model for F. Conclude that if such a formula has a model, it has a finite model of a predictable size; and that therefore there is a decision procedure for satisfiability for such formulas.

9.2.14. Show that if a closed formula F has a model $\mathcal{A}$ such that $|[\mathcal{A}]| = n$, then for each $m \geq n$, F has a model $\mathcal{B}_m$ such $|[\mathcal{B}_m]| = m$, and also F has a model with an infinite universe.

9.2.15. Show that, for every $n > 0$, there is a formula F_n that has a model with a universe of cardinality n, but that has no model with a universe of cardinality less than n.

9.2.16. Let F be a formula with free variables $x_1, \ldots, x_n$. Show that there is a structure $\mathcal{A}$ and function ξ such that $\mathcal{A} \models_\xi F$ if and only if $\exists x_1 \ldots \exists x_n F$ is satisfiable.

9.3.1. Prove Theorem 9.3.1.

9.3.2. Prove for the predicate calculus:

(a) one of the absorption laws;

(b) one of DeMorgan's laws.

9.3.3. Prove each of the following.

(a) $\neg \exists x F \equiv \forall x \neg F$

(b) If x has no free occurrence in G, then $(\exists x F \vee G) \equiv \exists x(F \vee G)$.

(c) $\exists x(F \vee G) \equiv (\exists x F \vee \exists x G)$

9.3.4. Give examples of formulas F and G such that:

(a) $\forall x(F \vee G)$ is not equivalent to $(\forall xF \vee \forall xG)$;

(b) $\exists x(F \wedge G)$ is not equivalent to $(\exists xF \wedge \exists xG)$.

9.3.5. Prove that if F and G are closed formulas, then $F \equiv G$ if and only if $(F \leftrightarrow G)$ is valid.

9.3.6. Find prenex forms of these formulas. Where several substantially different versions are possible, give them all.

(a) $(\neg\forall xPxy \vee \forall xRxy)$

(b) $\forall x(Px \longrightarrow \neg\exists yRxy)$

(c) $(\forall x\exists yPxy \leftrightarrow \exists x\forall yRxy)$

(d) $(\neg\forall x\neg\forall y\neg\forall zPxy \vee \neg\exists x\neg\exists y(\neg\exists zQxyz \longrightarrow Rxy))$

9.3.7. Prove carefully the following fact, which is used in the proof of Theorem 9.4.1: Every formula is equivalent to one in which no quantifier or negation sign is within the scope of any occurrence of a negation sign.

9.3.8. Here we consider closed formulas without function signs and with 1-place predicate signs only. Such a formula is in **miniscope form** if whenever $\forall xG$ or $\exists xG$ is a subformula, x is the *only* free variable of G. Show that every closed formula with 1-place predicate signs only is equivalent to one in miniscope form, and that there is an algorithm for making the conversion. (*Hint:* Consider first an innermost occurrence of a quantifier, that is, one in a subformula $\forall xG$ or $\exists xG$ where G has no quantifier. In the case of a subformula $\forall xG$, put G in conjunctive normal form; then apply the first rule in Lemma 9.3.1(c); then apply the first rule in Lemma 9.3.1(b). In the case of a subformula $\exists xG$, put G in disjunctive normal form and proceed analogously. For quantifiers that are not innermost, a similar procedure is followed, except that in forming a conjunctive or disjunctive normal form quantified subformulas must be treated as units—as though they were atomic formulas.)

9.3.9. Prove Lemma 9.3.2.

9.4.1. Find functional forms of each of the following formulas.

(a) $\forall x\forall y\exists z((Pxy \wedge Pyz) \longrightarrow \neg Pxz)$

(b) $\exists x(\forall y\exists zPxyz \wedge \exists z\forall y\neg Pxyz)$

(c) $\forall x(\exists yQxy \vee \forall y\exists zRxyz)$

(d) $\forall x(\neg\forall y\neg\forall zPyz \vee \neg\exists y(\forall zQxyz \longrightarrow Pxy))$

(e) $\forall x(\neg\exists xPxy \longrightarrow \exists xQxx)$

(f) $(\exists x\exists yPxy \leftrightarrow \forall x\forall yPxy)$

9.4.2. Exhibit truth-assignments verifying the Herbrand expansions of these formulas.

(a) $(\forall xPx \wedge \exists x \neg Px)$

(b) $(\exists x \forall yPxy \wedge \forall y \exists x(Pyx \rightarrow \neg Pxx))$

(c) $(\forall x(Px \vee Qx) \wedge \forall x \exists y(Px \leftrightarrow \neg Py))$

(d) $\forall x(\neg Pxx \wedge \exists yPxy \wedge \forall y \forall z((Pxy \wedge Pyz) \rightarrow Pxz))$

(e) $\forall x \forall y \exists z(Pxz \wedge \neg Pzy)$

9.4.3. Exhibit a finite, unsatisfiable subset of the Herbrand expansion of each of these formulas, of which no proper subset is also unsatisfiable.

(a) $(\exists x \forall yPxy \wedge \forall y \exists x \neg Pyx)$

(b) $\exists x \forall y \forall z \exists w(Pxy \wedge \neg Pyx)$

(c) $(\neg(\forall xGx \vee \exists y \neg Ny) \vee (\forall zGz \vee \exists w \neg Nw))$

(d) $(\neg \forall x(Gx \vee \exists y \neg Ny) \vee (\forall zGz \vee \exists w \neg Nw))$

9.4.4. For prenex formulas, the proof of the Expansion Theorem can be simplified. Give the most straightforward proof you can for this special case.

9.4.5. The functional form and Herbrand expansion, as here defined, are sometimes called the *satisfiability* functional form and the *satisfiability* expansion of a formula. Define analogously the *validity* functional form and the *validity* expansion of a formula in such a way that a closed formula is valid if and only if the disjunction of some finite subset of its validity expansion is a tautology of the propositional calculus.

9.4.6. (a) Let F be a prenex formula of the form $\forall y_1 \ldots \forall y_n \exists xG$, where $n \geq 0$. Let P be an $(n+1)$-place predicate sign not occurring in F, and let H be

$$(\forall y_1 \ldots \forall y_n \exists xPy_1 \ldots y_n x \wedge \forall y_1 \ldots \forall y_n \forall x(Py_1 \ldots y_n x \rightarrow G)).$$

Show that F is satisfiable if and only if H is satisfiable by constructing from any truth-assignment verifying $E(F)$ one verifying $E(H)$, and vice versa.

(b) Conclude that there is an algorithm that transforms any formula F into a formula G with prefix of the form $\forall y_1 \ldots \forall y_n \exists x_1 \ldots \exists x_m$, for some $n, m \geq 0$, such that F is satisfiable if and only if G is satisfiable.

9.4.7. Show that a formula F of the following form is satisfiable if and only if its matrix is satisfiable as a formula of the propositional calculus: F is prenex, and every atomic formula contains an existentially quantified variable whose quantifier is in the scope of each quantifier that binds some other variable occurring in that atomic formula. (For example, if F has prefix $\forall y_1 \ldots \forall y_n \exists x_1 \ldots \exists x_m$, then every atomic formula contains one of the x_i.) Conclude that there is a decision procedure for satisfiability for formulas of this type.

9.4.8. Under exactly what circumstances is a formula containing function signs the functional form of a formula without function signs?

9.5.1. Show that the Expansion Theorem provides an algorithm for determining satisfiability for formulas with the property that no positive occurrence of a quantifier has in its scope any negative occurrence of a quantifier. This is the case, for example, for prenex formulas without function signs with prefixes of the form $\exists x_1 \ldots \exists x_n \forall y_1 \ldots \forall y_m$ for some $n, m \geq 0$.

9.5.2. Suppose it is known in advance that a certain set S of formulas contains only unsatisfiable formulas and formulas with finite models (that is, models with finite universes). Show that there is a decision procedure for satisfiability for formulas in S.

9.5.3. Prove the following stronger version of Theorem 9.5.2. If $\mathfrak{A}$ is any model for a closed formula F, then there is a substructure $\mathfrak{B}$ of $\mathfrak{A}$ that has a countable universe and is also a model for F. By a **substructure of $\mathfrak{A}$**, we mean a structure $\mathfrak{B}$ for the same set of predicate and function signs as $\mathfrak{A}$ and such that

$[\mathfrak{B}] \subseteq [\mathfrak{A}]$;

$f^{\mathfrak{B}}(b_1, \ldots, b_n) = f^{\mathfrak{A}}(b_1, \ldots, b_n)$, for any n-place function sign f in the domain of $\mathcal{I}_{\mathfrak{B}}$ and any $b_1, \ldots, b_n \in [\mathfrak{B}]$;

$(b_1, \ldots, b_n) \in P^{\mathfrak{B}}$ if and only if $(b_1, \ldots, b_n) \in P^{\mathfrak{A}}$, for any n-place predicate sign P in the domain of $\mathcal{I}_{\mathfrak{B}}$ and any $b_1, \ldots, b_n \in [\mathfrak{B}]$.

9.6.1. The construction in the proof of Theorem 9.6.2 shows that satisfiability in the predicate calculus is unsolvable even for prenex formulas with prefixes of the form $\exists\forall\exists\forall$. Show that the same holds for the prefix forms $\forall\exists\exists\forall$ and $\forall\exists\forall\exists$. (The same also holds for the prefix $\forall\exists\forall$, but the proof is harder.)

9.6.2. (a) Show that satisfiability in the propositional calculus is $\mathcal{NP}$-complete even for formulas in conjunctive normal form. (This could be done by using Problem 8.5.10(a); however, it can also be done fairly simply by a direct modification of the construction in the proof of Theorem 9.6.1.)

(b) Show that satisfiability in the propositional calculus is $\mathcal{NP}$-complete even for formulas which are conjunctions of disjunctions of at most *three literals* each. (*Hint:* When faced with a "long" disjunction $(L_1 \vee \cdots \vee L_k)$, $k \geq 4$, introduce a new atomic formula A and replace $(L_1 \vee \cdots \vee L_k)$ by $(L_1 \vee L_2 \vee A) \wedge (\neg A \vee L_3 \vee \cdots \vee L_k)$.) (Compare this result with Problem 8.7.9.)

9.7.1. Convert to clause form.

(a) $\forall y(\exists x(Pyx \vee \neg Qyx) \wedge \exists x(\neg Pxy \vee Qxy))$

(b) $(\forall x(\exists y Pxy \wedge \neg Qyx) \vee \forall y \exists z(Rxyz \wedge \neg Qyz))$

(c) $\neg(\forall x \exists y Pxy \longrightarrow (\forall y \exists z \neg Qxz \wedge \forall y \neg \forall z Ryz))$

(d) $\forall x \exists y \forall z(\exists w(Qxw \vee Rxy) \leftrightarrow \neg \exists w \neg \exists u(Qxw \wedge \neg Rxu))$

9.7.2. Carefully spell out the final steps in the proof of Lemma 9.7.1.

9.7.3. What is $r(B_1, B_2; C_1, C_2)$ in each case?

(a) $B_1 = \{Px\}$; $B_2 = \{Ry\}$; $C_1 = \{Rx\}$; $C_2 = \{Ry\}$

(b) $B_1 = \{Pxy\}$; $B_2 = \{Rf(x)\}$; $C_1 = \{Qxy\}$; $C_2 = \{Qxx\}$

(c) $B_1 = \{Pxf(y)\}$; $B_2 = \{Qf(z)\}$; $C_1 = \{Rxf(x)\}$; $C_2 = \{Rf(z)u\}$

9.7.4. Find clauses A_1 and A_2 and a substitution θ such that $(A_1 - A_2)\theta$ is not a subset of $A_1\theta - A_2\theta$.

9.7.5. What are these atomic formulas?

(a) $Pxf(y)[x/f(y), y/x]$

(b) $Pxf(x)[x/f(x)]$

(c) $Pxyz[x/f(y), y/f(z), z/g(xyz)]$

9.7.6. Give a separating pair of substitutions for these clauses.

(a) $\{Pxyf(z)\}, \{Pyzf(z)\}$

(b) $\{Pxy, Pyz\}, \{Qyz, Rzf(y)\}$

(c) $\{Pxf(x)\}, \{Pxf(x)\}$

9.7.7. Apply the unification algorithm to these clauses and show how it progresses towards finding a most general unifier or concluding that the clause is not unifiable.

(a) $\{Pxy, Pyf(z)\}$

(b) $\{Payf(y), Pzzu\}$

(c) $\{Pxg(x), Pyy\}$

(d) $\{Pxg(x)y, Pzug(u)\}$

(e) $\{Pg(x)y, Pyy, Puf(w)\}$

(f) $\{Pxf(y)z, Pg(w)ug(w), Pvvg(w)\}$

9.7.8. Find all resolvents of these pairs of clauses.

(a) $\{Pxy, Pyz\}, \{\neg Puf(u)\}$

(b) $\{Pxx, \neg Rxf(x)\}, \{Rxy, Qyz\}$

(c) $\{Pxy, \neg Ryx\}, \{Rxx, Pyf(x)\}$

(d) $\{Pxy, \neg Pxx, Qxf(x)z\}, \{\neg Qf(x)xz, Pxz\}$

(e) $\{Pxf(x)z, Puww\}, \{\neg Pxyz, \neg Pzzz\}$

9.7.9. Establish by resolution the unsatisfiability of each of these formulas.

(a) $(\forall x\exists yPxy \wedge \exists x\forall y\neg Pxy)$

(b) $(\forall x\exists y\exists z((Py \leftrightarrow Px) \wedge (Qy \leftrightarrow \neg Qx) \wedge (Pz \leftrightarrow \neg Px)$
$\wedge (Qz \leftrightarrow Qx)) \wedge \exists x\forall y(Px \wedge Qx \wedge (Py \vee Qy)))$

(c) $(\forall x\exists y\exists z(Lxy \wedge Lyz \wedge Ay \wedge Bz \wedge (Pz \leftrightarrow Bx))$
$\wedge \forall x\forall y\forall z((Lxy \wedge Lyz) \rightarrow Lxz)$
$\wedge \exists x\forall y\neg(Py \wedge Lxy))$

9.7.10. Clause C_1 **subsumes** clause C_2 if and only if there is a substitution σ such that $C_1\sigma \subseteq C_2$. Give an algorithm for determining whether one clause subsumes another.

9.7.11. Prove that composition of substitutions is associative. Give an example that shows that it is not commutative.

9.7.12. Let S be a clause set and let $\mathfrak{a}$ be a truth-assignment to the ground instances of literals appearing in S. Let $R_0(S)$ be S together with all resolvents of pairs of clauses in S, at least one of which has a ground instance falsified by $\mathfrak{a}$. (That is, if C_1 and C_2 are in S but every ground instance of C_1 and C_2 is verified by $\mathfrak{a}$, no resolvent of these clauses is formed.) Define $R_0^*(S)$ in the usual way. Show that S is unsatisfiable if and only if $\Box \in R_0^*(S)$.

9.7.13. Let S be a clause set and let T be a subset of S such that $S - T$ is satisfiable. Say that a clause in $R^*(S)$ **has T-support** if it is a member of T or is a resolvent of two clauses, of which at least one has T-support. Define $R_1(S) = S \cup \{C \in R(S)\colon C \text{ has } T\text{-support}\}$, and define $R_1^*(S)$ in the usual way. Show that S is unsatisfiable if and only if $\Box \in R_1^*(S)$.

REFERENCES

Chapters 8 and 9 cover but a small slice of a very rich subject. They are not intended as a general introduction to mathematical logic; for that the reader is cheerfully referred to a text devoted wholly to that purpose. Two good ones are

H. B. Enderton, *A Mathematical Introduction to Logic*. New York: Academic Press, 1972 *and*

E. MENDELSON, *Introduction to Mathematical Logic*. New York: D. Van Nostrand, 1979.

The resolution method is due to

J. A. ROBINSON, "A Machine-Oriented Logic Based on the Resolution Principle," *Journal of the Association for Computing Machinery*, 12 (1965), 23–41

though it has its roots in earlier methods, for example

M. DAVIS and H. PUTNAM, "A Computing Procedure for Quantification Theory," *Journal of the Association for Computing Machinery*, 7 (1960), 201–215.

A full discussion of resolution can be found in

D. W. LOVELAND, *Automated Theorem Proving: A Logical Basis*. New York: Elsevier North Holland, 1978.

The Expansion Theorem has a long and complex history. For a discussion, see

B. DREBEN and W. D. GOLDFARB, *The Decision Problem: Solvable Classes of Quantificational Formulas*. Reading, Mass.: Addison-Wesley, 1979.

See that book as well for a full account of subcases of the predicate calculus for which satisfiability is a solvable problem. On the other hand, for subcases for which satisfiability is unsolvable, see

H. R. LEWIS, *Unsolvable Classes of Quantificational Formulas*. Reading, Mass.: Addison-Wesley, 1979.

The exposition in Section 9.6 is inspired ultimately on ideas of Büchi and Wang; see the citations at the end of Chapter 6. It was to show the unsolvability of the predicate calculus that Turing developed his notion of computation by automata, though Turing's proof looks much different from ours, since it does not rely on the Expansion Theorem. The satisfiability problem for the propositional calculus is the original $\mathcal{NP}$-completeness result, and is due to S. A. Cook; see the reference to Cook at the end of Chapter 7.

INDEX